DATE DUE

HISTORY OF THE ROMAN PEOPLE

PRENTICE-HALL, INC. *Englewood Cliffs, N. J.*

FRITZ M. HEICHELHEIM

University of Toronto , Canada

HISTORY OF THE ROMAN PEOPLE

AND   CEDRIC A. YEO

Caney College , Kentucky

A HISTORY OF THE ROMAN PEOPLE

BY HEICHELHEIM & YEO

© 1962, BY PRENTICE-HALL, INC. ENGLEWOOD CLIFFS, N.J.

LIBRARY OF CONGRESS CATALOG CARD NO.: 61-8225

PRINTED IN THE UNITED STATES OF AMERICA

39212-C

Second printing......July, 1962

Designed by Robert Kopelman and Andrew Zutis

In memory of a great master
and teacher of Roman history,
MICHAEL ROSTOVTZEFF;

and to GERTA,
for saving her husband's life

PREFACE

This book examines the historical evolution of Rome, from its earliest beginnings as a cluster of mud-hut villages on the seven hills to its days of glory as an empire embracing the entire Mediterranean region and huge segments of Europe, Asia, and Africa.

The survey of the prehistoric period in Italy and the discussion of Etruscan civilization were deemed an essential introduction to our subject, for the birth of Rome was not a precipitate phenomenon but the almost inevitable result of a long process—the beginning of which antedated by many centuries the legendary founding of the city itself.

Some readers may deplore the decision to end the book with the death of Constantine the Great. But an adequately detailed analysis of the fourth and fifth centuries, though significant and instructive, would have extended the book to a virtually unmanageable length. And which would have been the most suitable stopping point? The death of Theodosius the Great in 395? The deposition of Romulus Agustulus in 476? The death of Justinian I in 565? The reign of Heraclius I (575–642)? Or the capture of Constantinople by the Turks in 1453? A discussion of such events properly belongs—not to a history of the Roman people—but to the Late Roman Empire and the Middle Ages.

The disintegration of the Roman Empire has been attributed by various scholars to numerous single causes: soil erosion, slavery, rampant immorality, despotism, bureaucracy. Some of these "causes" are obviously absurd—all, taken singly, inadequate. The main objection is that not enough emphasis is placed on the Greco-Roman Empire in the East, which became the center and fulcrum of late Roman political and intellectual life. The power of the Eastern Empire suffered various temporary declines but was not destroyed until the fall of Constantinople in 1453. Even in the West, Roman glory still endured. Almost all the German princes who succeeded the Late Roman emperors became Roman magistrates (nor were the titles only empty honors) and never in the history of Roman warfare had military science and tactics achieved so high a level of excellence.

It was not until after the reign of Justinian I that the Western Empire foundered (to emerge later in the national monarchies of England, France, and Spain). Rome ceased to be the sole standard bearer of urban civilization, and as the Germanic, Celtic, Slavic, and Islamic peoples forged ahead to realize their national potential, Rome was forced to retreat to a more viable position. This retreat coincided in a vigorous age of intellectual and political efflorescence in the seventh and eighth centuries by the creation of a free peasantry in the East and the absorption and adaptation of Greco-Roman civilization by the Church. Thereafter, the Roman Empire occupied only a central position in a multiplicity of urban civilizations which extended from the Atlantic to the China seas.

There comes now the pleasant task of thanking the two persons who have done most to further the publication of this book: Mr. Richard M. Haywood of New York University, who read and criticized all the chapters as they came off the typewriter, and Miss Francesca Tillona of Prentice-Hall, who by careful and dedicated editing succeeded in removing many of the blemishes that marred the rewritten manuscript.

F.M.H.

C.A.Y.

CONTENTS

PART ONE / PRE-ROMAN ITALY

I

GEOGRAPHY AND CLIMATE OF ITALY 2

Geography, 4. Climate, 4.

II

PREHISTORIC ITALY 6

The Paleolithic Period, 8: *Lower Paleolithic Period, Middle Paleolithic Period, Neanderthal Man, Upper Paleolithic Period, Homo Sapiens, Upper Paleolithic Art, End of Old Stone Age.* The Mesolithic Period, 16. The Neolithic Period, 17: *The Village, Influence of Danubian Culture, The Culture of Vucedol and Arrival of the Indo-Europeans, The Lake-Dwellers and Bell-beaker Folk, The Terremare Culture, The Villanovans and Fossa People*

III

THE ETRUSCANS 26

Conquest of Etruria, 28: *Etruscan Expansion in Italy, Decline of Etruscan Power.* Etruscan Economy, 31: *Agriculture, Mining and the Metal Trades, Other Industries, Lumbering and Commerce.* Etruscan Culture and Religion, 33: *Sports, Religion.* Etruscan Art, 36: *Origin, Development, and General Features, Architecture, Sculpture, Painting.* Etruscan Family Life, 41: *A Typical Frontier Society*

PART TWO / THE ROMAN REPUBLIC

EARLY ROMAN SOCIETY 46

Latium and the Latins, 48: *Etruscan Cultural Infiltration*. The Rise of Rome, 50: *Economic Development, Historical Development of the Family, The Gens, The Pater Familias, Patricians and Plebeians*. Rome as a City-State, 57: *The King, The Senate, The Popular Assembly*. The Early Roman Army, 62: *The Servian Constitutional Reform*. Early Roman Religion, 65: *Magic and Taboo, Dynamism and Animism, Numen or Mana, Sacrifice and Prayer, Gods of the House and Fields, Jupiter and Mars, Italic Cults, Etruscan Influence, Greek Cults, The Roman State Religion, The Priesthood and the Priestly Colleges*. Early Roman Law and Moral Code, 73: *Virtue (Virtus)*

RISE OF THE ROMAN REPUBLIC 76

Sources of Information, 77: *The Early Annalists, Annalists from the Gracchan Age to Cicero, Livy and Dionysius, Minor Literary Sources, The Fasti, The Reliability of the Roman Historican Tradition*. From Kingship to Republic, 81: *Conflict of the Classes, Secession of the Plebs, The Plebeian Battle for Social Justice, A Period of Resurgent Liberalism, The XII Tables, The Post-Decemviral Reaction, Plebeian Triumphs, The Censors, The Questions, The Senate, The War with Veii*. The Sack of Rome, 91: *The Prehistoric Origin of the Celts, Early Celtic Art, The Celtic Invasion of North Italy*. Up from the Ashes, 98: *Constitutional Reform and Reorganization of the Government, The Conquest of Italy, The Samnites, The Old Latin League, The Great Samnite War (327–304/3 B.C.), The Third Samnite War, 298–290 B.C.* The Pyrrhic Wars, 107: *Pyrrhus' Sicilian Venture, 278–275 B.C., Reasons for Roman Success*

THE PERIOD OF THE PUNIC WARS 110

The Rise of Carthage, 112: *Carthage, a Hellenistic State, The Carthaginian Government*. The First Punic War: 264–241 B.C., 115: *Roman Intervention in Sicily, 264 B.C., Rome Builds a New Fleet, The Roman Invasion of Africa: 256–255 B.C., The War in Sicily, 254–241 B.C., Carthaginian Successes at Sea, Hamilcar Barca, The End: 241 B.C., Peace Terms: 241 B.C.* Between the Wars, 120: *Carthaginian Recovery, The Ebro Treaty, Roman Problems after 241 B.C., The Taxation of Roman Sicily, The Administration of Sicily, The Praetor, Gaius Flaminius, The Gallic Wars and Conquest of North Italy; 225–222 B.C., The Reform of the Centuriate Assembly, The Illyrian Wars: 229–228 and 220–219 B.C.* The Second Punic War: 218–201 B.C., 127:

PART THREE / THE ROMAN EMPIRE

THE PRINCIPATE OF AUGUSTUS 266

PRINCIPATE OF THE JULIO-CLAUDIANS 308

PART ONE

PRE-ROMAN ITALY

I
GEOGRAPHY AND

ROMAN HISTORY IS MORE THAN A RECORD OF THE CITY OF ROME.
It is a history of Italy, and of all the lands washed by the
Mediterranean. It is a history of the greater part of Europe and
immense areas of Asia and Africa which were welded by
Rome into a single commonwealth, a great universal state. It is
a history of the West, to which Rome bequeathed her language,
her culture, and her system of government. Roman history is, in
short, a history of the world.

Because the history of any state or region is in great measure
influenced by its particular physical environment, a study of
Rome must begin with an understanding of Mediterranean and
especially Italian geography.

The peaceful Mediterranean, usually calm under brilliant
skies, free of hidden shoals or treacherous eddies and studded

CLIMATE OF ITALY

with clusters of verdant islands, encouraged early man to sail from point to point, from inlet to inlet, from island to island. The Mediterranean became a highway linking together three continents. People of different races, languages, and cultures met—first, perhaps, to fight, later to trade, always to exchange ideas.

The Mediterranean, historically ancient, is nevertheless of recent geological origin. Although its area of more than 1,000,000 square miles makes it now the largest of all seas, as recently (geologically speaking) as one million years ago it was still divided in two

by an unbroken land bridge which joined Europe and Africa. A series of dislocations and sinkings later gave rise, in the north, to the mountainous formation known as the Alps and, in the south, established the present geological character of Italy, Sicily, and the Mediterranean itself.

The process of geological change is continuous: the Strait of Gibraltar is three times wider today than it was when it was known as the Pillars of Hercules. The Strait of Messina, once only about a mile wide, is now almost two miles across and its once perilous whirlpool of Scylla and Charybdis has subsided into a mere current. Like the Mediterranean, Italy is also geologically young.

It was not until around a million years ago that Italy began to acquire its present shape. The peninsula, much narrower and shorter than it is now, underwent a broadening and a lengthening process. The Po valley, once a vast extension of the Adriatic, was gradually filled in by alluvial deposits brought down by the Po, the Adige, and other rivers—a process that has made it one of the richest agricultural districts of Italy. Southern Italy and Sicily also rose above the sea and in places were elevated to a height of 4,500 feet. The same process of uplift aided by the action of volcanoes and by the development of river systems formed the fertile plains of Etruria, Latium, and Campania. Intense volcanic activity persists to this day on Vesuvius, Stromboli, and Etna.

From the continent of Europe Italy juts out into the Mediterranean like a gigantic pier. It falls into two parts: the northern, continental; the southern, peninsular. Together they occupy an area of about 91,000 square miles.

Geography

The part known as "continental Italy" is the northern plain, bounded by the Alps on the north and northwest and by the Apennines on the south. It is drained by the Po and the Adige that flow swiftly from the mountains towards the low-lying lagoon-filled coast of the Adriatic. From a shallow gulf-like extension of the Adriatic it became in early historic times a water-logged swamp fringed with thick woods. Here dwelt the lake-dwellers four thousand years ago. In later times it assumed its present aspect of a rich, well-watered, carefully tended garden, the best farm land in all Italy.

The peninsular part of Italy is dominated by the Apennines, which run from the southern French Alps to the coast of Liguria in the northwest (now a region of heavy rainfall, but in Roman times a backward, neglected mountainland of thick impenetrable forest). Southwards from Liguria and north-ern Etruria the Apennines fan out towards the Adriatic into a series of rugged limestone ridges running parallel with the shore line and cut up by narrow gorges. Of moderate height in the north (6,000 feet), the Central Apennines are highest in the Abruzzi, where the San Grasso d'Italia soars to 9,700 feet. They skirt the Adriatic shore so closely there is barely room for a road. Here the rivers are short, swift, and spasmodic, quite unsuitable for navigation. After the Apennines reach the wind-swept pasture-lands of Apulia, they veer over again to the west coast, which they follow all the way to the Strait of Messina.

Nature dealt more kindly with the west coast. Here are found the best harbors in Italy, and the longest rivers. The mountains are not so steep and recede further from the sea, leaving space for the wide lowland plains of Etruria, Latium, and Campania, which owe their fertility to the thick layer of ash and weathered lava ejected by the many once active volcanoes. These plains are drained by the Arno, the Tiber, the Liri, and the Volturno, which are easily navigated by small craft and whose valleys provide easy communication between the coastal region and the hill country in the interior. Because the west coast had the space and soil to support a thick population, first the Etruscans and then the Romans were able to flourish there and later extend their influence over the rest of the peninsula.

Climate

Except in the northern part, Italy has a typically Mediterranean climate generated by the interaction of the hot, dry winds of the Sahara and the cool, moist winds of the Atlantic. The former are dominant in summer, the latter in winter. The violence of this contrast is moderated by the Mediterranean, which cools the air by day and warms it at night. Autumns are long and warm; springs, long and cool. Thus Italy can grow cool season crops such as grain and vegetables, as well as grapes and olives, which require a late fall for ripening and drying.

The general characteristics of Italian climate are hot, dry summers and mild, rainy winters. Bright luminous skies—Italy has 2,300 hours of sunshine as compared with less than 1,500 hours in Britain—and a transparent atmosphere make things stand out in sharp profile.

There is much variation in temperature and rainfall from season to season and place to place depending less on latitude than on elevation and proximity to the sea. Potenza, which is 60 miles from the sea and whose elevation is 3,000 feet, has a mean winter temperature that is nearly 10 degrees lower than that of Naples. Certain Alpine districts have from 80 to 120 inches of rainfall; the Tavoliere table-land of Apulia has less than 20. Genoa, exposed to the rainbringing winds from the west, has an annual rainfall of 52 inches while Venice, on the Adriatic, has less than 30.

In Italy, especially in the south, rain comes down in a deluge. River beds, dry and wide all summer, become frothing torrents in a few hours of winter rain, and mountain slopes are stripped of soil. April gone, the rains come more infrequently.

Italy is a land of winds in both winter and summer. From the north, even under a hard and brilliant sun, the icy mistral blows dry and cold upon Genoa. Upon the Adriatic beats the bora, an icy blast from the eastern Alps. From the south blow two winds from the Sahara, called the sirocco. One is hot and humid and brings rain; the other is hot, dry, and scorching like the blast from a furnace, filling the air with a fine red dust.

It is to the remains of buildings and pottery, carefully preserved in the hot, dry Italian climate, that modern scholars owe much of their present knowledge of the prehistoric world. Most of the important phases of earth's history are represented in Italy in one region or another. The oldest rocks—limestone, gneiss, granite, and quartz—are to be found in the western and central Alps, in Sardinia and Corsica, in Calabria, and in parts of Tuscany. To the same early era belong the lead, zinc, iron, copper, and silver deposits of Sardinia. Iron is found on the island of Elba and some copper and tin in Tuscany, but in three basic ingredients of modern national power—iron, oil and coal—Italy is lacking.

Italy also possesses a wealth of stone for building and clays for pottery. Also noteworthy are the gray and white marbles of Carrara in Tuscany, and those of Piedmont, Liguria, and Verona. It is as if nature, though withholding the resources for modern industry, had lavishly bestowed in their stead the materials for art.

II

PREHISTORIC ITALY

THE BULK OF THE EVIDENCE ABOUT PRIMITIVE MAN COMES FROM Western Europe. Although archaeological investigations of exceptional importance have been carried on in France, Spain, Germany, and England, Italy also has recently contributed valuable evidence which indicates that it was inhabited several hundred thousand years before the founding of Rome. There is no foundation for the statement sometimes made that the original inhabitants vanished without a trace. Though their cultural influence upon later Italic peoples was small, their existence cannot be ignored. The oldest human inhabitants of Italy and western Europe may be traced back to the beginning of the Pleistocene or Quaternary Period, also known as the Ice Age. Believed to have lasted only some 275,000 to 600,000 years, it brought to a violent and convulsive end almost seventy million

years of warm and stable climate. For some unknown reason, temperatures dropped all over the northern hemisphere; snow piled up and froze into ice blocks of continental size and mountainous proportions. Propelled by their own enormous weight, they pushed down from the mountains of Scandinavia onto the plains of northern Europe. Minor glaciers inched down from the Alps, the Pyrenees, and the higher Apennines. Four times they advanced and retreated, each advance going through two or more secondary phases of advance and retreat. In the vicinity of the glaciers arctic weather prevailed all the time, but in France, Spain, and Italy summer, though wet and chilling, interrupted the bitterly cold winters. Each ice-front persisted for tens of thousands of years but finally receded giving way, as higher temperatures returned, to equally long interglacial pauses of semi-tropical weather. The second of these pauses, for instance, is believed to have lasted almost 200,000 years.

As the glaciers retreated, the warmth-loving animals returned to the north. Once more the southern mammoth and straight-tusked elephant roamed the woodlands of southern England; there, too, lived the hippopotamus, the broad-nosed rhinoceros, and the saber-toothed tiger. These tropical animals disappeared with the beginning of the Würm or fourth glaciation, which blanketed western Europe in ice and snow as far south as Spain and central Italy. The reindeer, the musk-ox, the cave-bear, the banded lemming, and the rhinoceros pressed south. Near Rome wandered the woolly mammoth and to the shores of Apulia came the great auk.

The Paleolithic Period

Man too reacted to the successive advances and retreats of the ice. During the warm interglacials, he lived out in the open, camping on hillsides or on riverbanks, where game was plentiful and flint for making tools could be found. Many campsites containing

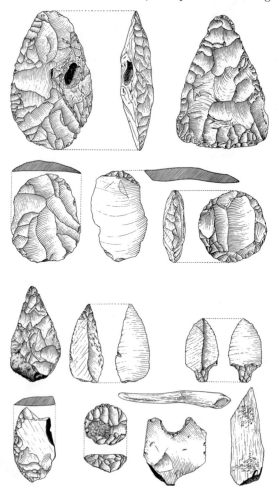

tools and animal bones have been excavated on the higher terraces of the Somme, the Seine, the Thames, and the Tiber. With the onset of the Würm glaciation (between 85,000 and 125,000 years ago) hunting tribes broke up into smaller groups and took shelter under over-hanging cliffs, in caves, or rock-shelter homes. These were the "cave-men" and so they remained for perhaps a hundred thousand years.

The millions of flint tools and animal bones excavated from river terraces, loess-beds, and especially caves are the main evidence of human culture for almost 99 per cent of man's earthly existence. That long span of pre-literate history we call the Stone Age. From the cultural standpoint we may divide the Stone Age into two main stages: the longer and more ancient period of chipped stone implements known as the Paleolithic or Old Stone Age, and the more recent period of polished stone implements known as the Neolithic or New Stone Age. Since in excavating caves and other sites one always finds the oldest layers of habitation at the bottom, we usually subdivide the Paleolithic into three periods: the Lower, Middle, and Upper Paleolithic.

Lower Paleolithic Period:

The Lower Paleolithic period is believed to have begun with the first ice-front (between 275,000 and 600,000 years ago) and ended with the third Interglacial (between 85,000 and 125,000 years ago). The Middle Paleolithic coincided with the approach and the first phase of the Würm or last glaciation (from 85,000 or 125,000, to about 35,000 years ago). According to reliable moraine and radio-carbon tests, the Upper Paleolithic extended from the beginning of the second phase of Würm (about 35,000 years ago) until the end of the third phase and the final retreat of the glaciers across Scandinavia and North America (between 10,000 and 8,000 years ago). The last Scandinavian glaciers vanished about 3,000 B.C.

Top series: *Typical Acheulian core tools.* Middle series: *Typical Levalloisian flake and core tools.* Bottom series: *Flake and bone implements.* (*Courtesy American Museum of Natural History*)

The European and especially the Italian stone industries of the Lower Paleolithic belong mainly to the core-biface tradition, although the so-called flake and scraper cultures of East and Central Asia, India, and East Africa were not unlike those then existing in Western Europe. Of these the Clactonian flake cultures, which existed side by side with the hand-ax cultures, were especially wide-spread.

The core-biface tool or hand-ax was used by the hunters and foodgatherers in European woodlands and forests for chopping, scraping, cutting, and hitting. It was made by knocking off flakes from a large almond- or pear-shaped flint with a small hammer stone so as to flatten it out on both faces and trim it down to a sharp cutting edge.

The hand-ax apparently first developed in the tropics, perhaps in East or South Africa, or in regions of luxuriant vegetation, where it was used for working wood and grubbing up roots and food from the ground. It has been found all over Africa, the Middle East, and India. In Europe it occurs everywhere west of the Rhine, in France, England, Spain, and Italy. Outstanding earlier hand-ax cultures are named *Chellean* and *Abbevillian,* a later one *Acheulian.* Acheulian hand-axes were neater, thinner, better chipped, and with straighter edges. So slowly did these industries evolve that 50,000 to 400,000 years may have elapsed between the oldest and the latest techniques. Some of the earliest Lower Paleolithic cultures appear to have discovered the art of fire-making.

In Italy hand-axes of the Lower Paleolithic tradition occur on the surface and in easily dated strata of caves and river terraces. They are found frequently in Umbria, the Marche, the Abruzzi, and the Matese. Excellent specimens have turned up in two Lucanian caves at Venosa and Matera, as well as in Apulia on the Gargano peninsula. Apart from sporadic surface finds, few appear in the North except at Imola, few along the west coast save on the island of Capri and in the valleys of the Tiber and the Liri. Though this early industry is abundantly represented in Italy, little is known about the tool makers themselves except that they were probably hunters who lived out in the open, used hand-axes or scrapers for skinning animals, and made clothing for themselves from skins punched with borers and sewn together with sinews.

Middle Paleolithic Period: Neanderthal Man

As the last Ice Age approached, a new toolmaking industry began to replace the core-biface and primitive traditions typical of the Lower Paleolithic. This was a flake industry usually called *Mousterian* from the site of its discovery, Le Moustier, a rock-shelter in southwestern France. Mousterian toolmakers used a heavy hammerstone to knock off broad thin flakes from a large flint core. By trimming the flakes down on one side with bone, horn, or wood, they made small hand-axes, side-scrapers shaped like a section of an orange, and a variety of borers and disks. Originating somewhere in central or southwest Asia, the Mousterian tool industry spread into central Europe and later into France, where it copied Acheulian methods of chipping and some tool forms. Such tools are found almost everywhere throughout the Italian peninsula, especially around Rome and in the lower valleys of the Aniene and the Tiber. Unlike Abbevillian, Chellean, or Acheulian artifacts, they are found most often in caves, where their makers had been forced to live by the severity of the climate.

The cavemen who made and used Mousterian tools owe their race name to the Neander Valley in Germany where a skeleton of the species was found in 1856. Their early habitat was central Europe. From there they migrated to France, Spain, and Italy, to escape the intense cold. More than a dozen skeletons have been dug out of caves in France. Others have been found in Belgium, in Spain, in Jugoslavia, in the Crimea, in Palestine, in China, and in Italy, not far from Rome. Of these the one discovered at La Chapelle aux Saints in France has become a "classic." The Old Man of La Chapelle, as reconstructed by the French anthropologist, Boule, is the cave man of popular conception: the beetle-browed brute who carried a club and dragged his wife about by the hair. He was about five feet three inches tall, with a short bull-like neck, a barrel chest, long arms and huge hands. His short, straight spine, crooked legs, and flat feet probably made him walk with a slouching, shuffling gait and unable to stand erect. His receding forehead, chinless jaws, flat head, and the huge bony ridge above his eyes, all gave him more the appearance of an ape than a man. Though he had a bigger brain case than modern man, his brain is believed to have been too little developed for sustained memory or logical thinking.

Not all Neanderthals looked like the Old Man of La Chapelle. Indeed recent excavations in Italy strengthen the hypothesis that there were two distinct Neanderthaloid types: the burly type just described, and a less rugged, more developed specimen who could stand erect and in several other respects resembled modern man. The former lived through the climax of the fourth ice front, the latter lived during the preceding interglacial, perhaps some 60,000 years earlier.

In a gravel pit at Saccopastore not far from Rome, workmen uncovered three skulls, one almost intact but for the lower jaw. As computed from the somewhat hypothetical curve of solar radiation, the skulls date back to some 125,000 years ago. Like their contemporaries at Steinheim and Ehringsdorf in Germany and at Krapina in Jugoslavia, the Saccopastore Neanderthals could stand up straight and were less rugged and heavy than the later cave-dwellers. An excellent example of the later but more conservative type was found a few years ago in a cave on Monte Circeo, which juts out from the coast of Latium. The Monte Circeo skull appears to be about 60,000 years younger than those found at Saccopastore. Probably as the weather got rougher in western Europe during the advance of the fourth glaciation, the Neanderthaloids degenerated into a specialized subrace that either died out or, as recent excavations on Mount Carmel in Palestine seem to show, was absorbed by later races of men.

The Neanderthals were hunters and food gatherers. They probably did little bird-hunting or fishing, for they lacked the proper equipment, but they were expert trappers of such big game as the arctic mammoth and the woolly rhinoceros. Considerable social co-operation must have been required to corner those huge animals or drive them into pitfalls and then drag the heavy carcasses to the mouths of the caves. A rudimentary social life must have developed as they huddled at night around the fire built up for comfort and as protection against savage animals. Of their religious life nothing is known except that they may have held ritual dances and made ritual sacrifices; they apparently believed in some sort of immortality, for they seem to have buried their dead carefully, after first cracking open the skulls and devouring the brains.

Upper Paleolithic Period: Homo Sapiens

With the advent of the Upper Paleolithic Period (now dated by radio-carbon tests as 35,000 years ago), there developed the present species of man, *Homo sapiens,* "wise man." The best known type of *Homo sapiens* is Cro-Magnon, named after a cave in the French Dordogne. Cro-Magnon men were tall, muscular, and of athletic build. They had massive skulls but clean-cut features, vertical foreheads, narrow noses, and prominent chins. It had been supposed that they originally came out of central or southwest Asia and entered Europe by way of either the Balkans or North Africa. There is now good reason to think that some branches of *Homo sapiens* are extremely old, their ancestry running back parallel with that of Neanderthaloids through the Pleistocene to the unknown beyond. The strongest support for this view comes from the recent discovery of two skulls in a cave at Fontéchevade in France. They have straight and almost vertical foreheads and their dimensions are comparable with those of living Europeans. They were found in a stratum containing tools of the early blade and scraper industries and animal bones dating back to the Lower Paleolithic. Of equal antiquity are three other European skulls of *Homo sapiens* type. One of them was discovered in England at Swanscombe, the two others in Italy, the one at Olmo near Arezzo, the other at Quinzano not far from Verona. Recent fluorine, nitrogen, and radioactivity tests have proved the

Swanscombe skull to have been at least as old as the Lower Paleolithic.

During Upper Paleolithic times Italy was inhabited by at least two types of *Homo sapiens*—the Cro-Magnons and the Grimaldi negroids. Among the sixteen skeletons found in the Grimaldi caves of Liguria there were two of markedly negroid characteristics; in body build and in the shape of their skulls they resemble the modern Bushmen of South Africa. How they happened to be in northern Italy is still a mystery. No trace of their presence has yet been found in southern Italy, in Sicily, or even in North Africa, which was then inhabited by a Caucasian race ethnologists call Afalou.

Life in that part of Europe not covered with ice and snow was still primitive during Paleolithic times. The new racial groups were much better equipped to deal with their environment than their predecessors had been. New skills and techniques for working on a wider range of materials produced tools more efficient for food gathering. From flint and obsidian, a kind of volcanic glass, Upper Paleolithic man made a variety of tools, among them long blunt-backed knife blades, beautifully edged gravers, chisels, spear points, arrow heads, barbs, and awls. Bone, horn, antler, and ivory, seldom used before as tool-making materials, were worked into needles as well as lance points, spear throwers, fish hooks, harpoons, and other hunting and fishing gear.

Archaeologically the Upper Paleolithic of western Europe can be divided into five main cultural stages, each distinguished by

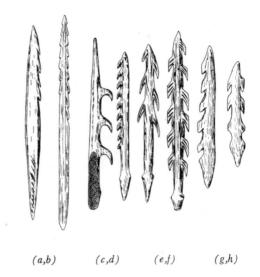

(a,b)   (c,d)   (e,f)   (g,h)

Evolution of barbed harpoons during Magda-lenian times. (a,b) Archaic prototypes. (c,d) Harpoons with single row of barbs. (e,f) Harpoons with double row of barbs. (g,h) Degenerate types of the final Magdalenian. (Courtesy American Museum of Natural History)

its own peculiar blade industry. All get their names from the French sites where first discovered. Chatelperronian, Middle Aurignacian, Gravettian, Solutrean, and Magda-lenian followed each other in that chronological order. Of these the Solutreans are most noted for their flint-work, the Magda-lenians for their bone industry and for their remarkable cave-paintings. Originating in Hungary, the Solutrean culture of the Bruenn men spread into western Europe, where they developed the most remarkable flint industry

Solutrean "laurel leaf" blade of the Paleolithic Period. (Courtesy American Museum of Natural History)

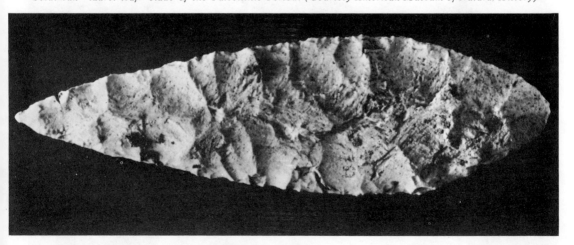

of the entire Stone Age. The best specimens of their flint work are the delicately flaked laurel-leaf and willow-leaf spear heads, which are as thin as steel blades and almost as sharp.

Two other cultures, Middle Aurignacian and Gravettian, are of interest to us simply because they are the only ones known to have spread into Italy. Originating in southwest Asia, Middle Aurignacian moved into central Europe and thence into France and Italy. Traces of it appear in the Ligurian caves and as far south as Tuscany and Latium. Gravettian, appearing first in South Russia as a horse- and mammoth-hunting culture, spread across Europe as far west as Spain. In Italy a local variant of it known as Grimaldian is found in the Ligurian caves, in the Pontine Marshes, and throughout southern Italy and Sicily. Southern Grimaldian is strongly impregnated with Capsian elements, a North African and Spanish blade

The cave paintings at Lascaux (Dordogne, France) are estimated to be some 20,000 to 30,000 years old. (Courtesy William Chapman)

Detail of the Lascaux paintings. (Courtesy French Government Tourist Office)

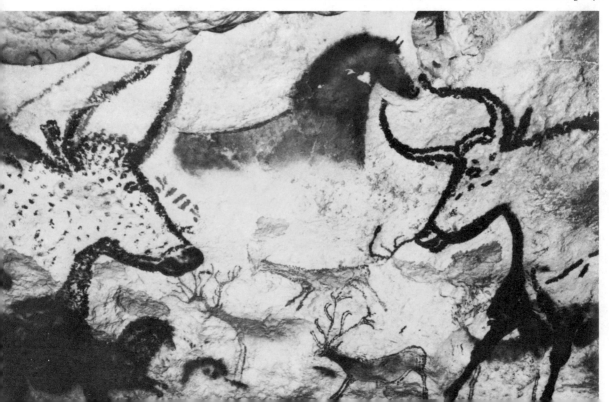

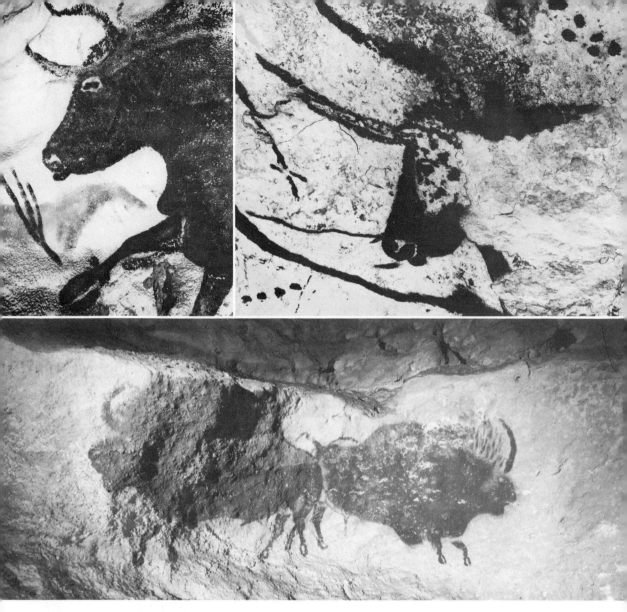

Top left: *The Great Black Bull of Lascaux. (Courtesy Archives Photographiques, Paris)*. Top right: *Bison's head: detail of the Lascaux paintings. (Courtesy French Government Tourist Office)*. Below: *Two bisons galloping away from each other: detail of the Lascaux paintings. (Courtesy Archives Photographiques, Paris)*

culture which was more or less contemporary with the Magdalenian. It is noted for its tiny crescent-backed blades, which were fitted into slotted hafts. Thus equipped, the Upper Paleolithic hunters went after the vast herds of mammoth, reindeer, bison, and wild horse that roamed the plains of western and central Europe. The charred remains of over 1,000 mammoths discovered at Predmost in Czechoslovakia and the bones of some 100,000 horses found at the great camp at Solutré give some indication of the success of these early hunters. So fond were the Magdalenians of deer hunting that the period from about 25,000 to 10,000 B.C. is often called the Reindeer Age. With bow and arrow, boomerang, and harpoon, the Magdalenians were able to capture geese, ducks and other wild fowls as well as salmon, trout, and pike. They supplemented their diet of meat, fish, and fowl with a variety of vegetable foods—nuts, berries, and wild honey. As the climate was still arctic or sub-arctic, they continued to live in natural caves, often improvising screens and windbreaks to provide more shelter. In open country they built round and oblong houses with floors sunk below the level of the ground, or wickiups covered with brush, sods, or skins.

Upper Paleolithic Art

The most amazing achievement of Upper Paleolithic man and especially the Magdalenians was not their successful battle with nature for survival and sustenance, but their art. A horse sculptured in ivory or carved in high relief on a rock, bisons modeled in clay, a herd of reindeer engraved on an eagle's wing bone, or a running stag incised on horn or stone are just a few examples of their skill as sculptors, carvers, and draftsmen. They covered the limestone walls and ceilings of their caves with engravings and paintings of individual animals in various at-

titudes. The animals most frequently sketched or painted were aurochs, bison, stag, reindeer, horse, mammoth, and ibex.

Practically all the animal engravings and paintings were done in profile; thus the problem of perspective arose only in drawing the feet, horns, or antlers. They solved that problem by the use of slewed or twisted perspective, whereby the feet and horns are seen from the front though the rest of the body is shown in profile. The colors used in cave painting ranged from yellow, orange, rose, vermillion, crimson, and violet-brown to black. They were all based on mineral oxides, red being derived from peroxide of iron, black from manganese. Sometimes the colors were applied to the dampened surface as pastels or sticks, but generally they were ground up and mixed with water or grease. After sketching the outlines of the animal with a sharp bit of flint, the artist applied the colors with his fingers or with brushes made from the tails of animals. Because the paintings were done at different times and by different artists, often one painting became superimposed on another.

Up to now more than forty painted caves

Bison: detail of the cave paintings at Altamira (near Santander, Spain) which are estimated to be some 15,000 to 20,000 years old. (Courtesy Spanish National Museum)

Unique composition of man, bison, and rhinoceros: detail of the Lascaux paintings. (Courtesy Archives Photographiques, Paris)

are known in central and southwestern France and about thirty-five in northern Spain. Of these the most famous are the Spanish caves of Altamira and Castillo and the French caves of Combarelles and Font-de-Gaume, all of which contain paintings of Magdalenian technique done during the so-called "Reindeer Age."

In 1940 five French boys, looking for their lost hunting dog, discovered the cave of Lascaux, a veritable prehistoric picture gallery. The paintings of this cave vary greatly in artistic merit: a few are said to be masterpieces. Among the animals represented at Lascaux, there are many horses with short legs and barrel-shaped bodies, shaggy little ponies, deer with delicate branching antlers, two charging bisons, a horse falling over a precipice, a jumping cow, a big sprawling, pregnant, black cow, an aurochs seventeen feet long, and several giant crimson bulls that look like Texas Longhorns. Some of these, like the bison of Altamira, are static, calm, and imposing; others surge with the life and brutal power of actual animals seen out on the steppes.

Despite its realism and impressionism, the art of Lascaux, like Upper Paleolithic art in general, makes no attempt at a composition showing a hunting scene or a conflict be-tween beasts and men. Only one has been found (at Lascaux) which tells a story. And this is the story: a man out hunting has wounded a bison; the bison charges and gores him to death. Along comes a wooly rhinoceros who with his murderous horn rips open the bison and slowly walks away leaving the bison with his guts sagging to the ground. And on a stick a little bird sits and looks on.

To explain the origin of prehistoric art, we need not invoke the familiar modern theories of totemism, sympathetic magic, or voodooism, whereby the hunter artist tried to put a hex on those animals so that they would allow themselves to be killed. Although magic undoubtedly played an important part in the lives of Upper Paleolithic people, it is also possible that some of the hunters enjoyed depicting the only life they knew and did so in the deepest recesses of their caves by the light of a mosswick lamp.

The first known examples of Italian engravings of the Franco-Cantabrian animal style were discovered in 1950 in a cave on the small island of Levanzo, 10 miles from the west coast of Sicily. The bulls, stags, and horses show the same vigor and realism as those engraved on the walls of French and

Spanish caves. Prior to this discovery the only example of cave art in Italy was a crudely engraved ox in the Romanelli cave in southern Apulia. The five soapstone statuettes found in the Grimaldi caves, besides the one found at Savignano near Modena and another quite recently at Chiozza in Emilia, all show the feminine figure with pendulous breasts, protruding buttocks, and the sex organs emphasized at the expense of the face, hands, and feet. The discovery of swaybacked, steatopygous or fat-rumped figurines have led some to infer an African origin for Grimaldian culture. This is quite improbable. More than ninety such figurines occur at Gravettian sites in both Europe and Siberia. Nor is it likely that these "Venuses" are cult objects of a fertility goddess. They

The Venus of Willendorf (ca. 30,000-15,000 B.C.). (Courtesy Prähistorische Sammlung, Naturhistorisches Museum, Vienna)

may rather be the product of masculine imagination, which attempts to express in art the things of greatest interest and desire.

The Grimaldians excelled, however, in the art of personal decoration. They made pendants from bone and ivory, bracelets and necklaces out of pierced stag teeth and tiny shells. They used thousands of these shells for making headdresses and as sequins for sewing on to their garments. The classic ground for these ornaments is the Riviera, the country of the Grimaldi caves.

End of Old Stone Age

After several thousand years, the brilliant culture of the Magdalenians came to an end, and with them ends the story of the Old Stone Age. Nevertheless the Neolithic or New Stone Age did not follow immediately. There intervened a span of about 5000 years between the two Italian stone ages, a period that was very short in terms of the Old Stone Age, but was as long as all recorded history. This interval is called the Mesolithic.

The Mesolithic Period

Around 10,000 years ago the last great ice-sheet was on its way north. The Sahara region, once a hunter's paradise, was drying up and its inhabitants had begun their trek toward the Nile Valley or the Atlantic coast. In western and northern Europe steppe and tundra gave way to forest. First birches and willows, then pines, and later the hazel followed by elms, oaks, and beeches invaded the old hunting grounds. With the change in the weather and the advance of the forests the park-tundra fauna—the mammoth, the bison, the horse, and the reindeer—disappeared. In their stead came the elk, the roe deer, the wild pig, and the squirrel. New hunting techniques, less socially organized and more individualistic than those of the Ice Age, now came into use against the smaller and more elusive animals of the forest. The hunting of small furred animals as well as auks, swans, geese, and ducks required the use of traps, snares, and arrows

tipped with tiny flints like those used in the earlier forest cultures of North Africa and southern Italy. Hooks, nets, funnel-shaped traps, and boats appeared for fishing in rivers and creeks. The gathering of limpets, mussels, and other shell-fish, the staple diet of many communities along the shores of Italy, Spain, France, and Denmark, gave rise to the manufacture of leather bags, wicker baskets, and possibly clay pots. Thus the changing environment of post-glacial Europe forced these hunter-fisher people of the Mesolithic to make some material progress. In some ways, notably in the making of pottery and the grinding of stone axes, they anticipated the Neolithic.

Left to themselves, they probably would in the course of time have hit upon a more systematic cultivation of plants or the breeding of animals. It was not among them, but somewhere in the Middle East that the first steps were taken to emancipate mankind from dependence upon external nature. The Mesolithic tribes of Europe were usually content to be hunters, fishers, and foodgatherers, and many of them remained this till around 2500 B.C., except where external influences had made themselves felt.

The Neolithic Period

Before 6500 B.C. or about 4000 years before Europe had even begun to emerge from savagery, there developed in the Middle East a series of basic changes which radically altered man's way of life for all time. The first and most important of these changes was the development of farming and stock raising, which made possible the production and control of the food supply. Unlike the hunters, fishers, and berry pickers of contemporary Europe, the people of the East now "stored" their meat on the hoof, their grain in jars or bins. Farming increased their security against famine, stimulated the growth of population, and gave them more time to do different things.

The agricultural revolution permitted an improved division of labor. While the children watched the flocks, the women made baskets, pottery, and hoed the crops. The men built houses, made tools, and mined, traded, hunted, and fished. Some specialized in the making of pottery and bartered their pots for food and clothing. Others took up weaving or tool-making. This development of the arts and crafts encouraged the rise of settled village life. Throughout the Middle East from Egypt to Iran and India there sprang up a string of village communities, like Jarmo in Kurdistan (radio-carbon date: 4756 ± 300 B.C.) or Jericho in Palestine (radio-carbon date: before 6500 B.C.), containing farmers, craftsmen, merchants, tribal leaders, and priests. Some of these settlements eventually became cities and centers of city states, governed by professional rulers and defended by professional soldiers. Thus the so-called "Neolithic Revolution" laid the ground work for brilliant urban civilizations in Egypt, Babylonia, India, and China.

Around 3000 B.C., the rays of Middle Eastern culture began to fall upon Europe. Passing from tribe to tribe and from region to region, the salient technical features of the Neolithic—farming, weaving, and the making of pottery—slowly became diffused over the European continent. They probably followed several paths of transmission: the shores of North Africa and thence Sicily and Spain, Crete and the other islands of the eastern Mediterranean, and around the Black Sea to South Russia and the Danube basin. By these routes came most of our domestic animals and cultivated grains. Wheat, for example, the most important cereal in Neolithic Europe, first started probably in the highlands of Iran and of Abyssinia, then spread into Egypt, Turkestan, and Afghanistan; thence westwards to South Russia, the Danube basin, Switzerland, and Denmark. Besides bread or common wheat, the two varieties of wheat most commonly cultivated in prehistoric Europe were emmer and dinkel. These, together with six-rowed barley, were transmitted from the East by way of North Africa and Spain or Asia Minor.

A group of farmers from Asia Minor found their way to the fertile valleys and plains of Thessaly and founded at Sesklo one of the earliest peasant communities on the European continent. Here they lived in small, unfortified villages of square or round huts built of reeds or sun-dried bricks. They hunted, fished, and tilled the ground with polished stone hoes. They grew wheat, barley, peas, figs, and pears, kept cattle, sheep, goats, and pigs. They could spin and weave. Their pottery, mostly of red monochrome ware, was thin and well made. The earliest pottery was the best in technique and decoration. Though they had carried with them the traditions of pre-Sumerian painted ware, they did not rigidly maintain these traditions, but worked out new designs in the form of squares, triangles, diamonds, and checks. Ray or flame patterns were also very common. Perhaps, because theirs was a frontier society, their pottery steadily deteriorated, the designs becoming cruder, the clay coarser, and the shapes more clumsy.

Offshoots from Sesklo and neighboring sites moved north into Macedonia and settled around Servia and Olynthus. Presently the entire valley of the Vardar northwards to the Danube and beyond was covered with villages of peasants, who lived by agriculture, stock-breeding, hunting, and fishing. Fishing was especially important along the Danube, where the settlers learned from the native Mesolithic population how to fish for sturgeon with nets, hooks, and double-barbed harpoons. One of these fishing villages was the famous site of Vinča on the south bank of the Danube just below Belgrade. Similar Danubian cultures combining farming with fishing developed and flourished between 3000 and 2300 B.C. in Romania and along the Körös and Theiss rivers in Hungary. We shall refer to these later in our discussion of Neolithic Italy.

Most experts on prehistoric Italy have abandoned the old theory of a gap between the Old and the New Stone Ages. Some nineteenth-century scholars, ignoring the existence of the Mesolithic, assumed that the Upper Paleolithic hunters evacuated the southern part of Europe and followed the mammoth and reindeer herds retreating to the North. In later times a horde of white invaders from Asia and Africa moved into the area and brought with them an advanced form of Neolithic culture. These invaders were short, dark, long-headed Mediterraneans.

These attractive theories rested on a rather fragile basis. One of them assumed that the invaders introduced from Egypt the practice of burying the dead in a curled up position. Actually the practice was not new. Nor were hut-dwellings, pottery, and the polishing of stone hatchets totally unknown. We now know that the Mesolithic descendants of the Cro-Magnons and Gravettians had not died out when cultural elements began to arrive from the Balkans, Africa, and the Middle East. The effect of this influence was neither sudden nor catastrophic. In many, perhaps all, excavated sites in both Italy and Sicily the use of some Paleolithic tools persisted throughout the entire Neolithic period. Undoubtedly the introduction of Neolithic civilization into Italy was a slow process of acculturation or cultural diffusion accelerated at isolated points by the movement of small bands of colonists and traders throughout the Mediterranean basin.

Some of the Neolithic inhabitants of Italy lived in caves, others in huts. Most of the cave-dwellers were confined to Liguria, the Eastern Alps, Malta with its unique and beautiful subterranean temples, Tuscany, the Abruzzi, parts of Apulia, northwestern Sicily, and Sardinia. The Italian cave dwellers lived by hunting, fishing, and herding, and like Polyphemus in Homer's *Odyssey*, drove their animals into the caves for the night. In these same caves they buried their dead. The hut-dwellers lived in the more fertile areas, especially the river valleys. They also hunted, fished, and kept cattle, pigs, sheep, and goats. In addition they cultivated the ground with stone hoes lashed to wooden handles. Hand-mills, found at several sites, indicate that they raised grain and made bread. Most huts were round or oval, but in eastern Sicily some were rectangular. They were generally erected over pits from three to seven feet deep and from seven to fifteen feet in diameter; around the pits posts were sunk and covered with wickerwork of brush plastered over with mud. In the South, where there was less need for protection against wind and cold, the huts were built on level ground. The huts were rarely isolated. They were usually found in groups of from twenty to forty.

The Village

In southern Italy both the individual huts and the villages were surrounded by ditches. Though dug almost 4300 years ago, the ditches are still visible from the air when the area containing them is covered with standing crops of grain. Air photographs of the Table-land of Apulia revealed nearly 200 Neolithic settlement sites. The settlements can be divided into three classes: a) the single homestead, b) the "patriarchal household" with 20 to 50 huts, c) the large village containing perhaps 270 family huts. The average single homestead was a farmhouse enclosed by three concentric circular ditches, the first about 160 feet in diameter, the middle one about 500 feet in diameter, and the outer one from 600 to 900 feet in diameter. The purpose of the third ditch no doubt was to protect the garden and crops from stray animals and mark the bounds of ownership. The village, similarly enclosed and measuring 2400 feet by 1500 wide, lay in one corner of a large oval-shaped area about three times its size. The enclosed field outside the village was either a pasture where animals grazed within sight of the villagers or more probably the most valuable cultivated ground worked on a communal basis. Both private enterprise and an elementary form of collectivism appear to have been practiced in Neolithic Apulia.

The Neolithic inhabitants of Apulia, now herdsmen and farmers as well as hunters, required pots for holding grain and milk, for making cheese, and for cooking. The art of making pottery, discovered in the Middle East, became known by 3000 B.C. to the people of Crete, Greece, the Balkans, and North Africa, and knowledge of this art soon reached Italy.

The pottery found in Apulian caves and villages are beautifully decorated vases, bowls, and cups, as well as the rougher, coarser wares. Apulian pottery can be divided into three main periods. Characteristic of Period I is the early coarse ware decorated before firing with random dots, strokes, cuts, zigzags, or kinky lines impressed with the fingernail, sharpened bits of wood or flint, or mollusk shells. This impressed ware was common in eastern Sicily and is similar to pottery found in North Africa, Spain, or in early Thessaly. The pottery of Period II with its highly polished vases painted red or dark brown on buff is called scratched ware because the designs—chevrons, cross-hatched triangles, zigzag bands, and checks—were scratched on the jars and bowls after firing. A thin white coating was applied over the patterns to make them stand out. This fine thin ware, often identified by its site's name of Matera, was in turn superseded after 2500 B.C. by the beautiful painted wares of Period III. Of the same pale fabric as the red-painted Matera ware, the cups and bowls of this period were decorated in purplish brown paint, with many designs—broad bands, triangles, zigzags, spirals, and meanders. While the spiral and meander patterns hint of Thessalian or Balkan origin and the tubular lug handles of vases often surmounted by bull or ram heads recall Egypt, it is probable that Apulian painted pottery developed from imitations of imported wares.

All three types of Apulian pottery made their appearance in the North. The painted ware, in particular, appeared on the island of Capri, at Ripoli in Abruzzo, at Chiozza in Emilia, in Tuscany, in the caves of Liguria, and in France as far north as Normandy. All of central and western Italy seems for a time to have been a cultural province of Apulia. This advance of Apulian culture to the North met a counter current of Danubian culture flowing in from the Northeast by way of the Julian Alps. That was the Theiss culture of Hungary.

Influence of Danubian Culture

Pushing north from Macedonia and the valley of the Vardar, bands of Neolithic farmers entered the plains of Hungary and settled along the banks of the Körös, where they taught the native survivors of Paleolithic society the use of the hoe in the cultivation of the earth. Sometime after 2600 B.C., the Körös culture gave way to another that sprang up along the banks of the Tisza or Theiss. Increasing wealth and population in this fine farming and fishing region enabled the Theiss people to dominate Danubian Europe for almost four hundred years and to extend their cultural influence as far west as the Rhine, as far east as the Dnieper, and southwards into Jugoslavia, Thessaly, and northern Italy. Some notable features of this Hungarian culture (as they appear in several sites recently excavated in northern and eastern Italy) are: a) square-mouthed vases; b) black-polished bowls with incised spiral and meander designs coated after firing with thick, powdery white, red, or orange paint, that is, "crusted" ware; c) ladles with hollow or socketed handles; d) pintaderas or clay stamp seals; e) clay figurines of naked female divinities; and f) stone-lined graves between the huts in which the corpse was placed curled up on its left side. Dogs are occasionally found buried with their masters.

The most important contribution of the Theiss culture to the development of Italy was the introduction of copper. The discovery at Vicenza (40 miles west of Venice) of an ax of pure copper along with a square-mouthed vase proves that Theiss cultural elements must have entered Italy soon after 2200 B.C., when the Hungarian Copper Age began. Prior to that time the Theiss people had been using copper as trinkets and ornaments. Their trading relations in the Aegean region and with the copper-using cultures of South Russia and Romania had led to the use of copper for tools and weapons in much of central Europe. During the final phases of Theiss cultural history, the knowledge of metal-working, first developed in the Ancient Near East, was transmitted to Italy at the close of the third millennium B.C.

The Culture of Vučedol and Arrival of the Indo-Europeans

About 2000 B.C., another Balkan culture, that of Vučedol in Jugoslavia, made its appearance in northern Italy, in Tuscany and in Latium. This Balkan culture included the stone battle-ax, the high-handled cup, the cross-footed vase, and the round-bodied cord-decorated pottery, all of which are associated with the warlike Indo-Europeans.

The original homeland of the Indo-European ancestors of the Indo-Iranians, Celts, Germans, Slavs, Greeks, Romans, and many other related national and linguistic groups has been long and hotly debated. Some writers have located it in Jutland, others, especially the linguists, between Kiev of South Russia, Saxony, and Thuringia of central Germany, others again in the region of the Kuban and the steppes of South Russia, whence came the oldest corded pottery and battle axes. Modern archeologists are inclined to challenge the assumption of a folk-migration from any single quarter. They would explain the emergence of grammatical forms, of refined declension and inflection, and the whole development of the European linguistic and social order after 3000 B.C. as the effect of the diffusion of Middle Eastern "food-producing" techniques among the Mesolithic hunters, and fishermen who formed a continuum across the plains of Europe from the Ural Mountains and the Black Sea to the English Channel. The final answer to this problem must await discovery of new archaeological material.

Two centuries or perhaps even more before the arrival of the Balkan influences, the entire lake country of northern Italy from the Maritime Alps in the west to Verona in the east was taken over by a people whose cultural history began in North Africa and Spain. From Spain, where a typically Neolithic society had been evolving under North African stimulus since the beginning of the third millennium B.C., colonists made their way into southern France and settled along the Rhône valley among the descendants of the Magdalenian reindeer hunters and salmon fishermen. Adopting the hunting and fishing techniques of the natives, they converted the region to an agricultural economy and created a vigorous civilization, which by 2500 B.C. had expanded into the lake districts of Savoy, western Switzerland, and northern Italy.

The Lake-Dwellers and Bell-beaker Folk

The communities making up this civilization were so well-organized and able to adjust to different environments that they could thrive in caves or fortified hill-top camps as in France or in lake-dwellings as in Switzerland and Italy. The Swiss lake-dwelling culture of Cortaillod and the Italian culture of Lagozza (near Milan) both stem from the Chassey culture of southern France.

The lake-dwellers were farming people who lived in villages of rectangular frame houses or oblong huts with thatched roofs. Their houses stood on platforms resting on piles driven into lake bottoms and the farmers got to their fields by means of light bridges or dugout canoes. To cut down trees for piles or clear land for farming they used stone axes and adzes mounted in tapered antler sleeves fitted into straight wooden handles. The discovery also of antler and stone hoeheads, plowshares, sickle flints, grain milling stones, and carbonized grains of wheat, barley, millet, peas, and flax, as well as of apple, pear, and poppy seeds, proves that agriculture was a major source of livelihood. Cattle, sheep, and pigs provided their meat supply, although hunting and fishing still bulked large in their economy. They made clothing from flax, hemp, and wool and brewed cider from apples and perhaps from poppies.

The pottery found in these Swiss and Italian lake-dwelling sites consists of simple round-bottomed pots and bowls, open, bag-shaped, and having string-hole lugs in place of real handles. In the Milan area the lake-dwellers made a very rough ware, but some of their unpainted red and black pottery was made of excellent clay, was well-fired and carefully polished. Further east, the lake-dwellers around Polada produced an inferior type of pottery, carelessly made and baked over open fires. This inferior pottery continued to be produced down through the years into the Bronze Age, which in Italy began shortly after 1800 B.C.

The close cultural relations established between North Italy and southwestern Europe in the middle of the third millennium B.C. were further intensified toward its close by the arrival in the Po Valley of bands of merchant adventurers from Spain known as the Bell-beaker folk. They owe their name to a large bell-shaped beer mug, which was made of a fine grit-tempered ware brick red to black in color and decorated with horizontal bands of "rouletted" hatchings put on with a short-toothed comb. They were a rowdy, hard-drinking group of traders who did much to open up commercial relations in Europe and diffuse knowledge of metallurgy. Armed with the bow and arrow, the flat-tanged dagger, and the halberd, they fought their way from one country to another. By sea they traded in copper, gold, and amber from Spain to Sicily and Sardinia and from Portugal to Britain and to the shores of the North Sea and the Baltic. Moving overland through France, they crossed the Rhine and settled in southern Germany and Bohemia, where they increased and expanded in every direction. A chemical analysis of the copper tools and weapons found in the famous North Italian cemetery of Remedello indicates that some of them migrated from Germany to northern Italy. In the Copper and Early Bronze Age northern Italy was a crossroads where cultures and people met coming from North, East, and West.

Development of Native Cultures: "Apennine." At the dawn of the Bronze Age around 1800 B.C. there were three main cultures in Italy: the lake-dwellers along the Alpine foothills, the round-hut villagers of the central Po Valley, and the inhabitants of the swamp lands further east. The rest of the peninsula, from Bologna to Taranto, that is, contained a third culture, which may be called "Apennine" to distinguish it from those of the Po Valley. Different cultures from these three prevailed on the islands of Sicily, Sardinia, Corsica, and Malta. During the late third and early second millennia B.C. Sicily was subject to Cretan and Mycenaean influences as well as to those emanating from North Africa and Spain. The tower structures of Sardinia, the so-called Nuraghen, and the equally famous underground rock chambers of Malta have caused much puzzlement. Thus similarly exposed to Balkan and Western influences, all regions of Italy had reached a common level of civilization by 1800 B.C. All practiced inhumation in disposing of the dead and shared in a common bronze industry, though North Italy, in closer contact with the metal-working centers of central Europe, produced better tools and weapons—swords, daggers, axes, and sickles.

The "Apennine" people excelled in decorated pottery, keeping alive the traditions inherited from Vučedol of double-line bands, spiral and meander motifs, and those curiously exaggerated jug handles surmounted by horns, crescents, volutes, and animal heads. Their fondness for small plastic animals and human figurines also betray Balkan influence, but they did not slavishly imitate these Balkan elements, integrating them instead with their own cultural traditions to form a culture distinctively Italian. The earliest remains found in the environs of Rome are "Apennine."*

The Terremare Culture

The Apennine culture, passing through several successive phases, persisted for more than a thousand years, and was contemporary with another, which existed in North Italy. Around 1700 B.C. there appeared in the Po Valley, probably from western Hungary, a typical fully-developed Bronze Age culture, commonly known as the *Terremare,* a name the peasants of Emilia in the nineteenth century gave to those mounds of black earth they spread over their fields. The mounds, four to eighteen acres in area and from ten to fourteen feet high, were built up by the refuse of centuries of living in that triangular region bounded by Bologna, Piacenza, and the southern banks of the Po and in a few districts north of the river around Mantua, Brescia, and Cremona. Here for almost 700 years the Terremare people lived in open villages of post-built huts of wattle and daub, at first round and later oblong in shape. Near the center of the village was an area which may have served as a market place or corral for cattle. The early villages were not built on piles like

lake or swamp villages nor were they laid out according to any regular plan. The pile-built settlement did not appear until about 1000 B.C., during the last phase of Terremare history, when the climate of Emilia became cold and wet and the region was subject to periodic flooding, a condition aggravated, according to some writers, by the gradual deforestation of the Apennine watersheds. Even then pile dwellings were required only on the lower plains; the villages set on high land or on hill tops have left no evidence of anything but hut posts.

The people of the Terremare are distinguished from the rest of the people of north and central Italy for their more advanced culture which showed close affinities with that of contemporary Hungary. They were superior farmers and breeders of live stock, especially cattle and pigs. The discovery of cartwheels made of bone, horn, or bronze and of bridle bits fitted with the Hungarian type of horn cheek-piece indicates that they were the first people in Italy to use horses for draft and perhaps for hunting purposes. Though not the first to introduce the bronze industry into Italy, they were the most skilled in the craft of bronze-casting and in the making of sickles, axes, chisels, daggers, swords, knives, razors, combs, brooches, and safety pins.

In the making of pottery the Terremare people showed the most skill and originality during the earliest phases of their settlement in Italy. The finest of their early wares were highly burnished gray and black vases decorated, in a style quite new to Italy, with fluted designs and with plastic warts or knobs surrounded by concentric circles. In the later period of the culture, Terremare pottery lost its originality and fell more and more under the influence of the Apennine tradition with its elaborate horned and crescent-shaped handles. The progressive decadence of Terremare pottery accompanied a general cultural decay precipitated by the harshness of the climate around 1000 B.C., which must have made life very miserable in the lower plains of Emilia.

Perhaps life had become hard enough to drive the later Terremare people into a primitive kind of communism. Without distinc-

* Recent archaeological excavations inside Rome have proved that Rome was inhabited by the "Apenninic" people at least seven centuries before the mythical date of its founding (753 B.C.). Penetrating about twenty feet below the surface, the excavators found twelve fragments of dark brown pottery decorated with incised dots and geometrical figures which were characteristic of "Apenninic" pottery.

tion of age or sex, wealth or class, the living probably worked for the community, and when they died the rough urns containing their ashes were placed in the common village cemetery, the "terremare of the dead." This form of burial-rite was probably confined to the later Terremare people; their predecessors undoubtedly buried the dead in the ground as did the other people of Italy and their European contemporaries of the Early Bronze Age. Though cremation has long been thought a hallmark of Terremare culture, actual evidence for the rite can be found in only three of sixty-two authentic sites and these three belong to the later period. Recent research has shown that the Terremaricoli adopted cremation as their burial rite after the mass invasion of Italy by cremation-practising folk from central Europe. The invaders cast Italy into a new cultural phase, in which the Terremaricoli played a role of only local importance.

The early centuries of the first millennium B.C. witnessed the arrival in Italy of the Indo-European speaking tribes either by way of the Alpine passes or across the Adriatic Sea. Coming in groups of varying size, they finally imposed their language and customs on the native population. The outcome of these invasions was the division of Italy east of the twelfth meridian into three linguistic zones: The western or "First Italic" zone extended along the west coast comprising southern Etruria, Latium, Campania, Calabria, and the eastern part of Sicily. Faliscan, Latin, Sicel, and related dialects were spoken in this zone. The central or "Second Italic" zone comprising the entire central part of the peninsula from Rimini to the northern borders of Lucania belonged to the Oscan-Umbrian linguistic group. The eastern zone, which extended along the Adriatic, encompassed an Illyrian linguistic group consisting of Venetic, East Italic, and Messapic dialects. That part of the peninsula lying west of the twelfth meridian belonged, on the whole, to the Etruscans and to the so-called "Ligurians," about whose racial and linguistic affiliations practically nothing is known.

The rise of the various Indo-European dialects in Italy seems to have been the result of the arrival of two large invading groups, probably from the Danube basin and the Balkans. These were the Villanovans and the Fossa people.

The Villanovans and Fossa People

The term Villanovan is derived from Villanova, a small hamlet five miles northeast of Bologna, where the Villanovan culture appeared in its most typical, and best known form. Here the Villanovans lived in villages of round huts. They cremated their dead and put the ashes into tall biconical urns of earthenware and, later, of bronze. The earthenware urn was a hand-made, smoke-blackened vase decorated with incised geometrical patterns—meanders, rows of chevrons, and swastikas. Covered with an inverted basin or bowl, it was placed in a round hole or rectangular stone-lined tomb. Various tools and weapons and small ornaments such as brooches, bracelets, and razors were placed inside and around the tomb. These objects are our chief source of information on the date and origin of the Villanovans. Unfortunately, the evidence is inconclusive. Where the Villanovans actually came from is still undetermined. Some scholars assume that they were descendants of the Terremaricoli because of the similarity of burial rite; others believe that they came down over the Alps, swept through the Po Valley without leaving a trace of their passage, and finally settled around Bologna. Against both opinions stands the fact that the first and oldest Villanovans lived not near Bologna, but in Latium and Etruria. These were the Southern Villanovans, many of whom may have fled northward to escape Etruscan domination.

The Southern Villanovans used two kinds of funeral urns: a) the standard biconical urn covered either with an inverted bowl as at Bologna or with a crested helmet of bronze or pottery, and b) a hut-urn, which was a miniature imitation of their round or quadrangular houses. Their oldest cemeteries are found at Allumiere, Vetulonia, and Tarquinii in Etruria, at Terni in western Umbria, under the Forum at Rome, and on the Alban Hills. The shape and decoration of their vases, brooches, swords, and razors have led recent archaeologists to be-

A typical helmet incinerary urn of the Villanovan period. (Courtesy Fratelli Alinari, Florence)

southwards to Calabria. These were the so-called Fossa people.

Although the Fossa people used the same cemeteries as the Villanovans or adjacent ones, they did not cremate their dead, but buried them in long rectangular pits or trenches lined with stones. Hence archaeologists call them Fossa or Trench-grave people. Their culture, a blend of many elements—Balkan, Sicilian, Greek, and native Italic—was quite dynamic in its influence upon the Southern Villanovans. Their water-jug was probably a prototype of the Villanovan burial urn and the geometric designs with which they decorated their pottery and scabbards—meanders, zigzag lines, swastikas, false spirals, and concentric circles—were freely used by both the Southern and the Northern Villanovans. This fact supports the hypothesis that the original home of the Northern Villanovans was Etruria, where they had come under the cultural influence first of the Fossa people and later of the Etruscans before migrating northwards to Bologna and Rimini.

Influence of the Etruscans on the Northern Villanovans. The Northern Villanovans, from the earliest time of settlement at Bologna, showed clear signs of the dynamic influence of the Etruscans, who seem to have first set foot on the shores of Tuscany early in the ninth century B.C. (See chapter III.) The Etruscans brought with them from Asia Minor the most advanced metal-working techniques of the East—the art of hammering designs upon bronze and of brazing or hard soldering. These techniques were new to the people of Italy, but the Villanovans learned

lieve that the Villanovans made their way over the Adriatic from the Balkans, later crossed the Apennines, and finally settled in Latium and Etruria sometime during the ninth century B.C. Here they lived peacefully beside another Indo-European people, probably also of Balkan origin, who had earlier settled along the west coast from Etruria

Two hut urns of the Villanovan period, discovered in the Alban Hills near Rome. (Courtesy Fratelli Alinari, Florence)

rapidly. As the eighth century B.C. opened, Bologna, at first probably a mere outpost of Etrusco-Villanovan culture, became the hub of the bronze export trade from Etruria to the Po Valley and the regions beyond the Alps, and later it became one of the busiest metal working centers in Italy. Perhaps some of the metal goods produced here such as rings, hairpins, brooches, wavy-bladed knives, and half-moon razor blades owed little to Etruscan craftsmanship, but the pails, buckets, and bowls wrought from hand-hammered bronze sheets as well as the girdles and helmets and the brazed snaffle bits were all reproductions of models originating in some Asiatic center. The snaffle bit with its interlocking rings and the cheek-piece in the form of a horse was a rather crude replica of snaffle bits common at Luristan in northwest Persia. The crested helmet and the broad lozenge-shaped belt closely resembled those worn by the Hittites, while the buckets with free-swinging handles were typical in Egypt and Assyria. Furthermore, the long-necked water bird and the double-headed duck were decorative artforms distinctive of both Asia Minor and Etruria.

Though these bronze wares and decorative motifs belonged to the earliest phases of the Villanovan settlement at Bologna, they had appeared among the Etruscans before. They emerged at Bologna before they became common in North Italy, and in North Italy before they did beyond the Alps. The movement of metallurgical techniques from South to North during the late Bronze Age and early Iron Age and the absence of any trace of an early Villanovan settlement in the Po Valley, whose fertile plains ought to have been more attractive to an invader than the rolling hills of Umbria, cast doubt on the familiar and almost sacrosanct thesis that the Villanovans first entered Italy by way of the Eastern Alps.

The familiar thesis that the Villanovan invasion of Italy occurred after the Iron Age had begun in Europe must also be discarded. Though the absolute chronology of the European Iron Age is hard to establish, it is now generally believed that central Europe did not enter the Iron Age proper until around 650 B.C., almost a century and a half after the Etruscans had begun to work the mines of Elba and Tuscany. If, as now seems probable, the arrival of the Etruscans preceded the migration of the Villanovans from Etruria to Bologna, we may with some confidence date the earliest Villanovan settlement at Bologna at 700 B.C.

During the next two centuries, the Villanovans had made notable progress from barbarism to civilization. Glass and amber were becoming abundant, and iron, at first scarce and rarely used, became exceedingly common. The wealth produced by agriculture, craftsmanship, and commerce led to the rise of a luxury-loving leisure class who rode horses, drove chariots, and adorned themselves with expensive jewelry. These economic and social changes are reflected in the tombs. While the older graves were uniformly poor in funeral furniture, the later ones showed a marked variation in the quantity and quality of the objects placed in and around the burial urns.

The Villanovans apparently never lived in a state of collectivism such as that practiced by the early Terremare folk. They were moving toward a new order of individualism and private property. How much of this social advance they owed to the Etruscans is hard to determine. It seems unlikely that the Etruscans ever attempted to dominate or absorb the Northern Villanovans until the closing years of the sixth century. By that time Villanovan society was breaking down and was soon to lose its identity.

III

THE ETRUSCANS

Most modern knowledge of the Etruscans, the first urban and highly civilized people of Italy, is derived from the ruins of their cities and, more particularly, their tombs. Tombs of all sizes, shapes, and types—the well and trench tombs of Villanovan times, the *tumuli,* those great mushroom-shaped, grass covered mounds with bases of hewn stone, the circular stone vaults built into hillsides, and the corridor tombs cut out of rock—all these, whether containing pottery, metal wares, furniture, jewelry, or wall paintings, enable us to describe the cultural life of the Etruscan people.

Other sources are of lesser value. Although nearly 10,000 Etruscan inscriptions (some dating back to the seventh century B.C., others as late as the age of Augustus) have been found and can be accurately translated, they have not yet shed much light

on early Etruscan history because only ten of them contain more than thirty words and nearly all of them contain only a repetitious monotony of proper names, religious formulae, dedications, and epitaphs. Nor have Greek and Latin writers been more satisfactory as sources. Cicero, for example, alluded merely to certain aspects of the religious life of the Etruscans, Livy to their military strength and their wars with Rome.

The historical origin of the Etruscans, endlessly debated since ancient times, cannot be established with certainty until more conclusive material is available. The archaeological sites in Etruscan Italy indicate a gradual change from Italian Bronze Age tools and customs to Etruscan practices. Some writers have, therefore, held that the Etruscans had been living in Etruria ever since the beginning of the Bronze Age; others that they migrated from central Europe some time before 1000 B.C. by way of the Alpine passes and settled first in the Po Valley and later in Etruria.

Archaeological evidence strengthens the hypothesis of an Eastern origin. The appearance, during the eighth and seventh centuries, of two types of Aegean or Eastern tombs, the corridor and the chamber tomb surmounted by a *tumulus,* suggests the arrival of the Etruscans themselves in two successive waves. It is most unlikely that burial traditions should have been transferred through ordinary commercial contacts. Nor can commerce alone account for the presence in Etruria of so wide a variety of Eastern cultural elements (see pp. 24–25)—the metal-working techniques, the snaffle-bit, the crested helmet, the lozenge-shaped belt, the bucket with free-swinging handle, and the use of long-necked water birds and double-headed ducks as decorative motifs. Furthermore, the practice of foretelling the future through the inspection of the livers of sacrificed animals shows that the Etruscans must have shared in the religious heritage of Babylonia and the Hittites. Finally, Etruscan ships were based not on Greek but on Oriental models.

Conquest of Etruria

According to oldest Greek tradition, as recorded by Herodotus (I. 94), the Etruscans sailed from West Asia Minor in search of food and land and finally dropped anchor along the shores of Etruria north of the Tiber.

Running their ships aground on the flat, gray-black beaches of Etruria, they seized the nearby hill-tops and fortified them with wooden palisades. With their superior armament and military organization, they easily overpowered or subjected to servitude or enforced friendship the more numerous Villanovans and other natives. Using some of the natives as slaves and training others as soldiers, farmers, smiths, stonemasons, and carpenters, the invaders established several strong states, each dominated by a rich and powerful city. For economic reasons, they built cities in fertile valleys or near navigable streams; for military reasons, on hilltops, whose cliffs made them easily defended. At first they fortified the cities by wooden palisades or earthen ramparts, but after the fifth century B.C. by walls of solid masonry thirty feet high and thirteen feet thick. These massive walls, constructed of polygonal stones or of rectangular blocks laid in regular courses, were set with towers and broken by three or more gateways usually spanned at the top with straight architraves, but occasionally, after the third century, with true or voussoir arches.

Inside the walls, the Etruscans appear to have laid out some of their cities on a regular plan with the two main streets intersecting

An Etruscan tomb at Arretium (Arezzo). (Courtesy Istituto Italiano di Cultura)

An Etruscan circular or tumulus tomb at Caere (Cerveteri). (Courtesy Fratelli Alinari, Florence)

at right angles like the *cardo* and *decumanus* of the later Roman camp. The first buildings to go up were temples for the gods and palaces for the king. Then, as the population increased, side streets were paved, drains dug, and places built for public entertainment. These cities, as in Greece, were the political, military, religious, economic, and cultural centers of the various states which sprang up between the Tiber and the Arno before the seventh century B.C. Along the coast were Caere, Tarquinii, Vulci, Vetulonia, Rusellae, and Populonia. These were the oldest. With the possible exception of Veii to the South, such inland cities as Volsinii, Chiusi, Perugia, Cortona, and Arezzo were founded later and illustrate the growth and expansion of Etruscan civilization.

A dozen of the leading Etruscan cities formed a league primarily for the joint celebration of religious festivals. The jealousy of the member cities and their insistence on rights of sovereignty prevented the formation of a federal union which might have acted to repel aggression that threatened to destroy them one by one. When events at last forced the cities to unite, it was too late.

During the early period, the executive power of the Etruscan city-state was in the hands of a king elected and assisted by a council of aristocratic chiefs of whom he was one. He was the symbol of the state, the commander-in-chief of the army, the high priest of the state religion, and judge of his people. He wore purple robes like those of the Hittite nobles and possibly a golden crown, and rode in a chariot inlaid with ivory. As he passed through the streets, heralds preceded him and lictors accompanied him bearing the fasces and double-bitted ax, symbols of justice and religion. Yet he was neither a hereditary monarch nor an absolute ruler. Sometime during the sixth or fifth century B.C., the nobles stripped him of his political, military, and judicial powers, and set up republics governed by aristocratic senates and headed, as in Rome, by annually elected magistrates. The real power in the state was at all times in the hands of a small circle of landowning families (*lucumones*), who enjoyed all the privileges of a warrior aristocracy and priestly caste. In some cities they were later forced to share the government with a small group of wealthy craftsmen and merchants. The middle and lower classes consisted of small shopowners, petty traders, craftsmen, foreign immigrants, and the descendants of the conquered Villanovans, who worked as serfs or slaves on the large estates and served as foot-soldiers in time of war.

Etruscan Expansion in Italy

By the middle of the seventh century B.C. the Etruscans had firmly established themselves in Etruria proper and were prepared to expand. They crossed the Tiber, seized Rome, and overran most of Latium. Early in the sixth century they broke into Campania, where they founded Capua and several smaller towns. In 540 B.C., with the help of the Carthaginians, they won a naval victory over the Phocaean Greeks near Corsica and forced them to withdraw to Massilia (Marseille) from that well-wooded island. Encouraged, doubtless, by that victory, in 525 they attacked Cumae in order to break the Greek hold on the Campanian coastal region. They failed.

During the latter part of the sixth century B.C., the Etruscans also began to expand towards the North. Crossing the Apennines, they founded, on the banks of the Reno, the city of Marzabotto. Seventeen miles further north, on the site of modern Bologna, they built Felsina, a strong base for the conquest of the Po Valley. Pushing northwards into the interior of the valley, they laid the foundations of Modena, Parma, Placentia, Mantua, and of Melpum, near Milan. Along the eastern seaboard they built Rimini, Ravenna, Spina, the port of Felsina, and Adria from which the Adriatic received its name. By the end of the sixth century the power of the Etruscans was at its height, their influence extended from the Alps to Salerno and from the east to west coasts. Their ships sailed both seas and disputed with the navies of Greece and Carthage the mastery of the Western Mediterranean.

Decline of Etruscan Power

Despite the speed and vigor of their colonial expansion, the Etruscans were unable to prevent armed uprisings by rebellious subjects or to defend their conquests against the Romans, the Greeks, the Samnites, or the Gauls. The basic weakness lay in their inability to establish a stable political organization and a unified military command. In the first place, Etruscan colonialism stemmed not from the concerted drive of an expanding

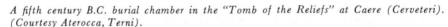

A fifth century B.C. burial chamber in the "Tomb of the Reliefs" at Caere (Cerveteri). (Courtesy Aterocca, Terni).

national state, but from the uncoordinated efforts of individual war-chiefs or conquistadores in whom love of adventure, desire for fortune, or dissatisfaction with domestic politics had generated a drive for conquest. The separate colonies they established were bound together by commercial, cultural, and religious ties rather than by a centralized political authority or firm alliance. They were unable to hold their easy conquests or to resist the attacks that brought their empire tumbling to ruins.

In 474 B.C. the Etruscans suffered a naval disaster at the hands of Hieron I of Syracuse, who later deposited an Etruscan helmet at Delphi as thanks for victory. That disaster broke Etruscan seapower and exposed Corsica, Elba, and Etruria itself to Greek attack. Rome, not content with the expulsion of her Etruscan rulers, passed to the offensive with an assault upon Veii. Finally, in 438 B.C., the Samnites took Capua and liquidated all Etruscan influence in Campania. At the beginning of the fourth century B.C., the Gauls burst into the Po Valley, seized Felsina, and marched south against Chiusi in Etruria. After 350 B.C. Etruria, her conquests lost, fought with Rome a losing battle for survival, which was to drag on for decades, and the political destiny of Italy passed forever out of her hands.

Etruscan Economy

The superstructure of Etruscan power and civilization rested on five solid economic pillars—agriculture, mining, manufacturing, lumbering, and commerce.

Agriculture

The Etruscan conquerors had put their subjects to work cutting the virgin forests and clearing land. The fields, with their rich deposits of volcanic ash and humus, produced excellent crops—grain for food and export and flax for making linen and sail cloth. An ingenious system of drainage tunnels (*cuniculi*) and dams won new land for the expanding population by draining swamps and checking erosion of the soil. On land not suitable for grain crops, they pastured cattle, sheep, and horses. On some terrains, like those around Orvieto, they planted vines and olive trees. Agriculture, then, did more than produce food and clothing for a dense population: it supplied the navy with sails, the army with horses, and the banquet hall with wines. It was, in short, the basis of Etruscan wealth, power, and luxury.

Mining and the Metal Trades

Since the Etruscans had already mastered the techniques of mining and metal working in their Asiatic homeland (see page 24), they followed up the conquest of the land with an energetic exploitation of the rich iron mines on the coastal island of Elba and the copper and tin deposits on the mainland. The most important center of the iron industry was Populonia, where the ore from Elba was smelted and some of the pig iron worked into finished wares, though the bulk of it was shipped to other metal-working centers in Etruria .or exported abroad. The mining and refining of copper was carried on around Volterra and Vetulonia; but Vulci, Perugia, and especially Arezzo played an important part in the forging and manufacture of iron or bronze wares such as helmets, weapons, chariots, urns, candelabra, mirrors, and statues. Besides equipping Etruscan armies, the metal industries bulked large in Etruria's foreign trade. In exchange for their metal exports, the Etruscans received amber, tin, lead, and other valuable raw materials from Spain, Britain, Gaul, and central and northern Europe. They imported from the lands of the Eastern Mediterranean a wide variety of luxury goods such as ivory, glass, scarabs, precious metals, jewels, delicate perfumes, rich tapestries, figured vases, pottery, and various metal utensils, all of which added to the elegance and splendor of the lives of the Etruscan upper classes.

Other Industries

The Etruscans did not confine their manufacturing to metal working. They made linen and woolen clothing, leather goods such as boots, harness, and hunting gear, delicate

jewelry and toilet-cases, and pottery both coarse and fine. Their pottery and jewelry deserve special mention. The early native pottery was a beautiful, shiny black ware known as *bucchero*. Whether made in molds or thrown with the wheel, it was baked in a closed kiln at a low temperature in order that the complete reduction of the ferrous oxides present in the clay would change the color from red to black. Besides bucchero, the Etruscan potters made excellent imitations of the beautiful black- and red-figured vases imported from Athens. The Etruscans remain unequaled as goldsmiths. The granulated gold fibula with twenty-eight figures, the massive necklaces and bracelets, the coronets and diadems are miracles of the goldsmith's art.

Lumbering and Commerce

Lumbering also contributed to the growth of Etruscan wealth and civilization. Virgin forests of beech, oak, fir, and pine supplied fuel for smelting and forging iron, wood for temples, houses, and furniture, and masts and beams for both fighting and trading ships.

Trade with Carthage, Sicily, Corcyra, Athens, Phoenicia, and Egypt kept Etruscan Italy in close contact with the advanced urban cultures of the Mediterranean world. It led ultimately to the introduction of money

economy in Italy and a standard coinage. The earliest coins found in Etruria were minted by Greek cities in Asia Minor. After 480 B.C. Etruscan cities began to issue their own silver, bronze, and gold coins, employing at first the Corcyrean variant of the Corinthian standard of weight and later the Attic standard which was at the time in circulation in both Sicily and the Athenian Empire. The reverse of most of these coins was blank (as those of Cyprus) but nearly all Etruscan coins have marks of value and grotesque heads and figures.

Etruscan foreign trade was mainly in luxury goods and high-priced wares. It enriched the trading and industrial classes and stimulated among the upper class a taste for elegance and splendor. Under Etruscan commercial leadership, the peoples of central

An Etruscan wine jug of Italo-Corinthian style (ca. 625–600 B.C.), showing a frieze of animals and monsters incised on a black background with touches of purple and yellow. (Courtesy Metropolitan Museum of Art, Fletcher Fund, 1925)

An Etruscan black-figured terracotta amphora (ca. 575–550 B.C.), showing banqueters, heralds and centaur, herdsmen and bull. (Courtesy Metropolitan Museum of Art, Gift of N. Koutoulakis, 1925)

Italy began to emerge from barbarism into the light of civilization.

Etruscan Culture and Religion

Etruscan literature must have come into existence sometime during the seventh century B.C., after the Etruscans had adopted for their own language a version of the Greek alphabet—probably from Cumae, a Chalcidian colony in Campania. Although Etruscan as a spoken language persisted as late as the second century A.D. and enough written materials survived till the first to enable the Emperor Claudius I (41–54 A.D.) to write twenty books on Etruscan history, all the Etruscan literary works are lost to us. There were probably many works on religion and the science of divination and, perhaps, annals of families and cities. There were also some rustic songs and liturgical chants. If the Etruscans composed dramas, or works on philosophy or science, no trace of them has been preserved or recovered.

If there was an intellectual vacuum in their society, the Etruscans redeemed themselves partially by their passion for music. They had a predilection for the flute, whose shrill strains accompanied all the activities of life—banquets, hunting expeditions, and athletic events, sacrifices and funerals, and even the flogging of slaves. As flutists, trumpeters, and lyre players they were renowned in Rome and throughout Greece. They also enjoyed folk and interpretative dancing. They danced at banquets, at religious festivals, and funerals. No matter what the occasion, they danced with ecstasy and abandon and with an almost orgiastic physical exuberance. This strange mixture of intense religious feeling with a brutal display of physical force was as baffling to their Greek contemporaries as it is to modern observers.

Sports

The tomb paintings show that outdoor sports assumed an important place in Etruscan life. Because of their association with religion and rites for the dead, sports were serious affairs and to neglect them was considered a sacrilege. There were also sociological reasons for the popularity of games. The growth of cities, the expansion of industry and commerce, and the rise of a wealthy leisured class gave the time, opportunity, and money for indulgence in sports of all kinds. Hunting and fishing, which for the prehistoric people had been a labor of necessity, became a form of recreation for the Etruscan rich. Next to hunting, riding and chariot racing were favorite sports. Organized athletic competitions, such as were common in Greece, were especially popular. They gave the upper class youth a chance to display their skill and prowess; they served also as a source of entertainment for the masses. Most illuminating in this regard is the great frieze in the *Tomb of the Chariots* at Tarquinii, which shows a vast stadium and a large number of spectators of both sexes applauding and cheering by turns the charioteers, the runners, the boxers, the wrestlers, and acrobats. Several paintings reveal the popularity of the equivalent of the Roman gladiator contest. This deadly sport, thought to have been a relic of the primitive custom of human sacrifices, formed part of the funeral games and must have been as thrilling as a Spanish bullfight or those bigger gladiatorial shows later offered at the Roman Colosseum.

Religion

Livy called Etruria the most religious of nations. Arnobius, the Christian writer, proclaimed her "the mother of superstitions." Of all the traditions which Rome inherited from the Etruscans religion resisted most firmly the flood-tide of Hellenism.

The clearest information on Etruscan religion comes to us from the Romans, who adopted many Etruscan beliefs and practices. Unfortunately the earliest pertinent Roman documents are as late as the last century of the Republic and these copy Etruscan sources that were not much older. Consequently, while the latest phases of Etruscan religious history are fairly well known, the early period is enigmatic. Most modern writers assert that the religion of the early Etruscans was pervaded with fear and gloom and dominated by a superstitious and authoritarian priesthood. This seems inconsistent with the evidence from the wall paintings of the tombs, which reveal the early Etruscans as a joyous, life-accepting people. They believed that the ruling powers of the universe—vague, impersonal, nameless, and incomprehensible—manifested themselves in every living thing: in men, in trees, in every flash of lightning, in lakes and streams, in the mountains and the sea. To penetrate their mystery, to make these powers speak, to wrest from them their

A large gold fibula with pendant, from the Regolini-Galassi tomb at Caere (Cerveteri). (Courtesy Fratelli Alinari, Florence)

A wall painting (ca. 500 B.C.), showing musicians in the "Tomb of the Leopards" at Tarquinii. (Courtesy Brogi, Florence)

secret, called for elaborate ritual. Once discovered, the will of the deity must be obeyed and executed with meticulous care. As time went on, Etruscan religion became more and more formal, theological, and legalistic, a vested interest of the priesthood, in whose hands lay the spiritual life of the people.

Under Greek influence the gods of the Etruscans became personalized and anthropomorphic. First among them was Tinia, later the Roman Jupiter, who spoke in thunder and hurled his lightning bolts across the sky. He executed the decrees of destiny, and with him were associated the two originally Italic goddesses, Uni or Juno and Minerva. Together they formed a celestial triad, whose temple (*kilth*) stood in every Etruscan city and on the Capitoline Hill at Rome. With nine other deities they formed the council of the Twelve Gods, six male and six female. A corresponding triad, the Etruscans believed, ruled over the lower world: Mantus (Hades), Mania (Persephone), and Tekum (Ceres), the goddess of the harvest. The Etruscans

also worshipped Vertumnus, the god of vines and gardens, and several other gods peculiar to certain cities and sacred places. In addition, there were the inferior deities or demons, of whom the most horrid was Charun, the conductor of the dead to the underworld fittingly represented in art with a big nose, pointed ears, bluish skin, and snakes crawling over his head and shoulders.

The most striking aspect of Etruscan religion was the so-called *disciplina*. This was an elaborate set of rules that aided the priests in their study and interpretation of natural phenomena to forecast the future, to know the will of the gods above, and to turn away the wrath of the malignant spirits beyond the grave. There were several kinds of divination, but the most important was the inspection of the livers of sheep and other animals slaughtered for sacrifice by special priests (*haruspices*). Thunder, lightning, and numerous other omens were also studied as tokens of the divine will, but the flight of birds, which the Romans studied with scrupulous care before battles, elections, or other affairs of state, was for the Etruscans of secondary importance.

This whole body of religious "science" was codified during the second century B.C., but none of it has come down to us, except the fragment which is preserved in Agram and inscribed on the linen wrappings of an Egyptian mummy of the late Hellenistic period, and, perhaps, an inscription from Capua. Of the ancient writers, Cicero was the only one to give any information on the subject, although for centuries the Romans turned to the Etruscan *disciplina* with implicit faith.

Etruscan Art

The art of the Etruscans was their most remarkable and enduring achievement. Religion gave it occasion and impulse. As in Greece, Etruscan temples and precincts were lavishly decorated with ornamental reliefs and paintings. Believing, like the Egyptians, in the survival of life after death, the Etruscans provided elaborate tombs for the dead, some of gigantic size such as the tumulus of Regolini-Galassi (about 158 feet in diameter), and spared no expense in their construction and decoration. In his grave the Etruscan noble or merchant prince had his chariot and hunting gear, his jewels and favorite Greek vases, his wines, his wife decked out in her costly robes and finery, and all the beautiful pictures to look at that evoked pleasant hours spent at home, in the country, and at the seaside.

In these tombs are preserved many masterpieces of both Greek and Etruscan art—black-figured vases imported from Athens, sarcophagi with sculptured lids, statues, silver goblets, gold and silver jewelry, engraved gems, and wall paintings. The desire to perpetuate the personality of the dead gave rise to the tradition of the sculptured portrait (later to develop among the Romans into the portrait busts that have preserved for us the likenesses of many illustrious Romans).

Origin, Development, and General Features

Three currents swelled the main stream of Etruscan art. The first was the contribution of the Villanovans, whose simple geometric designs persisted, especially at Chiusi and other inland centers. Secondly, the arrival of the Etruscans and subsequent commercial contacts with the East brought an influx of Oriental motifs—Assyrian, Hittite, Persian, and Egyptian. Of these the earliest and most notable were Assyrian hunting scenes, stylized horses, double-headed birds, long-necked water fowls, sphinxes, lions, and bulls. Even before the Orientalizing trend had reached its height (near 650–600 B.C.), there began to flow from Greece the third great current of influence upon Etruscan art, first from Corinth, then from Ionia, and later from Athens. Throughout the sixth century B.C. the creative genius and radiant energy of Greece exerted a powerful influence upon the art of Etruria and the entire Mediterranean world. Attic black- and later red-figured vases were imported in tremendous quantities and were much admired and imitated by the Etruscans. Numerous Greek artists and craftsmen appeared in the harbors and cities of southern Etruria. But the Hellenic influence was somewhat diluted by the multiplicity of local schools and traditions in Etruria and by the conservative tendencies of native artists, who during the sixth and early fifth centuries worked with considerable originality and creative freedom.

The next century (450–340 B.C.) witnessed both a weakening of Hellenic influence and a decline in the quality of Etruscan art production. The regression in art coincided with a political, social, and economic crisis probably brought on by the wars with Rome, the Gauls, and the Greeks. There was also a psychological reaction against classical Greek art. The Etruscans, preferring action to abstract thinking and the concrete and specific to the general and the ideal, found it difficult to understand or appreciate the idealism, restraint, perfection, and austere beauty of Athenian art in the age of Pericles. As they continued to reproduce the styles and motifs worked out in the preceding period, an artistic regression set in.

During the next century (340–230 B.C.), there occurred a renaissance of Etruscan art inspired, perhaps, by the peace with Rome and a general improvement in the social and political situation of the period. Cultural relations with the Greek world improved, particularly with Athens and South Italy. This renaissance in Etruria was preceded by changes in Greek art itself.

Even before Alexander's time Greek art had begun to lose some of the old ideals of perfection. As it became less restrained and austere and more freely expressive of sentiment and emotion, it more readily evoked appreciation by the Etruscans and invited imitation. From Etruria it passed to Rome, finally culminating in the grand art of the Antonines to the enrichment of the artistic experience of the medieval and modern world.

Architecture

The earliest architecture of Italy was Etruscan and upon it rested the great engineering and building tradition of the Romans. From the Etruscans the Romans first learned how to build gateways, bridges, and aqueducts. Even the ancient Roman house, with its *atrium* around which the living rooms were arranged, was modeled after the Etruscan house.

An equally important inheritance from the Etruscans was the principle of the true or radiating arch. Though the Etruscans made use of the arch and vault in the construction of city gates, sewers, bridges, and tombs during the later centuries of their history, they were probably not the first to invent them. The true arch was unknown to the builders of seventh century tombs, the vaulted roofs of which, as in the beehive tombs of Mycenae, were formed by corbeling out each course of stone over the one immediately below until the whole was finally arched over. In the crude keystones found in early Etruscan tombs, scholars have formerly seen the forerunners of the true or voussoir arch. It is now thought that the true arch and vault first appeared in Etruscan tombs of the third century B.C. at Chiusi and Perugia, that they came into Italy from the Hellenistic East after 300 B.C., and were used in the Greek cities of Cumae and Naples as well as in Etruria. To the Etruscans, apparently, the Romans owed not the invention of the arch, but its application in a wide variety of structures.

The Etruscan Temple. The Romans also adopted certain features of the Etruscan temple. As compared with the Greek temple, this was a rather low, squat, top-heavy building. It was usually set on a hill or, as at Orvieto, overlooking a precipice. Though it rested on a solid stone foundation, the structure itself was built of brick, the roof and columns of wood. A broad flight of walled-in steps led up to a deep columned porch almost as large as the main part of the building. Above the porch projected the steeply-

A clay sarcophagus (ca. 600 B.C.) from Caere (Cerveteri), showing a reclining married couple. (Courtesy Fratelli Alinari, Florence)

A clay statue of Apollo (ca. 500 B.C.) from Veii. (Courtesy German Archaeological Institute at Rome)

Arringatore or orator (bronze, ca. 150 B.C.). (Courtesy Anderson, Rome)

pitched saddle roof supported by a double row of columns each crowned by an early type of Doric capital. Neither the steps nor the colonnade ran all the way round the building as in Greek temples. The cella proper, almost square in plan, was divided by two interior walls into three cellas or chapels, one for each of a triad of gods. The brick and woodwork was sheathed with terracotta tiles brightly painted, or decorated with leaf moldings, acanthus scrolls, and other sculptured forms borrowed from the Greeks. The pediment was adorned with terracotta friezes and gable statuary. Despite such minor details, the total effect is not wholly pleasing. The façade, bedecked with many petty ornamentations, clashes with the plain unadorned columns below. Altogether it lacks Hellenic balance and symmetry; parts of it are excessively plain and severe, others are slightly garish. As reconstructed from excavated terracotta ornamentations and from its description by Vitruvius, the Etruscan temple appears like the work of an Orientalizing frontier people suddenly become rich—materialistic and ostentatious—who had failed to assimilate the various eclectic elements that entered into their cultural life.

The roaring chimœra (bronze, ca. 500 B.C.) from Arezzo, now in Florence. (Courtesy Fratelli Alinari, Florence)

Sculpture

Etruscan sculpture is truly outstanding and, though influenced at first by Near Eastern and later by Greek sculpture, it developed into a genuinely national art—vital and true to nature.

Clay, not marble, was the medium used by the early Etruscan sculptors in some of their best work. Their skill in handling this softish, plastic material is evident in the numerous sarcophagi of Caere, Volterra, and Chiusi, with complicated reliefs sculptured on the sides and figures of married couples on the covers. Solemn or gay, attractive or ugly, the faces of the men and women re-clining on these elaborate terracotta sofas belong to real people. The realism exhibited in this portrait sculpture and carried at times to the extreme of caricatured violence is as alien to Greek taste as is the naked physical strength and vigor of motion displayed in the celebrated *Apollo* of Veii. Except for the smile, typical of Greek archaic statues, the naturalism of the *Apollo* is apparent from the vigor of the god's stride and the tenseness of his powerful leg muscles as he advances boldly upon his enemy. It was from Veii, according to tradition, that Tarquin the Proud summoned Vulca to Rome to make a statue of Jupiter for the temple on the Capitoline.

The Capitoline she-wolf (fifth century B.C.). The infants, Romulus and Remus, are Renaissance additions. (Courtesy Gabinetti Fotografico Nazionale, Rome)

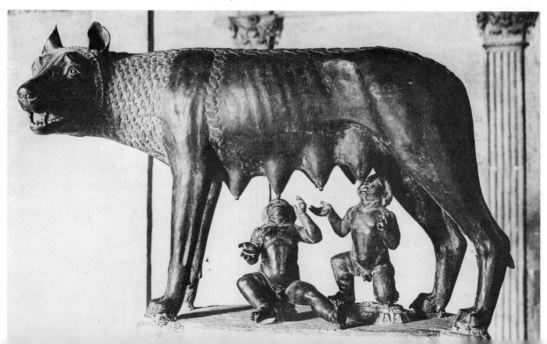

A wall painting (ca. 500 B.C.) in the "Tomb of the Augurs," showing wrestlers and a masked figure trying to beat down a dog. (Courtesy Fratelli Alinari, Florence)

A wall painting (ca. 475 B.C.) in the "Tomb of the Lionesses" at Tarquinii, showing a ritual dance. (Courtesy Brogi, Florence)

A larger section of the wall painting shown above. (Courtesy Fratelli Alinari, Florence)

The special forte of Etruscan sculptors was bronze. In this medium they created several masterpieces such as the celebrated *Capitoline Wolf* (sixth century B.C.) and the equally famous *Chimaera* of Arezzo (fifth century B.C.). These were once thought because of their merit to have been of Greek workmanship, but, though traces of Greek influence are there, the defiant glare of the wolf is undoubtedly Etruscan. And so is the *Chimaera.* Its realism is such that one can almost hear the roar of pain torn from the brute when he got hit by the deadly darts of Bellerophon. Two other genuine Etruscan works are the so-called *Capitoline Brutus* (a bronze head of the second century B.C.) and the famous statue, *Orator* (second century B.C.). The orator with his stern features and commanding personality has all the dignity of an Appius Claudius or Cato the Elder.

Painting

Painting, although perhaps not the greatest of the Etruscan arts, is the best preserved. It is preserved in the tombs, especially those of Tarquinii and Caere, which surpass even the tombs of ancient Egypt as repositories of ancient painting. Although the Greeks probably excelled in painting as they did in sculpture and architecture, their paintings (except those preserved on pottery) have been lost, dispersed, or destroyed with the buildings that housed them. The Etruscan works are therefore of particular historic importance, for they furnish the sole link between the lost Greek and later Roman paintings.

The drawings are bold and incisive; the colors are bright and achieve fine effects through juxtaposition and contrast. The themes, usually taken from life, are developed with direct and uncompromising realism and are often brutally frank. In the Tomb of the Augurs at Tarquinii (sixth century B.C.) one painting shows two wrestlers locked together in struggle. The brute strength of their hefty, well-built bodies finds parallel not in ancient or Renaissance painting but

A wall painting (ca. 525 B.C.) from the "Tomb of Hunting and Fishing" at Tarquinii. (Courtesy Fratelli Alinari, Florence)

in the modern prize-ring series of George Bellows, whose *A Stag at Sharkey's* displays the same savage and dramatic power. Another painting in the same tomb depicts a sport as brutal as the gladiatorial contests of the later Roman arena: a burly, thickset man, his head covered by a sack, is trying to knock down a savage dog whose leash is held by an opponent. If the man wins, he has his adversary at his mercy, if he loses, he will be left to the dog.

The festive side of life is a favorite theme in tomb paintings. In the *Tomb of the Lionesses* may be seen men and women reclining at a banquet, a massive bowl wreathed ·with ivy, and musicians playing. Everybody is in high spirits. A dancing girl has just thrown off her wraps and, with passion and abandon, is performing a lively and voluptuous dance. One of the male spectators, carried away with the excitement, leaps to his feet and takes up the rhythmic movements of the girl. Scenes of this kind are very commonly depicted in tomb paintings and, taken together, provide an interesting commentary on Etruscan social and religious life.

Etruscan Family Life

The most striking feature of early Etruscan society was a highly developed family life and the more or less equal status of women. Etruscan family life was unique in the ancient world and almost unparalleled in Europe till our own century. It was more comradely and integrated than the Greek, less patriarchal and authoritarian than the Roman, and not so inhibiting and ascetic as the early Christian. It was based on the legal and social equality of father and mother, on comradeship and mutual respect between husband and wife, and was therefore probably conducive to the growth of emotional maturity, which is the chief end of family life.

The Etruscan woman was not a chattel or household drudge confined to her part of the house or denied her husband's company or respect. Nor was she idealized or placed on a pedestal as in the romantic tradition of medieval chivalry or the Cavalier tradition of the aristocracy of England and the Virginia Tidewater. The Etruscan wife, on the contrary, was accepted as a person in her own right. She was her husband's equal, his partner and companion. She went to religious festivals with him; unlike her Greek counterpart, she reclined beside him at public banquets. Many Etruscan women also took a keen interest in sports either as active participants or as spectators. Their presence at public games, where male athletes sometimes contended in the nude, made them appear worse than immodest to the Greeks, who usually forbade their women to witness such exhibitions. The Greeks probably also disapproved of the wearing of transparent dresses by Etruscan women in public and their use of cosmetics, fine clothes, and jewelry to make themselves more alluring.

Children bore the names of both parents. The wife's tomb was often more splendid than the husband's; on covers of sarcophagi her portrait statue was sculptured beside his, the one not inferior to the other in dignity and self-assurance.

A Typical Frontier Society

The form of social and family life that evolved in Etruria was the product of two major experiences of the Etruscan people: the sea voyage from their original homeland of Asia Minor, and their settlement in an Italy not yet opened up to urban civilization and, except in magnitude, not unlike the early American frontier.

A cinerary urn, showing a married couple on a banqueting couch and a companion of Ulysses restored to human form. (Courtesy Fratelli Alinari, Florence)

A sea voyage, writes Toynbee, produces a dynamic effect on the life of any community. The migrating group is obliged to jettison all kinds of social accessories: institutions, customs, and traditions, as well as physical property. No doubt the Etruscan migrations, extending as they did over a considerable period of time, did much to obliterate the ties with their old homeland.

The impact of the frontier was vastly more decisive as a positive factor in shaping the social life and character of the Etruscan people. From the first moment of their arrival in Italy, they entered a new environment that called for new institutions and ways of life. The new land was comparatively rich in natural resources—soil, minerals, and forests, but their utilization required initiative, courage, and hard work. Now people who transform a country are often themselves transformed, whether they be Etruscans of the first millennium B.C. or pioneers of the American West. The Etruscan ceased to be an Asiatic, the American a European. For a time the Etruscan lived like a Villanovan, the American like an Indian. All intermarried with the natives, the Etruscans markedly so. Success was measured in terms of money, farms, houses, or shops. They had slight use for book learning or the niceties of high society during the first generations. This materialistic stamp on Etruscan character never entirely wore off even at the peak of their civilization. It persisted in their art and even in their religious institutions. In technical skill they were equal and occasionally superior to the Greeks. They were often better engineers and craftsmen. It was only in the fine arts that their taste was faulty and their execution often crude. They created nothing enduring in the way of literature or philosophy. Social equality of the sexes was another legacy of the frontier: where women are somewhat scarce and play a vital economic role, an inferior status is hard to maintain—an excellent illustration of the social working of the law of supply and demand.

On the other hand Etruscan society was not a classless society. The contact of an advanced dominant minority with a backward and subjugated people led inevitably

A banquet scene (ca. 525 B.C.) from the "Tomb of the Leopards" at Tarquinii.
(Courtesy Fratelli Alinari, Florence)

to the development of stratified social systems like those of Sparta or Norman England. The most acquisitive and aggressive seized the best and most land and became the landed aristocracy. Others equally enterprising won wealth and social standing through mining, craftsmanship, or commerce. Those who failed to succeed in the older communities along the coast became dissatisfied and restless and moved inland, across the Tiber into Latium and Campania, or eastwards into Umbria and the Po Valley to the North. Thus from one frontier to the next rolled the tide of Etruscan aggression until it engulfed major parts of Italy. Had the Etruscan people been able to rise above the individualism and sectionalism of the frontier, they might have kept their empire safe from the onslaughts of the Celts, Greeks, and Romans. But, as the dominant culture of Italy for several centuries, they nevertheless made a tremendous contribution to the future greatness of Rome.

PART TWO

THE ROMAN REPUBLIC

IV EARLY ROMAN

THE HISTORY OF THE ROMAN PEOPLE EXTENDS, STRICTLY speaking, from prehistoric times to the death of Constantine the Great in 337 A.D. It falls into three major divisions: 1) the Monarchy (from prehistoric times to the close of the sixth century B.C.); 2) the Republic (from the fall of the Monarchy to the Principate of Augustus in 27 B.C.); 3) the Empire (from 27 B.C. to the death of Constantine the Great in 337 A.D.). Monarchic Rome undoubtedly created and developed institutions and trends of great importance for the future life of the Roman people—the family, the concept of private property, social and political institutions, law, and religion. Unfortunately it is almost impossible to describe that period because of the unsatisfactory nature of existing sources of information.

The Roman historical tradition is a confused mass of truth

SOCIETY

and fiction, of legend and patriotic invention. The earliest extant literary sources, mainly the historians Livy and Dionysius of Halicarnassus, who wrote in the time of Augustus (last century B.C.), were so far removed in time from the events they attempted to narrate that their value is very questionable. They in turn depended upon sources relatively late, for it was not until the last decades of the third century B.C. that the earliest Roman historians—Fabius Pictor and Cincius Alimentus, and the poets Naevius and Ennius—attempted to reconstruct the first authorized version of early Roman history from

legend and folktale and from such written records as escaped the Gallic fire of 387/6 B.C. The later annalists, writing in the time of the Gracchi (133–123 B.C.) and Sulla (88–79 B.C.), further embellished their narratives by attributing to the remote past the ideals and institutions of their own age.

Yet the early annalists undoubtedly passed on some reliable information. They must have had access to a fair amount of written material, some dating from the time of the kings. It is known that the Romans had, by the middle of the sixth century B.C., acquired their alphabet from the Etruscans, the latter in turn probably from Cumae, a colony of Chalcidian Greeks. The Duenos Vase, which has on it a Latin inscription by its maker, the Lapis Niger or Black Stone inscription found in 1899 under the pavement of the Roman Forum, the inscribed gold brooch of Praeneste, the inscriptional texts in very archaic Latin of treaties extant, according to Dionysius of Halicarnassus, as late as Augustan times, as well as numerous archaic ritual songs and prayer formulae all prove a knowledge of writing in Rome and Latium before 500 B.C. In addition, the annalists probably had before them the full and ungarbled text of the XII Tables, which recorded the customs and unwritten laws of earlier centuries and were well acquainted with the traditions of ancient aristocratic families passed down from earliest times in oral or written form.

Recent archaeological investigations have, in some cases, helped us in our reconstruction of early Roman society, but unfortunately not much, since Rome has been inhabited for almost twenty-eight centuries and has been repeatedly rebuilt so that most of its early memorials have been swept away. A few prehistoric tombs contain pottery, bronzes, and other relics, but nothing like the wealth of material found in the Etruscan tombs of Praeneste, Caere, Conca, or Tarquinii. On the other hand, traces of the terracotta ornaments of about fifteen public buildings and temples, of which the most imposing was the Capitoline temple of Jupiter, indicate that sources have correctly represented monarchic Rome as one of the richest and most powerful cities of Italy.

Latium and the Latins

Latium lies between the slopes of the Apennines and the Tyrrhenian Sea, and extends along the coast from the mouth of the Tiber as far south as Cape Circeii and Terracina. Roughly triangular in shape, it is from 30 to 35 miles wide and about 60 miles long. The northern part, now known as the Campagna, is a rolling plain furrowed in all directions by valleys large and small and dominated by the Alban Hills, the highest of which, Monte Cavo, rises about 3,100 feet.

Through the Campagna flow the Anio and other, smaller, streams on their way to the Tiber, the great yellow-brown river which rushes seawards past Rome in a winding course between high green-bushed banks.

Though the land is in places rocky and barren, and the coastal region low and swampy, Latium produced excellent crops as soon as iron plowshares replaced the wooden ones of the Bronze Age. Between the Alban Hills and the Pontine Marshes lies one of the best wheat-growing sections in all Italy which supported more than a score of cities and was, during the fifth and fourth centuries B.C., Rome's chief source of food.

In the south lies the alluvial basin of the Liris. In the north, the land had in prehistoric times been deeply overlaid with volcanic ash. After the eruptions had ceased, the region, watered by rain and natural springs, became densely wooded and was annually fertilized by a layer of decaying leaves. By the eighth century B.C., Latium was ready for cultivation and settlement.

And settlers came, the southern Villanovans and the Fossa people (see p. 23). Though the Villanovans have often been identified with the Latins, and the Fossa people with the Sabines, archaeologists are inclined to distrust such identification.

The early Latins were apparently a hardworking people who lived by farming and stock-raising. They wore coarse, homespun clothing and made, by hand, a crude pottery. Except for some jewelry and bronze or iron tools, they seem to have imported few foreign goods. Their houses were round or elliptical wooden huts with thatched walls and roof held together by beams or poles. Smoke from the fireplace escaped through a hole in the roof and a single large doorway served for lighting and ventilation as well. The farms, though small, fostered the growth of many villages, which later developed into towns or cities. In the north was Tibur by the Anio and the fortress town of Fidenae overlooking the Tiber. Inland, lofty Praeneste guarded the road from Etruria to Campania and there was also Tusculum. Perhaps the oldest of all was Alba Longa, the religious center of Latium and legendary mother city of Rome. By the sea lay Lavinium with

Ardea close by. East of these stood Aricia, Lanuvium, and Velitrae. In the south, particularly in the rich Pontine district, there were clusters of towns such as Setia, Cora, Pometia, Suessa, Satricum, and Norba, many of which would have been totally forgotten save for their mention by Vergil and Pliny the Elder.

Etruscan Cultural Infiltration

The development of urban life in Latium was not without external stimulus. It came about partly as the result of Etruscan infiltration and domination and partly also because of the visits of Greek and Phoenician traders, especially after the Greeks had founded the Campanian city of Cumae* (sometime before 750 B.C.).

The first Etruscan settlers in Latium were probably not military adventurers but enterprising merchants, who were interested in Latium mainly because roads ran through it to the rich markets of Campania. The communities first to be Etruscanized lay along the two main routes between Etruria and Campania. The one followed the coast from Ostia to Ardea and Satricum, the other skirted the foothills of the Apennines. The more important inland route from Caere or Veii led across the Tiber at Fidenae to Tibur and Praeneste. Easily guarded from these strong points, it offered merchants a safer commercial route to Campania than was permitted by the storms, piracy, and enemy attacks likely on coastal trips.

Before the Etruscans established military and political control over Latium, their commercial activity had revolutionized its cultural life. To facilitate their trading activities, they taught the Latins the use of the alphabet, which they had learned from the Greeks of Cumae a few generations earlier. Craftsmen following close upon the heels of the merchants set up at Praeneste and other sites a flourishing industry in bronze and other metals. The Etruscans united the Iron Age hilltop villages of the Latins, thereby forming the so-called *oppida*, walled towns

---

* This was the northernmost Greek settlement in southern Italy, and one of the earliest.

or cities with fortified citadels. They taught the Latins to build timber-frame houses. They built temples and decorated them in the Etruscan style, made religion an organized institution and founded regular city-states. Thus by 600 B.C. the institutions, industries, and fine arts of Etruria were transplanted to Latium. The princely tombs of Praeneste with their hand-hammered cauldrons of bronze, their silver bowls, delicately carved ivories, and their exquisite gold ornaments were almost exact replicas of the famous Regolini-Galassi tomb at Caere. The temples at Satricum, Lanuvium, and Velitrae with their colored terracotta ornaments were scarcely distinguishable from those built in Etruria.

There soon developed in Latium the class distinctions of Etruria. The Etruscan merchants and warlords and perhaps some well-to-do Latin families constituted an aristocracy of wealth, which dominated the economic and social life of many Latin cities. Profit from trade or piracy not only enabled them to acquire large estates at the expense of small but formerly independent farmers, who were compelled to remain on the land as slaves, tenants, or serfs, but made it possible for them to live in princely splendor and adorn themselves and their homes with articles imported from Etruria, Greece, Egypt, and even the Baltic.

Agriculture continued as the chief occupation and main support of the population. And Latium was well cultivated during the period of Etruscan domination. As the population of the region increased, it became necessary to clear and plow more and more land, first the hillsides and eventually even the slopes of the mountains. Rains beating down upon those thin-soiled, denuded slopes soon peeled off the topsoil, carrying it down, along with gravel and other debris, to the lower plains. Rivers clogged with silt went on the rampage, flooded their banks, and left a mass of weeded, debris-tangled muck over once fertile fields as they receded. To save both the lowland and hillside farms, intelligent landowners with large capital and numerous tenants engaged engineers, probably Etruscan, to construct an elaborate network of so-called *cuniculi*, rock-cut drainage channels approximately five feet high and two feet wide. This remarkable drainage system, which must have required much engineering skill, an enormous expenditure of labor, and a numerous and well-disciplined population, preserved the agriculture of the Campagna for many generations. The so-called *emissaria* of the same period opened up several hundred acres of fertile agricultural land for new settlements on the shores of the Alban Lake and of Lake Nemi.

The Rise of Rome

While the lords of Praeneste and Satricum were living in princely splendor, Rome was still a loose aggregation of five or more drab pioneer villages with different languages and customs. One of these primitive settlements may have been the original Rome founded, according to later legend, in 753 B.C. Some of these settlements dated, in fact, back to the Bronze Age and were as ancient as any to be found in Latium.

Rome owed her future greatness in part to the excellence of her geographical site. For 250 miles the mighty Tiber roars southwards through the central Apennines. Fifteen miles from the sea it makes a sharp turn to the west. Here its course is slowed down somewhat by an island lying in midstream. Seven hills, ranging from two to three hundred feet above sea-level, rise above its left bank. The nearest ones are the Capitoline, the Palatine, and the Aventine, separated from each other by intervening valleys. Further to the east and enclosing them in a kind of arc stand the other four, the Quirinal, Viminal, Esquiline, and Caelian. On these seven hills stood the later city of Rome. Two other hills across the river, the Janiculum and Vatican, were ultimately incorporated.

Both modern historians and ancient Romans gave much of the credit for the greatness of the city to the presence of the Tiber. "Not without reason," Camillus, the fourth century hero, is quoted as saying (Livy 5.45.5), "did gods and men select this spot for founding our city: its healthful hills, the convenient river on which may be brought down the produce of inland districts and over which we receive the commerce of the seas, a position close enough to the sea for convenience, yet not so near as to be exposed to the danger of attack by foreign fleets, a central location in Italy, and a site uniquely adapted to the growth of a city." Yet the importance of the Tiber to the prehistoric Romans may easily be exaggerated. While it was a good source of fresh fish, a barrier against enemies attacking from the North, and a useful means for people living upstream to bring their produce down to Rome, it was not really a highway for sea-borne commerce. Its lower course was too winding for the effective use of sails and its current so strong that a crew could not row a seagoing boat from the river's mouth to Rome in less than a day and a night.* Even while Etruscan ships sailed the Mediterranean, Roman trade was confined largely to the southern neck of Etruria. There was probably no direct trade with Greece or the Middle East: the excavated Attic black-figured vases and Egyptian goods seem to have come second hand through Vetulonia or some other Etruscan port. The Tiber was not used much for maritime trade even after the Roman conquest of the Mediterranean, for the bulk of the imports from the East was landed at the Campanian port of Puteoli 138 miles south and from there transported to Rome by road. Even in imperial times, after the artificial port of Ostia was built, cargoes were transferred from seagoing ships to barges, which were then tugged by oxteams along the tow path to the city's docks. The Tiber was not therefore of major importance in Rome's political development. Rome possessed, as Livy said, "a site uniquely adapted to the growth of a city." There were excellent building materials nearby: tufa, peperino, and also travertine, all easily quarried and shaped with the simplest tools, selce for paving streets and pozzolana for making good concrete. She was not too near the sea to be raided or destroyed by pirates. Her central geographic position in Italy made her the focal point of the main road communications running up, down, and across the peninsula—communications which permitted her armies,

* Vergil, *Aeneid* 8.94 ff.

with minimum expenditure of effort, to strike in almost any direction at will. The seven hills upon which she made possible the observation of enemy movements and the proximity of the hills to one another facilitated the fusion of the several village communities into a single state, eventually the largest in area and population in all Italy.

The military and commercial advantages of the Tiber were of less immediate concern to Rome's early inhabitants than the fish they could catch in it, the nearby pastures, and the abundant good water in every season of the year. They had no occasion to study the potential advantages of their home, and the possibility of making use of Tiber Island for bridging the Tiber. The steep cliffs of the Palatine girdled by moat-like marshes gave them protection against wolves and human enemies. As long as the population remained small, the hilltops were large enough to grow all the beans and spelt they needed. Their wants were small. Excavations of the early huts and graves in the marshy land below Palatine Hill show their lack of metal wares and the crudeness of their hand-made pottery. They had no mines or industries and no trade save for the casual visits of peddlers with whom they bartered their wool and cheese for trinkets, pots and pans, or tools useful for farming. Such was the simple life of the primitive Romans.

Long before Rome was settled, people from the hill country of the central Apennines had been beating a path along both sides of the Tiber to and from the salt beds near the river's mouth.* (Salt was a valuable commodity in Europe even as late as the French Revolution.) It was the special treasure of the lower Tiber. While it was relatively simple to get down the river by raft, the strong current made it next to impossible to get back up again so trails along the banks were used instead. The trail along the right bank was less broken and irregular, and led to the best and most easily worked beds. When this trail came under the control of Etruscan Veii, independent salt miners and

* This idea was developed by L. A. Holland, "Primitive Roman Bridge," *Transactions of the American Philological Association*, 80 (1949) 281–319.

merchants had to use the Old Salt Road (*Via Salaria*), which ran along the left bank. When the Etruscans later crossed the river and seized the fortress of Fidenae, the salt men lost the use of this road also. To save their lives or escape the tolls, they had to bypass Fidenae by a wide detour inland via Nomentum on the Allia. Returning to the river at Antemnae, they followed the Old Salt Road to Rome. The vicinity of Rome provided the only safe and convenient place to cross the Tiber both because it was beyond Veii's range of control and because Tiber Island facilitated the building of bridges. The Sublician Bridge, once built and guarded from the Capitoline citadel, attracted many roads to it and made Rome a road center. Thus Rome gradually became a bridge town, a road center, a salt market, and a magnet of trade and population.

Economic Development

If it be true that economic factors can exert a determining influence upon the social life, the form of government, the class structure, and the legal system of a state, it seems logical, before attempting to describe the political and social life of early Rome, to survey its economic development.

Flocks and herds were undoubtedly the main source of livelihood of the early Romans. This fact is correctly inferred from their myths, religious customs, and language: Romulus and Remus were raised in a sheepherder's cottage; the festival of the *Palilia* on April 21st, celebrated clean-up day of stalls and stables; in honor of *Tellus* or Mother Earth, the primitive goddess of fruitfulness of animals as well as of crops, the early Romans twice annually celebrated the festival of the *Fordicidia,* at which they sacrificed a pregnant cow in the spring, a pregnant sow in early winter. Because of this pastoral tradition the Romans, like the Jews of the Old Testament, sacrificed animals to their gods: to Juno a goat, to Mars a bull, to Jupiter a white bullock. Traces of the same background is evident in the name given to one of their city gates, the "Lowing Gate" (*Porta Mugonia*), as well as in the words *egregius* meaning "out of the flock" and therefore

The Tiber: remains of the Sublician Bridge. (Courtesy Fratelli Alinari, Florence)

"excellent," and *pecunia,* meaning "wealth in flocks" but later "money" in general.

Even so, pasturage could not be pursued on a very large scale until the Romans had conquered wider grazing lands and seized command of the roads to summer pastures in the Apennines. Their battle for the trails with the Sabine mountaineers ended with a coexistence pact which gave to the Romans access to summer pastures in the mountains, to the Sabines winter pastures in the Lower Tiber Valley, and rights of intermarriage to both.

Meanwhile, the Romans had other sources of livelihood. They fished, raised pigs and chickens, and planted gardens of turnips, peas, beans, lettuce, and cabbage. In small plots of land adjacent to the house they cultivated spelt, a hard kind of emmer, which like durum was more suitable for making porridge than bread. They probably also gathered wild grapes and figs, which they either ate as fruit or brewed into wine.

A change in the primitive life of the Romans was not slow in coming. The Mediterranean world was then astir with commercial activity in which the Romans were soon to take part. To the shores of Latium came the Phoenicians and the Greeks. The Etruscans were crossing the Tiber and occupying Satricum and Praeneste as way stations along the road to Campania. Soon they would be coming to Rome via the Sublician Bridge. From the Sabine hills came buyers of salt; from Etruria, Capena, and Falerii came merchants to sell vases, arms, tools, jewelry, clothing, and other wares. From the surrounding countryside came farmers with their produce—livestock, wool, hides, and cheese. They all met at the Cattle Market, a trading post located near the approaches to the Sublician Bridge. Later, some of the farmers traded at the Vegetable Market, which became the first food market in this part of Italy.

Historical Development of the Family

One of the social institutions most influenced by the economic change was the family. The Roman family was not only the basic unit of Roman society—but the cradle of private law. Just as Roman public law developed out of the relations between citizens and the state, so private law, which persisted long after the fall of Rome, arose out of the organization of the family and interfamily relations.

The early Roman family was not primarily a genealogical concept. Though later texts often use the word 'family' in the sense of an association of blood relations, it was not a group of persons connected by ties of blood or marriage. It was rather an association of house-mates, some born in wedlock, others adopted, over all of whom the head of the household exercised absolute authority. It consisted of objects as well as persons, as is clear from the origin of the word. The Latin word *familia* is thought to have meant first "dwelling-place" or "house," then the "house-community." Thus it came to mean in a legal sense the "house-property." Both persons and property were at the disposal of and subject to the control of the head of the household, called the *pater familias.*

Under the guidance, control, and management of the *pater familias*, the Roman family was not only a community of work and property but a system of defense, law, and government—a miniature state. In the earliest Roman law it was recognized as a closed, self-sufficient, self-contained association, an economic unit operating under self-given rules within the larger frame-work of the economic system then prevailing and completely free from interference by the state. It was also a religious organization, a community of worship centered around the cult of the hearth and the cult of the dead.

The earliest form of family among the Romans, as among the other Indo-European peoples, seems to have been the great or joint undivided family, several generations living and working together. Linguistic evidence supports this view; comparative law and folklore justify it; and survivals of it down to historic times seem to confirm it. Plutarch tells us that one Marcus Crassus in early married life lived with his wife and two married brothers in his father's little house and all had their meals together at the same table. Likewise in his biography of Aemilius Paulus, he speaks of a family of sixteen grown men who with their wives and many children all lived together in one small house and worked a small farm near Veii. These instances are evidently the latest survivals of an earlier form of Roman family life. The cultivation of the hard tough soil around Rome with crude tools and primitive methods, and the herding of cattle made the joint, undivided family an economic necessity. In the days when slaves were few, even the married sons of the household helped provide for the family and care for the sick and helpless. Some-

times three or four generations lived and worked together. Long after social and economic changes had split up the joint family into individual families, traces of joint family practices persisted in Roman law.

During the Etruscan monarchy, if not earlier, the joint undivided family began to split up into separate or individual families. The rise of the state, which took over the functions of defense and internal order, rendered the continued existence of large kinship groups less imperative. Of even greater influence were economic factors: improved methods of farming, the increasing use of slave labor, the growth of trade and craftsmanship, also contributed to the dissolution of the joint undivided family.

Economic changes also modified the concept of property. The primitive Romans apparently did not make a sharp distinction between landed and movable property. They distinguished rather between real estate and personal property. Personal property consisted of things which the individual had made with his hands or had acquired by gift or capture such as dowries, spoils, and personal effects such as arms, hunting gear, ornaments, and clothing. Property of this kind was not heritable, but was placed beside the dead man in his grave or burnt upon his bier.

Unlike personal property (*res nec mancipi*), real estate was the common possession of the joint undivided family and passed down with that family from one generation to another, with the exception of family-approved cessions and transfers. We hear, in a Romulus legend and in a passage of the XII Tables, of a plot of one acre and a third, a *heredium* of two *iugera*, and, in other sources, of a larger fenced-in plot (*hortus*) as the characteristic property of the early Roman family. Property at the disposition of the joint family (*res mancipi*) apparently consisted of the house and adjacent garden patches, of some larger or smaller fenced-in grain fields, parts of which had to lie fallow in primitive rotation, and of the slaves and animals used in cultivating the land, and probably also the annual crops.

The family ordinarily had the use of land other than such family property. Land used mainly as pasture and often for grain production as well was originally not subject to either private or joint family ownership, but belonged, as *ager publicus,* to a village community or a *gens,* which distributed it among the individual families on an annual or terminal basis. The crops raised on this land were family property.

Sometime before the codification of the XII Tables, if not earlier, joint ownership of family property apparently had disappeared when the small individual family became legally recognized. Just when this much discussed development first began we do not know, but it could reasonably be dated back to the establishment of the 16 rustic tribes as part of the Servian constitution (see p. 64). Be this as it may, the economic unity and solidarity of the archaic joint family was not in principle thereby impaired. For the *pater familias* of the individual family had by the middle of the fifth century B.C. concentrated in his hands not only sole power of administering the family property as its custodian but full ownership of it as well.

The Gens

The origin and nature of the *gens* is obscure and much disputed. The Latin word itself, whose plural form is *gentes,* is etymologically connected with Greek *genos* and our word "kin" and is commonly translated "clan." It is usually considered a group of families united by a common name and by the belief of common descent from a single male ancestor (divine, human, or animal).

In early times every Roman had two names, a personal or given name (*praenomen*) and the name of his gens (*nomen*); later, as the *gens* became larger and was subdivided into families, a third or family name (*cognomen*) was added. Thus, for example, Gaius Julius Caesar had three names, Gaius the given name, Julius the name of his *gens,* and Caesar the name of his family within the Julian *gens.* The word "gens," therefore, meant to the Romans an association of families united by ties of blood, a social organization which has analogies in practically all Indo-European speaking peoples of antiquity.

Some modern writers hold, and perhaps rightly, that the region around Rome was originally settled by three tribes—the Tities, Ramnes, and Luceres of Roman tradition. As these tribes disintegrated, their settled territory became broken down into small rural administrative units known as *pagi.* Henceforth, the Romans were divided into rural *pagani* and urban *montani* (inhabitants of the seven hills). Within each *pagus* lived a *gens,* a territorial group originating in prehistoric times and composed of several neighboring families, which had banded together for mutual aid and defense. These families lived in hamlets, villages, or in isolated homesteads depending on the nature of the land and the security of the district. In time of danger they took refuge in walled fortifications (*oppida*), which tended to become local centers of government, or in small forts or citadels like the one on the Capitoline Hill. They pastured their stock on the community land, intermarried, became closely related in blood, and eventually acquired a common name, no doubt that of the largest or strongest family. In this way all members of the later *gens* came to feel that they had descended from a common ancestor.

Whatever its origin may have been, the early Roman *gens* seems to have existed before the city-state and passed on to it certain social customs and some archaic religious rites and festivals like that of the *Lupercalia* or "Wolf-festival" (see p. 65).

The *gens* was not only a religious community with its own guardian deity, special cults, sacrifices and festivals, and common burial grounds, but a social and political organization, whose members held meetings from time to time to decide on questions pertaining to wills, inheritances, the admission of strangers to membership, and the appointment of guardians for minors and mental defectives. It exercised jurisdiction and censure over its members, and within its own territory or *pagus* it fostered a spirit of solidarity and mutual assistance. After the formation of the city-state, the *gens* sent its leader into the senate, the advisory council of the king.

In primitive times, the *gens* had its own army, isolated survivals of which persisted even as late as the time of Marius. Territory seized from an enemy was not assigned to individual families, but was declared public land and reserved for occupation by the *gentes;* the residents of the conquered territory were reduced to vassals or clients. A very important element in the life of the *gens* was clientage, a primitive institution which existed among the Etruscans and Indo-European nations as well. Later on, the modified clientage (*clientela* and *patronatus*) was to influence strongly the pattern of Roman society throughout the world and even Western civilization up to the present day.

Clients may be defined simply as dependents of a *gens* and their relationship to it was very like that between a medieval feudal lord and his vassals, except that the clients in early and primitive Rome may not have been at first dependents of individual *patroni* or small single families, but rather of the *gens* as a whole. Their origin was varied. Some were non-Roman inhabitants of conquered territory, some were Romans unable to make a living as free men or to defend their lives and property; some were emancipated slaves; while others were strangers who voluntarily sought admission into the *gens* so as to be able to reside permanently on Roman soil and eventually to acquire Roman citizenship. This arrangement was advantageous to both *gens* and client. In return for a grant of land, for political and financial support, for protection in the courts, and for the privilege of sharing in the religious life of the *gens,* the client was expected to be loyal and cooperative, to render military service, to do field work, and to assist his patron (*patronus*) by voting for him in elections and by contributing to the payment of fines, ransoms, dowries, when called upon. In this way the client gained security, the *gens* acquired workers and soldiers. The mutual obligations were not enforced by law, but were founded on faith and sanctioned by religion and custom. Religion punished violations of this code as proclaimed by the XII Tables: "Cursed be the patron who has done his client wrong."

Later, during the fifth century B.C., as the state took over the functions of defense, police, and law enforcement, the *gens* ceased to exist as a true political and economic organization. Its influence lived on mainly as a religious community and as a bond of sentiment among families of the same name. The heads of the individual families, seeing its usefulness gone, tended to regard it as more of a nuisance than a source of protection. The clients were no longer dependents of the *gens* but of the rich and powerful families which had asserted their independence from the *gens.* And this continued to be their status during the Republic and Empire.

That the *gens* originally held some kind of property rights over the land seems implied by the Law of the XII Tables, which mentions the right of the *gens* to succeed to the property of a family whose head died without a will and without heirs. If this right of succession escheating to the *gens* when a family became defunct be not regarded as an abeyant right of original ownership by the *gens,* it is almost certain that even at the beginning of the Republic land was still an important adjunct of the *gens.* When the Sabine Atta Clausus, afterwards known as Appius Claudius, obtained Roman citizenship, he was granted an estate by the Anio for his *gens* and his five thousand dependents (Livy 2.26). We also know that the *gentes* of conquered cities were allowed to keep their lands (*agri gentilici*) when admitted to Roman citizenship. Mommsen has noticed still another proof. The sixteen oldest rural tribes allegedly created by Servius Tullius received their names from such land-holding *gentes* as the Cornelian, Fabian, and Aemilian. This Servian reform seems to have marked the breakdown of the *gens* as a political and economic organization and the rise of private ownership of farm land (cf. pp. 63–65). It is certain that by the middle of the fifth century B.C. the division of land among individual owners was well under way. For the XII Tables established the rule that ownership of land could be acquired after two years of continuous possession, a procedure technically known as *usucapio.*

It may be concluded that by the middle of the fifth century, if not before, three major developments had occurred or were already in progress: 1) the decay of the gens as a political and economic organization; 2) the disappearance of the joint undivided family and the advent of the individual family; and

3) the development of private ownership of landed property and its concentration in the hands of the all-powerful *pater familias*.

The Pater Familias

The *pater familias* was not necessarily a begetter of children. The phrase meant simply "master of the household." He might have no children of his own, he might even be a bachelor or a minor still under a guardian's care. The only qualification was that he be subject to no authority save that of the state, that he be legally independent and self-sufficient, and able to represent the family in its relations with other families and the state. In a legal sense he was the family and without him there was no family nor household. His power within the family was absolute, unlimited by the state or by any other social agency, and subject only to such moral and economic conditions as temporarily prevailed. He was accordingly the source of law within the family and there his orders were recognized by the community as having the force of law. His authority was based on ancestral custom of which he was sole judge and interpreter. He was the judge of the household and his rulings could not be set aside by any external authority, though he might kill, mutilate, expel, or sell into slavery his sons or house-mates, though he might break or dispose of the household property.

And he was priest. Each morning and evening the entire family, including the slaves, offered prayers and sacrifices to the dead. An essential element in Roman ancestor worship was the cult of the Genius of the living *pater familias,* in whom was incarnated the unity and perpetuity of the family. The Genius was more than a personification of his power of procreation. It was his guiding spirit, his inseparable companion, the source of his authority and strength, and the tie that bound him to his ancestors. He offered daily sacrifices to his departed ancestors at the family hearth whose ever-burning fire symbolized the unity and continuity of the family. As the representative and trustee of the family's blood, property, tradition, and name, he was duty bound to preserve its

unity and integrity, to hold together and increase its property. The moral and legal obligation of managing the household and of mobilizing its human and physical resources required the exercise of total power over all property—slaves, cattle, goods, chattels, and land. He administered not for his own personal benefit but in the interest of the family. Children born to him in wedlock as well as those adopted into the family were subject to his will as long as he lived, regardless of their age and status.

His sons were not absolved from his authority even after they had married and set up households of their own. Submission to his authority, however, did not take precedence over their rights and duties as citizens, as voters in the tribal lists, or as soldiers. Sons could contract legal marriages and acquire property, though in the eyes of early Roman law they could not fully own this property, or enter into contracts binding upon the family estate, or withhold for their own use any income accruing from their work.

Such was the power wielded by the *pater familias* in a society where law was based on custom and not enforced by any agency of the state. Respect for and obedience to tradition implanted by religious precept usually rendered his exercise of authority not a brutal display of force but a recognized distribution of the only justice that could be secured until the "moral imperative" was replaced later by the "legal imperative" established by the state.

Patricians and Plebeians

The early history of the Republic was dominated by the struggle between two distinct social and political classes, the patricians and the plebeians. The patricians were the native nobles, the plebeians the mass of common freemen and later immigrants. Though both classes had their origin during the kingship or earlier, the cleavage between them had gradually been widening. Both classes enjoyed rights of citizenship, but differed from each other in social and political privileges. The patricians monopolized the early senate and filled the priestly colleges and other offices. Social convention divided them into "founding" and "later" fathers, (*patres maiorum* and *patres minorum gentium*).

The plebeians had the right to trade (*commercium*), acquire property, and defend themselves in court. They also had the right to vote in the popular assembly though this meant little in the actual government of the state. The struggle between the two classes did not involve the question of citizenship, which both already had, but that of social and political equality within the state.

The origin of the plebeian class, though much discussed, has never been satisfactorily determined. According to Mommsen, the plebeians were former clients of the *gentes*. The main objection against this view is that the decay and breakdown of the *gentes* had not progressed far enough even by the beginning of the Republic to account for the existence of this large and independent social class. Some scholars have explained the difference between the patricians and plebeians as primarily one of race, the plebeians being the original inhabitants conquered by the patricians. The racial theory breaks down because the very patricians were of varied racial origin: Latin, Sabine, and Etruscan. The plebeians were also quite mixed. Other scholars have sought to explain the origin of the plebeians in terms of social and economic differentiation within the population and as a result of the heavy immigration of people in search of work and opportunity. It has recently been argued that the *plebs* was a Latin community, which had settled as a colony on the Aventine and was bound to Rome by treaty.

The widening cleavage between the two social classes—patrician and plebeian—was probably not an isolated phenomenon, but the outcome of the general and revolutionary transformation of Roman society in the Etruscan phase of the kingship. During the decay and disintegration of the *gentes* the most aggressive and enterprising persons would inevitably expand their estates and become the patricians, the weaker and less aggressive would lose their small holdings (*heredia, horti*), become the clients and dependents of the rich and powerful, and form the nucleus of the rural plebeian class.

Later the number of the plebeians would be swelled by immigrant merchants, tradesmen, craftsmen, and laborers, as well as by the inhabitants of outlying villages conquered and absorbed by Rome. The newcomers were not invariably people of inferior social status, but often members of well-to-do families denied admission into the Roman patriciate for one reason or another. This probably accounts not only for the origin of the plebeian class, which made up the bulk of the population of Rome, but for the division of that class itself into rich and poor.

On the other hand, comparative studies have demonstrated the existence among all early Indo-European societies of three primitive endogamic classes: priests, warriors, and a third estate consisting of small landowners, landless freemen, craftsmen, and traders. Such a class system is preserved in modern times only by the Hindus of India and in modern primitive societies. Whether or not these sharp class distinctions of early Roman society originated in prehistoric times, a social group which was the predecessor of the later plebeians may have formed part of the tribes that migrated into Latium during the first centuries of the first millennium B.C., for, as recently deciphered Mycenean documents have proved, such a social class is found similarly in Greece during Homeric times and no doubt earlier still.

Rome as a City-State

The story of Rome's founding and of her seven kings, according to Livy, Vergil, Dionysius of Halicarnassus, Plutarch, and Cassius Dio, is a strange mixture of truth and fiction, of ancient folklore, and pure invention designed to appeal to the vanity of a later age. Nevertheless, some of the legends are extremely old. The myth about Aeneas, for example, the first legendary Trojan ruler in Latium and the supposed ancestor of Romulus and of the Julian house, was current in Etruria as early as the first half of the sixth century B.C. Two clay statuettes recently found at Veii (dating probably from 470 B.C.) show Aeneas carrying his father Anchises on his shoulders.

Tacitus (*Annals* 1.1) seems to have been correct in his statement that in the beginning Rome was ruled by kings. So were Aricia, Tusculum, Lanuvium, and probably other city-states in Latium and Etruria. That kings ruled Rome during the sixth century B.C. is proved by mention of the word *rex* (RECEI) clearly inscribed on a mutilated stone pyramid found beneath the Lapis Niger (Black Stone), the oldest monument in the Roman Forum (early fifth century B.C.). The existence of kings is attested also by the survival in Republican times of the term *interregnum* and of the titles of *interrex* and the priestly *rex sacrorum* (the King of Sacrifices alluded to on the Black Stone). The *Regia* or King's House, which served in Republican times as the official residence of the Pontifex Maximus, may have been originally the palace of the kings.

The Roman historical tradition insisted on two phases of Roman kingship: a) the first four kings, who were Latin or Sabine, namely Romulus, Numa Pompilius, Tullus Hostilius, and Ancus Marcius and b) the last three, who were Etruscan, namely Tarquinius Priscus, Servius Tullius, and Tarquinius Superbus.

An apparently independent Etruscan tradition antedating the earliest Roman historical speculations corroborates the existence of the Tarquins. A fourth century wall painting in the François tomb near Vulci bears, among others, the name of Gneve Tarchu Rumach (Gnaeus Tarquinius of Rome). Macstrna (Mastarna) also named in this painting cannot, with absolute certainty, be identified with Mastarna (King Servius Tullius), although the name Caelius Vibenna (Caile Vipinas), the legendary friend of the Roman king, appears both here and on an Etruscan mirror. Other Etruscan inscriptions prove that the Tarchna or Tarquins belonged to a historical noble family in Etruria. An inscription at Vulci mentions the name of Tanaquil, the legendary wife of Tarquin the First and guardian of Servius Tullius.

Under Etruscan rule (from ca. 575 to 508 B.C., or later) Rome made rapid progress economically, culturally, and politically. Her territory expanded from approximately 58 square miles to 350 or more, her population

from 10,000 to more than 100,000. The city itself, now laid out as the *Roma Quadrata* ascribed to Servius Tullius by an extant fragment of an unknown Latin author, possibly Cato the Censor (Papyrus Oxyrhynchus XVII [1927] nr. 2088, lines 14–17), was surrounded by a ritually plowed furrow (the so-called *pomerium*). Laid out also with *cardo* and *decumanus* intersecting, according to Etruscan city planning, at right angles, the city contained numerous public buildings, a forum, drainage works, the grand circus, and the great Capitoline temple of Jupiter, which covered almost an acre of ground, was constructed and decorated by the finest architects and artists of Etruria and, according to the Greek historian Polybius, was dedicated in 509 or 508/7 B.C. to the triad of Jupiter, Juno, and Minerva, old Italic deities whose worship the Etruscans introduced into Rome.

The Etruscans also contributed greatly to Roman economic development. They cleared forests and bushland, drained swamps, and introduced better made iron plowshares and superior methods of cultivation as well as improved varieties of wheat, vines, and fruit trees. They introduced among the Romans the latest techniques of craftsmanship in metals, clay, leather, and wool, though Rome continued to import vases and metal wares from Tarquinii, Caere, and Veii, and especially from the Faliscan territory of southern Etruria. The text of a treaty signed with Carthage, as preserved in translation by Polybius, may, if authentic, reveal the extension of Roman trade outside of Italy towards the close of the Etruscan monarchy.

The Etruscan kings themselves probably did much to promote the economic development of Rome. Their building projects not only served to beautify the city but created a reservoir of skilled labor. Besides encouraging the immigration of traders and craftsmen, they made living quarters available to foreign merchants on the Aventine, to which annual fairs held in the precincts of the temple of Diana attracted people from all over Latium for both worship and trade, thus making Rome not only a religious but an economic and political center.

Both militarily and politically, Etruscan

Rome became the leading state of Latium. Her army, much enlarged and trained in the use of the efficient hoplite phalanx arms and tactics of Greece, enabled her to play a dominant role in the Latin League, which was a military organization. Rome owed her political predominance to the centralized character of her government, which was dignified by an elaborate state ceremonial and arrayed with awe-inspiring symbols of kingly power: lictors armed with rods and the double-bitted ax, the ivory eagle-headed scepter and golden wreath, the purple embroidered toga, the curule chair, and the triumphal four-horse chariot.

Unlike Egypt or Persia, whose absolute rulers exercised unlimited and divinely sanctioned power, the Roman government consisted of three branches each endowed with theoretically sovereign powers and so well balanced that, in the words of Polybius, no one could say for sure whether the constitution as a whole was a monarchy, an aristocracy, or a democracy. The three branches were the executive, the senate, and the popular assembly, and formed a system of "checks and balances" that is the prototype of modern European governments and that of the United States.

The King

The living symbol of the unity, power, and authority of the early Roman state was the king. Though he held his office for life, he acquired this neither wholly by direct inheritance nor by popular election. Some writers today, notably Italian, insist that he was nominated by his predecessor. The ancient opinion, influenced, no doubt, by the machinery set up in the Republic for the election of consuls, was that on the death of each king the right to predict the future (*auspices*), which bestowed upon royal authority its divine sanction, reverted automatically to the senate. Thereupon, the senate chose one of its members to serve for five days as "acting king," or *interrex*. He in turn appointed another senator to hold office for five days, and so on, until a ruler pleasing to both the gods and the senate could be selected. Then the last to act as *interrex* presented the nomi-

nation to the popular assembly for confirmation. The function of the assembly was simply to attend and witness the last taking of the *auspices,* to express approval of the new king by acclamation, and, upon his assumption of the royal command (*imperium*), to pledge him loyalty and obedience. This formal investiture of the king gave him almost unlimited sovereignty or "the power of life and death."

In the Etruscan period, the king's power was probably almost total, embracing three broad areas of function: command of the army, the administration of justice, and the priesthood. As chief of state and supreme commander of the army he had the power to make peace and war, direct foreign affairs, and conclude treaties with other states; to enforce military discipline, draft citizens into the army, and levy taxes in time of war; and to distribute booty among his soldiers or land among citizens in repayment of wartime loans. As director of internal affairs and administrator of justice, the king probably possessed both law-making and law-enforcement powers and issued edicts deemed necessary for the security and government of the state. Nevertheless he had little to do with the formulation of private or civil law since in early Rome that seems to have been created neither by royal decree nor by statute, but evolved out of use and custom and the social conscience of the community. He promulgated the so-called "royal laws" in his capacity of high priest. For at that time law, not divorced from religion and custom, was regulated by priests.

The king possessed extensive powers for carrying out his many duties as chief of state, commander-in-chief, chief justice, and high priest. He enforced the laws whether based on custom or decree through the agency of his lictors. Against violators of these laws he had various remedies such as corporal punishment, imprisonment, fines, and the seizure of movable property. He imposed the death penalty only upon those guilty of serious crimes against the gods or the state—treason, parricide, and sacrilege. He seldom intervened in private disputes unless called upon and even then limited himself to enunciating the general principle, leaving particular cases to be determined by regular judges or special arbiters.

The king's most important functions were religious, for religion was the foundation of royal power and with it was entwined the destiny of the state. As supreme head of the state religion the king's person was inviolable and sacrosanct. His duties were to represent the people in their relations to the gods of the state, to perform in person certain public sacrifices, to take the *auspices* and so learn the will of the gods, to appoint the priests and supervise their activities, to draw up the calendar, and proclaim the feasts acceptable to each of the gods. The gods must be consulted before every important act of state—the election of rulers, the calling of the people to assembly, and the departure of armies for battle.

The king entrusted the details of administration to his officials: to the prefect of the city, who governed when the king was absent; to the judges, who tried cases of treason and other public crimes; to the pontiffs, who supervised the sacrifices, fixed the calendar, and interpreted the civil law; to the augurs, who ascertained and interpreted the will of the gods; and to the Vestal Virgins, who kept aglow the city's sacred fires.

The Senate

The second branch of the early Roman government was the senate, a council of elders who exercised neither the executive powers of the king nor the legislative functions of the popular assembly. Yet it was probably more ancient than either for tradition carries its origin back to Romulus, who chose one hundred of the most eminent men in Rome to advise and assist him in the government. Mommsen's opinion is probably right that the earliest senate was a congress of clan leaders, one of whom later became the king. To maintain their control over the ever-growing multitude of clients, one of these clan leaders may even have organized the early Roman city-state around 650 B.C. following Etruscan and Greek models. The king must soon have become a permanent part of the government and, as his powers

increased, he made the senate a purely advisory council. He added new members, after the clans or *gentes* had broken up into a larger number of rich and powerful families. Sometime between 575 and 450 B.C. the royal and early Republican senate came to consist of three hundred members, a constitutional number which remained fixed till the time of Sulla (ca. 85-80 B.C.).

Powers and Functions of the Senate. The senate could not legislate and could give advice only when consulted by the executive (at first the king, later, the consuls). This advice was not always accepted although it was not politically "wise" for a king habitually to ignore or reject it, especially on major issues, since he was bound sooner or later to incur the enmity of the leading families and might, like the last Tarquin, even lose his throne.

The *auspices* seem to have reverted to the senate on the death of the king, and for five days thereafter any senator had the right to be chief executive until a new king was appointed. The senate possessed still another ancient source of authority summed up in the phrase *auctoritas patrum,* which gave it the power to ratify resolutions of the popular assembly before enactment. Thus even under the kings the senate was a link between the executive and legislative branches of the government.

The Popular Assembly

The third organ of the government was the popular assembly, traditionally known as the *comitia curiata.* Its origins are obscure and the functions usually attributed to it were probably based on reconstructions of later times. It was the oldest known assembly, as old, perhaps, as the unified Roman community itself, and was composed of all citizens capable of bearing arms including, probably, the plebeians as well as the clients of the patrician *gentes.* This assembly met only on summons by the king to transact business put before them by him. Marshalled in primitive times by heralds, but during the Etruscan period by lictors, they assembled regularly in the Forum, though occasionally for reli-

An Etruscan bronze helmet (ca. 650 B.C.), discovered near Capua (Italy). (Courtesy Metropolitan Museum of Art, Rogers Fund, 1908)

gious ceremonies on Capitoline Hill in front of the college of pontiffs. They lined up in groups called *curiae*, to which the assembly as a whole owed the name of *curiata*. Unlike the U.S. House of Representatives, the assembly did not vote by a simple counting of heads, but by *curiae*, each of which seems to have been a group of related families living in a given area and organized as a unit for religious, military, and political purposes as well as for taxation and voting. Ten *curiae* are said to have made up each of the three tribes—Ramnes, Tities, and Luceres—into which the Roman people are said to have been divided originally. Each *curia* seems to have provided the army with a quota of ten horsemen and one hundred infantry soldiers. The *curia* may have been the basis of the entire military and political organization of early Rome.

Functions of the Comitia Curiata. The role of the *comitia curiata* in government during the monarchy seems to have been a passive one. Legislation in primitive societies was rare (the law of custom seldom required modification or change) and the people assembled only on summons by the king and then not to speak but to listen. Though they are said to have possessed even then ultimate sovereign power (*maiestas*), that power was latent, theoretical, still in a state of development. (Nevertheless, the king was wise not to ignore it, if only to win the people's cooperation and consent to major changes in law and policy.) They participated in public religious functions celebrated by the king. They were present at his inauguration to witness the final *auspices* and to swear the formal oath of loyalty and obedience to him when he assumed the *imperium*. They heard proclamations concerning peace and war and other important matters of state. Besides these public functions, the assembly witnessed, if not authorized, wills and adoptions, and dealt with other matters connected with private law.

This primitive assembly became politically obsolete during the early Republic, if not before the end of the monarchy. It was superseded for legislative purposes by another assembly of the people in arms, known as the *Comitia Centuriata*. The new assembly

An Italic bronze breastplate (ca. 675 B.C.). (Courtesy Metropolitan Museum of Art, Rogers Fund, 1909)

may have owed its rise to a reform of the army and to the introduction of new types of equipment and tactics presently to be described.

The Early Roman Army

Among the early Romans were men no doubt as brave as Agamemnon or Ulysses, but no Homer sang of their arms or deeds in war. The lack of such a contemporary witness is not sufficiently made up for by archaeology to enable modern scholars to reconstruct the story of Roman warfare in the heroic age. Conjecture is no real substitute for evidence.

Before the close of the seventh century there seems to have been little organized fighting by masses of armed men. Like the heroes of the *Iliad*, the clan chiefs rode to battle in chariots, got off, and met their opponents in individual combat. Their arms were spears, swords or battle-axes, and large oblong shields protected their bodies from neck to knee. Behind each chief there followed on foot a crowd of retainers, who backed him up more by cheering than by fighting. Warfare came into being only with the rise of the state.

In the sixth century, the period of the Etruscan kings, there occurred a syndrome of changes—economic, social, military, and constitutional—more revolutionary in their impact upon world history than the fall of the monarchy and the birth of the Republic: the growth of Rome as a road center and trading post; its increase in area, population, and wealth; the rise of private property and the individual family; the decay of the clans as political and military units; and the incorporation of all such primitive organizations into a single city state. These important developments dictated a radical change in military tactics and in the composition of the army. The new army was a citizen army; its strength lay in the heavily armed infantry, which moved as a massive expression of the unity of the new-born state.

A similar pattern had earlier occurred in Greece. The rise of the city states had rendered the Homeric style of individual warfare obsolete. In its place came new arms and tactics, the most important of which innovations was a battle formation, the hoplite *phalanx*, in which heavily armed infantry troops advanced to the attack in tight ranks from eight to twelve lines deep. Each soldier now carried a long thrusting spear. He was protected by a small round shield fastened to the left arm, by helmets, corselets, and greaves all made of metal. First employed with increasing efficiency by the Lydians of the early seventh century B.C. and perfected by the Spartans, the *phalanx* soon developed into a machine of great striking power. Introduced into Italy by the Greeks during the last decades of the seventh century B.C., it gradually spread among the Italic tribes, and during the sixth century, as shown by the famous ostrich egg of Vulci, was adopted by the Etruscans, who passed it on to the Romans.

The first Roman hoplites were not ground troops but mounted infantry called *celeres*. Their horses carried them swiftly into battle and their heavy armor and new weapons gave them the fighting power of Greek shock troops or hoplites. Unlike real cavalry or the true *phalanx*, they fought not as a corps but individually like the charioteers of earlier times. On reaching the scene of combat, they dismounted and fought on foot. After the battle, they would ride away either in retreat or in pursuit of the enemy.

The *celeres*, according to tradition, consisted of three *centuries* (originally sixty, after Marius one hundred men) recruited from each of the three ancient tribes: Ramnes, Tities, and Luceres. The tribes also furnished 3,000 supporting ground troops divided into three corps or Thousands, each commanded by a military tribune. Most of these troops were probably clients belonging to the clans; some were possibly plebeians.

Sometime during the early phase of the Etruscan monarchy, possibly in the reign of Tarquin the First, the number of *centuries* was increased from three to six. At any rate both figures still seem to have been based on the three ancient tribes and must, therefore, have preceded the creation of the territorial tribes attributed to Servius Tullius.

The Servian Constitutional Reform

Tradition ascribes a complete military reform to Servius Tullius (sixth century B.C.). For the first time the infantry was drawn up in a more or less regular phalanx formation (a properly trained phalanx army did not come into being until the fourth century B.C.) and equipped with the armor of Greek hoplites—helmet, round shield, greaves, and breastplate, all of bronze. The offensive weapons were the long spear and the sword. The old army, divided into Thousands, was slightly increased to 3600 men and reorganized on the basis of centuries of sixty men. Thus came into being the first Roman legion of sixty centuries of front line men. And sixty remained the fixed number of centuries in all later legions. When the Servian legion was later split into two legions in order to give each of the two consuls a separate legion to command, the number of centuries remained the same even though there was not always enough manpower available to complete each century.

The purpose of the army reorganization was to enable Rome to meet her increasing military commitments. She seems to have been engaged in an exhausting struggle for supremacy in Latium. To replace battle losses required a larger body of citizens, who alone were eligible for the draft. Etruscan Rome was filled with immigrants willing to endure military service in order to acquire citizenship.

This Servian Constitution, commonly known as the Centuriate Organization, arose out of military necessity, but it was more than a simple reform of the army, for it transformed the state, as well. It was, apparently, a genuine political revolution, although many of the details ascribed to Servius Tullius by a late Republican tradition had to be worked out during the fourth, if not the third, century B.C. Its outcome was the city state based no longer on the ancient clans but on the citizen as a member of both the community and the army.

According to tradition, Servius Tullius redivided Roman territory into tribes, distributed the people into classes and centuries, and assessed the obligations and privileges of citizens on the basis of wealth or property. The five essential elements of this reform were eventually the tribes, the census, the classes, the centuries, and the popular assembly. The earliest and most basic of these seems to have been the tribes, since the creation of the four urban and sixteen rural tribes made citizenship depend more upon residence or domicile than upon membership in a clan or *curia*, as formerly. The new tribes served as districts for the registration of citizens and the assessment of their property and as units in the levy of recruits for the army, in the collection of taxes, and in the division of citizens into classes and centuries.

One of the most striking features of the Servian Centuriate Organization of Roman tradition was its timocratic character: the special privileges given to wealth. On the basis of their assessed wealth in land and other property, the citizens were divided into five property classes, and each class in turn into centuries of 60 men. (Some details obviously belong to the fourth century B.C.) To the first or richest class were assigned eighty centuries; to the second, third, and fourth, twenty each; and to the fifth, thirty. Ranking above all these were the eighteen centuries of cavalry, successors of the *celeres*. In addition there were four centuries of engineers, mechanics, and buglers and one century of the lowest, but the most numerous class of all, the proletariat, whose census was based on heads instead of property. In all there were believed to have been 193 Servian centuries, of which the ninety-eight centuries of the cavalry and the first property class not only constituted a majority in the fourth century B.C., but had the privilege of voting first in the new popular assembly. Special privileges were due to them, as a rule, throughout later history, because they were financially able to provide their own horse and armor, and upon them fell the heaviest burden of war and taxes.

The military character of this much discussed Centuriate Organization is revealed by the division into cavalry, infantry, and technical troops as well as by the subdivision of each of the five property classes into centuries, which served as recruiting units. In each class one half of the centuries consisted of *juniors* or men from seventeen to forty-six years old, the other of *seniors*, whose age ranged from forty-seven to sixty. The *seniors* formed the reserve, the *juniors* of the first three classes the hoplite infantry of the legion.

The organization did not lose its military character after the army had been separated completely from the Servian popular assembly, the so-called Comitia Centuriata, in the Samnite Wars. All through the Republic the ancient assembly retained the memory of its military origin. Summoned by a trumpet on orders of a magistrate with full executive power (*imperium*), it met at dawn on Mars Field in military formation outside the sacred wall (*pomerium*). During its meetings red flags flew on top of the Capitoline and Janiculum hills. The voting was by centuries, at least since the fourth century B.C., each century casting its single vote, which had previously been determined by a majority vote of its members. The centuries voted, perhaps early, in the order of their class, first the cavalry, then the highest property class, and so on until a majority of ninety-seven votes were cast. Whereupon the voting stopped. Only in the unlikely event of a tie would the fifth class, though representing the largest number of citizens, ever be called upon to vote. The system was far from democratic. For the rich with their ninety-eight centuries could always outvote the poor. The old could also outvote the young, since the *seniors*, though numerically inferior, had as many centuries as the *juniors*, who were subject to active military service. Thus the organization of this assembly, theoretically designed to represent citizens of all classes and citizens in arms, was actually plutocratic and conservative.

Functions of the Comitia Centuriata. The powers of the Centuriate Assembly may briefly be stated here though few writers would contend that they all go back to the monarchy or even the early Republic. During the fourth century B.C. and later it elected, upon nomination by their predecessors, the higher magistrates: the praetor-consuls, dictators, and censors. Their election ratified by the senate, these magistrates were solemnly invested with executive authority (*imperium*) before the Curiate Assembly. The centuries were also convened by a higher magistrate to accept or reject proposals affecting the interests of the state—the making of war and peace, the ratification of treaties, and the witnessing of trials for murder or high treason. One of its very early functions was, according to the XII Tables, that is during the later fifth century B.C., to act as a court of appeals for citizens condemned to death. But it probably did not possess the function of a truly deliberative assembly before the fourth or third centuries B.C.

Centuriate Reform. The existence in the fifth century B.C. of a centuriate assembly seems proved by the reference in the XII Tables to a *Comitiatus Maximus*. This Cicero repeatedly identified with the *Comitia Centuriata*. The actual existence of the Comitia Centuriata during the period of the Roman kingship is therefore considered as plausible as the existence of an Athenian hoplite *phalanx* army and of the Solonian and post-Solonian popular assembly in the more or less contemporary Athens of the tyrant Peisistratus and his sons. Much less certain, unfortunately, is an early or late dating of numerous details in the military and constitutional reforms ascribed to Servius Tullius. Therefore, although all ancient sources had, with one accord, assigned both the military and constitutional aspects of the reform to the sixth century B.C., some modern writers have found it difficult to agree. The many constitutional amendments from the fourth century B.C. to Sulla, obscure for us what may have belonged to constitutional reforms of the sixth century B.C. and especially to the period of Servius Tullius. Be that as it may, the army as a popular assembly is a recognized Indo-European institution of prehistory and was certainly, in the same function, not absent from the early Latin tribal settlements. Some pattern of army assembly existed in early Rome and subsequent army reforms and constitutional reforms were similarly interdependent in the Rome of the kings as in contemporary Greece.

Early Roman Religion

Religion played an important role in both the private and political life of Rome. A religion of home, farm, and pasture, it was concerned with present rather than with past or future needs. It inculcated the virtues of hard work, discipline, duty, courage, and loyalty. When the religion of the home became the religion of the state, it cemented the people together in a single community and gave the state an internal strength and cohesion which endured for centuries. Despite class struggles, changes of government, and foreign wars, it provided a common bond between rich and poor, patrician and plebeian, farmer and city dweller, and enabled the Roman state to face the world with unity and strength. Like other Italic peoples, the Romans had a varied religious inheritance from the past: from the prehistoric inhabitants of Italy, from the Indo-European immigrants of Central and Balkan Europe, from the Etruscans in the north and the Greek colonists of the south. As a result the Roman heritage contained elements of almost every known religious experience: totemism, magic, taboo, dynamism, animism, polytheism, and anthropomorphism. There are traces of totemism in the cults of the *gens*. Magic and taboo, though barred from the state religion, persisted among the common people throughout all Roman history.

Magic and Taboo

Magic, the mechanical use of certain materials, rites, formulae, or spells designed to force Nature, spirits, or other people to do one's will, survived during the classical period. The ceremony of the "Dripping-stone" (*lapis manalis*) was the use of sympathetic magic to bring rain. Another was the *Lupercalia,* which Shakespeare has popularized in his *Julius Caesar*. Two bands of youths with their brows smeared with the blood of a slaughtered goat and wearing goat skins around their thighs raced around the Palatine striking all the women they met with leather whips. The purpose of this rite was to dispel the curse of sterility. Charms and spells were commonly employed to drive away diseases, plagues, and foul weather, to fix broken bones, and to bring good crops and even success in war.

Allied to magic is another primitive survival usually known by its Polynesian name of *taboo*. In general it is a prohibition against persons, things, or acts regarded as dangerous to individuals or to the community. It was taboo for a woman to take part in the worship of Hercules, for a man to witness the rites of the Bona Dea, or for a horse to enter the sacred grove of Diana. A whole set of inexplicable ancient taboos fenced in the life and office of Jupiter's high priest. He might not see an army in battle gear nor do any kind of common work; never ride or touch a horse, a she-goat, or a dog; never cut his hair or nails with an iron knife; never wear an unbroken ring or have knots tied in his clothing; and never eat, among other things, wheat bread, raw meat, or beans.

Dynamism and Animism

The native religion of the early Romans is called *animism* by some scholars and *dynamism* by others. Dynamism, a term derived from the Greek word *dynamis* ("power"), is the belief that supernatural powers are synonymous with certain objects, places, natural processes, and living beings are inhabited by and indeed synonymous with supernatural spirits which are conceived of as impersonal, immanent, and pervasive. Animism, on the other hand, being derived from *anima,* the Latin word for "soul" or "spirit," regards these same objects to be inhabited by a discrete spirit which has a personal will, although it never attains the personality of a god of human form (anthropomorphic). Though dynamism is often regarded as a more primitive form of animism, actually both phases of belief existed side by side and were closely related.

The earliest form of animism was probably a vague belief in collective and undefined spirits usually thought of as hostile or malignant powers haunting persons, objects, and places like thick woods, dark caves, volcanoes, or old forest trees struck by lightning. These spirits aroused fear and had to be propitiated with offerings and prayers. As farm and family life became more settled and secure, certain spirits came to be regarded as friendly and helpful beings, if properly placated. They had their abode in such familiar objects in the house and on the farm as the house door (Janus), the fireplace (Vesta), the boundary stones that marked off one farm from another (Termini), and over all was Jupiter or the sky, the region of light, cloud, and storm.

The later animism recognized, in addition to the spirits of particular things and places, spirits presiding over definite human activities, especially the ones having to do with the making and storage of farm crops. Of these the most individualized and universal in their worship were Ceres, the spirit of grain crops; Consus, of the stored harvest; Saturn, of planting; Robigus, of rust or mildew; Flora, of flowers; and Pomona, of fruits. As religion became more highly organized, each separate operation of farm work had a special spirit (plowing, harrowing, sowing, weeding, harvesting, and storing). Each of these many functional spirits received offerings at the proper season of the year. When certain spirits were observed to be operating all at the same time in many places and for many families, they tended to become more real, more personal, and more human in form and personality. They gradually acquired names, had special priesthoods and rituals attached to their worship, and eventually attained the status of gods. Such a status Jupiter, a generally Indo-European high-god and sky spirit, seems to have attained in the third millennium B.C. So had Mars and Juno before Rome became a city.

Numen or Mana

The supernatural powers dwelling in certain sacred objects and places, in natural processes, in human activities, and in gods were thought of as possessing a mysterious force or influence which Latin writers of the Augustan age called *numen* (plural *numina*), but modern anthropologists identify by the Melanesian name of *mana. Numen* is essentially projected into external objects. It is both body and spirit. All things have an invisible as well as a visible existence. Nothing exists except by virtue of this mysterious force and without it no act can be performed. It is not the cobra which strikes but the *numen* within the cobra; it is not the spear that kills but the *numen* within the spear. Jupiter is the sky as well as the *numen* of the sky, Janus both the door and the spirit within the door. Like *mana*, *numen* connotes the triple idea of Power, Life, Will. As Power it brings about effects beyond human capability. As Life, it possesses a living consciousness. As Will, it can act for good or evil, if it wills. It was this mysterious Power-Life-Will association that evoked the feeling of religion (*religio*) in its primary sense of fear or anxiety and of religion in its secondary sense of a desire to establish right relations with the *numen* by prayer, propitiation, and ritual. *Numen* was not as yet conceived of as a single power immanent in the universe. Every object arousing fear or mystery and every act affecting the life and security of the worshipper had its own special *numen*. The world of animism was full of *numina*. Their number was legion. They were not gods. They were without human personality or form. They did not necessarily have name or sex. No statues represented them; no manmade temples housed them. Nameless, sexless, unhoused, and without mythology or image, they were yet the objects of worship, of sacrifice and prayer.

Sacrifice and Prayer

A Roman sacrifice was made in the conviction that it was good for the spirits as well as for the worshipper and the accompanying prayer *"Macte esto"* ("Be thou increased") reflects the belief that the offering increased the spirits' power to perform their special function for his benefit. Sacrifice replenished the store of *mana* consumed by the spirit. To restore the *mana* taken from Mother Earth by growing crops, the Romans held the annual spring festival of the *Fordicidia,* at which they killed a pregnant cow and made a burnt sacrifice of her aborted calf, thus "transferring" to the earth the fertility of a cow in calf. More than this, sacrifice was a means of conferring *mana* upon objects not possessing it before. To consecrate a new boundary stone between farms, the Romans used to make offerings of incense, grain, honey, and wine together with the blood of a lamb or sow.

If by sacrifice the *numen* or *mana* of a spirit could be increased, renewed, strengthened, or conferred, it was through prayer that the worshipper expressed his desire as

The Suovetaurilia (ca. 98–117 A.D.), in the Forum (Rome). (Courtesy Fratelli Alinari, Florence)

to the use and direction of that increased power. To make sure that his desires and petitions were clearly and fully understood, he worded his prayers in exact and unambiguous language. Any slip of the tongue made it necessary to start all over again. Having correctly and reverently performed the two chief acts of worship, sacrifice and prayer, the worshipper had done his part. The rest lay with the will of the unseen powers.

Gods of the House and Fields

The cults and festivals of house and field were the oldest and the most vital; they preceded the founding of Rome, they outlived her fall. In the time of her greatness some found expression in the wall paintings of Pompeii; many in the poetry of Vergil, Horace, Ovid, and Tibullus. Greek and Oriental cults did not completely supplant them; Christianity did not utterly destroy them. Under various names and disguises they have survived, to modern times, among the peasants of Italy and Spain.

The spirits of the house were few but all illustrate the various phases of animism previously outlined. They were partly local, partly functional in character. There was Janus, the spirit of the door, who represented the home in its insecure relation to the outside world. He faced both in and out, letting in friends and shutting out enemies. Family life began with Janus. At weddings it was the custom for the bride to smear his doorposts with wolf's fat and to be lifted over his threshold. At the birth of a child the threshold was struck with an ax, a pestle, and a broom to repulse wild spirits from the outside. When someone died in the house, the corpse was carried out feet first for fear that his ghost might find its way back in.

Inside the house was Vesta, the spirit of the fireplace, whose fire gave warmth and cooked the daily meals. She was pure spirit, the *numen* of the living flame. Of her no image or statue was made in early times. Yet she was the center of family life and worship. To her the head of the house presented his bride or new-born child. Before her hearth stood the dining table—it too a sacred object.

The salt dish was on it and the sacred salt cake baked by the daughters of the house. At dinner, the head of the family ceremoniously threw part of the cake into the fire. As Janus began, Vesta ended the roll of deities invoked in family prayer.

Not far from the fireplace was the pantry. Here dwelt a vague group of nameless spirits collectively known as the Penates. With Vesta they shared the offerings made at the fireplace because they guarded the food which Vesta cooked. In Latin literature they were a synonym for "home." So were the Lares.

Originally the Lares were probably not gods of the house but of the fields. As spirits of the fields, the Lares were worshipped at the feast of the Crossroads (*Compitalia*), a thanksgiving festival, in which even slaves took part. The plows were hung up as a sign that the season's work was done and everybody joined in the feasting and fun. Still more picturesque was the festival of the *Ambarvalia* held toward the end of May to secure divine favor for the growing and ripening crops. The farmer and his family, dressed in white with olive wreaths around their heads, solemnly drove a pig, a sheep, and a bull (*suovetaurilia*) three times around the farm. The three animals were then killed, opened, examined for omens, and burned upon the altar fire. There followed a long prayer for good weather and good crops to Mars, the primitive god of agriculture.

Besides the *Fordicidia* and *Terminalia* already described, there took place in spring the *Liberalia,* the *Cerealia,* and the *Robigalia,* at which a red dog was sacrificed to avert mildew or rust, which attacked wheat. Shepherds had their spring festivals too; the *Palilia* or feast of Pales, spirit of flocks and herds, took place in April just before the annual trek to summer pastures. At dawn the herdsmen sprinkled the animals with water, swept out the stalls, and decorated the barns with green branches. Then they lit a bonfire of straw, brush, and other stuff, through which both the flocks were driven and the shepherds leaped. After an offering of milk and cakes to Pales and a prayer for the health, safety, and increase of the flocks, they spent the rest of the day in sports, and in eating and drinking.

Two festivals held in late summer or early fall are noteworthy because they are coupled with the names of Jupiter and Mars, whose association with agriculture was, in later times, largely forgotten. The first was the Feast of Wine (*Vinalia Rustica*) held on August 19th in honor of Jupiter, whose high priest after the sacrifice of a ewe-lamb solemnly inaugurated the grape-picking season by cutting the first bunch of grapes. The other was the festival of the October Horse in honor of Mars in his dual capacity as god of war and god of farming. A chariot race was held. The near horse of the winning team, and a spear were sacrificed to Mars. The horse's tail was rushed over to the King's House, where its blood, still warm, dribbled upon the hearth. The head, cut off and decked with cakes, was fought over by the men of two adjacent wards in Rome, the winners being allowed to hang it up as a trophy in their ward.

Jupiter and Mars

Unlike most of the numerous spirits animating the world of the early Roman farmer, Jupiter and Mars entered history fully endowed with human personality and form. Conceived originally as the sky and the spirit immanent in the sky, as the source and giver of light and the unseen force in lightning, storm, and rain, Jupiter had long ago become a spirit of the vine also, and was associated with Venus, the primitive Italic spirit of vines and gardens. With the growth of political and urban life among the Latins and the Romans, Jupiter lost status as a farmer's god but came into his own as a god of cities and towns. He was the tribal deity of the Latins and the guardian of many Latin towns. In Rome he was the greatest of all gods, the symbol of the Roman state, the giver of victory, and the spirit of law and justice. Steadily increasing in majesty and power, he seemed on the way to becoming, like Jehovah, the supreme god of heaven and earth. Only he never quite became so. He was identified with the Roman state. His glory was the glory of Rome; his kingdom, the Roman empire. The military and political success of Rome made his help unnecessary on the one hand, and on the other it arrested his de-velopment towards the status of a universal god of righteousness. Even so, his exalted status, which he owed in part to the greatness of Rome, was a far cry from being a spirit of the sky and vine. Likewise did Rome exalt Mars. Once an Italic spirit of the forest, he became the protector of the farmer's crops and herds but later, as god of war, the defender of the Roman state against its enemies. Thus with the rise of Rome as a city and a state, Jupiter and Mars lost all connection with agriculture save the memory preserved in the rustic festivals just described.

The examples of Jupiter and Mars show that native Roman animism was capable of religious growth. Left to itself, it might even have developed something spiritually good and beautiful. It was not left to itself. Its potential good was buried beneath a tide of incoming foreign cults which influenced Roman religion both directly and indirectly —Italic, Etruscan, and especially Greek, for the Italian and Etruscan gods, long before their introduction at Rome, had come under the humanizing influence of the Greeks living in south Italy. The outward signs of this influence were temples and statues. Unlike the old Roman spirits, the new anthropomorphic gods had to have houses to dwell in and statues to embody them.

Italic Cults

After Rome had become a bridge town, a road center, and a trading post, she came into close contact with the cults of Latium and southern Etruria. She adopted as her own those which best filled newly felt needs. The most prominent and widespread of these cults was that of *Juno*, who was worshipped all over Italy and was a special favorite in Latium and southern Etruria. The growing popularity of her worship in Rome indicates that the city was becoming the cultural capital of the two districts lying on opposite sides of the Tiber.

From Falerii, a semi-Etruscan town higher up on the north side of the Tiber, came the cult of *Minerva,* an old Italian goddess of arts and crafts but worshipped under the name of *Menvra* in many Etruscan towns. Her worship in Rome, perhaps introduced by immigrant Faliscan workmen skilled in the pottery and metal trades, is clearly in line with the archaeological evidence of close commercial and industrial ties between Rome and south Etruria. The expansion of Roman commercial contacts is likewise pointed up by the erection in the Cattle Market of an altar to *Hercules,* the patron god of the Greek and Italian traveling salesmen. Politically the transfer of the worship of Diana from Aricia to the Aventine highlights Roman aspirations to leadership over the Latin League. So too does the coming to Rome of two other Latin goddesses both destined to have a great future; namely, *Fortuna* imported from Anzio and later identified with Tyche, the Greek goddess of luck or chance, and *Venus,* formerly worshipped at Ardea as a goddess of gardens and orchards but later identified with Aphrodite, the Greek goddess of love and beauty.

Of the deities just named all, except Hercules, had belonged originally to the spirit world of old Italy but had before their adoption in Rome, been transformed through Greek influence into gods of human personality and form. Even *Ceres,* the most earthy and the most native Italic of spirits, did not escape the effects of this transforming influence. Identified with *Demeter,* the Greek goddess of cereals, she had a cult more foreign than that of Hercules in the Cattle Market. Her temple on the Aventine was not only the Grain Exchange but, during the early Republic, the church of the dispossessed and the political rendezvous of the plebs, who at that time were excluded from the religious and political life of the state.

Etruscan Influence

Contact with the Etruscans gave an even stronger impetus to the influx of Greek anthropomorphic ideas among the Romans. Of the gods worshipped by the Etruscans Uni and Menvra were the Italic Juno and Minerva. Tinia, a truly Etruscan deity, was early identified with Jupiter. The temple, which the Tarquins built on the Capitoline to that triad of deities, must have been something new to the Romans, who had hitherto never set up for their gods anything more

elaborate or permanent than a rude altar of stones or sods. The elevation of its site, its massive appearance, and the beauty of its Greco-Etruscan ornaments provided the proper home for Rome's greatest deity. The Capitoline temple together with the two temples of Diana and Minerva on the Aventine firmly established temple building as a permanent feature of Roman religious life and powerfully reinforced the current trend from animism to the Greek anthropomorphic conception of deity.

Greek Cults

The introduction of Greek anthropomorphic ideas and cults through Etruscan and Italian contacts was followed before and after the fall of the monarchy by more direct contacts with the South Italian Greeks. The nearest, and oldest Greek settlement was Cumae, not far from Naples. From Cumae, quite early in the Republic, came the worship of *Apollo,* the god of healing and prophecy. Despite his unlatinized name, Apollo became, in later times, one of the greatest gods of the Roman pantheon. Cumae was also the home of the *Sibyl,* Apollo's inspired priestess, whose oracle must have been known in Etruscan Rome, though the story of Tarquin's purchase of the Sibylline books is probably pure legend. The earliest collection of Sibylline oracles seems to have been made at the beginning of the Republic. Kept in the temple of Jupiter and guarded in strictest secrecy by a special college of two priests, the oracles were consulted only by command of the senate in time of war, disaster, plague, or famine. Consulted in times of stress, the Sibylline books played a decisive role throughout the Republic in replacing the native animism of the past with a new Greco-Roman anthropomorphism. Consultation usually resulted in the introduction of some new Greek deity or form of worship. During the famine of ca. 496 B.C., a temple on the Aventine was promised and three years later dedicated to Ceres, Liber, and Libera, a triad of farm gods identical in almost everything but name with Demeter, Dionysus, and Persephone.

The following year saw the dedication also on the Aventine of a temple to another Greek god, Hermes, under the name of Mercury. Like Hercules, he was a god of traders and especially of the grain merchants in both Etruria and Greek Italy. His temple was a grain market as well as a rendezvous of merchants and traders. Sea-borne imports from South Italy seem to account for the early reception of Poseidon, the Greek god of the great open sea. He was identified with Neptune, though the latter was originally not a sea god but the spirit of springs and ponds and other small waters.

In addition to introducing new gods, the Sibylline books prescribed new forms of worship, some exceedingly spectacular and emotional and all quite foreign to the pious sober spirit of the early Roman religion. These innovations, both numerous and of great variety, consisted of funeral and secular games, stage plays and other dramatic performances, ritual dances, religious parades, banquets of the gods (*lectisternia*), and supplications. Perhaps the strangest of these was the *lectisternium*, at which images of the gods grouped in sex-pairs were publicly displayed reclining on couches before a table spread with food and drinks. At the banquet ordered in 217 B.C. there sat Jupiter and Juno, Neptune and Minerva, Mars and Venus, Apollo and Diana, Vulcan and Vesta, and finally Ceres and Mercury.

If the *lectisternium* implied a degrading conception of deity, it was not so emotional a spectacle as the supplication, in which men and women with wreaths on their heads and laurel branches in their hands paraded from temple to temple making prayers for deliverance from calamity or giving thanks for benefits received. In the latter days of the Republic a thanksgiving might last for fifteen days, the people all the while working themselves up to a high emotional fever of religious ecstasy.

The Roman State Religion

The foreign cults just described were not the only factors involved in the changing religious life of the Roman people. Equally important changes occurred when the primitive religion of house and fields became organized as the religion of the state.

The state itself was essentially a religious institution. It embraced and incorporated all the older and smaller social and religious communities such as the family, the clan, and the tribe. According to the legend, it had been inaugurated, with religious ceremonies, by Romulus. The *pomerium,* which enclosed the city, was a sacred boundary. As the city grew and expanded, it was the responsibility of the state to provide for the common religious life of all the people on behalf of the whole community.

The Romans showed little originality or inspiration in organizing a religion to meet the special needs of the state. The rustic cults and festivals had little meaning for an urban population. Household cults had more appeal because family life was very much the same in town and country. The most popular and successful were those of Janus and Vesta. Janus, the spirit of the house door, became the god of the Sacred Gateway at the northeast corner of the Forum. As the early armies probably marched through this gate on their way to war, it was kept closed only in peacetime. Another of the household deities to find a place in the state religion was Vesta, the Sacred Hearth, whose holy fire, relit only on March 1, the New Year's Day of the state, was kept burning by the Vestal Virgins. Unlike many of the old field cults and festivals listed in the state calendar, the worship of Janus and Vesta aroused genuine religious feeling among the citizens because it fostered a sense of belonging to one great national family. The cults which roused the strongest feelings of pride and love of Rome were those of Jupiter and Mars. Mars was the god of her triumphant armies, his altar the symbol of her military power. Jupiter, "Greatest and Best" of all gods, sent down upon Rome "the continual dew of his divine favor."

Neither the home fires of Vesta, the might of Mars, nor the transcendent glory of Jupiter saved the state religion from stagnation and decay. Its basic weakness lay not so much in its formalism and inappropriateness (field cults in an urban setting) as in the exclusive conduct of public worship by professional priesthoods. Since the state religion required nothing more of the people than to do no work on festival days, it failed to develop much popular interest. They had no need to concern themselves about the gods, for that was the job of the professional priest.

The Priesthood and the Priestly Colleges

During the Republic professional priesthoods, organized for the correct performance of public worship, played a larger and more independent role than they had under the kings, who were both rulers and chief priests. All priests and pontiffs then owed their appointments to the king and acted as his assistants and advisers. After the fall of the Monarchy, consuls and praetors took over his political and military powers, his religious functions being divided between the King of Sacrifices (*Rex Sacrorum*) and the Supreme Pontiff (*Pontifex Maximus*). In later times the powers of the former declined, those of the latter greatly increased. For the chief pontiff had acquired jurisdiction not only over the powerful college of pontiffs but over the Vestal Virgins and the special priests (*flamines*) assigned to the worship of Jupiter, Mars, and Quirinus, and of twelve lesser deities. Even the King of Sacrifices, though the nominal successor of the overthrown priest-kings and in the early Republic a personage of great dignity and prestige, was in actual fact subject to the jurisdiction of the Supreme Pontiff.

The members of the priestly colleges or associations were more important to the organized religion of the state than any of the individual priests or priesthoods. They were priests but not necessarily men of exceptional piety or endowed with special psychic or clairvoyant powers. They were rather men of learning, political experience, and high social rank. Their wealth enabled them to perform their priestly duties without financial reward. Some had been magistrates before becoming priests. Some were priests and magistrates simultaneously; and many were members of the senate. The chief qualification for membership in a priestly college was an exact knowledge of religious tradition, of divine law, and of correct ritual and ceremonial procedure.

Under the Roman constitution there were two main colleges, that of the augurs and that of the pontiffs. The college of augurs, consisting of three members (later increased to five and eventually to fifteen or sixteen), assisted the magistrates to take the *auspices* and thereby learn the will of the gods before undertaking any important public business such as the election of the higher magistrates and meetings of the popular assemblies. As the magistrate scanned the skies and reported to the blindfolded augur what he saw, the augur applied his expert knowledge of signs to determine and interpret the will of the gods. The signs were derived from thunder and lightning, the flight and cries of birds, the feeding of sacred chickens, and the behavior of certain animals and snakes. If the omens, especially those unsolicited, were pronounced as unfavorable, it was the duty of the magistrate to postpone the proposed action until the omens were right. In this way the augurs were in a position to exert considerable influence on politics during the Republic.

Still more important was the college of pontiffs. Originally the pontiff (*pontifex*) was a magician whose incantations were believed to give permanence to the flimsy bridges in early Latium. Though its function under the kings was purely advisory, the college assumed, from the birth of the Republic, a constantly growing all-pervading control over every aspect of the state religion except augury. The original three members were later increased to six, in 300 B.C. to nine, and by Sulla to fifteen. They held office for life, their functions were many and their influence great. They were the custodians and interpreters of the sacred law governing both the religious and legal relations of the community to the gods. They alone knew the exact formulae applicable in all legal transactions and the proper forms employed in the making of vows. They were the sole keepers of the temple archives, and prescribed the various rituals, prayers, chants, and litanies for use in public worship. They also supervised the dedication and the consecration of temples and altars, the burial of the dead, and the declaration of war and the making of treaties. It was they who organized the calendar that fixed the dates of festivals and the days on which the magistrate might not sit in court. The president of their college, judge and arbiter of things human and divine, had the power to convene and the right to preside over the Curiate Assembly. Since this assembly passed laws on adoptions and wills, the pontiffs exercised through it a dominant influence on the law of wills. Equally important was the influence of the pontiffs on the law of claims. As claims brought before the courts had to follow the precise meaning of the law on which they depended, they would best stand if drafted with the advice and assistance of the pontiffs, who held a monopoly of jurisprudence throughout the first two centuries of the Republic.

Early Roman Law and Moral Code

The pontiffs' superintendence of the state religion is overshadowed by their contribution to the field of early Roman law, which became, in the form finally given to it in the Justinian Code, the basis of European law and a prime element in the formation of modern Western civilization. This contribution to the development of law and legal science was not the result of their legislative activities (many of them had seats in the senate and acted as members of standing committees on religious and legal affairs), nor of their judicial function for, though magistrates frequently referred cases to them for judicial review, the pontiffs were not judges nor regularly practicing lawyers. Their contribution arose from their function as consultants and interpreters of the law.

Since it is impossible for even the wisest and the most gifted of law-makers to foresee all the possible needs of the future, as cases arise not covered by existing law, judges and interpreters must determine not only the exact meaning but the spirit of the law and be able to expand its details or to apply new meanings to old. The pontiffs based their interpretations on precedents, of which they alone had knowledge and whose mystery the

publication of the XII Tables had not yet entirely dispelled. To precedents based on ancestral custom (*mos maiorum*) they added interpretations or commentaries on the XII Tables, and formulae or instructions for the performance of legal acts, and especially opinions (*responsa*) on the legality of acts both contemplated and already performed. In step with the needs of the Roman state, the pontiffs began gradually the buildup of a body of jurisprudence which was based upon the principles of ancient unwritten customs and the XII Tables. Their achievement was not unlike that of English and American judges in the creation of the common law or that of the Supreme Court in the development of the Constitutional law of the United States.

The virtual monopoly of legal science by the college of pontiffs until the late fourth century B.C. and thereafter arose from the original lack of differentiation between Roman religion and Roman law. Criminal law was based on the principle that an offense against the community was an offense against the gods. In private lawsuits both parties swore oaths which, if violated, would provoke the wrath of the gods. The first Roman jurists of sacred, private, or public law came from the college of pontiffs, each assisted by a staff of secretaries, copyists, and recorders. Magistrates consulted the entire college on matters of religious and constitutional law; private disputes were referred to the pontiff appointed by the college to deal with such cases. This authority was not challenged until the later fourth or third centuries B.C., when knowledge of the law passed gradually into the hands of a wide circle of laymen.

Law was not the only by-product of the religious life of this period nor the sole legacy of Rome to the modern world. The religious ethics of the Roman family and clan also survive because the moral code of Rome has been transmitted in a modified and refined form by the Christian Church.

It is significant that most of the modern European names of moral concepts stem from Latin and some of them still retain their original meaning. The English words: virtue, prudence, temperance, fortitude, justice, piety, fidelity, constancy, and perseverance, stem from Latin roots. Of these "virtue" alone has a distinctly different meaning from that which it had in ancient Rome.

Virtue (Virtus)

The word "virtus" included everything which made up the true man and a useful member of society. It is virtue, says the poet Lucilius (ca. 180–103 B.C.), for a man to know what is good, what evil, what useless, shameful, and dishonorable; to be an enemy of bad men and customs, to be a friend and protector of those that are good; to place first one's country's good, next that of one's parents, and last that of one's self.

Virtue also meant a strong and healthy body, the ability to provide for one's family, interest in and devotion to the state, and heroism in war. If heroism was the greatest of these, it was not the individual heroism of Achilles or Hector. It was "virtue" only when used for the good and safety of the state. The ideal Roman hero was one whose courage and wisdom saved his country in time of peril. The virtues cited as examples in the moral education of the youths were drawn not from heroic poetry as in Greece but from history. Young men were taught that it was glorious to die for their country as did the heroes of the past. So important was *virtus* as an element of early Roman character that it has become the generic term for all kinds of human excellence in many modern languages.

Piety (Pietas). Four virtues were distinctively Roman and of great historic significance. They were piety, faith, gravity, and constancy. The first, piety (*pietas*), was a family virtue. It implied devotion and loyalty to the family group and a willing acceptance of parental authority, which gave unity and strength to the family. It further meant reverence and devotion to the gods as members of the family as shown in action by the exact performance of all required religious rites and ceremonies. Piety towards the state connoted obedience to the laws, faithful service, and patriotism consistent with justice, law, and the constitution. In this virtue Livy,

Propertius, and Vergil saw the prime reason for Rome's greatness.

Faith (Fides). Another virtue the Romans took pride in was faith, which Cicero called the "foundation of justice," Valerius Maximus the "supreme guarantee of human happiness." It had special importance within social units larger than the family—the *gens* and the state. It meant being true to one's word, the paying of one's debts, the keeping of sworn oaths, and the performance of obligations assumed by agreement. Based on religion and law, it was the foundation of public and private life. Violation of it was an offense against both the gods and the community. A patron, who broke faith with his client by unjust abuse of his power, was placed under a curse. A magistrate who broke faith by acts of injustice and oppression against the people gave the latter the right to rebel. Faith rooted in the social conscience was stronger than written law or statute as a force for holding all parts of the society together in a common bond of relationship.

Gravity (Gravitas) and Constancy (Constantia). Faith had to be supplemented by two other Roman virtues: gravity and constancy. The first meant absolute self-control, a dignified, serious, and unperturbed attitude towards both good and bad fortune. Cato the Censor, Cicero, and other writers give us some extreme examples of gravity, namely that no Roman was supposed to dance in public or to kiss his wife outside of his own home! The second virtue was constancy or perseverance, even under the most trying circumstances, in what seemed necessary and right until success was won. Of this virtue Rome herself was the greatest exponent, for in her long history she suffered many disastrous defeats. That she never broke under those defeats and often turned them into victories is no small tribute to Roman education.

It is clear that Roman education fostered a rather conservative type of human being, respectful to authority and loyal to ancestral custom (*mos maiorum*). Yet the conservatism of the Romans was resilient enough to respond to the necessity for change and, on occasion, could even be revolutionary.

Though it held fast to the ideals of order, simplicity, and discipline, it was dynamic, progressive, and responsive to the processes of history and the expansion of the state. The peculiar genius of the founders of the early Roman state lay in their ability to harmonize contrasting principles, to reconcile personal liberty with military discipline, the individual with the state, and to integrate these opposing elements into an order fixed in juridical norms, religious rules, and political regulations.

V

RISE OF THE ROMAN

THAT PERIOD OF ROMAN HISTORY KNOWN AS THE REPUBLIC
extended from the early part of the fifth century until the
principate of Augustus (27 B.C.). The name "republic" (*res
publica*) has come to mean a form of government, not necessarily democratic, but essentially different from that which exists
under a king or emperor. To the Romans the words *res publica*
("public affairs") meant simply the state or the affairs of the
state. Livy (II:3) expressed the difference between kingship and
republic in the following words: "The king is a man from whom
you may ask a favor, right or wrong; he can become angry with
you, but he can also forgive; he can distinguish between a friend
and an enemy. But law is a dumb, inexorable thing, healthier
and better for the poor than the rich; it has no indulgence or
forgiveness in it, if you overstep its limits; where there are so

REPUBLIC

many human errors, it is dangerous to have to live by innocence alone." Apparently, then, "republic" meant for the Romans a government of law rather than of men.

Sources of Information

It is impossible to describe or evaluate early Roman society and government without a survey of the sources of information (*see* p. 46).

The two chief literary sources for the history of this period as of the monarchy are Livy (Books 2–5) and Dionysius of Halicarnassus (*Roman Antiquities* 4–14). Both authors wrote in the time of Augustus and used as their main source the work of Aelius Tubero, who, in the time of Cicero (106–43 B.C.), wrote a history of Rome down to the Punic Wars based upon two other annalists of his time, Valerius Antias and Licinius Macer. Livy and Dionysius were familiar with their works either through Tubero or directly, sometimes preferring them to Tubero for certain facts. In addition to Tubero, Antias, and Macer, they also made use of older writers, namely, Calpurnius Piso, Cincius

Alimentus, and especially Fabius Pictor, all of whom wrote about the history of Rome from its founding to their own time (Piso in Latin, Cincius and Fabius in Greek). Their works, though lost to us, can be inferred both as to nature and content from a careful comparison of pertinent passages in Livy and Dionysius.

The Early Annalists

Of the early writers whom Livy and Dionysius used as sources, Piso was a consul (133 B.C.) and later a censor (120 B.C.); Cincius, a praetor (210 B.C.) and a general; while Fabius Pictor (ca. 220 B.C.), the earliest historian of Rome, was a senator, an ambassador to Greece, a soldier, a scholar, and a pontiff. These, and other writers of this period (who were almost as prominent socially and politically), seem to have intended their works as useful handbooks to keep magistrates, senators, and jurists informed about Roman laws and treaties. Some, such as Fabius, sought to justify Rome's ways to the Greeks. Although they included numerous legends and sagas in their accounts of the regal period, their treatment of the early Republic is much more factual.

Piso devoted two books to the first two hundred years of the Republic (or about ten lines a year). He probably mentioned the names of the chief magistrates, the dates of wars, the victories and defeats of Roman armies, fires, plagues, famines, earthquakes, and eclipses, all of which were contained in the priestly annals (*Annales Maximi*) published around 123 B.C. Piso probably had access to the lists of magistrates kept in the temple of Juno Moneta from the time of its dedication in about 344 until the middle of the first century B.C. as well as to the treaties stored in the Capitoline temple, which was destroyed by fire in the time of Sulla, the statutes kept in the temple of Saturn until the time of Caesar, and the acts of the senate kept in the temple of Ceres down to the age of Augustus.

A good deal of material must also have been available to Fabius who wrote, according to Polybius, a rather sketchy account of the early Republic. As a member of one of

Junius Brutus, a Roman patrician, with busts of his ancestors (marble, lifesize, first century A.D.). (Courtesy Fratelli Alinari, Florence)

the oldest and most illustrious of Roman families, Fabius probably knew all the best families of his time, saw the wax masks of their ancestors set up in the *atrium**, read the grave inscriptions, and probably attended funerals, where he heard speeches about the deceased and his ancestors, the temples and public buildings they had dedicated, the magistracies they had held, the triumphs won in war. Though some of these panegyrics contained not a few lies and exaggerations, they added background to those official lists of past magistrates in the possession of the consuls or to those to which he himself must have had access as a member of the college of pontiffs. He might also have read the Graeco-Sicilian historians, Timaeus (ca. 356–260 B.C.), Diocles and Philinus (ca. 250 B.C.).

* The living-room of the Roman house.

(Some of these western Greek writers of the third and second centuries B.C. had a fairly good knowledge of Roman conditions after 500 B.C.)

Annalists from the Gracchan Age to Cicero

Had Livy and Dionysius and their more immediate sources, Tubero, Antias, and Macer, used as reference only the earlier writers, their account of the monarchy and the early Republic would have been less lengthy, less legendary, and less entertaining perhaps, but far more factual and reliable. Unfortunately, the later annalistic tradition hinged largely upon the works of Cnaius Gellius and Claudius Quadrigarius. Of Gellius nothing much is known other than that he wrote sometime between 150 and 120 B.C. and that his annals were of extraordinary length. He devoted twenty books or more to the first two centuries of the Republic. (Piso, more factual, wrote only two books about that period.) Gellius probably embellished his account with entertaining legends, free reconstructions, and inventions. All the later annalists probably used his work, although Macer is the only one known to have done so. Gellius' greatest contribution, or rather his greatest disservice, to the annalistic tradition was his departure from the short, dry chronicles of the older annalists in favor of the fuller, more romantic, and more popular type of narrative. His influence is abundantly illustrated in the first ten books of Livy. So is that of Claudius, whose annals began in detail with the sack of Rome.

About 70 B.C. Valerius Antias wrote at least seventy-five books filled with sensationalism and patriotic romance. This element in his work made him the most popular and the most readable of all historians before Livy. A very interesting personality of the Sullan and Ciceronian period was Licinius Macer, a strong champion of the "popular" cause. He combined his own political experience with his historical studies to create a work setting forth his own radical convictions. His entire work was vitiated by false scholarship and pseudo-research.

Of all the annalists Aelius Tubero was perhaps the most polished writer. Unlike Macer, he belonged to an old distinguished family and was an ardent supporter of monarchy and aristocracy. His history of Rome began with the story of the Trojan Horse. Both he and Macer projected many of the events and political feelings of their time back into the past. To them Livy and Dionysius owed many of their facts and legends as well as some principles of the artistic historical style.

Livy and Dionysius

Both Dionysius and Livy followed Tubero as main source. Dionysius, who was by profession a rhetorician, was ambitious to write a work in the grand style of Thucydides or Aristotle yet lacked the courage to depart from the chronological arrangement used by Tubero and the other annalists. Sometimes he did rearrange his material but only because he wanted to create occasions for long-winded speeches and debates, of which he was very fond. Livy exhibited much more independence and literary style. He often used several other sources at a time preferring now one, now another, and arranged his material not exclusively according to consular years but around some central theme—event, idea, or personality. Of his second book, for example, the first twenty-two chapters center around the theme of liberty, the next ten around the class struggle, the next seven around the personality of Coriolanus, and the twenty-two after that around the agitation for agrarian reform. Any details appearing in his sources that seemed to him likely to obscure, destroy the unity of, or distract attention from his main themes he altered, compressed, or omitted altogether.

Livy as Historian. Today Livy would not be considered a scientific historian. Like Dionysius and all the annalists from Fabius to Tubero, he felt that Rome deserved as glorious a history as early Greece. Roman history was not a sequence of recorded events but the working out of some grand predestined design. The result is a compilation of truth and fiction, of lies and interpolations, of ideas and ideals carried over from Greek historiography and projected into the Roman past. Indeed some of the ideas which both Livy and Dionysius ascribed to Brutus and the other founding fathers of the Republic sound strangely modern.*

Minor Literary Sources

The remaining extant sources of the history of the early Republic consist of thirteen short chapters (25–37) in the second book of Cicero's *De Re Publica*, of the sixth book of Polybius on the theory and development of the Roman constitution, of a few papyrus fragments in Latin, and of a few facts about Roman affairs, some important, some not, which Diodorus of Sicily injects into five books (10–14) of his universal history written in Greek and published between 36 and 30 B.C. The most important contribution Diodorus has made to our knowledge is his list of consuls beginning with the year ca. 486 B.C. So important is this list that much attention has been devoted to his sources.

The Fasti

In ancient states, calendar years were not numbered in chronological sequence but named after one or more of the chief annual magistrates: in Athens after the head archon, in Sparta after the chief ephor, in Rome after the consuls. All such officials are known as eponymous ("year-naming") magistrates. Such a system made phenomenal demands upon the memory unless lists were handy for business, legal, and official purposes. During the fifth and fourth centuries of the Roman Republic many such lists must have been available to public officials, priests, and private individuals.

The oldest, perhaps, and certainly the most famous list of Roman magistrates was that kept by the pontiffs from the earliest years of the Republic. At the beginning of each year the head pontiff had a white-washed tablet set up in his office. Across the top of the tablet were written the names of the consuls, the other important magistrates, and the priests. Then followed a list of the feast or holy days (*nefasti*) and the regular days (*fasti*) on which it was right to do business or hold court. Opposite each day space was left for noting unusual events such as eclipses, earthquakes, plagues, prodigies, temple dedications, wars and triumphs, and the like. At the end of the year the tablet was stored away in the archives for future reference, but gradually decayed over the centuries and became completely illegible. It was probably from this primitive "card index" that lists of magistrates were compiled for public and private use.

Around 123 B.C. all the tablets were collected, edited, and published in a work of eighty volumes known as the *Annales Maximi*, an official document recording the names of the magistrates, the triumphs, and temple dedications from the beginning of the Republic. This was probably the chief source of the numerous lists in circulation during the last century of the Republic. It was the source of the *Fasti* of Diodorus, of Livy (the most complete), and of Dionysius (down to the year ca. 443 B.C.), as well as those compiled during the Empire, of the anonymous Chronographer of 354 A.D., of Hieronymus of 378, of Hydatius of 468, and finally of Cassiodorus of 519. The *Fasti* all together account for the names of 1,047 consecutive eponymous Roman magistrates from the Elder Brutus to Basilius Junior of 565 A.D.

The Capitoline Fasti. Another source of information are inscriptions. Of some thirty-five consular lists of varying completeness found on inscriptions at Rome, Ostia, Anzio, and other places, the most official and extensive is that commonly called the *Capitoline Fasti*, incised on marble, probably around 18 B.C., upon the Arch of Augustus in the Forum. Besides the list of consuls and other eponymous magistrates from the beginning of the Republic to Augustus, the *Capitoline Fasti* contained a list of all who won military triumphs since Romulus. The consular list, half complete, has fragments of no year earlier than 483 B.C. Though of capital importance, this list is not superior in reliability or author-

---

* The charges against Tarquin the Proud of having placed himself above the law, of having used spies and informers to destroy freedom of speech, of having abrogated the right of assembly, and of having converted the government into a tyranny may be compared with Locke's essay on civil government, or the Declaration of Independence.

ity to those of Livy or Diodorus. It is based upon the common stock of source material available in the last century B.C.

The Reliability of the Roman Historical Tradition

It is upon the soundness of the *Fasti* that the entire structure of historical tradition must rest. Beloch has established the interesting and important proposition that within the span of 185 years from 486 B.C., where Diodorus begins his list, to 302 B.C. Livy and Diodorus, though using entirely different sources, agree in 97 per cent of the consular names. The same consistency exists between Diodorus and the *Capitoline Fasti* within the same period.

Nevertheless Beloch damns as probably spurious, because of their plebeian names, twelve out of 48 consuls from 509 till 486 B.C.; and from 486 to the end of the century, six consuls, six decemvirs, and seven consular tribunes, whose names are preserved in the *Fasti*. Only one consular tribune with a plebeian name escaped detection and fifteen belonging to the first two decades of the next century were also rejected. Beloch concludes that in the early Republic, or until about 367 B.C., only patricians were really eligible to the consulship and the *Fasti* must have been interpolated and tampered with early in the third century B.C., when plebeians first began to take charge of the records in the office of the college of pontiffs. This radical theory of source criticism has been in vogue for quite a long time.

Other scholars consider the tradition essentially sound except for a few names that had become blurred and unreadable on the oldest tablets. Others, who hold that the names are all really genuine, have set out to prove that the patrician branch of some families later known only as plebeian such as the Junii, Minucii, Genucii, Sempronii, Veturii, and Volumnii may have died out in the meantime or lost their patrician status because of some stigma or calamity. Then again some names prominent in the consular annals of the first seventy-five years such as the Aebutii, Aternii, Cloelii, Curiatii, and Larcii were never heard of again. No one, it is argued, would have wanted to invent such names. On the other hand, many plebeian families of power and influence in the later centuries such as the Coruncanii, Fulvii, Livii, Decii, Marcii, and Fabricii never succeeded in getting their names in the list at all.

Recently Swedish Forum excavations have redirected critical thinking. Since the early Republican levels of Rome cannot possibly have been more than one or two decades earlier than 450 B.C., as Professor Gjerstadt maintains, the names of about 100 early Roman consuls in the *Fasti* must be spurious and interpolated. This is in principle a very strong argument in favor of Beloch and his successors, but not necessarily a decisive reason for rejecting single names or groups with the previous arguments. The history of the early Roman Republic can, under these circumstances, be reconstructed only with the utmost caution.

Temple Dedications. Temple dedications also furnish fairly important data for fixing the chronology of this period. The dedication date of the Capitoline temple, inscriptionally established as 507 B.C., has been pronounced by one of our most skeptical critics as the oldest datable event of Roman history, the cornerstone of Roman chronology. Although the pontiffs took pains in accurately recording such important events as temple dedications, the dates of some have been established independently of pontifical recording. For example, the year 431 B.C. has been verified by Greek sources as the dedication date of the temple of Apollo on the Flaminian Meadows.

From Kingship to Republic

The transition from kingship to republic is one of the most disputed questions of Roman history because of the unreliability of the literary sources and the scarcity of archaeological material. According to ancient tradition, the Romans overthrew Tarquin the Proud because of his tyrannical government and his son's rape of a nobleman's daughter. Her suicide, it is believed, set off a violent revolution which resulted in the expulsion of the Tarquins, the abolition of the monarchy, and the establishment of the Republic with fully developed institutions of government. Two annually elected consuls, each with equal executive powers and the right to veto his colleague's acts, assumed the command, *auspices,* and *fasces* of the king. This division and limitation of executive power was designed to guard against tyranny. The citizen was further protected against the exercise of arbitrary and despotic power by the right of appeal to the people. In times of crisis, one of the consuls could, with the approval of the senate, nominate a dictator, who would in turn appoint a master of the horse (*magister equitum*) as his chief assistant, to assume for six months the powers of both consuls. Unlike the consuls, the dictator was not accountable for his acts, could deny citizens the right of appeal, and exercised unlimited power and authority over the Roman state.

Nor were consuls always the regular or eponymous magistrates. In the years of the *Fasti* 451 and 450 B.C., they were replaced by two successive commissions of ten men (*decemviri*), who codified the laws known as the XII Tables; and in fifty of the seventy-eight years between 445 and 367 B.C. by military tribunes with consular power. After 367 consuls again became the chief magistrates and for the first time one of the two had to be a plebeian.

The traditional account contains many improbabilities and gives rise to difficulties almost impossible to solve: the character of the revolution which brought about the change of government, the time of its occurrence, and the nature of the executive authority that replaced the kingship.

Many scholars would reject the tradition of a sudden overthrow of the monarchy because it is doubtful that violent revolutions such as the French Revolution of 1789 or the Russian Revolution of 1917 occurred in ancient societies. It is more probable that the passage from monarchy to republic was the result of a slow evolutionary process, which may be called revolutionary only from the standpoint of its ultimate result. Another part of the tradition which must be rejected is the sudden appearance of a fully developed executive to replace the kings. The consulship with its equal division of powers, collegiality, and veto evolved probably only after a long period of experimentation and development.

It is agreed that the collapse of the monarchy resulted from social, economic, and political deterioration climaxed, perhaps, by military reverses. It is the climax which is disputed. It could have been around 509 or after 474 B.C. Some scholars still accept the traditional dating of the *Fasti* (509–507 B.C.). More recent scholars have argued for a much later date (from 474 until 450 B.C.).

According to independent Greek chronology, ca. 525 B.C. the Etruscans suffered a decisive defeat while attempting to seize the Campanian city of Cumae which resulted in a Latin revolt against domination by Etruscan Rome and the severance of land communications between Etruria and Campania. This, together with a simultaneous invasion of Latium by the Sabines and other mountain tribes, may have provoked an economic and political crisis in Rome and contributed to the eventual breakdown of the Tarquin regime, which probably had gradually lost its control over the army and its power to prevent some of the more powerful aristocratic families from seizing control of the state.

The crisis that provoked the fall of the Tarquin monarchy could also have occurred after 474 B.C., when the Etruscans incurred a decisive naval defeat at the hands of Hiero I of Syracuse which led to their final loss of Latium. The thesis that the Etruscan monarchy did not collapse until after this date is strongly supported by the results of the recent Swedish excavations in Rome, though these results have not yet been sufficiently conclusive to compel general acceptance.

Even more disputed is the nature of the executive that replaced the king. Some conjecture it was a dictatorship, some a triple praetorship, others again an embryonic form of praetor consulship. None of these conjectures, except perhaps the last, is free from objection; whether it be conflict with the *Fasti*, ancient tradition, or inherent probability.

Against those who hold that an annual dictator, whether called Master of the People (*Magister Populi*) or Supreme Praetor (*Praetor Maximus*), actually succeeded the kings as commander-in-chief of the army and chief of state, it must be pointed out that the term *Praetor Maximus,* which occurs in a passage of Livy (VII, 3, 4–9) in connection with the driving of a nail into the right side of Jupiter's temple to mark the number of years, was really not employed until around 367 B.C. and that the *Magister Populi,* though correctly identified with the traditional Roman dictator, was not, in historic times, a regular annual magistrate but an extraordinary one, who held office for a maximum term of six months in times of crisis or emergency. Dictatorships were comparatively rare in the first century of the Republic (there being only thirteen as compared with fifty in the next century). More important, the historic dictator was always accompanied by twenty-four lictors, twice as many as a king or a praetor-consul ever had, proof that praetor-consuls must have existed before dictators, since in time of emergency each one of them symbolically transferred to the dictator his twelve lictors, thus making a total of twenty-four. In short, dictators were never the immediate successors of the kings.

A few scholars have maintained that the immediate successor of the exiled Tarquin was the triple praetorship, a college of three praetors representing the commanders of the three original tribes, Ramnes, Tities, and Luceres, and that sometime after 367 B.C. two of the praetors became the later consuls, the third the city praetor, whose chief job was the administration of justice.

The main objection to this thesis is the number "three." According to the evidence now available, the three primitive tribes were no longer in existence at the beginning of the Republic, when the army probably consisted of a single legion, which was later split into two (*see* p. 63). Therefore, the commanders could have been one, or two, but never three.

Conflict of the Classes

The biggest fiction created by the annalistic tradition is that of the absolute and exclusive domination of the state by the patrician minority after the fall of the Tarquins. This fiction has become, both to the staunchest conservative defenders of the tradition and to its most radical skeptics, almost an unques-tioned article of faith. Contrary to the principles of sociology and in defiance of reason and even common sense, patrician domination of Roman society has been assumed as axiomatic even for the early shepherd squatters and fugitive slaves who dwelt one like another in mud huts on top of the Palatine!

Equally anachronistic and untrustworthy is the portrayal of Roman society in the first two decades of the Republic by the annalists. These represent the government of Rome as the exclusive monopoly of fifty or sixty patrician families in a period of war and uprising in Latium, internal unrest and confusion, with Sabine and Volscan tribesmen moving in to fill the power vacuum left by the Etruscans while the Tarquins struggled to restore the monarchy. It would have been practically impossible under these conditions for the patricians to maintain their control of the government without the support, co-operation, and partnership of some of the rich and powerful families of the plebeian class.*

It is probable that the patrician leaders sought the military and political support of the plebeian upper classes until they had consolidated their power and dispelled the danger of a restoration of the monarchy. When the crisis had passed and the support of the plebeians was no longer needed, the patricians apparently proceeded to establish a monopoly of office for themselves and become a closed social and political caste, from which they excluded families of the plebeian upper class. The leaders of that patrician reaction were probably members of the Fabian family which, according to the *Fasti,* held consul-

* Although the term "plebeian" has come to connote the masses of the underprivileged poor, it appears unlikely that a society as culturally and politically advanced as Etruscan Rome could have been composed solely of two rigidly defined classes: a small exclusive patrician minority at the top and a large, undifferentiated plebeian mass below. The plebeian class (p. 57) contained several classes differing in wealth, occupation, and social status: the rural and urban poor, clients of the rich, merchants and craftsmen, and some rich and powerful landowning families with clients of their own. The Servian centuriate reform (*see* Chap. 4, p. 63) seems to have given recognition to this class by the division of classes on the basis of wealth and the admission of the plebeian rich into the military and perhaps political life of the state.

ships for seven consecutive years. The reaction finally culminated in the prohibition of intermarriage between patrician and plebeian families and the prohibition was apparently legalized around the middle of the fifth century.

One method the patricians could well have employed to exclude the plebeians from public office or military commands was the refusal to present candidates, even those elected by the early Centuriate Assembly, to the Curiate Assembly for formal conferment of the *imperium,* without which no elected consul could take office.

The consequent organization of a mass plebeian movement confronted the patricians with the threat of secession and the creation of a new and separate state. The organization of such a movement was probably not too difficult because the demands of the masses for economic reforms must have been no less urgent than those of the plebeian leaders for admission to office. This struggle for political, social, and economic reform was to dominate the internal history of the Roman Republic for the next two centuries. Its outcome was the evolution of the Roman constitution itself as later shaped by the great legislative acts of ca. 367 and 287 B.C.

The collapse of Etruscan domination in Rome and Latium undoubtedly disrupted commerce and industry and precipitated an economic depression resulting in hardships for craftsmen, merchants and their families within the city. The small plebeian farmers were also in difficulties. Their farms, probably not more than an acre and a half in area, were too small to support their families. Worse still, they did not receive a fair share of the public lands they often helped to conquer. Forced to serve in the army, they had to neglect their farms and sometimes came back to find them looted by the enemy. They were also victims of the harsh debtor laws. In cases of default, money lenders could without legal action seize farms, sell farmers into slavery, or even put them to death.

Secession of the Plebs

In answer to stubborn patrician resistance to the demand for economic and social justice, the plebeians took the revolutionary step of seceding from the state. It was a non-violent movement, but exceedingly dangerous to the military security of Rome. According to tradition (though not a very reliable one), the victorious Roman army had just reached the gates of the city. Hearing that their demands for reform had just been rejected by the senate, the plebeian soldiers deserted their patrician general and headed for the Sacred Mount about three miles from the Anio. Knowing that without their help Rome was unable to fight any battles, they waited for the patricians to make the next move. They set up their own temporary organization headed by two tribunes and took oath to a constitution known as the Sacred Law (*lex sacrata*). The *lex sacrata* was a military oath well known in Italy, especially among the Sabines and Samnites: it declared the plebeian tribunes to be sacrosanct or inviolate. Anyone laying violent hands on a tribune would be placed under a curse and could be killed with impunity. All this is supposed to have happened in 494 B.C., certainly too early a date.

The first secession of the plebeians probably occurred around 471 B.C. on the Aventine, where they took the oath to the *lex sacrata,* organized an assembly known as the Tribal Council of the Plebs (*concilium plebis tributum*), and appointed a tribune for each of the city tribes. The historical number of plebeian tribunes was fixed at ten a few decades later, never to be changed again. The earliest tribunes were probably not elected, but rose to the top of the revolutionary heap through their power of leadership and were afterwards confirmed by acclamation. After the Aventine secession all tribunes as well as their assistants, the aediles, were elected by the Council of the Plebs. To be eligible for election a tribune had to belong to a plebeian family.

The Powers and Duties of a Plebeian Tribune. The duty and function of a plebeian tribune was to protect the life, person, and interests of all plebeians who called upon him for help against the arbitrary power of a magistrate. Always on call, he had to keep his house open day and night and never go outside the city limits. In order that he might perform his duties without fear, his person was declared inviolate or sacrosanct. Anyone laying violent hands upon him or willfully interfering in the performance of his duties was laid under curse or pain of death. The tribunes also had the power of intercession or veto over any bill passed by the popular assemblies, any decree of the senate, and any act of a magistrate (except a dictator) that was considered harmful to plebeian interests. This power was effective only inside Rome and one mile beyond city limits, and could not be employed to protect plebeians guilty of serious crimes. Though not based on specific constitutional law, the veto became accepted by custom and politically effective. Even the senate later recognized its effectiveness and encouraged the tribunes to employ it against trouble-making consuls.

Aediles. The auxiliaries of the tribunes as protectors of the common people were the two plebeian aediles, who were originally caretakers of the temple of Ceres on the Aventine, which was not only a marketplace and trading post but a center of early plebeian political agitation. Their functions became numerous and varied: they were custodians of the plebeian treasury and archives and, according to Livy (III:55), of the decrees of the senate from ca. 449 B.C. onward. In later times they acted as police and supervised marketplaces, weights and measures, public works, food and water supplies, and public games.

The Plebeian Tribal Council. The tribunes and aediles were elected by the Plebeian Tribal Council, which was usually convened and presided over by tribunes but occasionally also by aediles. Probably only plebeians attended the meetings, though there seems to have been no law prohibiting the presence of a patrician. Voting was by a simple majority of the tribes and the vote of each tribe was determined by a simple majority of voters. The resolutions (*plebiscita*) were not binding upon the whole state unless ratified by the Comitia Centuriata and perhaps not even then without the express approval of the senate. Only after 287 B.C. could it legislate for all the Roman people, when it probably merged with the Comitia Tributa. Some scholars have held that the Comitia Tributa

was another tribal assembly of the fifth century separate and distinct from the Plebeian Tribal Council and able to legislate for all the people. That idea now seems generally abandoned (p. 101).

The Plebeian Battle for Social Justice

Having proved themselves indispensable to Roman military defense, the plebeians became a power within the body of the state. They had their own public assembly and their own leaders and champions, to whom the patricians could do no violence. Their battle for social justice contributed in the development of the Roman constitution to the ultimate benefit of the patrician class itself. Before the middle of the fifth century B.C., that battle for law and justice was not yet won. Bigger hurdles were still in the way.

Around 462 B.C. (of the *Fasti*) C. Terentilius Arsa, a plebeian tribune, proposed that a board of five be appointed to write laws limiting the power of the consuls; for in the absence of a written code, the consuls could legislate as they pleased. The following year another tribune proposed that a commission of ten be appointed to legislate in the entire field of public and private law. Because these proposals aroused more patrician opposition than plebeian support they were not adopted.

About eight years later the tribunes suggested to the senate that a committee be chosen (representing both parties) to frame just and equitable laws. The senate turned down the suggestion of plebeian participation but did agree to send a commission over to Greece and especially to Athens to study Greek laws. It is probable that this expedition took place a decade or so before the terrible war between Athens and Sparta (433–404 B.C.).

A Period of Resurgent Liberalism

During the years the study commission was in Greece, two laws seem to have been passed under plebeian pressure. The first was the *Lex Icilia* setting aside land on the Aventine for a plebeian housing project. The other was the *lex Aternia-Tarpeia* limiting the fine that a consul could impose to thirty cattle and two sheep. Moderate consuls also seem to have returned to power. Five old consular names reminiscent of the early decades of the fifth century, the Veturii, and Minucii, reappear. If the official Roman *Fasti* are correct, there may also have been three plebeian consuls, namely Spurius Tarpeius and Aulus Aternius of the year 454 and Titus Genucius of the year 451 B.C. All three were connected at one time or another with the plebeian tribuneship. The decade just before the decemvirates appears to have been comparatively liberal, therefore, both in its legislation and consulship. Early Roman society was not as static as some modern interpreters of the literary sources believe. It was by turns liberal and reactionary.

The First Decemviral Commission. On the return of the study commission, it was decided to suspend the regular consuls and plebeian tribunes and appoint, with an Appius Claudius as chairman, a Board of Ten armed with full executive powers. One of the commissioners was a plebeian, T. Genucius, the consul. All through the year 451 B.C. of the *Fasti* (though possibly as much as a decade later), they governed with the utmost harmony, moderation, and justice. At the end of the year, after the ten laws presented to the Comitia Centuriata had been duly ratified, they resigned their commission. These laws were afterwards inscribed, it is said on bronze but more probably on wooden tablets, and set up in the Forum.

The Second Decemviral Commission. The following year a second commission, half patrician, half plebeian, was appointed to complete the work begun by the first. Appius Claudius was again chairman. According to Cicero, it was this commission that came up with the notorious prohibition of marriage between patricians and plebeians, a law which Livy fails to ascribe to this decemvirate but which Diodorus, who usually follows good sources, specifically attributes to the consuls of the year 449 of the *Fasti*, namely M. Horatius Barbatus and L. Valerius Poplicola. Both consuls are represented by the tradition as friends and champions of the people. At this point the record, as passed on by Livy and Dionysius, becomes a mixture of contradictions and improbabilities. Apart from the improbability of a half-plebeian commission formulating a law against mixed marriages, the personality of Appius Claudius himself seems to have undergone shocking changes. A model of justice and rectitude as chairman of the first commission, he seems later to have developed into a lust-driven scoundrel. The first decemvirate achieved great things in government and legislation, the second failed to accomplish anything constructive or beneficial to the state. It is difficult to discern the truth in the conflicting inventions of the several annalists.

The XII Tables

The Law of the XII Tables, while not among the most sublime achievements of the human intellect, was the seed from which Roman civil law grew to maturity and from which the system of Roman jurisprudence evolved through the interpretative applications of the pontiffs (p. 72) and later of the professional jurists (p. 73). Livy declared that it was the fountain of all private and public law, and Cicero, that it was the body of the entire Roman law. As the basis and source of law it may well be compared with the Constitution of the United States.

The Sources of the Existing Fragments. The original text of the XII Tables is said to have been lost in the Great Fire of 387/6 B.C. If so, it must have been easily reconstructed from memory; for private copies of it were still in use as long as the Republic lasted. Cicero tells us that in his boyhood schoolboys had to memorize it as part of their school work. It is estimated that about a third of the original is now extant. Most of the fragments, some quoted in the original words, some in context, others in paraphrase, are to be found in the works of Cicero, Aulus Gellius, Festus, of the jurists Gaius (160 A.D.) and Ulpian, and especially in scattered references appearing in the *Digest* of Justinian I.

Style and Content of the XII Tables. Though some Greek terms occur in the Twelve Tables and allusions to Attic and other laws, it is not certain how much the study commission learned from the law codes of Sparta, Athens, Sicily, and southern Italy. The style is archaic, not unlike that of the Elder Cato, simple, brief, harsh, but legally clear and exact, as in Table I. "If he calls him to court, go he shall; if he doesn't, plaintiff will call witness, then will take him"; or Table VII, "They will keep road repaired, if they don't cobble it, man may drive team where he wants to"; or Table VIII, "If burglary be done at night, if (owner) kills him, he shall be killed by law; if by day, not, unless burglar defends himself with weapon."

The XII Tables were neither a constitution nor a comprehensive code of laws. Though its main source was the old law of custom, it did not entirely replace primitive unwritten law. It served the more limited purpose of clarifying those problems which experience had proved to be most disturbing to the peace and harmony of the state. Its contents indicate that it gave most emphasis to the areas of greatest social and economic conflict, the exploitation of the poor by the rich, of the plebeians by the patricians. The first three tables deal with procedure in private law (preliminary hearings, trials, and the laws pertaining to debts), the next four with family and intra-family relationships (rights of fathers, wills and trusteeships, ownership and possession, and landed property), Table VIII with torts or penal law, Tables IX and X with public and sacral law pertaining especially to funeral extravagances; and finally Tables XI and XII with supplementary and miscellaneous regulations.

The law of the XII Tables, designed to maintain peace, harmony, and justice within the state, codified the pre-existing law of custom but was also capable through interpretation of meeting future needs. It elevated the position of women by allowing a common-law wife freedom from her husband's authority if she stayed away three days and nights a year from home. It reduced powers of the *pater familias* not required for the maintenance of family unity, guaranteed the right to property and testament, provided for the intervention of the state in civil disputes, the abolition of family revenge, and the referral of capital cases to the Comitia Centuriata. It also abolished torture as a means of obtaining evidence from free men. In short, the basic importance of the Twelve Tables was that they established in principle some equality in law between patrician and plebeian and, more or less, the equality of all free citizens before the law. This code was the

foundation of the Roman state, and more significant than a thousand military victories.

The Post-Decemviral Reaction

The confused and contradictory information concerning the fall of the second decemvirate reflects the bitterness of the struggle between the patricians and plebeians, a struggle that probably not only obstructed legislation, but was followed by a patrician reaction resulting in the restoration of the consulship by the patricians on one side and of the tribuneship by the plebeians on the other. The patrician reaction probably culminated in the legal prohibition of mixed marriages between the two classes (Diodorus 12.26.1).

The annalists have obscured the realities of the situation with many absurd inventions. The consuls of the year following the Second Decemviral Commission, L. Valerius Potitus and M. Horatius Barbatus, are represented as "friends" of the people, for whose benefit they are supposed to have introduced three laws: the first prohibited, under pain of death, the election of any magistrate whose decisions were not subject to the right of appeal to the people in capital cases; the second recognized the persons of the plebeian tribunes as sacrosanct and inviolate; the third decreed that resolutions (*plebiscita*) of the Plebeian Council were binding on the whole people. All three are probably fictions. The first two were unnecessary, one because the right of appeal had already been granted by the XII Tables, the other because the inviolability of the plebeian tribunes was based on a military and religious oath (*lex sacrata*), which the patricians could not defy without peril. (Though possible, it is unlikely that the patricians were willing to confirm tribune sacrosanctity by law.) The third "law" is an obvious anticipation of the two laws of 339 and of 287 B.C. and conflicts with everything Livy has to say on the subject in the next several books.

Plebeian Triumphs

About four years later, two facts served to help the plebeians in the see-saw conflict between the two classes. The most important was the critical military situation, which, as the patricians clearly saw, could not be met without plebeian goodwill and co-operation. The second was that one of the consuls of that year was M. Genucius, a plebeian. It was probably through Genucius that the plebeians were able to rescind the law against mixed marriages. The *Lex Canuleia* rescinding the older law was first proposed by the tribune, C. Canuleius, and passed by the Plebeian Council but could not possibly have became a state law unless presented to the Comitia Centuriata by a consul. An outgrowth of the class struggle was a compromise admitting plebeians to the supreme magistracy not as consuls but as military tribunes with consular power. This was evidently a shrewd maneuver by the patricians because it still guaranteed their real control of the state and at the same time secured plebeian military support by giving them a share in the government. Though the *Fasti* may indicate that plebeians had held the consulship before, the year of Genucius was the first year, according to annalistic tradition, that the supreme office was open to both classes (Livy 4.6.5).

Military Tribunes with Consular Power. For the next seventy-eight years of the *Fasti* between 445 and 367 B.C., consular tribunes held the highest office fifty times, consuls twenty-eight, the senate apparently deciding between the two. The number of consular tribunes varied from three to nine, at first usually three, sometimes four, later six. They had exactly the same military and executive powers as consuls. Eleven dictatorships occurred during their years of office. Had they not possessed the consular *imperium* they would not have been constitutionally able to delegate powers which they themselves did not possess. Yet they differed from consuls in that they did not have the right to a triumph nor to the rank of ex-consul with a seat in the senate after their term of office. Nor did they have the privilege of being buried in the royal purple toga. Each member of this college could participate in all the activities belonging to the office. Each had the power of veto though the magistracy as a whole may have operated in theory on the principle of unanimity. In practice there was a division of responsibility: one remained in the city

for the administration of justice and other executive functions, the others conducted the necessary military operations. Though military command was one of their more important functions, no correlation can be proved between years of war and their years of office. Just as many wars occurred when consuls were in office as consular tribunes. After 400 B.C. of the *Fasti,* fifteen plebeian names occur. In the years 399 and 396 B.C. five out of six consular tribunes were plebeian, in 379, five out of eight. The years 399 and 396 were years of war with Veii and it may well have been that in war years the plebeians were especially successful in breaking into the supreme magistracy. To reject all these names as interpolated is to reject solid and reliable parts of the Roman historical tradition.

The Censors

The year 443 of the *Fasti,* immediately following the establishment of the first consular tribuneship, saw the rise of another important magistracy, the censorship, which maintained itself with ever-increasing power to the time of Sulla, if not the Principate. The alleged purpose of the new office was the assumption of duties formerly performed by the consuls, especially the compilation of the census, which was the official list of Roman citizens for purposes of voting, taxation, and military service. To carry out these duties two censors were elected by the Comitia Centuriata every four or five years, but by a law passed in 434 of the *Fasti* they could serve only for eighteen months. At first the censors may have been rather unimportant people, not much better than clerks or secretaries. They did not have the *imperium* nor the right to the *fasces,* could not call the people or the senate to assembly, nor even nominate their own successors. Later their job of registering citizens and their property, of assessing their liability to taxes and military service, and of assigning them to tribes and centuries for voting eventually made their office, even without the *imperium* and the *fasces,* more feared and respected than the consulship itself. So eminent was the magistracy of a censor that when he died he was accorded the honor of burial in the full purple toga of royalty.

Their Powers and Functions. In addition to the job of making up the tax registers, the military registers, and the lists of voters, censors acquired after 312/10 B.C. the power of appointing senators and of removing them from the senate, if their moral life did not meet the standards of the Roman moral code. By putting a black mark opposite a man's name the censor could remove a citizen from his tribe, demote him to a city tribe, or take away his civil rights altogether for at least five years. To an equestrian or knight, i.e. a member of the Roman cavalry, thus stigmatized would be issued the command, "Go, sell your horse."

The censors were also concerned with the spending of funds appropriated by the senate or released by the consul. They drew up contracts for major public works such as roads, bridges, aqueducts, and public buildings. Control of the tax registers and of the state revenues gave them the knowledge required for making up the annual budget. They granted contracts for collecting such revenue, leased public lands, mines, salt works, and fishing rights, and arranged for the collection by speculators or publicans, of port dues and of taxes owed by squatters on public land. The only kind of revenue they had nothing to do with was that obtained from war booty.

The Quaestors

The origin of these minor but not unimportant officials is obscure. Most ancient sources carry them back to the monarchy, perhaps rightly so, though modern writers have seen their first appearance in the early Republic. In the early years of the Republic they may have been appointed by the consuls as assistants, but after 287 B.C. they were elected by the Tribal Assembly. At first two, and both patrician, they were increased to four in 421 of the *Fasti,* when the office was first thrown open to the plebeians, though it was not until the year 409 of the *Fasti* that plebian quaestors were actually appointed. Though their original function was to investigate murders, minor crimes against property also came under their jurisdiction.

Two of the four quaestors accompanied the consuls to the battlefield, where they served as quartermasters in charge of supplies and the payment of troops. The other two remained in the city to serve as keepers of the public treasury and prosecutors of tax delinquents. Since the state treasury was in the temple of Saturn, they were also in charge of the state records and documents kept in that building. A large staff of copyists and secretaries assisted in the discharge of these important duties.

The Senate

At the dawn of the Republic the consuls were probably, in fact as well as in law, more powerful than the senate, which acted, as it had for the kings (p. 60), merely as an advisory council. The power and influence of the senate increased as the constitution developed so that the consuls and other magistrates were obligated in practice, if not by law, to seek its advice on all major foreign and internal policies. They could safely neither oppose nor ignore this advice.

Several facts account for the growth of the senate's power. Unlike the kings, the consuls were annual officials, who at the end of their term of office might have to explain to the people any mistakes they might have made while going against the advice of the senate. Their political career might end in dishonor or find its reward in a lifetime seat in the senate. (For a plebeian a senatorial seat meant admission into the highest ranks of the nobility.)

The senate, on the other hand, was a permanent organ of the government. The kings were no more, their places taken by annual magistrates. Of the public assemblies, the Comitia Centuriata was of comparatively recent origin and had not even yet attained full maturity, while the Comitia Curiata was a decrepit body whose functions had atrophied into empty formalism. Only to the senate belonged the dignity of an antique tradition, unbroken from the earliest beginning of the Roman state.

Authority (auctoritas). The source of the senate's power was its so-called *auctoritas,* a concept which had both religious and constitutional connotations. In practice the term meant the prestige and esteem the senate possessed because of the dignity and outstanding qualities of its members. Constitutionally, it was the power to ratify laws passed by the Comitia Centuriata and to approve the election of magistrates. Without that ratification no bill passed by the popular assemblies could become law. Behind this authority lay the religious idea that all laws and resolutions must be pleasing to the gods. According to Cicero, some of the senators, who traced an ancestry reaching back to the dawn of history, pretended to possess an uncanny knowledge of divine will. Strange as it may seem to a more sophisticated age, such an absurd claim was widely accepted among the Roman people.

Control over Finances. The senate had complete control over finances except, perhaps, for funds expended at the command of the consuls. Even though first the consuls and later the censors held the keys to the treasury, it was actually the senate in both law and custom that decided what funds were to be ear-marked for war and public works. A soldier could not get his pay nor a victorious general his triumph unless funds for the purpose were made available by the senate. This control over finances gave the senate practical control over the government.

Advice-giving Function. The ultimate basis of senatorial control over internal and foreign affairs, the army, the treasury, and the government lay in its right to give official advice to the magistrates on all laws they wished to propose to the popular assembly. As long as the Republic endured, the senate never lost this advice-giving function, based not on statute law but on custom.

The advice given by the senate consisted of two parts: a) opinions (*sententiae*), which individual senators expressed about the matter on which the magistrate sought advice; b) the decree of the senate (*senatus consultum*) or the final form of the solution adopted in answer to the problem the magistrate laid before them. The *senatus consultum* was not a unilateral act of the senate but the joint act of the senate and the presiding magistrate. The latter alone made it legal, he alone could enforce it, modify it,

or revoke it altogether. It was strictly limited in its effect and time of enforcement. If revoked by a magistrate or vetoed by a plebeian tribune, it was then registered as a *senatus auctoritas,* as an expression of the authoritative opinion of the senate that such and such a course of action would be in the best interests of the state. The senate thereby absolved itself of responsibility for the consequences. If something then went wrong the magistrate who had ignored the advice would have to face the wrath of the people. Though not above the law, the senate could in times of crisis take extra-legal measures to ensure the safety of the state.

The War with Veii

Although the wars of the fifth century make up a large part of Livy's narrative from the beginning of the second to well past the middle of his fifth book, many of them are probably fictitious and at best were nothing more serious than minor skirmishes.

The enemies of Rome at this time were the Latins, the Sabines, the Hernici, the Aequi, the Volsci, and the Etruscans, all of whom the Romans conquered regularly, returning to Rome laden with enormous quantities of booty. There were occasional reversals of fortune. In the year 458 of the *Fasti* a Roman army is reported to have got trapped by the Aequi in the valley below Mount Algidus and would probably have been annihilated had not five horsemen broken out just in time to bring news of the disaster to Rome. The situation was so alarming that a delegation from the senate went out to see Cincinnatus, who was plowing at the time on his four-acre farm. At their insistence he accepted the offered dictatorship and administered to the Aequi a shattering defeat, after which he resigned his dictatorship, went back home, and yoked up his ox.

The Roman struggle with Etruscan Veii, near the end of the century, ended a long period of rivalry. Veii was a big old town, rich and well fortified about fifteen miles from Rome and on the other side of the Tiber. In an early conflict with Veii the Romans suffered a defeat at the Cremera, which almost annihilated the Fabian clan. After a forty-year truce, fighting again broke out over possession of Fidenae, a river town of strategic and commercial importance. This time Rome won. Some time after 407 B.C. war broke out again. In an account worthy of slight respect Livy describes a tunneling operation, which enabled the Romans to capture Veii in 396 B.C. (of the *Fasti*). They destroyed Veii, sold its inhabitants as slaves, and annexed its territory, thereby almost doubling the area of the *ager Romanus*.

The dictator Camillus, the victor of Veii, his face and hands painted red like the statue of Jupiter, rode in triumph in a four-horse chariot through the streets of Rome quite unaware of the war clouds even then gathering in the North.

The Sack of Rome

While Camillus was celebrating in Rome his triumph over Veii, the Celts were pouring over the Alps. Within a few short years they would be roaring down the peninsula leaving death and havoc wherever they passed. Rome, directly in the path of their advance, would not escape.

The new invaders, whom the Romans called Galli, spoke Celtic, an Indo-European language to which Latin and Italic have closer affinities than to German or even Greek. Celtic was then spoken in many parts of the British Isles, in most of France, and in many parts of Spain, as well as in wide areas of central Europe. Today it is confined largely to the Bretagne, Ireland, Wales, Canada, and the Highlands of Scotland.

The Celts who then lived in western Europe all came originally from Central Europe. Some arrived hundreds of years earlier than others. This accounts in part for the present differences, for example, between Irish and Welsh. Similar dialectical differences existed when the invaders burst through the Alps: the Celtic they spoke was more like that spoken in South Germany, France, England, and the Highlands of Scotland.

When we speak of Gaul and of Gauls or Celts, we think first of France, but the Celtic invaders of Italy before and after 400 B.C.

probably did not come from France. Celtic tribes had not yet permanently occupied all of southern France which would have furnished them with a much easier outlet for expansion than Italy. Nor is there any archaeological evidence to support the theory that they crossed the Western Alps or arrived in Italy from that quarter. There are strong reasons for believing that they came instead from central Europe. First, the Rhineland, southern Germany, and Austria had not only been the original home of all Celts, but was still the heart of the Celtic world and the propulsive center of expansion from the Atlantic to the Black Sea. The workshops and creative centers of Celtic art were in districts from the Rhine to the Middle Danube while those of southern France were still poor and barren. Italic, Etruscan, and Greek traders and goods had been passing over the Alps from North Italy to central Europe for more than a century. The same routes were equally open for invasion. And at this time the Celts of western Germany were under pressure from the Teutons moving into the Rhineland and southern Germany from the North and East. Also the pressure of population had been forcing migrations from the Rhineland to France and Spain. These migrations were to continue for another century or more.

The Prehistoric Origin of the Celts

The prehistoric origin of the Celts is still most problematic despite much archaeological and linguistic research. The theories accepted twenty or thirty years ago have now for the most part been discarded. Celtic, a technical term embracing the entire complex of Celtic civilization, is now thought to have originated from one or the other of two prehistoric cultures in late Neolithic and early Bronze Age Europe: Saxo-Thuringian and Lausitz.

Saxo-Thuringian Culture. Saxony and Thuringia seem to have been the meeting ground of two older cultures. The first was that of the Beaker Folk (p. 21), who are said to have originated in Spain (we are no longer sure, since more Beaker remains have been found in central Europe than in Spain).

The other was that of the pig herders and hunters, who wandered into central Germany from Galicia and the South Russian steppes. Distinctive of the former were the bell-beaker, the bow and arrow, the flat-tanged dagger and the halberd; of the latter, single burial in pits lined with wood or stone and surmounted by mounds or *tumuli,* perforated stone battleaxes, and globular amphorae ornamented with impressions of cord or string. Graves containing most of these elements have been found in Britain. Therefore, Celtic may be traced to the Saxo-Thuringian culture.

Lausitz Culture. A more probable source of Celtic was the Lausitz culture of eastern Germany and western Poland, into which wandered a group of warlike farmers and herdsmen from southeastern Europe bringing with them a culture, probably of Asia Minor origin, which spread, before 1000 B.C., through the Balkans and thence all over Europe from the Bug in the East to the Rhine in the West, from Switzerland to the Black Sea, and westwards into central France, Britain, and Spain. Carrying along in its current some elements of the older Baden and Vučedol cultures (cf. pp. 20–22), the culture of Lausitz pushed its way into the Po Valley giving rise there to the civilization of the Terremare (cf. pp. 22–23). Possible Lausitz offshoots appeared also in Latium, the home of the Southern Villanovans (*see* p. 23f.).

This dynamic and expansive culture, whose nucleus was in east-central Europe, is chiefly distinguished by its urnfields or cremation cemeteries of flat graves containing ash urns such as the late Terremare or Villanovan peoples used. The other distinguishing marks are knob- or wart-decorated pottery, cylinder-neck urns with string and groove decoration, violin bow fibulas, poppy-head pins, and antennae swords. Bosch-Gimpera, the Spanish archaeologist, maintains that some urnfield people, at least in France and Spain, spoke Celtic. Therefore their language cannot have been exclusively Illyrian, as earlier scholars suggested. If the urnfield people were not Celtic, their civilization must have been a common link between different Old European language and dialect groups, as was the case with Hallstatt later on.

The extensive urnfield cemeteries bespeak stable populations and so do the substantial houses grouped in usually fortified villages. The people lived by farming the rich bottom lands of river valleys unlike the earlier Barrow or Corded-ware folk, who pastured their animals on the less fertile uplands. The urnfielders also made extensive use of bronze, fashioning swords, helmets, bridles, and possibly chariots. The Lausitz culture in Moravia, Silesia, Brandenburg, and Poland was, around 500 B.C., weakened and eventually destroyed by a Scythian invasion from the East.

Hallstatt Culture. The expansive energy of the Lausitz culture had carried urnfield people during the Late Bronze Age into southwestern Germany, the Rhineland, and eastern France, where they mixed with the older Tumulus people. Both cultures continued to co-exist for some time, but by 700 B.C. or later they became blended, forming a new culture known as Hallstatt, a site near Salzburg, Austria, whose name is synonymous with Europe's First Iron Age. The Rhineland, the Upper and the Middle Danubian regions had now become meeting places of peoples, great melting pots, the concentration points of cultural currents from many directions, and as a result dynamic, propulsive, outgoing centers radiating their influence east and west and sending forth large groups of population into France, Spain, England, and elsewhere. Here Iron Age Europe's first metal working revolution began. Here the historical character of Celtic civilization first took shape, as did that of Old Slavic civilization in what is now Poland; Celtic, Slavic, and other European language groups having first appropriated the economic superstructure of Hallstatt civilization.

The chief stimulus to the Hallstatt industrial revolution probably was the expansion of Etruscan technology into North Italy. The large foundries of Bologna and Este exported metal wares to all parts of central and western Europe and imported scrap metal for recasting even from the British Isles. Many products of Etruscan shops and factories, jewelry, urns, buckets, belts, bridles, and swords were exported to the Hallstatt area at this time. Hallstatt may well be called a metal working province of Etruria up to a point, not the other way round as some archaeologists have too frequently asserted. This will become more apparent in our discussion of Celtic art.

Hallstatt civilization presents a multitudinous variety of burial rites, pottery, weapons, and ornaments. Its most distinctive feature is the long Hallstatt sword of bronze or iron with leaf-shaped blade and blunt point, which was carried in a wing chape scabbard. It was a cavalry weapon and is said to have marked the first appearance of mounted warriors in central Europe, though we may point out that these are represented on Hallstatt urns and swords imitated from Etruscan models. Although these swords may not, in fact, herald an influx of mounted warriors of the Andronovo and Karasuk civilizations of the Eurasian steppe, they do represent a new independent advance in the art of warfare on the European continent.

Hallstatt society was organized on an aristocratic if not on a feudal basis. Small local units were incorporated into clans, larger tribal organizations, or even petty kingdoms. The class distinctions are shown by the different burial rites: the common people practised cremation, but the chiefs were buried in well-timbered houses with their swords, their valu-

The famous Etruscan bronze situla (sixth century B.C.), discovered near Certosa (Italy). (Courtesy Fratelli Alinari, Florence)

Top: The Great Iron Sword of the early Hallstat period (seventh century B.C.). Bottom: Hilt of the Hallstatt Sword. (Both photos courtesy Württembergisches Landesmuseum, Stuttgart)

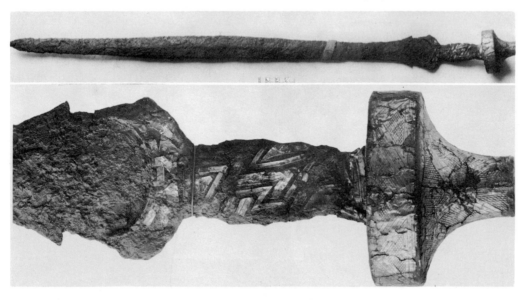

able and often imported jewelry and bronze vessels, chariots, and wagons all found in elaborate surmounting mounds or *tumuli*. The homes of the chiefs were set inside strongly fortified ramparts, often of enormous extension and always big enough, in time of danger, to afford protection to quite a large population and their livestock too. Gradually permanent settlements developed around some of these circumvallations, a few becoming towns as modern excavations have revealed.

The La Tène Phase of Celtic Civilization. Around 500 B.C. Hallstatt was succeeded by a new phase of Celtic culture known as La Tène which lasted until the birth of Christ or later. La Tène is the name of a site discovered in 1857 at the eastern end of Lake Neuchâtel in Switzerland, where there once must have stood a toll station with large stores and warehouses. Though the amount of archaeological material found here was smaller than later discoveries in the French regions of the Marne and the Somme, in western Germany, Austria, and Bohemia, La Tène remains as the type site of post-Hallstatt Celtic civilization.

The Celts of the La Tène period were the inventors of horse drawn carts, the hood, the cowl, and improved methods of making butter. La Tène finds usually consist of finely tempered short swords or daggers used in hand-to-hand combat for slashing or stabbing, large round or oval shields of wicker or metal, heavy bladed knives or machetes, bronze helmets studded with coral, long spear heads of willow leaf shape, various types of brooches, girdle clasps, collars or torcs, bracelets, finger rings, belts, and large bronze pails or cauldrons with swinging handles modeled after Etruscan imports.

Most important of all in war was the light chariot, a construction of Etruscan type, and especially the invention of nailed horseshoes, well-stratified specimens of which have recently been found in levels of the late fifth century B.C. both near Salzburg and at Enserune in the Pyrenees. Tiring out the unshod horses of their enemies, the Celts were able to push as far west as the Atlantic and eastwards to the Black Sea. In 278 B.C. they invaded Asia Minor and permanently settled in Galatia, a region afterwards made famous by the Greek sculptured figure of the *Dying*

Left: *An imported Etruscan bronze stamnos.* Right: *A beaked bronze flagon of Celtic manufacture, copied from an Etruscan import. (Note the animal heads decorating the handle). (Courtesy Württembergisches Landesmuseum, Stuttgart)*

Two Celtic gold drinking horns with ram's heads as finials. (Courtesy Württembergisches Landesmuseum, Stuttgart)

Gaul and by St. Paul's *Epistle to the Galatians.*

Early Celtic Art

The Celts were the first people of western and central Europe to create art of future significance. It later dominated the minor arts of France and other northern provinces of the Roman Empire, and is virtually our sole source of information about the spirit and psychology of a people who played a large role in history from Roman times down to the present day.

The older and more advanced art of the Greeks had little or no direct influence upon the development of Celtic art. Although the Celts had received long before the close of the Hallstatt period some of the finest Greek vases and bronze works through the port of Marseilles and the Rhone Valley, they did not understand them nor attempt to imitate or copy them. Celtic art found its models and sources of inspiration elsewhere.

Sources. There were three sources of Celtic art. One was a diluted or bastard form of Etruscan art that continued to survive in the retarded and backwater areas of northern Italy at Este and other places along the Alpine foothills. Another was the Scythian art of South Russia. The third was a late form of Persian art. In the final analysis all three sources reflected some influence from Greek art but remained basically Oriental.

North Italian or Etruscan Components. Some of the important Italian contributions are: 1) The so-called Hallstatt ducks used singly as decorative motifs and in paired or antithetic groups; 2) the chief types of gold and bronze brooches and finger rings ornamented with embossed human facial masks or animal heads in addition to beak-flagons, stamnoi, basins, buckets, tripods, helmets, and chariot parts; 3) Celtic geometric ornaments have the same components as those of the earlier Etruscan Orientalizing style; 4) Etruscan influence appears both at Hallstatt and La Tène in temple architecture and in burial customs.

Scythian or South Russian Components. The Scythian influences reached Celtic territory not via Hungary, where Celtic archaeological material is rare or late, but through Silesia and northeastern Germany, which the Scythians invaded around 500 B.C. These consist of: 1) some characteristics of the South Russian animal style, which spread westwards into Celtic territory and eastwards into Siberia and China; 2) drinking and hunting horns often decorated with ram finials; 3) shining bronze horse trappings and gaily colored harness ornamented with coral and enamel, (the use of enamel being typical of the Kuban and the Caucasus); 4) a certain open work and animal palmettes commonly used as cheek pieces of bridle bits.

Persian Components. The Celts probably derived the fashion of wearing gaily colored

A silver-coated iron torc with bulls' heads as terminals (middle La Tène period). (Courtesy Württembergisches Landesmuseum, Stuttgart)

pants and collars or torcs from Persia as well as the use of man-eating lions as decorative motifs on flasks and torcs.

The Rise and Character of Celtic Art. The external sources of Celtic art do not explain its genesis. Some of its closest analogies are to be found in faraway Siberia and China. Apparently the Celts consciously imitated none of the Etruscan, Sythian, or Persian originals, but selected and absorbed them, infused them with their own spirit, and transformed them into a living art of native inspiration thereby creating a new symbolistic style, mature, and truly Celtic, seemingly without beginning, preparation, or precedent. It seems to have burst suddenly into life.

Celtic art is almost exclusively an art of ornamentation of useful articles—swords, helmets, flagons, brooches, and torcs. The only sculpture, confined to southern France, is late, primitive, and poor. The clumsily sculptured objects are in strong contrast to the excellence of the metal work and the exquisite fineness of the jewelry, almost microscopic in some of its details and decorated with stylized human facial masks, entire animals or birds or their heads, also with tendrils, spirals, palmettes, leaves, floralized animals or animalized plants. Rams' heads ornament the terminals of a torc, two herons the cheek-piece of a helmet, a pair of ducks lie asleep on a brooch.

The Use of Animals in Celtic Art. In its use of animals or parts of animals for decorative purposes Celtic art was a Western derivative of the Scythian and Etruscan animal styles, with which it shared many peculiarities. The animal figure, for instance, is used solely for the ornamentation of useful objects (the unattached animal is extremely rare). Animals are rarely used in groups to form scenes, but the entire animal figure, realistically treated, often forms the handle of a jar or flagon and parts of animals or birds serve as finials or terminals of drinking horns and torcs. Animals, usually with their heads turned back, are frequently used to fill up open spaces. Not unlike Scythian art after it came under the influence of Ionian Greek art, Celtic art abounds in fantastic animals (often confronting each other and sometimes with heads turned back) such as lion-griffins, rampant dragons, rams with eagle beaks, double animals with a single head or a single body with two heads. Similar animals are often used to form open-work plaques, palmettes, lyres, and even whirligigs.

Though Scythia and Persia were the immediate source of all such animal ornaments, neither invented them. They borrowed them directly from the Assyrians, who had inherited them ultimately from the art of Sumer and Elam of the third millennium B.C.

Celtic Art in Italy. The Celtic invaders of Italy produced little art. The finds are few and show little originality or initiative: evidently the invaders were too busy marching, fighting, and looting.

A Celtic whirligig, found in Bulgaria. (Courtesy The Trustees of the British Museum)

The Celtic Invasion of North Italy

The Gauls passed over the Alps. Five great tribes with their women and children, flocks and herds, chariots, wagons, and pack animals fanned out over the plains. Etruscans were able to put up little resistance in the open country. Although Bologna held out till 350 B.C. and Marzabotto was not taken without a long and bitter struggle, the rest of the country was occupied without much difficulty. Many of the invaders finally settled down and became good farmers, peaceful, contented, hardworking, and prosperous. The entire country from Como to Ancona, from Milan to Verona was one continuously populated Celtic territory.

The Senones, who arrived with the last wave of invaders, found the best land already taken in the North, marched southward, and

Left and Right: *Two so-called Lorraine flagons (Celtic, early fourth century B.C.), found together with a fifth century B.C. Etruscan stamnos (middle) in a grave at Basse Yutz in the Moselle region (France). (Courtesy The Trustees of the British Museum)*

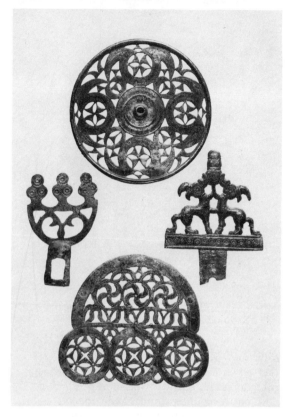

Four ornamental objects from a La Tène chariot burial, discovered at Somme Bionne in the Marne region (France). (Courtesy The Trustees of the British Museum)

burned everything except the Capitol, which was reportedly saved by the alarm raised by the cackling of Juno's sacred geese and the valor of Marcus Manlius.

After besieging the Capitol for seven months, the Gauls learned that the Veneti had invaded their lands in the Po Valley. Eager to go back home, they readily accepted a ransom of a thousand pounds of gold (about a quarter million dollars) and marched away.

The battle of the Allia caught the attention of the Greeks. Theopompus, Heracleides, and even Aristotle took notice of it, which enables us to date this event precisely in the years 387/6 B.C. The reputed fighting ability of the Gauls put them in great demand as mercenaries thereafter. Dionysius I, the tyrant of Syracuse, engaged their services and so did the Spartans later on.

Up from the Ashes

Rome was badly damaged, her defenses smashed, the wealth of her citizens exhausted, and her prestige in Latium at a low ebb.

When the Romans returned to rebuild their ruined city, they recognized the need for strong defenses. Having learned how impregnable to direct assault were the walls of Veii, they decided to build similar walls of the same grayish yellow *tufa* quarried at Grotta Obscura near Veii. This stone was superior to any they had previously used, and they continued to use it in all squared-stone masonry till the end of the second century B.C. It was cut into rectangular blocks of uneven dimensions and laid down so that rows of headers alternated with stretchers. In this way was built the so-called "Servian Wall" about twelve feet thick, twenty-four feet high, which extended around the entire city, including the Aventine, a distance of five and a half miles.

After the Gauls had departed from Roman territory, some Latin cities, especially Tibur, Velitrae, Praeneste, Anzio, and Satricum, began to assert their independence and even to show hostility to Rome. The rest seem to have remained loyal to their alliance, which

about 390 B.C. descended upon the Etruscan town of Clusium (Chiusi). The uneasy Romans sent envoys up there to negotiate, but one of the envoys became involved in a fight with a Gallic chief and the negotiations broke down. All hope for peace was gone.

The Allia. Since Rome was not well fortified, the Romans marched out to intercept the Gauls. On the 18th of July, 387 B.C., they made contact with the Gauls near the Allia, a small stream flowing northwards into the Tiber about eleven miles from Rome. The Gallic iron-shod cavalry and infantry armed with long, well-tempered swords struck the stiff, slow-moving Roman phalanx of spearmen. Their lines broken, the panic-stricken Romans swam across the Tiber to Veii. The road to Rome was open.

Hearing of the disaster at the Allia, the Romans fled across the river to Caere. The Gauls marched into the deserted city and dated back to the time of Spurius Cassius in the early Republic (*see* p. 103). To make matters worse, the Etruscans, Aequi, Hernici, and Volsci, all of whom Rome is supposed previously to have conquered, invaded what was left of Roman territory. Camillus beat back their attacks with tremendous success, so it is reported, but it is useless to repeat the details because the tradition, with its confused chronology, its duplications, and inventions, is obviously unsound. Nevertheless, it is probable that Rome succeeded in stabilizing the situation in Latium at this time.

More real, perhaps, than the danger from invasion was the fear of dictatorship. Under similar circumstances a Greek state might easily have succumbed to the appeal of a strong-man government as the most efficient way of getting things done in a hurry, especially in a time of emergency. Not so Rome. The Republican tradition of liberty seems to have been too firmly set against it.

There was no lack of candidates; among them was no less a figure than Camillus himself, the hero of many battles and the chairman of the committee in charge of rebuilding the city walls. In spite of his splendid record of achievement and his immense personal prestige, he was driven into exile. Two other top military and political leaders with similar ambitions were executed.

Constitutional Reform and Reorganization of the Government

About 376 B.C., with the military danger lessened, two plebeian tribunes, C. Licinius Stolo and L. Sextius Lateranus, both very able and dynamic leaders of the new plebeian nobility whose wealth, social position, and marriage to women of the ancient patrician aristocracy gave them the power to break down the bars of exclusion from the highest political office, introduced before the Plebeian Council three proposals: 1) that interest already paid on debts be deducted from the principal, and the remainder of the debt, if any, paid within three years in equal instalments; 2) that no one be allowed to have more than 300 acres of public land; 3) that the consular tribuneship be abolished and only consuls be elected of whom one *must*

be a plebeian. Ten years later, we are told, these proposals were enacted into law.

Livy's account of the enactment of these laws is filled with absurdities, contradictions, and improbabilities. It is a mixture of two historical traditions, one old, simple, factual, and genuine, the other slanted, contradictory, and absurd. Among the improbabilities is the story that the patricians prevented the passage of the laws by persuading the eight other tribunes to interpose the veto. That could have happened in the Gracchan period but probably not in the fourth century. Another is the statement that between the years 375 and 370 B.C. Rome was without a government.

The laws themselves, except that relating to debts, are open to suspicion, especially the one stipulating that one of the consuls *must* be a plebeian. Such a law was unnecessary because there never was a law saying that a plebeian could not be a consul. The *Fasti* seem to have proved that plebeians were consuls or consular tribunes many times during both the fifth and the fourth centuries. Furthermore, the reported passage of a law (ca. 367 B.C.) that one of the consuls *must* be a plebeian is proved false by the fact that in the years 355, 354, 353, 351, 345, and 343 of the *Fasti* both consuls were patrician. It is unlikely that the Romans, traditionally a law-abiding people, would permit such an open and flagrant violation of a recent plebiscite.

There is, nevertheless, no denying that this year 367 B.C. was a turning point in Roman constitutional history. It was the year in which the government was reorganized to promote greater administrative efficiency. The multiple consular tribuneship was abolished and the dual consulship restored. A differentiation of function was required and at the same time a centralization of authority and responsibility. From then on, consuls, whether patrician or plebeian, held the supreme military command and general control over the government of the state.

The New Praetorship. To promote greater administrative efficiency and differentiation of function, a new office was created, the *praetorship,* probably not to compensate the patricians for the presumed loss of one of the consulships, but to relieve the consuls from the administration of justice. The consuls could now give their undivided attention to military and foreign affairs.

Next to the restoration of the consulship, the most important constitutional innovation was the new praetorship. The praetor (*Praetor urbanus*) was entrusted with the administration of justice within the city, and was later made responsible for the loyalty and the maintenance of law and order in other cities as they came under Roman control. Like the two ancient praetors (henceforth called consuls) he was elected annually by the Centuriate Assembly. As a junior colleague of the consuls, he possessed the *imperium,* and could, if necessary, assume command of an army. Although he ordinarily convened and presided only over the minor assemblies he could, in the absence of the consuls or if deputized by them, summon meetings of the Centuriate Assembly or the senate and perform all the executive functions of a consul. He had the *fasces* and six lictors, the purple bordered toga, the *curule* chair, and all the other insignia of a higher magistrate.

The Curule Aedileship. Another office, the curule aedileship, was created at this time to assume some of the functions of an expanding municipal administration. The curule aedileship was so called because the two new aediles had the right to the curule chair. The first curule aediles were patrician, but plebeians were later eligible in alternate years. Their functions were the same as those of the plebeian aediles previously described (p. 85). The increase in the number of aediles from two to four is evidence of the expanding functions of municipal administration.

Laws Relating to Debts, Interest Rates, and Mortgages. Among the pressing problems which the legislative activity of this period attempted to solve were those relating to debts, interest rates, and mortgages. Around 357 B.C. the maximum rate of interest as fixed by the Twelve Tables at $8\frac{1}{3}$ per cent was re-enacted. Apparently creditors had been charging a higher rate than that set by the old law. In the year 352 of the *Fasti,* the consuls appointed a board of five commissioners empowered to assist debtors in two ways: 1) by loans from the state bank secured by mortgages and 2) by permission to liquidate their debts by declaring bankruptcy. Five years later (about 347) the interest rate was reduced to $4\frac{1}{6}$ per cent with three years to pay. In 342 of the *Fasti* all loans at interest were abolished by law and enslavement for debt was made illegal. As creditors had been permitted by the law of the Twelve Tables to enslave or imprison debtors, the law of 342 was both misunderstood and disregarded until rendered more explicit by a law making enslavement for debt illegal for all time. This *Lex Poetelia Papiria* of 326 has rightly been called the charter of personal liberty.

Admission of Plebeians to Religious Offices. Another legislative reform was the admission of plebeians to a share in the responsibility of looking after and interpreting the Books of the Sibyl. This had hitherto been an exclusive prerogative of the patricians, who made use of it to block plebeian proposals for social, political, and economic reform. A new commission of ten men, five of whom had to be plebeian, was set up to take charge of these books. One of the last patrician bulwarks was the priesthood. In the year 300 B.C. the *Lex Ogulnia* increased the number of the pontiffs to eight and of the augurs to nine, of whom four pontiffs and five augurs must be plebeian. The only priestly offices still reserved to the patricians were the King of Sacrifices, the special priesthoods (*flaminats*) of Jupiter, Mars, and Quirinus, and the college of the Salii or Leaping Priests.

Concord of the Orders. The main grievances of the plebeians were now satisfied. As a symbol of harmony a temple of Concord was vowed and dedicated. There still remained a few constitutional reforms to be made to complete the great reform movement begun in 367 B.C. The year 356 of the *Fasti* saw the first plebeian dictator, 351 the first plebeian censor, and 337 the first plebeian praetor. To give more plebeians a chance to be elected to these offices it was made illegal for a magistrate to hold more than one curule office during any one year or the same office twice within a ten-year period. In 339 of the *Fasti* all bills proposed by the consuls had to have their form and constitutionality confirmed by the senate before presentation to the Centuriate Assembly for final enactment. This law increased senatorial control over the magistrates while decreasing it over the people.

The Hortensian Law of 287 B.C. The Hortensian Law of 287 might be called a landmark in the history of the Roman constitution. It marks not only the last full measure of equality between the patricians and plebeians, but probably also the birth of a new public assembly, the *Comitia Tributa*. For it gave resolutions or plebiscites of the Plebeian Council the full force of law. The Plebeian Council (*see* p. 85) became for the first time a regular public assembly of all the people.

The Tribal Assembly (Comitia Tributa). After 287 B.C., Rome had three public assemblies, the Curiate, Centuriate, and the Tribal. The first was now a ghost of the ancient assembly of the early kingship. The *Comitia Centuriata*, which began to function in the early fifth century as the supreme law-making body of the whole people and was referred to in the XII Tables as the *comitiatus maximus*, still retained in the third century B.C. all its ancient majesty, but had in the meantime become a clumsy, unwieldy body assembled only for the most important functions and on the most solemn occasions. It continued to elect the highest magistrates—consuls, praetors, and censors, to decide questions of war and peace, and to hear appeals in capital offenses involving the death penalty. But it had become the conservative stronghold of entrenched wealth.

The Tribal Assembly had been growing important even before 287 B.C. Its importance may be seen in the eagerness of the city masses to register in and control the voting of as many rural tribes as possible and in the equally strong determination of the landowners to keep them out. When Appius Claudius, the censor of 312/10 B.C., let them in, the opposition of the farm bloc forced the censors of 304/3 to restrict their registration to the four city tribes. After 287 B.C. it became the newest and youngest of the assemblies and perhaps the most important law-making body. Being easily assembled and having the simplest voting procedure, it passed a great batch of laws or plebiscites,

which only sticklers for legal niceties were later able to distinguish. The average person saw no difference between them. For it met in the Forum as the Plebeian Council had. Voting was by simple majority of the tribes, of which there were thirty-five by 241 B.C. The only apparent difference between the Tribal Assembly and the Plebeian Council was that the former was assembled by a regular magistrate of the people, the latter by a plebeian tribune.

The Conquest of Italy

With the passage of the Hortensian Law in 287 B.C. the program of constitutional reform was virtually complete and Rome, having put her own household in order, could face the problems of Italy in unity and strength. The internal cohesion and solidarity of the Roman people enabled them later to turn even the most disastrous defeats into ultimate victories.

It may be granted that the reorganization of the government begun about 367 B.C. permitted greater efficiency in administration and at the same time removed friction between the two dominant social classes of the community, the ancient patrician aristocracy and the new but powerful plebeian nobility. It may be taken for granted that foreign problems were among the most compelling reasons for governmental reorganization and political equalization of the two social classes. To say that the reform movement was expressly designed for the future conquest of Italy would be an extreme exaggeration. But once Rome had correctly appraised and met the crises of the fourth century B.C. she had once and for all successfully set her course for the conquest not only of Italy, but of the Mediterranean world. Her future as a world state was then largely determined.

Besides Rome the chief military powers in Italy in 350 were the Gauls, the Etruscans, and the Samnites. Of these the Etruscans and the Gauls were the least to be feared.

The Etruscans were a moribund league of cities unable to do anything really effective, though still capable of making trouble. By 474 B.C. they had lost Campania to the Greeks and Samnites, by about 400 the North to the onslaught of the Gauls. Now they were squeezed in a vise between the Gauls from the North and the waxing might of Rome in the South.

The Gauls had never been able to repeat their performance of the Allia. Walled cities were proof against their attacks, though later raids into Latium and Apulia revived old memories of their wild terror. When they came back about 349 B.C., the Romans easily routed them. They actually helped rather than hindered the Roman march to final conquest for they revealed to Rome her lack of defense against attack, and her need for governmental reform. They had helped to eliminate the Etruscan threat and, by the savagery of their attack, their indiscriminate killing, and wholesale plundering, had driven many Italian communities to look to Rome for leadership and protection. Finally, because of their spasmodic, uncoordinated, and ineffectual operations, they had left the fate of Italy to be decided between the Romans and the Samnites.

Though the life or death struggle between the Romans and the Samnites did not occur till after 327 B.C., it was perhaps obvious even in the middle of the century that they would be future enemies. To postpone the inevitable and to have time to prepare, Rome signed a treaty of alliance with the Samnites about 354 B.C. Both sides probably welcomed the treaty because of their common fear of the Gauls.

The Samnites

The Samnites were a mountain people living in the southern Apennines. Their territories extended from a point on the Adriatic coast due east but slightly to the north of Rome as far south as the Gulf of Tarentum (Taranto). In their own language they were called Sabines, but Greek and Roman writers have perpetuated the name Samnite. Their language was Oscan, an Italic dialect similar to Latin. They lived under primitive conditions without very marked differences of class. Flocks and herds supplied their livelihood, supplemented by whatever agriculture the mountains would permit. These sources of income were never enough to support their

expanding population and they were compelled to push down into the fertile plains of Campania to the west or into Lucania in the south. Their constant pressure behind the Volscans had long been forcing the latter to invade Latium and wage endless wars with the Romans. To the Greeks of South Italy they had been a constant and unnerving menace. It was clear to the Romans, even though protected by distance and sheltered behind their fortress on the Tiber, that they would some day have to fight with them the battle of Italy.

Around 350 B.C. the Samnites seemed much stronger than the Romans. They held more than three and a half times as much territory (8,300 as opposed to 2,300 square miles) and had more than double the population (perhaps 650,000 as opposed to probably 317,400). Even these figures do not convey the initial weakness of the Romans, because they include territories and populations already unreliable and hostile, which ten years later were at war with Rome. Nevertheless, before the end of the century Rome owed her victory over the Samnites to her superiority in manpower and resources. With each succeeding decade Rome expanded and gained in strength while the Samnites grew weaker.

On the other hand, Samnite expansion into Campania and Lucania did not increase Samnite war-making power. Many of the original Samnite settlers had become rich and had risen to a position of leadership among the local aristocracy. As they did not want the status quo upset by a mass invasion of their have-not kinsmen, they were inclined to line up behind the Romans.

Similarly, the Lucanian Samnites, or at least the dominant faction, had turned their backs upon their northern kinsmen and wanted to play a big role in the world of the Greek city states. From time to time they made alliances with the Romans against their own people.

Even more serious and dangerous were the relations of the Samnites with the people of their own race living on their northern borders, the Marsi, Paeligni, and Marrucini. When the Romans made alliances with the latter they were able to carry the war right into the heart of Samnium. Though the Samnites were brave fighters and passionately devoted to the defense of their mountain homeland, they were too clannish to cooperate with people outside their immediate neighborhood.

The Samnite homeland itself was divided into four main tribes forming, in time of war, a loose confederacy liable to come apart when unity and cohesion were most required. The confederacy lacked a national assembly, which might have enabled the Samnites to formulate a clear, long-range war policy. Their most brilliant victories failed to produce any permanent results.

The Samnites could and did give the Romans many painful lessons in mountain fighting. From their many encounters with the Greeks the Samnites had learned that the hoplite *phalanx*, though irresistible on level ground, was a distinct liability in mountainous terrain. After a while the Romans mastered the secret of mountain fighting, but the Samnite failure to copy Roman political and diplomatic methods spelled the difference between final victory and defeat.

The First Samnite War, 343–341 B.C. About 343 the Samnites attacked the Sidicini, an insignificant state south of Capua. Capua appealed to Rome for help, which the Romans readily gave because it made them allies of Italy's second biggest city and gave them a foothold in Campania. The war itself was not a serious one and the battles recorded are undoubtedly fictitious. Some scholars would reject this war altogether, but without it it seems hard to explain the presence of the Romans in Campania and some of the events which followed.

Capua was saved; but the Roman soldiers, failing to understand why they had to fight so far from home, mutinied. The Romans were glad to make peace and so were the Samnites who feared Archidamus, the Spartan king who had landed in Italy in 343/2 B.C. in response to an appeal for help from the Greek city of Tarentum. The peace terms of 341 B.C. acknowledged the Samnite right to occupy the Sidicini territory and the Roman alliance with Capua.

The Latin War of 340–338 B.C. The Latin and Campanian allies of Rome regarded the treaty of 341 as a shameful betrayal of the Sidicini and when the Samnite occupation of that small state began about 340, they took up arms in its defense contrary to the wishes and advice of Rome. For years the Latins had been chafing against their Roman alliance, which seemed to them another form of domination. As the Gauls were no longer a menace after 349 of the *Fasti* they saw in the Samnite occupation a chance to make their bid for freedom and independence. They were already at war with Samnium and their insubordination brought them also into a war with Rome. The war gave the Romans a chance to settle the Latin problem (with the help of the now-friendly Samnites) before they got involved in any major conflict.

By 338 of the *Fasti* the bitter conflict was over. The Campanians had already accepted the generous terms offered them and had deserted their allies. The Latins and the Volscans were soon afterwards crushed never to rise up again, and the Old Latin League was dissolved. From now on the future of the Latins would be determined at Rome's pleasure.

The Old Latin League

The Old Latin League dissolved around 338 B.C. had had a long history. It had grown out of one of the ancient religious leagues formed for the joint celebration of common festivals. It acquired a political and juridical status by the treaty concluded by perhaps Spurius Cassius (*see* pp. 59, 99) between the early Roman Republic of the one part and perhaps thirty Latin cities of the other. It had been renewed about 358 B.C. with some added provisions tightening Roman control.

In the original treaty ascribed to Spurius Cassius, which established an offensive and defensive alliance, Rome had formally renounced all claims to domination over Latium. The terms were that peace should exist between the two parts forever, that the enemies of the one be the enemies of the other, that both contribute equal numbers of troops for war, and that booty taken in wars fought in common be divided equally.

There were also provisions relating to the private rights of citizens known as Latin Rights. These were specially important.

The rights, which Roman citizens were to enjoy in each of the allied Latin cities and Latin citizens in Rome and in each of the other Latin cities, were intermarriage (*conubium*), the right to do business and make legally binding contracts (*commercium*), and the right to change residence. The children of a Roman husband or wife married to a Latin inherited Roman citizenship and both their parents' property. Latin citizens doing business in Rome could sue or be sued in Roman courts and could enjoy the benefits of the Roman law of sale and of succession. All contracts could be enforced only in the courts of the place where originally drawn up. In early times Latin citizens had the mutual right of changing residence and afterwards of acquiring citizenship. A Latin moving to Rome would vote in the tribe he had drawn by lot.

Latin Rights after 338 B.C. of the Fasti. When the Romans scrapped the Old Latin League, they did not leave a vacuum for underground hostility or sullen resentment to fill. At least six Latin cities or municipalities (*municipia*), on losing their old independence, were incorporated into the Roman state with full rights of citizenship, including the right to vote and hold office. Local government in these cities still continued to function. The colonies founded by the League received the same rights. The rest of the Latin cities and some trusted Etruscan allies received limited Roman citizenship without the right to vote, but with the obligation to furnish troops for the Roman army when called upon. They were allowed the right to local government, but might not formulate an independent foreign policy or form leagues among themselves. They were also prohibited from the rights of intermarriage and of making contracts among themselves: these they could enjoy only with Rome.

They were now fully protected against foreign attack and were assured the full benefits of Roman civil law in all their business enterprises. In addition they could still enjoy the privileges of local government. Many of them were no doubt grateful for the benefits already given and hoped to prove themselves worthy, by loyal cooperation with Rome, of

admission later to the privileges of full citizenship. Thus did Rome bind to herself with ties of loyalty and hope all her defeated Latin enemies. The wisdom and success of this policy was vindicated; for they remained faithful even in the darkest hours of defeat against all the allurements of the Samnites, of Pyrrhus, and of Hannibal.

Extension of Latin Rights to Italian Communities. The settlement of the year 338 of the *Fasti* was not only epoch-making in the history of citizenship in general and of working relationships between conquered communities and the center of power, but it set the pattern for the conquest first of Italy and later of the Mediterranean world. It was a stroke of political genius unique in the ancient world and, as a weapon of conquest, was worth more than many legions. Prior to 338 a conquered city was usually either completely destroyed, as Veii had been by the Romans themselves, or left to smolder in discontent ready to burst into rebellion the moment the conqueror had relaxed his grip. The Romans instead devised the municipal system of government within the Roman super-state.

Municipia. Municipia (municipalities) were cities and towns in Latium, Etruria, and Campania, whose inhabitants had the full burdens of Roman citizens without the rights of voting and acquiring property in Rome. They were required to furnish troops or money contributions for war and were prohibited from making war against or concluding treaties with other states. Otherwise they could conduct their local affairs as they had done in the past according to their own constitutions, laws, and traditions. Because they enjoyed the Latin rights of intermarriage and the benefits of Roman civil law, their status may be said to have been halfway between complete independence and full Roman citizenship.

Colonies. Another Roman device was the planting of colonies at strategic points throughout Italy. The idea was not a new one, for the planting of colonies was one of the joint activities of the Old Latin League, the purpose of which was to hold down conquered territory and at the same time serve as an outlet for surplus population. Two such colonies were founded in southern Etruria on land conquered from Veii. A number of other colonies were established on conquered Volscan territory. Nine such colonies were in existence at the time of the break-up of the League.

It was not till after 338 of the *Fasti* that the planting of colonies became established Roman policy. During the next fifty years, colonies were founded at Ostia, Antium, Terracina, Sinuessa, and Minturnae to guard harbors and waterways or defend the coasts of Latium (Rome then had no permanent fleet). Other colonists were sent to Campania and Apulia to occupy key points and forge a ring of fortresses around Samnium, to Umbria and other points North to keep the Gauls in check.

There were two kinds of colonies: Roman citizen colonies and Latin colonies. Latin colonies were by far the more numerous. Up till the First Punic War twenty-one Latin colonies were founded, but only nine Roman citizen colonies. The two types differed not in the colonists since both Latins and Romans could be accepted for either, but in the size of population and constitutional status. Until 194 B.C. or later, Roman citizen colonies were limited to 300 families while Latin colonies varied between 2500 and 6,000 families. It is said that one at Venusia, thirty miles north of Tarentum, consisted of 20,000. Roman citizen colonies were too small to form a state and the colonists never ceased to be full Roman citizens. Latin colonies had the status of Latin allies or ordinary *municipia*. They had the right of local self-government with their own laws, elected magistrates, census, and coinage. If a Latin colonist moved to Rome, he could become a Roman citizen, provided he left in his place a son of military age.

Roman citizen colonies were simply small garrisons sent to places that were of strategic importance, but unattractive and incapable of economic or community growth. The Latin colonies often became, especially in North Italy, the first foundations of some very large cities.

Alliances. Another method the Romans used in their policy of Samnite encirclement was the formation of a system of alliances with Greek and Italian city states, who felt threatened by the Samnite menace. Rome signed treaties with them differing according to mutual need, dependence, and the gravity of the military situation. All allied states were commonly required to place their military forces at Rome's disposal and agree to leave the conduct of foreign affairs in her hands. In return she agreed not to impose taxes upon them and to allow each allied city to raise, equip, and command its own troops, who would fight under the command of a Roman general. Rome would also provide the allied troops with food and subsistence pay at her own expense and would share with them the spoils of war. Furthermore, all allied cities could enjoy the Latin Rights of Roman civil law and intermarriage. At the same time they would be permitted local self-government under their own laws and political institutions.

The Great Samnite War (327-304/3 B.C.)

The war against the Samnites, for which the Romans had long been preparing by all the various methods just described, broke out at last around 327. The battle for Italy had begun. The immediate cause of this long-awaited and long-lasting war is not clear. A trivial incident occurred in Naples when a Roman and a Samnite faction squabbled over control of the city. The Roman faction won, Naples became a Roman ally, and the war between Rome and Samnium began.

The military history of this war is obscure. Most of the battles the annalists record are unimportant even if they did take place, except the battle of the Caudine Forks which took place in 321 of the *Fasti*. The Romans, attempting to march from Campania to Apulia, were misled by false information into a trap at the Caudine Forks, where they were compelled to surrender, give hostages, and agree not to renew the war. Stripped down to single garments, they were ignominiously driven under a yoke, which consisted of two spears stuck in the ground and united at the top by a third. To pass under the yoke was a token of complete defeat and unconditional surrender.

New Military Tactics. The battle of the Caudine Forks made clear to the Romans that they needed to learn about mountain fighting. They used the peace to good advantage by reorganizing the legion so as to form three lines separately trained, differently armed, and able to maneuver independently. The new formations could better operate in mountainous terrain and some troops were armed with Samnite javelins instead of *phalanx* spears. Now able to put four legions into battle instead of two and to fight on the plains as well as the Greeks, and in the mountains as well as the Samnites, the Romans found an excuse in 316 of the *Fasti* for repudiating the peace treaty and renewing the war.

The very next year the Romans suffered another serious defeat at Lautulae near Terracina, a coastal town in southern Latium. This reverse almost caused the Campanian allies to run out of their alliance, but strong pressure soon brought them back into line. The Latins stood firm, partly because the Samnites were getting too close to home and partly because the Romans had dealt with them so fairly after 338 B.C.

Stabilizing the situation on the Campanian front both by the recovery of lost ground and by setting up colony bases at key points, the Romans shifted their attention to the Apulian front, where they had established earlier a big base at Luceria. At the same time they

continued their policy of Samnite encirclement. They concluded military alliances with the Lucanians in the south and with the Marsi, Marrucini, Paeligni, and Frentani in the north, all close kinsfolk of the Samnites.

This offensive strategy in the north came none too soon. For the Samnites began to copy Roman diplomatic tactics and persuaded some southern Etruscan cities whose treaties with Rome were about to expire to create a second front against Rome. There was also a danger that they might induce the Gauls to effect a junction with their army. The Gauls made no move and the Romans continued to create a broad buffer zone across central Italy, from which they were able to make devastating raids into the heart of Samnium. By this show of force they also compelled the Etruscans to renew and observe their treaties.

The man who is thought to have masterminded this astute military and diplomatic strategy was the old censor of 312/10 B.C., Appius Claudius the Blind. It was he who hoped to increase patriotism in Roman territory by introducing a more democratic system of tribal voting (p. 101). It was also his idea to run a highway, later stone-paved, from Rome to Capua, over which troops

The Old Appian Way. (Courtesy Istituto Italiano di Cultura)

could be swiftly moved in any kind of weather. This was the famous Appian Way.

In spite of the brilliance of their strategy and their constancy and doggedness in danger and defeat, the Romans did not easily win the Second Samnian War. Despite the constant increase of Roman military strength, both sides were still fairly evenly matched in territory and population. Each side had unreliable allies. Some Roman allies considered defecting to the Samnite side when they saw Rome becoming too strong for their own future security. The war was long and bloody, the victory was by no means absolute, as the peace of 304/3 B.C. clearly shows. The Samnites lost none of their original territory, none of their independence, and none of their capacity to fight again.

The Third Samnite War, 298-290 B.C.

The balance of power had been shifting steadily in favor of Rome. After 304/3 B.C., she controlled an area of 9,242.77 square miles and a population of some 927,000, as compared with 5,676.13 square miles and 498,000 population of the Samnites. The danger of the growing disparity had become clear to the Sabines, the Etruscans, the Umbrians, and even the Gauls, who all joined forces with the Samnites in 295 B.C. in the hope of stopping Rome. They fought the Romans at Sentinum in Umbria. The consul Decius Mus, a Roman hero, was killed but the Romans won the battle for Italy. The Samnites, knowing that all hope was gone, surrendered and sued for peace. Their lands were annexed and they accepted the status of Roman allies. The Etruscans and Gauls fought their last battle at Lake Vadimo in 283 B.C. After that the Roman conquest of Italy would have been complete except for a mopping-up operation, had not Pyrrhus suddenly arrived in Italy.

The Pyrrhic Wars

Pyrrhus, the king of Epirus, had landed in response to an appeal from Tarentum. He was the last of the many Greek adventurers, who had come to help Tarentum against her Italian enemies. The first was King Archidamus of Sparta, from 343/2 to 338 B.C., next Alexander of Epirus, the uncle of Alexander the Great, from 334 to 331/30, then another Spartan king, Cleonymus in 303/2, and after him Agathocles of Syracuse (298–289 B.C.). Not one had succeeded either in making Tarentum a strong power or in carving out an empire for himself.

In 285 B.C., Thurii, a Greek city not far from the western shore of the Gulf of Tarentum (Taranto), under attack by the Lucanians, appealed to Rome for help rather than to her ally, Tarentum. Perhaps the Thurians held the belief that Rome was stronger than Tarentum, and more reliable as well as less dangerous. With some misgivings the Romans answered the appeal, defeated the Lucanians, and stationed a small garrison in Thurii. Rhegium, Locri, and probably Croton also asked for and received Roman protection.

Roman interference in the internal affairs of Greek Italy aroused the suspicion and enmity of Tarentum. So, when a Roman naval squadron of ten ships, cruising about in the Gulf of Tarentum in violation of the treaty of 334 of the *Fasti*, happened to put in at the port of Tarentum shortly after the Thurian incident, some hotheads from the city went down, sank four ships, and killed the admiral. Then the Tarentines fitted out an expedition, marched to Thurii, drove out the Roman garrison, and sacked the town. When ambassadors from Rome came to seek redress and reparations, they were publicly insulted, ridiculed for their bad Greek, and refused a hearing. The Tarentines might have been more disposed to listen and make amends had not Pyrrhus arrived upon the scene.

Pyrrhus was king of Epirus, a small mountainous country in northwestern Greece. The ambitious Pyrrhus, educated in Egypt, had married a Ptolemaic princess, and had for some years been subsidized by Ptolemy II. He had been king of half of Macedonia in 288/5 B.C. The invitation from Tarentum presented a real opportunity to establish the empire he craved, especially as both Ptolemy Ceraunus, the murderer of Seleucus I and king of Macedonia from 281 to 279 B.C., and

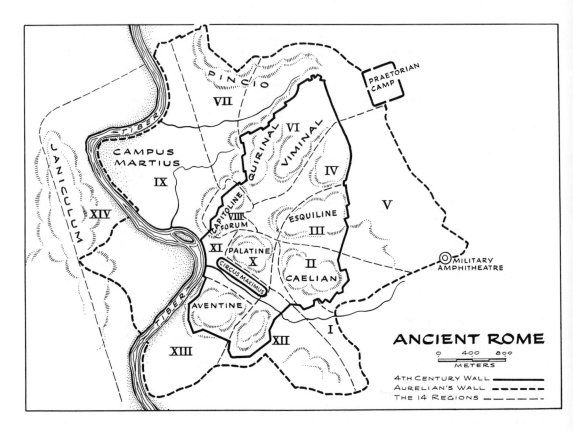

ANCIENT ROME

0   400   800
METERS

4TH CENTURY WALL ——————
AURELIAN'S WALL ▬ ▬ ▬ ▬ ▬
THE 14 REGIONS — — — — —

Ptolemy II of Egypt were prepared to assist him in this venture.

The Greek cities of South Italy were fairly rich at the time and he hoped to unite them and use them as a base to take over Sicily and later, perhaps, the Carthaginian empire in Africa. No longer beholden to subsidies from Egypt, he could then expand into Spain, southern France, North Italy, and might later on add to his dominions Macedonia, Tripolitania, and maybe Egypt itself.

In the spring of 280 B.C. he arrived in Italy with 25,000 mercenaries, many of whom were veterans of the slain Seleucus I. Pyrrhus had hired 20,000 heavily-armed phalanx men, and purchased 20 Indian war elephants. Shortly after landing, he met the Roman army at Heraclea. He found to his surprise that his hoplite *phalanx* was unable to make a break through the Roman legions which were equipped and drilled in Samnite style and always able, after giving ground here and there, to close their ranks. For the first time since Marathon, the *phalanx* had met its match.

Pyrrhus was a keen general and an able tactician. Instead of using his elephants like modern tanks to make a break through the center of the Roman lines, which might have let the elephants through and then closed before the infantry could follow, he adopted the unorthodox tactics of attacking both flanks with elephants and cavalry.

The encircled Romans lost 7,000 men and were forced to retreat. But Pyrrhus himself lost 4,000 men and won only a tactical victory. (Such an outcome has since been known as a "Pyrrhic victory.") With most of South Italy under his control, Pyrrhus next tried to force a decision by a lightning attack upon Rome. He marched as far as Praeneste, within forty miles of the capital, but he found to his surprise that the Roman allies upon whose help he had depended did not flock to his colors. He then tried a peace offensive and when that also failed he was forced to get ready for another battle. He met the Romans in battle at Asculum in Apulia. The first day the Romans fought on rough ground, where the Pyrrhic *phalanx* was ineffective; the next day Pyrrhus feigned a retreat to more level ground. The Romans followed. His elephants broke through the Roman center lines. This victory too was costly: a loss of 4,000 men. It was then that Pyrrhus is said to have declared: "Another such victory and I am lost!"

Pyrrhus' Sicilian Venture, 278-275 B.C.

His costly victories over the Romans dissuaded Pyrrhus from further attempts to establish an empire in Italy. Besides, opportunities had opened up elsewhere. The Celts had invaded Macedonia in 279 B.C., and killed Ptolemy Ceraunus. Pyrrhus, if he was strong enough, might go there as champion of the Greek world and win back the Macedonian throne. Sicily, about to be conquered by the Carthaginians, offered still another possibility. Hard-pressed Syracuse sent envoys begging for his help. He decided, perhaps after some prodding from Egypt, to try out his luck in Sicily. Peace talks were begun with the Romans and would have gone on smoothly for him, had not Mago, the admiral of a large Carthaginian fleet anchored off Ostia, suddenly appeared offering to supply Rome with ships, money, or anything reasonable she might want, if she would keep Pyrrhus occupied in Italy. Finally Pyrrhus was obliged to leave half of his army in Tarentum to defend his allies and set sail for Sicily in the fall of 278 B.C. without any definite commitment from Rome.

His successes in Sicily were immediate and colossal. He had driven the Carthaginians off the mainland and was besieging their last stronghold, the small island of Lilybaeum, when Carthage sued for peace. Just then there loomed up before Pyrrhus the possibility of making a lightning attack upon defenseless Carthage and, with the aid of a fifth column, of conquering Egypt. These dreams never materialized. In some mysterious way the Sicilian city states suddenly found the encouragement to declare themselves neutral. Only Syracuse remained faithful to

him and even she was divided by civil strife. The Sicilian venture had failed. There was nothing else to do, but to return to Italy.

Pyrrhus lost part of his fleet in a naval battle with the Carthaginians during his attempt to get back to Italy in 276 B.C. In Italy he afterwards captured a few Greek towns, plundered the treasures of the temple of Persephone at Locri, and made his way to Tarentum. Regrouping his forces he marched northwards into Samnium. He lost several of his prize elephants during an indecisive battle with the Romans near Beneventum, and finally withdrew to Tarentum to avoid getting caught between two consular armies. Though he had never lost a land battle, his entire Italian campaign had been a failure. He returned to Greece in 275 B.C. and again became king of Macedonia in 274. Two years later he lost his life on a street in Argos, where some woman dropped a pot on his head from a second story window.

Pyrrhus gone, all Italy from Pisa and Rimini in the north to Brundisium (Brindisi), Tarentum, and the straits of Messana in the south came under the undisputed domination of Rome.

Reasons for Roman Success

Part of the reason for Rome's success was the reorganization of the government around 367 B.C. and her unity in the face of external danger. Her success was due in large part to her willingness and ability to fulfill all her treaty obligations and to the statesmanlike quality of her leadership. Her strong but generous policy towards her Latin allies had secured their loyalty which never wavered. Also, most Italian communities regarded the Samnites in the south and the Gauls in the north as a greater menace to their security than Roman supremacy. Rome wisely refrained from annexing any territory in the north until her victory over the Samnites was assured. At the end of the Samnite wars she controlled sixty times more territory and six times as many people.

THE PERIOD OF THE

Immediately after her conquest of the greater part of the Italian peninsula, Rome made her appearance upon the larger stage of Mediterranean and world affairs. In size, strength, and military capability she was already a great power, as her victory over Pyrrhus had proved, but she had not yet actually moved into the mainstream of Hellenistic civilization, which then dominated the political, economic, and spiritual life of the world from the Himalayas in the East to the Atlantic seaboard in the West.

It was not Egypt, Syria, Macedonia, or any of the other heirs of the vast conquests of Alexander the Great that compelled Rome to emerge from isolation, but Carthage, the mighty African empire of the West. Carthage, though never conquered by Alexander nor an inheritor of any part of his conquests, was

PUNIC WARS

economically and militarily a great Hellenistic power.

There are for the first time fairly reliable sources of information. Of the early annalists, whom Livy and the Greek writer, Polybius, used as sources, Fabius and Cincius were well past middle age before the Second Punic War began and had either witnessed themselves the events of the First or learned them directly from those who had.

Polybius himself, whose works Livy had used, came to Rome just a century later than the outbreak of the First Punic War. His brief account of the First Punic War and

his detailed description of the Second is as reliable as one would expect from a keen and interested observer of Roman military and political history. Unfortunately, his work is intact only to the year 216 B.C. and after that only in fragments, but Livy, whose work is complete from 219 onwards, makes up for part of this loss. In addition, there are some biographies of Cornelius Nepos and especially Plutarch dealing with the events of this period and the accounts of Diodorus and of Appian, who, though living in the second century A.D., was a careful compiler and used excellent sources of information.

Besides the works of the writers just mentioned, a number of Greek writers whose works are now lost were interested observers of the events of this period and must also have contributed to the building of a reliable historical tradition. Nor can the written primary sources, coins and inscriptions be ignored, which now become ever more numerous and enlightening.

The Rise of Carthage

About the tenth century B.C., if not before, the Phoenicians, traders and seafarers from time immemorial, had begun to frequent the shores of the Mediterranean Sea. Cyprus and Egypt, Greece and Italy, Africa and Spain knew their ships and the goods they carried in them—the latest arms and weapons, linen and woolen fabrics, purple dyes, painted vases, glassware, and ornaments made out of ivory, gold, or precious stones, all products of the famous workshops of Sidon and Tyre. In exchange they carried back to Phoenicia copper, lead, tin, silver, gold, and other raw materials. They found copper and silver in Spain, and may have sailed to Britain in search of tin.

To facilitate this exchange of goods, they established small trading posts on both the Mediterranean and the Atlantic shores of Spain and all along the coast of North Africa. These trading posts served also as way stations or stopping-off places on long voyages. One of the earliest established was Gades (now Cadiz) on the Atlantic side of southern Spain. Here they loaded their ships with the silver brought down from the headwaters of the Guadalquivir and copper from the famous Rio Tinto mines. From here they sailed to Cornwall for tin.

The home land, Phoenicia, was a narrow strip of territory beside the sea. Crowded together in this small country between the two great powers of Egypt and Assyria, the Phoenicians sought outlets for their surplus population. Since the coastal regions of the eastern Mediterranean were already occupied and thickly settled, they turned to the West and especially to Spain, North Africa, Sardinia, and Corsica, where small trading posts had already sprung up. The arrival of colonists from Tyre and Sidon must have been a pleasing sight to the native populations of all these regions, for the Phoenicians brought with them science, craftsmanship, new agricultural methods, and metalworking skills, as well as a knowledge of medicine. Colonization was a mutual benefit to the Phoenicians and the people of North Africa and Spain.

The most famous, though not the oldest, of the Phoenician colonies was Carthage. The story of its founding, like that of Rome, is encrusted with legends, but archaeological discoveries prove that most of the men came from Tyre, some of the women and certain of the gods from Cyprus. Carthage, founded probably between 673 and 663 B.C. and not, as formerly conjectured from uncertain evidence, between 860 and 814, was situated on a small tongue of land jutting out into the Gulf of Tunis almost midway between Egypt and Spain and across the sea from Sicily. In strategic position at the narrowest part of the Mediterranean and with access to either end, Carthage was an ideal location for a naval power. After she had occupied the island of Malta, she was able to exclude the Greeks from the western half of the sea.

Situated at the head of a long, narrow bay with hills frowning down upon it and a narrow entrance from the outer sea, Carthage possessed a secure roadstead for anchored ships sheltered both from the north winds and attacks of pirates. In the center of the city rose the Byrsa or strongly fortified citadel, which afforded protection against the attacks of hostile natives living round about. Behind the city stretched miles of potentially rich farming land, some of it still covered with heavy stands of fine shipbuilding timber. In the entire Mediterranean basin it would be hard to find a site at once more strategic and more easily defended, economically more favored and scenically more beautiful. In more ways than one Carthage deserved the title of "Queen of the Seas."

For several decades Carthage remained an obedient daughter of Tyre, but during the seventh century the mother city became subject to Assyria and afterwards to Babylon and Persia. Tyre now was unable either to control or protect the Phoenician colonies of the West. That duty fell upon Carthage, but instead of making the Phoenician settlements loyal and cooperative allies as Rome had done in Italy, she forced them to pay for protection and to become tribute-paying subjects of her empire, which eventually extended from Bengasi in the East to Gibraltar and Portugal in the West and included Sardinia, Corsica, parts of Sicily, and the Balearic Islands. At the same time she was creating a navy second to none in the whole Mediterranean.

As a result of this short-sighted imperialistic policy, she failed to win friends and, during her struggle with Rome, was forced to stamp out numerous revolts among her Spanish and North African subjects, a distraction which seriously hampered her prosecution of the war. As events later proved Carthage could ill afford such policies in spite of her enormous wealth and overwhelming naval power. The only people who received moderately good treatment from Carthage were the Sicilians because she was competing for their loyalty first with Syracuse and later with Rome.

Apart from tribute imposed upon unwilling subjects and vassal states, the amazing wealth of Carthage before the Punic Wars was chiefly derived from mining, shipping, sales monopolies, and agriculture.

Mining. Carthage controlled by far the richest mining resources of the Mediterranean basin. Sardinia had relatively small resources of mineral wealth, but of remarkable variety—lead, zinc, copper, iron, and silver. The mines of Spain were richer and even after two and a half millennia of continuous working Spanish mines produce millions of tons of iron ore besides lead, zinc, mercury, copper, gold, and silver. When the Phoenicians first found silver at the headwaters of the Guadalquivir, their eyes, it is said, almost popped out of their heads. Hannibal is said to have been able in later times to get out 300 pounds a day of almost pure silver. The copper mines of Rio Tinto were worked then just as they are today.

The Carthaginians also had access to other sources of mineral supplies. Leaving Gades they would sail north to Cornwall, as the

Phoenicians probably had done long ago, and load their ships with valuable cargoes of tin. From the same port other expeditions passed along the West coast of Africa as far south as the Gold Coast, the Cameroons, and even Gaboon, from which they brought back gold, ivory, Negro slaves, and war elephants. The expedition of Hanno is especially famous. He brought along 30,000 colonists, whom he settled at six different points along the northwest African coast. Never again did Mediterranean navigators venture so far south of Gibraltar until the time of Bartholomew Diaz (1486) or of Vasco da Gama (1497).

Shipping and the Carrying Trade. Not all the mineral cargoes carried in Carthaginian ships were utilized by the metal foundries of Carthage. Many of them were rerouted to the Hellenistic East. For several centuries prior to the First Punic War, the carrying trade from West to East was virtually a Carthaginian monopoly since Greek, Etruscan, or Roman shipping was excluded from almost half of the western Mediterranean by treaty or by naval force. Any Greek ship caught in western waters was usually sunk.

Sales Monopolies. The mercantilistic policy of Carthage, probably copied from that of Ptolemaic Egypt, excluded foreign competition in all parts of her empire, except possibly Sicily. This policy enabled Carthaginian merchants to sell within that area cheaply manufactured goods at monopolistic prices. The only Carthaginian manufactures which might have competed in a free market were textiles, especially the purple dyed fabrics which enjoyed a good reputation in all parts of the Mediterranean world.

Agriculture. The contribution that the Carthaginians made to scientific agriculture and especially to the development of the slave-worked plantation is usually ignored. It was they who taught the Romans the techniques of organizing large masses of slave labor on agricultural estates or plantations for the production of single marketable crops or staples. Although the slave trade and the limited use of slaves as farm hands and shop workers were known in Greece and other ancient countries, slave labor was never able to compete with native free labor in Greece, in the Seleucid Empire, or in Ptolemaic Egypt. It remained for the Carthaginians, while relying on Greek and Hellenistic treatises for the scientific cultivation of specific farm crops, to work out a system of plantation management involving the large scale use of slave labor.*

Large estates were built up by the Carthaginian nobles throughout the vast African empire. The breeding of cattle, sheep, and especially horses was developed to a fine art. Carthage itself was surrounded by a wide belt of vineyards and olive plantations producing for the expanding markets inside and beyond the Carthaginian empire. Thus while Carthage was a pupil of Hellenistic agricultural science, she alone up to this time had the space, the capital, and the markets for the application of that science on a large scale.

Carthage, a Hellenistic State

Carthage was a Hellenistic state, i.e. a state in which non-Greek people overlaid their native culture with a veneer of Greek culture. The upper classes adopted Greek methods of government, warfare, farming, manufacture, architecture, and town planning, Greek styles of dress, and even the Greek language itself. The borrowing of such externals does not imply that the ruling aristocracy, much less the masses of the population, understood the essence of Greek culture.

Nevertheless, Carthage, while remaining more or less out on the periphery or fringe-area of the Hellenistic cultural world, adopted many of the externals of Greek civilization. Greek methods of manufacture were copied and Greek industrial products,

* Shortly after the destruction of Carthage in 146 the senate expressly ordered, no doubt for the use of rich landowners in Italy, a translation of Mago's classic work of thirty-two volumes on Carthaginian agriculture, perhaps the only part of Punic literature they thought worthy of preservation and study. The influence of this work on later Roman writers about agriculture can scarcely be overestimated. Nor did its influence die with them. It was transmitted indirectly to the Moors of medieval Spain and probably to the Spaniards, who established slave-worked plantations in the New World.

such as pottery, jewelry, statues, and all kinds of metal wares were imported, imitated, mass produced, and sold throughout the Carthaginian commercial empire.

The Carthaginian Government

Another Hellenistic importation was the Carthaginian form of government. As described by Aristotle, it consisted apparently of four branches: an executive of two annually elected *Shophetim* or Judges, a senate of three hundred members, a popular assembly, and a supreme court of one hundred and four members. With the possible exception of the popular assembly, which did not have much actual power, the government was an oligarchy of rich businessmen, merchants, and landowners. The two Judges and all the generals, though elected by the Assembly, were invariably men of substantial wealth and belonged to the inner circle of this exclusive oligarchy.

The real power of government lay in the hands of two bodies: the Supreme Court and a Council of thirty men chosen by the Assembly to act as a committee of the Senate. The Council, of which the two Judges were members *ex officio,* prepared the agenda for the deliberations of the Senate. The members of the Supreme Court were also members of the Senate, but unlike the Council were selected not by the Assembly, but by a cabinet of five executive heads dealing with finance, army, and navy, whom Aristotle called Pentarchs. The Supreme Court, though originally intended to check dictatorial tendencies, gradually became itself one of the most dreaded bodies in the state and, working together with the Pentarchs, the most venal and corrupt. Such was the government of Carthage until its reformation by Hannibal.

The Navy. Before the First Punic War the pride of Carthage was her large navy, needed to guard her trade monopoly of the western Mediterranean, enforce embargoes, protect her colonies, and prevent piracy. Taking no chances with disloyal and half-hearted crews, she manned her ships with her own citizens commanded by naval experts.

The Army. The army, on the other hand,

contained few citizen troops, and was composed largely of men conscripted among the natives of Libya, Sardinia, and Spain, troops hired from the allied but independent chiefs of Algeria and Morocco, and mercenaries picked up in every part of the Mediterranean. It was difficult to whip so heterogeneous a group into an efficient fighting machine. The general's task was not only difficult but dangerous: if he won too many battles, he might be accused of dictatorial ambitions and be hauled up before the Supreme Court. But if he lost too many, he might be nailed up on the cross.

The First Punic War: 264–241 B.C.

In Sicily, Rome and Carthage, the two great republics of the western Mediterranean, one strong on land, the other at sea, fought a war which neither wanted. Neither had yet done anything to hurt or offend the other and both scrupulously avoided any incident which might bring them into conflict. Their relations up to 264 B.C. had been diplomatically correct, if not friendly, and if a third but stronger power had threatened the existence of either, they probably would have quickly joined forces to repel the danger. For the want of a common enemy they became locked in a deadly conflict, which generated much hatred and propaganda.*

The Mamertines were a group of Campanian mercenaries who named themselves after Mamers or Mars, the god of war. They had been hired by Syracuse, but in 289 B.C. deserted and seized the strategic town of Messana in the northeastern corner of Sicily quite close to the straits of Messina. Like the Roman legion, who during the Pyrrhic War had deserted and seized the town of Reggio on the Italian side of the straits, the Mamertines killed off all the men of Messana, took their wives, and made plundering raids upon Syracusan territory.

* It was said, for example, that the Carthaginians were faithless, cruel, and licentious, and that they regularly sacrificed little children to Moloch.

To exterminate this menace, Hiero II, the young and able king of Syracuse, attacked Messana in 265 B.C. and was on the point of capturing it when the Mamertines appealed for help to the admiral of a nearby Carthaginian fleet, who came ashore with a strong force to prevent the Syracusans from getting control of so strategic a location. Frustrated, Hiero abandoned the siege and went home.

The Mamertines, though grateful to the admiral for his assistance, feared the Carthaginians were intending to remain in Messana permanently. They appealed to the senate for Roman military aid and an alliance with Rome. The conservative majority in the senate feared that an alliance with the Mamertines might mean war, which they particularly wanted to avoid because wars in the past usually made it easier for plebeians to get elected to higher office and secure seats in the senate. They also argued that it was beneath the dignity of Rome to ally herself with the Mamertines, a lawless gang of deserters, cutthroats, and thieves and that to go to their aid might lead to a war with Carthage which Rome without a navy was unprepared to wage against the strongest naval power of the Mediterranean. Faced with this difficult decision, the senate decided to do nothing.

Appius Claudius, son of the Censor, and his friends were unwilling to let the matter drop so easily. They brought it up before the people who, though sick of war, were persuaded to accept the alliance, probably by the argument that to rebuff the Mamertines would give the Carthaginians a permanent base for future attacks upon Italy, that complete Carthaginian occupation of Sicily would hurt the trade of the south Italian Greeks and turn them against Rome, and that to take a strong line now might prevent war in the future.

Roman Intervention in Sicily, 264 B.C.

The Mamertine alliance approved and accepted, two legions under the command of Appius Claudius marched down to Reggio in 264 prepared to relieve Messana. He sent an advance guard across the straits meeting only token opposition from the Carthaginian fleet at Messana. The Mamertines had meanwhile requested the Carthaginian admiral to withdraw his garrison from the town and he foolishly complied, and let the Romans march in unhindered, an error for which he was afterwards crucified.

The loss of Messana stung the Carthaginian government to action. They sent an army over to reoccupy it and persuaded Hiero II of Syracuse to make an alliance with them. The allies now joined forces to attack and blockade the town. Appius Claudius managed to sneak his main force across the straits under cover of darkness. When the Carthaginians rejected his demand that they raise the siege, he attacked first the Syracusans and then the Carthaginians and easily defeated them in turn. His action saved Messana, but resulted in war with both Carthage and Syracuse.

It may have been true that the Romans had reason to fear the presence of a Punic garrison in Messana as a potential threat to Italy but in expelling the garrison they had broken a treaty signed with Carthage in 306 B.C. forbidding Punic intervention in Italy and Roman intervention in Sicily. Roman historians, who laid so much emphasis on faith (*fides*) and were ready to accuse others of perfidy, found it difficult to explain this treaty. They either denied its existence, for Rome "never" broke a treaty nor committed an act of aggression; or else they invented the lie that the Carthaginians had already broken the treaty in 272 B.C. by their alleged attempt to seize Tarentum, which the Romans were then besieging. The invention of this lie by the later annalists proves that they regarded as fraudulent the attempt of the older annalists to deny the existence of the treaty. The best that can be said on behalf of Rome is that she was guilty of justifiable aggression.

Carthage was not prepared for this war: most of her ships had been lying in the docks ever since the Pyrrhic War; rowers had to be hired and trained, a matter requiring considerable time. Even with the available ships the admirals ought easily to have been able to prevent Appius Claudius from slipping across the straits. Their failure to do so angered Hiero II and helped to break up his alliance with Carthage. When the Romans

attacked Syracuse in 263 with an army of 40,000 men, Hiero, becoming alarmed at Carthaginian lack of support, capitulated, made an alliance with Rome for fifteen years, and agreed to help finance the war against Carthage.

With the help of Hiero II, the Romans next attacked and besieged Agrigentum (Girgenti), the second largest Sicilian city, where the Carthaginians had a strong garrison. After the defeat of a Carthaginian relief army, the city was stormed, captured, destroyed, and its inhabitants enslaved for work in Roman war industries. They were the first people of a civilized city to be so treated by Rome, but they were not the last.

After the fall of Agrigentum, the Romans saw the possibility of driving the Carthaginians out of Sicily altogether. The obstacle was the Carthaginian fleet which had sailed into Sicilian waters in 260 B.C., all ready for action. Such a fleet could cut communications with Italy and starve the Roman army into submission and surrender. It could also raid the Italian coastal cities without hindrance. Rome realized that she must at all costs build a navy or else get out of the war.

Rome Builds a New Fleet

The first Roman attempt to create a navy was in 311 B.C., when they built twenty *triremes,* fast, light vessels, but not too seaworthy. The trireme was propelled by 150 oars in groups of three, one man to an oar. Even this puny navy was allowed to lapse into decay after 278. Rome depended entirely on her allies in south Italy who, although they had nothing available better than a trireme, supplied the ships that enabled Appius Claudius in 264 B.C. to put his army across the straits. Perhaps it was just as well that Rome had no navy in 260 B.C. She might have been tempted to use the trireme, which had become an obsolete and worthless type of vessel for naval warfare on the high seas.

The pride of the Carthaginian navy was the *quinquereme,* now believed to have been a one-deck ship of from fifty to sixty oars, five men to an oar. In a task force of a hundred ships the Carthaginians would have some 88 quinqueremes and 12 triremes. The only exception, and it was unique, was the *hepteres*, also a single deck ship but probably with seven men to an oar. This particular ship was the flag ship of Pyrrhus, captured by the Carthaginians during his attempt to get back to Italy after his Sicilian fiasco. The quinquereme was heavier and slower than the trireme, but more seaworthy. What counted most was its weight because the usual tactic then used by the Carthaginian navy was ramming. In order to sink enemy ships by ramming, weight was essential. The trireme was inadequate for this purpose and had become obsolete.

The Romans had no ships like the quinquereme and had probably never even seen one until they happened to find one stranded on the shore not far from the straits. Using this as a model and with the help, perhaps, of Syracusan shipbuilders they built one hundred quinqueremes in addition to twenty triremes in about sixty days. Building ships was not as hard a problem as finding crews to man them. They had to recruit most of their trained oarsmen from the Greek seaports of south Italy. There were never enough of them. While the building of ships was in progress, they had to set up wooden stages on land in order to train raw recruits to row.

It was indeed fortunate for the Romans that the trireme had become obsolete because every rower on board a trireme had to be a skilled oarsman. On a quinquereme where there were five men to an oar, only one or two of them had to be skilled.

There was another reason why the quinquereme was well suited to Roman needs. In order to convert sea fights into land battles, the Romans installed, in their new quinqueremes, a device, which in Roman naval slang was known as the *corvus* or raven. The Athenians had once thought it up during their ill-fated Sicilian expedition, but failed to use it successfully. This was a hinged, but more probably a slotted bridge or gangway with a heavy grappling spike at the end. From this spike or beak came the name of *corvus*, crow, or raven. The bridge was fastened to the mast by a rope running through a pulley and could be raised or let fall upon the deck of an enemy ship which was held fast as the spike embedded itself deep in the planks. The Romans then rushed

over the bridge and fought just as on land. Such a device would have been out of the question on a light ship such as the trireme, since it rendered even heavy ships like the quinquereme much less seaworthy. If the Carthaginian admirals and captains had not been so devoted to ramming as a naval tactic, they would not have lost so many naval battles.

With his brand new fleet consul Duilius put to sea and met the Carthaginians off Mylae not far from Messana. The mediocre admiral of the Punic fleet, anticipating an easy victory, launched a reckless frontal ramming attack, but many of his best ships were grappled by the raven, boarded by the marines, and captured. After 31 ships had been captured and 14 sunk, he broke off the engagement and escaped with 85 ships. Duilius celebrated his triumph in Rome, where in his honor a column was erected on the Forum ornamented with the rams of the ships he captured. Since the seapower of Carthage was severely damaged, Corsica and Sardinia were now exposed to Roman attack. After losing another sea fight near Sardinia in 258 B.C., the incompetent Carthaginian admiral was promptly crucified.

The Roman Invasion of Africa: 256-255 B.C.

After their unexpected victories at sea, the Romans decided to end the war quickly by an invasion of Africa. In 256 the consuls, Regulus and Vulso, set sail with 250 warships and 80 transports and about 100,000 men. They engaged the Carthaginian fleet off Cape Ecnomus on the east coast of Sicily. Hasdrubal, the Punic admiral, feigned retreat in the center of his line to draw in the Romans while the rest of his ships, dispersed in echelon formation, were to turn around and attack from behind. This plan might have worked had it been understood, accepted, and carried out by his two rear-admirals. Instead the Romans won a third victory. They captured 50 ships and sank 30 others with a loss of only 24. Though Carthaginian seapower was temporarily broken and Carthage herself was open to invasion, the Romans knew that Hasdrubal had found the answer to the raven and after 255 B.C. they never made use of it again.

Regulus landed in Africa in the fall of 256 B.C. He inflicted a minor defeat on the Carthaginians and, thinking that they were just about ready to give up, offered them terms of peace so harsh that they were rejected. Though winter would have been the best season for African fighting, he decided to wait till spring.

Meanwhile, Carthage had not been idle. She had engaged the services of Xanthippus, a Spartan strategist and an expert in elephant tactics. New mercenary troops were hired and many citizens of Carthage volunteered for service. All that winter the work of preparation and training continued unabatedly.

In the spring of 255 B.C. Regulus decided to begin the Battle of Carthage. He advanced into the valley of the Bagradas, but found the enemy was already waiting for him. Here Xanthippus threw his *phalanx,* elephants in front and cavalry on the wings. In vain Regulus strengthened his center; the elephants broke through anyway, trampling the massed legionnaires to death as the Punic cavalry outflanked and encircled them. The entire Roman army was destroyed, except for a remnant of 2,000 men, who escaped to the coast to be rescued by the navy. Regulus himself was taken prisoner. Thus the Romans suffered as severe a defeat on land as the Carthaginians had at sea.

In 255 B.C. luck began to run against the Romans at sea. An armada of 250 ships sent for the blockade of Carthage met and defeated a Carthaginian fleet of 200 ships off Cape Hermaea, capturing some and ramming many others against the shore. After taking on board the remnants of Regulus' army, they put out to sea. As they were approaching the shores of Sicily, a sudden squall caught them and all but 80 vessels were lost. Two years later another fleet returning from a raid on Libya was wrecked off the northern shores of Sicily. These unexpected catastrophes ended for a time Roman naval superiority in the Mediterranean.

The War in Sicily, 254-241 B.C.

From 254 to the end of the war Sicily and its surrounding waters remained the sole theater of military operations. After their capture of Panormus (Palermo) in 254, the Romans had driven the Carthaginians almost out of the island except for two strongholds at the western tip, Lilybaeum and the naval base of Drepana, both of which they blockaded by land and sea. The Carthaginians seemed content merely to hold their naval bases in Sicily, meanwhile concentrating their main effort on expanding their empire in Africa and stamping out native revolts. That vast expenditure of effort on African expansion proves that the big landowners were momentarily holding the whip hand in Carthaginian government and administration.

Carthaginian Successes at Sea

Despite the lack of interest in naval affairs on the part of the home government, the Carthaginians were able, for the first time since the outbreak of the war, to win some minor successes at sea. Their ships were swift and well built compared with the slow, lumbering Roman vessels. Though the Romans had rebuilt their navy after the disasters of 255 and 253 B.C., they had lost the initiative at sea. Since 255 they had been forced to abandon their best offensive weapon, the raven, partly because the Carthaginians had devised successful defensive tactics against it and partly also because its weight made their ships very vulnerable to storms at sea. Moreover, the admirals now in command of the Roman fleet were not in the same class with Duilius, the victor of Mylae, nor even with Regulus of Ecnomus.

Claudius Pulcher, a violent, hot-headed, blasphemous bully, was in command of a Roman fleet of 120 ships engaged in the blockade of Lilybaeum. Knowing that Adherbal with one hundred ships at Drepana would shortly be reinforced by 70 new ships of the latest type from Carthage, he made up his mind to strike before these reinforcements arrived. His expedition was inauspicious in more ways than one. The sacred chickens refused to eat, a very bad omen and most disconcerting to the crews. On receiving this report he exploded, "Throw the damn chickens into sea; if they won't eat, let them drink!"

He also made a number of tactical blunders. He set sail at midnight in the hope of catching the Punic ships by surprise at daybreak in the harbor like sitting ducks. His fleet sailing in line ahead, he placed himself in the rear of the line, so as to hustle the laggards instead of at the front to direct maneuvers. When Adherbal saw the leading ships approaching the mouth of that long, narrow harbor, he at once pulled out his entire fleet. When Claudius became aware of what had happened, he ordered the ships in front, which had by this time entered the narrows, to put about and sail out again. In making the sharp turn the ships ran foul of each other, had their oars broken, and much confusion arose. At this point Adherbal attacked and destroyed 93 Roman ships. That was the first real naval defeat the Romans had suffered since the beginning of the war.

Their second defeat followed soon thereafter. The other consul sailed out from Syracuse with eight hundred transports escorted by one hundred twenty warships. This enormous fleet was completely destroyed partly by Carthaginian attack and partly by storm. For the next few years the Carthaginians had undisputed mastery of the sea. They were now able to break the Roman blockade of Lilybaeum, cut communications between Rome and Sicily, and make raids upon the Italian coast itself.

Hamilcar Barca

Never had the war picture looked brighter for Carthage, especially after she had sent to Sicily in 247 B.C. the young Hamilcar Barca, the most brilliant general of the war, whose lightning moves behind Roman lines and daring raids upon the Italian coast made him the terror of Rome. Well did he merit the name of Barca, which in Punic meant "Blitz" or "Lightning."

The End: 241 B.C.

Despite the brilliance of Hamilcar Barca and the amazing successes of the Carthaginian navy, Carthage lost the war, chiefly because of her inability to deliver the final blow when Rome was staggering in defeat.

Rome's ultimate victory was not wholly due to her doggedness, perseverance, and superior moral qualities, which the classical scholar too often harps upon, but to the weakness of the Carthaginian state itself, the internal division, and the fatal conflict of interest between the commercial tycoons and the powerful landowning nobility.

At the very moment when the Carthaginian navy and the generalship of Hamilcar Barca seemed about to win the war, the landowning group headed by the so-called Hanno the Great came into control of the Carthaginian government. To them the conquest of vast territories in Africa of great agricultural productivity was of more importance than Sicily, the navy, and the war against Rome. That the dominant faction in the Carthaginian government was not interested in winning the war is clearly evident from the fact that in 244 B.C. the entire Carthaginian navy was laid up, demobilized, and its crews, oarsmen, and marines were transferred from the navy to the army of African conquest.

Meanwhile Rome saw that her only chance for survival lay in the recovery of her naval power. She persuaded her wealthiest citizens to advance money for the construction of a navy, promising to repay them after victory. In 242 a fleet of 200 Roman ships of the latest type appeared in Sicilian waters. In the following year one stormy morning it brought to action, near the Aegates Islands, a Carthaginian fleet of untrained crews and of ships undermanned and weighted down with cargoes of grain and other supplies for the garrison at Lilybaeum. The result was a disaster which cost Carthage the war. The garrison at Lilybaeum could no longer be supplied and would soon be starved into surrender. There was no alternative but to sue for peace.

Peace Terms: 241 B.C.

The Carthaginian government empowered Hamilcar Barca to negotiate peace terms with the Consul Lutatius Catulus, the victor of the recent naval battle. Both sides were exhausted and weary from the long, continuous, and bitter struggle. The Romans, knowing by how slight a margin they had won, were disposed to make the terms relatively light. Carthage was to evacuate Lilybaeum, abandon all Sicily, return all prisoners, and pay an indemnity of 2200 talents in twenty years. These terms seemed too lenient to the Roman people. They increased the indemnity to 3200 talents ($3,840,000) to be paid in ten years. The Carthaginians were also required to surrender all islands between Sicily and Italy, to keep their ships out of Italian waters, and to discontinue recruiting mercenaries in Italy.

The war had been costly to both sides. The losses of Rome were approximately five hundred ships and 200,000 men, those of Carthage heavier still. The sea power of Carthage was broken and her control of the western Mediterranean was ended for all time.

Between the Wars

No sooner had Carthage made peace than she had to fight with her own mercenaries, a war of the utmost cruelty and barbarity. Upon their return from Sicily, the mercenaries, 20,000 of them, Libyans, Spaniards, Celts, Ligurians, Greeks, demanded from the government their accumulated pay and the rewards promised to them in Sicily by Hamilcar Barca. These reasonable demands were rejected by the Carthaginian government, which was then dominated by reactionary landlords such as Hanno the Great. The mercenaries mutinied and marched on Tunis. They were joined by the oppressed natives of Libya, by the Libyphoenicians from the East and the Numidians of the West. The deadly revolt flared up everywhere. The mercenaries became masters of the open country, from which Carthage was isolated. It was a war without truce. A similar revolt subsequently broke out in Sardinia.

For the first time in their lives the citizens of Carthage really had to fight. Hanno assumed command of the army, but his "greatness" failed to achieve any military success. The situation deteriorated until Hamilcar Barca took command. After three years of the bloodiest fighting, during which all manner of atrocities, crucifixions, and inhumanities were committed on both sides, Hamilcar finally stamped out the revolt.

In her terrific struggle for survival Carthage received the unexpected sympathy and help of Rome, who furnished her with supplies while denying them to her enemies, and permitted her to trade with Italy and even recruit troops there. Rome also rejected appeals for alliance from the rebels of Utica and Sardinia.

After the revolt against Carthage had been stamped out in Africa, Rome suddenly changed her attitude from sympathy to hostility. As Hamilcar was moving to reoccupy Sardinia, she decided to listen to the appeal of the Sardinian rebels, declared war on Carthage, and robbed Carthage of both Sardinia and Corsica in addition to demanding an additional indemnity of 1200 talents (about $1,600,000). She was able to commit this act of international piracy with impunity because Carthage had no fleet and could not fight back, though the natives of Sardinia fought ferociously against Roman occupation, which was not fully completed until 225 B.C. The two islands became the second Roman province administered by an annually elected praetor as governor.

Carthaginian Recovery

Shortly after the loss of Sardinia and Corsica, Carthage made a strong recovery mainly because of the genius and energy of Hamilcar Barca, who vanquished the mercenaries and reinstated Carthage as a great Mediterranean power. The loss of the two islands was more than offset by the reconquest of Spain. During the First Punic War and later the Truceless War, Carthage had lost most of her Spanish possessions except Gades to native rebellions and most of her trade to the encroachments of Marseilles. Hamilcar recovered those possessions and much more besides. Landing at Gades in 237 B.C., he conquered all of southern Spain and by a judicious mixture of war and diplomacy founded a bigger and richer empire than Carthage had ever possessed.

Hamilcar Barca was unfortunately drowned in 229 B.C., but his son-in-law, Hasdrubal, continued the work of empire building. He founded New Carthage, now called Cartagena, which became the capital, the navy and army base, and the arsenal of the Carthaginian empire in Spain. All the important mining districts were now brought back under Carthaginian control.

For several years Rome had been watching these developments with growing suspicion and alarm. What chiefly stirred her apprehension was the knowledge that the Barca family, sworn to eternal hate and vengeance against Rome, had under their control that vast empire in Spain, a small but modern navy, a fine army composed of Carthaginian citizens and the flower of the manhood of North Africa and Spain, well equipped and undergoing intensive training in constant warfare against the Spanish tribes. In addition, the mines of Spain furnished them an annual revenue of between 2,000 and 3,000 talents, or between three and four million dollars. This enormous revenue at their disposal enabled the Barca family to wield almost kingly power in both Spain and Carthage.

Nevertheless, the Carthaginian expansion in Spain did not affect the economic interests of Rome as directly as it did those of Marseilles. Marseilles, long bound to Rome by ties of friendship (and probably by this time by a formal alliance), complained to the Romans of the Carthaginian threat to her colonies and especially to her trade, which she had expanded at the expense of Carthage during the First Punic War. About 231 B.C. the Romans sent a mission to Spain to investigate, but they came back apparently satisfied with Hamilcar's explanation that he was only trying to explore new sources of revenue to enable Carthage to pay her indemnity to Rome.

The Ebro Treaty

The continued Carthaginian expansion in Spain evoked ever louder complaints from Marseilles. At last the Romans, in 226 B.C., negotiated with Hasdrubal the famous Ebro Treaty, which prohibited him from crossing the Ebro River with warlike intent, but allowed him a free hand south of the river.

As the Ebro flows eastwards into the Mediterranean across the northern part of Spain, this treaty gave him control over almost seven-eighths of the entire peninsula. Marseilles was probably less satisfied, although she was guaranteed the security of her two coastal colonies lying between the Ebro and the Pyrenees and was not excluded from peaceful trade with Carthaginian Spain.

Unfortunately, the exact terms of the treaty, though drawn up in both Latin and Punic, were never quite clear either to the ancient Romans and Carthaginians or to modern scholars.

Roman Problems after 241 B.C.

Rome's most pressing inter-war problems were: the administration of her two newly acquired provinces of Sicily and Sardinia plus Corsica; the reform of her government to satisfy the claims of the middle class farmer, who had shouldered the heaviest burdens of the war; the conquest of North Italy to secure her northern frontiers against future Gallic attack and at the same time to open up more lands for farm settlement; and the suppression of piracy on the Adriatic Sea.

The conquest of Sicily presented Rome with the entirely new problem of governing a country outside of Italy. She naturally first tried out her old Italian policy of making the newly conquered cities her allies, giving them local self government in return for military and naval assistance in time of war. Similarly in Sicily she entered into alliance with Syracuse and Messana and later on with two other cities. She afterwards discovered that it was impossible to apply this policy to that part of the island which the Carthaginians had formerly controlled.

The Sicilians had never been used to the Roman form of government; their traditions had been entirely different. Military help would be unwillingly given, small in any case, and probably quite useless. Rather than be called upon to fight they preferred to pay tribute in the form of money or farm products, as they had always done, and be left alone. This policy, though foreign to her own traditions, was the one Rome decided to adopt. It seemed expedient for the first time in her history to fall in line with a policy long practiced in the East by the Hellenistic monarchies and later adopted in the West by Carthage and Syracuse.

From time immemorial Egypt and other states of the ancient Near East had held the theory that all land belonged to the deity and, therefore, to his earthly representative, the king. A farmer no more "owned" a piece of land than one living in a hotel owns his room. He was allowed the use of it, provided he paid his tithe: one-tenth of the harvest. This theory had been adopted by Alexander the Great and all the Hellenistic kings after him, and later Carthage and Hiero II of Syracuse.

The ancient Oriental theory of state ownership of land was alien to the Romans, who believed in private ownership of land, except public land (*ager publicus*) confiscated by the state from an enemy. After their conquest of Sicily they adopted the Oriental practice, but regarded the revenue collected from farm land in Sicily not as rent but as a tax levied to defray the expenses of administration and defense, later calling it tribute (the name of the property tax collected from Roman citizens in time of war).

Those parts of Sicily which had formerly been under the rule of Carthage or Syracuse had very much the same system of taxation and planned economy as Hellenistic Egypt. The Romans applied the Syracusan (or Hieronic) system to the other parts of the island, with the difference that they permitted the farmers to plant whatever crops they pleased, whereas under Hiero II, just as in Ptolemaic Egypt, they had been told just what crops they had to plant each year. The *Lex Hieronica,* a revised Latin translation of the laws of Hiero II, was used by the Romans not for crop planning but for taxation purposes only.

The Taxation of Roman Sicily

In an agricultural province such as Sicily the principal source of provincial revenue was the tithe (one-tenth of such harvested crops as wheat or barley and one-fifth of garden produce and fruits). Until the year 212 B.C. only about half of Sicily was required to tithe to the Roman provincial administration. The rest of the province was exempt: the five cities (Centuripae, Halaesa, Segesta, Halicyae, and Panormus), which were rewarded for their help during the war by being left free and independent, and the four other cities (Messana, Syracuse, Tauromenium, and Leontini), which, as allies of Rome, were obliged to furnish military or naval assistance at Rome's request.

After 212 B.C. Syracuse, together with the cities dependent upon her, lost the privileged status of a non-taxpaying ally as a result of her unsuccessful revolt against Rome and became subject to the tithe. In addition, some of the land controlled by these rebellious communities was confiscated and declared public land (*ager publicus*), which was rented out either to former owners or to others at an annual rental of one-third of the harvested crops.

The system of tithe collection, which Carthage and Syracuse had both used in the past, and which Hiero II of Syracuse had worked out in the *Lex Hieronica,* was adopted by the Romans. Each year the magistrates of Sicilian cities subject to the tithe took a census of all the farmers in their surrounding territory, both owners and renters, recording the size of the farms, the acreage under crop, and the amount of seed sown. The records, signed under oath, were filed in the records office of local administrative centers and were open to inspection by contractors (either private individuals or agents of tax-collecting firms) preparing to make their bids for the collection of the annual tithe. On the basis of these census returns they would complete their estimates of the crop prospects and would appear before the Roman quaestor, the provincial treasurer, on the day appointed for the auctioning of contracts and make their bids, which were based on $10\frac{2}{5}$ per cent of the estimated crop, of which 10 per cent went to the treasury, the remaining fraction to the contractor. The highest bidder, after receiving the contract and after paying the treasury in advance, would go to the farmers and draw up signed agreements specifying both the amount of the tithe and the date of its delivery at the public warehouses. These agreements would be

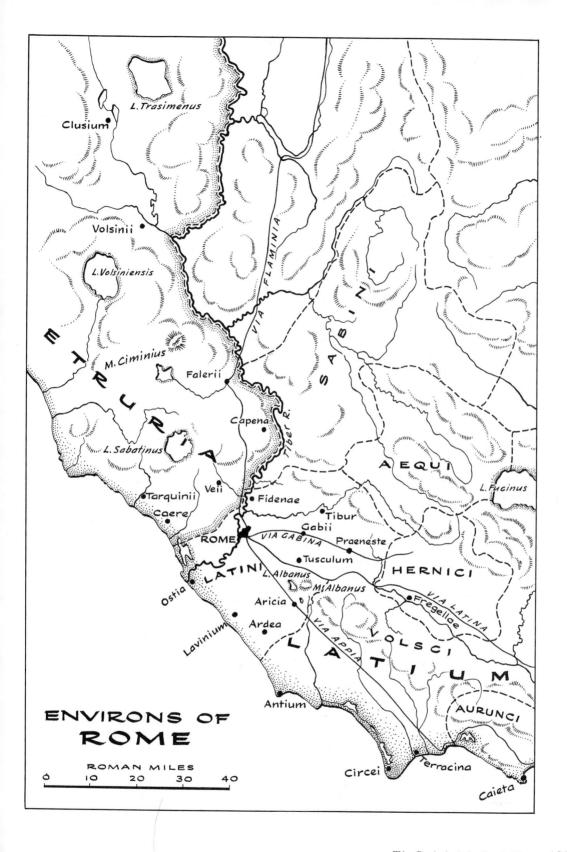

ENVIRONS OF ROME

ROMAN MILES

0   10   20   30   40

L. Trasimenus

Clusium

Volsinii

L. Volsiniensis

ETRURIA

M. Ciminius

Falerii

VIA FLAMINIA

SABINI

Capena

Tiber R.

L. Sabatinus

Veii

Tarquinii

Caere

Fidenae

Tibur

Gabii

ROME

VIA GABINA

Praeneste

AEQUI

L. Fucinus

HERNICI

Tusculum

L. Albanus

Ostia

LATINI

Ms Albanus

Aricia

Fregellae

VIA LATINA

Ardea

VOLSCI

Lavinium

VIA APPIA

LATIUM

Antium

AURUNCI

Circei

Terracina

Caieta

filed in the offices of the local magistrates, who were held responsible both for their enforcement and for the delivery of the tithe to the provincial treasury.

The other sources of provincial revenue were customs dues (*portoria*) levied at the rate of 5 per cent on all imported and exported goods; the *scriptura,* paid in cash on each head of grazing stock on pasture land; rentals on public lands of one-third of the annual crop; and royalties on mines and quarries.

The Administration of Sicily

The Romans first attempted to govern Sicily directly from Rome by quaestors responsible to the magistrates of the city. Fourteen years of experience taught them that Rome was too far away for direct administration and that a magistrate with full executive powers was required in the province to deal with such problems of defense and the maintenance of law and order as arose. A quaestor did not have sufficient authority; only a magistrate possessing the *imperium,* such as a consul or a praetor, would do.

Accordingly, after 227 B.C., the Roman assembly annually elected two praetors, one as governor of Sicily, the other for the province of Sardinia-and-Corsica. That praetors rather than consuls should be elected seemed a logical consequence of the step taken in 242 B.C. of adding another praetor (*praetor peregrinus*) to deal with the legal disputes, too numerous for the city praetor to handle, arising between Roman citizens and the foreign immigrants then entering Rome in large numbers. In this growing cosmopolitan city foreigners ignorant of Roman law were often taken in by dishonest Roman citizens. From 227 B.C. on four praetors were elected, two for the city and one for each of the provinces.

The Praetor

Though the Roman Senate laid down the general principles governing provincial administration, it left the details to be filled in by the praetor as governor of the province. Each newly elected praetor on taking office would publish an edict similar to that of the city praetor, setting forth the rules and regulations he intended to follow during his year of office. The edict would specifically state the rules of procedure he would apply in his administration of justice. These varied little from year to year and were changed only under special conditions. They were based partly on the civil law of Rome and partly on the law of nations, which applied to all mankind.

In this way there was gradually built up a system of international law, a large part of which has persisted down to our own times. The edicts of the city and provincial praetors, especially those of each new praetor peregrinus in Rome, contributed to the creation of a body of law, which was not only incorporated in the Justinian Code and in the Code Napoléon, but has become the basis of modern international law. The best authorities on international law today are found in France, Holland, Switzerland, Italy, and especially the Latin American countries, whose civil law is based largely on that of Rome.

The provincial praetor was assisted in administration by one or more quaestors, who served as treasurers and receivers of revenues derived from taxes. Three legates or lieutenants of senatorial rank, who were nominated by him and appointed by the Senate, acted not only as liaison officers between the praetor and the senate, but as his advisers and often as his deputies. He had with him also a number of comrades or young family friends who, as members of his staff, might gain an insight into the workings of provincial administration. In addition, he had a staff of clerks and secretaries as well as numerous household servants.

Duties and Powers. The functions of the provincial praetor were many. He commanded the armed forces within the province, supervised the quaestors in their financial administration, and was responsible for the administration of justice in all civil and criminal cases involving Roman citizens and for the arbitration of disputes arising between the subject communities.

Inside the province the powers of the praetor were practically absolute: there was no colleague of equal rank to oppose his decisions or acts, no plebeian tribune to interpose his veto in defense of private individuals, no senate as in Rome to exercise by its higher authority a moral restraint over his abuse of arbitrary power, and no popular assembly to pass laws, which he had to obey. As subjects of a foreign power, the people of the province had neither the right of appeal nor legal guarantees of the rights of life, liberty, and property. Although some cities had charters granted them by the Roman senate guaranteeing local liberties, these could easily be circumvented. Although his term of office was theoretically limited to one year, it was sometimes longer than that because of the failure through neglect or corrupt influence to elect a successor. Theoretically, too, the provincials had the right to bring charges against the praetor for misgovernment and extortion, but they were rarely known to have done so until the time of Cicero (70 B.C.), and then only under the most unusual circumstances and for the most flagrant crimes of extortion and tyranny.

Gaius Flaminius

The period after the First Punic War was an age not only of imperial expansion but of reform—social, economic, constitutional, and legal. This reform movement arose as a result of popular agitation and the resumption of the old struggle between the plebeian and patrician classes. The plebeians who tilled small farms around Rome and in Latium were particularly dissatisfied with their lot. Subject to the draft and forced to fight long campaigns far from home, they had to neglect their crops, their sole means of livelihood. During the war many of them had fallen into debt and afterwards were unable to raise the money to pay back their loans, since the price of wheat was falling as a result of competition with wheat imported from Sicily. Another cause of grievance was the lack of newly conquered land suitable for distribution and settlement, since the new provinces of Sicily and Sardinia offered no opportunity for colonization. These and perhaps other grievances led to political agitation and the demand for reform.

The leader of the reform movement was Gaius Flaminius. As plebeian tribune in 232 B.C. he forced through the Tribal Assembly, without previous consultation with the senate

and in spite of its violent opposition, a plebiscite requiring that the public lands (*ager Gallicus*) confiscated south of Ariminum (Rimini) a half century before from the Gauls be cut up into small farms and distributed among plebeian families. The unorthodox disregard of senatorial authority and privilege set a precedent followed by other champions of the popular cause a century later (*see* p. 174).

The Gallic Wars and Conquest of North Italy: 225-222 B.C.

A doubtful aristocratic tradition (preserved by Polybius) alleges that the land distributions after 232 B.C. alarmed the Gauls of North Italy, who had been peaceful farmers ever since 283 B.C., and provoked them to invade central Italy. Since the lands distributed had been in continuous Roman possession for sixty years, it would have made little difference to the Gauls whether they were distributed among small farmers or leased in large sections to senatorial landlords, and furthermore, the unrest had begun as early as 236 B.C., when the Boii joined up with fresh swarms of Celtic invaders from over the Alps in an abortive attack upon Ariminum.

In 225 B.C. an army of Gauls, estimated at 70,000 men, crossed the Apennines and pushed down into Etruria, plundering as they went. Faced with this menace, the Romans took a census of their available manpower in central and southern Italy. The census, according to Polybius (II, 24), showed roughly 700,000 infantry and 70,000 cavalry, of which 250,000 infantry and 23,000 cavalry were Roman. From this large reserve of manpower they raised two powerful consular armies, which converged upon the Gauls near Cape Telamon and almost annihilated them.

After this victory the Romans resolved to end the Gallic menace for good by the conquest of north Italy. During his consulship of 223 B.C. Gaius Flaminius subdued the Insubres by a decisive victory, which led by 220 B.C. to the submission of all the Gauls (except the Taurini of the Piedmont and a few other sub-Alpine tribes). During his censorship in 220 B.C. he arranged for the construction of the great military highway, the Flaminian Way, which ran northeast from Rome to Ariminum on the Adriatic and was the predecessor of one of the most important rail lines and motor roads in modern Italy. In the same year (or slightly later) he founded Latin colonies at Cremona and Placentia (Piacenza) both to control crossings of the middle Po and provide outlets for land-starved Roman farmers.

The Reform of the Centuriate Assembly

During the career of Gaius Flaminius, probably in his censorship of 220 B.C., there took place a reform of great constitutional importance, the reorganization of the Centuriate Assembly, which had long since become the stronghold of entrenched wealth. In 241 B.C. two new voting tribes had been added, bringing the number of tribes to a final total of thirty-five. As a result of the reorganization the tribes became purely administrative divisions to which newly enfranchised citizens were assigned regardless of place of residence.

Hitherto, the richest people controlled the majority of votes in the assembly: eighteen centuries (distributed on the basis of tribes) had been assigned to the cavalry or equestrian class and eighty to the first of the five property classes, the other four had only twenty, twenty, twenty, and thirty centuries respectively. After the reform the cavalry retained its eighteen votes and the proletariat its five, but the five property classes were each assigned seventy votes divided equally between juniors and seniors (men over forty-five years old), thus making a total of 373 votes. Furthermore, the right of casting the first vote was now transferred from the cavalry to a century of the first property class, chosen by lot for each meeting. These changes struck a blow against the rich by giving the middle class farmer a stronger voice in the government.

The Claudian Law of 218 B.C. Perhaps another attempt to counteract the influence of wealth on Roman political life was the Claudian Law of 218 B.C., which the tribune Q. Claudius proposed at the instigation of Gaius Flaminius, making it illegal for a senator to own or operate ships large enough to use in overseas trade. This law was so easily circumvented that senators did not bother to have it rescinded.

Legal Reforms. Following the trend set by Appius Claudius the Blind, the censor of 312/310 B.C., and of Gnaeus Flavius, the aedile of 304/3 B.C., Tiberius Coruncanius, who was the first plebeian ever to hold the office of Pontifex Maximus (254 B.C.), announced that he was prepared to give free advice to any person, even though not involved in a lawsuit. In the age of Gaius Flaminius, the learned jurist, Sextus Aelius Paetus Catus, had begun work on his famous commentaries on the Twelve Tables together with the legal interpretations handed down by the pontiffs. After the publication of this work in 204 B.C., anyone, poor or rich, could inform himself about Roman laws.

The Illyrian Wars: 229–228 and 220–219 B.C.

The two Illyrian wars were the first wars fought by the Romans in the eastern half of the Mediterranean. They were easily-won police actions rather than wars of defense or imperial expansion.

During the First Punic War, Agron, the ruler of Illyria, which embraced most of the coastal regions of Yugoslavia as well as Albania, had greatly expanded his kingdom by warring upon his neighbors to the south. After his death his wife, Queen Teuta, continued the aggressions, conquered Epirus, and extended her conquests to the Corinthian Gulf.

It was not the aggressions of Queen Teuta that caused the Romans to interfere, it was rather her inability or unwillingness to curb the piracy which the Illyrians had been engaged in since time immemorial. And no wonder, for the rugged, broken, and deeply indented coast of Illyria with its myriads of small islands seemed intended by nature just for the pursuit of this profitable business. Their light and speedy craft would waylay many a passing merchant ship. With the Greeks grown weak, they roved the seas at will and attacked not only Greek but Italian ships, capturing or killing their crews. Growing ever bolder, they ransacked towns along the Adriatic shores of southern Italy. The complaints of merchants and pillaged towns at last compelled Rome to act.

In 230 B.C. two Roman envoys arrived in the Illyrian capital of Scutari to lodge complaints, but Teuta was busy waging war at the moment and had no time to listen to silly complaints about what her subjects had a natural right to do. The protests were insolently rejected, and the envoys haughtily dismissed. On the way back one of the envoys was killed.

Rome was not slow to respond. In the summer of 229 B.C. a fleet of 200 ships appeared off the island of Corcyra (Corfu). Demetrius of Pharos, whom Teuta had charged with the defense of the island, betrayed her and surrendered to the Romans without a fight. The fleet then sailed north to support a Roman army of 22,000 men engaged in attacking the towns of Apollonia and Dyrrhachium (Durazzo). Teuta, unable to resist, was compelled to sue for peace. She was permitted to retain her crown on condition that she renounce her conquests in Greece, abandon all claim to islands and coastal towns captured by the Romans, and agree not to let more than two Illyrian ships sail past Lissus, the modern Albanian town of Alessio. As a reward for his treachery, Demetrius was granted his native island of Pharos to govern as well as some mainland towns.

Now Demetrius could not be true to anyone, not even to the Romans. Conspiring with Antigonus Doson, the acting king of Macedonia, who looked askance upon Roman interference in Balkan affairs, he stealthily extended his kingdom after Teuta's death over all Illyria, invaded Roman protectorates, attacked Greek cities further south, and made pirate raids far into the Aegean.

The Romans could not overlook these activities and in a speedy campaign, they conquered the Albanian kingdom of Demetrius, who fled for refuge to the court of Philip V, the youthful king of Macedonia. Here he remained for several years all the while whispering plots of revenge into the young king's ear. The Romans could not further pursue their Illyrian campaign, for at that moment ominous news began to come in from the western end of the Mediterranean.

The Second Punic War: 218–201 B.C.

After Hamilcar Barca died, Hasdrubal, his son-in-law, had brought under Carthaginian control almost all of the Spanish peninsula south of the Ebro River. Hasdrubal, assassinated by an enraged Celt in 221 B.C., was succeeded by Hannibal, the eldest son of Hamilcar Barca.

Hannibal

Not much is known about Hannibal's character. Livy and Cornelius Nepos tell us that Hamilcar consented to take the nine-year-old Hannibal with him to Spain only on condition that he go to the altar and swear eternal hatred to Rome. From then on Hannibal spent his entire life in the army. Even after he had become a general, he ate with his men and dressed like them; he slept on the same hard ground between the sentries and the outposts, covered only with a cloak. His power of leadership must have been exceptional, for he commanded for fifteen unbroken years an army composed of Africans, Spaniards, Gauls, Phoenicians, and many other races and never once in all those years were they known to mutiny or rebel, though he led them on long, fatiguing marches, across wide rivers, through swamps, and over the snow-capped Alps.

Now at the age of twenty-five he began a military career which was one of the most brilliant the world has ever seen. The tactics he employed in the battle he won at Cannae have been minutely studied by military experts down to our own time and those devised for the battle lost at Zama were employed in tank battles of World War II.

After two years of preparation, Hannibal advanced along the road to Salamanca and conquered several tribes of the Upper Tagus and the Douro. South of the Ebro only Saguntum (Sagunto), a town perched on a rocky plateau overlooking the Mediterranean, remained unconquered. It had become an ally of Rome sometime between 230 and 219 B.C.*

In 219 B.C. Hannibal besieged Saguntum because of what he termed its unprovoked attacks upon neighboring tribes subject to Carthage. After a desperate siege of eight months the town fell. With its fall began the Second Punic War, the most crucial war, perhaps, in all history because its outcome determined whether Rome or Carthage should rule the Mediterranean and give law to the world. The fall of Saguntum marks, therefore, not merely the outbreak of the Second Punic War but the birth of the Roman empire and the genesis of Western civilization.

Rome sent ambassadors to Carthage demanding both the evacuation of Saguntum and the surrender of Hannibal for trial in Rome as a war criminal. After the rejection of the demands, the leader of the Roman embassy held up two folds of his toga saying: "Here I give you peace or war; choose which you will." When the Carthaginians replied that the choice was up to him, he dropped the folds of his toga and declared: "Then I give you war."

Hannibal's War Strategy

Hannibal had command of a splendid army, loyal, well trained, and equipped with the best Spanish swords and spears, but no navy to complement and assist it. Roman naval superiority was so great that Carthage could neither safely transport and supply large armies by sea nor prevent the Romans from establishing beachheads wherever they chose. Their seapower permitted them to wage war on several fronts simultaneously, to invade Africa and Spain, and land several armies in both countries at the same time.

Since Hannibal's only strong base and source of manpower and supplies was Spain

* Saguntum and Marseilles had both assimilated the weights of their silver coins to that of the Roman Victory coin (*victoriatus*), which was first introduced from Illyria around 231. Since no mention was made of Saguntum in the Ebro Treaty of 226, Saguntum possibly became allied with Rome sometime after 226, no doubt at the insistence of Marseilles.

and since he had only one really well trained and reliable army, his sole chance of success lay in establishing a single front, preferably in Italy; for so long as Rome was in danger, the Romans would be compelled to concentrate the bulk of their forces in Italy. Only an invasion of Italy would enable him to seize the initiative. Only an invasion of Italy would render useless the great Roman navy.

An even stronger reason behind Hannibal's decision to invade Italy lay in his hope of cutting at the roots of Roman military power, which was potentially six or seven times that of Carthage. Only by wrecking the Roman system of alliance and her Italian confederation could he hope to paralyze and destroy that enormous war potential. He knew that the Gauls of North Italy were already at war with Rome and would rally around him, and he also hoped that her confederate allies in central and southern Italy would break away from their confederation and join him as their liberator.

Roman War Plans

The Romans planned to wage an offensive war. Their unchallenged naval superiority would enable them to seize at once and hold the initiative and to choose the theater of military operations. One army under the consul Publius Cornelius Scipio actually landed at Marseille for the invasion of Spain, another assembled in Sicily for an invasion of Africa. The decision to land at Marseille was theoretically good strategy, since it offered alternate objectives: an invasion of Spain or the interception of Hannibal in France should he decide to invade North Italy. It also permitted the possibility of using the fleet of Marseille for operations in Spanish waters. The Romans partially achieved only two of these objectives, since they landed at Marseille too late to intercept Hannibal. He was already on his way to the Alps.

The March to the Alps

Around the first of May in 218 B.C. Hannibal set out from New Carthage with about 40,000 infantry, 6,000 cavalry, and some 60 elephants. He crossed the Ebro, passed over the Pyrenees, and in the middle of August reached the Rhone, which he crossed before Scipio was able to intercept him. When Scipio discovered he had arrived too late, he ordered his brother to lead the army into Spain while he himself sailed back to Italy in order to lead the two legions in Cisalpine Gaul against Hannibal as he came down the Alps.

Meanwhile Hannibal crossed the Durance, and then, perhaps, the Aygues. On his ascent towards the Alps he may have passed through the Col de Grimone, marched along the middle reaches of the Durance and entered the pass known as the Col de la Traversette (10,000 feet high). None of the many brilliant victories he afterwards won has stirred the imagination of mankind as this crossing of the Alps. The way was not easy: he suffered great losses because of the dangerous passes, the deep snows and biting frost of the late autumn, and most of all the treacherous attacks of the mountain tribes. By the time he reached the sunny plains of North Italy he had left only about 26,000 infantry, 4,000 cavalry, and 20 elephants. The Insubres and the Boii, already at war with Rome, eagerly joined his army and made up for the losses of men. The elephants, of course, could not be replaced. After a short rest his army met the Romans at the Ticinus.

The Battle of the Ticinus, 218 B.C.

The battle of the Ticinus was a minor cavalry engagement in which Hannibal's Numidian cavalry encircled and defeated Scipio's cavalry, which was inferior in speed, equipment, and training. The consul himself was wounded,* and the Romans were forced to retire south of the Po.

Even this minor defeat was serious enough to compel Rome to abandon the planned invasion of Africa and to transfer the other consul, Titus Sempronius Longus, and his army to North Italy. Although the Romans had been able, before their transfer to Italy, to seize Malta, which controlled communica-

* He would have been taken prisoner had he not been rescued by his own seventeen-year-old son, the future conqueror of Carthage and victor over Hannibal.

tions between Africa and Sicily, Hannibal's attempt to maintain a single front was already succeeding.

The Battle at the Trebia: 218 B.C.

The two consuls, Scipio and Sempronius, with a combined force of over 40,000 men held a strong position on the eastern or right bank of the Trebia, a small southern tributary of the Po. On a bitterly cold December morning, Hannibal sent over the river a cavalry detachment weak enough to be easily defeated and compelled to retreat. Encouraged by their easy victory, the Romans waded in pursuit across the rain-swollen river to the other side. There they were at once attacked and encircled by Hannibal's men, who had lain concealed in heavy underbrush. Only 10,000 Romans succeeded in breaking out of the encirclement and in reaching Placentia (Piacenza). The entire Po Valley fell into Hannibal's hands.

The loss of north Italy infuriated the peasant middle classes, who now controlled the Centuriate Assembly, and who saw the land they had fought so hard to win for settlement not a decade ago slipping away because of the bungling of the senate and the poor generalship of the consuls. Rage and frustration impelled them to elect as consul for 217 B.C. Gaius Flaminius, who in his consulship in 223 B.C. had subdued the Insubres and placed the Cisalpina under Roman control. Gnaeus Servilius, a nominee of the senate, was the other consul. New legions were called into service and the new consuls were instructed to hold the line and, if possible, recover North Italy.

The Battle of Lake Trasimene: 217 B.C.

Servilius took the road to Ariminum, Gaius Flaminius to Arretium (Arezzo) in Etruria in order to block Hannibal's invasion of central Italy. Hannibal did move down into Etruria but by an unexpected route: a pass which was most difficult and which, therefore, had been left unguarded. After leading his army through terrain flooded by the Arno and losing many men and horses on the way, he reached Etruria, where

Flaminius began to hang closely onto his rear. He tried to coax the Romans into battle by exposing his flank as he marched past. Flaminius refused the bait but followed closely in his tracks. When widespread looting and the burning of peaceful homes also failed to bring on a battle, Hannibal adopted an ingenious ruse: he made it appear as if he were going to march against Rome itself. Suddenly veering eastwards towards Perugia, he passed along the north shore of Lake Trasimene, where a ridge of fairly steep hills descends almost to the water's edge leaving for the most part a narrow road or passage way along the shore except where they retreat to form a small plain about five miles long. He concealed his men in the hills above the plain and waited. Into this plain early one foggy morning Flaminius marched with his army of 36,000 men. Suddenly Hannibal's men came thundering from the hillsides. In the ensuing two-hour battle most of the Romans were either killed or captured and Flaminius himself was killed.*

The news of Trasimene filled Rome with fear of imminent siege. The fear was groundless because Hannibal knew that the siege of a large fortified city without siege engines and a strong supply base would have been foolhardy. Also, the Romans still had field armies capable of intervening. Hannibal had another plan.

This brilliant battle tactician was also a politician and a master of grand strategy. He had invaded Italy in the hope that he might find chinks in the Roman alliance system which he might pry open, widen, and exploit. Victorious battles were only means to this end, but since they had so far produced satisfactory results only in the North and not in Etruria or central Italy, he crossed the Apennines to see what could be accomplished further south.

Fabius Maximus Cunctator: 217 B.C.

The defeat at Trasimene, the fear of a siege, the daily meetings of the senate, the death of Flaminius, the people's idol, and

---

* The same fate afterwards befell 4,000 cavalry-men, whom Servilius had sent down the Flaminian Way, perhaps to support the legions wiped out at Trasimene.

the eclipse of their party, the return of the aristocrats to power—all served to revive the dictatorship, an office defunct for thirty years, and to cause the advent of the strange, enigmatic figure of Quintus Fabius Maximus of illustrious lineage and decidedly conservative views on politics and war. His elevation to office was most unusual and to him in particular most unsatisfactory.

It was the ancient custom in times of crisis for the consuls to transfer, for six months, their lictors, their military commands (*imperia*), and executive powers to a dictator who would then appoint his own master of horse. Now that one consul was dead and the other cut off from Rome, Fabius owed his appointment to the Centuriate Assembly, which appointed also his master of horse, M. Minucius Rufus, a rash, impulsive, headstrong person and always in disagreement with Fabius over the conduct of the war.

Fabius worked out and adopted an original but somewhat negative strategy which did not consist of any new battle tactics (he avoided battles because the Roman cavalry was much inferior to Hannibal's), but was rather a kind of psychological warfare based on attrition and exhaustion. It called for the avoidance of all pitched battles until Hannibal should inadvertently work himself into an impasse and be forced to fight under highly unfavorable conditions. Meanwhile Fabius kept his army always on hilly terrain where Hannibal could not use his superior cavalry to advantage, and attempted to wear him down by constantly dogging his heels, hampering his movements, and preventing him from acquiring allies, feeding his army, or establishing bases. By this frustrating strategy Fabius hoped to prevent Hannibal from achieving the chief objective of his campaign, the destruction of the Roman system of alliance.

The cautious strategy of Fabius is to this day known as "Fabian" and, in his own time, earned for him the title of Cunctator or Delayer. Minucius hated his tactics and so did many others whose minds were incapable of grasping their military significance. Naturally the strategy of attrition is a double-edged weapon and puts as hard a strain on the user as on the enemy.

On one occasion Fabius used his favorite

tactic where the situation seemed rather to call for an immediate attack. While marching through unfamiliar country in Campania, Hannibal had been treacherously guided into a place enclosed by mountains. Before Hannibal discovered his danger, Fabius had occupied Callicula Pass, the only suitable pass for escape. Minucius urged an immediate attack but Fabius delayed. One dark night Hannibal ordered his men to drive 2,000 cattle up the mountain side with blazing bundles of tar-smeared sticks tied to their horns. When the Romans saw all the darting, flaring lights, they left the pass to investigate. And Hannibal led his army out of the pass to safety.

While Fabian tactics undoubtedly saved the Roman alliance system from collapse, thus frustrating Hannibal's main objective, they were very unpopular and a strong reaction set in against them. It was a dangerous reaction, for the men elected to succeed Fabius went to opposite extremes.

In 217 B.C. Minucius appeared before the assembly convened to elect new consuls and in a ringing speech declared that Rome had not yet brought her full force to bear against Hannibal and urged the election of men who would seek a speedy end of the war. The newly elected consuls, Terentius Varro and Lucius Aemilius Paulus, were expected to make short work of Hannibal.

The Battle of Cannae: 216 B.C.

The two consuls, with an army of 80,000 men, set out to reach Hannibal in Apulia in the vicinity of Cannae, a small fortress but important supply base near the river Aufidus. They placed their infantry in the center in three lines, closer together than usual. The right wing cavalry, commanded by Paulus, stood between the infantry and the river Aufidus, the left wing under Varro stood out on the open plain.

Except for the cavalry on the wings, Hannibal arranged his troops in a less conventional manner than the Romans. His front line, composed mainly of Gauls and Spaniards, bulged forward. Behind them in an echelon formation he posted his heavily armed African veterans.

Under a blazing morning sun, the Roman infantry advanced against Hannibal's front line, which for some time resisted stubbornly but was slowly forced by the weight and pressure of the Roman attack to give ground and sag inwards. Still they did not permit a breakthrough. The African troops on the wings stood firm. The more deeply the Romans pressed into this slowly sagging pocket, the more closely they became packed together.

All this time a cavalry battle was in progress. The Punic left wing attacked and easily destroyed the Roman right wing, which was somewhat cramped for space between the legions and the river. Wheeling around, the victorious cavalry wing attacked the rear of Varro's left wing now engaged by Hannibal's right and completed its destruction. With both wings of the Roman cavalry gone, the Punic cavalry was free to attack the rear of the Roman infantry.

The Roman infantry soldiers had already wedged into so tight a pocket that they were no longer able to use their weapons—a helpless mass unable to prevent the horrible massacre that followed. When the battle ended, 70,000 Romans, including numerous senators and nobles and the consul Aemilius Paulus, were left dead on the field. Only a small remnant of the Roman army managed to escape. These included Varro, the consul, and two others, Marcellus and Scipio Africanus, who lived to fight Hannibal again. Hannibal's victorious tide had now reached its crest.

Hannibal's victory at Cannae remains a classic example of battle tactics for it depended not only on an unorthodox disposition of troops but on timing and coordination. If. his crescent-shaped front line had retreated too fast or had permitted a Roman breakthrough, his army would have been cut into two easily defeated segments. If his cavalry had not completed the destruction of the Roman cavalry in time to strike at the rear of the Roman infantry, the results of the battle might have been entirely different.

The Aftermath. The effect of this bloodiest of all Roman defeats was more serious than that of Lake Trasimene. The Romans were so fearful of a march on Rome that they made feverish preparations for defense, enrolled all citizens above the age of sixteen and even organized two slave legions.

More serious still was the fact that Hannibal almost achieved his war aims. The Roman allies were exhausted; some began to waver in their loyalty. Several towns in Apulia and most of Lucania and Bruttium went over to Hannibal. The big cities of Capua in Campania and Syracuse in Sicily revolted against their alliance with Rome and opened their gates to him. He captured Tarentum. Even some of the Latin towns and colonies began to complain against taxes and the terrific drain on their manpower and economy. More serious still, Philip V of Macedonia, who was eager to drive the Romans from their bridgeheads in Illyria, concluded in 215 B.C. a mutual assistance pact with Hannibal. Never did the war picture look brighter for Carthage than in the years between 216 and 212 B.C. After Cannae, the Romans returned to the Fabian strategy of attrition and the avoidance of battles such as Cannae. They now began to concentrate upon keeping their Italian allies loyal and winning back the cities that had gone over to Hannibal, preventing Hannibal from provisioning his army in Italy or obtaining reinforcements from Carthage, and prosecuting with vigor the war in Sicily, Illyria, and Spain. These tasks required the expenditure of enormous sums of money and manpower, for a fleet of at least 200 ships had to be maintained, and twenty-five legions at home and abroad fed and supplied.

Because of their enormous manpower and resources the Romans were able not only to check Hannibal but to reconquer the disloyal cities. Without reinforcement from Carthage or Spain, Hannibal could not protect his Italian allies and, at the same time, keep his army intact. He was forced to stand helplessly by and watch the Romans reconquer one by one his new allies. His helplessness neither increased his prestige nor encouraged other cities to revolt against Rome.

The Romans won back the Apulian cities, then laid siege to Capua. Hannibal could neither supply Capua with arms and food nor defend it by attacking the Romans. At last he tried to relieve Capua and force the Romans to abandon the siege by a pretended attack upon Rome. When the ruse failed, he had to leave Capua to its fate. The fall of Capua in 211 B.C. restored all Campania to Roman control. Two years later the Cunctator occupied Tarentum, which Hannibal had captured in 213 B.C.

The Siege of Syracuse

The year before Capua's defeat, Syracuse fell after a long siege led by the famous Roman general, Marcellus. Ever since the year of her revolt from Rome (214 B.C.), Syracuse had been able to defend herself by means of artillery and other devices invented by the mathematician and physicist, Archimedes. During the siege Carthage gave Syracuse little effective support except a feeble attempt to lend naval assistance. The city was finally betrayed by a Spanish army captain. It was looted after its capture, its art treasures shipped to Rome, and its independence destroyed for all time. After the fall of Agrigentum in 210 B.C., all Sicily fell under the Roman yoke.

The First Macedonian War: 215–205 B.C.

After his alliance with Hannibal, Philip V of Macedonia attempted to open a second front against Rome in Greece and the Balkans. In 214 he attacked Roman protectorates and naval bases in Illyria hoping, with the help of a Carthaginian fleet, to invade Italy and assist Hannibal. The expected Carthaginian fleet did not arrive but a Roman flotilla of 50 ships did. The Romans easily recaptured the naval bases and some of their former protectorates. In order to prevent Philip's intended invasion of Italy, they created an anti-Macedonian coalition in Greece by an offensive alliance with the Aetolian League and with other Greek states. Though Philip conducted four brilliant campaigns against the Greek coalition, the Greek war served Rome's purpose well by keeping Philip occupied so that he was unable to give Hannibal any effective assistance in Italy. Thus in both Italy and the Balkans a balance of power was established which prevented for a time a definite conclusion of the war.

The War in Spain: 218–209 B.C.

It was in Spain that Hannibal lost the first round of the war. His opponent was the consul of 218 B.C., Publius Cornelius Scipio, who, though not a good battle tactician, understood the meaning of grand strategy. Unable to prevent Hannibal's crossing of the Rhone, he had sent his brother Lucius to Spain, where he joined him after the defeat of his own army at the Trebia. The purpose of this Spanish campaign was to deprive Hannibal of his main base and source of manpower and supplies and to prevent Hannibal's brother Hasdrubal from bringing reinforcements to Italy.

The success of the Spanish campaign hinged upon Roman naval supremacy in the Spanish coastal waters. This was established by a naval encounter in 217 B.C. and by the help of Marseilles. In 215 B.C. the two Scipios met Hasdrubal in battle near Ibera on the Ebro. Though Hasdrubal employed exactly the same tactics as Hannibal had at Cannae, he lost the battle because his center was too weak to prevent a Roman breakthrough before the wings could close in and complete the encirclement. His army was split into two segments, each easily destroyed, and the Scipios followed up their success by the capture of Saguntum in 212 B.C. The Carthaginian position in Spain was further weakened by the recall of Hasdrubal to North Africa to suppress the revolt of Syphax, a treacherous and unprincipled king of the Numidians.

After Hasdrubal's defeat, many Spanish tribes went over to the Romans but the Scipios later learned how treacherous and unreliable their Spanish allies could be. In a later battle with Hasdrubal, the Spaniards deserted, the Roman army was destroyed and the Scipios slain. Thus died the Scipios, who with meager forces had powerfully contributed to the final victory of Rome.

Scipio Africanus

Scipio Africanus, the son and nephew of the slain Scipios, had rescued his father at the battle of the Ticinus. He was at the battle of Cannae, after which he persuaded the remnants of the Roman army to fight until death. After the death of his father in Spain, he was appointed by the Centuriate Assembly at his own request as commander of the Roman forces in Spain. Though a private person, having held no rank higher than that of a curule aedile, he was granted the *imperium* and the rank of a pro-consul.

Scipio had had a good Greek education, was more individualistic than most Roman aristocrats, and had a better sense of humor. He showed an unusual degree of kindness and clemency to defeated enemies. As a general, he possessed courage, resourcefulness, self-confidence, and the power to inspire confidence in his men.

In Spain, Scipio replaced the short Italian sword (useful only for stabbing) with a longer Spanish one, which with its well tempered steel point could be used either for stabbing or slashing. It is probable, though not absolutely certain, that he also introduced the Spanish javelin (*pilum*). He broke away from the close order of the old Roman legion which was drawn up in three lines, each composed of ten maniples. So heavy a formation could advance with terrific force, but could not easily wheel or turn, and so might be readily outflanked, as at Cannae. Also, it tended to act as a whole and did not permit the individual soldier to fight separately or in smaller units. Scipio also modified the old triple line formation and adopted a new formation similar to that used by Hannibal at Cannae and one capable of expanding or contracting quickly, if required to do so. These innovations required much more drill and training than ever given to Roman armies in the past. The new Roman soldier soon became an efficient instrument of conquest.

After taking command, Scipio struck a heavy blow at Carthaginian power in Spain by a lightning advance through enemy country. He ordered a bold frontal attack on New Carthage from the land side and at the same time sent a wading party equipped with scaling ladders into the lagoon on the north side of the town to scale the neglected and undefended walls. Ordinarily this feat could not be accomplished, but a strong north wind happened to be blowing at the time and lowered the level of the lagoon just enough to make the operation a success. Cicero asserts that a great general must have luck in addition to his other qualities, and this was no doubt a piece of pure luck. His soldiers thought him divinely inspired and from then on carried out his orders with blind faith.

The capture of New Carthage gave Scipio a fine military base as well as access to the local silver mines. In addition, he captured eighteen ships and immense quantities of booty, money, arms, and weapons. In the town there were 10,000 hostages, mostly Spanish. By generously sending them back to their homes with some of the captured loot he was able to win friends among the Spanish tribesmen. Thus the capture of New Carthage gave Scipio a valuable opportunity to wage political and psychological warfare against the Carthaginians.

With a well drilled and well equipped army numbering between 35,000 and 40,000 men he advanced into southwestern Spain and fought a battle at Baecula with Hasdrubal, who had an army of about 25,000 men. The battle was a tactical victory for Scipio, but actually a strategic victory for Hasdrubal, who was able to out-maneuver Scipio, extricate the bulk of his forces, and march away to join Hannibal in Italy.

Scipio's Conquest of Spain

Now that Hasdrubal was gone, it was not too difficult for Scipio to defeat the other Carthaginian generals in Spain, especially since they did not get on well with each other. Carthaginian power finally collapsed after the battle of Ilipa in 207 B.C., in which Scipio proved himself a master of encircling tactics. Soon the whole of Spain was in Roman hands and even the ancient Phoenician colonies of Gades (Cadiz) and Malaga voluntarily became Roman allies.

The Battle at the Metaurus and
Death of Hasdrubal: 207 B.C.

The years just before Hasdrubal's crossing of the Alps had not been good for Rome. With so many farmers in the army, agricultural production had declined, many

fertile districts had been repeatedly devastated, and famine was widespread. Had Rome not succeeded in obtaining some wheat from Egypt the food problem would have been acute. Some of the Roman and Latin allies were so exhausted by the war that they refused to supply Rome with any more men or money.

Had Hasdrubal succeeded in effecting a junction with Hannibal's army Rome might have lost the war, but Hannibal did not attempt to join his brother in north Italy for fear of losing Bruttium, his only good base in Italy. He did advance as far north as Apulia but found his way barred by four Roman legions commanded by Claudius Nero.

Unfortunately for Hasdrubal the message he sent his brother asking him to march into Umbria and meet him near Rome was intercepted. The Romans now knew exactly where he was. Four Roman legions were waiting for him in the North. Then Claudius Nero, leaving a small part of his army behind to watch Hannibal, quietly set out for the North and six days later reached the Metaurus. Suddenly and unexpectedly Hasdrubal found himself matched against the superior strength of two Roman armies. He tried to retreat over the river but it was too late. His splendid army was destroyed and he himself was killed. Several days later his severed head was thrown into Hannibal's camp. Hannibal knew then that he had lost the war and sadly withdrew to Bruttium.

Two other misfortunes followed swiftly: in 205 B.C. a Punic fleet bringing reinforcements and supplies was lost in a storm; that same year Hannibal's brother Mago who had landed at Genoa with an army, was defeated, wounded, and compelled to withdraw again to Genoa, where he received orders from Carthage to set sail for home. During the voyage, he died.

The End Approaches

After Scipio's return from Spain in 204 B.C., the Senate debated how to end the war. Scipio, who had already made a deal with two petty kings of Numidia, Massinissa and Syphax, wanted to invade Africa. Fabius, the leader of the Senate, who did not like the young upstart, his Greek ideas, his air of superiority, and his reckless strategy, vigorously opposed the African venture. "Why don't you apply yourself to this and carry the war directly to where Hannibal is instead of chasing off to Africa expecting him to follow you?" he asked.

Finally Scipio obtained the Senate's reluctant permission to go to Africa, but not to raise troops. He appealed directly to the people for volunteers for the African expedition, and about 7,000 enlisted. These, together with the two legions already in Sicily, made up the African Expeditionary Force.

Fabius, apparently for spite, saw to it that a rather pedantic and narrow minded quaestor named Cato, the later Censor, was sent to accompany Scipio to keep an eye on his expenditure of public funds. When Cato objected to Scipio's lavish spending on his soldiers and officers funds not properly allotted, the two men quarreled. Cato returned to Rome in a rage and remained Scipio's lifelong enemy. Fabius' certainty that the expedition would fail did not take into account Scipio's extraordinary luck.

In 204 B.C. Scipio landed near Utica in Tunisia and immediately became mixed up in the quarrels of two Numidian kings, Syphax and Massinissa, both of whom were in love with Sophonisba, the beautiful daughter of Hasdrubal Gisco, the Carthaginian governor of Numidia. Syphax, the stronger of the two petty kings, won the hand of Sophonisba, deposed his rival, and allied himself with Carthage. Massinissa, now a king without love, land, or throne, found refuge in Scipio's camp.

Scipio had entered into peace negotiations with Carthage and Syphax for the sole purpose of lulling their suspicions and learning the nature and disposition of their camps. Having learned what he wanted to know, one night he surrounded Syphax's camp, which was constructed of osiers and reeds, and set it on fire. The Carthaginians, thinking that the fire was accidental, rushed out to help, and both armies were attacked and destroyed. Scipio had now proved himself the master of Syphax and Massinissa in guile and treachery. He would soon be Hannibal's master in battle.

Massinissa then captured Syphax, married Sophonisba, and returned to Numidia in triumph having won for himself love, land, and throne. In exchange for benefits received from Scipio, Massinissa was requested to provide the Roman army with cavalry. Later Scipio began to fear Sophonisba might charm her husband into an alliance with Carthage. By conferring upon Massinissa a curule chair and certain other specious honors and benefits he persuaded him to get rid of Sophonisba by adding a little poison to her wine.

The Carthaginians, imitating Scipio's guile, perfidy, and treachery, opened peace negotiations with him and at the same time recalled Hannibal from Italy. Before leaving Italy, Hannibal inscribed on a bronze tablet, which he deposited in the temple of Hera Lacinia near Croton, a chronicle of all his deeds since crossing the Alps. (Polybius declares he read this.) After Hannibal's arrival in Africa, the peace talks suddenly ceased. The war continued until a battle was fought at Naraggara, which was three days' march west of Zama.

The Battle of Zama: 202 B.C.

Not even at Cannae had Hannibal devised a more ingenious plan of battle than at Zama and he never made a more brilliant and lasting contribution to military science and tactics. The two most original ideas worked out for this battle and employed for the first time in history were the principles of the fighting reserve and of the "hedgehog" or islands of defense, which can still offer resistance even after being overrun by the enemy.* In view of these facts it is no exaggeration to assert that in purely logistical strategy Hannibal was greater than Napoleon.

At Zama Hannibal posted his two cavalry wings to protect the flanks of the infantry. The real innovation was the arrangement of the center. First came elephants, next the light infantry units, then a screen of heavy infantry units, then an empty space, then another screen of heavy infantry, and placed

* "Hedgehog" tactics were extensively employed in tank battles of World War II especially by the Russians. The principle of the fighting reserve is standard in most modern armies.

back some distance in the rear stood his veterans from Italy as a fighting reserve. The first three lines of infantry were to be sacrificed in the absorption of the initial Roman attack and used later to attack the Roman rear.

The Roman battle order also consisted of two cavalry wings. The main innovation was that the legions, as at Baecula and Ilipa, were subdivided into small units with space between for the elephants to run through without breaking up the formations. Massinissa's cavalry was of supreme importance to the Romans in this battle.

In the actual battle Hannibal's elephants had little effect upon the Roman lines but did a great deal of damage, when they stampeded, to his own cavalry wings, which, weak to begin with, were soon put out of action by Massinissa's cavalry.

Hannibal's first line, consisting of some 12,000 mercenaries—Ligurians, Celts, and Moors, resisted the initial Roman attack long and valiantly, but when the second line of Libyans and Carthaginians did not come to their support as quickly as expected, they thought themselves deserted and retreated in panic, only to be cut down by the second advancing line. Hannibal was therefore forced to bring his reserve units forward earlier than he had planned in order to stabilize the front lines. Hit in the rear by a strong cavalry attack, the reserve units were unable to resist the second phase of the Roman offensive and the Carthaginian resistance was broken. The weakness in cavalry had been Hannibal's undoing. It was ironic that Hannibal, whose tactics have been successfully employed in tank battles of the twentieth century, should have been defeated by an opponent using tactics of the third century B.C. Thus ended the battle of Zama.

Peace Terms

It was Hannibal himself who advised Carthage to ask for peace, even though he knew that the terms would be hard. In 201 B.C. Carthage was compelled to surrender all territories outside of Africa, to recognize the independence of Numidia and Massinissa's alliance with Rome, to agree not to wage war outside of Africa and not even within Africa without Roman permission, to reduce her fleet to ten light triremes or coastguard vessels, and to pay an indemnity of 10,000 talents, the equivalent of 12,000,000 gold dollars, payable in fifty years. The power of Carthage as a state was broken forever. Peace declared, Scipio returned to Rome in triumph and upon him was conferred the proud title of Africanus.

Hannibal as Administrator

Like Julius Caesar and Napoleon of later history, Hannibal revealed, as proved by his postwar career, unusual talents as an administrator. In the half-dozen years after Zama, he tackled the job of reconstructing the Carthaginian state with courage and energy. Carthage, he knew, had lost the war mainly because she had been governed by a corrupt, venal, and pusillanimous oligarchy, whose divided policies and petty jealousies obstructed the war effort when victory was in sight. After the war the same group proceeded to wring taxes from the poor to pay the indemnity exacted by Rome.

When elected Suffete or Judge, Hannibal established a system of taxation based on income and ability to pay and made the government accountable to the people for its expenditures. The financial administration was so efficient that in 191 B.C., only ten years after Zama, Carthage offered immediate payment of the forty remaining installments of her war indemnity (Rome refused the offer). Commerce and industry revived as never before and Carthage again became one of the busiest ports of the Mediterranean. Unfortunately Carthage soon lost the benefits of efficient administration. Rome became alarmed at the remarkable recovery of Carthage and, acting upon the accusation by his political enemies of planning another war, demanded the surrender of Hannibal as a war criminal. To save his life, Hannibal escaped from Carthage and took refuge in the East.

Reasons for Roman Success

Even if Hannibal had won the battle of Zama, Carthage would still have lost the war, for its outcome had been determined in Italy by Hannibal's failure, despite his victories at Trasimene and Cannae, to wreck the Roman confederate alliance, the destruction of which was the main objective of his total war strategy and his sole hope of ultimate victory. If so, the prime mover and chief architect of Roman victory was not Scipio Africanus, the victor at Zama, but Fabius Maximus Cunctator, whose favorite tactics of attrition and exhaustion frustrated Hannibal's main design and afforded time for the mobilization of Rome's enormous war potential. He saved the state by his delaying (*cunctando restituit rem*).

Feebly supported by his own government, Hannibal had attempted the heroic but impossible task of conquering a state composed of free citizens fighting in defense of their homeland. They defeated Hannibal, as they did the Gauls, the Samnites, and Pyrrhus before him, because Rome had since 338 B.C. gradually developed and consolidated a system of alliances founded on justice and mutual benefit. Perhaps the war had really been won earlier still, in 367 B.C., when Rome resolved the long struggle of the classes by granting the plebeians political equality with her ancient aristocracy, and faced the world with new unity and strength.

THE CONQUEST OF VII

No sooner had Rome conquered Carthage and won dominion over the western Mediterranean than she was drawn into conflict with the Hellenistic powers of the Balkans and the Middle East. Since she had no vital interests or obligations in that area and since not one of the Hellenistic powers had ever attacked, injured, or threatened her in any way, modern historians have been at a loss to explain why she carried on unprovoked and aggressive war against them. It would be useless to discuss the various suggested explanations without an understanding of the political and military conditions existing in the Mediterranean area at the close of the third century B.C. and after that a very brief description of the state of mind prevailing in Rome at the end of the Second Punic War.

THE MEDITERRANEAN

The empire created by the military genius of Alexander the Great had originally embraced Macedonia, Greece, most of Asia Minor, Egypt, and the entire Middle East, extending from the Mediterranean to central Asia and northern India. After his death in 323 B.C. that empire had fallen apart in the struggle for power among his generals, not one of whom was able to establish himself as sole ruler and preserve its unity. Before 275 B.C. three dynasties, descended from three of his generals, had established powerful kingdoms. The Antigonids, descended from An-tigonus the One-eyed, ruled over Macedonia and from time to time over large parts of Greece; the Ptolemies over Egypt, Cyrene, bridgeheads along the Red Sea and East Africa, Phoenicia, several islands in the Aegean, and some cities along the coast of Asia Minor and the Gallipoli peninsula; the Seleucids over most of the old Persian empire embracing the western and southern parts of Asia Minor, northern Syria, Mesopotamia, and Persia, and at one time also northwestern India and Afghanistan, and Turkestan in central Asia.

Among the minor Hellenistic states was Pergamum, in the northwest corner of Asia Minor. Its founder, Philetaerus, a satrap first of Lysimachus (ruler of Thrace after the death of Alexander), and later of Seleucus I of Syria, had surreptitiously made it an independent principality in 283 B.C. and had embezzled the equivalent of ten million gold dollars entrusted to his care. At his death in 263 B.C., he was succeeded by Eumenes I, who was in turn succeeded in 241 B.C. by Attalus I, the first king of the Attalid dynasty. Under his rule Pergamum, enriched by agriculture and a flourishing foreign trade, blossomed into a center of art and literature and a champion of Hellenism.

Another important small state was the island republic of Rhodes, which lay off the southwestern tip of Asia Minor. Like Pergamum, it too was a brilliant cultural center, but it owed its material prosperity solely to sea-borne trade, which it guarded by a small but efficient navy. For more than a century the Rhodian navy had policed the sea lanes of the Aegean against the pirates of Cilicia and Crete. Rhodes was also famous for one of the seven wonders of the ancient world, the Colossus, the enormous statue of Apollo which stood at the mouth of the harbor until knocked down by an earthquake in 227/6 B.C. Long after Rhodes had lost its importance as a shipping and banking center, it remained an art and cultural center. (Here Cicero and Caesar studied oratory and philosophy.)

There were two political and military league federations in Greece, which Isocrates had long ago advocated as the salvation of Greek unity and prosperity. One was the Aetolian League of small townships and rural communities, which, by 250 B.C., embraced most of central Greece north of the Gulf of Corinth. It contained no large cities, no capital or leading power, but was a loose and rather primitive confederacy centered around the temple of Apollo at Thermum, where assemblies were held to decide on a common military and foreign policy. The other was the rival Achaean League, which included the minor cities of the Peloponnesus except Sparta, Elis, and Messenia. At its peak of power it was led by Aratus of Sicyon (245–213 B.C.), who through fear of Sparta and the Aetolian League had allied himself closely with Antigonus Doson of Macedonia (229–221 B.C.) and later with Philip V (221–179 B.C.).

The Balance of Power

The existence of the small Hellenistic states depended upon the balance of power established between 277 and 225 B.C. among the three major powers of Egypt, Syria, and Macedonia. If one of the major powers succeeded in expanding its influence and territory, the other two combined against it. Though not one of the three liked this balance of power, it was the salvation of the kingdom of Pergamum, the republic of Rhodes, the Achaean and Aetolian Leagues of Greece, and, towards the end of the century, of Egypt itself. When it was finally disturbed, Pergamum, Rhodes, the Greek Leagues, and Egypt all made repeated appeals to Rome to help restore the balance, never dreaming that eventually all, both great and small, would become subject to Roman domination.

Antiochus III of Syria

While the Second Punic War was raging in the West, the balance of power was being disturbed in the East by the ambitions and warlike activities of two young monarchs, Antiochus III of Syria and Philip V of Macedonia.

In 223 B.C., when Antiochus became king as a youth of eighteen, the Seleucid empire had already crumbled into almost total disruption. Most of Asia Minor, which had once been part of the early Seleucid empire, was now either in revolt or in the hands of Attalus I of Pergamum. In the East, Mesopotamia was in revolt, northern Iran had been lost to the Parthians, and Bactria, which embraced Afghanistan and the Russian Republic of Uzbek, had become independent.

A man of energy and initiative, he first suppressed the revolts in Iran, Mesopotamia, and Asia Minor. He next invaded Phoenicia (then held by Egypt). Undaunted by the crushing defeat inflicted upon him by the Egyptian king at Raphia in 217 B.C., he completed the conquest of large areas of Asia Minor and then began his historic march to the East. Between 212 and 205 B.C. he reconquered Armenia, northern Iran and, marching eastwards along the southern shores of the Caspian, compelled the Greek ruler of Bactria to recognize his overlordship, but wisely and generously permitted him to rule Bactria as an eastern outpost of Hellenistic civilization, and as a buffer state against the restless tribes of central Asia. Antiochus then crossed the Hindu Kush mountains and pushed down into the valley of the Indus, where he received 150 valuable war elephants as tribute. On his way back to Antioch, he assumed the title of Antiochus the Great and his exploits were hailed throughout the Greek world as second only to those of Alexander.

Meanwhile, Egypt, an ally of Rome since 273 B.C., had fallen into decay. The export market for wheat and textiles had contracted, inflation had been rampant since 220 B.C., the treasury was empty, and the Egyptian army and navy had suffered neglect. A social revolution was in progress. The native Egyptians, recruited to help fight the battle of Raphia, felt now a new sense of power and were no longer willing to put up with the exploitation they had endured in the past. Moreover, in 205/4 B.C. the king had died and the new king was only a child, surrounded by a group of corrupt and degenerate advisers.

Now, if ever, came the chance for Antiochus to avenge Raphia. He attacked and defeated the Egyptians at Panium in northern Palestine (200 B.C.). Seven years later, he had a marriage arranged between the young Egyptian king and his daughter, Cleopatra, the first of a famous line of Cleopatras extending down past the time of Julius Caesar and Mark Antony.

Most of Asia Minor reconquered, some Thracian possessions and islands of the Ptolemies seized, the revolts in the East suppressed, and Egypt itself subject to Seleucid influence, Antiochus had almost succeeded in destroying the balance of power. Nothing now stood in the way of the resurrection of the vast empire of Alexander the Great except Philip V of Macedonia and Rome far off in the west.

Philip V of Macedonia

The stupendous successes of Antiochus III stirred the envy of Philip. He, too, was an excellent soldier whose reign had been largely spent on the battlefield. Yet, although he had shown the speed and dash of an Alexander (and was almost as good in siege warfare), he had made no important acquisitions.

In order to compete successfully with Antiochus, Philip needed money and ships. He had none. There was only one thing to do: seize some of the Aegean islands and a few rich cities of Asia Minor. Since many of these islands and cities were controlled either by Egypt or by Rhodes, Philip enlisted the aid of one Dicaearchus, a professional pirate from Aetolia. Here was somebody he could use as his secret agent to capture trading ships, wring money from the islands, and assist the Cretan pirates (who were at war with Rhodes because she had tried to interfere with their source of livelihood). He sent another secret agent to set fire to the dockyards and arsenal at Rhodes. The raiders were highly successful in the performance of their appointed tasks, Dicaearchus particularly so, since he came back with enough loot to enable Philip to build 50 new warships and a number of lighter craft.

With his new fleet Philip sallied forth into the Aegean and recklessly attacked cities on both sides of the Dardanelles and the Sea of Marmara, forced some to become his allies, annexed others, and even destroyed and enslaved a few. The occupation of these cities gave Philip control of the Black Sea grain trade, which was of vital importance to Athens and Rhodes. Rhodes declared war and persuaded Attalus I of Pergamum to do likewise.

Philip was not at all surprised at the action taken by Rhodes, but he was furious with Pergamum. He accused Attalus I of unprovoked aggression, since he had done nothing to injure Pergamum. Angrily he marched against Pergamum and defeated a small force sent to oppose him but, unable to storm the city, he turned his wrath upon the statues and shrines outside the walls, cut down a sacred olive grove, and destroyed, among other buildings, the temple of Aphrodite.

After a number of naval engagements Attalus and the Rhodians concluded that they were unable to defeat Philip without outside help. In 201 B.C. they appealed to Rome and sent embassies to wait upon the senate. The senate was in a more receptive mood than it had been the year before when it had rudely rebuffed an Aetolian embassy bringing complaints against Philip.

The ambassadors charged Philip with aggression against Pergamum and, taking advantage of the hysterical and jittery feelings engendered among the Romans by the Hannibalic War, they accused Philip of having made a secret pact with Antiochus III to carve up the foreign possessions of Egypt and insinuated that the pact was ultimately aimed at Rome. Though this "pact" may have been a propaganda lie concocted to scare the Romans, it served to make the senate believe that Philip and the mighty conqueror of the East might some day make a landing on the shores of Italy. And what if Hannibal should be given command of their armies!

Their mission accomplished, the envoys returned home. In the fall of 200 B.C. P. Sulpicius Galba, a professional slave catcher, whose brutalities during the First Macedonian War had become notorious, was elected consul for the second time and given Macedonia as his province. He laid before the Centuriate Assembly a proposed declaration of war against Macedonia which was overwhelmingly turned down. The Roman people did not want another war. They had learned to hate war. Their minds had not yet been fully contaminated by propaganda when the war bill was first presented. It would take time to make them fall in line. Meanwhile, the matter would be taken out of their hands and they could do nothing about it.

Even after the assembly had rejected the request for war, the senate sent a commission of three of its members ostensibly to investigate the situation in the East but really to provoke Philip into war by presenting him with demands unauthorized by the Roman people. The commission demanded that he should not attack any Greek city and ordered him to pay reparations to Attalus I as if he, and not Attalus, had been the original aggressor. Since Philip could not honorably accept

these outrageous demands, he continued his military operations. Actually war between Rome and Philip was a foregone conclusion before the assembly met for the second time to vote on a formal declaration. Thus a few determined war mongers had involved two nations into a war which neither wanted and for which there was little cause.

The Senate's Motives for War. Historians have suggested many single motives to explain why the senate wanted to wage an unprovoked and aggressive war against Philip. Some have suggested the desire for territorial expansion, but Rome already had more land in North Italy and Spain than she could use.

Commercial imperialism cannot be so easily ruled out. The East was a lucrative field for investment and exploitation, and a source of the world's most skilled and intelligent slaves. That some senators were already interested in foreign commerce is proved by the Claudian law of 218 B.C. (*see* p. 126).

Far less plausible is the suggestion that Rome waged war in the East because of her sentimental desire to preserve the Greek way of life. Except for a few such as Scipio Africanus, Titus Flamininus, Aemilius Paullus, and some others, most of the Fabian group did not have any particular admiration for the Greeks, not the Claudians, not Cato, nor any of the other conservative groups, who dominated the senate when it declared war against Philip.

One other fairly obvious suggestion is that some members of the higher nobility saw in war a road to military glory and later political advancement. See how soon after Zama Scipio rose to the exalted position of leader of the senate!

Perhaps the dominant motive, if there was one, was the fear, real or imaginary, that the Hellenistic powers, if left unchecked, might eventually combine against Rome and invade Italy. Hannibal's invasion must have left many senators fairly sensitive on that score. The Rhodian and Pergamene ambassadors must have either sensed this fear or had been informed that their best talking point was the possible danger of Antiochus allying with Philip. The same point was made by the war mongers, who addressed the Centuriate Assembly.

The Second Macedonian War: 200–196 B.C.

The Romans landed in Illyria in the fall of 200 B.C., but did little fighting until the next year and even then fought no important battles. Their only success was in persuading the Aetolians, inveterate enemies of Philip, to enter the war. The other Greeks remained neutral except the Athenians, whom Philip had earlier attacked. Perhaps the Greeks distrusted the commanders of the Roman armies during the first two years of the war.

Titus Quinctius Flamininus. The new consul, Titus Flamininus, arrived to take command in 198 B.C. He spoke Greek with a faultless accent and could write it well too. He understood and sincerely admired and appreciated Greek culture. Besides, he was a soldier with a brilliant military career. He had fought under Marcellus, one of the best Roman generals, against Hannibal. At the age of 23 he had been placed in command of the Roman garrison at Tarentum with the rank of pro-praetor. His magnetic personality, his enthusiasm, and natural wit befitted the true diplomat. His somewhat careless and unkempt appearance served to bring out the charm of his personality. He was above all a master of the propaganda slogan. No sooner had he arrived than he electrified the Greek world with the slogan of "Freedom and self-determination of all Greeks." This was indeed a most unusual Roman.

Flamininus maneuvered Philip out of nearly all Greece except the key fortresses of Demetrias in Thessaly, Chalcis in Euboea, and Corinth in the Peloponnesus. Philip, now confined to Thessaly, sought a peace conference with Flamininus. Although the two men understood and admired each other, the conference itself achieved nothing, and broke up over Philip's refusal to surrender the three fortresses, which he had inherited from his ancestors.

The Battle of Cynoscephalae: 197 B.C.

The war was decided at Cynoscephalae or "Dogs' Heads," a ridge of hills in Thessaly. The two armies were about equally matched but the Macedonian hoplite phalanx, after a brilliant breakthrough, was destroyed because it was taken in the flanks. It could smash its way in a solid frontal charge on level ground but became a helpless, floundering mass if taken on hilly or rough ground. The Romans had learned this at the battle of the Caudine Forks with the Samnites (321 B.C.), as well as in their battles with Pyrrhus. Philip owed his defeat to what Toynbee would call the worship of an ephemeral technique.

Peace Terms. Philip had lost the battle of Cynoscephalae and the war. He had no other army, Macedonia was exposed to invasion, peace had to be obtained at any price. The terms were better than expected, for Flamininus did not want to destroy the Macedonian state (as the Aetolians demanded) since it served as a buffer against the restless Balkan tribes to the North. Also, Philip might be a useful ally to Rome some day, perhaps more useful than the Aetolians.

Philip was compelled, late in 197 B.C., to recognize the freedom and independence of the Greeks, to withdraw all his garrisons from Greece, the Aegean, and Illyria, to surrender his fleet, reduce his army to 5,000 men, and pay an indemnity of 1,000 talents (or 1,200,000 gold dollars) half to be paid at once, the rest in ten annual installments. The infuriated Aetolians demanded the whole of Thessaly as their share of victory, but Flamininus would concede them only Phocis and the western part of Thessaly and, even worse, allowed Philip to make jokes at their expense during the peace negotiations.

The Proclamation of Flamininus. In July of 196 B.C. Flamininus made a grand appearance at the Isthmian Games at Corinth and, as proconsul, proclaimed in the name of the Roman senate the promised freedom and independence of the Greek states: they were to be subject to their own laws, without garrisons, without tribute. A pandemonium of joy and thanksgiving broke loose unparalleled since the day Alexander proclaimed the right of all Greeks to return to their homes. Gold coins, imitating the famous staters of Alexander, were struck bearing the portrait of Titus Flamininus. (In some cities he was even worshipped as a god, the first Roman ever to receive divine honors.)

For a while some of the Greeks, especially the pro-Roman aristocrats, enjoyed their newly proclaimed freedom enormously. Flamininus understood and admired the aristocrats of Greece and desired to perpetuate their domination of the masses. He knew little about the poor and cared less. He regarded their struggle for the cancellation of debts, the redistribution of land, and other social and economic reforms as subversive activity.

Flamininus was prevailed upon by his aristocratic Greek friends to declare war upon Sparta, the only state in Hellenistic Greece which attempted to carry out a program of social justice and reform. Nabis, the king of Sparta, whose character biased sources have sought to blacken, was an able and energetic man, who in 206 B.C. had resumed the reform program begun by Cleomenes III twenty years before. He abolished the malignant plague of debt, broke up the large estates, distributed the land fairly, enfranchised the helots, and proclaimed liberty to captives and slaves. His kingdom had become a refuge to homeless exiles. Though Sparta had in a short time become a fairly strong power, she was unable to resist the might of Rome.

Flamininus, in his exuberant optimism, could not foresee that once the Roman army had departed, the Greeks, plagued by their petty jealousies and meannesses, would fall out with each other and with Rome or that, in exasperation, the Romans would finally remove the newly bestowed freedom and blanket all Greece under the darkness of tyranny and oppression, yet only a few years after the proclamation of Flamininus, the Greek masses were prepared to join any uprising to remove the hated Roman power. The occasion for such an uprising was not far off.

The War with Antiochus the Great: 192–189 B.C.

No sooner had Flamininus pulled his legions out of Greece and celebrated a glorious triumph in Rome than the senate became alarmed at the activities of Antiochus III. After he had confirmed his peace with Egypt by the marriage of his daughter Cleopatra I

to Ptolemy V, Antiochus began to annex the few still free coastal cities of Asia Minor. He occupied Ephesus, though it had been held by Egypt for more than a century. In 196 B.C., he crossed the Dardanelles and occupied several towns in Thrace. Since all these cities had once belonged to the empire of Seleucus I, Antiochus felt he had a perfect right to reoccupy them.

The attempt of Antiochus to recover the empire of Seleucus I alarmed Pergamum, which had also once formed part of the old Seleucid empire. The new king, Eumenes II, decided to follow his father's example of appealing to Rome and it was not until near the end of his reign in 167 B.C. that he realized that Rome, once having vanquished all her enemies, would then deprive Pergamum and all the other small states of their freedom and independence.

In response to the appeals of Eumenes and of some Greek cities in Asia Minor, the senate authorized Flamininus to negotiate with Antiochus. Flamininus warned the king to keep his hands off the independent Greek cities in Asia Minor, not to cross the Dardanelles, and to evacuate all towns recently taken from Egypt. The king replied that Flamininus had absolutely no right to speak on behalf of the Greek cities in Asia Minor and that, if the Romans would leave him alone, he, Antiochus, would gladly leave them alone.

About this time (196 B.C.), Hannibal, forced into exile from Carthage (p. 136), arrived at Ephesus. To the king's query, Hannibal replied that the only chance for victory against Rome lay in the creation of a united front of all her enemies. Antiochus would have to come to terms with Philip V, with Egypt, with Pergamum—perhaps, even, make concessions.

Antiochus thanked Hannibal for his sage advice and ignored it. He decided to ally himself instead with the little powers of Greece, a decision which was to prove extremely unwise.

Antiochus III Invades Greece: 192 B.C.

In Greece, the disgruntled Aetolians had become violently anti-Roman, particularly because the peace settlement restricted their favorite occupation: plundering their neighbors. They tried to enlist Philip's help in throwing off the hated Roman yoke but he, remembering how they had urged Flamininus to dismantle his kingdom, rejected their overtures. Antiochus was so ill-advised as to accept their invitation: he landed in Greece in 192 B.C. with a puny force of 10,000 men and was promptly elected Aetolian commander-in-chief.

The Romans secured Philip's help by offering to cancel the unpaid balance of his war indemnity and promising him any Thessalian cities he might capture from the Aetolians. This is a good illustration of the typically Roman policy of *Divide et Impera* ("Divide and Rule").*

Allied with Philip, Pergamum, Rhodes, the Achaean League, Numidia, and even Carthage, the Romans had little trouble in defeating Antiochus, whose last stand was at Thermopylae, a position historically impossible to hold. After his defeat at Thermopylae, Antiochus made his escape to Chalcis and set sail for Ephesus.

The Results of the War. The failure of Antiochus had two important results: the invasion of Asia Minor by the Romans, and the immediate resurgence of the Scipionic group in Roman party politics.

The spectacular successes of Flamininus naturally gave the Fabian faction (to which he probably belonged) immense prestige although Scipio Africanus was most critical of the peace settlement. Later events seemed to justify Scipio and in the years 191 and 190 B.C. only pro-Scipionic consuls were elected.

In view of the probable magnitude of the coming struggle with Antiochus it would have been advantageous to elect Scipio Africanus, the greatest living Roman general, to the consulship. Since Africanus had been consul in 194 and was not eligible for re-election until ten years later (*see* p. 100), the people elected instead his younger brother, Lucius Cornelius Scipio, in the expectation that the latter would appoint him as legate and permit him to assume actual command. Lucius did just that.

Early in 190 B.C. the Scipios sailed from Brindisi with a small army, took command of the larger army already in Greece, and began their march through Macedonia to the Dardanelles. Under the Roman policy of *Divide et Impera,* the Scipios secured Philip's active assistance. Philip allowed the Romans to pass through his country and helped them by supplying provisions, building bridges, and repairing roads.

The conquest of the East would have been impossible for the Romans without command of the sea, which they secured partly through the tactical skill of their admiral, Gaius Livius, and the effective assistance of the Rhodian and Pergamene navies and partly through the stupidity of Antiochus himself.

The first decisive naval battle was fought off Cissus between Ephesus and Chios, the next off Side, Pamphylia. Antiochus committed the inexplicable blunder of placing Hannibal, one of the greatest land generals, in command of the fleet! He was defeated by the smaller but more efficient Rhodian fleet. A few weeks later Antiochus' main fleet was destroyed off Myonnesus, between Teos and Samos, and Scipio's army crossed the Dardanelles without naval opposition.

Antiochus Offers Peace Terms. Antiochus offered to abandon Thrace, break off relations with the Aetolian Greeks, and recognize the independence of the Greek cities in Asia Minor, as Flamininus had demanded seven years before. In addition, he agreed to pay half the costs of the war. There was a time when the Romans would have made peace with him, had he merely agreed not to cross the Dardanelles and refrain from attacking the cities of Thrace. Now his far more sweeping offers came too late. Nothing would satisfy the Scipios short of the surrender of all Asia Minor north and west of the Taurus Mountains and payment of the entire costs of the war, which terms Antiochus rejected.

The Battle of Magnesia. The battle for Asia took place near Magnesia on the Sipylus in 190 B.C. It was easily won by the Romans despite the absence of the Scipios because of illness. Antiochus lost the battle because of poor generalship, poor equipment, and the lack of coordination among the various units of his huge but ill-assorted army. He contributed greatly to his own defeat by repeating the mistake which cost him the battle of Raphia in 217 B.C. Taking personal com-

* Cato served as advisor of the consul.

mand of a fine squadron of Iranian cavalry, he routed the Roman cavalry. Then, instead of reining in and attacking the rear of the Roman infantry, he pursued the Roman cavalry too far. By the time he returned he found that his main army had been defeated by a second-rate Roman general, the ex-consul Cn. Domitius Ahenobarbus, with the assistance of Eumenes II of Pergamum. And Hannibal had once again been placed in command of the Seleucid navy.

The Peace Treaty of Apamea: 188 B.C. At Magnesia Antiochus lost the war and the Seleucid empire lost its power. The king was obliged to give up all his possessions in Asia Minor north of the Taurus Mountains and west of the Halys River, to surrender his navy, and to pay 15,000 talents (or 18,000,-000 gold dollars), one of the largest indemnities exacted in ancient times. Hannibal managed to escape.

Some of the vast territory in Asia Minor surrendered by Antiochus (Rome was not yet prepared to assume the administration of so large an area) went to the Greek cities in return for their help, more to the Republic of Rhodes, but the lion's share to Pergamum, whose original size was increased tenfold: an area almost equal to that of Great Britain. The new kingdom of Pergamum, writes Polybius, was now inferior to none.

The Aftermath

Antiochus the Great was assassinated when caught robbing a temple of Susa in 187 B.C. He had robbed temples before but this time he did not get away with it.

After Magnesia, Hannibal escaped first to Crete and afterwards to Bithynia, then at war with Pergamum. He won a naval battle for his friend, Prusias I of Bithynia. Flamininus finally hunted him down and compelled Prusias to promise his surrender. Hannibal frustrated the plan by taking poison in 183 B.C., dying as proudly as he had lived.

Earlier in the same year died his great opponent, Scipio Africanus. Cato, jealous of Scipio's military achievements, had never forgiven him for dismissing him from his quaestorship in Sicily twenty years before. In 187 B.C. he instigated two tribunes to demand in the senate that Scipio's brother, Lucius, give an account of the 500 talents ($60,000) received from Antiochus after Magnesia. Africanus knew that the attack was really aimed at himself, but instead of calmly vindicating his brother by showing that the money paid by Antiochus was actually booty to be used at the general's discretion and not war indemnity for which an account had to be rendered to the senate and the people, in a wild outburst of temper, he tore up the account books in the presence of the senate.

The senate let the whole matter drop, Cato did not. He caused another tribune to demand an account from Lucius before the people, and himself delivered a ringing speech of denunciation. Lucius did not condescend to reply. The tribune then fined Lucius for refusing to render an account and would have had him arrested and imprisoned had not another tribune, Tiberius Sempronius Gracchus, intervened. It was shortly after this that Africanus retired to his country estate and died.

It is not easy to explain why the hero of Zama and conqueror of Spain, Africa, and Asia should have ended his days under a cloud of unpopularity nor why, for later generations, he seems to have lacked the glamor of Hannibal, of Titus Flamininus, and of his two illustrious grandsons, Tiberius and Gaius Gracchus. Even Flamininus—vain, theatrical, flamboyant, and at times somewhat cheap—seems to have had a stronger appeal.

Philip V had done comparatively well since his defeat at Cynoscephalae, although he did not reap many permanent advantages from his disgraceful alliance with Rome against Antiochus. He received only a few paltry talents and the promise of a few towns in Thessaly—a promise that the Romans ultimately failed to keep. He did try, when it was almost too late, to cultivate good relations with the other Hellenistic states—Egypt, Syria, and even Pergamum. He changed the Macedonian constitution to permit the towns under his rule the right of local self-government so that he might pose as the champion of the oppressed masses in Greece.

In Macedonia, Philip set about building up the economic life of the country. He encouraged agriculture, sank new mines, reopened old ones, and encouraged the people to raise larger families. To increase the population still more, he brought in Thracian settlers from the Balkan regions he had recently annexed. These measures were intended to increase the military power of his kingdom.

Philip's last days were far from happy. He had put his own son Demetrius to death on charges of treason later found false. After learning the horrid truth, Philip, tortured with remorse, could no longer sleep and fell an easy victim to illness. He died in 179 B.C. and his eldest son, Perseus, succeeded to the throne.

Even Philip, for all his sins and cruelties, cuts a better figure than Eumenes II of Pergamum. Eumenes posed as the champion of the Greeks and the defender of their liberties but in the end no one had done more to destroy those liberties than Eumenes by his betrayal of the Hellenistic world to the Romans and his constant complaints to the Roman senate against other Eastern kings. The Romans used him as their spy, informer, and lackey but they evidently had little respect for him. When they had conquered the last of their great Hellenistic enemies and had no further use for him, they refused to listen to any more complaints. Early in the winter of 167-166 B.C. he arrived in Italy but was met at the dock by a quaestor bearing a senate message that the Fathers had decreed that no more kings were to be permitted to come to Rome and if he had any communication to make to them he was to pass it to the official and then leave Italy at once.

On one of his trips to Rome Eumenes had presented a list of complaints against Perseus of Macedonia. On the way back from Rome Eumenes was severely injured at Delphi, where rocks were rolled down upon him as he was going through a mountain pass. He was nursed back to health at a hospital in Aegina, but this incident was later used as propaganda against Perseus, the young Macedonian king.

The Third Macedonian War: 171–167 B.C.

The Third Macedonian War was caused partly by the awakening power of Macedonia, partly by the knavish intrigues of Eumenes, and partly by the chaotic conditions in Greece after the dismal defeat of Antiochus and the Aetolians. The Greeks had perverted the freedom proclaimed at the Isthmian Games into chaos and anarchy, a danger to themselves and a constant source of worry and annoyance to the senate.

Greece was torn apart by the class struggle between the haves and the have-nots. The petty and venal aristocracy, whom Flamininus hoped might guide the Greek cities onto the path of freedom and self-government, were as much responsible for the anarchy as the demagogues, who kept fanning the smoldering embers of popular discontent. In vain Eumenes tried to persuade the Greeks to preserve law and order by pretty phrases and prettier gifts of gold. His gifts were spurned with contempt, the statues formerly erected to him were broken in pieces, and the metal tablets inscribed in his honor were melted down. In disgust many able and upright men in Greece began to turn from Rome to Perseus. At last the exasperated senate was provoked into war with Perseus.

The first three years of this war provided a pitiable exhibition of incompetence on both sides. The Roman commanders marched to and fro to no purpose and made mistakes which a more resolute and daring enemy than Perseus could have turned into defeats as disastrous as those of the Caudine Forks, Trasimene, or Cannae.

Perseus was a good soldier but no general. In time of peace he might have been a good king, though he lacked the energy and decisiveness of his father. His 43,000 men were twice as many as Hannibal had when he rocked Rome to its foundations. Moreover, Perseus had in his treasury the equivalent of almost 12,000,000 gold dollars (after his defeat he still had about $7,000,000 left which fell into the hands of the Romans). He could have hired twenty or thirty thousand Celts, had he been willing to spend money. He might even have bought the support of Eumenes II, not to mention that of the Greeks. His excessive caution prevented him from taking these opportunities.

Lucius Aemilius Paullus and the Battle of Pydna: 168 B.C.

Lucius Aemilius Paullus belonged to the Scipionic circle and had a sincere appreciation of Greek art and culture. He had been consul in 182 B.C. and accepted the second consulship only on condition that his conduct of the war not be hampered by unsolicited and unwanted advice.

The battle of Pydna was a repetition of Cynoscephalae. The Macedonian phalanx, charging forward in solid mass on level ground, pushed the Roman legions back but, carried forward by its own momentum, jerked itself apart on the higher and rougher ground. Into the gaps thus opened and around its flanks, the Romans penetrated and cut the disordered Macedonians down. This battle once more demonstrated, as did those at the Allia, at the Caudine Forks, at Heraclea, at Cynoscephalae, and at Magnesia, that the phalanx, supreme in the days of Epaminondas and Philip II, was now a thoroughly obsolete battle formation.

Perseus, a most pathetic figure, was brought to Rome as a prisoner and was forced to walk, clad in black, in the triumphal victory parade of Aemilius Paullus. He was afterwards interned for life and died, still captive, around 165 B.C.

Macedonia after Pydna. In Macedonia the Romans decided to try an experiment apparently modeled after the Greek leagues. They abolished the monarchy and replaced it by four independent republics, separate, disarmed, and deprived of the rights of alliance, intermarriage, or trade with each other. The Romans also made the royal mines and domains the property of the Roman state, closed the royal gold and silver mines for ten years, forbade the export of timber, and exacted an annual tribute of 100 talents, which was half the amount of the land tax formerly paid to the kings.

The Macedonians were far less concerned about having their form of government changed than about the unity of their country. They had never regarded their monarchy as an oppressive evil but as the symbol of their national unity. Macedonia more nearly resembled a nation than any other state in the ancient world. It was not a land of city states like Greece or Italy, it was not a loose confederation of cities like the Achaean League, nor was it a universal state held together solely by the monarchy like the

empire of the Seleucids. It was one people in race, language, religion, customs, and government. The Roman experiment violated the very nature and traditions of the Macedonian state.

It is little wonder, then, that within two decades the Roman experiment failed. Andriscus, an upstart pretender, probably the son of a clothmaker, was able to convince the people that he was the son of Perseus and they rallied around him. He restored the monarchy in 149 B.C., reunited the kingdom, and even overcame a small Roman army sent against him. After defeating him with a larger army, the Romans converted Macedonia into a province in 148 B.C. thereby ending the political existence of Macedonia for all time.

Greece after Pydna. The Roman treatment of Macedonia was mild compared with the punishment inflicted upon Greece. In Aetolia, the Romans lent troops to their contemptible henchmen to carry out a purge of Macedonian sympathizers, probably the most intelligent and democratic elements of the population. In Achaea, they deported to Italy one thousand of the leading citizens, including the historian Polybius, whose names they found among the papers that Perseus had neglected to destroy. For sixteen years the Achaean hostages were kept interned without a trial or hearing and were not released until after seven hundred of them had died. The most horrible and revolting brutality was inflicted upon Epirus, where seventy towns were destroyed and 150,000 people were dragged off to the slave market.

The worst was yet to come. In 146 B.C. Lucius Mummius arrived in Corinth. To punish this city and the Achaean League for rebellion against Rome, he turned his troops loose upon it, sacked it, and razed it to the ground. He massacred many of its inhabitants, sold many more as slaves, and shipped its priceless art treasures to Rome.

After the destruction of Corinth, the Romans in 146 B.C. dissolved the Achaean and most of the other leagues, breaking the last desperate but hopeless attempts of the Greek people to win back their freedom and independence. They destroyed the militant democracies and set up petty tyrants or aristocratic oligarchies in their place. Each city state now had separate relations with Rome, but the governor of Macedonia was empowered to intervene, to settle disputes, and preserve public order. A century later, Augustus made Greece a separate province.

Rhodes and Pergamum after Pydna. The hand of Rome fell heavily also upon Rhodes, the proud and wealthy republic, which for a century had kept the eastern seas free of pirates. Rhodes had appealed to Rome for help against Philip V and had later given Rome valuable naval assistance in the war against Antiochus III. This faithful friend at last made one mistake. Just before Pydna she tried to mediate between Rome and Perseus not so much because of sympathy towards Perseus as fear that Rome might become the unbalanced power in the eastern Mediterranean. Rome took offense at this attempted mediation. A praetor even proposed a declaration of war and war it might have been had not old Cato stood up and made a strong plea in defense of the Rhodians.

Although Rhodes humbly repented of her mistakes, dragged the pro-Macedonian leaders to the scaffold, sent Rome a massive golden wreath in thanksgiving for deliverance from war, and begged for an alliance, she did not escape Roman vengeance. She was stripped of the territories in Asia Minor given her after Magnesia (an annual loss of 130,000 gold dollars) and prohibited from importing shipbuilding timber from Macedonia. Delos was given to Athens in 167/6 B.C. and made a customs free port. The artificial competition of Delos reduced the income of Rhodes as a banking, shipping, and commercial center from 200,000 to around 30,000 gold dollars annually. The loss of revenue from her Asiatic possessions and from harbor dues and banking so crippled the finances of Rhodes that she was compelled to reduce her navy and was no longer able to keep piracy in check in the eastern seas.

Eumenes II, king of Pergamum, who had done so much to betray the Hellenistic world into the ruthless hand of the Romans, incurred the senate's displeasure because of suspected collusion with Perseus. He was punished by confiscation of territory and hounded by hostile Roman commissions sent to Asia Minor to gather evidence against him. Thus did Rome reward her most devoted and servile ally in the Middle East.

Aside from his misguided collaboration with the Romans, Eumenes had done many good things during his long reign both for his own city and for the Greek cities in Asia and Europe. He beautified Pergamum with many magnificent buildings and temples all adorned with the most splendid sculptures. He built one of the finest libraries in the Hellenistic world and by the patronage and encouragement he gave to scholars, poets, and artists, made Pergamum the Athens of Asia. He gave money and grain to a number of Greek cities, among them Miletus, Athens, Cyzicus, and Delphi, and erected temples and theaters for them. His gifts and donations were more numerous and magnificent than those of any other contemporary monarch.

The last years of Eumenes' reign were filled with remorse, anxieties, and troubles. Living under a cloud of Roman suspicion and hostility, he had the intelligence to realize at last the disastrous results of Roman intervention in the East which he had labored to bring about and saw with increasing anxiety the decline of Hellenism in the Seleucid Empire after Magnesia. Everywhere throughout that empire the small islands of Hellenism were being engulfed by the mounting tide of Orientalism, which was spilling over into Armenia, into Asia Minor, and even into the domains of Pergamum itself. In the vain attempt of stemming that tide Eumenes devoted himself to building up a Greek united front and to promoting a crusade of Greek solidarity, which might be called a form of Greek cultural imperialism. As the leader of this movement, he cultivated close relations with all Greek rulers and was instrumental in placing Antiochus IV on the throne of the Seleucids.

When Eumenes died in 159 B.C., he was succeeded by his brother, Attalus II, who followed Eumenes' policy of friendship and subservience to Rome and of philanthropy towards the Greek city states. He continued also to promote Pergamum as a cultural and intellectual capital and maintained the Greek cultural offensive against the Oriental menace. He was followed in 138 B.C. by Attalus III, whose parentage is uncertain. Like Louis XVI of France, he preferred his studies and hobbies to being a king. He did serious research on botany, zoology, medicine, scientific agriculture, and gardening. Having no direct heirs, he bequeathed his kingdom to the Roman people thereby closing with his early death in 133 B.C. the history of Pergamum as a separate state.

The Seleucid Monarchy

After Magnesia in 190 B.C., the defeated empire of the Seleucids had rapidly disintegrated. Everywhere the Oriental peoples were on the march—the Arabs, the Jews, the Iranians, the Parthians, and the Hindus. Even the Greek colonies of the East were becoming increasingly Oriental in spirit, religion, and government. The blow Rome struck at Magnesia against the stability of the Seleucid Empire served to accelerate the inevitable process of Orientalism. This blow was all the more damaging to Hellenism because of the very nature and character of the Seleucid monarchy itself.

The Seleucid Empire was not a national state like Macedonia nor a city state like Athens or Rome. It was rather a universal state consisting of many races, languages, and even forms of government. All were more or less loosely held together by the military prestige, personality, royalty, and divinity of the Seleucids, the heirs of Alexander the Great and of the Persian kings. The power of the king and his claim to royalty and even to divinity rested ultimately upon military victory, a sign both of royal virtue and divine favor. Defeat in war signified the loss of royal virtue and divine power, and tended to destroy the claim of the Seleucid monarchy to the loyalty and allegiance of the various regional rulers, provincial governors, satraps, and native kings. Thus the defeat of Antiochus III at Magnesia dealt a shattering blow to the unity and stability of the Seleucid Empire.

Most of Asia Minor had gone to Pergamum and Rhodes. Armenia broke away. The Parthians seized large areas of Iran. Further to the east, the huge kingdom of Bactria broke away, having snatched the eastern portions of Iran. Two decades or so later a new Jewish state sprang up in Judea. New Arab kingdoms arose in southern Palestine, Transjordan, and southern Syria.

The Age of Antiochus IV: 175-164 B.C.

Antiochus IV, a younger son of Antiochus III, had been a hostage at Rome for several years and lived in Athens for a long time. His foreign experiences convinced him of the need to modernize the Seleucid army and that Syria must not again attempt to cross swords with Rome. His stay in Athens had developed in him an enthusiastic admiration for Greek culture and his long friendship with Eumenes II made him a strong advocate of Greek cultural supremacy in the Middle East. As the legitimate heir of Seleucus I and of Alexander, Antiochus IV commanded the allegiance and religious devotion of his subjects (his royal title *"Epiphanes"* meant "the god manifest on earth"). In 170 B.C., his cousin, Eucratides, set forth with a well-equipped army trained to fight in the manner of the Roman legions, recovered the lost Iranian provinces and conquered Bactria and a large part of India. Antiochus' ambition to revive the dying world of Hellenism was shattered by an unwanted war with Egypt.

At this time the two sons of Ptolemy V, nephews of Antiochus, were not yet of age and Egypt was governed by two worthless and unprincipled regents, the one, a eunuch of the royal harem, the other, a Syrian slave accountant. To divert attention from their maladministration and a serious financial crisis, the regents made war on Antiochus IV, who defeated and killed them in battle. Early in the fall of 170 B.C. Antiochus invaded Egypt and at Memphis signed a treaty of peace and friendship with his nephew, Ptolemy VI Philometor, the king of Egypt. Infuriated by the high-handed interference of Antiochus in Egyptian internal affairs, the Alexandrian mob revolted against Philometor and declared allegiance to his younger brother, Ptolemy VIII, commonly called Ptolemy Physcon ("Potbelly").

After Antiochus had withdrawn his troops

from Egypt, the two young kings made a pact with each other and planned a joint invasion of Syria. Infuriated at this development, Antiochus again invaded Egypt in 168 B.C. and was just about to make an assault upon Alexandria when there arrived from Rome Gaius Popilius Laenas, who sternly handed him a decree of the senate commanding him to stop the war. When Antiochus replied that he would have to consult his generals, Popilius took a stick and drew a circle in the sand around the king and ordered him to make up his mind before stepping out of the circle. Antiochus IV gave in and then, so the story goes, embraced Popilius as an old friend.

Though his death in 164 B.C. prevented Antiochus from realizing his dreams of conquest, nevertheless, his achievements were remarkable. The Greek cultural offensive, though possibly planned by Eumenes II, was actually carried out by Antiochus. He had done much to Hellenize his empire by promoting Greek cultural life, the worship of Greek gods, and the adoption of Greek customs and styles of dress. Richer than any Seleucid before him, he used his vast wealth to found new Greek cities and Hellenize many old ones, of which Babylon with its Greek theater, gymnasium, and city government was the best example. To inhabit the newly founded cities and strengthen the Greek element in the provinces, he brought many settlers from Greece, particularly from Athens.

The religious overtones of Hellenization brought Antiochus into conflict with the Jews, though he desired not so much to stamp out the worship of Jahweh or Jehovah as to create a strongly Hellenized Jewish city state as a buffer between Egypt and Syria. When Jason, a Jewish aristocrat, suggested to him in 175 B.C. the idea of assisting the Hellenized Jews to establish a Greek city state in Jerusalem, the king readily agreed.

As chief priest of the temple of Jahweh and the spiritual leader of Judaism, Jason endeavored to Hellenize Jewish life and to create a separate Jewish community under the political constitution of a Greek city state. This program aroused some discontent among the Jews, but no open revolt occurred until Antiochus decided to devote the temple of Jahweh to the worship of Baal Shamin

("Lord of the Heavens"), a universal deity, whom the Greeks identified with Olympian Zeus and the Hellenized Jews with Jahweh. Simultaneously, he revoked the decree of his father, Antiochus III, which had permitted the Jews to live and worship according to the law of Moses.

A priestly landowner named Judas Maccabaeus aroused the Jews to rebellion, gathered together an army, and inflicted a series of defeats upon the king's troops. Antiochus IV, preoccupied with his eastern campaigns, agreed, in 164 B.C., to restore the worship of Jahweh to the Jews. Not reconciled, Judas occupied the temple by force in the same year and purified it by the removal of statues, shrubbery, and every other kind of Greek ornamentation. Aided by the death of Antiochus IV (late in 164 B.C.) in Armenia and the subsequent disruption of the Seleucid empire the Maccabees rooted out every last vestige of Hellenism in Jerusalem and restored the ancient temple state. In 161 B.C., as the result of a treaty with Rome, the Jewish temple state gained recognition as an ally and in 129 B.C. became completely independent.

The Results of Roman Imperialism in the East

One of the motives of Roman intervention in the East was the fear that the combined Hellenistic powers might become strong enough to threaten the political existence of Rome. However dominant, that fear was probably groundless because neither Philip V nor Antiochus III ever had any serious intention of invading Italy since their political interests were confined to the East. Nor would they have worked together because each feared that the other might attempt to restore the universal empire of Alexander the Great.

If fear had been the dominant motive of the Romans before Cynoscephalae and Magnesia, that fear was surely dispelled after the defeats of Macedonia and Syria. Their later subjugation of the Hellenistic states was not a policy of self-defense but of imperialism. Some modern writers have argued that Rome was not imperialistic because she never annexed, until later, a single foot of ground in Asia or the Balkans but this argument implies that the annexation of territory constitutes imperialism. Recent history has proved that imperialism can be economic and political as well as military and territorial. In the modern sense of the word, the Roman policy after the battle of Magnesia, if not before, was definitely imperialistic.

Rome ruined the Hellenistic states economically, disintegrated them politically, and greatly accelerated the social and cultural destruction of Hellenism in the Middle East. Rome's victory also probably hastened the social, political, and cultural deterioration of the Greek and Oriental masses.

While Rome was waging war in the East, she was able at the same time to recover the territories she had lost in North Italy during Hannibal's invasion. She subdued and colonized these territories between 197 and 175 B.C., occupied and colonized Milan in 196 B.C., and in 190 reinforced the two early colonies of Placentia (Piacenza) and Cremona, both vital strongholds during the Second Punic War, with a total of 6,000 Roman and Latin settlers. The following year saw a Latin colony of 3,000 settlers established at Bologna and in 183 B.C. Parma and Modena each received 2,000 Roman colonists. Small market towns and administrative centers rapidly sprang up as the country became settled by the many individual farmers who were encouraged to move North and take up land.

After the conquest and settlement of the central region of North Italy, the Romans turned to the coastal areas. In 181 B.C. they founded a Latin colony at Aquileia, at the head of the Adriatic, which served as a springboard for the later conquest of Istria and the Dalmatian coast. During the late Republic and early Empire, Aquileia was one of the busiest shipping and commercial harbors of Italy.

On the west coast or the Italian Riviera, the conquest of the hardy but culturally backward Ligurian tribes was a long and difficult operation attended by several Roman defeats, some victories, and some atrocities. Throughout the early part of the second century B.C. the Ligurian country had been a happy hunting ground for Roman generals looking for triumphs, to obtain which they would sometimes make war upon friendly and inoffensive tribes. The two notorious slave catchers, Marcus Popilius Laenas and his brother Gaius (p. 162), had a peculiar weakness for such wars.

By 172, after a series of campaigns, the Romans had brought both the Italian and the French Riviera under their control as far as the borders of Marseille. They had founded colonies at Pisa in 181, perhaps at Luca in 178, and at Luna (now the Italian naval base of La Spezia) in 177 B.C. While these Roman and Latin colonies were being planted along the Ligurian coast in the North, 40,000 Ligurians were moved south and settled on vacant public land near Beneventum in central Samnium.

The building of roads was equally important for the occupation and settlement of the North. A very active road builder as well as colonizer was Gaius Flaminius, the consul of 187 B.C. Following in the footsteps of his famous father, who was killed at Trasimene, he built the New Flaminian Way from Arezzo to Bologna. Not to be outdone, his consular colleague, Aemilius Lepidus, built the famous Aemilian Way, which ran from Ariminum (Rimini), the terminus of the Old Flaminian Way, through Bologna as far as Placentia (Piacenza).

Several years later (171 B.C.), the Cassian Way was built from Rome to Arretium (Arezzo) where it joined the New Flaminian Way, thus providing a strategic throughway to North Italy as far as Aquileia. About two decades later, another important road, the Postumian Way, was constructed across North Italy connecting the cities of Genoa, Piacenza, Cremona, and Verona. Many secondary roads were built and, in a short time, North Italy had become an integral part of peninsular Italy. The wars ceased and the use of the Latin language spread. Rome was rapidly becoming the capital of a united Italy.

The Subjugation of Spain

When the Romans had driven the Carthaginians from Spain in the Second Punic War, they decided to hold on to that country in order to prevent any other state from using it as a base for another attack on Italy. They were also influenced by tales of its fabulous mineral wealth and the remarkable fertility of its soil. They hoped to extract enough wealth from Spain to pay for the costs of its occupation and recoup the staggering losses they had suffered from the Second Punic War and, perhaps to finance future wars as well.

The Romans encountered unexpected difficulties. There were in Spain no large self-governing states or kingdoms, which could be held responsible for the collection of tribute or the maintenance of law and order. The Romans were therefore compelled to undertake this duty themselves. Large areas in the interior and in the western part of the peninsula had never been subdued by the Carthaginians or even explored. The tribes living in these backward areas had long been in the habit of raiding the richer and more civilized parts of Spain formerly controlled by the Carthaginians and now by the Romans. To protect their recent gains the Romans were obliged to make further conquests.

But Spain was cut up by its mountains into thousands of small communities and as many separate clans. Communications between them were difficult and access to them all was practically impossible. The Romans could not conquer them in a few pitched battles as they had Macedonia or Asia Minor because the Spaniards formed small armed bands skilled in making sudden raids and vanishing as rapidly as they came. (It was probably from them that Hannibal had learned the tactics of ambush and lightning attack.) The Romans were completely baffled by the guerilla warfare, which the Spaniards loved to wage. War raged almost continuously until 133 B.C. and even then, Spain was not fully subdued until the time of Augustus.

Hither and Farther Spain

For purposes of administration and defense, the senate decided in 197 B.C. to divide Roman Spain into two separate provinces known as Hither and Farther Spain, each to be governed normally by a praetor but, in time of war and crisis, by a magistrate of consular power. The Mediterranean seaboard from the Pyrenees to a point slightly south of Cartagena comprised Hither Spain, rich in silver mines but agriculturally somewhat poor. Farther Spain, roughly coextensive with Andalusia, embraced the fertile Guadalquivir valley as far north as the silver mining region of the Sierra Morena range. Neither province extended very far into the interior and both were quite well known, having been visited from the Late Bronze Age onwards by Phoenician, Greek, and Etruscan traders and sailors.

The costs of provincial administration and defense were defrayed by revenue derived from tribute and regular taxes. The tribute (*stipendium*) was imposed on all tribes, semi-urban communities, and a few municipalities such as Malaga and Cadiz. It was not collected by tax farmers as in other provinces but by government agents (prefects). It consisted sometimes of farm products such as wheat or barley but more often of payments in silver or gold, partly in bullion and partly in coined money. Up till the year 195 B.C., the amount of the tribute varied from year to year according to the needs of the provincial government and the rapacity of the governor. As a rule, it was too high for primitive rural communities and often provoked unrest and rebellion. The regular tax, on the other hand, was fairly low, being only a twentieth of farm crops, payable in kind. In addition to tribute and taxes, all communities were required to furnish troops to the Roman army.

The year, in which the two provinces were created, war broke out in both because of the extortions and tyrannies of the Roman praetors, as the Romans, who had been welcomed as deliverers, proved more faithless and cruel than the Carthaginians had ever been. Even Cadiz and Malaga, finding themselves denied the promised status of allies, supported the inland tribes in the fight for independence.

Cato's Governorship of Hither Spain. In 195 B.C. Cato, the consul, arrived in northeastern Spain with an army of 50,000 men. Though he was successful in stamping out the rebellion in his own province and even subdued the region as far west as the headwaters of the Tagus, his military achievements were not as outstanding or as permanent as his economic and administrative reforms (which applied to both provinces since he was the senior magistrate). He did not reduce the tribute but fixed it once and for all for each administrative district so that the people would know long in advance what they would have to pay.

More important, he reopened the mines which had been shut since the Carthaginian defeat and placed most of them under public ownership, operation, and control, thus providing new income for the provincial administrations and employment for the poorer people living in Cartagena and other mining districts. Many of the regulations he then put into effect were probably embodied later in the laws promulgated by the emperors Vespasian and Hadrian. According to two famous imperial inscriptions, each mining district was made a self-contained economic community, in which concessions were leased to the highest bidder for the exclusive right to sell certain products and to operate bathhouses, barber shops, pressing and cleaning establishments, and shops for the making and repair of shoes. These regulations, adapted no doubt from Carthaginian models and Hellenistic practice, are of historic importance. Analogies are still to be found in West Virginia and in other mining regions of the United States.

Tiberius Sempronius Gracchus: 180-178 B.C. Tiberius Gracchus, son-in-law of Scipio Africanus and the father of Tiberius and Gaius Gracchus, was another governor whose fame rests not on military achievements but on his reforms, fairness, and sympathy. To remove the causes of unrest, he founded many new towns and villages and gave the peasants and workers in Hither Spain good land for settlement. The faith and confidence he inspired among the people kept them contented and peaceful for twenty-five years.

The peace and order which Tiberius Gracchus had established in Spain were destroyed by the brutalities of the later governors. The senate refused to punish their crimes, in spite of bitter denunciations by Cato and the repeated appeals of the Spanish people.

In Hither Spain war broke out reportedly because the senate, swayed by the selfish interests of the large landowners in the province, suddenly decided to deprive the small farmers of the land granted to them by Tiberius Gracchus. The renewed slave-hunting activities of the Romans also helped to goad the people into acts of desperation. Marcus Claudius Marcellus might have been able in 152 B.C. to restore peace in the province had the just peace terms he had arranged with the Spanish people been ratified, but the corrupt senate majority rejected the terms. The war continued for another twenty-five years and the resentment of the Spanish people until after the time of Augustus.

The successor of Marcellus, L. Licinius Lucullus, savagely attacked a peaceful, inoffensive tribe, captured a town by treachery, and marched west into Further Spain to assist his colleague, Sulpicius Galba, in the butchery of 7,000 Portuguese soldiers, whom he had persuaded by false promises to lay down their arms. For this act of treachery and cold-blooded murder Galba was brought to trial in Rome, but he escaped punishment by a clever use of money extorted from the Spanish people and by the tears of his little children. The eighty-five-year-old Cato was one of the chief prosecutors of this despicable culprit.

Viriathus

Fortunately, one of those who escaped from Galba's murderous hand was Viriathus, whose name, even after two thousand years remains synonymous with freedom. Viriathus was a shepherd and a hunter who knew the mountains, glens, and winding paths through which he led 10,000 soldiers rescued from Galba's murderous clutches. For eight years he and his followers held the Romans at bay cutting down one army after another. Again and again he would attack and then fade away into the darkness by paths the Romans could never follow.

In 141 B.C., Viriathus had entrapped a Roman army of 50,000 men whom he spared in return for a treaty respecting the freedom and independence of his people. He could not know to what depths of infamy the senate majority had sunk: the treaty was ratified and, the next year, broken. The Romans bribed two traitors to slit the throat of the sleeping Viriathus, and the Portuguese, left without a leader, submitted to the enslaving power of Rome. In 138 B.C. the consul Junius Brutus brought an army and a fleet against the leaderless Portuguese and within two years had completely subjugated them. Lisbon, at the mouth of the Tagus was made a fortified stronghold. A large part of the population was transported to form a Latin colony at Valencia, where they could not easily resist Roman authority.

The Siege of Numantia. The war in Hither Spain raged around the fortress town of Numantia. Even for its small garrison of about 4,000 men Numantia was easy to defend because of its situation on a hill at the junction of two rivers, which flowed between deeply cut banks through thickly wooded valleys.

During the siege of Numantia, the Roman commander Mancinus saw his army of 20,000 caught in an ambush by 4,000 Spaniards and forced to sign a treaty, which the youthful Tiberius Gracchus had persuaded the Numantines to accept. This treaty of 137 B.C., which saved a large Roman army from utter destruction, was later shamelessly broken.

After several such defeats, the Romans in 134 B.C. sent to Spain the best general of his time, Scipio Aemilianus, who reformed and retrained the demoralized Roman army, drove away the plunder buyers, bootleggers, and prostitutes, and built around Numantia a double ring wall five miles long set with towers and guarded by seven camps. He then proceeded to starve Numantia into unconditional surrender.

After a siege of eight months, one hundred starved survivors staggered forth, half naked, filthy, haggard, sick, and too broken even for use as slaves. Scipio set the town on fire and the flames mounting to the skies were witnessed by many famous men: by the historian Polybius, by Gaius Gracchus, the brother of Tiberius, by Gaius Marius, the later illustrious Roman general, by Jugurtha, the Numidian prince, with whom Rome later waged war, by the poet Lucilius, and by two future historians of the Spanish wars, Asellio and Rutilius Rufus.

Thus ended the Spanish wars until the first century B.C., when once more the banners of revolt would fly.

The Destruction of Carthage: 146 B.C.

Even after Zama, Carthage had continued to prosper. She was still a busy shipping and industrial center and controlled all the trade between Africa and the Hellenistic world. Now that peace and order prevailed in North Africa, she enjoyed a better market for her industrial products than ever before. The crops grown on her farms and plantations were the envy of the world. Her commercial and diplomatic relations with Rome had steadily improved. In an effort to please and cooperate with the Romans, the Carthaginians had scrupulously observed all their treaty obligations. They had disavowed Hannibal, and had supplied grain for the Roman armies on numerous occasions. They had helped Rome wage war against Philip V, Antiochus III, and Perseus by furnishing both military and naval assistance. Perhaps they would have remained on good terms had it not been for the ambitions and aggression of Massinissa.

Massinissa

Massinissa, who had fought with Scipio in the battle of Zama, appeared at first to be nothing but an unscrupulous killer. Later he proved to be a strong and imaginative ruler who established peace and order and welded the large kingdom of Numidia into a well-governed and centralized state.

He lifted his people up from banditry and nomadism into a settled life of agriculture, and promoted trade throughout the formerly backward interior. He encouraged the growth of municipal self-government in scores of inland towns; and did more during his half century of kingship to encourage the spread of Punic and Hellenistic civilization than the Carthaginians had done in all preceding centuries. Had he realized his ambition of incorporating Carthage into his kingdom, he might well have been able to defy the might of Rome and change the course of Mediterranean history. He failed to achieve that goal because Carthage resisted annexation and Rome stepped in to prevent it.

Massinissa is remembered chiefly for his aggressions against Carthage. The treaty between Rome and Carthage after Zama left Carthage in possession of many ports and trading posts along the African coast but confined her to the northern half of Tunisia within frontiers known as the Phoenician Bounds, which enclosed an area of about 30,000 square miles. Massinissa, on the other hand, was permitted to occupy any land which either he or his ancestors had previously held. Another clause forbade Carthage to wage even defensive war without the consent of Rome. Massinissa took full advantage of both clauses of the treaty.

Massinissa had seized one by one most of the Carthaginian coastal colonies from Morocco to the western frontiers of the Cyrenaica. Around 160 B.C. he took the area near Tripoli, a territory that was prized for its grain fields and olive plantations and contained three important coastal towns, one of which is said to have contributed a fabulous revenue to Carthage. He also stepped within the Phoenician Bounds time after time and appropriated large sections of territory. Not permitted to resist these aggressions by armed force, Carthage appealed to Rome who sent commissions to arbitrate. These sometimes decided in favor of Massinissa and sometimes left the dispute unsettled fearing, no doubt, to upset the balance of power between the king and the Republic of Carthage.

Around 154 B.C., Massinissa seized the Great Plains in the upper valley of the Bagradas or Medjerda river, the best wheat-growing land Carthage had left and a region of large estates. By this time, Massinissa had whittled Carthage down to about 5,000 square miles or one-sixth of her former area. In answer to an urgent Carthaginian appeal, the Romans sent a boundary commission headed by Cato. The commission left the matter undecided but, before returning to Rome, made an inspection tour in and around Carthage.

The proud city, overflowing with wealth and luxury, teeming with fighting men, filled with arms and military supplies, and its busy shipyards piled high with shipbuilding materials, stirred in Cato an unreasonable hatred. On his return, he demanded an immediate declaration of war, and thereafter ended all his speeches, regardless of the subject, with the hysterical refrain: *Carthago est delenda* ("Carthage must be destroyed!").

Cato's Foreign Policy

Cato's blind rage against Carthage defies explanation. He was an experienced and widely traveled man, having been a soldier, a general, and the governor of two provinces. For fifty years he had taken part in most of the senate debates on foreign affairs and his ideas were listened to with much respect.

He had been neither a warmonger nor an imperialist. He favored military intervention in the East only when Roman security seemed directly menaced. Though he feared a powerful Macedonia as a threat to Italy's eastern flank, he opposed making Macedonia a province. He was especially opposed to meddling in Greece. He made a strong and effective speech against the resolution calling for war on Rhodes. In it he condemned wars for aggressive and imperialistic purposes. His demand for the destruction of Carthage seems strangely inconsistent with his earlier foreign policy.

There is no proof for the theory that his motives were economic. The ripe fig he is reported to have held up before the senate and picked near Carthage just two days before, was not meant to symbolize the thriving agriculture of Carthage, but her dangerous proximity to Rome.

Cato is usually thought of as a farmer because he wrote a famous manual on agriculture but he made most of his money from investments, from lending, and from his partnership in shipping firms and companies engaged in foreign trade. (He used a dummy to get around the Claudian Law of 218 B.C. which forbade senators from engaging in foreign trade.) He may have considered Carthage a competitor in his more profitable enterprises.

Did he really believe that Carthage could again be a serious menace to a power that had struck down Macedonia and Syria or did he fear that on the death of Massinissa, now approaching his ninetieth year, Numidia would fall apart and that Carthage would then be able to destroy the balance of power in Africa? To these questions there is no certain answer.

The Third Punic War: 151–146 B.C.

In Carthage, democratic leaders, exasperated by the aggressions of Massinissa and the indifference of Rome, had seized power in 151 B.C. They exiled the adherents of Massinissa and attacked his sons who had been sent to demand the restoration of the exiles. In 150 B.C. war broke out between Carthage and Massinissa with disastrous results to the poorly trained and badly led Carthaginian army. Worse still, in waging war against Massinissa, the Carthaginians had violated the treaty of Zama and gave Rome a convenient excuse for declaring war on Carthage.

Hearing that the Romans were preparing to send an army to Africa, the Carthaginians made haste to undo the mischief they had done. They returned their oligarchs to power, executed the popular leaders, and sent ambassadors to Rome to request peace terms. The ambassadors were told that Carthage would be permitted to retain her territory and independence provided that she surrendered three hundred noble hostages and carried out all future orders of the consuls. The consuls demanded the surrender of all arms and weapons. After receiving the surrender of the war engines and military equipment, the consuls grimly announced the senate's secret final terms: the Carthaginians must abandon and destroy their city and rebuild at least ten miles from the sea—a death sentence for people who made their living by commerce.

The Siege of Carthage

Beside themselves with fear and rage, the Carthaginians prepared to defend their beloved city. Supplies of food were hurriedly gathered from the surrounding countryside and brought into the city where the people were toiling day and night to make new weapons. Prisons were opened, slaves freed,

and even the temples were turned into factories as the Carthaginians frantically prepared for siege. Two Hasdrubals were named commanders; one, a recent exile now welcomed back, the other, a grandson of old Massinissa.

The siege lasted three years. Carthage was situated in an excellent defensive location and its walls were enormously thick and strong. The Romans received no help from old Massinissa, hostile at this usurpation of the fruits of a lifetime of ambition and intrigue. The badly disciplined Roman armies were led by incompetent commanders. One young lieutenant distinguished himself. He was Publius Cornelius Scipio Aemilianus, the son of Aemilius Paullus and the adopted grandson of Scipio Africanus.*

So impressive were his exploits that when he returned to Rome in 147 B.C. to stand for election as curule aedile (he was only about thirty and ineligible for any higher office), a special law was passed clearing the way to his election as consul and placing him in command of the besieging army.

The young consul finally took Carthage by storm in the spring of 146 B.C. For six days and nights the struggle raged inside the city from street to street, from house to house until the beautiful old city was a sea of flames. The last to fall was the citadel, from which emerged 50,000 people. All were sold as slaves, and Carthage became the province of Africa Proconsularis. On the site of Punic Carthage a new Roman Carthage rose in 28 B.C.†

* He had also served Rome well when he was asked in 148 B.C. by the dying Massinissa to arrange the future of Numidia. Scipio divided Numidia among the old king's three sons thereby averting the menace of a strong, united kingdom to the future security of Rome.

† The common belief that the city was leveled to the ground and a plow run over it is based on the exaggerated account of the late writer Orosius (Fifth Century A.D.). Actually, the ruins remained for centuries afterward. In fact, Plutarch tells us that Marius once sat among them. And they remained on an immense scale. For centuries the old walls, temples, and other buildings were a quarry of ready dressed stone. Far more thorough agents of demolition than Scipio's soldiers were the builders of Roman Carthage and the insatiable stone hunters of later centuries.

VIII

THE AGE OF THE

ROME HAD ESTABLISHED BY WAR AND CONQUEST HER DOMINION over the Mediterranean world. The political and economic unification begun by Alexander the Great and continued by the Hellenistic monarchies was complete. In less than a century and a half, she had passed from city state to empire. Zama, Cynoscephalae, Magnesia, and Pydna mark the triumph of Rome's armies in three continents. She had reduced the most powerful kingdoms to vassalage and subservience. Vast streams of gold, silver, slaves, and other tribute flowed into her hands. Before her nations trembled. Such a phenomenon of world conquest and expansion had begun, even before the age of the Gracchi, to create revolutionary effects upon the economic, social, political, and moral life of the Roman people. The most spectacular transformation occurred in agriculture.

GRACCHI

Agriculture

In the early centuries of the Republic, agriculture was not only the principal occupation of the Roman people, it was also a way of life. To its influence Cato the Censor attributed all the moral virtues of the early Romans. The early consuls and dictators, Cincinnatus and Manius Curius, whose example Cato loved to imitate, worked with their hands as did the other farmers of their time.

With the help of his sons and perhaps a slave or two, the farmer was able to produce all the food his family required as well as most of their clothing, shoes, and other necessities. The occasional sale of a few bushels of grain or a couple of pigs would enable him to buy what he could not produce on the farm.

By the middle of the second century B.C. farm life in Italy had undergone a radical change. This change had been hastened by Hannibal's invasion. For fourteen years Punic and Roman armies marched up and down the peninsula, living off the land, seizing or destroying crops, killing livestock, and burning down thousands of homes and farm

Posta di Colle. *Part of a farm recently excavated in Italy, with a range of rooms and an enclosure ditch in the foreground. (Courtesy J. S. Bradford, Oxford, England)*

buildings. Malaria had become endemic in the swampy districts.

The human losses were terrific. The 290,000 Roman citizens listed before the First Punic War had declined to 137,108 by the year 209 B.C. and to 143,704 in 194. This decline reflected not only battle losses but the large number of men serving in the armies abroad, the majority of whom had come from the farms. Many of the farmer-soldiers would never return. The security of army life, the sight of strange and exciting places were more pleasant for some than the dull farm routine. Others returned to find homes ruined and fields overrun with briars and weeds. Not a few farms had been seized for debt or by some greedy neighbor. Returned soldiers lucky enough to find houses and fields intact could not raise money to buy the necessary oxen, tools, and seed. Many, discouraged, drifted into Rome hoping to find employment. Others went back into the army or returned to the provinces where looting and trading paid better than farming.

The decline of the farm population is again revealed by the census lists of the second century. In 164 and 136 B.C. the number of Roman citizens were respectively 337,452

and 317,933, a loss of almost 20,000 or 8 per cent at a time when the population of Rome itself was growing by leaps and bounds.

Despite the enormous property and man-power losses, the family size farm of ancient Italy could have been restored within a few decades (the ravages of ancient wars were superficial and not permanently ruinous to fertile regions), had not the Roman conquest of the Mediterranean basin generated new economic forces that proved destructive of the primitive agricultural regime in all but the most backward and mountainous sections of Italy. The flow of capital and cheap slave labor from the conquered provinces, especially those of the Hellenistic East, brought about the ruin of the small Italian farmer and the rise of the cattle ranch and the plantation. The cattle ranch predominated in southern Italy, in Etruria, and in some parts of Latium; the plantation in other parts of Latium and especially in Campania.

The Plantation

The word "plantation," in its standard and classical sense, meant a capitalistic type of agricultural organization, in which money capital of large amount was invested in land, labor, and equipment for the purpose of achieving, under unified management and control, the specialized production of certain single or staple crops for sale in local or foreign markets. In the Southern United States before the Civil War, the staples were sugar, rice, cotton, and tobacco; in Cuba, sugar and tobacco; in Brazil, coffee and cotton; in Roman Italy, wine and olive oil.

Wherever the plantation developed, it depended upon five main elements: abundant capital and land, cheap labor, special equipment, efficient organization and management, and expanding markets.

The Roman conquests with the wholesale plundering of the provinces started an unprecedented flow of capital to Rome. Enormous commercial expansion followed, and additional wealth poured into the Roman treasury from war indemnities, provincial taxation, the sale of slaves, and the exploitation of lands, seized and declared public, mines, quarries, forests, and fisheries. Enormous sums also filled the pockets of private individuals. Generals and military governors made money from the sale of army promotions, exemptions, and furloughs, sometimes from the embezzlement of military funds, but more often from the extortion of money from cities and private persons unfortunate enough to fall under their power.

Even bigger fortunes were made by the knights (*equites*) or equestrians who received government contracts for supplying equipment to the army, for the construction of roads, bridges, harbors, and temples, for the collection of provincial taxes and rents, and for the exploitation of lands, pastures, mines, forests, and other natural resources seized and owned by the state in Italy and the provinces. Operating sometimes singly, but more often in partnerships, syndicates, or joint stock companies, the knights set up banking monopolies, which lent money to private persons, cities, and states at usurious interest rates and financed industrial and commercial enterprises throughout the empire. Merchants sometimes operated independently, but more often as business agents of individual senators, arranging the sale of the produce of the large senatorial estates. They also engaged in shipping and, particularly in the East, in banking, real estate, and slave trading.

Land. Some of the acquired capital was invested in shipping, commerce, and industry, but most was invested in real estate (especially farm land) since it was for senators the only kind of investment permitted by the Claudian Law of 218 B.C., and for members of the equestrian class the main road to political advancement and social recognition.

The so-called Licinian-Sextian legislation which restricted the growth of the large estate had never been strictly enforced and was almost completely ignored after the Second Punic War. The state encouraged such investment, for it had some 14,000,000 acres of land (most of it confiscated after the war) at least 9,000,000 acres of which were good farming land. Since the state found it easier to deal with large investors, it leased most of the public land for long terms at small stipulated rents to rich and powerful landowners, who after a few generations came to regard the leased lands as private property and even ceased paying rent to the state. The rough and mountainous areas in the South were often used for cattle and sheep ranches, whereas in western and central Italy it was not ranching, but another type of capitalistic organization that displaced the small grain producing farmer: the wine and oil plantation.

The growth of the plantation in Campania, southern Latium, and parts of Etruria was favored by two separate government policies: the importation of wheat from Sicily and Sardinia and the colonization of the North for purposes of defense. Wheat imported by sea from the provinces as tribute (Rome exacted from Sicily an annual tribute of a million bushels before the Second Punic War), as rent collected from tenants on arable land confiscated by the Roman state, or as the result of outright grain confiscations by powerful Roman officials could be sold in Rome at prices with which the small and medium size grain growers of Campania and Latium could not compete. Lacking the capital to engage in the more profitable forms of agriculture, many sold or abandoned their farms and took advantage of the government's colonizing program in the North and Northwest. These abandoned farms were bought up at extremely low prices by rich investors, who consolidated them into plantations ranging at first from sixty to two hundred acres, and later to as many as five hundred acres. The risk of crop failure, crop surplus, or insufficient labor at harvest time encouraged planters to acquire several plantations located in different regions rather than to operate an extremely large one.

Slave Labor

The wars of conquest solved the labor problem they created by subsituting for the depleted free manpower the hundreds of thousands of war prisoners. During the second century B.C., the Italian labor market was flooded with thousands of Greeks, Macedonians, Asiatics, Spaniards, Ligurians, Gauls, and Carthaginians. Indeed, some modern writers refer to some of the wars of that century as vast slave hunting expeditions.

In the time of peace pirates and kidnappers kept the slave markets supplied. The greatest contribution to the success of plantation agriculture was made by the pirates of Cilicia, whose skill in the art of kidnapping and slave hunting was unsurpassed. The Asiatic slaves they caught were at a premium because of their intelligence, submissiveness, and their skill as vinedressers, winemakers, and cattle breeders.

Technique of plantation management was based on the earlier experiences of the Carthaginians who had made important contributions to scientific agriculture and to the techniques of organizing large masses of slave labor. These principles of plantation management and organization were embodied in Mago's famous treatise which the senate ordered translated into Latin for the benefit of the Italian planters and which greatly influenced Cato, Varro, Columella, and even later writers on agriculture.

Use of slave labor encouraged the cultivation of such crops as required attention all year round yet which involved the simplest processes of cultivation so that even the dullest hands could learn by routine and such crops as permitted maximum concentration of labor in the smallest possible area in order to reduce the high cost of supervision. Sugar, rice, oil, wine, coffee, and, to a lesser extent, cotton and tobacco, are ideal plantation crops. Wheat and barley are not suitable because they have a relatively short growing season, require a great deal of labor at planting and harvest time, and do not permit use of the gang system, whereby a single supervisor can direct the work of the greatest number of slaves in the smallest possible area. (Some wheat was grown because the plantation aimed to achieve the ideal of self-sufficiency but it was rarely produced as a staple.) The production of wheat was rendered further unprofitable in the coastal areas of ancient Italy by the importation of wheat from the provinces as tribute. The provincial wheat competed with home grown wheat in feeding the city of Rome and possibly other coastal towns as well as in supplying the Roman army.

The use of slave labor not only determined the crops but encouraged the growth of large estates since, in order to be profitable, slavery must be organized on a large scale. The big plantation operated more economically because a larger number of slaves could be organized under a single supervisor. The heavy cost of equipment required for the processing of rice, sugar, wine, or olive oil always calls for a sufficient amount of land and labor to distribute fixed capital costs. The large operator also enjoys other advantages over small and middle-sized producers, the advantages always incidental to large-scale organization, namely superior financial credit, superior marketing and purchasing power, and the benefit of influential connections.

The competitive advantages of organized slave labor were many. It was a stable supply of manpower, always available when and where needed, and easily replaced. Slaves, unlike tenants, could not be drafted for military service. Still more important, they could be organized, concentrated, and combined in any way the owner saw fit. Because the owner could appropriate any physical or value surplus earned by slaves, he was able to produce at price levels only slightly above the cost of maintaining them.

The Marketing of Farm Products

Rome's conquests and her political unification of the Mediterranean world contributed as much to the development and expansion of markets as to the mobilization of capital and labor. We have already alluded to the important role of the *negotiatores* and other traveling businessmen as sales agents of the senators for the marketing of the tremendous volume of farm and derivative products produced on their Italian estates—immense quantities of wine, oil, fruit, hides, meat, and wool as well as bricks, iron and bronze tools, bronze vessels, and pottery. From these estates came most of the meat, leather, wool, and flax used by the Roman army and navy.

As early as 167 B.C. and as late as the time of Sulla (87-80 B.C.), Italian wine and oil were exported to Delos and to other islands as well as cities in the eastern trading area. Though the volume of these exports was at first probably small, they do show that by the middle of the second century B.C. Roman farm products had begun to compete in markets hitherto the exclusive monopoly of the Greeks.

The chief market for Italian farm products was western and northern Europe. Wine exporting to France, where a six-gallon jug cost as much as a slave, must have been a very lucrative business, and began surprisingly early. The remains of a Greek ship, which probably foundered around 230 B.C. was recently discovered among a group of islands south of Marseilles.* It was laden with Campanian tableware and about 10,000 large jars of wine, some of Greek vintage but most of it red Latian produced on the Sabine hills. It seems likely, therefore, that Italy began the production of wine for the export trade much earlier than hitherto believed. Exports continued until France began to produce on a large scale, some three centuries later.

Italian wine was later shipped to Germany, Carthage, Egypt, South Russia, to East

* See the *National Geographic* issue of January, 1954.

Africa, and as far away as eastern India and perhaps even Indo-China.

The most surprising fact about this export trade is its volume. In Carthage alone more than a thousand jars have survived (they had been used to shore up a wall on the citadel). Some of them, as shown by their stamps, must have come from estates which also produced many of the stamped Campanian bricks. Thousands of other such jars have been found in Switzerland and France. In a small section of the French river Saône, over which a railroad bridge was constructed in 1869, 24,000 jar ends were dredged up. These accidental discoveries are only an indication of what must have been the extent and volume of the Roman export trade.

Far larger than the export trade, of course, was the local consumption of wine, oil, and other farm products. The demand in Rome and other cities must have grown apace with the influx of wealth and the ever-rising standard of living. As recent well-documented studies have shown, the city of Rome alone had a population close to a half million as early as the second century B.C. In the latter part of the second century A.D., the annual consumption of wine in Rome has been estimated at about 20,000,000 gallons, 90 per cent of which was produced in Italy.

Other cities also were growing in size, population, and wealth. The Campanian cities were becoming industrial centers. Bronze wares from Capua were exported as far north as Scotland and Sweden and as far east as South Russia and the Caucasus. Most of the silver plate, glassware, and dinnerware found in Germany and in other countries of northern Europe from Norway to Poland was made in Campanian shops. The port of Puteoli was beginning its spectacular growth as an industrial center and a gateway of world trade. The large number of wineshops and bars in the small (25,000 people) city of Pompeii just before its destruction in 79 A.D. gives some idea of the quantities of wine and other farm products which must have been consumed in the larger cities of Capua, Puteoli, Naples, and, of course, Rome. It is written, for example, that Lucullus on his return from Asia in 80 B.C. distributed in gifts as many as 100,000

A wine tavern in Herculaneum. (Courtesy Istituto Italiano di Cultura)

jars or 650,000 gallons of wine from his cellar.

Social, Political, and Moral Effects of the Slave Plantation. The well organized plantation was an unqualified success as a source of wealth for both the owner and for the state. Unfortunately, it contributed to the creation of social and political problems which led finally to the breakdown of the Republic.

These problems began with the wars of conquest which emptied the countryside of its free citizens, formerly the backbone of the state. The resulting military weakness alarmed farsighted and patriotic citizens such as the Gracchi. The dispossessed farmers flocked into Rome where they lived in shacks or in badly built tenement houses and formed an unemployed, discontented proletariat, dangerous to the peace and order of the state.

Rich and unscrupulous politicians bought their votes and organized them into mobs to influence elections, create riots, or kill political opponents. The violence and anarchy thus introduced prevailed in Roman politics till the downfall of the Republic.

The moral effects of the Roman slave system seems to have permeated all levels of society. Slaves were treated with the utmost cruelty and inhumanity. They were literally worked to death and when sick or too old to work, if the brutal advice in Cato's manual on agriculture was followed they were turned out to die. Many of those who worked in the fields toiled in chains and at night were penned up in foul underground prisons. The treatment inflicted upon the slaves was dehumanizing to those who gave it as well as to those who received it. It is not much wonder that the senate during the second century treated foreign peoples such as the Spaniards with the utmost disregard for human life.

Social and Economic Decay of the Near East

After Pydna, there was a drop in military efficiency and a general decline of national performance. One by one the men reared in the old hard school of war had died and with the death of Cato their voices ceased to be heard in the senate. The minor wars of this period were not won by military strategy but by starving cities into submission, by the violation of treaties, and by assassination.

Yet the age had no lack of problems—problems perhaps more complex and difficult than the wars against Syria and Macedonia. The free farmers, backbone of the old Roman state, were being replaced by slaves. Vast estates were spreading out over the body of Italy like a cancerous growth. Rome itself was overrun with swarms of unemployed, starving men living in shanties or rickety tenements, dependent on the handouts of rival politicians, and a potential and unpredictable menace to the stability of the state. The food supply of this great mass of humanity was at the mercy of the sea, the slaves of Sicily, and the locusts of North Africa.

War, conquest, and the expanding slave economy had even more ruinous effects upon the population of the Hellenistic East. The extent of the damage is mainly revealed by

Above: *the* victoriatus, *a silver drachma of the third century B.C., showing on the obverse side (left) the head of Jupiter and on the reverse side (right) a victory crowning trophy—ROMA. Below: the quadrigatus, a silver didrachma of the third century B.C., showing on the obverse side (left) the young Janus, and on the reverse side (right) Jupiter (holding a thunderbolt) and victory in a quadriga— ROMA. (Courtesy The American Numismatic Society, New York)*

papyri, inscriptions, cuneiform documents, archaeological material, all excellent primary sources of information on the fluctuations of prices, wages, rents, and population. Between 201 and 136 B.C., Greece, Egypt, Syria, and other parts of the Near East may have lost as much as twenty to twenty-five per cent of their population. Houses fell into decay, large tracts of land lay fallow or were turned into pasture for want of labor. From 210 to 160 B.C., while wages remained low, the prices of food, rent, and other necessities rose and in times of crop failure, even skyrocketed. Prices finally went down again because of the lack of buying power but not before the people had undergone intense suffering. Poverty-stricken parents were forced to abandon new-born children. It is believed that the health of some eighty per cent of the population was seriously impaired.

The Monetary System

A good indication of the general malaise was the increased value of silver and gold in terms of copper. It has been estimated that the Romans took out of the East about 31,000 pounds of gold, almost 700,000 pounds of silver and around 25,000,000 dollars in indemnities. Before the conquests, silver had had sixty times, gold 750 times the value of copper. The removal of precious metals from circulation together with the temporary shutdown of mines in Spain and Macedonia and the paralysis of normal trade throughout the Near East, India, and Africa, doubled the price of silver and greatly increased that of gold.

A clear proof that silver was now worth about 120 times the value of copper was the introduction in 217 B.C., or slightly later in the course of the Second Punic War (not in 269 B.C., as formerly concluded from less reliable evidence), of a new Roman silver coin known as the *denarius* (worth around twenty cents), which was tariffed at ten bronze sextantal (two-ounce) *asses* so that its value-ratio to copper was 120:1. By 170 B.C. the *denarius* had superseded as the standard silver coin of Rome the older *quadrigatus* (probably equal to twenty *asses* of 72 scruples each after 209 B.C.), a didrachma of Greek style introduced ca. 269 B.C. with

Two illustrations of the denarius, *introduced in 217 or 215 B.C., showing on the obverse side (a) the head of Bellona and on the reverse side (b) Castor and Pollux on horseback— ROMA. (Courtesy The American Numismatic Society, New York)*

types Janus-Jupiter and Victory in *quadriga,* and to some extent also its half, the *victoriatus* (with types Jupiter-Victory and Trophy), which continued to be struck beside the *denarius* for trade with South Italy, Sicily, Spain, and, particularly, Illyria.

The reform of 217 B.C. gave Rome a coin useful for local, Italian, and also for foreign trade especially with the East after the *denarius,* slightly reduced in weight (retariffed in 122 B.C. at 16 one-ounce *asses* instead of ten two-ounce), was accepted at par with the Attic *drachma.* In 184 B.C. Egypt adjusted its currency to the *denarius* to be followed by one state after another so that by the first century B.C. the *denarius* currency and its reintroduced half, a reduced *victoriatus,* was used directly or indirectly all over the Mediterranean trading area—a truly imperial and international coinage.

Of great importance for making small change was the silver *sestertius,* a *denarius* quarter worth two and one-half *asses* (approximately five cents) and marked IIS.

The Slave Revolts

Proletarian and slave revolts began breaking out after 138 B.C. In Italy, the revolt of these miserable wretches was suppressed after the crucifixion of 450 of them at Minturnae, 150 at Rome, and 4,000 at Sinuessa. An uprising at the great slave market of Delos was put down by force of arms, another at the silver mines of Laurium near Athens, where for some months the revolting slaves had set up an independent state and even issued their own coinage. In Pergamum, the war (132-129 B.C.) of Aristonicus, the bastard son of Eumenes II, and his Stoic "Sun-state" against Rome was simply a major revolt of slaves, proletarians, and soldiers. Worst of all was the slave revolt in Sicily, where normal slave thuggery and mugging had swelled into full scale war near 136 B.C. under the leadership of a Syrian slave named Eunus, who by vomiting fire and uttering oracles was able to persuade his 70,000 (some say 250,000) followers that he was Antiochus, the king of the Syrians. Only after several years of hard fighting, the murder of many landlords, and much damage to property, were the Romans able to crush this

dangerous revolt, extinguishing its last sparks in 131 B.C.

The Senate

The senate had emerged from the Second Punic War as the most powerful organ of government in the state. The military triumphs of the second century B.C. further confirmed its supremacy and widened its functions. Its control over finance, military and foreign policy, and even the courts was unchallenged until the time of Tiberius Gracchus. It often reduced the consuls and other magistrates to obedient executors of its will. The tribunes, formerly the champions and protectors of the people, now were the senate's willing tools and accomplices. The popular assemblies, theoretically the supreme lawmaking bodies in the state, now ratified senate decisions without question. Not even the powerful censors, except the aggressive Cato, ventured to challenge its authority.

The success of the senate lay in its efficiency and experience. A compact and permanent body, it could assemble if necessary at a moment's notice to make quick decisions. Though it consisted of rival factions competing for leadership and power, its members, magistrates and ex-magistrates, had a common background of political experience.

The *Lex Villia Annalis* had been passed in 180 B.C. setting twenty-eight as the minimum age for holding the quaestorship and establishing a two-year interval between each of the higher offices. Office was to be held in the following sequence (*cursus honorum*): quaestorship, aedileship, praetorship, and consulship. Two other laws, the *Lex Fufia* and the *Lex Aelia,* both passed in 153 B.C., established the right of magistrates and tribunes to obstruct meetings of the assemblies by announcing unfavorable auspices. These laws were intended to keep the senate free from dangerous radicals and to maintain its hold upon the government.

Despite the adherence of many senators to the ideals of the Roman moral tradition, the corrupting influence of sudden wealth, of a slave economy, and of power politics, showed itself in the brutal destruction of Corinth, Carthage, and Numantia, and the treachery toward the Spanish people. Having transformed itself into an exclusive and arbitrary oligarchy, the senate exposed itself to the attacks of the Gracchi. Their efforts to reform the Roman government led to social disorders, civil war, and the final destruction of the Republic.

The senate was controlled by a small group of fifteen or twenty noble families. Few of them (the Fabii, Claudii, Cornelii, Aemilii, and Valerii) actually belonged to the ancient patrician aristocracy. The others were of plebeian origin, but just as jealous of their privileges as the ancient patriciate had been. Into their closed ranks new men now seldom gained admittance. Cato was one of the very few to do so. Even he, rich as he was, made the grade only through the backing of an aristocratic family.

The handicaps a new man (*novus homo*) had to overcome to gain the higher offices and a seat in the senate were numerous and difficult. Only a rich man could stand the expense of an election campaign and hold an office for which he was paid no salary. His chances of getting elected were slim if opposed by a member of an old and illustrious family supported by numerous clients, powerful friends, and influential connections. Then again, he might not be presented to the assembly for election, if the presiding magistrate disapproved of him. It was difficult enough to reach the quaestorship, which in Sulla's time entitled him to a seat in the senate. To reach the consulship, which gave the rank of noble, was almost impossible. Only men of exceptional ability and personality like Cato, Marius, and Cicero could burst the bars of exclusion. Such was the closed caste that ruled the senate.

The Knights or Equites

By the third century, the term "knight" was extended to citizens of full birth whose income was equal to that of knights enrolled in the equestrian centuries. These comprised the capitalistic middle class, which made money by taking contracts to build roads, bridges, temples, and other public works, to supply the army with military equipment and supplies, by exploiting the resources or collecting the taxes of Italy and the provinces, by banking, shipping, and commercial enterprises. Some members of this class were almost industrialists, such as those who made the beautiful "Samian" or red glazed pottery known as *terra sigillata*. Others were book publishers, the most outstanding of whom was Cicero's friend, Titus Pomponius Atticus.

Although members of the middle class could lend money to the aristocrats, act as their business agents, and marry well-endowed daughters into impoverished noble families, they could not shed the stigma of inferior social status.

The Italians

Even worse off than the unemployed city proletariat (*see* p. 164), were the Italians who, no longer needed to help Rome fight for freedom and security, were treated almost as conquered subjects. Roman generals gave their Italian allies a smaller share of the captured booty and subjected them to scourging and execution, against which Roman soldiers had been protected by law since 199 B.C. Roman magistrates behaved most rudely on their travels through Italy.

Religion and Philosophy

Although Rome permitted the Italians to trade in the conquered East, she denied them the right of citizenship, and the Roman senate began interfering in Italian internal affairs, particularly religion. The most striking instance of senatorial interference in Italy was the decree issued in 186 B.C. against the cult and secret mysteries of Dionysus or Bacchus whose worship, with its wild drinking and sex orgies, had spread from south Italy to Rome. In order to stamp out the wave of immorality, drunkenness, and crime, the decree forbade, under penalty of death, more than five persons to assemble and meet together for worship in Rome or Italy without permission from the praetor.

Not all the Oriental cults were similarly restricted or outlawed. Some had been at first even encouraged by the state. The Romans, after consulting the Books of the Sibyl, introduced in 205 B.C. the worship of Cybele, the Great Phrygian Mother. The famous black stone brought from Pessinus was depos-

A Bacchic inscription (2nd century A.D.), found on what probably was a statue base in the Roman Campagna. (Courtesy The Metropolitan Museum of Art, Fletcher Fund, 1926)

ited first in a shrine on the Palatine and later in a temple built in 191 B.C. on the same hill for the worship of the goddess.

The Roman conservative element was horrified at this outlandish, disorderly cult, with its gorgeously clad priestly eunuchs, riotous outdoor parades, wild dances to the beat of drums and cymbals, and castrations and mutilations performed at the climax of religious ecstasy. The cult of the Great Mother centered around the death and resurrection of the god Attis, who was both her son and husband. The rite symbolized the annual withering and rebirth of grass, flowers, and other vegetation. Although Roman citizens were forbidden to participate, Oriental cults kept coming into Rome especially from Egypt and Syria. Their arrival seems to have co-incided with periods of great social and economic stress and upheaval.

While the Greek and Oriental cults helped divert the attention of the depressed and exploited masses from their sufferings, Greek philosophy replaced the lost faith in the old Roman gods and mythologies for the intellectuals. These turned to such as Euhemerus, a Sicilian philosopher and novelist, who had soon after Alexander the Great propounded the doctrine that the gods were simply human beings who, like Hercules, had by their superhuman deeds become saviors of the world. The work of Euhemerus on the origin of the gods was also available in a Latin translation by Ennius. More lasting and influential were the philosophies of Epicurus and the Stoics.

Epicureanism

Unlike Stoicism, which appealed mainly to the Roman aristocracy, Epicureanism was originally a rural and suburban philosophy which had become popular in Italy before arriving in Rome. Epicureanism did not appeal strongly to the aristocratic Roman because it was centered on the individual rather than on the state. It advocated the renunciation of political ambition and the avoidance of publicity. It seems to have been largely a missionary philosophy which passed from person to person, unlike Stoicism which was introduced by imported teachers such as Panaetius of Rhodes.

Epicureanism was the philosophy of Epicurus (341-270 B.C.), who returned in 306 B.C. to his native city of Athens to write and teach. Of the many books and letters he wrote, only three short essays and some fragmentary scrolls in Herculaneum are preserved. Much of the present knowledge of his teachings is derived from the great Roman poet Lucretius (99-55 B.C.) who revered him as the deliverer of mankind from ignorance, superstition, and fear.

Epicureanism is a system of ethics under which the individual might lead a full and happy life free from the fear of misfortune and death. The material world, according to Epicurus, consists of indestructible atoms, whose various weights, shapes, and sizes account for the different physical objects. These atoms fall with equal and uniform velocity through empty space, in accordance with natural law. They may swerve or deviate from the perpendicular and, as they swerve, they unite to form solid bodies in which they continue to vibrate. Death occurs when the atoms separate and drift out into empty space. Epicurus believed that the gods do possibly exist, but asserted that they do not interfere with the laws of nature or with human affairs.

The truth of the ethical ideas of Epicurus does not rest on the accuracy of his scientific theories. He based his ethics on the proposition that humanity has neither a pre-existence nor an afterlife. There is only one life and life is the greatest good. That good he called pleasure (a term which has been frequently misinterpreted both in ancient and modern times). Actually, some Epicurean principles are reflected in the writings of St. Paul.

Epicureanism, with its misunderstood doctrines of pleasure and materialism, its denial of Divine Providence, and its hatred of superstitions, has always offended the orthodox, the conservative, and the upholders of caste and respectability.

One adherent was the banker and brilliant business executive, Titus Pomponius Atticus, with whom Cicero carried on a long and friendly correspondence. Caesar himself had strong Epicurean sympathies while his father-in-law, L. Calpurnius Piso, distinguished senator and provincial governor, was the patron of the Epicurean philosopher, Philodemus, whose books have been rediscovered in Herculaneum. Another prominent Epicurean was Titus Manlius Torquatus, a man of illustrious ancestry, whom Cicero chose as spokesman for the sect in his philosophical work *On the Definitions of Good and Evil*.

Philodemus extolled abstention from politics, but failed to convince all his pupils and friends. A few Epicureans were devoted followers of Caesar but many others, such as Cassius Longinus, active defenders of Republican ideals.

Of the Epicurean virtues—wisdom, temperance, fortitude, justice, honesty, faith, love of mankind, friendship, hope, and gratitude—the greatest is honesty (frankness, sincerity) and, next, friendship. The truth derived from honesty not only makes us free but contributes most to securing the greatest good, which is the fullness of life. The full life depends on freedom from fear, peace of mind, happiness, and pleasure which are achieved by living virtuously and courageously in the present, each individual being "master of his fate and captain of his soul."

Stoicism

Stoicism made an even stronger impact than Epicureanism on Roman society in the second century B.C. It derived its name from Stoa, the Porch or colonnade near the Athenian marketplace, where Zeno (336-263 B.C.), a Phoenician from Cyprus, began to teach (some time after Epicurus). Zeno taught that the universe is animated and governed by a Supreme Power variously called Universal Law, Divine Reason, World Soul, or God. The universe, itself both rational and divine, is the handiwork of this Supreme Power. According to Stoicism, human beings are endowed with reason, which governs the body and restrains all the feelings, desires, and passions that hinder us from knowing and doing the will of God. True happiness, secured by virtue (of which the greatest is duty), consists in achieving harmony with reality, or the governing power of the universe. Duty alone enables the individual to harmonize free will with that Supreme Power. "Reason" and "duty" are, therefore, key concepts in Stoic philosophy.

Zeno advanced the idea of a federal world state, in which all good men would share universal brotherhood through their common participation in universal reason. The replacement of the existing society of small city states and royal empires with one universal state under natural law was a magnificent concept suggested, perhaps, by the world conquests of Alexander. In the ideal state the citizens would be emancipated from all existing conventions and moral standards but bound together by divine reason and nurtured by common law. The Utopia of Zeno was too splendid and gave way to others less sublime but equally unattainable. In the third century, Iambulus, a Hellenistic novelist, envisioned on isles of the Indian Ocean a truly modern Utopia, the Sun-state, a classless society in which people would work together in perfect concord and bliss, equal in wealth, in social status, and even in wisdom.

The philosophical ideas of later Stoicism are almost as numerous and various as the individual philosophers that held them. Soon after the conquest of the East, there came to Rome Panaetius of Rhodes, the founder of the so-called Middle Stoa and friend of Scipio Aemilianus. Panaetius acclaimed Rome the perfectly balanced state of Stoic philosophy, the only one capable of ushering in the Sun-state throughout the world. Like Polybius, he praised the Roman constitution because it contained the principle of checks and balances between its monarchic, aristocratic, and democratic elements. He identified the Roman moral code with Stoic ethics, adapting the latter to fit the former. (What Zeno would have said about compromises of this kind is not difficult to imagine.) In turn, the Roman aristocrats welcomed the practical philosophy of Panaetius' brand of Stoicism with its catchwords of "virtue," "fortitude," and "duty."

Stoic Influence upon Roman Politics. The Stoic philosophers had at Rome a unique opportunity to influence politics. Their patrons were aristocratic statesmen, in whose homes they lived, whose children they tutored, and with whom they discussed logic, ethics, and politics. Among the Romans who seriously accepted Stoic teachings were Scipio Aemilianus, Q. Aelius Tubero, P. Mucius Scaevola, the consul of 133 B.C., and his son, the consul of 95 B.C., Sextus Pompey, M. Porcius Cato Uticensis, and many learned jurists of the second and first centuries B.C. Two of these men, the younger Scaevola and the younger Cato, put Stoic principles into actual practice. As governor of Asia, Scaevola paid his personal expenses out of his own pocket, and was an incorruptible administrator of justice and protected the people from exploitation by the knights. Cato's own policy on provincial administration was similarly the practical application of Stoic principles.

Literature

Though the Roman people had a language and a history as old as those of the Greeks, they were many centuries later in creating a literature. When Rome first began, in the third century B.C., to create a literature in imitation of the Greek, the great age of Greece was long ago past. The only prose the Romans had during the early Republic consisted of the Twelve Tables, the priestly commentaries, a few laws and treaties, and speeches delivered in the senate or at funerals. Early poetry was confined to the hymns of the Arval Brethren, the litanies of the Salii or Jumping Priests, lullabies, wedding songs, funeral dirges, ballads sung at banquets, and the chants of workers in the fields and women at the loom. Most of these songs were in the Old Italic Saturnian meter, a rude kind of verse, alternating stressed and unstressed syllables.

Livius Andronicus: 284–204 B.C.

The father of Latin literature was Livius Andronicus, a Greek war captive brought from Tarentum to Rome as a slave. He learned the Latin language well enough to be able to translate Homer's *Odyssey* into Latin. This epic, composed in Saturnian verse, though clumsy and rude, began a glorious succession of epics culminating in Vergil's *Aeneid*. In 207 B.C. he was asked to compose a processional ode (*carmen saeculare*) for a religious festival. He also wrote tragedies and comedies, largely translations from or adaptations of the Greek.

Naevius: 270–199 B.C.

Naevius was born in Campania. He was a plebeian by birth and frequently attacked the nobles by satire and invective. He, too, wrote tragedies based on Greek originals but also introduced the historical play. He wrote numerous comedies, some based on the Greek New Comedy, others on Roman life, all witty, caustic, and frankly outspoken. Most famous is his epic poem in Saturnian verse on the First Punic War. He set a pattern in his legends about Troy and Carthage, which was later followed by Ennius and Vergil.

Ennius: 239–169 B.C.

Ennius, a half-Greek born in Calabria, served as a soldier in Sardinia until brought to Rome by Cato in 204 B.C. where he later won the friendship and admiration of Scipio Africanus and Fulvius Nobilior. Ennius spoke three languages, and was well acquainted with the philosophy of Pythagoras, Euhemerus, and Epicurus. He wrote comedies, many Euripidean tragedies, and several satires. His fame as the father of Latin poetry rests on his *Annals,* an epic poem of eighteen books describing in Homeric or hexameter verse the story of Rome from her origins until 172 B.C. This was Rome's first national epic, and established the fame of Ennius as the Roman Homer.

Plautus: 254–184 B.C.

Plautus, unlike the writers just mentioned, was exclusively a comic writer. He was a man of humble birth from Umbria. His early life in Rome was hard, for he worked first in a flour mill and afterwards as an actor and a stage hand. He wrote about 130 plays, of which 21 are preserved. All except one are complete. They are based on the writers of the Attic New Comedy, especially on Philemon and Menander, whose plays have been lost, except for the substantial papyrus fragments of the latter author found in Egypt. The Greek prototypes have as characters the young callow lover, the cranky old man, the parasite, the prostitute, the white-slave dealer, the swaggering but cowardly soldier, and frequenters of barrooms or brothels. By introducing numerous Roman allusions, customs, and colloquialisms, Plautus produced farces very different from his Greek models. His slapstick humor abounded in slave beatings, door-bangings, profanity, noisy dialogue, and other forms of buffoonery. Some of his plays are comedies of intrigue, others are based on mistaken identity such as the *Menaechmi* (which Shakespeare imitated in his *Comedy of Errors.*)

Terence: 195–159 B.C.

Terence, six comedies of whose still survive, was a freed African slave. Terence is less coarse, more refined, more subtle, and much less funny than Plautus. His skillfully constructed plots are inclined to be monotonous and were probably appreciated only by a select and intelligent audience, for whom the neatness and elegance of his language must have had an added charm. Some of his neatly turned expressions still live: "Fortune favors the brave"; "While there's life, there's hope"; and "Each man to his own opinion." Though several ancient literary critics regarded his language as the best in Latin literature, it was too elegant for the common people to appreciate. It is said that they walked out in the middle of his play, *The Mother-in-law,* to watch the rope-dancers and the gladiators!

Lucilius: 150–103 B.C.

Gaius Lucilius, a leading member of the circle of Scipio Aemilianus, was the father of satire, an original literary creation of the Romans. Satire is probably derived from the old Italian word *satura* meaning a medley or a mixture of different things. As used by Lucilius, it meant a miscellany or a collection of poems on various subjects and in various meters. His thirty books of satire written in a rather hasty and colloquial style quite befit the title he gave his poems: "Conversations" (*sermones*). They expressed his feelings and opinions about people, events, travels, politics, literature, the follies and vices of the time, the stupidities of the Roman government, and the Roman habit of aping the Greeks. His harsh and often scurrilous value judgments on people and their faults established the present meaning of satire. His poems were popular in both his own and later times. Some Roman literary critics went so far as to pronounce him the greatest of all Latin poets. His two greatest imitators were Horace and Juvenal.

Cato: 234–149 B.C.

Artistic Latin prose developed later than poetry. Up to the time of Cato the Censor, all Roman historians had written in Greek. In 149 B.C. Cato published a Latin work called *Origines,* which described the history of Rome from the earliest times. The few fragments that still survive show that Cato had a much lower opinion of the deeds of his political opponents than of his own. He had a strong dislike of aristocrats in general and particularly of Scipio Africanus.

Cato wrote several other works on various subjects, of which the only one extant is his *De Agri Cultura,* a farmers' handbook written in an extremely simple, terse style. In all his literary works and public speeches, he seems to have followed the excellent advice he once gave his son: *Rem tene, verba*

sequentur ("Grasp your subject, the words will follow").

Tiberius Gracchus

The revolt in Sicily was only a warning of things yet to come. The Roman conquests had already produced an economic and social upheaval that had reduced the constitution to a sham and was driving the Republic towards inevitable disaster. A few thoughtful men weakly tried to stave off the coming disaster. No doubt Scipio Aemilianus was able to trace the growing military weakness of Rome to the growth of the large estates and the depopulation of the countryside. His friend Gaius Laelius, the consul of 140 B.C., proposed a tightening up of the Licinian-Sextian Laws of 367 B.C. which limited estates created from public lands to 320 acres and provided for the resettlement of people who had lost their farms. He quickly dropped this proposal when he saw the angry reaction it produced in the senate. Five years earlier C. Licinius Crassus had, during his tribuneship, drawn up a similar land reform bill, only to have it vetoed, probably at the senate's instigation, by a fellow tribune. Appius Claudius Pulcher was thinking along the same line. Clearly the senate majority was violently opposed to reform.

At last a reformer came forward who was determined to save his country despite the senate. Tiberius Gracchus was descended from a long line of fearless champions of the people. His great-grandfather and namesake once fined Claudia, the sister of the consul of 249 B.C., for making a nasty remark about the plebeians and, as consul of 238 B.C., used the money collected from similar fines to build a temple of Liberty on the Aventine. Tiberius' own father had had a long and illustrious career, had twice been consul, had won two triumphs, and during his censorship in 169 B.C. was as stern as Cato in his censure of the vices of the nobles. He was beloved in Spain for his land distributions and his social and administrative reforms. Of the four distinguished Romans who bore the famous name of Tiberius Sempronius Gracchus, the young tribune and reformer of 133 B.C. was the most illustrious.

The strongest influence on Tiberius was that exerted by his mother, Cornelia, the daughter of Scipio Africanus. One of the most remarkable and best-educated women in Roman history, she spoke and wrote with the utmost elegance and grace. To her sons, whom she called her "jewels," she imparted the elements of that unusually simple yet deeply moving eloquence, which swayed the masses more powerfully than the oratory of Cicero ever could. She secured for them the best of teachers: Diophanes of Mytilene taught them rhetoric; Blossius of Cumae, Stoic philosophy. The training received from these two teachers probably reinforced the political ideals of their family.

At fifteen Tiberius accompanied his brother-in-law, Scipio Aemilianus, to Africa. He was the first to scale the walls of Carthage. Impressed by the youth's courage and discipline, Scipio spent many a quiet hour discussing with him the politics of the day and the future of Rome. His next tour of duty was in Spain, where as quaestor under the notoriously incompetent consul Mancinus, he found himself performing the duties of commander-in-chief because the Spaniards, who had ambushed and entrapped the Roman army, would negotiate only with a Gracchus. The treaty, which saved from destruction an army unable to save itself, was later torn up by the senate. Only the gratitude of the Roman people helped soften his anger against the perfidy of the senate.

Before becoming tribune, Tiberius married the daughter of Appius Claudius Pulcher, the president of the senate. Appius belonged to one of the oldest patrician families which had yet been one of the most radical and eccentric, ever since the days of Appius Claudius the Blind of 312/10 B.C. When the senate refused Appius the honor of a triumph after his victory over the Salassi, he celebrated one at his own expense. Equally unconventional was the betrothal of his daughter to Tiberius. At a banquet of the augural board, to which Tiberius had been elected in spite of his youth, Appius broached the question of marriage to his daughter. Tiberius gladly accepted the proposal and old Appius, in his joy, fairly danced all the way home. His unsuspecting wife met him at the door and, beholding his excitement, calmly said: "Appius, why all the fuss, unless you've found young Gracchus for our daughter." (Plutarch, *Tiberius Gracchus*).

The Tribuneship of Tiberius Gracchus: 133 B.C.

In the year 133, one of the most memorable in the history of the Republic, the 30-year-old Tiberius Gracchus took office as tribune of the people. His first act was to introduce before the Tribal Assembly his famous agrarian bill designed to break up the large estates created out of public land and to divide them among the landless poor of Rome. In his campaign speeches he had spoken of the scenes of desolation he had seen as he passed through the Maremma of Etruria on his way to Spain and of the slaves working on the huge plantations. The men who had fought Rome's battles in the past all came from the small, family size farms. Who, he asked, will defend the Roman empire? Slaves cannot be drafted for military service, neither can the men who have lost their farms and now live in squalor in the city. Unemployed, starving, they are worse than useless, they are a menace to the state. "The wolves and the bears," said Tiberius to the plebeians, "have dens and places to rest and sleep. The men who fight their country's battles have nothing but air and sunlight. Their generals ask them to fight for their homes; they have none. You fight and die only for the wealth and luxury of others. You are called the masters of the world but you have not a foot of ground to call your own." (Plutarch, *Tiberius Gracchus* 8.4).

The bill introduced by these stirring words was most conservative and less stringent than the old law of ca. 367 B.C. It had been drafted not by Tiberius, who was merely its spokesman, but by Appius Claudius, the president of the senate, and by two learned jurists, P. Licinius Crassus and P. Mucius Scaevola, the consul of 133 B.C. It ordered the state to repossess all public land in excess of 320 acres plus an allowance of 160 acres for each of two sons. The holders of estates between 320 and 640 acres were guaranteed clear title unencumbered by taxes or rent, and reimbursement for any improvements they had made in the way of buildings or plantings on the land to be repossessed. The repossessed land was to be assigned to landless citizens in lots varying in size probably from nine up to eighteen acres and was to be subject to a nominal rent payable to the state. The allotments were inalienable and entailed against sale or transfer.

The Gracchan land law was not only conservative (being a re-enactment of the ancient but still existing Licinian-Sextian Law*) and very generous to the illegal occupiers of public land, it was also a salutary measure designed both to alleviate the unemployment crisis in Rome and to repopulate Italy with a sturdy peasant class, which would provide suitable recruits for the Roman army.

Some recent writers have condemned Tiberius for failing to consult the senate before presenting his bill to the popular assembly, but his action was neither unprecedented nor unwarranted, since he had before him the example of Gaius Flaminius who had enacted *his* land law of 232 B.C. without prior consultation of the senate (*see* p. 125). Furthermore all the more recent attempts to resume land settlement in Italy had been blocked by the determined opposition of the senatorial aristocracy (*see* p. 172).

The Land Bill Vetoed. On the day of the vote, the farmers flocked in from the country in unprecedented numbers. After a moving speech, Tiberius ordered the clerk to read the bill to the people. Suddenly Octavius, a fellow tribune, interposed his veto on behalf of the senate, which had in the past successfully used this device to block radical legislation. Tiberius adjourned the assembly hoping Octavius would change his mind before the next meeting. The following day Octavius again vetoed the bill. Because the assembly was on the verge of a riot, friends persuaded Tiberius to submit the bill to the senate. When the senate angrily rejected it and

raised a clamor of abusive criticism, Tiberius came away determined to unblock the veto by removing Octavius from office.

The Deposition of Octavius. At the next meeting of the Tribal Assembly, Tiberius urged the people to decide between Octavius and himself. Eighteen votes would decide. When seventeen tribes had voted against Octavius, Tiberius held up the voting for a moment to appeal to his colleague to change his mind. The latter remained obdurate. The voting resumed and Octavius was divested of his tribunate and forcibly removed from the tribune's bench.

The constitutional issue raised by the deposition of Octavius has evoked the most divergent opinions. Upholders of the senate have argued that the tribunate had undergone considerable change of purpose and function since its inception. With the successful outcome of the plebeian struggle for office and seats in the senate (by 179 B.C. the senate probably contained 216 plebeians and only 88 patricians), the tribunes were no longer needed as protectors of the plebeians and the sole justification for their existence was their service to the senate as a check on dangerous legislation by volatile and irresponsible popular assemblies. By overriding the tribunician veto, which the Tribal Assembly itself had long ago made absolute, Tiberius had removed that check. By using force against the sacrosanct person of a tribune he had flouted the constitution and laid himself open to impeachment at the end of his year of office.

Gracchan adherents have argued that the senate was acting unconstitutionally in making the tribunate serve functions alien to its original institution; that although the plebeian aristocracy no longer required tribunician protection, the masses of unemployed and starving plebeians did; and that tribunes elected to defend and serve the people had no moral right to betray the people by serving as lackeys of the senate, a corrupt oligarchic machine bent on thwarting the sovereign will of the popular assemblies and on blocking all reforms necessary to prevent the state from sinking into social ruin and military impotence.

The Agrarian Commission. To carry out

* The Licinian-Sextian Law of ca. 367 B.C., though often ignored and frequently violated, had never fallen into disuse or oblivion, since it had been repeatedly re-enacted, as proved by Cato's allusion to it in his speech of 167 B.C. on behalf of the Rhodians.

the provisions of the land act, Tiberius asked the people to appoint a commission of three members consisting of himself, his younger brother, Gaius, and his father-in-law, Appius Claudius. The commission was later granted full judicial powers with *imperium* to determine what lands were public and what private, to repossess all public land not exempt by the law, and to distribute it to new settlers. Ample funds were required to pay the salaries of surveyors and other officials as well as to help the new settlers make a start by providing them with housing, tools, work animals, and seed, as well as subsistence till the crops were harvested. The senate, which held the keys of the state treasury, had provided for operating expenses only thirty cents a day.

The Pergamene Treasure. Attalus III of Pergamum had upon his death willed his personal fortune and kingdom to the Roman people (*see* p. 150). Tiberius, casting about for new sources of money, at once requested the people to make these funds available for the use of the commission.* Thus thwarted, members of the senate began to make ugly threats against his life. To prepare the ground for violence, they circulated the rumor that he was planning to declare himself king and had retained for the purpose the diadem, scepter, and royal vestments of the Pergamene kings.

Tiberius Campaigns for a Second Term

To protect his legislation from annulment, and to save himself from certain prosecution and probable death, Tiberius offered to run for a second term, a step contrary to recent custom but not unconstitutional, since the sovereign people could re-elect him in spite of law or custom just as they had, in violation of custom, elected his grandfather, Scipio Africanus, to supreme command during the Second Punic War.

The senatorial machine was bent on his defeat and destruction and Tiberius had not

yet won the support of the middle class or the city voters. The country voters who supported him might be too busy with their crops to turn up on election day. In his campaign speeches he hastily endeavored to win the majority he needed by promising, it is said, to shorten the term of military service, to extend the right of appeal from the courts to the people, to admit jurors of equestrian rank to the court established by the Calpurnian Law in 149 B.C. to try governors for extortion in the provinces,* and to compensate the Italian allies for losses suffered through the land reform law. Although these promises have often been considered pure demagoguery, they held out the hope of reforms that were badly needed. Apparently, they were not radical enough to win the overwhelming support of the city voters. They were too few and too late.

Even so, the early voting ran so strongly in his favor, that the partisans of the senate interrupted the voting by vetoes and bogus religious "omens." Just when the assembly seemed about to break out in open riot, Fulvius Flaccus pushed his way through the milling throng to inform Tiberius that the senate was holding an emergency session in the temple of Faith. The senate, he said, had accused Tiberius of wanting to be king and had invoked an ancient law under which Tiberius was to be killed as a tyrant!

Scaevola, the consul, had refused in horror to take part in the murder but Scipio Nasica and some other senators rounded up a mob of sympathizers and slaves, and hurried to the Forum. The tribunes of the people, who might have interposed their sacred persons between Tiberius and the mob, scurried out of the way like rabbits. Picking up legs of broken chairs and benches, Scipio and his men rushed towards Tiberius and clubbed him and three hundred of his followers to death. They threw the bodies into the Tiber. While the bodies of the slain were floating

* It is not completely certain whether such a bill was ever passed or whether the mere threat to deprive the senate of control over provincial revenues caused that body to open up the state treasury for the use of the commission.

* The *Lex Calpurnia* of 149 B.C. instituted a standing court composed of fifty jurors drawn entirely from the senate and presided over by a praetor to try cases for the recovery of damages from governors and other officials accused of extortion in the provinces (*quaestio de rebus repetundis*).

down the Tiber, Popilius Laenas, the consul of 132 B.C., set up a special court to try the Gracchan partisans. The more outspoken ones were executed. To forestall popular retribution Scipio Nasica was whisked out of danger and sent on a diplomatic mission to Pergamum, where, as Head Pontiff, he safely performed his pontifical duties in absentia. There, in 132 B.C., he died—too soon to see the consequences of his act: the vicious class war that was to come and the massacres of Marius and Sulla.

The Land Commission

Though Tiberius Gracchus was slain, the land commission set up to administer the Sempronian land law was allowed to function with undiminished vigor. A less astute body than the senate might have further risked the people's wrath, but with the death of the author, the senate was unwilling to undo his work. The consul Popillius Laenas even boasted of what he had done to carry out the law. On a milestone in Lucania he caused the statement to be inscribed that he was "the first to compel the shepherds to make way for the plowmen."

The commissioners appointed after the death of Tiberius were two active leaders of the Gracchan party, M. Fulvius Flaccus and C. Papirius Carbo. They worked with zeal and energy, and within six years the commission settled over 75,000 men, an increase of twenty per cent in the manpower available for military service. The Gracchan land law temporarily achieved its objective of strengthening the military power of Rome.

The work of the commission was hard and thankless, and probably involved some injustice, for it was seldom easy to determine what land was public. Some tracts had been leased from the state, others acquired by purchase, others by illegal occupation. Some of the public land had been in the possession of the same family for so long that the state had ceased to collect rent. Some lands had been bought, sold, mortgaged, or bequeathed so many times that the present occupants were not the original violators of the law. Title deeds, if they had ever existed, had been lost; and the old landmarks had long

ago been swept away. However conscientiously the commissioners consulted the old land registers and summoned neighbors to testify, probably in some cases they seized private property and in other cases confiscated the only good land the owners possessed. The complaints must have been numerous and bitter, but the commission could not permit them to impede the execution of its task.

The grievances of the Latin and Italian allies could not be brushed aside so easily. To ignore the complaints of the federated allied states might constitute a violation of their treaty rights with Rome, disturbing peaceful relations, and perhaps even inviting revolt. To the allies, whether as individuals or as communities, Rome had assigned public lands by lease or by outright grant. When the commission seized some of these lands, of which the Italian poor received no share, the allies looked for a patron to champion their interests. They found one in Scipio Aemilianus, the destroyer of Carthage and Numantia. Realizing the value of their military help, he gladly consented to press their claims before the senate and succeeded in having the judicial powers of the commissioners transferred to the consuls, at least as far as the Latin and Italian allies were concerned. If the consuls preferred to go off on long campaigns to avoid involvement in irksome land disputes, the work of the commission would be brought to a standstill.

Scipio's meddling with the land problem in 129 B.C. did not help his popularity with the Gracchan party. In fact his popularity had waned since he spoke before the Assembly against Carbo's* bill to legalize re-election to the tribuneship. In the course of the debate, Carbo asked him what he thought of the murder of Tiberius Gracchus. Scipio replied, "If Gracchus intended to seize the government, he has been justly slain." When the crowd greeted this remark with jeers and catcalls, Scipio roared, "I have never been scared by the shouts of the enemy in arms.

---

* Though Carbo failed to get this bill passed, he had succeeded two years earlier in passing the secret ballot law (131 B.C.). No bill was more potent in breaking up the senatorial machine.

Shall I be frightened by your outcries, you step-sons of Italy?"

In May, 129 B.C., Scipio announced that he was going to make a speech about the Latin and Italian allies. It is not known whether he intended to talk about the land law or about the granting of Roman citizenship. He went home early to work on his speech. The next morning he was found dead in bed. Whether he died from natural causes or was, as rumored, the victim of foul play either by one of the Gracchans or by his plain and unloved wife was never known.

Fulvius Flaccus took up the cause of citizenship for the Italian allies. As consul (125 B.C.), he proposed the grant of citizenship to any of the allies that wanted it. When all classes opposed his idea—especially the people, who did not want to share their privileges with the Italians—Fulvius dropped his bill and went off on a campaign in southern France to conquer new lands for farm settlement, a scheme dear to the hearts of democrats since the days of Gaius Flaminius.

The departure of Fulvius from Rome and the failure of his proposal was a severe blow to the hopes of the Italians. Their overt agitation in Rome made them quite unpopular and at the suggestion of the senate a tribune pushed a bill through the assembly legalizing their expulsion. The refusal of citizenship and the alien exclusion bill provoked such anger in the hitherto loyal Volscan town of Fregellae that its people broke out in open rebellion. The revolt was crushed, and Fregellae destroyed. Feeling in Rome ran high against both the Italians and the democratic leaders who were suspected of having inspired and encouraged the revolt. Even Gaius Gracchus, who had just returned from Sardinia, was accused, but was able to prove his innocence.

Gaius Gracchus

The powers and capabilities of Gaius Gracchus were known and feared years before he became tribune. The senate considered him a menace because of his membership in the land commission set up by his brother and his influence over crowds. His enemies were naturally relieved when it fell to his lot in 126 B.C. to go as quaestor to Sardinia, whose pestilential climate, it was hoped, might do him no good. The plan to keep him there for at least five years was frustrated by his sudden return to Rome in 124 B.C. Far from impairing his health, the seclusion of Sardinia had allowed him to form a plan of action. In spite of the oligarchic machine, he campaigned for the tribuneship and was elected. Once more the country voters poured into the city as they had done ten years before to support his brother. They voted him into power again in 122 B.C., although he was not an official candidate at that time.

The Tribuneships of Gaius Gracchus:
123–122 B.C.

The two years of the tribuneships of Gaius Gracchus were the most memorable years of the Roman Republic and perhaps the most crucial in the history of the Roman people. He converted the tribuneship, hitherto an agency of the senate, into an instrument of almost absolute power, thereby creating an example for the future. A century later (23 B.C.), the Emperor Augustus strengthened the principate by invoking not the powers of a consul but those of a plebeian tribune (*tribunicia potestas*).

Outside the office of Gaius Gracchus waited callers of every rank, nationality, or walk of life, some singly, others in smaller or larger groups. They came from Rome, from Italy, the provinces, or from foreign countries. Laborers came, looking for work, road superintendents for instructions, businessmen for contracts, magistrates for advice, foreign emissaries for his mediation. Such was the prestige acquired by the tribuneship of Gaius Gracchus.

It is difficult to do justice to a political luminary of the magnitude of Gaius Gracchus. He was unsurpassed as a reformer, as an executive, as a popular leader, or as a mob orator.

Mob ortatory was indispensable to the politician or statesman. The eloquence of Gaius Gracchus was simple and direct, unadorned by the artificial trappings of rhetoric. He played upon the emotions of crowds much as an expert musician plays on a violin: he could make them laugh; he could make them weep; he could overwhelm them with pity and overcome them with joy.

During his two short years of office he passed at least seventeen major laws, all highly damaging to the power and prestige of the senate. This flood of legislation was possible because of his personal magnetism and the control he exerted over the Tribal Assembly, a control which rested upon a keen intelligence, a gift for impassioned oratory, and the disarming freshness of youth.

The Reforms of Gaius Gracchus

Upon taking office, Gaius Gracchus proceeded to stir the fury of the people against his brother's murderers, who had violated the sacrosanctity of a tribune, and against the Court, which had, under Popillius Laenas, condemned his brother's followers to death without appeal to the people. The assembly responded by passing a law which prohibited the senate from creating extraordinary tribunals to condemn political offenders without appeal to the people. Under a retroactive provision of this law Popillius Laenas was condemned and exiled.

The Purpose of the Gracchan Reforms. Revenged, Gaius Gracchus proceeded to carry out his more constructive program of reform, the ultimate purpose of which was to create a system of government capable, as the senatorial oligarchy was not, of dealing intelligently and realistically with the social and economic problems generated by the Roman conquests. The most pressing problems concerned the spreading unemployment and slums, the periodic fluctuations in food prices, the decline of military strength and efficiency, the frequent slave revolts, and the continuing problem of provincial administration and dissatisfied allies.

To implement his program of reform, it was necessary for Gaius to break the senatorial monopoly of government and to neutralize the power of the oligarchic machine that had insidiously acquired control of elections and the popular assemblies. Lacking military force, he attempted to organize a coalition of the middle class, the proletarian city voters, and the farmers.

The Farm Vote. To win the farm vote, Gaius revived and amplified his brother's legislation. He restored to the land commission the judicial powers, which Scipio Aemilianus had perhaps justly persuaded the senate to remove. Most of the public land had by now been assigned, but he was able to benefit the farmers by an extensive roadbuilding program, under which a network of secondary roads was created linking farms with markets, villages with towns, and towns with Rome. These roads not only enabled farmers to obtain employment but permitted them to move their crops more easily and cheaply to markets, thus improving trade, and by facilitating attendance at assembly meetings, promoted a fuller participation in popular government. The extraordinary speed with which this project was completed under Gaius' personal direction further increased the fears of the senate.

The City Vote. To gain the political support of the city masses, Gaius persuaded the assembly to pass the famous *lex frumentaria* or Grain Law, which provided that the state should buy and import grain from overseas for sale on demand in fixed monthly amounts to citizens residing in Rome at six and one-half *asses* per *modius* (a price which has been estimated as equivalent to 32 cents a bushel), a price not far below the average market price in Rome and often much higher and never below the regular producer prices in such surplus areas as Egypt, Sicily, Upper Italy, and Spain. This law, the most severely criticized of all the Gracchan reforms, did not constitute a dole; it was passed solely to promote price stabilization for the benefit of the consumer (not, as now, for the producer). A considerable amount of the wheat consumed in Rome came in as tribute and cost the state only the expenses of transport, naval convoy, and storage. The Grain Law also provided for the construction of warehouses and wharves in Rome, a measure designed to relieve unemployment.

The Grain Law had a negative and more subtle purpose. It was designed to counteract the age-old evil of clientage, upon which the senate relied as the source of its power and wherein lay one of the chief strengths of the senatorial machine. In periods of high food prices senatorial candidates had regularly bought votes by the provision or promise of cheap grain. The Grain Law helped to restore the independence of Roman citizens and rendered more effective the secret ballot law of 131 B.C.

Some other important laws were passed whose purpose was not merely to win voters. The Military Law (*lex militaris*) required the government to clothe and equip Roman soldiers without deductions from their pay, shortened the term of military service, and forbade the call-up of boys under seventeen years old. This law was intended to improve army morale, always a concern of the Gracchi, and to win the political support of soldiers, allies, and voters with small incomes. In 122 B.C., as has been established (*see* p. 166), the weight of the denarius was reduced. This measure not only meant that the Roman citizens had to pay lower money taxes, but also significantly reduced the tribute of the Roman allies without special legislation.

His laws authorizing commercial and agricultural colonies in Italy and across the sea were intended to relieve the overpopulation in Rome and provide economic opportunities for farmers, traders, craftsmen, and small businessmen unable to make a living. The sites selected were Capua, Tarentum, and Carthage. The most ambitious of these projects, as authorized by the Rubrian law, was the founding of Junonia near the cursed site of Carthage, where 6,000 colonists drawn from Rome and the rest of Italy were to be settled on farms of 125 acres. Gaius went to Africa to supervise in person the initial stages of the settlement, which first established officially the principle of emigration.*

His Appeal to the Middle Class Voter.

* The senate was strongly opposed to Junonia and, by the use of mendacious propaganda and the appeal to superstitious fears of the curse of 146, managed to persuade the people after Gracchus' death, to repeal the Rubrian Law authorizing the scheme. Had it been completed, it would have been one of the greatest of the works of Gaius Gracchus. He had anticipated by almost a century the policy of Augustus and the later emperors.

In a further effort to drive a wedge between the equestrian middle class and the senate, Gaius appealed to the cupidity of the middle class by two important laws, both of them easily interpreted as purely demagogic and pernicious unless viewed in light of his entire reform movement.

The middle class (businessmen and the tax farmers in particular) was already irked by the senate's control over finance, provincial administration, and especially over the rich revenues of the new province of Asia. After Attalus III had willed his kingdom of Pergamum to Rome in 133 B.C. (*see* p. 150), the senate decided to collect direct taxes of fixed sums payable by the communities to the governor and by him in turn to the Roman treasury. Gaius had a law passed overturning this arrangement and directing instead that the taxes of Asia take the form of a tithe as in Sicily (p. 122). Unlike the system employed in Sicily, where the tithe was collected locally, the Gracchan law stipulated that the censors should auction the lucrative contracts for the tithes of Asia to tax-collecting companies in Rome for five-year terms.

The new system of taxation provided the Roman treasury with immediate funds and was less burdensome to the provincial taxpayers than fixed taxes, since payments in kind would fluctuate with good or poor crops. It was also beneficial to the Roman tax collectors, since clauses were added protecting them against losses due to war and other calamities. It naturally benefited the richest men of the middle class, for the right to bid was open only to those owning property in excess of 400,000 sesterces (20,000 dollars). This Gracchan law increased the economic power of the middle class and simultaneously weakened the control of the senate over public finance.

Jury Service

Another move which tended to divide the middle class and the senate into mutually hostile camps was the Acilian Law, which excluded senators, the relatives of senators, and all curule magistrates from the juries of the standing courts established under the

Calpurnian Law of 149 B.C. to try provincial governors for extortion.*

The transfer of jury service from the senate to the wealthy middle class achieved its intended purpose of widening the breach between the two classes and of "throwing daggers into the Forum," but it punished good governors for preventing the wholesale exploitation and plundering of the provinces by the knights and businessmen. As an enlightened statesman, Gaius Gracchus should have anticipated the evil effects of this legislation, which became most apparent shortly before the time of Sulla.

The Italian Question

In his second term as tribune, Gaius Gracchus introduced a bill which proves that he was not an opportunist but a courageous statesman willing to risk his life and career on a measure he knew to be dangerously unpopular. The bill, which proposed to extend Roman citizenship to the Latins and Latin rights to the rest of the Italians, was scuttled by the selfish ignorance of the Roman populace and the malice of the senate. Had it been enacted into law, it would have averted the destructive civil war that was to come in the next generation. It might have led, as Professor Frank once suggested, to the evolution of a representative form of parliamentary government simply because of the necessity of securing the expression of a widely scattered electorate. It might even have prevented the failure of the Republic and welded Rome and Italy into a unified national state capable of governing a great empire.

Livius Drusus. During the seventy days Gaius was in Africa laying the groundwork of the colony of Junonia, the senate had been planning the destruction of both the Italian citizenship bill and its author. They found in the tribune, M. Livius Drusus, a brilliant agent of their diabolical scheme. An eloquent speaker but an outrageously unscrupulous demagogue, Livius Drusus pampered the self-

ish interests of the Roman populace and threatened to veto the Gracchan bill to extend citizenship to the Italians. That threat prevented it from being brought to a vote. Livius then presented a bill to protect Italian soldiers from mistreatment by Roman army officers, which was an important advance, but a shabby substitute for the citizenship bill. He then introduced a bill which promised to found twelve colonies in Italy, each to consist of 3,000 colonists selected from the poorest class. The land was to be rent free. He also proposed to release from payment of rent the settlers who had been allotted land under the law of Tiberius Gracchus. The proposal to found twelve colonies in Italy was never intended to be carried out since there was not enough public land left in Italy to permit so ambitious a scheme. After it had achieved its purpose of destroying Gaius Gracchus, it was speedily dropped. Had Livius Drusus been sincere, he might have become one of Rome's greatest benefactors.

The Fall and Death of Gaius Gracchus

When Gaius returned from Africa, he discovered that Livius, acting in collusion with the senate, had succeeded in undermining the democratic party and even in splitting the once solid ranks of the city electorate. Too long had Gaius stayed in Africa; too late did he realize the extent of the conspiracy against him. His immense popularity had made him over-confident. Fulvius Flaccus, whom he had left in Rome to look after his interests, was a violent and tactless man who had done a great deal of damage to the Gracchan party by his reckless and turbulent acts. Gaius was defeated in his attempt to run for a third term. Only his membership in the African commission (granted *imperium* by the Rubrian Law) stood in the way of the senate now resolved to take his life.

To remove the protecting power of the *imperium,* the senate hastened to bring about the annulment of the Rubrian Law authorizing the founding of Junonia. Though still holding an official position as commissioner, Gaius lacked the authority to summon the people or the power to resist the threatened repeal. He wished to avoid acts of violence,

---

* The justification for the Acilian Law was the charge that the senatorial juries had recently acquitted governors commonly believed guilty.

which might give his enemies the excuse for declaring martial law but the newly elected consul, Lucius Opimius, the destroyer of Fregellae and a violent reactionary, deliberately provoked an incident. As Opimius was preparing to offer a sacrifice in the porch of the Capitoline temple, one of his attendants, who carried the utensils required for sacrifice, stood opposite Gaius and cried out the traditional formula ordering all "bad citizens" to leave the porch. A Gracchan follower thereupon cut the man down with his sword, thus giving Opimius the pretext he had been seeking.

Armed with a final decree of the senate (*senatus consultum ultimum*), virtually declaring a state of martial law, he organized a posse of senators and their slaves and, assisted by a force of Cretan archers, attacked the Gracchan followers, who had taken refuge on the Aventine. Here the Gracchans were routed and 250 of them killed. Fulvius Flaccus was killed as he attempted to escape. Gaius also attempted to escape but, seeing the hopelessness of his position, ordered his slave to kill him. His severed head was filled with melted lead and brought to Opimius, who paid its weight in gold. Afterwards pseudo-legal trials resulted in the execution of 3,000 Gracchan followers.

Thus died Gaius Gracchus, who in his two years of office as tribune of the people had temporarily broken the senate's monopoly of government and permanently impaired its authority. He had concentrated in his hands many executive powers and functions. He had supervised the distribution of grain to the populace, selected the juries of the courts; awarded contracts for and superintended the construction of highways, presided over meetings of the senate, supported and campaigned for candidates to the consulship, and converted the tribuneship into an office more powerful than the consulship itself. Some of his reforms were truly measures of enlightened statesmanship. Others were dictated by political necessity and must be described as frankly opportunistic. But since it is impossible to separate the means from the ends, it is equally impossible to evaluate a particular reform exclusively on its own merits. Each must be considered in terms of the larger purpose they were intended to serve.

In death the Gracchi were mightier than in life. By killing them, the senate had unwittingly exalted the two tribunes into figures of heroic proportions. Allowed to live they might have been the sooner forgotten. Instead statues were erected to them in public places and the spots where they had fallen became hallowed ground. Prayers and sacrifices were offered to them as to gods. Even the proudest noble, regardless of his private opinions, dared not speak of them in public except in respect and veneration. The common man revered them for having brought hope into his world of misery and exploitation.

IX

THE AGE OF MARIUS

The hope of the senatorial oligarchy that the death of Gaius Gracchus and the bloody suppression of his party would once more permit the state machine to run smoothly along in its old tracks was destined to be shattered within the next few decades. Violence and terror could not solve the problems of the age shouting for reform, as the oligarchs themselves tacitly admitted when they accepted with slight modifications the constitution created by the men they had killed.

For fear of the city masses they did not repeal the Grain Law, for fear of the middle class they changed neither the selection of jurors for the extortion courts nor the administration of provincial taxes set up by Gaius Gracchus. Even the land laws, even those pertaining to the founding of colonies, though modified, were not overtly overthrown. It was far easier to kill

AND SULLA

Gaius Gracchus than to overturn what he had done or to invent newer and better solutions to the problems of the age.

The reign of terror that followed the slaying of Gaius Gracchus seems to have completely cowed the popular assembly. When Opimius was prosecuted for murder before the people, he was acquitted and his acquittal confirmed the legality of the senate's final decree (*senatus consultum ultimum*), which proclaimed a state of martial law enabling Opimius to put citizens to death without appeal to the people. Popillius Laenas, who had been exiled by the people for killing the fol-

lowers of Tiberius Gracchus, was now allowed to return to Rome.

Three successive laws halted the Gracchan land settlement reforms. The first, enacted probably in 121 B.C., permitted the settlers to sell the farms allotted to them by the Gracchan land commission. This law tended to nullify the purpose of the Gracchan legislation and permitted the rich proprietor to buy or force the sale of small family-size farms. The second land law (passed perhaps in 118 B.C.), abolished the land commission, whose work was probably already done, halted further division of public land in Italy, and guaranteed legal possession of lands already distributed on payment of a small rent to the state. Finally in 111 B.C. a third law, probably the *lex Thoria,* partially preserved in an inscription, abolished all rentals ordered by the law of 118 B.C., declared as private property all public lands assigned by the Gracchan commission up to 320 acres, and guaranteed to colonies and municipalities secure tenure of lands already granted. It also forbade further encroachment on public pastures and strictly regulated the number of animals the stockmen could run on those lands.

The Gracchan program of land settlement in Italy was strongly reinforced both before and after the tribunate of Gaius by the conquest, colonization, and settlement of lands beyond the borders of Italy, particularly in southern Gaul (thousands of Roman colonists still remained around Carthage even after the abrogation of the Rubrian law). The Romans first intervened in southern Gaul in 125 B.C. during the consulship of M. Fulvius Flaccus who, in answer to repeated complaints from Marseille, crossed the western Alps and subdued first the Ligurians and then the Saluvii, who dwelt north of Marseille between the Isère and the lower Durance. Their subjugation gave the Romans control of a road leading from Italy to the Rhone valley, which they dominated from a strongly fortified base established in 122 at Aquae Sextiae (Aix) by the settlement of Roman veterans.

The pacification of southern Gaul was largely the work of Gnaeus Domitius Ahenobarbus. After decisively defeating two powerful Celtic tribes, the Allobroges and the Arverni, in a great battle at the confluence of the Rhône and the Isère, Domitius occupied all southern Gaul, exclusive of the small territory of Marseille, from the Alps to the Pyrenees and in 120 B.C. organized it into the Roman province of Gallia Narbonensis. He also constructed a permanent military highway, the *Via Domitia,* from the Rhône to the Spanish Pyrenees. On this route a Roman citizen colony of discharged veterans was established in 118 B.C. at Narbo, the first Roman colony, apart perhaps from Junonia at Carthage, to be founded outside the Italian peninsula. The founding of Narbo not only provided the commercially minded equestrian class a trading center in southern Gaul, but fulfilled a dream of the Farmer's Party cherished since the days of Gaius Flaminius: the finding of new lands for settlement by the small farmers of central Italy.

The Jugurthine War: 111–104 B.C.

Nothing revealed more clearly the weakness and incapacity of the senatorial oligarchy than the series of events known as the war with Jugurtha. The war occurred in the North African kingdom of Numidia between the years 111 and 104 B.C.

After the death of Massinissa in 148 B.C. (p. 157), the kingdom of Numidia was ruled for a time jointly by three of his sons and, on the death of two of them, by the surviving Micipsa until his death in 118 B.C. He ruled the kingdom in peace and justice; he promoted agriculture and made his capital city of Cirta (today either Constantine or El Kef) an important trading center, where many Italian merchants came to live. At his death he willed the kingdom jointly to his two sons, Adherbal and Hiempsal, and to Jugurtha, his nephew, whom he had adopted several years earlier. Adherbal and Hiempsal were rather weak, inoffensive creatures but Jugurtha was able, energetic, and aggressive. Like his grandfather, Massinissa, he was a lion of the desert, a good athlete, a skilled rider and hunter, and a born soldier. He had fought under Scipio Aemilianus at the siege of Numantia and had become acquainted with many young Roman officers, from whom he learned all he needed to know about the state of Roman society.

After a brief attempt at joint rule, the three princes agreed to split the kingdom. Jugurtha plotted instead to take the whole of it for himself. He had Hiempsal murdered and made war on Adherbal, whom he defeated and drove out of Numidia. Adherbal fled to Rome and appealed to the senate. Though many of the senators listened to his words with politeness and sympathy, they were reluctant to interfere. Others were strongly in favor of Jugurtha, especially after they had been contacted by his agents, who came plentifully supplied with gold. After some debate the senate decided to partition Numidia and in 116 B.C. appointed a commission to go to Africa to arrange the details. The commission awarded the eastern part with its capital city of Cirta to Adherbal and the western part, which was larger and richer in both its soil and its soldiers, to Jugurtha.

Three years later, Jugurtha again attacked Adherbal, first by plundering raids and then by invasion. In an early morning attack, he surprised and defeated Adherbal's army and laid siege to his capital, Cirta, which was vigorously defended by the Italian merchants. Though the city occupied an almost impregnable position on a towering cube of rock encircled by a river, it could be starved into surrender. Again Adherbal appealed to Rome. The senate, unwilling to involve Rome in an African war in view of the alarming situation beyond the Alps and in the East, merely sent two investigating commissions to remonstrate with Jugurtha. The commissions succumbed to Jugurtha's diplomacy and accomplished nothing. Cirta was starved into surrender, Adherbal was tortured to death, and the Italian merchants were massacred.

The massacre of the Italian merchants set off an explosion of anger in Rome. Enraged by the slaughter of members of their own class and by the loss of business opportunities under Jugurtha's rule, the middle class once more, as in the time of Gaius Gracchus, united with the city proletariat. Gaius Memmius, the tribune of 111 B.C., openly accused some senators of receiving bribes from Jugurtha and attacked the senate so vigorously that it was forced to declare war against Jugurtha. The consul, L. Calpurnius Bestia, raised an army and invaded Numidia.

The Phony War and the Peace

The war, which the senate declared with reluctance and under pressure, was waged with little zeal or vigor. Jugurtha seemed to understand the senate's half-heartedness for after permitting the Romans to win enough successes to appease the populace in Rome,

he allegedly again resorted to bribes, and sued for peace, which Bestia gladly granted, receiving a small indemnity in token of the sham surrender. Jugurtha was permitted to keep his entire kingdom. Bestia returned to Rome firmly convinced that he had ended the war and was bringing back peace with honor.

In Rome the people were not deceived. The bringer of peace with "honor" was greeted with a storm of protest. Bestia's peace reeked of bribery and corruption. The middle class was no less bitter in their rage and frustration. They had hoped to see Numidia develop into a secure and profitable area for trade and investment. By leaving a rabid nationalist like Jugurtha in control of all Numidia, Bestia had dashed their hopes to the ground. To these hatreds, and frustrations, Memmius, the tribune, gave loud and vehement expression. He demanded a thorough investigation and asked the Tribal Assembly to pass a bill ordering that Jugurtha be brought to Rome in person, under safe conduct, to testify.

In due course Jugurtha arrived in Rome and appeared before the assembly. After reciting the catalogue of his crimes and murders, Memmius asked him to reveal the secret partners of his bribery. Before he could answer, another tribune, suborned to interpose his veto, forbade him to speak. Memmius had failed, but Jugurtha made good use of his visit. He hired gangsters to kill his cousin Massiva who lived in Rome and had been prevailed upon to present before the senate his claim to the throne of Numidia. The murder was traced to Jugurtha and he was obliged to leave Rome. To allay the suspicion of collusion with such a scofflaw, the senate repudiated Bestia's peace and renewed the war.

The Failure and Defeat of the Roman Army: 110–109 B.C.

After rapid but elaborate preparations, the consul Spurius Postumius Albinus set sail for Africa in command of an army of some 40,000 men. With his undisciplined and demoralized army and a foe so crafty and elusive as Jugurtha, he was able to accomplish nothing. He too tried to persuade

Jugurtha to surrender and was likewise suspected of accepting bribes. Finally Postumius returned to Rome to preside over the elections and left in command his equally incompetent brother, Aulus Postumius, who whether for glory or gold marched, in the depth of winter, against Suthul, where Jugurtha kept his treasure. There he was lured into a trap and his badly defeated army was forced to pass under the yoke. The peace terms stipulated that Rome should evacuate Numidia within ten days and acknowledge Jugurtha as an ally.

The news of this disaster further enraged the people. The humiliating peace terms were at once rejected. A tribune named Gaius Mamilius Limetanus put through a bill setting up a special court composed of jurors selected from the middle class, but presided over by the distinguished noble M. Aemilius Scaurus, to investigate those accused of corruption or collusion with Jugurtha. The court condemned Bestia, Spurius Postumius Albinus, and Lucius Opimius and sent them into exile.

Quintus Caecilius Metellus: 109–108 B.C.

The African command was at last assigned to a competent general: Metellus, the consul of 109, who though a rigid aristocrat and perhaps even an unscrupulous one, was incorruptible and an excellent disciplinarian. His first duty was to whip a thoroughly demoralized and undisciplined army into an efficient fighting machine. Only then did he invade Numidia, making forced marches under the burning desert sun.

Jugurtha retreated, hoping to lure Metellus into ambush. Finally Jugurtha launched his surprise attack, which was beaten off with heavy losses. In Rome the failure of Metellus to capture Jugurtha was misunderstood. The businessmen hoped for a speedy termination of the African war but they did not understand the difficulties of desert warfare. Neither, of course, did the people. They were inclined to accuse Metellus of prolonging the African war for his own glorification.

This unjust accusation was not only entertained in Rome but was sedulously encouraged by the activities of Gaius Marius, one of Metellus' senior officers. He urged the merchants of North Africa to write letters to their friends and agents in Rome protesting against Metellus' conduct of the war.

Gaius Marius

If the Roman people did not understand the difficulties of North African warfare, Gaius Marius did and was calculating and unscrupulous enough to exploit them to his own advantage. Born outside of Arpinum, the son of an upper middle class farmer, Marius remained a true plebeian even at the height of his fame. Even after he had become the commander-in-chief of the Roman army, he slept on the same hard ground as the common soldier. He seemed also to have capitalized on his rough and shaggy appearance, which together with his poor education and bad grammar, made him popular with the mob and the common soldier.

He had been with Scipio Aemilianus at the siege of Numantia. His courage, his physical endurance, the care he took of his horse and equipment, and the attention he gave to details about the camp attracted the general's notice and led to his becoming a member of Scipio's general staff. He had only distaste for the aristocracy, but for the sake of his future military career he became a client of the powerful Metelli family. After the military tribuneship and the quaestorship, he became, for 119 B.C., a tribune of the people and won the esteem and admiration of the proletariat by his defiance of the senate and the arrest of his own patron for opposing his bill to reform the ballot. Though defeated in his campaign for the aedileship, he managed with some difficulty to get elected to the praetorship in 115 B.C., after which he was sent as a propraetor to Farther Spain, his first military command. His praetorship entitled him to admission into the ranks of the nobility and his humble birth was no longer a bar to his marriage into the ancient patrician family of the Julii (his wife was the aunt of the future Julius Caesar). No further promotion came his way until Metellus appointed him as chief-of-staff in Africa. Even so, the consulship would have been

The execution dungeon of the Tullianum under the Capitol. (Courtesy Fratelli Alinari, Florence)

beyond his reach, except perhaps under most unusual circumstances—circumstances he set about creating.

Marius Campaigns for the Consulship. Whatever gratitude Marius may have felt towards Metellus for appointing him chief-of-staff and any admiration the two men may have had for each other as soldiers rapidly disappeared when Metellus scornfully refused to grant Marius leave to go to Rome to campaign for the consulship. Marius had been encouraged to seek the consulship by the words of a priest at Utica, "Ask and ye shall receive, seek and ye shall find," and by the flood of letters sent by the merchants of North Africa to their friends and agents in Rome complaining about the slow progress of the war and urging the election of Marius to the consulship and to the Numidian command. Finally, to get rid of a disgruntled officer, Metellus granted him leave to go to Rome, where Marius was not only elected consul (107 B.C.) by the Centuriate Assembly but was given the North African command by the Tribal Assembly against the will of the senate.

In recruiting troops for service in North Africa, Marius broke all precedents by accepting as volunteers all who were physically fit regardless of property qualifications. (The political results of this revolutionary innovation became evident only later.) Before leaving for Africa, Marius, disregarding his antipathy for the aristocracy, selected as his quaestor and chief-of-staff the capable Lucius Cornelius Sulla.

In Africa Marius made no move until he had trained his raw recruits. The training completed, he made long and fatiguing marches through the hot waterless wastes capturing many towns and fortresses until he had reached the extreme western borders of Numidia, fully six hundred miles from his original base. There he seized Jugurtha's war treasure stashed away on the lofty summit of an almost unassailable rock, and compelled Jugurtha and his ally and father-in-law Bocchus, the king of Mauretania, to fight pitched battles with the Romans. In two bloody battles Marius broke the military power of Numidia and Mauretania and turned king Bocchus to thoughts of peace and friendship with Rome. Still the war could not be considered won until he had captured Jugurtha himself. He entrusted this highly dangerous task to Sulla, who persuaded Bocchus to lure Jugurtha into an ambush. Marius brought the captured Jugurtha to Rome to walk in royal robes and in chains before his triumphal chariot and had him killed a few days later in the horrible dungeon of the Tullianum. As a reward for his treachery, Bocchus received the western and major part of Jugurtha's kingdom, the eastern part going to Gauda, the half-witted brother of Jugurtha. The middle class was satisfied at last. Numidia was a safe and secure field for investment and exploitation.

The War with the Cimbri and the Teutons

After the Jugurthine war Marius was immediately needed to repel the far more serious threat of war in the North. He was elected consul for the year 104 B.C. and for the next four years thereafter, sometimes in his absence from Rome and always in violation of the law requiring a ten-year interval between consulships.

What drove the people to violate both law and precedent in the election of Marius? —the threat of an invasion by the Cimbri, the Teutons, and the Ambrones, who had by their mass migrations convulsed central and western Europe for more than a decade. Driven from their homelands of Jutland and Schleswig by overpopulation and tidal inundations, the three Germanic tribes loaded their families into leather covered wagons and migrated southwards. Fairhaired giants equipped with copper helmets, tall, narrow shields, and long iron swords, they were accustomed to rush into battle in serried ranks linked to one another with chains.

These homeless hordes marched in search of land or plunder. Streams and mountains proved no barrier to their ceaseless advance. They surged down through the Elbe valley and entered Bohemia. Turned aside by the Boii, they poured over the Danube and entered the passes of the Carinthian Alps, where the consul Cn. Papirius Carbo, with disastrous results to his own army, tried in 113 B.C. to lure them at Noreia to their destruction. Deflected more perhaps by the dreaded name of Rome than by Carbo's vain treachery, the three nations turned westward. After a four year trek around the foothills of the northern Alps, they crossed the upper reaches of the Rhine and passed over the Jura mountains bringing with them the Tigurini of Switzerland, who had befriended them and had given them food and rest.

From eastern France the Cimbri, the Teutons, and their allies approached the Roman province of Gallia Narbonensis, where they attacked and broke the army of consul M. Junius Silanus in 109 B.C. Before the battle they had requested the senate to grant them land for settlement, offering to serve in the Roman armies as mercenaries. These reasonable requests, which the Roman emperors of a later time would gladly have granted, the senate rejected.

Two years later, the Tigurini, having crossed the Rhone, moved into southwestern France, where they met, defeated, and killed the consul L. Cassius Longinus and sent his army under the yoke. After the Tigurini had evacuated southwestern France, the people of Toulouse rebelled and placed the Roman garrison in irons. In 106 B.C. the proud aristocratic consul, Quintus Servilius Caepio, recaptured the city by treachery and looted the temple of 100,000 pounds of gold and 110,000 pounds of silver (a sum probably equivalent to some 50,000,000 dollars). This treasure was later lost, either hijacked on the road to Marseille or embezzled, as he was accused, by Caepio himself.

The Battle of Arausio: 105 B.C.

The Germans again begged land for settlement and permission to enroll in the Roman army. Again the request was coldly rejected. Alarmed by the German invasion of the Province and the threat of an invasion of Italy, the senate ordered Mallius Maximus, the consul, to join forces with Caepio. Caepio the aristocrat refused to cooperate with or take orders from Mallius. This refusal was a huge factor in the subsequent defeat of the Roman army with losses estimated at some 80,000 men. The disaster revived memories of the Allia and the Sack of Rome. The "Cimbric terror" of 105 B.C. swept Marius into power and kept him there for five years, in violation of all constitutional precedent.

Marius Reorganizes the Army

Marius had introduced army reforms of the greatest importance. Because of the lack of property-owning recruits, he had thrown the army open to volunteer enlistment of the city proletariat, farm hands, and debt-ridden farmers. The city volunteers were attracted largely by the pay, those from the country by the prospect of getting out of debt or of securing farms of their own after discharge. The army was thereby converted from a conscript militia into a standing army of professional soldiers serving continuously from sixteen to twenty years whether in peace or war.

The New Legion. Another reform instituted by Marius was the reorganization of the legion. Before his time the legion normally consisted of 3,000 regular infantrymen and 1,200 lightly armed skirmishers. He abolished the skirmishers and increased the legion to between five and six thousand men, all heavily armed. The old division into three distinct lines of *hastati, principes,* and *triarii* had practically lost its meaning and Marius, if he retained them at all, probably amalgamated them in the *cohort,* a new tactical unit of from five to six hundred men or one-tenth of a legion. He also abolished the old maniple of 120 men or of two centuries of sixty men each as a separate legionary unit. Three maniples, each composed of two full centuries—each corresponding to the three old battle lines, now united to form the new cohort. The cohorts of Marius may be called supermaniples strong enough to fight separately but numerous enough to be deployed in various tactical combinations. Thus without losing its flexibility, the legion acquired a compactness and cohesion symbolized by the new standard Marius introduced, the famous silver eagle.

Each legion was commanded by a professional lieutenant-general, or *legatus,* not, as formerly, by a senatorial amateur. The soldiers were trained to fight as duellists in the cut-and-thrust technique used by gladiators. They were toughened up by long marches and by a great deal of fatigue duty, such as ditch digging. Thus by a mixture of hard training and a rough and ready camaraderie, Marius created a formidable military machine which could also become an effective political weapon.

The German Strategy of Invasion. The Germans planned to attack Italy on three widely separated fronts: the Teutons and Ambrones by way of southern France, the Cimbri, after circling around the northern slopes of the Alps, by way of the Brenner Pass and the valley of the Adige, and the Tigurini by way of the Julian Alps and Venetia.

The Battle of Aquae Sextiae: 102 B.C. When Marius was ready, he attacked first the Ambrones, then the Teutons near Aquae Sextiae (today Aix-les-Bains) in a valley where they had little chance of retreat. Using the tactics of Hannibal, Marius provoked the Teutons to attack him in front and then hurled his reserve force against their rear. The carnage was terrific. More than 100,000 are said to have been slain and as many taken prisoners.

The Battle of Vercellae: 101 B.C. Meanwhile the Cimbri had successfully negotiated the Brenner Pass and the valley of the Adige and had forced the consul Q Lutatius Catulus, more renowned for his love of culture than his knowledge of war, to withdraw from his fortified positions on the Adige and retreat to the south of the Po. In 101 B.C. Marius joined forces with Catulus and under the burning midsummer sun brought the Cimbri to battle near Vercellae, which is believed to have been not far from Turin in the Po valley. The Cimbri succeeded in breaking through the Roman center but were attacked from both wings and annihilated. The Tigurini, on learning the fate of the Cimbri, abandoned their planned invasion of Venetia and returned to their old homes in Switzerland. The trek of the Teutons, Ambrones, and Cimbri for land and homes had ended in slavery and death.

The Slave Revolt in Sicily: 104-99 B.C. Had the Germans invaded Italy and set at liberty a million slaves or more, the consequences might have been similar to the revolt of the slaves in Sicily which took five years to suppress. In 104 B.C. Marius asked the Roman client-kings of Asia Minor to send troops to assist in the defense of Italy against the Germanic invaders. When the kings sent back word that most of their subjects had been kidnapped and sold as slaves by the pirates and that many of them were in Sicily, Marius and the senate ordered the governor of Sicily to release the slaves held illegally. After the release of several hundred persons, the governor allowed himself to be browbeaten by the landowners and harshly ordered the rest of the slaves applying for freedom to go back to their masters. They did not go back; instead they took to the hills and prepared to resist. Under the leadership of Tryphon and Athenion, the slave revolt swelled into full scale war and for four years (104-101 B.C.) the slaves had control of the country. Before the end of the Cimbrian war released enough troops to put down the rebellion, 100,000 lives had already been lost.

Piracy in the Eastern Mediterranean. Even before the suppression of the Sicilian slaves, the Romans had to deal with another pest: piracy in the Eastern Mediterranean. Ever since the destruction of Rhodes as a naval power, the pirates and slave traders of Cilicia and Crete enjoyed unrestricted freedom of the seas and conducted kidnapping raids upon the coastal regions of Syria and Asia Minor to supply the great slave market of Delos (where ten thousand slaves are said to have been sold every day) and the plantations of Italy. Finally in 102 B.C., two years after King Nicomedes III of Bithynia had complained to Rome about the abduction of one half of his able-bodied subjects, the popular assembly passed a law commissioning the praetor Marcus Antonius (grandfather of the famous Mark Antony) to attack and destroy the chief bases and strongholds of the Eastern pirates. After destroying the pirate strongholds, he annexed the coastal part of Cilicia as a Roman province and base of future operations against the pirates. These measures may have checked but did not destroy the evil of piracy, for in 100 or 99 B.C. the Romans had to close to pirate ships all ports and harbors under their control.

The Failure of Roman Government. The power to govern had in the last decade of this century slipped from the senate's feeble grasp. There was no one to take its place for by their very nature the popular assemblies were incapable or unwilling to accept the task of governing except when they became angry about something. They attacked individual oligarchs for baseness and incapacity, but did not attempt to replace the corrupt oligarchy itself.

Even less capable of governing was the uncertain coalition of the middle class and the city proletariat which Gaius Gracchus had attempted to create. It held together only so long as both groups were in conflict with the senate. During the war with Jugurtha, they had come together because of a common opposition to war policies. The weakness of the senate and the inability of the popular assemblies to assume responsibility left no other possible source of government but Marius.

The Political Incapacity of Marius. Just returned from glorious victories, Marius was the object of adulation and even worship: he was "another Camillus"; he was the savior of Rome. He enjoyed the unfailing support of a devoted army,—the perfect instrument for seizure of dictatorial power— and found before him a populace that cried out for leadership. Few men have been presented with better opportunities for leadership than Gaius Marius.

As a politician Marius was most inept. He could face the fiercest enemy in battle, but before the senate or the popular assembly he often could only stammer forth a few incoherent words. Worse than his lack of eloquence was his indecisiveness. He had his animosities but no particular party loyalties or ideals. Gladly would he have escaped from politics, had he not had a strong urge to be always in the limelight. Besides, he owed it to his army to stay in politics. He was under obligation to find land for his veterans. He had held five consulships, he wanted his sixth and his seventh. When the senate frustrated his desires, he was driven to cooperate with two radical leaders, Gaius Servilius Glaucia and Lucius Appuleius Saturninus, neither of whom he really liked.

Lucius Appuleius Saturninus: 103–100 B.C.

Saturninus was an eloquent speaker, an able, courageous, and sometimes unselfish man. He had his reasons for hating the senate, though he himself was of noble birth. As quaestor in 104 B.C., he had had charge of the grain administration at Ostia. When through no fault of his grain prices rose and a famine was imminent because of the Sicilian slave revolts, the senate removed him from his job and replaced him with one of its own party men, thereby alienating him forever.*

When Saturninus entered upon his first tribuneship in 103, he sponsored a law assigning 66 acres of land in Africa to each of Marius' African veterans. A colleague of his, acting on behalf of the senate, attempted to veto the bill but after a shower of stones promptly withdrew his veto. Saturninus had no patience with obstructive tactics or legal technicalities. Fists and stones were more effective than vetoes or religious "omens."

During his first tribuneship, Saturninus introduced a law, which made it a criminal offense to compromise, injure, or diminish the honor or dignity (*maiestas*) of the Roman people. This was very dangerous legislation. Under it Saturninus brought action against Caepio and Mallius for losing the battle of Arausio in 105 B.C. In the case of Caepio the law was needed since the old law against treason (*perduellio*) did not cover insubordination of legally constituted authority thereby jeopardizing the safety of the army and the very existence of the state. Caepio was an extremely unpopular person for other reasons. During his consulship in 106 B.C., he secured the passage of a law, later repealed in the tribuneship of Glaucia in 101, restoring senators to the juries of the extortion courts. He was also held responsible for the mysterious disappearance of the sacred treasures seized at Toulouse. When Caepio was tried before the people for these crimes and misdemeanors, two tribunes, who attempted to veto the proceedings, were driven off by violence and Aemilius Scaurus, the leader of the senate, was hit on the head with a stone.

* Another whom the senate had alienated was Cn. Domitius Ahenobarbus, a tribune of 104 B.C. Angry because he was not coopted into the college of pontiffs to succeed his father, he brought Aemilius Scaurus to trial for the improper performance of sacred rites. When he failed to convict him, he secured the passage of a law (the *lex Domitia*) which made all the priestly offices elective by seventeen tribes, chosen by lot, instead of by priestly nomination. This law removed from the senate the power to block democratic reforms by the pretense of having discovered unlucky signs in the entrails of sacrificial animals and in flights of birds in the sky. The author of this bill was the first Supreme Pontiff to be elected by the people.

In 100 B.C., the year of his second tribuneship, Saturninus embarked upon a full program of social legislation. This included a grain law (possibly dating back to his first tribunate of 103), which restored the regular monthly grain distributions suspended after the death of Gaius Gracchus at a selling price undoubtedly below the market rate but probably not at the absurdly low rate mentioned in a single and probably corrupt source of five sixths of an *as* per *modius* (one-eighth that fixed by the Gracchan law of 123 B.C.). The bill seems to have been carried over the vetoes of his fellow tribunes and the violent opposition of the quaestor in charge of the treasury. His second bill provided for the founding of veteran colonies in Sicily, Greece, Macedonia, and possibly Africa. A third law assigned land once occupied by the Cimbri and Teutons in Gaul (possibly Gallia Narbonensis) to veterans who had fought under Marius.

Lastly, Saturninus proposed a general mobilization of Roman forces against the Cilician pirates and against Mithridates VI of Pontus. To this batch of laws, Saturninus appended a clause requiring all senators to take oath within five days to obey these laws—on pain of loss of their seats, exile, and a fine of twenty talents. In spite of vetoes, "omens," and violence, the laws were passed.

To most of these laws the senate offered strenuous and determined opposition. They suborned tribunes to interpose vetoes, which Saturninus brushed aside with, "Let the voting proceed." Then by courier the senators informed the presiding magistrate that they heard thunder in the distance, a religious "omen" long employed by the senate to block necessary legislation. Saturninus asked the courier to advise the senate to keep quiet lest the thunder turn into hail.

The Fall of Saturninus and Marius

All eyes were fixed on Marius to see if he would take the oath of obedience appended to the bill assigning land in France to his veterans. At the last minute he did take the oath to observe the law "as far as it was legal." This express reservation turned the law into a farce and all the senators who took the oath could make the same reservation. Marius' blunder lay in his indecision. He wanted to cooperate with the popular leaders but at the same time he did not like to offend the senate. Though he probably disapproved of the methods Saturninus used to pass the law, he did not hesitate to accept its benefits.

Before the end of his second tribuneship, Saturninus had lost the support of both the middle class and the city masses. The middle class disliked his radical and revolutionary methods and feared he might next attack the sanctity of private property. The city voters turned against him because his agrarian law of 100 B.C. had granted too many benefits to the veterans, many of whom were Italians. The senate was not slow to take advantage of the mistakes, vacillations, and petty hatreds of Marius, Saturninus, the middle class, and the city voters and to involve them all in a common ruin. The popular leaders, particularly Saturninus and Glaucia, naïvely supposed that they could with impunity imitate the senate in violence and assassination.

Knowing that their lives were worth nothing the moment they stepped down from office, Saturninus and Glaucia campaigned successfully for the tribuneship and consulship, respectively, in defiance of the Villian law requiring a two-year interval between the offices of praetor and consul (see p. 166). In order to rid himself of a possibly successful opponent, Glaucia hired gangsters to kill the former tribune Gaius Memmius. The senate declared a state of emergency and ordered Marius to take action.

Marius did not want to injure or destroy Saturninus, Glaucia, and the other democratic leaders, to whom he and his veterans owed so many benefits. To save their lives he locked them up in the senate building. An angry mob of nobles and knights climbed up to the roof, ripped off tiles, and pelted his prisoners to death. Marius was ruined. Distrusted by the nobles and the senate and despised for his weakness by his democratic friends, he was obliged to look on helplessly as the senate declared the laws of Saturninus null and void.*

* He suddenly remembered that he had to go to the East to fulfill a vow he had made.

The Decade of Reaction

The stormy opening of the last century of the Republic soon died down. It was followed by a decade of inaction and stagnation. The slave revolt in Sicily that began in 103 B.C. was triumphantly suppressed in 99 B.C. A Spanish uprising of 97-93 B.C. was also brilliantly handled. The veterans of Marius were still unsatisfied and the demand of the Italians for citizenship was answered by their expulsion from the city in 95 B.C. In the interest of conservative reaction a law was passed in 98 B.C. requiring an interval of seventeen days between the publication of a law and its enactment by the Tribal Assembly. The new law also forbade the enactment of an omnibus bill (*lex satura*) that included more than one subject in its provisions, such as Saturninus may have tried to pass. Finally in 92 B.C., P. Rutilius Rufus, who assisted Mucius Scaevola as deputy governor of Asia, was tried and convicted for extortion. His "offense" in the eyes of the equestrian jurors was that he had assisted the stern and righteous governor in drawing up a model edict and in preventing the tax-farming companies from plundering the people of the province. The conviction of this upright man seems to have proved that it was dangerous for a provincial governor to be other than an opportunist. Such were the main events of this passive and melancholy decade prior to the rise of the Younger Livius Drusus.

The Attempted Reforms of Livius Drusus: 91 B.C.

The monotony of this uneventful decade was broken by the tribune, Livius Drusus the Younger. He was more brilliant and idealistic than his father, who in 122 B.C. had helped to bring about the downfall of Gaius Gracchus. Livius Drusus had two main objectives: 1) the revival of the power and prestige of the senate; and 2) the extension of Roman citizenship to the Italian people. All his proposals and reforms were subordinate to these two objectives.

To strengthen the senate he proposed to double its membership by the admission of

300 of the richest and most prominent men of the middle class or equestrian order. This reform had as its aim the fusion of the two highest classes representing nobility and wealth. To remove the chief source of friction between these two classes, he proposed that jurors for the extortion court be chosen partly from the enlarged membership of the senate and partly no doubt from the knights enrolled in the first eighteen centuries of the Centuriate Assembly. To his proposed reform of the courts he added a special clause making corruption or the acceptance of bribes a criminal offense.

These proposals naturally met with a chilly reception from the senate and the united opposition of the middle class, and could not possibly be carried through the assembly, unless Drusus succeeded in winning the support of the masses. To gain this support he proposed the public distribution of grain at low prices, the founding of colonies in Italy and Sicily (as his father had once proposed), and the renewed distribution of public land to individual colonists. To defray the expenses of his grain law he proposed to debase the silver coinage with an eighth part of copper. All these laws seem to have been passed but whether separately or in an omnibus bill is uncertain.

Nor is it certain how, if, and when he introduced the bill to extend Roman citizenship to the Latin and Italian allies. As a separate law, it stood no better chance of passage than it had in the time of Fulvius Flaccus or of Gaius Gracchus. The urban voters were just as strongly opposed to it as ever; the knights did not want to share their control of the courts or tax-gathering privileges in the provinces with the Italian middle class; nor the senate its office-holding rights with the Italian nobility. It is more likely that Drusus hoped to be able to tie it in with other more popular proposals. Of the need, wisdom, and justice of the law there can be little question. The Italian allies had supplied more than half the soldiers who had fought Rome's battles but had no share in the Roman higher offices, no say in determining Roman policies, had received no benefits that Roman citizens enjoyed in the distributions of public lands, no protection against the abuse and tyranny of Roman generals and officers, and no right of appeal in cases tried by Roman judges.

In the end the rest of the legislative program of Livius Drusus fared no better than the abortive proposal to extend the Italian franchise. The court law was enacted by the assembly and seemed at first to meet the general approval of the senate, though the conservative right wing which bitterly opposed the admission of the wealthy capitalists to their exclusive, aristocratic body, had wanted nothing less than a repeal of the Gracchan law and the full restoration of jury service to the senate. Other members, who had been able to profit from the financial speculations of the knights, did not want the Gracchan law disturbed. At last the senate opposition led by the consul L. Marcius Philippus grew strong enough to declare the laws of Livius Drusus null and void on the ground that they had been passed through violence and unconstitutional methods.

The Death of Livius Drusus. Even after the nullification of his reform laws, Drusus seems to have been determined to bring before the assembly a special law granting citizenship to the Italian allies. But before he was able to bring the bill to a vote, he was stabbed to death near the entrance of his house by an unknown assailant who vanished into the night. Thus died Livius Drusus, an enlightened statesman and the last of Rome's great civil reformers. The justice he tried to procure for the Italian people by legal means they were to win for themselves by a war which drenched their land in blood.

The Italian or Social War: 90–88 B.C.

Never since the Samnite and Pyrrhic Wars, not even in the blackest days after Cannae, had Roman supremacy in Italy been more violently shaken than in the months that followed the stabbing of Livius Drusus. With his death vanished the last hope of the Italian allies of securing the rights and freedoms of citizenship by peaceful means. The praetor Gaius Servilius Caepio went to the Abruzzi and addressed the people of Asculum (Ascoli) in a violent harangue against their agitation for citizenship and their revolutionary societies. The Asculans, enraged by the insolence of his threats, tore apart Caepio and his lictors, and massacred all the Romans who lived in the town. The war which Livius Drusus had tried to prevent had begun.

The revolt spread like wildfire through the Abruzzi down into the southern Apennines. First rose the Marsi to arms, then their neighbors, the Paeligni, Marrucini, and Frentani; in the North, the unenfranchised Picenes and Vestini; in the South, the Samnites, the Lucanians, and Apulians. From the Po to the straits of Messina the Italian people rose up in arms. Only the landlord-ridden sections of Umbria and Etruria did not, nor the more civilized Latins and Campanians, the Greek coastal cities from Naples to Tarentum, or the colonies and settlements already awarded the rights of Roman citizenship.

Preparation for War

Among the insurgents the Marsi and the Samnites were the fiercest. Together with their allies they declared their independence and set up a confederacy they called Italia, whose capital was at Corfinium in the Abruzzi about 75 miles due east of Rome. Their government, modeled on that of Rome, consisted of a senate of 500 members representing the various tribes and towns and of two consuls and twelve praetors elected annually by their senate. The new state issued its own coinage showing usually on one side either Bacchus or a female head representing Italia and on the other a swearing in of troops or the Italian bull goring the Roman she-wolf.

The Italian confederacy raised an army of 100,000 men, many of them hardened soldiers trained in the tactics and discipline of the Roman army. They had as their commanders two excellent generals, the Marsian Q. Pompaedius Silo, and the Samnite C. Papius Mutilus. In the spring of 90 B.C., the Italian armies advanced westwards, the Samnites against Campania and the Marsians against Latium in order to cut Rome off from the south.

In waging war against the Italians, the Romans had several important advantages. Their control over the ports and harbors of Italy as well as their command of the sea gave them access to the manpower and resources of the provinces and enabled them to recruit Gauls, Spaniards, and Numidians. In a short time they were able to raise and equip about 150,000 men. Another advantage they enjoyed was their ability to operate within interior lines of communication, and their control of the road system enabled them to shift troops from one point to another more quickly than the insurgents. Within insurgent territory the Romans held strong enclaves of resistance, which could impede or threaten the Italian war effort.

Military Operations

Even with these advantages the Romans fared badly in the first year of the war. Some of their defeats arose from the senate's hostility and spite towards Marius, the greatest general of the age. It recalled him from Asia but instead of placing him in command of the army sent eastwards against the Marsians it made him serve as a *legatus* or deputy commander under the consul P. Rutilius Lupus, who had little military skill or experience. The consul, rejecting Marius' advice to take time to train his troops, attacked immediately, and was defeated and killed. Only the military genius of Marius saved the main Roman army from complete disaster. Even then he was obliged to share the supreme command with Q. Servilius Caepio, who was later lured into an ambush and killed.

On the southern front the Romans also suffered serious reverses. In 90 B.C. the army, led by the consul L. Julius Caesar with L. Cornelius Sulla second in command, was sent to check the Samnite advance into Campania and there suffered several defeats and failed to prevent the Samnites from overrunning most of Campania and breaking through to the coast. Caesar finally defeated the Samnites at Acerrae, inflicting on them a loss of 6,000 men. Even then Rome was still in serious danger of being cut off from the rest of Italy, and new revolts began to flare up in Etruria and Umbria.

The Roman Grant of Citizenship to the Italians

At last Caesar found a way of turning military reverses into political victory. He returned to Rome and carried through the assembly a bill called the *lex Julia* to confer citizenship on all Latins and Italians still loyal to Rome and to those who would at once lay down their arms. In 89 B.C. the tribunes, M. Plautius Silvanus and C. Papirius Carbo, put through a more comprehensive bill, the *lex Plautia-Papiria*, granting citizenship to all free persons resident in any allied community who would register before a Roman praetor within sixty days. A third law, the *lex Pompeia,* proposed by Cn. Pompeius Strabo, a consul of the same year, extended citizenship to all free persons residing in the Cisalpina south of the Po and Latin rights to those living north of the river. The revolts began to collapse.

Before his consulship, Cn. Pompeius Strabo (author of the *Lex Pompeia* and father of the future Pompey the Great), had suppressed a revolt in Picenum by organizing a private army among his numerous clients. As a reward for his services to Rome, that powerful landowner of Picenum was elected consul for 89 B.C. and placed in command of the army besieging Asculum, which he captured late in the year. He put the inhabitants to the sword as punishment for the massacre of Roman citizens just before the war. Just before the capture of Asculum, he had been the victor in a great battle, involving 75,000 Romans and 60,000 Italians. His consular colleague, L. Porcius Cato, was less successful. Unable to discipline his unruly troops, he nevertheless attacked the Marsians and after a minor initial success was defeated and killed. It was then left to Pompeius Strabo to finish the war against the Marsians and their allies in central Italy.

On the southern front, Sulla, after taking over the command from Lucius Julius Caesar, decisively defeated the Samnites under Papius Mutilus in southern Campania. After sweeping all the Samnite forces out of Campania, he carried the war into Samnium. His victorious march was checked finally by a reverse at the hands of the famous Marsian general, Pompaedius Silo, who later met death in a battle with Q. Metellus Pius. The death of the great Marsian marked the end of the war except for sporadic local resistance. The longest to hold out was Nola in Campania, which lay besieged for many years.

The Aftermath of the Social War

The war had exacted a heavy price for shortsighted senatorial policies. The human and property losses must have been almost as great as those inflicted by Hannibal. The economic hardships were extremely severe. Food was scarce and prices high; rich and poor were oppressed by debts they had no means of paying and the city was crowded with Italian refugees. The city praetor of 89 B.C., A. Sempronius Asellio, attempted to give the debtors some relief by issuing an edict which revived the fourth century B.C. law prohibiting interest. He was killed by a mob of angry creditors.

The senate seemed to have profited little from the experience. With the war almost over, it attempted to withhold the concessions made and condemned the Italians to second class citizenship by enrolling them in eight or ten of the thirty-five tribes so as to limit their influence in the assemblies.

Nevertheless, the war produced some good results. It added almost 500,000 new citizens to the rolls. From the Po river to the straits of Messina all free men were now Roman citizens and all the many different racial elements would in time be fused into a single nation. Local self-government was permitted and all communities and municipalities enjoyed the right to elect their own boards of four magistrates (*Quattuorviri*). Gradually they would adopt Roman private and public law as well as a common Latin language. The grant of universal Roman citizenship was a giant stride towards national unification and the development of a common Latin culture.

The First Mithridatic War

In granting citizenship to the Italians, the senate had been prompted not only by the adverse military situation, but by the aggressive actions of Mithridates VI, king of Pontus.

Since 281 B.C., most of Asia Minor had formed an integral part of the Seleucid Empire of Syria. After the battle of Magnesia in 190 B.C. and the Treaty of Apamea in 188 B.C., Rome had become the dominant power, especially after her annexation of the province of Pergamum in 129 B.C.* Beyond her range of influence were the kingdoms of Armenia and Parthia. The latter, had become the domain of a nomadic tribe that had once lived near the Caspian Sea.

Taking advantage of the breakdown of the Seleucid Empire, the Parthians had by 140 B.C. overrun Iran, Mesopotamia, Afghanistan, northwestern India, and, for a time, Bactria. They were too far east either to invite Roman interference or to challenge Roman domination of western Asia Minor. Northwest of the Parthian Empire lay the large kingdom of Armenia, which had been ruled since ca. 94 B.C., by Tigranes II. Still farther north was the kingdom of Pontus, a mountainous region but fertile and beautiful, which extended along the southern shores of the Black Sea. Pontus had been an unimportant state until its rulers, who claimed descent from the Persian royal family, succeeded in subjugating some of the Greek colonies along the coast.

The three mighty kingdoms of Parthia, Armenia, and Pontus were at this time strategic buffer states between the Western World and the Far East. They were under pressure simultaneously from the Romans of the West and from the Sakas, the Sacrucae, and the Tocharians of the northeast, who were being pushed westwards by the relentless and inexorable pressure of the Huns, who were pressed in turn by the Chinese. To protect Parthia from sudden attack from the East, the king encouraged his provincial governors

* The Roman province of Pergamum (see map, p. 198) lay along the coast of the Aegean Sea south of the Dardanelles. Along the southern shores of the Black Sea to the east lay first Bithynia, Paphlagonia, and Pontus. South of these were situated first Galatia, then the huge kingdom of Cappadocia, and finally that of Armenia, which extended eastwards as far as the Caspian Sea. Southeast of Armenia lay the large kingdom of Parthia.

and the landowning military aristocracy to keep themselves and their horses in constant readiness so that they might, on their own initiative and at a moment's notice, be able to repel any such aggression. While they were not under obligation to seek the king's authority to act in time of emergency, they were bound to him by oaths, gifts, and fiefs. It is indeed most interesting to observe that the kingdoms of the Middle East were compelled by the necessities of national defense to anticipate the feudal system of Western Europe by many centuries.

Mithridates VI Eupator: 120–63 B.C.

About 120 B.C., the crown of Pontus descended to a young prince named Mithridates VI, later known as Mithridates the Great. At eleven, he had already run away from his legal guardians and spent several years wandering from place to place. He lived by his hunting and his wits. Like Massinissa and Jugurtha of Numidia, he was an excellent athlete, hunter, and soldier, but as a statesman and administrator, was to leave much to be desired. When he came of age in 115 B.C. and returned to Sinope, the Pontic capital, his first act was to kill his mother and his brother, with whom he had shared the throne.

Sometime between 110 and 106 B.C. he enlarged his kingdom by annexing the Greek cities of the Crimea and the Taman peninsula, which had invoked his aid and protection against the attacks of the Scythians and Sarmatians of the South Russian steppes. He later made alliances with these tribes and with the Bastarnians and Thracians in the Balkans, and by 100 B.C. had brought under his control the entire coastal region of the Black Sea from the Straits of Kerch to the mouth of the Danube. After his conquest of the Colchians at the eastern end of the Black Sea, he had converted that sea into a Pontic lake and gained access to one of the richest sources of wheat, shipbuilding supplies, and manpower known in the ancient world. The conquest of this region enabled him to recruit enormous armies and to build a fleet of 300 ships.

Rich in natural resources, the conquered regions were backward, uncivilized, and lacking in people with the skill, education, and culture required for the development of a strong empire. The citizens Mithridates sought were to be found in Asia Minor, the conquest of which now seemed essential to the future growth of his kingdom. Nor did the conquest appear difficult, for Rome, the only deterrent, was occupied with the Teutonic and Cimbrian war. Furthermore, the neighboring states of Cappadocia, Galatia, Paphlagonia, and Bithynia, nominally Rome's allies but actually her vassals, had submitted to their status with the deepest resentment.

Mithridates agreed with Nicomedes III of Bithynia to partition first Paphlagonia, which had fallen into anarchy, then Galatia. In neither conquest did Rome interfere. Next came the large kingdom of Cappadocia, a most valuable acquisition, whose king, Ariarathes VI, was assassinated at Pontic instigation. This time Nicomedes II betrayed Mithridates, invaded Cappadocia, drove out the heir, Ariarathes VII, and married his widowed mother—a sister of Mithridates. The outraged Mithridates wrested Cappadocia from Nicomedes' grasp and restored Ariarathes to the throne. But he later quarreled with the uncooperative puppet king and killed him in a duel. He gave the throne to one of his own sons, but the Cappadocian people finally rebelled. With Roman approval, they elected Ariobarzanes I instead.

Fearing Roman intervention at this point, Mithridates persuaded his ally, Tigranes II of Armenia, to whom he had given his daughter in marriage, to invade Cappadocia and drive out Ariobarzanes. For the first time Rome interfered and in 92 B.C. instructed Sulla, then governor of Cilicia, to restore Ariobarzanes to the throne and extract from both Mithridates and Tigranes an agreement to leave Cappadocia alone. Mithridates broke the agreement around 90 B.C. and brought not only Cappadocia under his control but Bithynia as well. In response to the appeal of the two ousted kings, the senate instructed Manius Aquilius to compel Mithridates to withdraw from both kingdoms and recognize Ariobarzanes as the lawful king of Cappadocia and Nicomedes IV, son of Nicomedes III, as king of Bithynia. This done, Aquilius did a very foolish thing. He incited Nicomedes to raid Pontus in order to seize enough loot to reward the Romans for their intervention in Bithynia.

Mithridates Makes War on Rome

When Aquilius persuaded Nicomedes to invade Pontus (88 B.C.), Mithridates, after several unheeded protests, decided to strike. Quickly defeating Nicomedes, he swept the weak Roman forces aside and invaded Pergamum. He captured Aquilius and paid him the money he had demanded by pouring molten gold down his throat. All Asia Minor welcomed Mithridates as a deliverer and a savior and seized the chance of making the Romans pay dearly for their forty years of oppression. In one day they slaughtered 80,000 Italians, mostly tax agents, money lenders, and merchants.

The conquest of Asia Minor was not enough. Mithridates would not feel secure unless he added Greece to his dominions. He knew that the Romans were hated in Greece almost as much as in Asia and had sent his agents to Athens and other cities to make propaganda for his cause. Meanwhile his powerful navy had broken out into the Aegean and made a descent on Delos, where he ordered the massacre of 20,000 Italian merchants and slave dealers. That massacre and the seizure of property permanently destroyed the prosperity of the island. Athens, too, was ready for revolt and, under the leadership of the philosophers Athenion and Aristion, overthrew its pro-Roman oligarchic government and made common cause with Mithridates, whose general, Archelaus, occupied the Piraeus (port of Athens) and from that base conquered most of southern Greece. Another Pontic army was entering Greece from the North. Such was the dangerous situation in the East as Rome slowly rose from the ruins of the Social War.

The Rivalry of Marius and Sulla: 88 B.C.

Two well known and experienced Roman generals, Marius and Sulla, were most eager for the command in the war against Mithridates. Marius wanted to recover the popularity he had enjoyed after

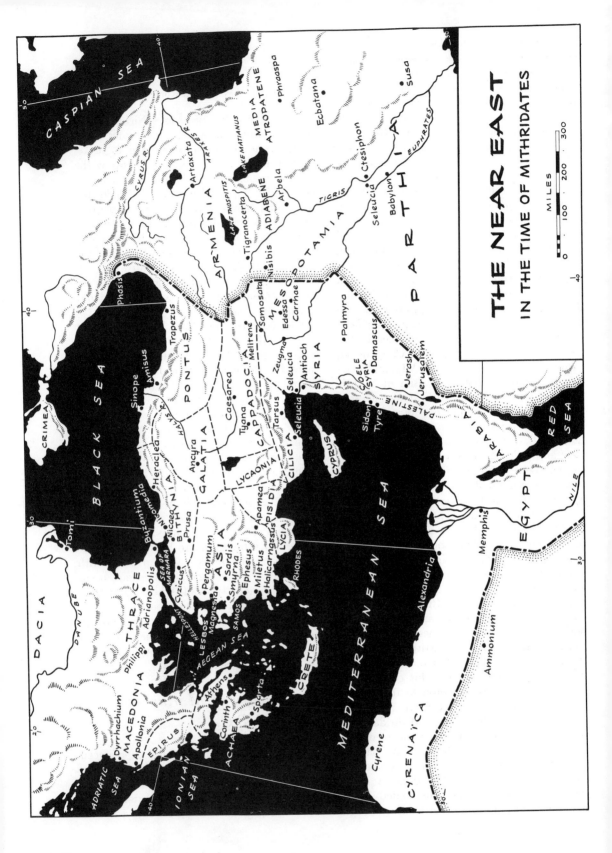

THE NEAR EAST
IN THE TIME OF MITHRIDATES

the Jugurthine and Cimbrian wars but had later lost (*see* p. 190). Sulla wanted the command because he believed the war would be easily won and a source of power, fame, and especially fortune, for he loved pleasure, and was a hard drinker, a heavy spender. The senate awarded the command to Sulla.

The Tribuneship of P. Sulpicius Rufus: 88 B.C.

The rivalry between the two generals might well have been settled by the senate's decision had it not involved the political aims and ideals of the tribune, P. Sulpicius Rufus, a close friend and admirer of Livius Drusus the Younger, and like Livius a fairly conservative demagogue. Sulpicius had strongly opposed the senate's restriction of the newly enfranchised Italians to eight of the thirty-five tribes. Though a member of one of the most ancient and illustrious patrician families and an heir to immense wealth, Sulpicius had given up his patrician status (88 B.C.) in order to qualify for election as tribune. Like Gaius Gracchus, he was an orator of remarkable power, a little inclined to be showy perhaps but, Cicero declared, by far the best he had ever heard.

As tribune of the people, Sulpicius Rufus made four proposals which seem to have been presented in one omnibus bill: 1) to enroll the new Italian citizens as well as the freedmen in all the thirty-five tribes; 2) to recall all exiles; 3) to exclude from the senate all members owing bills in excess of 2,000 denarii (about 500 dollars) in order to prevent bribery and corruption; and 4) to replace Sulla with Marius in the command against Mithridates. The first law was the least acceptable. He was able to muster the support of twelve tribes (he needed eighteen): the four urban ones, to which Aemilius Scaurus had, in 115 B.C., assigned the freedmen, and the eight in which the Italians already had votes. To gain the support of the six other required tribes, he had to make a deal with Marius, who might, in exchange for the command against Mithridates, be able through the votes of his veterans to swing the six needed tribes required for a majority. The bill became law though not without considerable opposition and violence.

Sulla's March on Rome

At first Sulla tried to prevent the passage of these laws by declaring religious holidays in order to suspend all meetings of the assembly. Exasperated by the repeated use of that religious weapon, Sulpicius and his armed followers rioted. Sulla escaped by taking refuge in the house of Marius. After Sulla had publicly revoked the religious holidays, Marius, like an old soldier doing a good turn for another, allowed him to escape from his house by the back door expecting that he would go into exile. Instead, Sulla hastened to his army which was then besieging Nola, and persuaded them to march on Rome.

During the ensuing reign of terror, Sulla set fire to all the sections of the city which offered resistance and put to death many innocent people. Sulpicius attempted to escape but was betrayed. He was murdered and his head stuck up on the rostra in the Forum. Marius also fled and got as far as Minturnae, where he was found hiding in a coastal marsh, up to his waist in mud. He was conveyed to the civil authorities for execution, but when the executioner, a Cimbrian slave, entered his cell, Marius fixed his flashing eyes on the slave and in a haughty voice asked whether he dared to kill Gaius Marius. The slave, quite unnerved, dropped the ax and fled. The city magistrates, ashamed that Marius, the great savior of Rome, should be more honored by a slave he had conquered than by the citizens he had saved, set him free and let him take ship for Africa.*

The victorious Sulla rescinded the laws of Sulpicius Rufus. Although he introduced a law for the relief of debtors reducing the maximum rate of interest to ten per cent, he then made a number of reactionary changes. At his behest, the Centuriate Assembly reappropriated the legislative powers of the Tribal Assembly. The Assembly also reorganized it-

* During the reign of terror, Sulla attempted to disarm one of the best generals of the Italian War by transferring the command in the central Apennines from Pompeius Strabo to his more co-operative colleague, Pompeius Rufus, whose death warrant he thereby unintentionally signed. The soldiers killed Pompeius Rufus when he attempted to take command.

self so that the centuries of the senatorial and upper middle class and those of the first assessment class had a clear majority. Another reactionary step was the requirement that magistrates consult the senate before introducing new legislation.

Sulla's attempt to interfere with the consular elections failed, though he did manage to extract a promise from one of the newly elected consuls, Lucius Cornelius Cinna, not to tamper with any of Sulla's constitutional changes already made. After Sulla had carried out these changes, he departed for the East to make war against Mithridates.

Cinna's Consulship

Hardly was Sulla out of sight of Italy's shores than the democratic and dynamic Cinna annulled the laws of Sulla and re-enacted those of Sulpicius. He enrolled the Italians in all thirty-five tribes against the opposition of the senate and of his colleague, Gnaeus Octavius. After some violent rioting, Octavius drove Cinna from the city and had him declared a public enemy by the senate. In so doing the senate committed a very serious blunder for it gave Cinna the opportunity of appealing to the Italian voters and winning the support of the army still besieging the Campanian town of Nola. He recalled Marius from Africa and, imitating Sulla's example, marched on Rome.

Marius and His Reign of Terror

Recalled from Africa, the Elder Marius, now well over seventy, stormed Ostia, the seaport of Rome, cut off the food supplies of Rome, and starved her into surrender. Marius, brutalized by years of war and slaughter, embittered by ingratitude and neglect, and maddened by his recent experiences in Italy and Africa as a hunted outlaw, gave full vent to his rage and lust for blood. For days he ranged the city like a raving lunatic. His followers struck down all the nobles and senators he hated. Their mutilated corpses littered the streets and their heads, dripping blood, decorated the rostra. Their houses and property were confiscated and auctioned. His outrages made even Cinna quail, and he

finally put a stop to them. In 86 B.C. Marius at last achieved his long cherished ambition of a seventh consulship. Unfortunately he fell ill and died a few days after taking office.

Sulla's Operations against Mithridates

In 87 B.C. Sulla landed in Greece with an army of about 30,000 men. From Epirus he advanced into Boeotia, where he defeated the forces of Aristion and Archelaus and drove them from the open country. He then invaded Attica and laid siege to Athens, which did not fall until the following spring. His soldiers killed every tenth Athenian, and looted the town, carrying off many rare books and works of art. After more hard fighting and severe losses, he occupied the Piraeus and destroyed its docks and installations.

After the capture of Athens and the Piraeus, Sulla hastened north to meet a large Pontic army of 100,000 men that had come down through Thrace and Macedonia and had penetrated into Boeotia. It was a poor army of badly disciplined barbarians, and Sulla was able to destroy it at small cost. His victory is less amazing in light of the fact that eastern rulers, still untaught by the disasters at Cynoscephalae, Magnesia, and Pydna, continued to employ the hoplite phalanx formation and tactics now obsolete for at least two centuries. Sulla won at Chaeronea with the help of trench fortifications in 86 B.C., a feat which he repeated the next year at Orchomenus in Boeotia.

It was after Chaeronea that Lucius Valerius Flaccus, whom Cinna had sent to take over the command from Sulla, arrived in Greece. He lost some of his men at sea in encounters with the fleet of Mithridates, he lost still others by defection to Sulla. When Sulla refused to surrender his command, Flaccus, after an oral agreement, promptly set out for Asia by way of Macedonia and Thrace. No sooner had Flaccus crossed the Hellespont and arrived in Bithynia than his soldiers mutinied at the instigation of Flaccus' own legate, C. Flavius Fimbria, and murdered him. Elected by the soldiers' council to take over the command, Fimbria exhibited surprising energy and talent. In a night attack he defeated the army of Mithridates' son and marched against Pergamum. Mithridates, realizing that he had already lost the war not only because of the defeats of his armies but because of the revolts stirred up in Asia Minor by his despotism and tyranny, sued for peace.

Sulla wanted peace so as to be free to get back to Italy and take revenge on the followers of Marius and Cinna. The peace he made in 85 B.C. at Dardanus in the Troad was the softest a Roman was ever known to make, especially with an enemy like Mithridates, who had robbed and murdered at least 100,000 Roman and Italian citizens. All Mithridates was required to do was abandon all his conquests in Asia Minor, surrender eighty of his warships, and pay the trifling indemnity of 2,000 talents (two and a half million dollars). Far harsher terms were imposed on the province of Asia, from which was exacted an indemnity of 20,000 talents (twenty-five million dollars), and five years' back taxes. Sulla billeted his army on the towns during the winter of 85-84 B.C. requiring them to pay each soldier sixteen drachmae a day, which apart from the food and clothing also required of them must have amounted to at least another $25,000,000. To raise these vast sums the province had to turn to the Roman money lenders and fell victims to a crushing burden of debt.

Sulla's Return to Italy: 83 B.C.

After making peace with Mithridates, Sulla took over the army of Fimbria, who later committed suicide in Pergamum. Placing that army under the command of L. Licinius Murena to serve as a permanent garrison in the province of Asia, Sulla set sail for Italy. Accompanied by his army of from 30,000 to 40,000 men, more loyal to him than to their country, he stepped ashore at Brundisium in the spring of 83 B.C. To oppose Sulla the ex-consul Carbo had raised two armies of 50,000 men, mostly raw recruits, undisciplined, and not very loyal or reliable. They were also poorly led, for the two consuls in command, L. Cornelius Scipio and C. Norbanus, knew little about war. Sulla defeated the army of Norbanus with little trouble, Scipio's deserted to him. The

only anti-Sullan who might have defeated him was Quintus Sertorius but the party leaders found him too disturbing a critic and at the earliest opportunity shipped him off to Spain instead.

The army leaders who joined Sulla after his arrival in Italy were much superior to their opponents in military capacity and experience. The first was his brother-in-law, Metellus Pius, who brought with him a number of recruits from his hiding place in Liguria. Next came the young Marcus Licinius Crassus at the head of a small army returning from Spain. An even more valuable addition was Pompey both in the number of troops he brought and in military skill. On his own initiative he had raised three legions in Picenum and on reaching Sulla was hailed, young as he was, with the flattering title of *Imperator* and even as "The Great," a title that stuck to him for the rest of his life.

To bolster their tottering regime, the anti-Sullans elected as consuls for 82 B.C. Cn. Papirius Carbo and Gaius Marius, the adopted son of Marius the Elder. Neither one was a first class general though both were fairly successful in gathering recruits, especially in Etruria and Samnium. Carbo went south and rallied thousands of Samnites to his cause, while Marius attracted many veterans by the magic of his father's name. Choosing separate combat areas, Carbo directed operations in the north, Marius outside Rome. In his efforts to block Sulla's advance up the Appian Way, Marius fought a hard but losing battle and was forced to take refuge in Praeneste. Sulla immediately dashed north and met Carbo at Clusium (Chiusi) in Etruria. Although he did not win a decisive victory, he succeeded in breaking the morale of Carbo's army, already somewhat undermined by the successes of Metellus in North Italy and of Pompey and Crassus in Umbria. Carbo, seeing the futility of further struggle, escaped to North Africa.

Carbo may have given up too quickly. The war was far from being over and even victory might still have been won. Had Carbo had the military sense of a Marius, he might have, even with his battered army, followed Sulla as he hastened south to meet a huge Samnite army outside of Rome. At the battle of the Colline Gate the Samnites, fighting with insane fury far into the night, crumpled the left wing which was under Sulla's personal command and had Crassus, in command of the right wing, not been victorious Sulla might never have become dictator of Rome. Carbo's arrival at that crucial moment might have spared Rome the horrors of a Sullan triumph.

Sulla's Reign of Terror: 82 B.C.

The bloody battle at the Colline Gate ended all effective resistance in Italy. Then a reign of terror began, during which thousands of persons suffered death often accompanied by torture. Next door to the temple of Bellona, where Sulla was addressing a meeting of the senate, 6,000 Samnite prisoners, whose only crime was that they lost a battle for what they believed was freedom and justice, were tortured to death. As the screams of the dying broke into his speech and distressed some of the senators to the point of fainting, Sulla grimly explained that only some criminals were punished at his orders.

The Proscriptions. To ruthlessness he added method. He posted lists of his intended victims, some carefully selected by himself, others suggested by his henchmen; some were listed for political reasons, others to avenge private injuries and others for no other reason than that the proscribed owned large and valuable properties. The proscribed were to be hunted down as outlaws, murdered, and a price set on their heads. Sulla confiscated their property and revoked the citizenship of their children. Among the thousands he doomed to die were 90 senators, 15 men of consular rank, and 2,600 knights, whose property was distributed among his supporters and veterans. As beneficiaries of his murders they would, when required, rally around him or loyally support the oligarchy, whose power he proposed to restore. He secured additional supporters by freeing 10,000 slaves which had belonged to his victims. He generously rewarded some freedmen. One, for example, was allowed to buy an estate worth $300,000 for $100.

Unfortunately, the murder and spoliation of rich individuals failed to provide enough money or land to enable Sulla to redeem his promises of pay, pensions, and farms to his discharged veterans. He compelled cities, towns, and other communities to contribute their share to the cause, especially those suspected of having resisted his seizure of power or of having supported his enemies. Their punishment was in proportion to the duration and strength of their resistance and opposition. The cities that offered only mild opposition were required to pay fines, have their walls torn down, and surrender most, if not all, of their territory. Others, such as Praeneste in Latium or Florence in Etruria, which resisted him long and stubbornly, were destroyed and their inhabitants sold into slavery. He thus turned the richest and most thickly populated districts of Samnium into a desert. Although the confiscations and enslavements were heaviest in Etruria and a few other parts of central and northern Italy, Samnium remained for long a desolate waste. Such were the atrocities of one of the most savage dictators ever to befoul the pages of history.

Sulla's Changes of the Constitution

In 82 B.C., a few days before his arrival in Rome, Sulla had demanded and secured the formal passage by the Centuriate Assembly of a law known as the *lex Valeria* to appoint him dictator for an undefined period for the purpose of drafting laws and "reconstituting" the state. The assembly, confirming that which had already been established by military force, revived an office held only once since the middle of the third century (by Fabius Maximus Cunctator in 217 B.C.), and legalized his murders, confiscations, and other atrocities.

Unrestrained by law or custom, by the right of appeal, or by tribunician veto, Sulla's dictatorship could be terminated only by his death or resignation. He had the power of life and death and his *imperium* was absolute.

In 81 B.C. Sulla increased the membership of the senate, which had been somewhat reduced by the civil war and the series of assassinations conducted by Marius, and by

Sulla himself. The 300 new members came from the first eighteen centuries of the Centuriate Assembly and from the rich, land-owning knights of the Italian municipalities. To maintain the senate's membership at a level of 500 or more, he increased from twelve to twenty the quaestors, who were eligible for seats in the senate after their term of office. The main object of expanding the senate's membership was to make a larger number of persons available for jury service, which he transferred from the knights to the senate. In expanding the membership of the senate and in making senators alone eligible as jurors, Sulla was actually carrying out a proposal of Livius Drusus.

Sulla's Reform of the Courts. In his reform of the courts Sulla went much further than Livius Drusus. He abolished trials before the popular assemblies and replaced them with trials by jury, thereby giving the senate control over the administration of justice. He raised the number of special jury courts for the trial of major crime to seven (namely: the *quaestio de repetundis* dealing with extortion; *de maiestate,* with treason; *de ambitu,* with bribery in elections; *de falsis,* with forgery; *de peculatu,* with embezzlement of public property; *de sicariis et veneficis,* with murder; and *de vi publica,* with assault and battery). To provide enough judges to preside over these standing courts he increased the number of praetors from six to eight. The reform of the courts was the greatest and the most permanent of Sulla's reforms. It clarified and recast the law dealing with serious crimes and laid the foundation of Roman criminal law.

Changes in the Magistracies. To regulate the system of office holding, Sulla re-enacted, in a considerably modified form, the *lex Villia Annalis* of 180 B.C., which prescribed a regular order of holding office (*cursus honorum*): first the quaestorship, then the praetorship, and finally the consulship. He re-affirmed the rule prescribing an interval of ten years between successive consulships. His revised law advanced the minimum age for the quaestorship to 30, for praetorship to 40, and for consulship to 43. During their year of office the eight praetors and two consuls were to remain in Italy and were prohibited from raising armies. In the following year the senate would assign them provinces to govern as proconsuls and propraetors.

Changes were made in the tribuneship which destroyed the effectiveness of that office. Sulla crippled it most by disqualifying a tribune from holding any higher office, in order to make it unattractive to able and ambitious men. He limited the veto power of a tribune to the protection of personal rights and restricted or abolished his right to propose laws or prosecute cases before the Tribal Assembly. He removed another check upon the senate's control of the government by abolishing the censorship.

The Reorganization of the Provinces

Before the time of Sulla there were nine provinces, six in the West (Sicily, Sardinia-and-Corsica, Nearer Spain, Farther Spain, Africa Proconsularis, and Gallia Narbonensis), and three in the East (Macedonia, Asia, and Cilicia). Cyrenaica, though accepted in 96 B.C. as a legacy from its king, Ptolemy Apion, was not formally organized as a province till 74 B.C. The tenth province was created by Sulla, who detached Cisalpine Gaul from the rest of Italy and sent a governor and a garrison to guard it against the raiders who periodically descended from the Alps.

It was also to provide enough governors for the ten provinces that Sulla had increased the number of praetors from six to eight. They, like the two consuls, would automatically become provincial governors after their year of office in Rome. To further fortify the power of the senate and prevent ambitious governors from creating personal armies strong enough to seize control of the state, Sulla limited the term of governor to one year and prohibited him from making war beyond the frontiers of his province without express authorization from the senate. He hoped thus to give the senate full control over the armed forces and limit the war-making potentiality of consuls and praetors in both Italy and the provinces. In the case of a major conflict the senate would raise the armies, choose the general, and grant him "extraordinary command." What Sulla did not foresee was that the real danger to the future of senatorial control would arise not from the provincial governors but from generals given the "extraordinary commands."

Sulla's Consulship, Abdication, and Death

After Sulla had fully reorganized the government to his own satisfaction and had restored the oligarchy to power, he stood for election as consul for 80 B.C. and headed the government both as consul and dictator. The following year he resigned his dictatorship and retired to his country estate near Puteoli (Pozzuoli) in Campania, where he hoped to pass the rest of his life in ease, luxury, and pleasure. He did not enjoy himself long. In 78 B.C. the 60-year-old Sulla died of a stroke and was cremated in Rome after a most magnificent funeral. Before his death, he had dictated the epitaph to be inscribed upon his tomb, "I have always rewarded my friends with good, my enemies with evil."

Sulla had named himself Felix, which means "Lucky." He was even more fortunate in death for he never saw the utter futility of the major part of his work. He died in the happy belief that he had restored the oligarchy to the power it had possessed in the fourth and third centuries B.C. The constitution he had tried to reconstruct, though it had such good features as the reform of the courts, the expanded membership of the senate, and the administration of the provinces, was hopelessly reactionary and doomed to failure from the start. As it turned out, the oligarchy he had restored to power was no more capable of governing than the one that had preceded it. Hardly had the ashes of his funeral pyre cooled than the whole rotten structure he had tried to prop began to give way and finally collapsed in ruin. It is a pity that his futile attempt should have involved so great a cost of human life.

The Decay and Fall of the Sullan Constitution

In 78 B.C. Sulla was dead. A decade later his constitution—which had briefly restored the oligarchy to absolute power—was dead too. The most bitter enemies of the restored oligarchy were the sons, relations, and friends of the men who had suffered proscription,

exile, or death. In the forests of Etruria roamed bands of once-peaceful and well-to-do farmers whose lands had been confiscated by Sulla for distribution among his veterans. In the city of Rome, the starving masses had been deprived of their subsidized food. The middle class had suffered financial ruin and had been denied the right of jury service in the extortion courts.*

As the years passed, no group was more frustrated and rebellious than Sulla's own veterans who had been given confiscated land but no knowledge of farming. They were soon enmeshed in debt and became one of the most discontented and potentially dangerous elements in Roman society. Hatreds, frustration, and the desire for revenge could not have found expression without leaders. And leaders came.

The Rebellion of Lepidus: 78 B.C.

The first attacker of the Sullan oligarchy was Marcus Aemilius Lepidus, the consul of 78 B.C. and a member of a most ancient and aristocratic wealthy family. Once a conservative, he had belonged to Sulla's inner circle. He had increased his wealth by buying at cut rates the property of those proscribed by Sulla. Afterwards, as governor of Sicily, he so shamelessly plundered that province that he narrowly escaped impeachment, the threat of which thrust him into the leadership of the rebel opposition.

Hardly had the torch kindled Sulla's funeral pyre than Lepidus proposed the recall of all exiles, the resumption of cheap grain distributions to the poor, the return of all confiscated properties to the former owners, and the restoration of the powers of the tribunes. The first two proposals the senate somewhat unwillingly accepted, the last two vigorously and successfully opposed. Soon the exiles began to return; first came Marcus Perperna, then the young Lucius Cinna, and a young man named Gaius Julius Caesar. Political clubs sprang up and the barrooms

---

* Small compensation was the presentation of senate seats to 300 of the richest men of the middle class: the rest had as little contact with these as with the nobility.

and whorehouses of the city hummed with political plots and conspiracies.

The senate was in a difficult position. To eliminate Lepidus, they sent him to northern Etruria to suppress an armed rebellion near Florence, where the evicted farmers had emerged from hiding and had driven the Sullan veterans off their lands. To carry out his assignment Lepidus went to Cisalpine Gaul and raised an army. Leaving his legate, M. Junius Brutus, in charge of North Italy, he marched to Etruria where, instead of suppressing the rebels, he invited them to join his army and marched on Rome. To the senate's order that he disband his army he replied with the demand of a second consulship and the restoration to the tribunes of their abolished powers.

The senate responded by sending the loyal consul Catulus to oppose Lepidus and Pompey to fight Junius Brutus. Catulus, with the aid of Sulla's veterans, drove Lepidus away from Rome back to Etruria, while Pompey defeated Brutus and put him to death. Pompey then moved down into Etruria and defeated Lepidus at Cosa. His cause lost, Lepidus escaped with the remnants of his army to Sardinia, where he soon afterwards died. His legate, Marcus Perperna, took the army to Spain and joined Sertorius, who had been waging full-scale war against the Roman government since 80 B.C.

Quintus Sertorius

Quintus Sertorius was unquestionably one of the greatest military commanders in the history of Rome. Under Marius he had fought in the Cimbrian and Social Wars and had learned how to train and discipline troops. For eight years, with units made up of a few Roman officers and some temperamental Spanish troops, he had repeatedly vanquished the mightiest armies Rome could throw against him.

Had the democratic leaders, who had mismanaged the war against Sulla in 83 B.C., only utilized the military and political talents of Sertorius instead of shipping him off to Spain, they might have changed the history of the Republic. Had Sertorius been in command of those brave Samnite fighters at the Colline Gate, Sulla would probably never have become dictator of Rome. Militarily, there could have been little doubt of the result. The political outcome must be assumed in view of what Sertorius did in Spain.

Sertorius in Spain: 82-72 B.C. Following the provincial policies of Fulvius Flaccus and Gaius Gracchus, Sertorius attempted to Romanize the provincials and make them standardbearers of Roman civilization. He accepted many Spaniards and Portuguese as Roman citizens, admitted some of their leaders into his opposition senate, and established a school for the education of the upper class youth.

By war, diplomacy, and sheer force of personality, he had acquired an authority over the Spanish people such as no native chieftain (not even Viriathus) had ever wielded. He taught the thousands who flocked to his standards to fight as Roman soldiers without destroying their natural aptitude for guerrilla warfare. He appealed to their superstitions by pretending he received all his secret information from a white fawn, a gift of Diana, which followed him everywhere. By tact, justice, and moderation, he won the devotion of the Spanish people, controlled the major part of the country, and defeated Sulla's generals, even the great Metellus Pius, in battle after battle.

Despite his battles against Roman armies, Sertorius never felt he was really at war with Rome or the Romans but only with Sulla's government. After Sulla's death he was eager for reconciliation, but the senate, determined to fight, had found a competent general. Pompey, in command of an army which he refused to disband, had practically demanded that he be sent to Spain. The senate agreed most reluctantly, fearing to entrust so dangerous a weapon as an army into the hand of a youth not old enough to hold even the lowest political office. With misgivings the senate passed a decree conferring upon Pompey proconsular power and the chief command in Nearer Spain.

Pompey was the son of Gnaeus Pompeius Strabo, who had fought in the Social War. He was, as his father had been, the largest landowner in Picenum. A good athlete, and an excellent swordsman, he was only twenty-three when he raised an army for Sulla who jokingly, but with real admiration, gave him the title *Magnus* ("The Great").

He was cautious and even timid in war, in business, and in human relations. Although he loved his wife and children, he lacked the nerve to defy Sulla's command that he divorce her (she belonged to the "wrong" family politically). Nor did he dare speak up for his friends, who had helped him in trouble, when Sulla struck them down before his very eyes. In battle he seldom attacked unless assured of overwhelming numerical superiority. His one act of bravado was to insist that Sulla accord him a triumph after his destruction of the Marian rebels in Sicily and Africa.

As a statesman, Pompey was somewhat inept and shortsighted. He spoke poorly and awkwardly and often fell back on silence—partly because he could not think of anything to say. Although the Sullan constitution was often contrary to his personal interest and ambitions, he had joined Sulla and fought on his side out of disgust with Marius and Cinna. Such was the man into whose hands the senate thrust so much power. Had he known how to use it, he might have become the first Roman monarch.

Pompey in Spain: 76-71 B.C. When Pompey arrived in Spain in 76 B.C., he found the military situation more formidable than he had expected. Sertorius, a superior tactician and field general, succeeded in defeating him twice, even with fewer men. On one occasion, only the timely arrival of old Metellus saved Pompey's army from annihilation. Pompey sent off a bitter letter to the Roman senate demanding strong reinforcements, which finally arrived. With their help and after the treacherous assassination of Sertorius by Perperna in 73 B.C. Pompey at last wound up the Spanish campaign.

Though a less skillful tactician than Metellus, Pompey seems to have been a better advertiser, for when the war was over public opinion gave Pompey the victory. The triumphant Pompey promptly executed Perperna for the murder of Sertorius. Yet he wisely followed the example of Sertorius and dealt with the Spanish people with great justice. His honorable peace terms restored prosperity to Spain and were long and gratefully remembered by the Spanish people.

The Great Mithridatic War: 74–63 B.C.

The eastern end of the Mediterranean was also ablaze with war. In 75 B.C., the childless king of Bithynia, Nicomedes IV, bequeathed his kingdom to the Roman people. The senate accordingly declared Bithynia a Roman province. This action provoked Mithridates VI of Pontus, who feared that Roman control of Bithynia would block his access to the Aegean Sea. Mithridates moved swiftly and occupied Bithynia before the Romans arrived, and eleven years of uncertain peace came to an abrupt end.

This long expected Mithridatic War erupted sooner than either side desired. Mithridates had begun to make preparations when the senate showed unwillingness to ratify the treaty of Dardanus, which he had made with Sulla in 85. He had engaged Roman exiled officers to modernize his army and made alliances with his son-in-law, Tigranes II of Armenia, with the pirates of Crete and Cilicia, and with Sertorius of Spain.

When war broke out with Rome, the pirates flocked to Pontus and helped Mithridates build up a formidable navy. Sertorius had sent some of his officers to drill and train the Pontic army to fight with Roman tactics. Tigranes did nothing, at least not yet.

Lucullus: 74–66 B.C.

Lucullus, consul of 74 B.C., was of a very old aristocratic family which had fallen into poverty. After his consulship, he was slated to be governor of Cisalpine Gaul but contrived to have himself transferred to the provinces of Cilicia and Asia and the command of the Roman army in the war against Mithridates. His consular colleague, M. Aurelius Cotta, received Bithynia as his province and command of the fleet. At the same time Marcus Antonius (father of Mark Antony), was given an extraordinary command to suppress the pirates of Crete and Cilicia, the naval allies of Mithridates. He failed most miserably. The pirates of Crete compelled him to sign a disreputable treaty, which the senate repudiated. He afterwards died in Crete. Cotta, in his first year, also got involved in difficulties. Hoping to carry off a big victory before Lucullus should reach the battle area, he impatiently began military operations against Mithridates, who attacked by land and sea, killed 3,000 of Cotta's men, burnt or captured nearly seventy of his ships, and shut him up in Chalcedon, a city on the Bosporus opposite Byzantium, now Istanbul.

Lucullus arrived and, with fewer than 30,000 infantrymen and 1,600 cavalry, he forced Mithridates to raise the siege of Chalcedon and won a magnificent series of victories against tremendous numerical odds. Had Mithridates at once retreated to the familiar mountain terrain of Pontus, he might have lured the Romans into ambush. Instead he suddenly bolted westwards and laid siege to the big city of Cyzicus, where he was himself trapped and where he lost most of his enormous army.

His communications cut, Mithridates ran short of supplies. He had allowed his army to get pinioned between the almost impregnable walls of Cyzicus and the immovable Roman army. Storms destroyed his siege works; disease broke out among his men; defeat followed defeat. Only his fleet enabled him to rescue a small remnant of an army said to have once numbered 200,000 men.

Lucullus was as good an admiral as he was a general. Near Lemnos he attacked and completely destroyed a Pontic fleet of fifty ships carrying 10,000 select troops (many of them Roman exiles) which had broken out into the Aegean.

The Battle of Cabira: 72 B.C.

After chasing Mithridates out of Bithynia, Lucullus invaded Pontus in the fall of 73 B.C. with his small army and even smaller cavalry. Bypassing Sinope, he crossed the Halys and besieged the large town of Amisus. After defeating the Pontic cavalry, Mithridates' pride, he brought the king to battle at

Cabira in 72 B.C. There followed panic, headlong flight, and terrific carnage. Mithridates fled to Armenia, without army or kingdom.

Leaving his lieutenants to besiege the stubbornly resisting coastal cities of Pontus, Lucullus took time to relieve the sufferings of the cities of the province of Asia crushed by the burden of Sulla's indemnity and by the debts they had contracted to pay it. Loans of 20,000 talents ($25,000,000) had, because of the high interest rates charged by money lenders, grown to six times the amount of the principal. The cities were on the verge of ruin and enslavement.

Lucullus took drastic steps to help the cities. He assisted the city treasuries by imposing a tax of 25 per cent on crops and special taxes on houses and slaves. He fixed the maximum interest rates on loans at 12 per cent, disallowed two thirds of the debts giving four years to pay them without interest, and issued a ruling that no debtor had to pay more than one quarter of his income. These regulations rapidly restored the economic health of the province, but infuriated the bankers at Rome.

The Armenian War: 69–66 B.C.

By the year 70 B.C. the Romans had gained control over all of Asia Minor, but they could not consider the war really won so long as Mithridates was at large and able to fight again. Lucullus accordingly demanded that Tigranes surrender his father-in-law. When Tigranes refused, Lucullus led his army across the Euphrates and invaded Armenia.

The invasion of Armenia had not been authorized by the senate, which might have hesitated to make war on a monarch apparently so formidable as Tigranes. On the strength of his alliance with Mithridates, Tigranes had attacked and occupied several disputed provinces of Parthia, Mesopotamia, the decrepit Seleucid Kingdom of Syria, and finally Cappadocia. Within a few years, he had become a great Oriental king of kings. From the lands he had conquered he had shifted hundreds of thousands of people to his newly founded capital of Tigranocerta near the headwaters of the Tigris. A more cautious man than Lucullus might have hesitated to risk an army in a country of steep mountain ranges so remote and isolated from the rest of the Middle East. To achieve this dangerous feat he had hardly 18,000 men, battleweary and disgruntled soldiers, to pit against forces maybe ten or twenty times as large. Disregarding all the dangers and difficulties, Lucullus boldly pushed forward against the mighty city of Tigranocerta with its seventy-five-foot walls partly surrounded by a river and laid it under siege.

The Battle of Tigranocerta: 69 B.C. When Tigranes appeared with his enormous army and saw the tiny Roman force, "too few for an army, too many for an embassy," he forgot Mithridates' urgent advice against attacking the Romans and saw no risk in a battle. In a few minutes of fighting, Lucullus drove an enormous Armenian troop of mail-clad cavalry crashing into the center of their own infantry, which broke and fled in wild confusion without striking a blow. The rest was slaughter. Tigranes escaped but the city of Tigranocerta fell with its vast stores of grain and gold.* Rarely in Roman military annals were tactics more brilliantly conceived and executed nor the destruction of the enemy more complete.

Elated by this brilliant victory, Lucullus set out on a long, painful march against Artaxata, the second capital. He never got there. The hard march through the mountains, the heavy snows of an early fall, and the iron discipline of Lucullus at last broke the morale and endurance of his officers and men. Almost within striking distance of Artaxata, they stopped and refused to go on. He fell back from Artaxata and wintered his army in Mesopotamia, where he won his last victory in the brilliant siege and capture of Nisibis and all the rich booty it contained.

Even while Lucullus was falling back from Artaxata, Mithridates was gathering a force of 8,000 men. He advanced into Pontus as liberator and avenger and easily destroyed the small Roman garrisons stationed there.

---

* The gold not only covered the expenses of the war but there remained enough for distribution among the soldiers, each receiving the equivalent of 165 dollars.

In the spring of 67 B.C., Mithridates defeated the legate Valerius Triarius, killing 7,000 men. The weak and feeble Tigranes, after reoccupying Armenia, again invaded Cappadocia. Lucullus could do nothing. His men refused to fight. He appealed to Rome for more men but got none. He appealed to the new governors of Cilicia and Asia, who also refused. The disastrous effects of the mutiny nullified eight glorious years of victory. Finally, Lucullus was relieved of his command and Pompey appointed in his place.

The humiliation of Lucullus was an unbelievable ending to his almost miraculous military achievements. He had transformed demoralized troops into a hard-hitting military machine. He had destroyed enormous armies with the most trifling losses to his own. He had permanently shattered the military power of the two proudest kings of the East. All without taking a single denarius from the Roman treasury.

His failure resulted in part from his relations with his own men. He had driven them to the limit, never once relaxing his discipline. He scorned to imitate Sulla, who rewarded his men by allowing them to loot captured cities. Lucullus, preoccupied with vast schemes of conquest, had no time for the common soldier. An unbending aristocrat, he lacked the earthy humor of Marius and the magnetism of Caesar.

Yet the soldiers of Lucullus might have brought the war to a glorious conclusion had not the middle class investment bankers, infuriated because he had checked their extortions and swindles in Asia, sent agents to incite mutiny among the men. Lucullus, cheated of victory by the cruel spite of the money lenders, betrayed by a weak and cowardly oligarchy, and thwarted of a triumph he richly deserved, found consolation in his wine cellar, his fish ponds, and his cherry trees.

Spartacus and the Slave War in Italy: 73–71 B.C.

While wars were raging at both ends of the Mediterranean, a dangerous slave revolt broke within Italy itself. In 73 B.C., Spartacus, a Thracian slave possibly of royal descent, led a band of gladiators out of the barracks of a training school at Capua. They fortified themselves in the crater of Vesuvius and called upon all farm slaves to join them in a fight for freedom. Many thousands did, especially the Gauls and Germans Marius had captured in the Cimbrian war. They were a dangerous and desperate lot, big brawny rascals brutalized by hard labor and harsh treatment on the plantations. The cowhands and shepherds, who came to Spartacus from the big ranches in the South, were well armed. The others soon obtained arms, buying them from the pirates and unscrupulous traders or capturing them from the Roman armies sent to subdue them. Their force grew to 70,000, as they ranged over the country, breaking open the slave prisons and arming the slaves.

The government, which had thought the slave revolt would be easily quelled, soon learned that Spartacus commanded a large army and was a master strategist as well. Defeat followed defeat. After Spartacus had vanquished the armies of four praetors and two consuls, the senate in desperation appointed Marcus Licinius Crassus to take command and assigned him six new legions in addition to remnants of the four consular legions Spartacus had shattered.

Marcus Crassus

Like Pompey and Lucullus, Crassus had been a Sullan partisan and a chief factor in Sulla's victory at the Colline Gate. Sulla had repaid him by his proscriptions, for Crassus was always on hand to buy up the properties of the victims. He later added to his millions by the acquisition of plantations and mines, as well as by his legal and banking business. In none of these activities did he show more initiative than in his real estate business in Rome. He operated a kind of private fire department and owned gangs of slaves skilled in the building trades. Whenever a fire broke out, his firemen would quickly appear but would never put the fire out until the owner had first signed an agreement to sell his property at a much reduced figure. As a result

of these numerous interests, Crassus became the most celebrated Roman millionaire. His wealth may be estimated from his own statement that nobody should be called rich, unless he was able to support an army on his income.

Though money provided him with a powerful political weapon (half the senate was in debt to him), Crassus yearned for the security of political office and especially military power. The Slave War provided Crassus the greatest opportunity of his life since the battle at the Colline Gate.

After he had trained his men, Crassus pursued Spartacus to the southern part of Bruttium and tried to fence him off by a walled entrenchment 35 miles long across the peninsula. One dark winter night Spartacus broke out through that barrier and marched into Lucania. Crassus was discouraged and the senate, more frightened than ever, recalled Pompey from Spain. Crassus was determined to do something before Pompey arrived and stole all the glory. The enemy unintentionally helped him, for the Germans and Celts, feeling that they were superior fighters to the Thracian and Asiatic followers of Spartacus, insisted on detaching themselves from the main army and attacking the enemy alone. They were promptly defeated. Subsequently the power of the revolt was easily broken, and Spartacus, who had created an army out of herdsmen, farm hands, and outcasts, had supplied them for two years with food and arms, and had defeated nine different Roman armies, was killed.

Pompey, on his way back from Spain, encountered and slew 5,000 slaves in Etruria. This minor feat of arms enabled Pompey to claim credit for ending yet another war.

The Consulship of Pompey and Crassus: 70 B.C.

Pompey and Crassus, both victors, marched to Rome and encamped their armies outside the gates. Each expected a triumph, both demanded the consulship. Crassus, praetor in 72 or 73 B.C., was eligible for the office. Pompey was six years too young to be a consul and had not yet held any of the lower offices the law required for a consular candidate. The senate could grant Pompey's demands only by scrapping the Sullan constitution, on which their power was based. Yet they could not reject the demands without the risk of having legions enter Rome. The hope of playing Crassus off against Pompey was equally vain. Although the two disliked each other, neither had any liking for the oligarchy or loyalty to the constitution. To avert a civil war, they agreed to form a coalition and adopt the reform program of the democratic agitators, who seemed more amenable. The coalition of Pompey and Crassus, their alliance with the democratic leaders, and the fear inspired by the encamped armies compelled the senate to award an ovation or minor triumph to Crassus, to Pompey a triumph, and to both the right to stand for the consulship.

The consulship of Pompey and Crassus completed the ruin of the Sullan constitution, which had been under attack for several years. In 75 B.C. the consul C. Aurelius Cotta had carried a law permitting the tribunes to hold higher offices. The consuls of 73 B.C., a year of scarcity and high prices, sponsored a bill to distribute five pecks a month to 45,000 citizens at the price set by Gaius Gracchus. Pompey now proposed and carried a law to restore to the tribunes all the powers taken away by Sulla. (Pompey hoped that the tribunes would later help him to secure desirable commands. They did not disappoint him.) The tribunes then proposed a law to restore citizenship to all who had fought under Lepidus and Sertorius. The consuls revived the censorship dormant since Sulla's time and the newly appointed censors promptly ejected from the senate sixty-four of Sulla's partisans.

Near the end of this historic consulship, the praetor, L. Aurelius Cotta, drafted and carried a law to break the senatorial monopoly of jury service and to draw jurors in equal numbers from the senate, the knights, and the *tribuni aerarii* ("tribunes of the treasury"). About the tribuni aerarii we know almost nothing. They were probably inferior to the knights in rank, but like the knights belonged to the middle class, which henceforth supplied two-thirds of the jurors.

The Trial of Gaius Verres: 70 B.C.

Cotta's court reform bill, strenuously resisted by the senate, won easier passage after the famous trial of Gaius Verres, the ex-governor of Sicily, who was tried for extortion, murder, and other heinous crimes. He had been a democrat in pre-Sullan days but had with sure instinct deserted to join the Sullan conservatives. The rewards were handsome. He became praetor for 74 B.C. and for three years thereafter governor of Sicily, which he plundered outrageously.

The trial was of unusual significance. Not only Verres, but the senatorial jury system, the Sullan reaction, and the oligarchy itself were on trial. Accordingly, powerful friends rallied to his support. Hortensius, the famous lawyer, undertook his defense. The most ingenious tricks and dodges were employed in a vain attempt to quash the indictment or postpone the trial. A "friendly" prosecutor was later brushed aside and a real prosecutor, Marcus Tullius Cicero, appointed.

Marcus Tullius Cicero: 106–43 B.C.

Cicero, the son of a knight, was born in 106 B.C. at Arpinum. Though from a middle class family of modest means, he had received a fine education, had traveled extensively, had studied philosophy and rhetoric in Athens, Asia, and Rhodes, and had trained himself for the Roman bar. He became one of the world's most renowned orators and greatest literary figures. His writings consist of many legal and political speeches, of which his *Pro Cluentio, In Catilinam,* and *Philippics* are the most famous, essays such as that *On Old Age* (*De Senectute*) and *On Friendship* (*De Amicitia*), many philosophical and political treatises, of which the best known are the *De Legibus* (*On the Laws*), *De Re Publica* (*On the State*), and *On Duties* (*De Officiis*), and works on oratory such as the *De Oratore,* (the *Orator*), and the *Brutus*.

More important from the historical standpoint are his *Letters*. They inform us of the events of this period not only from year to year but often even from day to day. It is doubtful whether any period of history has been so carefully recorded until the advent of the modern daily newspaper. Cicero's letters are more than historical documents: they reveal the soul of a man as well, his deepest feelings, his weaknesses, and his strength of character. And strength of character he had. For not many men have had the courage, the basic assurance, and the honesty to reveal themselves, unless it be St. Augustine in his *Confessions*. On the basis of these *Letters* he has been unfairly judged by modern historians. Yet it is true that he never rose above the ideals of his time: he was not an apostle of the common man.

Throughout his lifetime Cicero continued to unveil the offenses and scandals of the oligarchy though never wholly deserting them or ceasing to look up to them. Nor was he a political coward. In 80 B.C. he defended a young man who was threatened by one of Sulla's henchmen. He had a genuine sympathy for the oppressed people of the provinces. For that reason he undertook the case against Verres and marshalled such a mass of damning evidence against him that the great Hortensius gave up the case and Verres took himself off to exile. He left Rome for Marseille, where the mullets were delicious and the climate delightful. Not a really harsh punishment for a man who had robbed the Sicilian people of millions and had even crucified a Roman citizen.

Cicero's second Verrine oration, never delivered but published as a pamphlet, describes how Verres was able to amass a fortune by plundering his province. He made false accusations against well-to-do persons and intimidated the judges to hand down verdicts of confiscation against the property of the accused, which he then seized for himself. He sold justice as well as priesthoods and municipal offices to the highest bidder. He made partnerships with the tax collectors to extort without redress as much money as the traffic would bear. He lent public money at scandalous rates of interest and paid little or nothing for the wheat he bought from the Sicilians for resale to the Roman government at regular market prices. His extortions extended to works of art, which he collected from individuals, cities, and even from temples. All who resisted or opposed his thefts and extortions he imprisoned, or crucified.

The disclosure of the iniquities of Verres supplied Cotta with all the ammunition he needed in his daily harangues against senatorial juries. The senate yielded to the popular clamor and the bill passed. Thus the main pillar of the Sullan constitution tottered to its fall. After Pompey and Crassus had completed their program of reform, the constitution had for the most part been restored to its pre-Sullan state (*see* p. 202).

POMPEY, CICERO, AND

AFTER THEIR HISTORIC CONSULSHIP OF 70 B.C., BOTH POMPEY and Crassus retired to private life, Crassus to make a few more millions, Pompey to wait for an important military command. Pompey never attended meetings of the senate, where he was most unwelcome, but he was always accompanied on his rare appearances at the Forum by a mass of clients and retainers, to the mingled awe and pride of the populace. He was their idol and the mighty protector of their rights.

The next two years were peaceful and uneventful. A decade earlier it had been treason to praise Marius or Cinna in public. In 68 B.C. Caesar, as quaestor, dared to display their images and extol their virtues at the funerals of his aunt, the wife of Marius, and of his own wife, Cornelia, the daughter of Cinna. The oppressive age of Sulla had passed and a new era of freedom and democracy had dawned.

CAESAR

The restoration of the powers and privileges of the tribunate in 75 and 70 B.C. attracted to the office two able and upright men: Aulus Gabinius and Gaius Cornelius, proposers of many excellent laws.

The first law of the tribune Cornelius obliged praetors to administer justice according to the principles they had laid down in their edicts on taking office—an enactment of supreme importance and the foundation of common law and equity throughout the empire. His second law imposed a fine and future exclusion from office for persons guilty of bribing the electorate. His third, as finally passed, made it illegal for the senate to exempt individuals from the laws unless a quorum of two hundred members were present. Of his other proposals, later carried by his colleague Gabinius, the first forbade the lending of money to foreign and provincial envoys to enable them to secure audience in the senate by bribery, the second compelled the senate to give priority to the reception of embassies during its February meetings to protect the Roman allies against dilatory political tactics. These excellent and salutary laws, enacted in spite of the violent opposition of the senate, seemed to justify the freeing of the tribuneship from the restrictions imposed by Sulla.

The fame of Gabinius rests largely upon the passage of a law in 67 B.C. to deal with the scourge of piracy in the Mediterranean. Previous attempts to suppress it had proved ineffective (*see* p. 190) and the menace had recently reached dangerous proportions. With a thousand or more fast ships, the pirates swarmed all over the sea from one end to the other; had captured, by siege or storm, four hundred cities; had attacked large coastal cities in Italy itself; had destroyed a large Roman fleet near Ostia; and so infested the waters around Sicily that grain ships supplying the city of Rome no longer ventured to sail. Food prices had risen and the people, threatened with famine, resolved to clear the seas.

The bill Gabinius laid before the assembly provided for the appointment of a supreme commander of consular rank to take command with extraordinary powers for three years over the waters and coasts of the Mediterranean basin and gave him an authority superior to that of the provincial governors over all coast lands extending fifty miles from the sea. As finally enacted, the law authorized him to draw from the public treasury 6,000 talents, raise a fleet up to 500 ships, if necessary, recruit an army of 120,000 infantry and 5,000 cavalry, and appoint a staff of 24 subcommanders (*legati*) of praetorian rank and two quaestors.

The consul C. Calpurnius Piso and the senate strenuously opposed this bill because of the enormous powers it gave to one man, but the populace mobbed the consul. One of the tribunes vetoed the bill but withdrew his veto when threatened with the treatment Tiberius Gracchus once dealt out to Octavius. The bill passed. After it became law the senate appointed Pompey to take the command. They had little choice; for there was no one else of equal competence and, although not expressly named in the law, he was the person the assembly had in mind.*

Pompey threw himself into the campaign against the pirates with tremendous energy. He divided the Mediterranean and Black Seas into thirteen naval districts, each under one of his subcommanders, so that any pirates able to slip out of one net might get caught in another. His excellent organization and the vast concentration of ships, men, and supplies enabled him to sweep the western Mediterranean clean in forty days. Sailing into eastern waters, he forced the pirates to fight a naval battle off the shores of Cilicia and there completely destroyed them. Before three months had passed, he had not only swept them off the seas but had destroyed all their bases, strongholds, and installations on land.

Pompey owed his swift victory over the pirates not only to the overwhelming superiority of his armaments but also to his treatment of captives. Instead of following the usual Roman practice of crucifying or selling them into slavery, he adopted the more humane methods which Sertorius had introduced in Spain: he settled all those who surrendered on farms or in villages in Asia Minor. Many of the basic social and economic causes of piracy were thus eliminated, and the resettled pirates later became some of Rome's most loyal and useful subjects. Some were among the first in the East to receive Roman citizenship.

For some time the war against Mithridates had not been going well. Lucullus, despite his brilliance as a field commander, had been unable, because of his mutinous troops, to prevent the Pontic king from reoccupying his kingdom. The newly appointed governors of Cilicia and Bithynia were so incompetent that Lucullus retained the command. Pompey, who was already in the East with a large army and fleet, was the logical successor. While the senate was trying to make up its mind about giving him the appointment, the tribune Gaius Manilius proposed his famous law, the *Lex Manilia*, conferring upon Pompey the supreme command of all Roman forces in Asia Minor. Caesar was in favor of the law and Cicero delivered on its behalf a famous oration which he later published as a pamphlet. The assembly unanimously adopted the resolution amid wild enthusiasm, for Pompey was now the idol of the populace as well as of the capitalistic middle class. Though the senate opposed the sweeping

* So great was the confidence in his leadership that grain prices fell the very day he received the command.

provisions of the law and some of the democratic leaders had their private fears too, no
one dared to speak in public against the
appointment of this very popular general,
Pompeius Magnus.

Pompey's Conquest of the East: 66–62 B.C.

Like a buzzard come to enjoy another's kill, Pompey arrived to take over the
command of Lucullus, who had already shattered the armies and destroyed the prestige
of Mithridates and Tigranes. With an army of
50,000 men, about double as many as Lucullus ever had, and a navy cruising about in
the Black Sea, Pompey overtook and destroyed the inferior forces of Mithridates, who
fled first to Armenia and, when refused haven
by Tigranes, to the distant Caucasus. Pompey
did not attempt immediate pursuit.

Pompey next invaded Armenia and advanced upon Artaxata, where he accepted
the abject surrender of Tigranes and acknowledged him as an ally and friend of the
Roman people. In the spring of 65 B.C. he
attempted the pursuit of Mithridates, whom
he failed to overtake. He advanced as far as
the Caucasus and conquered the Albanians
and Iberians, who dwelt between the Black
and Caspian seas. Abandoning his attempted
march to the Caspian, he returned to Pontus,
which he divided into two parts, joining the
western part as far as the river Halys to the
province of Bithynia and assigning the eastern
part to an allied prince.

Meanwhile Mithridates had made his way
through the Caucasus to the Crimea. Here
that persistent but ineffectual king attempted
to raise a huge army for the invasion of Italy
by way of the Balkans and the eastern Alps,
a grandiose idea carried out five centuries
later by Attila the Hun. By the inhuman
cruelty of his conscriptions Mithridates provoked his subjects to rebel. Shut up in his
palace, with all hope of escape or mercy gone,
he murdered his wives and daughters and
then took his own life. His son, Pharnaces II,
turned the body over to Pompey, who buried
it in the tombs of the Pontic kings.

Pompey in Syria: 64/3 B.C.

News of the death of Mithridates
reached Pompey in Syria, where he was fighting to stamp out the anarchy which had
reigned there since Lucullus had driven out
Tigranes II and restored Antiochus XIII to
the decrepit throne of the Seleucids. Tyrants
had seized control of the cities; robbers and
pirates harassed the people. Pompey disposed
of these nuisances and annexed Syria and
Phoenicia as a Roman province.

Turning south into Palestine, Pompey
found two brothers, Hyrcanus and Aristo-
bulus, fighting over the throne of the Maccabees. Both rivals gave him presents and sought
his favor. In Rome's interest he took the side
of the rather feeble Hyrcanus, who was supported by the Pharisees, against his more
able pro-Parthian brother, the leader of the
Sadducees. In making this choice Pompey,
who knew nothing about Jewish theology,
unwittingly contributed to the ultimate triumph of the Pharisees over the Sadducees.

The Sadducees, composed mainly of the
rich landed aristocracy and of the priestly
caste, were conservative fundamentalists who
accepted literally the text of the Written Law
contained in the Torah or first five books of
the Bible. The Pharisees accepted the Written
Law too, but included a mass of interpretations and oral traditions handed down by the
Scribes. The Pharisaic Rabbis or Teachers
later produced the great commentaries of the
Law known as the Mishna and the Talmuds.
In deciding in favor of Hyrcanus on purely
political grounds, Pompey may have set the
future course of Judaism.

Pompey's Achievements in the Near East

Pompey's work in the Middle East was
done—a work which long endured. Because
the existing records are poor and barren,
little is known of his military strategy and
tactics, and only the main outlines of his
achievements are even dimly visible. Rapidly,
smoothly, but with overwhelming force, he
completed the task begun by his more brilliant but highly erratic predecessor. Pompey
did not attempt the impossible, as Lucullus

had done. Parthia's hostility did not provoke him, nor did Egypt's weakness invite him. Few generals with the forces at Pompey's disposal ever acted with more self-restraint.

Yet his command in the Middle East was historic and his achievements solid and enduring. He extended the Roman empire from the Mediterranean to the Euphrates. He poured into the Roman treasury more revenue from a foreign war than any of his predecessors. In return for the taxes and indemnities he imposed upon the people of the Middle East, he gave such peace and security as they had never enjoyed since Alexander. He cleared the seas of pirates and made them safe for commerce, delivered Syria from anarchy, and all Asia Minor from the scourge and fear of war. More important still, he encouraged city life, granting privileges to numerous existing cities and restoring or founding scores of others.

During Pompey's absence the senate had been bitter and resentful towards him. It prosecuted the tribunes who had proposed the bills giving him his commands. Gaius Manilius was indicted twice. The hatred of Marcus Crassus was even more intense because it was personal and mixed with envy and fear: Pompey might return with his powerful army and, like Sulla, draw up a proscription list. Whose name would more likely head the list than that of Crassus? His millions made him an attractive victim.

Crassus did not turn to the senate for help not only because he knew it resented his joint consulship with Pompey, but also because it lacked an army to protect him. He therefore sought the support of the democratic leaders, the *Populares*, who had procured for Pompey his military commands and might help him too. Necessity made a "democrat" of Crassus, the multi-millionaire, the man of many clients, and creditor of half the senate. Among the leaders of the *Populares* the most eloquent and effective was Gaius Julius Caesar.

Gaius Julius Caesar: 102–44 B.C.

Caesar was born on July 12, 102 B.C. into a family which was very ancient, very

patrician,* but which had for centuries been politically obscure. He had strong revolutionary antecedents. His aunt Julia had been the wife of Marius; an earlier Julia, the wife of Fulvius Flaccus (consul 125 B.C.). His own wife was Cornelia, Cinna's daughter, for love of whom he had once defied Sulla's command to divorce her (*see* p. 206).

Caesar's later fame has led many historians to exaggerate the importance of his early career. His exploits and narrow escapes belong to biography rather than to history. He may have spoken in favor of the tribuneship restored in 70 B.C., but he had little to do with the overthrow of the Sullan constitution. In 68/7 B.C. he went to Spain as a quaestor, but his political career did not really begin until his alliance with Crassus in 66 B.C. Crassus had the money, Caesar had the charm, eloquence, and a gift for influencing and managing people. Together they might build a strong democratic machine. Control of an army might follow.

The elements required for the creation of a united democratic faction were present: the common people (proletariat) whom Caesar and Crassus are accused of having "debauched" through the sale at low prices of five *modii* of grain per month—ordinary prison rations. Victims of economic forces over which they had no control, many had lost their farms because of wars, slave labor, proscriptions, and debts and had come to Rome, where they seldom had enough to eat. Naturally they voted for anyone who promised them relief. Many hoped to sell their votes but the only ones lucky enough to do so were those who voted in the equivocal rural tribes.

Besides the proletariat there was a group of impoverished nobles and knights who were willing to sell their votes as well as those of their clients. Nor must Sulla's veterans, who had failed to make a living on the farms allotted to them, be forgotten, or those unfortunates whom the dictator had driven into destitution. Such were the elements out of

* According to Suetonius, *The Divine Julius* (6.1), Caesar boasted of his descent from the immortal gods and from King Ancus Marcius (*ab Anco Marcio*).

which an able and wealthy politician could build an effective democratic machine.

The Censorship of Crassus and the Aedileship of Caesar: 65 B.C.

In 65 B.C. Crassus took office as censor, together with Q. Lutatius Catulus (a senator of extremely reactionary views but a man of rare virtue and integrity), and Caesar as aedile. Two of their followers, P. Cornelius Sulla (a nephew of the dictator) and P. Autronius Paetus, had been elected to the consulate. A crisis was precipitated when the two consuls were convicted of bribery under the so-called Calpurnian Law of 67 B.C. The culprits were called upon to relinquish their recently acquired offices. But since bribery of the electorate had by this time become standard procedure which, if not condoned, was at least usually ignored, the convicted consuls angrily refused to resign and conspired with Lucius Sergius Catiline to murder their consular rivals, L. Aurelius Cotta, an uncle (or cousin) of Caesar and L. Manlius Torquatus on New Year's Day (65 B.C.). The plot, known as the First Catilinarian Conspiracy, failed.* Crassus exerted his influence in the senate to have one of the conspirators, Cn. Calpurniüs Piso, sent to Nearer Spain as governor. There he unwisely insulted a Spaniard and got stabbed to death.

Meanwhile Caesar was winning popularity and entertaining the multitude with money supplied by Crassus. For their delectation he had the Forum decorated, exhibited 320 pairs of gladiators, and armed the criminals condemned to fight the lions in the arena with weapons of pure silver. Early one morning, people entering the Forum saw gleaming gold statues of Marius and his trophies set up everywhere. The old veterans gathered around, tears of pride streaming down their cheeks. Caesar's efforts had begun to bear fruit.

Crassus' ultimate purpose in building a democratic machine was to create an army. Because one of the best recruiting grounds was North Italy, he proposed to enroll as

* Later attempts to connect Crassus and Caesar with the conspiracy also came to nothing.

full citizens, in all the voting tribes, the people of the Cisalpina living north of the Po. His colleague effectively blocked the proposal and, in order to prevent any future attempt of the same kind, persuaded the senate in 64 B.C. to order the expulsion of all Gauls from the city. Even so, the proposal won for Caesar and Crassus the gratitude of the people north of the Po and future armies were easily recruited there.

Another of Crassus' schemes concerned Egypt, which was said to have been bequeathed by will to the Roman people in 80 B.C. He drafted a bill declaring Egypt a province which cleverly appealed to several groups. It would have given Crassus or his agent Caesar the right to raise an army, the Roman populace a rich source of grain, and the middle class a store of untapped wealth. Nevertheless it was foiled through the efforts of his own colleague, Catulus, and of Cicero, who was then one of Pompey's staunchest supporters.

The Elections of 64 B.C.

Foiled, frustrated, and now out of office, Crassus and Caesar sought to gain control over the executive machinery of the Republic by backing Catiline and one C. Antonius Hybrida, who were now running against Cicero for the consulship of 63 B.C.

Catiline was already a man of some fame, or rather, notoriety. Although descended from an ancient and illustrious lineage, Lucius Sergius Catiline was (if Cicero's accounts are to be believed) a scoundrel, a murderer, and a master of every known vice. Yet he was also a man of extraordinary talents and prodigious energy. He had a respectable military record and seems to have been a born leader whose influence over the masses may be compared only with Caesar's. In 67 B.C., while serving as propraetor of the province of Africa, Catiline was accused of extortion and brought to trial.* Bribery secured him an acquittal, and he went on to stand for the

* The prosecutor at the trial was Publius Clodius Pulcher. Like Catiline, he too was descended from an ancient and distinguished family, and he too had achieved a reputation for viciousness and dedicated debauchery.

consulship. But at the last minute Catiline alarmed the electorate by his violent behavior and his radical talk about the cancelling of debts, and Cicero won the election by a large majority. Antonius was a successful but poor second, Catiline a close third. Although the success of one of his candidates (Antonius) made the election seem at first to be a partial triumph for Crassus, it had actually been a total defeat: Cicero soon won the allegiance of Antonius by asigning him to Macedonia, a far richer consular province than that Antonius had originally drawn.

The Rullus Land Bill: 63 B.C. The defeated but irrepressible Crassus and Caesar conceived another scheme, a land law tremendous in scope and extremely radical, too radical for them to openly propose themselves. They entrusted that task to an obscure tribune, P. Servilius Rullus, ragged, dirty, and unshorn. Among its many vague and complicated clauses the bill provided for the appointment, by 17 tribes chosen by lot out of the 35, of ten commissioners of praetorian rank. They were to be vested for five years with final legal authority to terminate leases on the rich revenue-producing public lands of Campania for distribution to the poor and to purchase other lands for the same purpose from state funds accruing from the sale of public properties acquired in Italy and the provinces since the year 88 B.C. and from the seizure of recent war booty including that from Pompey's prospective conquests in the East. The law also empowered the commissioners to adjudicate titles to land and compensation thereof, to found colonies, to enroll and equip troops, and to occupy Egypt by military force. Its real purpose was to provide Crassus and Caesar with an immense amount of patronage and the power to raise armies.

On the first day of his consulship Cicero attacked the Rullus bill with arguments both sound and specious, employing devastating ridicule, misrepresentation, and alarmist propaganda. Using all the tricks of a demagogue, he even persuaded the people in whose interests the bill was supposedly framed that it was too dangerous to vote for. The bill was voted down.

At this point, one of Caesar's partisans entered the arena. Titus Labienus, a tribune

of 63 B.C., carried a bill to bring suit against Rabirius for treason (*perduellio*), in fact for the murder of the tribune Saturninus in obedience to the final decree of the senate (*senatus consultum ultimum*) 37 years earlier. Caesar had nothing against Rabirius, who was an old obscure senator. His object was to attack the validity of the final decree, under which the consuls had put to death declared enemies of the state without an appeal to the people. Convicted in a special court permitting appeal to the people, Rabirius was tried before the centuriate assembly. Cicero made an eloquent plea on his behalf (*Pro Rabirio Perduellionis*). Since Caesar did not want either the old man sentenced to death nor the validity of the *senatus consultum ultimum* upheld by his acquittal, he instructed a praetor, just before the voting was to begin, to raise the red flag over the Janiculum, thereby dissolving the assembly. The old man was allowed to go home in peace. His trial proved nothing. Two victories for Caesar and his party broke the long series of popular defeats. Labienus carried a law to restore the election of priests to the special tribal assembly of 17 tribes, as under the *Lex Domitia* of 104 B.C. (*see* p. 191) which Sulla had revoked. Caesar supported the bill and the popularity he thereby gained helped him in his election as Pontifex Maximus. This was a triumph for so young a man especially since one of his opponents was Quintus Lutatius Catulus, the distinguished elder statesman and one of the most respected members of the senate. Yet another reverse followed the triumph: Caesar's proposal to recall and reinstate the Sullan exiles was blocked by Cicero.

The Catilinarian Conspiracy: 63 B.C.

Catiline again ran for the consulship, in the elections for 62 B.C., this time without the backing of Crassus, who probably feared the effects of his agitation for a general scaling down of debts. While proposals of this kind repelled bankers and capitalists, they had a strong attraction for debtors, ruined aristocrats, Sulla's veterans, and the sons of the persons Sulla had proscribed. The more support Catiline received from idlers, hoodlums, criminals, and exiles, the more he caused the well-to-do and respectable citizens to fear him as a public nuisance, if not a dangerous enemy. Cicero did his best to whip up the fear that Catiline, if elected, would resort to violence and revolution.

Shortly before losing the election, Catiline, frustrated and desperate, formed a conspiracy to overthrow the government, rumors of which reached Cicero. More definite information arrived through the wife of one of Catiline's accomplices.

Still, Cicero's first denunciation of Catiline before the senate was based largely on surmises. Even when he reported that Catiline's lieutenant, Manlius, was busily recruiting an army of malcontents in Etruria to seize control of the government, his evidence was dismissed as incomplete by the senate, which nevertheless hastily issued a *senatus consultum ultimum*—an emergency declaration of a state of siege.

But Catiline did not strike on the day predicted by Cicero and the public fear was compounded with confusion. Wild rumors circulated. Was Catiline a conspirator, or was Cicero lying? Crassus secretly visited Cicero and entrusted to him a number of compromising letters which he had received from the conspirators. To this indisputable evidence was added the news, which arrived in Rome a few days later, that Manlius had recruited a substantial army in Etruria. Cicero had not lied.

Cicero refrained from using the emergency decree, waiting instead for Catiline's next move. Catiline called a secret meeting of his fellow-conspirators to make the final arrangements. He assigned some to start fires within the city, others to foment uprisings through Italy, and he named the day on which Manlius was to march. Two knights volunteered to carry out the assassination of Cicero and other important political leaders.

But the wife of the false accomplice reported the plans to Cicero. When the would-be assassins arrived at his house, he was ready for them. That same day he called an emergency session of the senate and delivered his First Oration in the presence of Catiline himself. The following night Catiline left Rome to join Manlius in Etruria. The senate thereupon declared him a public enemy.

Catiline was gone, but dangerous men still remained in the city. They could have been even more dangerous had they had the energy and daring of Catiline. Cicero knew their identity, but lacked the evidence to place them under arrest until they made their supreme blunder. They made overtures to envoys from a tribe of Allobroges from Gallia Transalpina in the hope of enlisting cavalry support for Catiline. The envoys betrayed the conspirators by securing signed agreements from them, which they promptly turned over to Cicero. Acting with great speed, Cicero ordered the conspirators arrested and brought before the senate, where he made them acknowledge their signatures and secured their confessions.

The news of the arrest and confession of the five conspirators spread through the city. Every time Cicero appeared in public he got a thunderous ovation. Next morning throngs waited outside the senate house to hear the prisoners' fate. The democratic faction and its leaders—even Caesar—were in danger.

The Debate in the Senate. Even the senate was in turmoil. Silanus, the consul elect, moved that the prisoners be put to death and at first the majority were in favor of the motion. Then Caesar rose. He acknowledged the guilt of the prisoners but wondered if execution might not be both illegal and politically dangerous. He moved that they be imprisoned for life in some Italian municipality instead and their property confiscated. His eloquence persuaded a majority of the senators to change their opinions. Even Cicero seemed on the point of voting for Caesar's motion. Then Cato took the floor and attacked the weakness and irresolution of his colleagues. So stinging were his words that a majority of the senators finally voted for the death penalty. That same day the conspirators paid for their crimes in the gloomy torchlit prison of the Tullianum.

The Death of Catiline: 62 B.C. The executions brought the conspiracy to an end. Two thirds of Catiline's army melted away. The 3,000 who were left fought and died on the plains of Pistoia (northwest of Florence) around their proud standards, the eagles of Marius. Catiline was among the slain.

Cicero

Cicero of Arpinum had attained sudden glory. For delivering Rome from danger he was voted a thanksgiving festival and given the title of "Father of his Country." Without the support of a proud family name, wealth, military talents, or strong political following, he had reached the consulship and entered the senate—a proud achievement, particularly to one as sensitive and vain as Cicero. The experience must have had its uncomfortable moments: he was admitted, but not accepted; admired for his eloquence, but ridiculed for his self-adulation. The first *novus homo* ("new man") since Marius, Cicero cannot but have been hurt by the aloofness of his colleagues, by their tacit assumption of superiority, and by their frequent rudeness.

Difficult as it must have been for so proud a man to accept such treatment, Cicero was nevertheless convinced that the preservation of republican government depended on maintaining the supremacy of the senate. The ancient nobility was to give it prestige and continuity with the past, and new men—like Cicero himself—were to bring to it energy, intelligence, and an awareness of present problems. Peace, stability, and freedom depended on the continued harmony (*concordia ordinum*) between the senatorial aristocracy and the wealthy middle class. In a slightly expanded form, the concord of the orders was an alliance of all good law-abiding citizens against revolutionary attacks upon property and the status quo. He also insisted upon the *consensus Italiae,* by which he meant that Rome should conduct her affairs in conformity with the interests and sentiments of Italy as a whole.

Of the ideals underlying all Roman political life Cicero was the most eloquent spokesman and supplied the vocabulary. The greatest of these was *libertas,* the spirit and practice of constitutional government, under which a man belonging to the governing elite could pursue a career to which birth entitled him as a right, maintain his *dignitas* (rank, prestige, and honor), practice freedom of speech, and display the virtues of honesty, independence of spirit, and generosity to friends and clients (*magnitudo animi*). In short, *libertas* was almost a form of government, which respected law and constitutional forms and perpetuated the special privileges of the governing class. When *libertas* obtained, then *otium cum dignitate;* peace, tranquillity, and security for all classes and for each its own dignity and influence.

Cicero's concept of the ideal state was one governed according to law. To the magistrates was to be allotted executive power, to the senate, authority, to the people, liberty. It was to be a state in which the people might live and work in peace and security, and the governing class find fulfillment worthy of rank and dignity. All classes were to flourish, undisturbed by social strife or civil war. Such a state, Cicero believed, could be neither a monarchy nor a democracy (which Cicero mistakenly identified with mob rule), but only a free aristocratic republic.

The Crises of the Republic

Towards the end of 62 B.C. Pompeius Magnus, the conqueror of the East, landed at Brundisium. He at once disbanded his powerful army, with which he might have seized dictatorial power, as Sulla had done. His action belies the monarchic ambition sometimes attributed to him by modern scholars. This fiction is based upon the literal and serious acceptance of *rex* and *regnum,* two terms of political invective freely and loosely hurled. They were used to arouse hatred against such popular leaders as the Gracchi, Saturninus, and Cinna. They were hurled at Sulla, though he restored the supremacy of the senate and, at the end of two years, more or less voluntarily relinquished his dictatorship; at Crassus, who sought only to protect himself against Pompey; and even at Cicero, who was maliciously called "the first foreign king at Rome since the Tarquins."

Against no one has the charge of monarchic ambition been more frequently hurled than against Julius Caesar, who has been described as having perversely dedicated his whole life to the goal of kingly power. He probably never had such a long range program but more immediate goals: the acquisition of money to pay his debts (he owed 75,000,000 denarii before he went to Spain) and as a source of patronage; the maintenance of his *dignitas*; and the winning of *gloria* in politics and war. When a Roman achieved those goals, he did not need or want the useless and invidious *ornamenta* of a king. To Caesar, to Pompey, and to every other Roman *nobilis* the very name of king was still anathema.

The opening days of the year 61 B.C. looked bright for the future of the Republic. The senate had shown unexpected strength and resolution in dealing with the Catilinarian conspiracy. The middle class had, in Cicero, a brave and eloquent spokesman, whose *concordia ordinum* seemed an answer to social and civil strife, although not a substitute for needed reforms. A most hopeful sign was Pompey's dismissal of his army and his refusal to seize dictatorial power. Cicero might yet have saved the Republic, could Pompey but have been induced to support the *concordia* policy.

But these were empty hopes: the jealousy of Crassus, the hostility of the senate towards Pompey, Pompey's own ineptness, and Cicero's unconquerable vanity all contributed to the breakdown of the tenuous harmony. Pompey entered the senate meeting, expecting to be hailed as another Alexander. Crassus solemnly rose and, pointedly ignoring Pompey, dramatically declared Cicero the savior of Rome. Cicero, his vanity flattered, promptly forgot all about Pompey and went on to speak at great length of his own illustrious deeds instead. The resentful Pompey stalked out. Cicero had unwittingly shattered his own hopes of reconstructing the Republic.

Pompey's modest demands, when finally presented to the senate, met unexpected opposition. He wanted simply land for the settlement of his veterans and ratification of his *acta* or dispositions made in the East. The consul Metellus Celer opposed them and so did the consul of 69 B.C., Metellus Creticus, who held a grudge against Pompey. Lucullus, emerging from his princely gardens, vindictive and rancorous, insisted on debating them in detail, not *en bloc* as Pompey requested. He had the support of Crassus and Cato.

Cato the Younger

Not one of the conservative reactionaries opposed Pompey's requests with more rancor than Cato the Younger, whom Mommsen once described as one of the sorriest caricatures of this melancholy age. Narrow-minded and pedantic, yet honest and fearless, he was one of the few Stoics who lived by the philosophy they professed. In the vice-ridden capital, he reflected almost to the point of parody the harsh virtues of his ancestor, Cato the Censor. Although he was still only one of the lowliest senators—a group which Cicero scornfully called *pedarii* ("footmen")—Cato's moral courage soon gained him recognition as the spokesman of the reactionary conservatives and his forceful character won him a power greater than that of any other member of the senate. Because of Cato's obstructive tactics, ratification of Pompey's *acta* was delayed.

Crassus and the Senate

After destroying the good will between Pompey and the senate, Cato proceeded to alienate Crassus and the knights by blocking passage of a bill for the relief of tax-collecting companies which had optimistically bid too high for the taxes in Asia and were now requesting a reduction of their contract payments to the treasury. Cicero, though he privately considered the petition outrageous and impudent, had nevertheless supported the bill for the sake of his policy of *concordia ordinum*.

Cato further antagonized the knights by forcing passage of a bill which declared as criminal offense the acceptance of bribes by knights serving on juries (it had long been so for senators). Again Cicero betrayed one principle for the sake of another: although he thought the bill a fair measure, he opposed it as being detrimental to harmony.

Caesar and the Senate

Cato's next object of attack was Julius Caesar. Caesar, on his return from Spain, had requested the right to stand for the consulship *in absentia*, in addition to receiving the triumph already voted for his military successes. It was legally impossible for him to have both: a recent law compelled candidates to appear in person before the assembly, but to cross the city limits would have meant the forfeiture of his triumph.

When Caesar learned that Cato opposed the petition, he decided to forego the triumph and stand for the consulship instead. Fearing that Caesar might win the election and thereby be eligible for a province and control of a provincial army, Cato persuaded the senate to assign the mountain roads and forests of Italy as the provinces of the consuls of 59 B.C. If Cato had deliberately set out to destroy the Republic, he could not have been more successful.

The First Triumvirate

Caesar, personally popular, had the added support of the old followers of Marius. After his governorship of Spain, he seems also to have had fairly abundant funds of his own for bribery, in addition to those provided by his running mate, Lucceius. The senate, determined to defeat Caesar, decided to raise its own fund (to which even the incorruptible Cato contributed) to ensure the election of Bibulus, a stubborn and somewhat dull-witted man but a son-in-law of Cato. Caesar also secured the aid of Crassus and Pompey, both of whom had, like himself, been thwarted and injured by the senate. The three privately swore that each would seek only those ends not objectionable to the other two, and this informal coalition became known as the first Triumvirate.* As the mediator between the still-smouldering jealousies of Crassus and Pompey, Caesar soon became the dominant member of the coalition. He further strengthened both the coalition and his position within it by marrying his daughter, Julia, to Pompey. The personal aims of the three were fairly clear: Pompey wanted land for his veterans and ratification of his *acta* or peace settlements in the Middle East; Crassus desired a reduction of the contracts of his eques-

* Perhaps in the hope of adding eloquence and respectability to the group, Caesar had invited Cicero to be a fourth member. Cicero refused.

trian friends; Caesar sought command of a province and an army.

Thus supported, Caesar had little trouble winning the election (though Lucceius lost to Bibulus). Caesar began his term by being studiously polite both to the senate and to his colleague, Bibulus. He consulted them on all matters, accepted their suggestions and amendments, and proposed only moderate bills. His friendly behavior may have been interpreted as weakness, or Caesar himself may have tired of the cautious approach, for he soon resorted to more direct methods. When even his moderate bills were endlessly debated and obstructed in the senate, Caesar had Cato, the leader of the opposition, arrested. Upon reflection, however, he apparently decided not to turn the righteous Cato into a martyr, and had him set free.

As a last resort, Caesar presented his land bill for the settlement of Pompey's veterans to the assembly. Bibulus promptly vetoed it, and the last constitutional path for the triumvirs had thereby been cut off. Caesar bided his time and gathered his power. One of his partisans, the tribune Publius Vatinius, secured passage of a bill which granted Caesar immediate proconsular power for five years over the provinces of Cisalpine Gaul and Illyricum and an army of three legions. Caesar began at once to recruit his army and held it in readiness near Rome. The senate was powerless: it could have declared the law null and void if summoned by a magistrate, but no one summoned it. Nor could it pass a *senatus consultum* (thereby declaring a state of emergency) for there was no one to enforce it except Bibulus, and Bibulus had no troops.

Now Caesar presented his land bill to the assembly a second time. The Forum was filled with eager spectators, most of them Pompey's veterans. The law was proposed; three tribunes interposed vetoes. The crowd's murmur rose to an angry roar. Dramatically, Caesar halted the voting and asked Pompey what other action he was prepared to take. Pompey placed his hand on his hip and declared that he would not hesitate to draw his sword. Bibulus, who had pushed his way into the Forum, jumped to his feet. But before he could say a word, the angry mob had broken his fasces and someone dumped a basket of filth over his head. In the face of a possible riot, the prudent assembly passed the bill, and Caesar declared it carried.*

The humiliated Bibulus retired from public life and spent the rest of his term shut up in his home. Some wag acutely observed that from then on the names of the two consuls were no longer Bibulus and Caesar, but Julius and Caesar.

Now unopposed, Caesar carried out the rest of his legislative program with speed and efficiency. A law was passed which provided for the distribution of Campanian public lands among 20,000 needy citizens—the only requirement being that each have at least three children. A bill was passed to ratify *en bloc* all Pompey's settlements in the East; another bill remitted one third of the contract payments that the Asia tax collectors, Crassus' friends, had to submit to the treasury.

Neither senate nor nobles dared oppose any of these measures for fear of incurring Caesar's wrath. Those who still attended senate meetings became more considerate and polite: when the governor of Transalpine Gaul suddenly died they voluntarily assigned that province to Caesar.

One of the most enlightened of Caesar's early laws ordered the publication of the *Acta Diurna*, a daily bulletin which contained the texts of all currently enacted laws as well as condensations of the debates and proceedings of the senate and popular assemblies (*Acta Senatus et Populi Romani*). Sold in the streets, posted in the Forum, and sent to all the towns of Italy and to provinces, this publication kept the people informed about foreign and domestic problems.

The most statesmanly law of Caesar in 59 B.C. was the *Lex Julia de Repetundis*, which regulated the administration of the provinces, drastically controlled extortion, and forbade governors, under pain of heavy penalty, to accept presents, sell or withhold justice, transgress the limits of their provinces without authorization, or fail to deposit their official edicts: two copies in the provinces and one at Rome. This excellent law served to protect the people of the provinces from oppression and promote their well-being and prosperity.

The Banishment of Cicero: 58 B.C.

Before leaving for Gaul, Caesar wanted to make sure that the senate would not venture to annul the Julian laws of 59 B.C. In an effort to prevent Cicero from freely speaking his mind, Caesar offered him a remunerative position in the Land Commission. That offer rejected, Caesar then invited Cicero to accompany him to Gaul as his legate. When Cicero turned down this and other offers, Caesar decided to leave Cicero to the devices of the tribune Clodius.*

Loose and dissolute, clever and audacious, Publius Clodius, the most radical and violent of all the eccentric Claudians, was one of the most clever rabble rousers in Roman history. His armed gangs ruled the streets of Rome.

Clodius had a very special reason for hating both Cicero and Cato.

Late in the year 62 B.C. Roman women were celebrating at the house of Julius Caesar, the Pontifex Maximus, the annual festival of the Bona Dea, from whose rites men were rigorously excluded. Clodius, alleged to have been the lover of Caesar's second wife, Pompeia, at the time managed to enter the house disguised as a woman. His presence was detected and a scandal ensued, as a result of which Caesar divorced Pompeia declaring that "Caesar's wife must be above suspicion." Instead of treating the escapade as a joke (Cicero privately regarded it as such), Cato brought Clodius to trial on a charge of sacrilege. When called as a witness, Caesar refused to testify, but Cicero, testifying at the trial, ruined Clodius' attempt to establish an alibi. Conviction seemed certain, but the wealthy Crassus bribed the jurors to vote for acquittal. Clodius never forgave Cato for bringing him to trial, or Cicero for testifying against him.

* The authors of the bill had foresightedly included a clause, similar to that inserted into his land bill of 100 B.C. by Saturnius, which required all senators to swear obedience to the law. They all did, including Cato.

* Born into a patrician family, Clodius had to be formally adopted by a plebian family in order to qualify for election as tribune of the people. Clodius easily won the election and took office late in 59 B.C.

One of the first bills Clodius carried abolished the use of "omens" for the obstruction of legislation. Another of his laws provided for the distribution of free grain to the needy. But Clodius is remembered for the notorious law which was part of his revenge against Cicero: it forbade the use of fire and water to all persons who had put Roman citizens to death without trial or appeal to the people. The law attacked not only Cicero, who had ordered the execution of the Catilinarian conspirators, but also the *senatus consultum ultimum,* the senatorial decree whose legality had been debated since the time of the Gracchi. Cicero, who had believed himself immune from attack, was stunned: he and his friends vainly pleaded with the consuls, Piso and Gabinius, to intercede. He appealed to Pompey, who had once promised him protection but the cautious Pompey, according to Plutarch, slipped out of his house upon Cicero's approach. His pleas denied, Cicero had no choice but to leave Italy. As he departed the city, many citizens sadly accompanied him to the gates.

Clodius next disposed of Cato: he assigned him to govern the distant island of Cyprus, dryly observing that Cato was the only man in Rome honest enough to administer the royal treasures of that new province.

The removal of his two ablest opponents ensured for Caesar the perpetuation of the recently enacted Julian Laws of 59 B.C., and he finally set forth for his proconsular provinces.

The Gauls

Caesar, waiting outside Rome for Cicero to be exiled, now hurried north, took command of the legion stationed in the Province* and suddenly appeared at the banks of the Rhone opposite Geneva. The Province, shaped somewhat like an inverted "L", followed the Mediterranean shoreline from the Alps to the Pyrenees, whence its northern boundary swung around in an arc to Geneva about two hundred miles north of the sea.

North of the Province lay free or "long-

* The eastern part of which is now Provence, in southeastern France.

haired" Gaul (*Gallia Comata*). It embraced what is now all central and northern France, Belgium, and most of Holland and the German Rhineland. According to Caesar, this territory was divided into three parts: the first was Aquitania, which lay in the southwest between the Garonne and the Pyrenees. Its people were related to the inhabitants of the Iberian peninsula (probably the modern Basques) with a considerable Celtic admixture.

The second part embraced all central and northern France and the neighbouring German regions as far east as the Rhine, not including the northeastern area. The people were almost purely Celtic, who had been coming over the Rhine from South Germany, Austria, and Bohemia, probably from the seventh century B.C. onwards and had either driven out or absorbed the original inhabitants. The third was the northeastern region extending from the Seine and the Marne to the estuary of the Scheldt and the Lower Rhine. There lived the warlike Belgians, a mixed race of Celts and some Germans, most of whom had crossed the Rhine late in the second century B.C. The three Gallic nations differed from one another in race, language, customs, and institutions.

Economy

Agriculture. The three regions differed also agriculturally. Aquitania was noted for its cavalry horses, large, fast, and strong. The Celtic invention of horseshoes sometime during the fifth century B.C. further enhanced the natural superiority of these horses in battle. The Celts in the central region raised both livestock and grain. The hill country in the south had long been famous for its cattle and sheep. Good wheat crops were raised on the plains between the Garonne and the Loire, in the valley of the Rhône, and in northern Gaul too. Oats were grown, and much barley, which was brewed into beer (*cervesa*), the national drink. Wine was not produced and only the rich could afford the expensive imports from Marseille, Greece, and Italy.

Belgic Gaul, a land of dismal swamps and thick forests, was nevertheless a good meat-

and wool-growing region. From their lanky, coarse-wooled sheep, the Belgians made the cloth for their famous bright-colored hooded cloaks, as well as other textiles. The region was also noted for its salted pork and cured hams. Large herds of fierce, half-wild swine roamed the swamps or fattened on acorns in the oak forests of the Ardennes.

The Gauls, in general, took pride in their livestock and field crops. They imported well-bred horses from southeastern Europe to improve the native stock. Their work oxen were highly esteemed in Italy. Their advanced agricultural practices astonished the Romans. Not only did they use such artificial fertilizers as lime and marl, but they practised some rotation of crops. Their farm implements were surprisingly good—hand tools made partly of iron, mechanical reapers, and wheeled plows.

Crafts. The making of farm implements, war equipment, horseshoes, and even house keys indicates some skill in mining and craftsmanship. Rich, easily worked iron mines in many parts of Gaul and abundant supplies of hardwood for smelting favored the development of metal working, and the growth of such craft centers as the town of Bibracte. Sizable communities also grew up around the mines of Lorraine, Périgord, and Bourges. Gold, silver, copper, lead, and tin were of secondary importance and less abundant.

Forestry and Woodworking. One of the most important natural resources of Gaul were the forests, which supplied fuel for warming houses and smelting ore, and material for the construction of houses, ships, log roads, bridges, and mine props. The Gauls were skilled in woodworking and developed a variety of tools, such as hammers, saws, axes, and chisels. They excelled in the manufacture of carts, wagons, and carriages. The ships they built for trading and for the transport of metals from Britain were among the sturdiest and most seaworthy in the ancient world.

Commerce. Commerce between Gaul and the Mediterranean countries began after the founding of Marseille by the Greeks around 550 B.C. and the conquest of North Italy by the Etruscans in the late sixth century B.C. Much of the early trade was in wine, Ionian pottery, Rhodian wine flagons, and bronze wares. It passed through Marseille up the Rhône and the Saône into central Gaul and by way of the Belfort Gap to the Upper Rhine.

In the early La Tène period (500–450 B.C.) some of the trade was still in Greek hands but much was Etruscan. It consisted of coral, ivory, glass and, of course, wine and all the pottery and bronze vessels used in carrying, storing, mixing, and drinking it. The most numerous of the objects found are Etruscan bronze flagons with beaked spouts, but large bronze containers (*stamnoi*) and Attic wine cups also form part of this luxury trade. An enormous bronze vessel of Greek manufacture has been discovered recently in the grave of a late Hallstatt princess at Vix in mountainous East-central France.

By the middle of the third century B.C. or later, Italy had begun to export wine and fine black-glazed Campanian tableware (*cf.* p. 163).

Greek traders also made their way through Gaul to Britain to procure tin. Of the three routes they commonly took one was via Narbonne, the Garonne and the Gironde; another up the Rhône to the Loire; and the third was by way of the Saône, the Marne, and the Seine.

Even before the age of Caesar the Belgian aristocracy had begun to import Italian wine and oil, together with silver cups, bronze wares, glass, and red-glazed Arretine ware (made at Arezzo in Etruria). Through trade the upper class was gradually becoming somewhat Romanized despite the efforts of some tribes such as the Nervii, who lived along the Scheldt, to keep out the traders.

In exchange, the Gauls exported hides, skins, woolen goods, horses, mules, work oxen, grain, salted pork, cured hams, iron, and slaves.

Coinage. A knowledge of the coinage of a people is valuable for the light it can throw on trade relations. The study of Gallic coins is very difficult. A genuine native coinage did not arise, apparently, before the beginning of the third century B.C. In prehistoric Europe trade was conducted by barter, later, as among the Romans, by bars of raw copper or bronze weighed in the balance or by the use of bronze bracelets, brooches, and other trinkets.

The earliest Gallic coins were those minted at Marseille, electrum and silver coins of the late sixth or fifth centuries B.C., small silver coins of the late fifth or early fourth centuries, B.C. Sometime during the second century, B.C., if not earlier, central and northern Gaul began to imitate the gold staters of Philip II of Macedonia (ca. 350 B.C.) It is not clear how the Gauls obtained the originals (probably through the Balkans rather than by way of Rome or Marseille). They issued many local imitations of the staters, as well as some bizarre adaptations. After the conquest of the Province in 121 B.C., Roman *denarii*, with their local imitations, and some original bronze coins came into common circulation.

A few early Celtic towns, such as Bourges and Bibracte, were manufacturing or mining communities, but the majority were trading posts which had sprung up at the mouths and elbows of rivers and at road junctions.

There were Paris and Rouen on the Seine, Nantes and Orléans on the Loire, Bordeaux and Toulouse on the Garonne, Amiens on the Somme, Besançon on the Doubs, Lyons at the confluence of the Saône and the Rhône, while Reims on the Marne was also the junction of six roads. Some of these river settlements, such as Besançon, were also natural fortresses.

In the interior some towns, Bibracte, Gergovia, and Alesia, for example, were steep-sided hilltops, easily defended places of refuge, occupied in time of danger but often afterwards abandoned unless of industrial or commercial importance. A few survived as religious or administrative centers. Nevertheless it is unlikely that many of the Gallic towns ever became genuine cities until Gaul had become part of the Roman Empire. It was Caesar's conquest that first brought Gaul under the urbanizing influence of Mediterranean civilization.

Political Organization

The Gauls, though the most gifted and economically the most advanced people north of the Alps, were yet the weakest and the most unstable politically. They had the strength neither of barbarism nor of civilization, and only vague sentiments of national unity.

Their constitution was based on the tribal state (*civitas*), a loose confederation of more or less independent clans, each with its own magistrate and army. The largest and strongest of these tribal states, of which there were nearly a hundred, were the Aedui, the Arverni, and the Sequani of central Gaul; the Helvetians of Switzerland; the Nervii of Belgium; and the Veneti of Brittany.

Perhaps the strongest of all Gallic states were the Arverni, who before their defeat by the Romans in 121 B.C. had succeeded in dominating the greater part of central Gaul. The Aedui, their closest rivals, attempted to strengthen their position by an alliance with Rome. When the Aedui made war on and defeated the Sequani, the latter invited in 61 B.C., a powerful Germanic king, Ariovistus, to come over the Rhine and help them. After decisively defeating the Aedui, he refused to go back home, robbed the Sequani of one third and then another third of their land to provide homes for his Germanic followers who continued to stream over the Rhine. To the Sequani and the Aedui alike his aggressions were becoming ever more unbearable, especially after Ariovistus had been made a Roman ally.

To make matters worse, most of the Gallic states had overthrown their kings about a half century before Caesar's arrival and had not yet worked out a stable form of government. Meanwhile they had fallen prey to a feuding oligarchy. The powerful nobles, with their thousands of clients, debtors, serfs, and slaves, held the people in bondage and kept the states in turmoil by their perpetual feuds and petty wars. Every state, tribe, and clan was torn apart by faction. One group was for monarchy, another for a constitutional oligarchy; one was for the Romans, another for Ariovistus. The resulting confusion and disorder made the Gauls vulnerable to conquest either by the aggressive barbarism of the Germans or the imperialist civilization of the Romans.

Caesar's Conquests

Such were the political conditions in Gaul when the great proconsul arrived in the Province. At that moment the Helvetians of western Switzerland were ready to set out on a long projected trek across Gaul to the West, to a land richer and more spacious than their own and far away from the aggressions of Ariovistus and the Germanic tribes in southwestern Germany. They had burnt their homes and villages behind them and, in the spring of 58 B.C., stood poised on the banks of the Rhône.

Here was an opportunity for Caesar to display his military talents. A decade earlier, as governor of Spain, he had visited the temple of Hercules at Cadiz and, it was said, tears of envy fell from his eyes as he gazed at the statue of Alexander the Great who at the age of thirty-three had conquered the world.

As the Helvetians were assembling by the tens of thousands, upon Caesar, as proconsul and representative of the senate, rested the duty of upholding the interests and honor of Rome. The Helvetians must not be allowed to reach their intended destination, where they might harass the Gauls and threaten the security of the Province. Nor must they leave their own country to the Germans, who might later use it as a springboard for an invasion of Italy.

Accordingly, when the Helvetians sent their envoys across to ask the proconsul's permission to pass through the Province, he told them that he would give them his answer two weeks hence. In the meantime he fortified the banks of the Rhône to make sure they could not cross. When their envoys appeared at dawn on the appointed day, he told them that he was unable to grant their request and would employ force should they attempt to cross against the will of the senate and the Roman people.

There is a pass that winds around the Jura mountains along the right bank of the Rhône, a route narrow and difficult, where ox-pulled wagons may pass only in single file. After being repulsed on the Rhône, the Helvetians took that road intending to follow the Saône before crossing and swinging west. They moved most slowly and the proconsul let them go. Leaving his legate, Labienus, in command of the Tenth Legion to guard the Rhône, he hurried down to Cisalpine Gaul to join the two legions he had ordered enrolled and to summon another three in winter quarters at Aquileia.

Meanwhile the fifteen-mile-long Helvetian column marched through the land of the Sequani, cutting a wide path of destruction as it passed. As it reached the banks of the Saône (Arar) in Aeduan territory, a pro-Roman Aeduan delegation appealed to Caesar for assistance. They promised to supply provisions and 4,000 light cavalry, which Caesar badly needed. Caesar agreed to strike.

Word came that though three of the Helvetian tribes had crossed the Saône, the fourth, the Tigurini, was still on the eastern bank. Caesar moved swiftly. Under cover of darkness his legions slashed their way through the forest to the river. Then, with trumpets blaring fiercely in the night, they fell on the Tigurini and cut them down. Only a few Helvetians managed to escape into the forest.

The next morning the proconsul ordered his engineers to throw a pontoon bridge over the Saône, a feat which the Helvetians would have taken three weeks to perform. The Helvetians correctly surmised that a man who could march so swiftly, strike so hard, and build bridges so quickly might more easily be appeased than defeated, and sent an embassy headed by Divico, an old warrior.

When Divico demanded that the Helvetians be granted new homes in Gaul and Caesar insisted that they return to their former homes, no compromise was possible, and the war was resumed. After a series of minor skirmishes, the two armies clashed in a gigantic battle during which the Romans all but destroyed the Helvetian army. Caesar compelled the survivors to return to their native homeland.*

Ariovistus. There began almost immediately a procession of envoys from many states

---

* Except the Boii, whom he allowed to settle in Aeduan territory, at the request of the Aeduan leaders.

of central Gaul to Caesar, some to offer congratulations for his recent victory, others to implore his aid against Ariovistus, who had already reduced two states to vassalage and whose aggressions were daily growing more menacing. Caesar at once began negotiations with the king in whose rudeness and arrogance he found a plausible pretext for war. Bold, swift marches, a few skillful maneuvers, and a single battle ended in the utter rout and destruction of the Germans. Thus, in one brief summer, Caesar had destroyed two major enemies and had made Rome the arbiter of Gaul. After quartering his legions at Besançon for the winter, he hastened to Cisalpine Gaul to hold the November assizes and recruit two more legions for another campaign.

The Belgic War: 57 B.C.

Caesar's selection of eastern Gaul for winter quarters aroused the fears and hostilities of the Belgians. A letter from Labienus about their warlike preparations sent the proconsul hurrying back over the Alps with two more legions. In two weeks he had crossed the Marne. One Belgic tribe, the Remi, (from which Reims received its name) surrendered at once and became a firm ally of Rome. Caesar sent his Aeduan allies to ravage the country of the powerful Belgic tribe of the Bellovaci, just east of the Lower Seine, while he marched north, crossed the Aisne, and took up a strong position opposite the Belgian army which numbered (according to Caesar's somewhat exaggerated account), three hundred thousand men. The Belgian force proved too unwieldy for unified command and soon ran short of supplies. Torn by mutual jealousies and dissension, the Belgians broke up and dispersed after only one minor skirmish. Caesar could now subdue the Belgian states one by one.

The only tribe to offer effective resistance was the warlike Nervii. That tribe prepared a gigantic trap for Caesar on the banks of the Sambre, surprised, and almost defeated him. Caesar, with consummate skill, rallied his weary and outnumbered forces and attacked. Man after man fell beneath javelin and sword. Higher and higher rose the heaps of the dead. Calling his men by name, Caesar took up a sword and fought alongside the common soldiers, driving on steadily to victory.

Meanwhile young Publius Crassus, the triumvir's eldest son, whom the proconsul had sent with one legion to western Gaul, had compelled all the tribes along the English Channel and the Atlantic seaboard to submit to Rome. Gaul was prostrate at the feet of the conqueror. Even the Germans beyond the Rhine sent hostages and promised to obey his orders. On receiving report of these triumphs, the senate decreed a public thanksgiving of an unprecedented fifteen days.

The Political Situation in Rome: 58–56 B.C.

While Caesar was winning battles, Rome itself was the scene of disorder and violence. Constitutional government had broken down. The senate was too weak to govern, Pompey the Great too inept. Clodius had by his free grain law made himself the idol of the slums and his armed gangs ruled the streets. They besieged and burnt down houses, hissed at or spat upon political opponents, pelted them with stones or stomped them to death.

No sooner had Caesar left for Gaul than Pompey and Crassus began to quarrel. The former, in order to restore his ebbing popularity and win the support of the nobility, began to agitate for the recall of Cicero from exile. Clodius, aroused to fury, incited a series of riots, and the ensuing jeers, insults, and threats, drove the general from public life temporarily and confined him to his house. Crassus, who had no liking for Cicero and kept Clodius supplied with funds, chuckled over his rival's discomfiture with malicious glee.

Clodius, as tribune, could veto every proposal for the return of Cicero and continued to incite his followers to riot whenever such a bill came up before the assembly.

Pompey returned to the political arena during the summer of the Belgic war: he entered into correspondence with Caesar, and began to attend assembly meetings in the Forum once more, usually escorted by a large group of followers (many of them veterans of his eastern wars) headed by the tribune,

Annius Milo. Pompey called upon Cicero's brother, Quintus Cicero, to guarantee that the orator, if permitted to return, would do nothing to upset either the triumvirs' rule or the Julian laws. Pompey's efforts bore fruit and that same autumn a bill for Cicero's return passed the assembly with uproarious acclaim. The success of the bill had depended somewhat on the victory of Milo and his followers during a bloody scuffle with the followers of Clodius.

Cicero's return was met with thunderous applause from the watching throngs who scattered flowers in his path. The senate undertook to rebuild (at public expense) his house, which had been destroyed by the followers of Clodius.*

After Cicero's return a sudden and dangerous shortage of grain compelled the frightened senate to place Pompey in charge of the food supply. He was given command of a fleet to transport the grain from Egypt. They would have given him an army had he not solemnly demurred, deceiving nobody. They simply took him at his word and gave him less than he secretly desired. His friends, though exasperated by his lack of frankness, saw a good opportunity for him to acquire an army when Ptolemy the Fluteplayer, driven from his throne by the citizens of Alexandria, formally requested Roman aid. Unfortunately for Pompey's ambitions, someone took the trouble to consult the books of the Sibyl and found it there forbidden to use an army to restore a king of Egypt. Much relieved, the senate let the matter drop.

Caesar was undoubtedly kept informed of the political situation in Rome through correspondence with Pompey, Crassus, and others. He knew that Cicero and Clodius (the latter with the connivance of Crassus) were both attacking the Julian laws of 59 B.C., though for different reasons. He knew that Pompey, with Cicero's encouragement, was veering heavily over to the nobility. With the triumvirate about to collapse, the time had come for Caesar to act. He therefore summoned Pompey and Crassus to a conference at Luca. The meeting, because of the immense amount of patronage involved, was also attended by members of the senate.

The three men deliberated behind closed doors and settled their differences. It was agreed that Pompey and Crassus should stand for the consulship of 55 B.C., that Pompey should afterwards be governor of the two Spains and Cyrenaica for five years with six legions, that Crassus for an equal period should be governor of Syria with the right to wage war against the Parthians, and that Caesar's proconsulship be renewed for another five years. They also agreed that Cicero's acid speech-making be curbed and the mobs of Clodius and Milo restrained. The conference over, Caesar swept off for Transalpine Gaul.

The Gallic Wars

Caesar found the Veneti of Brittany in full revolt. A shipbuilding and seagoing people who lived by trading with Britain, they presented a formidable naval threat. Their flat-bottomed ships of seasoned oak were able to sail among shoals and withstand the Atlantic swells. High in the bulwarks, they were proof against archers, and so strong that the ram was useless against them.

The Roman fleet, commanded by Decimus Brutus, was bewildered by the sail-driven giants of the enemy. It was not until the battle was underway that Decimus thought of an ingenious device: the swift Roman ships drew alongside the Venetans and extended long poles tipped with grapnels to catch the rigging. A vigorous tug brought yard, sail, and mast crashing to the decks and the Venetan ships rolled helplessly on the waves. Roman soldiers, swords in hand, climbed aboard to finish the job. First one, then another of the Venetan ships fell victim to this ingenious tactic. The seapower of the Veneti broken and the conquest on land rapidly completed, the proconsul turned east to meet a new menace emerging from the wilds of Germany.

In the late fall of 56 B.C., two German tribes pushed savagely westwards by the advance of the Suebi, crossed the Rhine. Their numbers have been exaggeratedly reported as 400,000. Probably not more than 100,000 of

* Unfortunately the same hoodlum drove away the workmen, demolished the reconstructions, and set fire to his brother's house, next door.

these were full-grown fighting men; the rest were women and children. The Romans entered into negotiations with the leaders of the tribes, but a treacherous attack by the German cavalry provoked Caesar to arrest the still-negotiating German chiefs and lead an overwhelming Roman attack which resulted in the ruthless slaughter of the leaderless tribes.

To strike even more terror into the hearts of the Germans, Caesar determined to invade their homeland and set his engineers to building a forty-foot bridge across the Rhine. His feat amazed the Germans and filled them with fear. Many of them hid in the woods and refused to come out and fight. Caesar took advantage of their absence by energetically burning fields and villages. After eighteen days of this activity, he recrossed the Rhine and burnt the bridge behind him.

It was in the late summer of 55 B.C. that Caesar invaded Britain, an event more memorable in British history than in Roman. He may have had several motives: curiosity, a desire to punish the Britons for helping the Gauls or impress Roman society by conquering, like Alexander the Great, a land of mystery at the edge of the world, and perhaps to pacify the conquered Gallic leaders by making them partners in the invasion of Britain.

Caesar's force was small, the season late; his fleet was battered by a storm. Though his expedition was of little military value and meant no expansion of Roman power, it so flattered Roman pride that the senate decreed another public thanksgiving, this time lasting twenty days.

The next year Caesar again invaded Britain. With a new fleet of specially constructed ships, he landed five legions and 2,000 cavalry on the shores of Kent. He pushed inland swiftly. But disaster struck: word arrived that wild storm winds and high tides had pounded his anchored fleet upon the beach. Encouraged by the news, the Britons rallied for a counterattack under the leadership of their famous war-king, Cassivellaunus, skilled in ambush and guerrilla tactics. Caesar repulsed the British attacks and, again driving inland, crossed the Thames, stormed and captured the king's main stronghold. The

Britons sued for peace. Hostages, and a formal promise of tribute were the terms, and Caesar returned to Gaul to deal with the new and dangerous unrest brewing among the Gallic chiefs.

The Gallic Revolt

In the fall of 54 B.C., Caesar called a meeting of the Gallic leaders at Samarobriva (Amiens). There he learned that their chief complaint against Roman authority was that it cramped their age-old right of warring upon and plundering their neighbors. Proud of their glorious past, they were galled by Roman subjugation. Moreover, Caesar's perpetual demands for grain in a year of poor crops were driving them to desperation.

Sensing their dangerous mood, Caesar dispersed his legions in a wide arc among the Belgians. The dispersion of the legions strongly tempted the tribes to revolt and in the late fall of the same year, the Nervii, Treveri, and Eburones attacked the legions encamped in their lands. Ambiorix, the lying and treacherous chief of the Eburones, lured the gullible Roman legate, Sabinus, to lead an entire legion and five cohorts out of their well fortified camp into a trap from which few escaped. The Nervii tried the same trick on Quintus Cicero, but he refused the bait and held out until the proconsul brought relief. The Treveri attacked the legion of Labienus with results most disastrous to themselves. Upon the Eburones Caesar later inflicted pitiless punishment.

Vercingetorix

Caesar's savage reprisals against the Belgians, his execution of certain Gallic leaders, the oppressive severity of his rule, and the encouraging reports of turmoil in Rome, aroused the tribes of central Gaul. In 52 B.C., under the leadership of Vercingetorix, the son of a former Arvernian king, the Gauls began their war for independence.

The revolt began with frightful massacre of Italian merchants at Orléans and spread rapidly over all Gaul. It aroused the Aedui, Rome's oldest and strongest friends. It threatened the Province. Returning in haste from the Cisalpina, Caesar found himself cut off from his legions stationed for the winter in the North. After arranging for the defense of the Province, he made a fast but painful march through deep mountain snows into the home state of Vercingetorix, a strategy which diverted the latter from his original plans and indirectly enabled Caesar to recover the initiative and join his legions in the North.

Realizing that his armies were hopelessly inferior to Caesar's veteran legions, Vercingetorix devised and at first carried out guerrilla and scorched-earth strategy—the burning of towns and villages, the disruption of communications, the capture of convoys, the destruction of foraging parties, and hit-and-run attacks on the Roman army.

Had the Gallic leaders permitted Vercingetorix to pursue his strategy consistently, he might have paralyzed Caesar's army and perhaps even driven him out of Gaul altogether. They could not bear to see their beautiful town of Bourges either fired or captured and when Caesar besieged it with gigantic siege-works and circumvallations, he took it by storm and destroyed a large Gallic army. Then Caesar again invaded the home province of Vercingetorix and besieged the hill fortress of Gergovia, where the Romans suffered their first defeat of the war.

As Caesar marched north to join Labienus (to whom he had earlier assigned the task of suppressing revolts around Paris and among the Sequani), he heard the Aedui had revolted, seized his grain stores, treasures, hostages, and horses, had massacred Roman merchants, and cut down bridges over the Loire. Caesar's own narrative, which moves forward at this point with feverish intensity, reveals that he felt the conquest of Gaul—his life's work—imperiled. He met the crisis with courage and intelligence, coolly exploiting his opponent's every mistake. Emboldened by his victory at Gergovia, and partly to placate his jealous and recalcitrant Aeduan allies, Vercingetorix abandoned his own guerrilla tactics and adopted those of open warfare. He began by throwing his cavalry against the oncoming Roman army without the benefit of infantry support. But Caesar had not only recently recruited German cavalry but had also devised new tactics. Vercingetorix

next led his army to the hill fortress of Alesia, which Caesar promptly besieged by setting his men to work with pick and shovel to dig entrenchments nine miles long and studded with twenty-three redoubts.

The Siege of Alesia: 52 B.C.

Failing to hamper Caesar's siege works, Vercingetorix ordered his cavalry, with muffled hooves, to steal away one night, each to his own part of the country and there recruit a relief army in the cause of national independence. Informed by spies, Caesar had an elaborate second line of circumvallation constructed to keep the relieving army out—wide and deep river-inundated trenches interspersed with bastions and towers; beyond and further out, innumerable turf-concealed pits and booby traps, the most ingenious system of defense works ever constructed till the wars of the twentieth century.

The Gauls answered the call for help. From almost everywhere men kept streaming toward the appointed marshaling center. A vast assembled host marched to Alesia. Day after day raged the battle of Alesia, the battle of Gaul to decide the future of Europe. Cavalry engagements, sorties by the besieged army inside of Alesia, assaults upon the outer defense works by the relieving army occurred simultaneously or in rapid succession. The Romans, hard pressed at times everywhere, were in one particular sector almost overwhelmed. A hard-riding messenger breathlessly told Caesar of the breakthrough; the defenders weary, exhausted; the defense works collapsing under the weight of the mass attack. Into that salient Caesar threw six cohorts, then seven more, and hurried himself to the spot with more reinforcements. The cavalry was ordered to follow; additional cavalry units were ordered to hit the enemy rear. Labienus threw in every available man. The legionaries, exhausted and on the point of surrender, caught sight of Caesar's scarlet battle cape fluttering in the wind, took heart, and pressed home a furious attack. The enemy broke and ran, vanishing into the night. Except for some minor (though at times rather difficult) mopping up operations, the battle of Gaul was over.

THE CIVIL WAR

THE TRIUMVIRS, POMPEY, CAESAR, AND CRASSUS, HAD MET AT Luca none too soon. The government they had established in 59 B.C. was rapidly disintegrating. To complicate matters for the crumbling triumvirate, Cato and Cicero were both returned from exile. The more dangerous of these was Cato, who hastened, by virtue of his uncompromising nature, the downfall of the Republic he sought to preserve.

Crassus and Pompey came away from the conference with enlarged powers and renewed strength. Both would again stand for the consulship and would again command armies and provinces: Pompey, the two Spains; Crassus, Syria. Their enemies were stunned: Cicero, bound to preserve the peace, turned quickly from invective to softer words of praise and thanksgiving. With the proconsul himself Cicero kept up a frequent corres-

pondence; borrowed money from him; and sent him his latest works, the *De Oratore* perhaps, which he could admire, as well as some poems, which he could not. Had his friendship continued, the Republic might have been saved.

In the last years of the Republic four things clearly mattered—the consulate, the armies, the tribunate, and the role of the elder statesmen which many aspired to play —above all Cicero, Cato, Pompey, and Caesar. All strove for prestige and power; none desired to precipitate violence or revolution.

Politics and Literature

During the consulate of Pompey and Crassus, the tribune C. Trebonius carried a law (the *Lex Trebonia*) assigning the consuls their provinces for five years as agreed upon at the Luca conference. Pompey did not go to Spain but decided, perhaps on Caesar's advice, to remain in the vicinity of Rome to watch the course of events. At last he could recruit legions. Some he would send to Spain, others retain in Italy. Never again would he make the mistake of disbanding them as he had in 61 B.C. after his return from the East.

Pompey's rival and colleague lost no time in setting out for his province. Even before the end of his consulate Crassus left Rome for Syria and, early in the spring of 54 B.C., invaded Mesopotamia with an army of 35,000 men. He crossed the Euphrates, captured and garrisoned a few border towns, and returned to winter quarters in Syria. He took advantage of the pause in military operations to replenish his war chest by looting the temple at Jerusalem and other rich shrines in the province.

In the spring of 53 B.C., Crassus again crossed the Euphrates; his objective: a full-scale invasion of Parthia. Knowing little about Parthian topography or war tactics, Crassus rejected the idea of attacking Parthia through Armenia and boldly struck out across the desert of northern Syria. Day after day, the weary Roman soldiers trudged across the pathless, burning sands. Thirsty and exhausted, they fell into an ambush set by a mass of heavily armored Parthian cavalry near Carrhae. At first the Romans resisted bravely, but when encircled by thousands of mounted archers shooting arrows into their tightly packed ranks, they died like flies.

Young Publius Crassus, who had been one of Caesar's ablest lieutenants in Gaul, fell first. The sight of his severed head impaled on a pike struck terror into the Roman army. A day or so later his father fell, and his grisly, bleeding head was displayed at the Parthian court during the performance of the *Bacchae* of Euripides. Seven legions met destruction, their proud eagles set up in Parthian temples. Of an army of almost 40,000 men only 10,000 made good their escape into Syria through the skill of Cassius Longinus.

The Dissolution of the Triumvirate

One of the triumvirs was dead. The other two, Pompey and Caesar, kept drifting steadily apart. The personal bond which had been sealed by Pompey's marriage to Julia, Caesar's only daughter, was broken in 54 B.C.

by the untimely death of that charming and tactful lady.

The proconsul's meteoric rise threatened Pompey's prestige and dominance. To maintain his position, Pompey needed the support of the senatorial leaders. Their hope of wedging the two strong men apart seemed about to be realized. To close the ever widening breach, Caesar asked for the hand of Pompey's only daughter, and was coldly rebuffed. Pompey himself married Cornelia, the daughter of Metellus Scipio, an aristocratic lady who was good looking as well as rich.

Meanwhile disorder prevailed in Rome, corruption and electoral bribery without restraint. The year 53 B.C. began without consuls, 52 likewise. Violence and rioting made the streets unsafe. Milo was running for the consulship, Clodius, with Pompey's support, for the praetorship. The bribes were lavish. Blood flowed. For the sake of decency and order, the tribunes vetoed the elections. The year expired. No elections and no magistrates. Authority had broken down. Rome was in anarchy.

The Death of Clodius: 52 B.C.

One mid-January afternoon, as Milo was driving down the Appian Way accompanied by many gladiators and slaves, he met Clodius with a few followers returning to Rome. The two leaders had passed each other when their followers came to blows. Clodius, who turned back to see what was going on, was wounded in the shoulder. He took refuge in a roadhouse nearby. One of Milo's men went in after him, lugged him out, killed him, and went on his way leaving the body on the ground.

Two hours later, a certain senator passing that way found the body and brought it to Rome. The news spread. That night the populace swarmed out into the streets and milled about in the Forum. The young widow Fulvia, red-haired, passionate, violent, displayed her husband's wounds and addressed the people, lashed their mounting anger into seething fury. Milo, Cicero, Pompey, and all the senators remained discreetly out of sight.

At dawn the mob carried the bloodstained

corpse into the Forum. First the tribunes mounted the speakers' platform, then Fulvia. Words of sorrow for the dead, of anger against his enemies alternately drove the populace into grief or rage. The mob surged forward carrying the body into the senate house, where they piled up chairs and benches and set on fire that august chamber as a fitting pyre for their beloved champion. Several adjacent temples also went up in flames.

Smoking ruins, riot, pillage, murder furnished cause for Pompey's third consulship, a unique consulship without colleague, and therefore a virtual dictatorship. In alarm the senate declared an emergency, instructed Pompey to recruit troops in Italy. The streets rang with the legions' tramp. All else was quiet. Laws followed, laws against violence and corruption, retroactive to the year 70 B.C., (the year of Pompey's first consulate.) Special courts of 360 jurors of high repute— senators, knights, tribunes of the treasury— brought rioters and murderers to justice, among them Milo, even bribers and corruptors of the electorate. Consuls and praetors must wait five years for assignation to provinces after their term of office. Few could afford to bribe and afterwards wait that long.

Milo's trial began. Pompey posted pickets in the Forum and its approaches to prevent attempts to intimidate the jury. The prosecutors spoke, the jurors listened. Then Cicero rose on behalf of the defense. The eloquent Cicero, who was later to write the masterly *Pro Milone* (*In Defense of Milo*), sensed the stern mood of the jury. He became flustered, and sat down. Milo was convicted, but received a light sentence: exile to Marseille.

Towards the end of his consulship, Pompey accepted as colleague his ignorant and debauched father-in-law, Q. Metellus Scipio. Pompey's pretended friendship with Caesar was a sham. He had renewed for another five years his own governorship of Spain, to which he had never gone, but underhandedly attempted to annul the Law of the Ten Tribunes (passed in 52 B.C.), which had given Caesar the right to stand for the consulship *in absentia*. So clumsy a manipulator fooled nobody. Certainly not Caesar, whom the law had permitted to pass directly from army command to consulship without risk of prosecution as a private citizen for acts which the vindictive Cato had proclaimed as illegal or unconstitutional. Caesar had obligations to his own veteran soldiers. Their security was bound up with his own political future. Pompey must have known this.

Pompey's recent attack against Caesar was not unique. Even before Luca, the edicts of Bibulus, the speeches of Domitius Ahenobarbus and of the elder Curio were in circulation.

More subtle and more difficult for Caesar to combat were the lampoons of two gifted literary men, the brilliant poet Gaius Valerius Catullus and his friend, C. Licinius Calvus, a passionate lyric poet as well as a fine orator. Calvus, like Caesar, was an exponent of the Attic style, which was terse and abrupt— quite different from the ornate and abundant styles of Cicero and Hortensius. In the courts Calvus had repeatedly and sometimes unjustly maligned one of Caesar's followers, Vatinius, the tribune of 59 B.C. Although effective at the time, neither his speeches nor his lampoons survive. The lampoons of Catullus survive, however, chiefly because most of them were obscene and, besides being quoted in smart society, were also inscribed on appropriate walls.

The proconsul, always sensitive to slander, was probably hurt by those indecent epigrams but was enough of a connoisseur to appreciate them. He even invited Catullus, the son of an aristocrat of Verona in Cisalpine Gaul, to dinner. He really admired Catullus, who poured out his feelings of love and ecstasy, of jealousy and hate in simple and melodious language. He could readily understand the poet, hot-blooded and passionate like himself, and his infatuation for Clodia, a beautiful and voluptuous sister of Clodius, his own political agent in Rome. What he thought about that series of poems about Clodia's pet sparrow, the proconsul never revealed.

Lucretius

Of the writers who lived through the turmoil and violence of the dying Republic, none was greater than Lucretius. In the *De Rerum Natura (On the Nature of Things)* a didactic poem of six books, Lucretius undertook to explain the world and the problems of human life in the light of the philosophy of Epicurus (p. 171), who adopted the atomic theory of Democritus as the basis of his ethics.

As an atomist, Lucretius held that the universe is made up of empty space and atoms—solid yet invisible particles, infinite in number and differing only in size and shape—which swerve and collide as they fall through space, and cluster together to form all animate and inanimate things: the earth, the stars, plants, animals, the bodies and even the souls of men. All things, even the human soul, must come from something or become something else; for, as the individual object dies or disintegrates, its constituent atoms—themselves eternal and indestructible—separate and drift away into space once more. Death, even that of the soul, being nothing but atomic separation, is a process of nature—inevitable, but not to be feared.

Nor, maintained Lucretius, are the gods to be feared who, though they do exist, dwell apart in celestial space and do not concern themselves with human affairs.

Thus did Lucretius, a philosopher of deep religious insight, attack through reason the ancient Roman religion and the superstitious cults from the East. Cicero admired him as a poet although he personally had little liking for Epicurean ideas.

Esteemed as a poet even in his own time, it was not until the twentieth century that Lucretius came to be appreciated as a philosopher, as well.

Cicero

Cicero's influence upon post-Renaissance European thought and literature has been stronger than that of Plato, Aristotle, or Lucretius. Cicero's conservative ideas, his urbanity and humanism appealed to the aristocratic and cultured classes of western Europe. Perhaps his most enduring achievement was his skill in making the Latin language a vehicle for popularizing the best in Greek philosophy. His own philosophical essays were, for the most part, copies or adaptations of Greek works (as Cicero himself frankly admits in a letter to Atticus). But they were enlivened by anecdote and written in a supple and polished style which has caused them to be read and re-read over the centuries.

Among them are *On the Definitions of Good and Evil,* in which he discussed Epicurean, Stoic, and Platonic philosophy; the *Tusculan Disputations,* a discourse on the essentials of human happiness; *De Natura Deorum (On the Nature of the Gods),* which deals with Stoic physics. The best known of his treatises are the two short dialogues, *De Amicitia (On Friendship),* and *De Senectute (On Old Age).*

Cicero's enlightened philosophy, worthy of the name *humanism,* deals with man, his nature, the validity of his perceptions and his place in the universe. From Cicero's insistence on proper regard for all men stems the idea that all men are created equal.

Cicero wrote two treatises on political science the more important of which, *De Re Publica (On the State),* is an imaginary dialogue between Scipio Aemilianus and his friends. Its unfinished sequel, *De Legibus (On the Laws),* was a discussion by Cicero, Atticus, and Quintus Cicero. Both treatises set forth political theories based partly on Stoic teachings and partly on the scepticism of the New Academy as outlined in the *De Officiis* and other philosophical works.

The New Academy upheld the doctrine of its founder, Carneades (ca. 214-129 B.C.), that some ideas are more probable than others. Although Cicero was an avowed adherent of the New Academy, he was strongly attracted to Stoicism because he saw in it a close affinity to the Roman moral code. He admired the Stoic doctrine of duties and its sublime belief in fortitude. Cicero unreservedly accepted Reason as the governing principle of the universe and the foundation of natural law. True law, or reason in harmony with nature, is superior to civil or international law. It is the basis of human brotherhood and it is based, in turn, on the natural concept of universal justice implanted in the hearts of men.

Cicero's battle for the Republic was consistent with his philosophical ideas. He held that a state guided by an enlightened magistrate *(princeps)*, with a senate and citizenry observing their separate functions would guarantee a form of government not only stable but capable of reconciling individual freedom with social responsibility. Such a state would combine the best features of monarchy, aristocracy, and democracy and in it all social classes would work together for the common good.

Sallust

Though he lived in the Ciceronian age, C. Sallustius Crispus was quite different from Cicero. One of the greatest of the Roman historians, Sallust was a member of Clodia's fast set and, like her brother Clodius, a radical democrat. A strong partisan of Caesar, he was elected tribune of the people in 52 B.C. Two years later he was expelled from the senate, allegedly for "immorality" but more probably for his radical views and for the leading role he had played in the burning down of the senate house after the death of Clodius.

In two open letters to Caesar*, the first written before 49 B.C., the second some time later, Sallust recommended reforms to relieve the widespread poverty. He urged that new citizens be admitted and that the senate membership be increased. He also suggested that the senate abandon the vote by voice in favor of the secret ballot, and that people from the poorer classes be allowed to serve as jurors.

Many years later, in the same spirit, he wrote three historical works, *The Conspiracy of Catiline, The Jugurthine War,* and the *Histories* in five books. The first two are extant, some fragments of the third remain. His concise style was far removed from Cicero's. His vocabulary archaic, his sentences brief and abrupt, are more reminiscent of Thucydides, Cato the Censor, or Tacitus.

Less edifying was his somewhat subjective judgement of men and events. Though he professed to be a moralist, he lacked the faith of Cato or the ideals of Cicero. In attributing the decay and breakdown of the Republic to greed, luxury, corruption, and immorality,

* Both letters are now considered genuine.

Sallust may have blazed a false trail which moralists have followed ever since. The decay of morals may well have little or nothing to do with the decline of a civilization. The downfall of individuals is a different matter.

Caesar as a Man of Letters

Early in 50 B.C., and not in 51, Caesar had published the first seven books of *De Bello Gallico (On the Gallic War)*. *De Bello Civili (On the Civil War)*, in three books, was probably written in late 48 or early 47 B.C., but was not published until after Caesar's death.

Caesar's description of these wars was a unique combination of history and commentary. Unlike the dry, factual military reports which had prevailed since the time of Alexander the Great, Caesar's commentaries were elegant, rhetorical, and vigorous. No historian has been able to rework them without sacrificing their author's personality and genius. The purpose of *De Bello Gallico* has never been clear. Mommsen held that it was the military report of the democratic general to the people who had given him his command. Most scholars no longer share this opinion; they hold that Caesar was more likely seeking to impress members of his own class. The common modern view—that Caesar wrote to justify his war in Gaul as a defensive measure—seems hardly correct. No justification or apology was required for a war against barbarians. In waging it the proconsul fulfilled his major duty: the maintenance and extension of the power and dignity of the Roman Empire. If the commentaries have a motive other than military, it is not apology but more likely self-glorification.

The Civil War was different in both tone and purpose. The consciousness of war guilt is evident, for civil war is the worst of crimes in a society where the state is all-important, and it must be shown to have been waged only under extreme provocation. According to Caesar's account, a small group of ultrareactionaries had perversely driven him to defend his honor and dignity and the good name and best interests of the Roman people. The men are shown as cruel and vain, cowardly in battle and ignominious in defeat.

They begged for mercy; he spared their lives. There are no outrageously false statements in the account, but the truth may be said to have been tested for elasticity.

The Gathering Storm

The dissolution of the triumvirate, the death of Caesar's daughter, Pompey's wife, the defeat and death of Crassus in Syria, the murder of Clodius, the conviction and exile of Milo, the vacillation of Cicero, and the devious and ambiguous policies of Pompey all contributed to push Rome over the brink of civil war.

Envious of Caesar's successes in Gaul, Pompey determined to check his rival's rise to power. He called upon all arms-bearing men in Italy to tender their military oath to him personally and induced the senate to prolong his own proconsulship for a third five-year term. He also pushed passage of a law which forbade consuls to govern provinces until five years after the end of their term. (He was exempt.) Among the several eligible and hopeful ex-consuls was Cicero, who was sent to govern Cilicia. Bibulus went to Syria. None was more eligible than L. Domitius Ahenobarbus to succeed Caesar as governor of Gaul. Domitius was a wealthy ranchowner, an unrelenting oligarch, and a bitter enemy of Caesar.

Pompey's new law would have permitted Domitius to take over the province at any time and exposed Caesar to certain prosecution were he to resign his army command before entering upon the consulship promised him at the Luca Conference (p. 231).

In the year 51 B.C., one of the consuls, the ultrareactionary M. Claudius Marcellus, attacked Caesar's grant of citizenship to people living north of the Po by having a man from that region publicly flogged. This act repelled even Cicero. The zealous consul was deterred by the more cautious Pompey from his attempt to deprive Caesar of his province and command, as well as his right (granted by law) of running for the consulship.

The consul of 50 B.C., Aemilius Paullus, and the tribunes seemed to favor Caesar. The most brilliant of the tribunes was C. Scribonius Curio, an eloquent speaker and a master of intrigue who had married Fulvia, the beautiful widow of Clodius. He was recklessly extravagant and some sources allege that Caesar won his support by paying his huge debts. Bribed or not, Curio was Caesar's subtlest weapon and could, under pretense of neutrality, block all action unfavorable to Caesar.

Three other clever young men, Caelius, Dolabella, and Marcus Antonius supported the proconsul. Like Curio, Caelius was a fine speaker, worldly and sophisticated. He had been Clodia's lover and Cicero's friend. Dolabella, debauched and sinister, was Cicero's son-in-law. Marcus Antonius, though pleasure-loving and licentious, was a brilliant soldier and strategist and was well-liked by Caesar, whom he had followed over the mountains and through the plains and forests of Gallia Comata.

The major reactionary attempt to cripple Caesar, in March of 50 B.C., failed. The consul Paullus, in collusion with Curio, faked a noisy and angry debate over the provinces and thereby forestalled the discussion of all other matters. The "non-partisan" Curio astutely demanded that both Caesar and Pompey relinquish their commands and surrender their armies for the security of the Republic. He became a popular hero overnight.

Although irked by Curio's tactics and frustrated by his vetoes, Pompey refused to admit defeat. He persuaded the senate that troops were needed in the East to fight the Parthians, and that body accordingly decreed that he and Caesar should each supply a legion. Although ostensibly fair, the decree actually profited Pompey, for he had to give up nothing while Caesar was forced to relinquish two legions: one of his own and one lent him two years earlier by Pompey for service in Gaul. When the troops arrived in Italy, Pompey decided they were no longer needed in the East and stationed them (under his command) at nearby Capua instead. The reactionaries were willing to endanger the Republic in their frantic struggle to destroy Caesar.

On December 1, the consul Gaius Marcellus appeared before the senate and moved that Caesar be stripped of his command.

Denarius of Julius Caesar illustrating his clemency. (Left, obverse) A temple of four columns with closed doors, possibly the Temple of Janus, but probably the new Temple of Clementia in view of the inscription: CLEMENTIA . CAESARIS. (Right, reverse) A horseman (desultor) riding the nearer of two galloping horses. P. SEPULLIUS MACER (mint master). Struck approximately 44 B.C. (Courtesy The American Numismatic Society, New York)

Curio did not interpose the expected veto. The motion carried. With mounting confidence, Marcellus then proposed that Pompey be permitted to retain his command. Again Curio remained silent; again the motion passed. Then Curio rose: he too had a proposal. Condemning all military dictatorships, he pointed out the injustice of penalizing only Caesar, and proposed that both Caesar and Pompey be made to step down. His motion carried by an overwhelming 370 to 22. Enraged, Marcellus cried, "Have it your way, since you want Caesar for your master!" and he stormed out of the senate. Curio then went to the Forum to address the assembled populace. His eloquence served him well: he was wildly applauded and pelted with flowers by his enthusiastic audience.

Next day Marcellus summoned a special meeting of the senate. He spoke of rumors of Caesar's arrival in Cisalpine Gaul and of a possible march on Rome. The senate must act at once, he urged, to proclaim a state of emergency and declare Caesar a public enemy. The two legions stationed at Capua must march to defend the capital. Curio, insisting the rumors were false, vetoed the motion. Marcellus in turn moved a vote of censure against Curio as a subversive and an obstructionist. When the motion failed to pass, the consul took it upon himself to go to Pompey. He handed him a sword and commissioned him to lead the two legions against Caesar. Pompey accepted the commission, but with a singular lack of enthusiasm.

One crisis followed another: debates in the senate, public mediation, private negotiations. Caesar offered to resign his command provided Pompey would resign his. But the senate ignored the proposal, declared him a public enemy, and proclaimed martial law. The new tribunes, Marcus Antonius and Quintus Cassius, their veto censured and their very lives in danger, fled the city with Curio and Caelius and went to join Caesar.

Caesar Crosses the Rubicon

Meanwhile Caesar had arrived in Cisalpine Gaul with one Roman legion and some detachments of German and Gallic cavalry. He set up his headquarters at Ravenna, a small town on the Adriatic shore and awaited the arrival of the two legions he had summoned from Further Gaul. When Caesar heard of the senate's action, he decided to act without further delay. He had camped on the bank of a small stream, the Rubicon, which separated the Cisalpina from Italy. As he stood with his assembled troops on the northern bank, the significance of what he was about to do became clear to him. Once across the river there would be no turning back: the invasion of Italy would have begun. Resolutely he declared, "The die is cast," and led his men across the Rubicon.

His decision to invade Italy with only one legion and in the dead of winter was a calculated risk: the mobilization of Italy had just begun. The hastily recruited troops which were being sent against him would be untrained and perhaps unwilling to fight. He also knew that Pompey had only two trained legions and they were the ones that had served under Caesar in Gaul: they might be counted on to desert.

Caesar swept down the eastern coast, taking town after town without a fight. Large districts surrendered to him, even Picenum, Pompey's own barony. As he advanced, his army increased. Pompey's own recruits surrendered and joined Caesar. At Corfinium Domitius Ahenobarbus, defying Pompey's orders, pigheadedly attempted a stand in the hope that Pompey would come to his relief. Pompey did not appear. Instead came Caesar, his army now augmented by the enlistment of many Pompeian recruits and the arrival of the two legions summoned from Further Gaul. The siege of Corfinium was brief. The garrison of 15,000 men mutinied and Domitius himself surrendered. Caesar let the man go.

Caesar's swift advance, his easy capture of Corfinium (considered a strong base) created a panic among the followers of Pompey. They had abandoned Rome weeks before and sped to the coast neglecting, in their haste, to take the state treasure. Pompey hastened to Brundisium with all the troops he could muster and embarked for Greece.

Caesar arrived too late: the army had already escaped to fight again on other fronts. Caesar left Brundisium and started for Rome.

Caesar's swift conquest of Italy had been made possible in part by the fact that he enjoyed absolute and uncontested command of his forces. No consuls or senators annoyed him, as they did Pompey, to advise, to expostulate, to divide and confuse. Caesar was therefore able to embark on precipitate action: his fast marches had broken up Pompey's concentrations. He had enrolled captured troops in his own army after freeing their commanders and officers. He had protected the civilian population and spared their lives and property, thereby endearing himself to them. His acts of clemency alone facilitated many victories.

The tasks ahead were stupendous, for Pompey, with undisputed command of the sea, could cut Rome off from the grain supplies of Sicily and North Africa and starve her into submission. Pompey had many battle-hardened legions in Spain and could also draw upon the vast resources and manpower of the East, where he had made and unmade kings. With these forces he could launch a two-pronged attack on Italy. And what if Gaul, recently conquered and weakly held, should raise up another Vercingetorix? Such were the problems confronting Caesar as he hurried to Rome.

Before reaching Rome, Caesar stopped off to call on Cicero and beg him to come back to Rome and support the new regime by lending it both dignity and prestige. Not quite sure yet which side would win and repelled by the reprobates Caesar had on his staff, Cicero refused. Much disappointed, Caesar went on his way.

Caesar Reorganizes the Government

Caesar entered Rome for the first time in nine years and at once set about reorganizing the government. Summoning all senators still in Rome, he invited their cooperation to avoid bloodshed. Some responded willingly, others less so. They did accept the law granting citizenship to the people living north of the Po, to whom Caesar owed much.

Caesar speedily arranged for the temporary administration of Rome and Italy. He appointed the praetor M. Aemilius Lepidus, son of the radical leader, whom Pompey slew in 77 B.C., to take charge of affairs in the city. He made Marcus Antonius governor of Italy and commander-in-chief of all the armed forces. He sent Curio to secure the grain supplies of Sicily and North Africa and Dolabella and Gaius Antonius, younger brother of Marcus, to Illyria to block a possible attempt by Pompey to invade Italy from the northeast. Caesar ordered the doors of the state treasury opened and unceremoniously removed the obstreperous tribune who attempted to intervene. The administration of Rome thus assured, Caesar set out for Spain.

Caesar in Spain: 49 B.C.

Caesar had first to break the opposition of Marseille which not only endangered the line of communication between Spain and Italy but which might also encourage the resurgence of rebellion in Gaul. Here he found Domitius and Vibullius, the two officers he had released at Corfinium, busily working against him. He therefore ordered Trebonius to besiege the city with the three additional legions he had pulled out of Italy and Decimus Brutus to attack it by sea.

He himself with six legions and 7,000 cavalry hurried on to Spain. Having crossed the Pyrenees, he advanced to meet a Pompeian army of five veteran legions, 5,000 cavalry, and about 15,000 native troops, encamped in and around Ilerda (Lérida) on the right bank of the Segre, a northern tributary of the Ebro. Ilerda was a natural fortress and the well-trained Pompeian forces were commanded by two able and experienced officers, Afranius and Petreius.

A series of initial reverses almost brought Caesar to disaster, but his excellent Gallic and German cavalry finally cut off the city's grain supplies. When the enemy attempted to escape across the Ebro, Caesar headed them off, fenced them in on a waterless hill, and compelled them to surrender without even a battle. He enrolled some of the captured officers and men in his own army, the rest he allowed to go back to their homes. Within forty days he had subdued all the Pompeian forces in Spain including the two legions in Farther Spain which were commanded by M. Terentius Varro, a fine scholar, linguist, and historian, a great authority on agriculture, but not a good general.

On the way back, Caesar accepted the surrender of Marseille forced by the sea victories of Decimus Brutus and the siege works and engineering skill of Gaius Trebonius. As punishment for their aggression he confiscated their colonies and territory, demanded the surrender of ships and arms, and the payment of a small indemnity. Marseille became virtually a part of the Roman empire.

News of Caesar's victories in Spain aroused wild enthusiasm at Rome and greatly increased his political power. A special law, proposed by Lepidus, had invested him with a temporary dictatorship. The populace rejoiced, his followers triumphed.

The Death of Curio. The death of Curio in Africa turned triumph into sorrow. The young and eloquent tribune, Caesar's fiery and fearless partisan, had gone at Caesar's orders to Sicily and North Africa to wrest from Pompey's hands control over Rome's food supply. In Sicily, Curio had accomplished his mission easily (Cato had refused to fight).

In Africa, Curio's assignment was harder, for Attius Varus, who had usurped the governorship, and Juba, the Numidian king, were both zealous adherents of Pompey and rabid enemies of Caesar. Curio easily defeated Attius but, when he then set out to attack Juba, he fell into an ambush and was trapped with all his army on a sunburnt plain near the Bagradas. Curio could have escaped and saved his own life but he chose not to desert the army Caesar had entrusted to his command and fought alongside his men, dying with his sword in his hand. Asinius Pollio (who was later to write a history of this period) gathered the surviving remnants of Curio's army and led them back to Sicily.

Two important matters engaged Caesar's attention in Rome—the consular elections and social reforms. Dictator for eleven days in December, he secured his own election as consul for 48 B.C. with P. Servilius Isauricus, a moderate aristocrat, as his colleague.

Caesar's most pressing problem was the relief of debtors and the revival of credit and business undermined by the civil war. For many, the grain dole was the sole salvation.

For the relief of debtors Caesar had enacted a law to the effect that creditors be obliged to accept real estate at pre-war valuations, that all paid interest be deducted from the principal (a loss to creditors of roughly twenty-five percent) and that all interest payments be suspended for one year. In order to make money circulate more freely and encourage lending at twelve percent interest as decreed by the senate in 50 B.C., he re-enacted an old law forbidding the hoarding of more than 15,000 denarii ($3,000).

The most humane and enlightened of Caesar's acts was the recall of persons exiled by Pompey and the restoration of civil rights to victims of Sulla's cruel proscriptions. Proposed by praetors or tribunes, the laws rectifying long-standing injustice were duly passed by the Tribal Assembly. The procedure was regular, correct, quite constitutional in fact.

Pompey Prepares for War: 49 B.C.

While Caesar was winning control of the West, Pompey had built up a large force in Greece and Albania. By the end of 49 B.C. he had nine Roman legions under training and two others on the way from Syria. From the provinces and dependent peoples of the East Pompey, "the king of kings," had impressed an additional force of 3,000 archers, 1,200 slingers, and 7,000 cavalry, a fleet of

500 warships, numerous transports, and a huge magazine of grain and war materials. With this enormous army and vast armada Pompey stood poised for the invasion of Italy when Caesar suddenly struck across the Adriatic and landed in southern Albania.

Brundisium and Dyrrhacium: 49–48 B.C.

One evening in late December Caesar left Rome and with Marcus Antonius as his aide went down to Brundisium. Seven legions were waiting at the docks, three had been stationed nearby the year before, four others had arrived after his return from Spain. Only twelve warships were available for convoy duty against Pompey's powerful flotilla, which had absolute control of the Adriatic.

At dusk on January 4, Caesar put to sea leaving Antony behind to lead across the four legions now on their way to Brundisium. He slipped past Pompey's patrols and landed safely south of the Albanian port of Dyrrhachium (Durazzo). The speed and success of the crossing surprised the methodical and slow-moving Pompey, who was on his way to occupy Dyrrhachium as a springboard for his invasion of Italy. Both generals raced to that strategic port. Pompey won.

Failure to seize Dyrrhachium was not the last of Caesar's troubles. Pompey's admiral, Calpurnius Bibulus, the consul of 59 B.C. and an old enemy of his, had waylaid, captured, or burnt many of his transports, crews and all, on their way back to Brundisium to bring over Antonius' legions. Caesar's half-starved army, cut off from sea-borne supplies, had to march and fight on empty bellies. Plague and malaria threatened. Clearly everything favored Pompey—command of the sea, a larger army, superior cavalry, and accessible supplies.

At last Marcus Antonius with four legions and 800 cavalry managed to slip through the naval blockade and land at Alessio, some thirty miles north of Dyrrhachium, and joined Caesar.

Caesar began the siege of Dyrrhachium by constructing miles of trenches around Pompey's camp at Petra, a rocky plateau nearby. Pompey succeeded in forcing Caesar to overextend his lines and then broke through them at their weakest point. Four months of back-breaking labor were lost, and

Caesar suffered a severe reversal. To deprive his opponents of their naval support, Caesar decided to transfer the war inland.

The Battle of Pharsalus: 48 B.C.

By a strategic retreat and long, fast marches, Caesar moved into central Thessaly and encamped at Pharsalus. Instead of seizing this opportunity to invade undefended Italy, Pompey chose to follow. Pompey was confident of victory: Caesar had only 22,000 men, Pompey had 47,000 and a cavalry seven times the size of his opponent's. Caesar was equally confident: his army, though smaller, was well-trained, experienced, and imbued with purpose.

The armies met on a sultry summer morning. Caesar ordered his men to charge. Seeing no move on the other side, they halted midway to get second wind, then went on. Coming within range they hurled their javelins and closed with drawn swords. The two armies locked in combat. Pompey dispatched his armored cavalry to turn Caesar's flank. Caesar had anticipated such a move: instantly six cohorts, drawn up obliquely in echelon formation behind the main lines quickly advanced with their *pila* fixed as bayonets and cut down the front riders. The others reined in sharply and, confused, bolted off the field. Meanwhile, Caesar's own cavalry, which had been brushed aside, turned and, with the six cohorts, struck Pompey's army in flank and rear. Then Caesar, using tactics Hannibal had devised at Zama, flung into action his strategic reserve. The enemy line buckled; broke. In scattered confusion they fled to camp. Pompey himself was already there.

In his tent waited Pompey, slumped over in despondency. When he looked up and saw Caesar's men breaking into his camp, he pulled off his scarlet battle cape, mounted a horse and rode away. His destination was Larissa, then Tempe, whence he sailed for Lesbos to see his wife, Cornelia Metella.

A battle lost and many a brave soldier dead, Pompey's great army surrendered. Caesar's men, dog-tired and sweating, had slain 15,000 of the enemy and taken 24,000 prisoners whom Caesar enrolled in three new legions and sent to Asia. He then set out to find Pompey.* He never found Pompey alive.

Pompey sailed from Lesbos with Cornelia Metella, young, rich and beautiful,† and his young son, Sextus, Ephesus, Rhodes, and Syria would have none of him; Africa, where the dauntless Cato had joined Juba for a last stand, seemed too far away. Egypt alone would welcome him as a former benefactor. There some of his old soldiers still lived; there he might find money, help, and new opportunity to recover his lost power.

He arrived in Egypt at a most unfortunate time: the country was convulsed by civil war. Two young rulers, Ptolemy XIV, a boy of thirteen, and his co-regent, elder sister, and nominal wife, Cleopatra VII, were fighting over a throne left them by their father, Ptolemy the Flute-player. The harmony of the early years of their dual reign had been shattered by the efforts of the eunuch, Pothinus, young Ptolemy's vizier, who had prevailed upon the boy king to drive Cleopatra off her throne and banish her from Alexandria. She fled to Syria, where she raised an army, and had returned to fight for her inheritance. The two armies were about to engage when Pompey cast anchor at the mouth of the Nile and requested the king's permission to land.

The Death of Pompey: 48 B.C.

The king's advisers invited him to land. As he was stepping ashore a renegade Roman stabbed him in the back. The advisers cut off his head and pickled it in brine as a gift to Caesar and left the body to rot on the shore. Three days later Caesar arrived.

Caesar in Egypt: 48–47 B.C.

When Caesar came ashore, he appeared wih the dread *fasces* of a consul showing that Egypt was now subject to the

* Exactly why is not known. He probably did not intend to kill him for he had liked and occasionally admired Pompey. He may have desired to offer him a new coalition, and in that case Pharsalus would have been Caesar's last battle. It was not.

† Cornelia believed herself to be the bringer of misfortune.

authority of the Roman people. Presented with Pompey's head he turned away in disgust. He wept, ordered the head reverently buried and the perpetrators of the murder executed for daring to do violence to a leader of the Roman people.

The consul's arrival with the *fasces*, his occupation of the royal palace, and his dictatorial flouting of Ptolemy's majesty raised a roar of anger in Alexandria. Egyptian soldiers and civilians thronged streets and docks in an ugly mood; muggings and knifings of Roman soldiers in the streets and dark alleys of that great metropolis were of nightly occurrence.

The consul took no chances. He at once summoned two more legions and ordered both Ptolemy and Cleopatra to appear before him in the palace to adjudicate their father's will. Ptolemy obeyed reluctantly, Cleopatra with eager anticipation. Cleopatra was conscious of her powers and proud of her illustrious Macedonian ancestry. She was now in her early twenties and, it is said, though not beautiful, her elegance and her intelligence made her a woman of great charm and fascination. Caesar at once fell in love with her and married her, though he already had a wife in Rome.

The marriage was quite legitimate though Roman law did not permit bigamy nor recognize marriages between Romans and foreigners who had not received the right of *conubium*. Caesar and Cleopatra got married not under the laws of Rome but under those of Macedonia, of ancient Persia, and of the Seleucid and Ptolemaic empires, where bigamous marriages were entirely legal, as papyri and parchments from Egypt and Syria abundantly prove.

Caesar's preemptory restoration of Cleopatra to the throne and his collection of an old debt owing to him from her father so angered Pothinus and other advisers of Ptolemy XIII that they ordered out the royal army and kept Caesar under siege for several months. Unable, with his one small legion, to cope with an army of 20,000 men as well as with the mobs of Alexandria, Caesar was in dire peril until the arrival of the two legions he had earlier summoned. The last one to arrive was a mixed force of Jews, Syrians, Arabs, and Cilicians hastily collected by Mithridates of Pergamum, reportedly one of the many bastard sons of old Mithridates VI of Pontus.

When Mithridates, advancing from Syria, had reached the Nile, Caesar took over command and crushed the Egyptian army. Ptolemy fled and was drowned in the Nile. The Alexandrians submitted. The crown passed to Cleopatra and another brother, Ptolemy XIV, who became her dynastic husband. In the spring of 47 B.C. Caesar left Egypt.

From Egypt Caesar passed through Syria, Cilicia, and Cappadocia on his way to Pontus, where he planned to settle accounts with Pharnaces, son and killer of Mithridates VI (p. 217). Taking advantage of the civil war, that despot had emerged from South Russia, had overrun Pontus, Lesser Armenia, and Cappadocia, and had committed mayhem and other outrages upon Roman citizens. He had recently defeated Cn. Domitius Calvinus, the governor of Asia. In a five-day campaign Caesar tracked him down and annihilated his army at Zela. In a letter written to his friend Matius in Rome Caesar proclaimed this swift and decisive victory with the laconic *"Veni, Vidi, Vici"* ("I came, I saw, I conquered"). After rewarding Mithridates of Pergamum for his services in Egypt, in South Russia, and Asia Minor at the expense of Pharnaces, and settling other affairs in Asia Minor, the conqueror hastened back to Italy.

Caesar in Italy: 47 B.C.

Many tasks awaited Caesar's hand on his arrival in Italy in the summer of 47 B.C. after an absence of eighteen months. He had to restore order, solve several social and economic problems, find ways and means of raising money, restore discipline among his own mutinous legions, and finally take an army over to Africa to subdue the large Pompeian forces assembled for an eventual invasion of Italy.

After Pharsalus Caesar had sent Marcus Antonius to Italy to act as his deputy or master of the horse, but had not taken time to specify what he wanted done. Antonius, a dashing, swashbuckling cavalry officer, courageous and resourceful in battle, felt somewhat inadequate and lacking in authority when dealing with some of Caesar's own revolutionary and obstreperous followers.

Among these was the brilliant young Caelius Rufus, who, though a close friend of Cicero's, had joined Caesar for partly selfish, partly idealistic reasons. Feeling that Caesar had not done enough for the relief of debtors, Caelius, when praetor in 48 B.C., proposed a moratorium on debt payments and interest for six years and the abolition of house rents for one year. His proposals came to nothing. Even the populace was apathetic. Expelled from his praetorship, he tried to rouse the lower classes of southern Italy to revolt. He died in the attempt.

The next to take up the debtors' cause was Dolabella, Cicero's divorced son-in-law. Elected tribune for 47 B.C., he proposed the repudiation of all debts and the abolition of rents. Riots and murders followed. Acting on complaints of the creditors and a decree of the senate, Antonius' troops quelled Dolabella's followers, leaving eight hundred dead in the Forum. Even these drastic measures did not stop Dolabella.

Another problem Antonius was unable to handle was the mutiny of the legions Caesar had sent back to Italy after Pharsalus. When they got their orders to embark for Sicily for the coming African campaign, they wanted to get out of the army and be paid the money and bonuses Caesar had promised them. They had already begun their march on Rome when Caesar arrived.

On the arrival of the dictator a sudden stillness seemed to descend upon the city. The mobs disappeared from the streets at once. Peace and order reigned within the city but outside the mutinous legions were camped on Mars Field. To their surprise Caesar suddenly appeared and addressed them. Crowding around the speaker's platform, they saluted. He asked them what they wanted. To be discharged, they replied. This demand he immediately granted, then went on to say he would fulfill his promises and more on the day of his triumph. After addressing them as "Fellow citizens" instead of as "Fellow soldiers," he turned on his heel to go. Stung by the rebuke, they stood mute, repentant, ashamed; then began to beg and implore him to take them back as his soldiers. He relented and gave them their orders to march.

Turning next to social and economic problems, the cause of the recent disorders, the dictator neither disapproved of Dolabella's attempt to solve them nor strongly condemned Antonius' drastic action against the attempt, though he quietly chose Lepidus as his next master of horse, an older and more level-headed politician. His program of debt relief was a moderate adaptation of Dolabella's. He remitted for one year all house rents up to 500 denarii in Rome and 125 in Italy and deferred for a year all interest in arrears since 49 B.C.

The African Campaign: 46 B.C.

After Pharsalus Cato had regrouped Pompey's shattered forces and taken them to Africa. Forced by a storm to land in the Cyrenaica, he led his army for hundreds of miles through the desert from Benghazi to Tripoli and thence to Tunisia, where he joined Varus and Juba. After this astonishing military feat, Cato misguidedly resigned the command in favor of Metellus Scipio, Pompey's father-in-law, a higher ranking officer but one of demonstrated incapacity. Scipio, with 50,000 infantry and Labienus with 18,000 cavalry, stood together with Juba's forces to contest Caesar's mastery of the world.

In the fall of 47 B.C. Caesar sailed from Sicily to Africa with five legions and 2,000 cavalry. A storm scattered his transports and prevented him from landing more than 3,000 troops and 150 cavalry. He established a small beachhead near Hadrumetum (Sousse) in eastern Tunisia, seized two small ports nearby, and waited for the rest of his transports. Though Labienus at once attacked his old commander-in-chief with an enormous cavalry force, Scipio was unable to drive him back into the sea. Caesar escaped and reached his base without major losses. He remained on the defensive until reinforcements arrived.

Caesar must have been grateful for an opponent such as Scipio. Scipio could either have retreated into the desert and lured Caesar into a death trap like Carrhae (p. 236) or detached some of his forces for an invasion of Italy. He had the men to do it. Either strategy would have meant defeat for Caesar or prolongation of the war, both equally ruinous. Instead Scipio chose to fight Caesar where he was. That was a serious blunder, but a bigger one was yet to come.

When Caesar became strong enough to go on the offensive, he put himself in a seemingly exposed position. Scipio could not resist the temptation. Thapsus, a town Scipio had strongly fortified, lay at the tip of a peninsula easily sealed off from the mainland. Caesar led his army to attack this town, which Scipio must defend to save face. Scipio did, hoping to pin his enemy between his army and the town and starve him into surrender. All odds seemed in Scipio's favor except that there was no room to deploy his greatly superior cavalry. He set his men to work digging trenches.

Before Scipio could complete either his entrenchments or formations, Caesar's legions attacked with devastating force. It was a day of butchery and Caesar's own losses, though minor, were not insignificant.

The Death of Cato: 46 B.C.

When Cato received news of Thapsus, he saw the approaching end of the free state.

Although he might have obtained Caesar's pardon, he could not bring himself to ask, and preferred to take his own life instead. His suicide was a cruel blow to Caesar and took some of the glory from his triumph. "O Cato," he exclaimed, "I envy you your death; You denied me the chance to spare your life." Cato became a legend, his martyrdom a cult; even the despots of the later Empire were wont to array themselves in the robes of that self-slaughtered saint.

Caesar's Homecoming and Triumph: 46 B.C.

The news of Thapsus had preceded Caesar's return to Rome. His followers were in ecstasies. The Forum rang with jubilation. The senate decreed a thanksgiving of forty days and voted seventy-two lictors to attend him at his triumph—three times the usual number. They renewed his dictatorship for ten years and appointed him Prefect of

Morals for three years with powers of a censor. He received the right to express his opinion in the senate first, so that every timid and self-seeking politician could take his cue. His statue, cast in bronze, was to stand on the Capitol opposite to that of Jupiter himself. He rejected most of the other religious and monarchical honors allegedly showered upon him. Some of them are of late report and fictitious, undoubtedly suggested by the history of later Caesarism. The thesis that Caesar consciously set out to establish a Hellenistic monarchy finds no support in Caesar's own latest work, the *De Bello Civili* (written probably in late 48 or early 47 B.C. and published after his death), which does not reveal the slightest trace of an intention to destroy the republic and establish a monarchy. Nor do the coins struck in 44 B.C., the year of his assassination, indicate indisputably any claim to kingship simply because they bear the head of Caesar. On the other hand, coins struck in 45 and 44 B.C. show an Etruscan crown, a royal diadem, and other symbols of kingship. Caesar was dictator and wielded the powers of a monarch, but may have neither needed nor desired the odious name of king, as indicated by his contemptuous refusal of the diadem:

"Caesarem se, non regem esse." Within two years after his death Marcus Brutus, the archtyrannicide and liberator of the Republic, issued coins of the Roman state bearing his own head on the obverse and on the reverse the daggers and cap of Liberty of the Ides of March.

Soon after his arrival, Caesar celebrated his long-awaited triumphs. There were four, each celebrated on a different day, over the Gauls, the Egyptians, over Pharnaces and Juba (but none over Pompey or Scipio). Gigantic parades, the distribution of the equivalent of seventy million dollars among soldiers and civilians, 23,000 tables loaded with food and wine for the plebs, elaborate shows, games, and gladiatorial combats, a naval battle in an artificial lake, and a mock battle between two armies on Mars Field were among the highlights of the grandest display ever seen in Rome.

The Spanish Campaign: 45 B.C.

Late in 46 B.C. Caesar embarked for Spain with eight legions. The southern part of that country was in revolt and had defected to the Pompeians because of the greed and tyranny of Q. Cassius Longinus, whom Caesar had appointed as governor in 49 B.C. Taking advantage of the uprisings, Pompey's two sons, Gnaeus and Sextus, had succeeded in recruiting fifteen legions, composed partly of veterans who had served in Spain under their father, partly of refugees brought over from Africa by Labienus, but mostly of native troops.

Failing to draw the Pompeians into a battle by attacking their fortified towns, Caesar finally caught up with them at Munda (between Seville and Malaga), where his men had to deliver their attack uphill. The battle was one of ferocious savagery as fear and hate on both sides supplied energy to their desperate valor. Superior discipline and generalship at last gave Caesar the decision. Labienus died in battle and Gnaeus Pompey was caught three weeks later.* This was Caesar's hardest battle, his last. He was now the undisputed military champion of the world.

Caesar's Work of Reconstruction

If by war Caesar had saved his life, honor, and dignity, he must now save the Roman state from chaos and ruin, heal its wounds, and give to it such peace, justice, and stability as it had not known for almost a century.

Armed with the powers of the ancient Roman dictator and with those of a tribune of the people, which Gaius Gracchus had shown so well how to use, he undertook the task of transforming the Roman empire into a world state. Unlike Sulla he did not attempt to resurrect the pre-Gracchan constitution now quite withered and dead. Not a destroyer of the past but a forerunner of the future, he resumed the work of Gaius Gracchus and Livius Drusus and blazed trails which Augustus and his successors were later to follow.

Some of Caesar's reforms were administra-

* Sextus lived to fight years later against Caesar's successors.

tive or governmental, some social and economic; others belonged to neither category. Some affected Rome alone, some Rome and Italy, others the empire as a whole. The overall effect of his reforms was to reduce the absolute dominance of the city of Rome and to integrate Rome with Italy and Italy with the rest of the empire.

Before he even began his work of reform Caesar had removed one fatal weakness of the late Republic: separate control of the armies and the provinces. Caesar was both chief executive of the state and commander-in-chief of the army. After his rise to supreme power, no governor of a province could act the tyrant, no victorious general would dare to use his army as a personal or private instrument for the overthrow of the constituted civil authority of the state. In his own person as chief executive Caesar had at once united the civil and military authority of the state.

Administrative Reforms

The most important of Caesar's administrative reforms had to do with the senate. Traditionally and constitutionally the senate had been a purely advisory council serving first the kings, later the early consuls. During and after the Punic Wars it had gradually and surreptitiously usurped executive and even legislative functions, an usurpation not only unconstitutional but conducive to the decay and breakdown of the Republic. In restoring to the senate its ancient, proper, and constitutional function, Caesar was not a radical destroyer of the Republic, but rather a true conservative, the most Roman of the Romans.

Nor was it in an attempt to humiliate that august chamber that he raised its membership from six to nine hundred. The increase of quaestors from twenty to forty, of praetors from eight to sixteen was not mainly to reward his followers or pack the senate, but for purely administrative reasons. Into the senate he had also admitted some Italians and Gauls. Without exception all the new Italian senators were able to boast of an old and distinguished ancestry. In admitting the newcomers into the senate, Caesar had broken down the barriers between Rome and Italy. Rome and Italy for the first time became one, the dominant partners within the Roman empire.

Caesar took a giant stride towards the unification of Rome and Italy when he drafted the Julian Municipal Law (*Lex Julia Municipalis*) which was divided into three parts and first enforced after his death. Two of its sections refer to Rome, the first dealing with the reduction of free grain recipients from 320,000 to 150,000, the second with the upkeep and repair of streets and roads in Rome and suburbs. The third relates to the Italian towns, specifically to the age and other qualifications of municipal councillors or senators and to the taking of the local census. The law provided for local self-government and relieved the Roman city praetors of the burden of law enforcement throughout Italy. It laid the basis for·the later extension of the municipal system of government to the provinces.

Social and Economic Reforms

Some of Caesar's social and economic reforms affected Rome, some Italy, others the empire as a whole. The immediate purpose of many of the reforms was to provide useful employment for those he had cut off from the grain dole and to relieve the congestion of population in Rome (then approaching 700,000). He also had to provide for his war veterans. In a society whose industrial capacity was low, Caesar had only two alternatives—public works and colonization.

The object of Caesar's building program in Rome was not only to provide unemployment relief but to make Rome the beautiful and magnificent capital of a great empire. The chief architectural achievements of the period were the Basilica Julia, a covered hall to house the law courts, and the Forum Julium with galleries all around it and a temple of Venus Genetrix in the center. He had plans drafted for a new senate house, a large meeting place for the popular assemblies, a fine

public library, a splendid theater, and an enormous temple of Mars.

Even more gigantic were the projects planned for Italy: an artificial harbor at Ostia for sea-going ships (a project later undertaken by Claudius), a road across the Apennines to the head of the Adriatic and the draining of the Fucine Lake and the Pontine Marshes (a feat often attempted later but never accomplished till modern times).

To promote still more the economic recovery of Italy, he compelled by law all wealthy citizens to invest half their capital in land and also enacted that at least a third of the cowhands and shepherds employed on cattle and sheep farms be men of free birth.

Colonization

To relieve unemployment, remove excess population from Rome, and find homes for a large number of war veterans, he resumed, on a much larger scale, the colonizing work of Gaius Gracchus outside Italy. In all he founded no less than twenty colonies and provided homes in the provinces for at least 100,000 Roman citizens. In Spain the chief colonies were Hispalis (Seville) and Tarraco (Tarragone); in France, Arelate (Arles), Nemausus (Nîmes), and Arausio (Orange); in Africa, Cirta and Carthage; in Greece, Corinth; in Switzerland, Geneva. To promote the commercial importance of the new Corinth, he planned to have a canal cut across the isthmus. Further east, he founded colonies at Sinope and Heraclea on the Black Sea.

The majority of these colonies were commercial or industrial, since most of the colonists had urban backgrounds and few were able to yoke an ox or run a plow, to look after a pig or milk a cow.

The Romanization of the Provinces

In his work of integrating the provinces with Rome and Italy, Caesar also resumed the Romanizing policy of Sertorius, the second great democratic statesman of the Roman people (p. 207). Following too the example of Marius, he granted citizenship to the soldiers he had recruited in southern Gaul. He enfranchised doctors, teachers, li-

The Palatine Gate and Statue of Julius Caesar. (Courtesy Italian State Tourist Office, New York)

brarians, and scholars who came to Rome from the provinces, and granted Roman or Latin status to many provincial towns—full Roman citizenship to Cadiz and Lisbon (Olisipo), Latin rights to thirty other Spanish towns, to Toulouse, Vienne, and Avignon in France, and to all the towns of Sicily. He also founded schools and public libraries in many towns of the western provinces, whence came a century or so later some of Rome's greatest writers.

Even these works do not encompass all that Caesar did for the provinces. In the East he reduced the burden of taxation and transferred, as far as possible, the right of collection from the harsh and corrupt Roman tax-farmers, hitherto the curse of provincial

administration, to the municipal governments. In Asia and Sicily he replaced the traditional tithe by a land tax of fixed amounts. To stimulate the growth of a true money economy in the provinces, he supplemented the silver *denarius* with a new gold coin worth 25 *denarii* called the *aureus*, which was destined to play an important economic role in the empire of the future.

√Reform of the Calendar

The most lasting of all Caesar's reforms was a new calendar based, not as formerly on the phases of the moon with a year of 355 days beginning on March 1st, but on the sun, with a year of 365¼ days beginning on

January 1st. The new calendar, worked out by the Egyptian astronomer Sosigenes, is still in use with a few minor corrections added in 1582 by Pope Gregory XIII. In honor of Julius Caesar the senate decreed that the month of his birth formerly called Quintilis (the "Fifth") be named July. Later Sextilis (the "Sixth") became August in honor of Augustus, Caesar's heir and successor.

Had Caesar lived longer, he might have accomplished his greatest work, the codification of Roman law, a task destined to await another six hundred years and the hand of another organizing genius, the Emperor Justinian I. Even as the Napoleonic Code was the greatest and the most enduring of Napoleon's achievements, the codification of Roman law might have been Caesar's.

The Assassination of Julius Caesar: 44 B.C.

Among history's greatest reformers and administrators, Caesar was still a soldier. The last act of his military career was to be a campaign against the Dacians, who lived north of the lower reaches of the Danube, and against the Parthians in the East, who had defeated and destroyed the army of Crassus at Carrhae in 53 B.C.

But he had made enemies. Some sixty senators, led by Gaius Cassius Longinus and Marcus Junius Brutus, incensed at his growing power and his unfailing popularity with the people, plotted to kill him as he rose to address the senate. It is said that a soothsayer stopped him on his way to the senate building and warned "Caesar, beware the Ides of March!" Undaunted, Caesar continued on his way. As he rose to speak, the plotters crowded closely about him, ostensibly to hear him. Before he could say a word, their daggers flashed and Caesar fell, bleeding from countless wounds, at the foot of Pompey's statue. It was the fifteenth of March, 44 B.C.

The Last Days of the Republic

The murdered Caesar lay wrapped in his blood-stained toga. The silence of fear descended upon the city. The senators adjourned in distracted alarm and stole away to their homes. The two arch-conspirators, Brutus and Cassius, still exulting, still exalted by their grim but noble deed, arrived to address the populace, and found the Forum almost deserted. The few who lingered there were sullen, hostile, and apathetic, and listened to their words in a dazed and stony silence. The uneasy conspirators retired to the Capitol and there barricaded themselves in to plan their future moves. Nobody knew exactly what to do. Even Marcus Antonius, stout-hearted and fearless in battle, remained in hiding until he found courage to put on his consular robes and with lictors and soldiers march into the Forum.

The first fears of Antonius were not well founded. Lepidus, Caesar's master of horse, had brought an armed legion into the Forum. Caesar's old soldiers were also there awaiting promised pensions and farms. They would take orders from Antonius. So would Lepidus, never sure either of himself or of the loyalty of his troops. There too was Fulvia, Antonius' own wife, passionate, violent, and unscrupulous but faithful.

At Fulvia's insistence Antonius went to Caesar's house and from Calpurnia received Caesar's private papers and fortune. He then held secret conferences with Lepidus and other Caesarian leaders, meanwhile keeping in touch with the conspirators. Both factions also kept in communication with Cicero, the elder statesman who had declared for Caesar's murderers immediately after the killing.

The outcome of the various conferences was a meeting of the senate on March 17th, over which Antonius presided. He remained cool and shrewd, reasonable, objective, and conciliatory. Many of the senators wanted Caesar condemned as a tyrant, his assassination approved as necessary and just, his body flung into the Tiber, and all his acts declared null and void. Briefly replying, Antonius urged them to reject such measures as extreme, unwise, and impractical; proved to them that they owed to Caesar offices, provinces, and political future; hinted at the danger of uprisings in Rome, Italy, and the provinces; and appealed to them to open their ears and listen to the people outdoors howling for vengeance and the blood of the conspirators. The appeal to fear and self-interest prevailed. Even the adherents of Brutus and Cassius in the senate voted to give all Caesar's acts the force of law, to proclaim an amnesty for the conspirators, and to grant Caesar the honor of a public funeral.

After the meeting Antonius invited the conspirators to a banquet. The toasts they drank seemed to proclaim more loudly than senatorial resolutions that at last an era of peace, concord, and good feeling had dawned.

March 20th was the day of Caesar's funeral. Marcus Antonius delivered the traditional oration. His speech was brief, factual, and undramatic.* A reader recounted Caesar's mighty deeds, his benefactions to the Roman people: gardens across the Tiber bequeathed as a public park and 300 sesterces (about $15) in cash to each Roman citizen. The chief beneficiary of Caesar's recorded will was not Antonius but Octavius, Caesar's grandnephew and adopted son. Decimus Brutus, one of the assassins, was mentioned jointly with Antonius as a minor heir.

With consummate showmanship, Antonius displayed Caesar's bloodied toga and a wax image of the corpse with its oozing wounds. The angry crowd went completely berserk and surged forth into the streets to find the conspirators. (By mistake, they tore apart one innocent bystander.) Returning to the Forum, the mob burned Caesar's corpse and the senate house too, and far into the night they kept vigil over the ashes of their hero and benefactor.

Such being the mood of the populace, the Forum was not a safe place for the conspirators. Nor was Rome. Still playing a cool and cagey game, Antonius allowed them to proceed to the provinces Caesar had allotted them, Decimus Brutus to the Cisalpina, Trebonius to Asia. Cassius and Marcus Brutus had not yet gone to their provinces, but lingered forlornly among the towns of Latium in a vain effort to recruit support for their cause.

Antonius' Bid for Power

At this time it seemed Antonius would succeed Caesar. Though disappointed that

* Quite unlike that popularized by Appian, Plutarch, and later by Shakespeare.

Caesar had not made him his heir, he profited much from his possession of the Dictator's private funds, papers, and rough drafts, much more still from his own skillful diplomacy, wise statesmanship, and conciliatory spirit. He was not a rabid Caesarian partisan nor a violent enemy of the conspirators. He had some liking for Marcus Brutus. He accepted Dolabella as his consular colleague and procured for Lepidus the high pontificate. He reluctantly permitted Dolabella to demolish an altar and pillar set up in the Forum for Caesar's worship and had the office of dictator forever abolished. Not for twenty years had Cicero's dream of a concord of the orders come so close to full realization. Such appeared to be the aim and desire of Antonius.

Antonius was an ambitious man, who could brook no rivals. He sent Lepidus to Spain to thwart the successes of Sextus Pompey, now a most successful pirate and later a capable general against Caesar's governors of western Spain. He assigned to Dolabella, in accordance with Caesar's wish, the province of Syria and to himself, the senate concurring, the province of Macedonia with all the legions Caesar had mobilized for his intended invasion of the Balkans and of Parthia. Brutus and Cassius having left for the East, Lepidus departing for Spain, and Dolabella acquiescent, Antonius was virtually master of Rome.

Antonius now set about raising an army, not a difficult task since 6,000 of Caesar's veterans needed his help to obtain the promised pensions and farms. Antonius, in turn, needed them to serve as his bodyguard, to suppress rioting and disorder in Rome, and, if necessary, to intimidate the senate.

The more Antonius thought about his political future, the more dissatisfied he was at having Macedonia as his province. It was too far from Rome. The Cisalpina, the "Acropolis of Italy," to which Decimus Brutus had gone as governor, was much more advantageous both in location and as recruiting ground for soldiers. He resolved to obtain a plebiscite ordering Decimus Brutus to surrender the Cisalpina in exchange for Macedonia. Antonius would also take the Comata, which Caesar had conquered, and transfer to both provinces the legions Caesar had stationed in Macedonia for his Balkan campaign. Antonius probably expected Brutus would never accept and would fight for the Cisalpina even in defiance of the sovereign will of the Roman people. Antonius might have to fight for the Comata as well, for Plancus, a fellow Caesarian, had already taken command there. Nevertheless by a combination of conciliation, diplomacy, skillful maneuvering, and some naked force Antonius was already within sight of his goal of supreme power, when an unexpected rival came trooping out of the East.

Octavianus

The new rival was Gaius Octavius Thurinus,* the grandson of a rich banker from the small Latin town of Velitrae. Caesar's sister Julia was his grandmother and the Dictator had adopted him as his own son.

At the time of Caesar's death, Octavianus, a handsome but rather sickly youth of eighteen, was at Apollonia (a coastal town in Albania), engaged in the study of oratory while awaiting orders to accompany Caesar on the Balkan or Parthian campaigns. Not until after the reading of Caesar's will did Octavianus learn of the adoption. Whether the Dictator intended to make him his successor is open to question. Against the advice of parents and friends, Octavianus at once set out for Italy to claim his inheritance, wisely omitting for the present an appeal to the legions stationed in Albania.

He also wisely refrained from entering Rome until he had first contacted the right people—Balbus, Caesar's former secretary, Hirtius and Pansa, the designated consuls for the year 43 B.C., and other Caesarian leaders. Nor did he confine his attentions to one party. While staying in Campania, he went to Cumae to call on Cicero. Possibly Octavianus, a student of Greek rhetoric, felt strongly drawn at first to Ciceronian eloquence and ideals of government.

* After his adoption he acquired the legal name of C. Julius Caesar Octavianus, but for political and propagandistic reasons he preferred the name of C. Julius Caesar and after 38 B.C. that of Imperator Caesar.

Having thus prepared his ground, Octavianus entered Rome at the end of April, 44 B.C. A halo appeared around the sun on the day of his arrival and was instantly received as an augur of future royalty. He addressed the people; then he confronted Antonius with a demand for Caesar's money. Antonius countered with evasions and delays, but finally refused to relinquish the funds or to explain why he had let the conspirators go unpunished. With this exchange, the two became deadly enemies.

Antonius had surely underestimated the power and ambition of Octavianus. The pale, callow youth had belied his looks, and turned out to be a master of intrigue and propaganda.

To win over the populace, he held lavish games and festivals. Even the heavens gave him timely help. A comet appeared in the northern sky. The superstitious immediately acclaimed Caesar as a god and Octavianus had a star placed on the head of Caesar's statues.

Next he set out to gain the support of the veterans. Going to Campania, he gave to each veteran that joined his army 500 denarii (double the annual pay of a regular soldier), and promised in the event of success 5,000 more. He thereby quickly but illegally raised 3,000 soldiers for a march on Rome. It is not certain where he got the money: some perhaps from the sale of his own properties, some from rich banker friends, but the bulk of it probably from funds Caesar had transferred to Brundisium and Albania for his Balkan and Parthian campaigns. That Antonius had embezzled and squandered all Caesar's fortune is most improbable, Ciceronian invective notwithstanding.

Cicero's Philippics

To this period belongs some of the world's finest oratory. Antonius had criticized with perfect justification Cicero's neglect to attend meetings of the senate. In reply Cicero delivered his *First Philippic,* a mildly critical speech but irritating enough to provoke Antonius to an angry attack upon Cicero's past career. Cicero in turn wrote and published an undelivered speech known as the *Second Philippic,* in which he branded Antonius as a tyrant, ruffian, drunkard, and coward, a man who flouted morality by kissing his wife in public. Twelve other invectives followed, an eternal monument to Cicero's eloquence, but filled with misinformation and misrepresentation. Antonius did not hear them all. He had other things to do.

Rome had become unbearable for Antonius. Down to Brundisium he went to meet the four legions he had summoned from Macedonia, intending to send them north to drive Decimus Brutus out of the Cisalpina. His consular year (44 B.C.) was near its end. Should he delay, he might be left without a province or legions to command. Brutus and Cassius had proceeded East to take over rich provinces and the large armies stationed there. Cassius had defeated Dolabella and had driven him to suicide. Lepidus in Nearer Spain was a shifty and precarious ally; Plancus in Gallia Comata and Pollio in Farther Spain were even less dependable. To make matters worse, Octavianus had marched on Rome and two of Antonius' Macedonian legions, seduced by bribes and promises, had declared for the young revolutionary.

The Siege of Mutina: 44–43 B.C.

Antonius hastened north and entrapped the recalcitrant and unyielding Decimus Brutus in Mutina, to whose relief the senate sent the two new consuls, Hirtius and Pansa, and at Cicero's clamorous demand also the young Octavianus, twice armed with propraetorian power and adlected senatorial rank. He was promised rich rewards: money and land for his legitimized troops, and for himself the right to stand for the consulship ten years before the legal age.

The three armies finally forced Antonius to abandon the siege of Mutina, but were unable to prevent his retreat across the Alps into southern Gaul, where he hoped to gain the dubious support of Lepidus and Plancus. Both consuls lost their lives at Mutina, Hirtius killed in battle, Pansa later dying of his wounds. Their deaths left Octavianus master of the field.

Mutina was a day of glory for the Republic. Triumph, exultation, delirium! The enemy was on the run. The armies of the Republic would shortly track him down. Dolabella dead, the entire East fell into the hands of Brutus and Cassius. Decimus still held the Cisalpina; and Sextus Pompey was supreme at sea. Soon the Republicans would close the ring and dispose of Octavianus too. Then would come the day of the glorious restoration of the Republic and of constitutional government. History decided otherwise.

After Mutina, the senate declared Antonius a public enemy. For the soldiers, the living and the dead, who had fought for Decimus Brutus and the Republic, they decreed a thanksgiving of fifty days, never until then decreed in a war of Roman against Roman. Upon Brutus and Cassius they conferred superior command (*imperium maius*) over all Roman magistrates in the East. To Decimus Brutus they voted a triumph and supreme command over all the armies in Italy. Even to Sextus Pompey, though really nothing but a successful pirate, they extended a vote of thanks and an extraordinary command over the Roman navy; but for Octavianus, who had rescued Decimus Brutus from siege and defeat, they proposed only a minor triumph or *ovatio* and an inferior command. Even this they finally voted down, refused to reward his troops, and repudiated the promised consulship. Through their own folly they drove Octavianus back into the arms of the other Caesarians.

Octavianus punished the slights and studied disdain of the senate by imperiously demanding a triumph, the consulship promised to him, and rewards for his troops. The senate refused. Octavianus marched on Rome. He had eight legions, and when the two legions brought over from Africa to defend the senate declared for him, all resistance collapsed. Octavianus entered Rome and had himself elected consul with Quintus Pedius, an obscure relative, as his colleague. Octavianus was not yet twenty.

The first act of the new consuls was to rifle the treasury to pay each soldier 2,500 *denarii* (about $500), the next was the passage of a law instituting a special court to try Caesar's murderers as well as Sextus Pompey. At the same time Octavianus, who needed allies, had the senate's decree against Antonius revoked. That done, he hastened north to meet Antonius.

Meanwhile Antonius himself had not been idle nor unsuccessful. The debacle at Mutina had brought out leadership, courage, endurance, and self-discipline. After a hard and painful march into southern Gaul, he confronted the far larger army of the aging Lepidus, the governor of Nearer Spain and of Narbonese Gaul, who maintained control over his men solely because of his professed loyalty to Julius Caesar. The two armies lay encamped on either side of a small river.

Begrimed, haggard, and thickly bearded, Antonius stole into the camp of Lepidus and addressed the men. Thereafter, the two armies began gradually to fraternize and soon Antonius was in real command. He used the same tactics in approaching the army of Plancus, the governor of Comata, and returned to Italy with twenty-two legions. He occupied the Cisalpina without opposition, for the defending army of Decimus Brutus deserted. Brutus himself attempted to escape to Macedonia, but he was trapped and slain by a Gallic chief.

When Antonius and Lepidus returned to the Cisalpina, they found Octavianus already there with eleven legions. They could easily have overwhelmed the young pretender but they did not even try. Their men might refuse to fight against one who bore Caesar's magic name. Lepidus arranged a conference instead.

The Second Triumvirate

After some preliminary negotiations, the three leaders met on a small island in a river near Bologna and agreed upon a joint policy. Carefully avoiding the emotionally charged name of dictatorship, they declared themselves an executive committee with absolute powers for five years for the reconstruction of the Roman State (*tresviri rei publicae constituendae*). The consulship survived in name with traditional prestige, title, and conferment of nobility but with greatly reduced powers. Octavianus agreed to resign the office and two nonentities took his place.

Octavianus was not the dominant member in the triumvirate, as the division of provinces reveal. Antonius secured the Cisalpina and the Comata, Lepidus Gallia Narbonensis and the two Spains. Octavianus received a more modest and doubtful portion—North Africa and the islands of Sicily, Sardinia, and Corsica, all disputed, some already seized by the outlawed adventurer, Sextus Pompey.

The Proscriptions: 43 B.C.

Before taking office on the first of January, 42 B.C., the triumvirs sent a chill of horror through Roman society by a proscription as cold-blooded and loathsome as that of Sulla and with little better excuse. Among their victims were 130 senators and perhaps 2,000 knights. The excuse alleged was the avenging of Caesar's murder, but the real reason was the confiscation of wealth and property in order to raise money for their forty-three legions and for the campaign against Brutus and Cassius. When the triumvirs found that the wealth of their victims was insufficient for their needs, they imposed a capital levy upon opulent females, laid crushing taxes upon the propertied classes in Italy, and set aside the territories of eighteen of the richest cities in Italy for veteran settlements.

In addition to their greed and rapacity the triumvirs desired to wipe out political enemies. Their most distinguished victim was Cicero. Unlike some of the proscribed, he lingered until too late and died on the seventh of December, 43 B.C., a martyr to the cause of the dying Republic.

To buttress their regime of frightfulness and violence, of confiscation and proscription, the triumvirs packed the senate with men of low and infamous origin and occupation, with ruffians, and even escaped slaves. They made the consulship the reward of graft or crime, nominating, within a single year, several pairs of consuls. To the praetorships, which Caesar had increased to sixteen, they added fifty more.

Formally taking office on the first of January, 42 B.C., the triumvirs compelled the senate and the magistrates to swear an oath to observe Caesar's acts, dedicated a temple to him in the Forum, and by a special law elevated him among the gods of the Roman State under the name of the Divine Julius. Octavianus could now call himself *Divi Filius* ("Son of a God").

Philippi: 42 B.C.

After crushing all resistance in Italy, the triumvirs determined to make war on Brutus and Cassius, who by a systematic and ruthless looting of the Eastern provinces had accumulated a huge war chest. With nineteen legions, some of them Caesarian veterans, and with numerous mercenaries, the conspirators had taken up at Philippi on the Macedonian coast a strong position flanked on the north by mountains, on the south by a marsh. Their navy dominated the seas.

Eluding the Republican naval patrols, Antonius and Octavianus landed in Greece with twenty-eight legions and advanced to Philippi, where in the fall of 42 B.C. two battles took place. In the first, Brutus defeated Octavianus, but Antonius defeated Cassius. Thinking all was lost, Cassius fell on his sword. The loss of Cassius, by far the abler general, was ruinous to Brutus. Instead of letting winter and famine destroy the enemy, he yielded to the impetuous clamor of his officers and offered battle three weeks later. It was a fatal mistake. After a hard and bloody battle, the triumvirs emerged victorious. Brutus took his own life. Antonius when he came upon the corpse, pulled off his purple battle cape and reverently laid it over his fallen enemy but former friend.

Philippi was a decisive victory. It laid the Roman world at the victors' feet. To Antonius, the real victor, went the glory and the major share of the spoils. Lepidus, on the other hand, who was reported to have been secretly negotiating with Pompey, now began his sudden slide to impotence and obscurity. Accusing him of disloyal intrigues with Sextus Pompey, Antonius robbed him of Gallia Narbonensis, Octavianus, of the two Spains. Then they agreed to shunt him off to Africa provided he could prove his loyalty and conquer the province. Antonius thus had control over the entire East and all the Gallic provinces, though he later surrendered the Cisalpina for annexation with Italy. Octavianus had still

to reconquer his original provinces of Sicily and Sardinia, which Sextus Pompey had seized.

After the reassignment of provinces came the more unpleasant tasks, the hardest and most unpopular of which fell to the lot of Octavianus. He had to return to Italy to disband the troops and by confiscation find land for the resettlement of over 100,000 veterans. Antonius elected to go to the East to regulate its affairs and raise the money promised to the legions. The more calculating and far-sighted Octavianus had clearly perceived, no doubt, that Italy was still the key to empire and to ultimate supremacy.

Antonius and Cleopatra

Antonius had an assignment more pleasant than he had anticipated. After his arrival in the East, he had extracted considerable money from the rich cities of Asia arranging for nine years' tribute to be paid in two, and had set up or deposed kings, proving himself a very capable administrator. Finally he came to Tarsus in Cilicia, where Cleopatra, whom he had earlier summoned to explain why she had aided and financed the conspirators, was soon to arrive. She arrived in a splendid barge with silvery oars and purple sails, decked out in gorgeous clothes and redolent with exquisite perfumes. Without requesting explanation of her past policies, Antonius quickly succumbed. There followed days and nights of revelry and ecstasy. So absorbed was Antonius that the winter was already over before he could tear himself away to undertake more serious tasks. He was not to see Cleopatra again for another four years.

The Siege of Perugia: 40 B.C.

Unlike Antonius, Octavianus was beset with difficulties in Italy. He arrived weak, ill, despondent. The eighteen cities previously earmarked for soldiers' settlement proved insufficient to satisfy the veterans and the evicted owners angrily protested. Expanded confiscations further increased the ground swell of discontent. The populace of Rome was also in a disturbed and angry mood. Sextus Pompey, who still controlled the seas, had begun to shut off grain supplies. Discontent, confusion, insecurity, and want threatened the stability of the state. Soldiers and civilians were at each other's throats. Octavianus himself once almost fell into the clutches of a battling mob.

Intrigue aggravated the difficulties, unpopularity, and danger of Octavianus. The firebrand, Fulvia, the wife of Marcus Antonius, and his brother Lucius, the consul, attempted to whip up against Octavianus the suspicion and hatred of both veterans and landowners. In so doing, Fulvia and Lucius hoped to destroy Octavianus and catapult the absent and unsuspecting Antonius to supreme power. They well knew that Antonius would disavow their acts and would refuse to repudiate his agreements with Octavianus but they hoped to force his hand. They eventually went too far and drove Octavianus to make war on them. He maneuvered them into Perugia and put them under siege. Antonius, ignorant of their aims and doings, made no move. His marshals gave them no concerted or effective help and starvation quickly forced them to surrender. Octavianus generously spared their lives and even sent Lucius as governor to Spain, where he soon died. He allowed Fulvia to visit her husband in Greece. There she too soon died, but her evil deeds, later amplified by mendacious defamation, lived after her without redemption or defense.

Perugia was not the end of troubles for Octavianus. Pillage, fire, and mass executions had not solved his problems nor made him safe from danger. His atrocities served only to increase the loathing and horror in a land still seething with revolt and held in the grip of famine, turmoil, and despair. Hostile fleets menaced Italy's coasts, assailed the provinces, interrupted grain shipments. Octavianus seemed doomed, caught up in the web of his own duplicity, trapped, and destroyed at last.

In his extremity Octavianus sought accommodation with Sextus Pompey, master of the seas, apparently unaware that Antonius, taking Fulvia's advice, was also making overtures. To make his negotiations appear more sincere, Octavianus put aside Clodia, Fulvia's daughter, whom he had earlier married, and took instead Scribonia, many years his senior but an aunt of Sextus Pompey's wife.

Finally fortune began to smile on Octavianus. In Gaul the governor died who had been Antonius' appointee and his weakling son surrendered to Octavianus that entire province and eleven legions. Octavianus gladly then placed his own governor in command. Now virtually in control of all western Europe, Octavianus, towards summer's end, hastened to meet Antonius at Brundisium.

The Pact of Brundisium: 40 B.C.

Serious reasons had moved Antonius to desert Cleopatra's bed and speedily depart from Egypt. News had reached him that the Parthians, led by Quintus Labienus, son of Titus, Caesar's famous lieutenant in Gaul and later enemy, had overrun Syria, Palestine, and parts of Asia Minor. Not yet prepared to fight the Parthians, Antonius sailed for Greece. There Fulvia had persuaded him to receive envoys from Sextus Pompey and accept the proffered alliance. Only then did Antonius proceed to Italy to recruit legions for war against the Parthians.

By previous agreement Antonius and Octavianus were to use Italy as a common recruiting ground. How worthless that agreement was Antonius discovered when he found Brundisium closed against him. Frustrated and angry he landed troops and besieged that port. Simultaneously his Republican ally, Sextus Pompey, struck against southern Italy. When Octavianus appeared at Brundisium to oppose his colleague, Caesar's old legions refused to fight and fraternized instead. There followed negotiations, conferences, and finally a new agreement known as the Pact of Brundisium, which renewed the triumvirate. A redistribution of provinces left Octavianus in control of Illyricum as well as of all the western provinces, Antonius of the East, and Lepidus of Africa. Italy was to remain, theoretically at least, a common recruiting ground for all triumvirs.

To seal the pact Antonius married Octavia, the fair and virtuous sister of Octavianus. The covenant between the two powerful rivals filled Italy with joy and thanksgiving. All Rome rejoiced. A golden age of peace and concord seemed near. So men hoped. So wrote Vergil in his Fourth or Messianic Eclogue in words reminiscent of the prophecies of Isaiah.

The rejoicings were premature. Sextus Pompey, who felt that Antonius had played him false, was threatening Rome with famine. Taxes, high prices, and food shortages provoked riots. The people clamored for bread and peace. When Antonius and Octavianus prepared to attack Sextus, popular reaction was such that they were forced to negotiate with him.

At Misenum the triumvirs met with Pompey, argued, bargained, and banqueted. They agreed to let him retain Sicily and Sardinia, which he had already seized, and gave him Corsica and the Peloponnesus besides. They also allowed him compensation for his father's confiscated lands and promised him a future augurship and consulate. In return he agreed to end his blockade of Italy, supply Rome with grain, and halt piracy on the high seas.

The Predominance of Antonius: 39–37 B.C.

The power and popularity of Antonius was now at its height. His influence was especially strong among the senatorial and equestrian orders, old line Republicans, and most men of property throughout Italy, while that of Octavianus was stronger with the Roman populace and the veterans. Time was on the side of Octavianus. Years of absence in the East caused the influence of Antonius to wane in the West.

For the present the West looked bright to Antonius. Pompey would surely counterbalance the growing power of Octavianus. So thought Antonius as he set out for Athens in company with Octavia, his young and loving bride. There he spent two winters enjoying to the full domestic happiness and the culture of that old university town. From there he directed the reorganization of the East. To the Balkans he sent Asinius Pollio to subdue the Parthini, to the East Ventidius and Herod, since 40 B.C. king of Judea, to drive out the Parthian invaders of Syria, Palestine, and Asia Minor. Moving with the speed of Caesar, Ventidius shattered the Parthians in

three great battles and rolled them back to the Euphrates. There Ventidius stopped.

Having restored Roman prestige in the East, Antonius moved to subjugate the Parthians and avenge Carrhae. In 37 B.C. he sent Canidius, another of his great marshals, to pacify Armenia. Canidius obeyed but carried Roman arms beyond Armenia to the Caucasus. Returning to Armenia, he awaited the arrival of Antonius. He waited long; for new troubles in the West compelled Antonius to postpone his invasion of Parthia. Octavianus was the cause.

To Italy the Treaty of Misenum had brought peace and a brief respite from piracy, shore raids, and famine but to Octavianus even greater benefits. Exiled Republicans were returning home, aristocrats of ancient lineage, allies worth his while to court and win. The peace was of short duration. Octavianus did not want peace. Sextus Pompey was an enemy to be destroyed. His first act of war was to accept the province of Sardinia from a traitor, whom Pompey had failed to liquidate; his second was to divorce Scribonia.

For love and politics Octavianus promptly married Livia Drusilla, young, beautiful, rich, politically astute, and proud of her descent from the illustrious Claudian line. She had already been a wife and the mother of two sons, one of them Tiberius Claudius Nero, the future emperor Tiberius. Marriage to Livia brought several ambitious aristocrats to his support. He was sure to get still more. Soon the snobs, the time-servers, and other chiselers would come flocking to his side. He would eventually undermine the predominance of Antonius in Italy.

The Treaty of Tarentum: 37 B.C.

Octavianus was unable to finish alone the war he had started against Sextus Pompey. His attempted invasion of Sicily in 38 B.C. was a fiasco and Pompey destroyed two of his fleets. These reverses compelled him to recall Agrippa from Gaul, the most talented military man of his generation, and to invoke the aid of Antonius. Though angry at Octavianus for his unprovoked aggressions and for delaying his own campaign against the Parthians, Antonius loyally came to his aid and left Athens with a large fleet. The two triumvirs met at Tarentum, both resentful and suspicious of each other. Through the patient diplomacy of Maecenas and the alleged good offices of Octavia, they concluded an agreement and renewed their triumvirate for another five years. In exchange for the 120 ships Antonius contributed for the war against Pompey, Octavianus promised 20,000 Roman soldiers for service in the East. Antonius never got them.

The Defeat and Death of Sextus Pompey: 36 B.C.

The ships lent by Antonius and added to those constructed and equipped by Agrippa enabled Octavianus to mount a three-pronged amphibious attack upon Sicily: Octavianus and Agrippa sailed from Puteoli, Statilius Taurus from Tarentum, and Lepidus from Africa. The operation proceeded according to plan except for a crippling defeat suffered by Octavianus at sea. Agrippa and Lepidus both landed and quickly overran the island, while Agrippa forced Pompey to fight a sea battle at Naulochus near the Straits, perhaps the largest and most decisive naval engagement in ancient history. His fleet destroyed, Sextus escaped to Asia Minor, where he was later killed by a lieutenant of Antonius.

Octavianus had already overcome one rival, soon he would another. Lepidus, with twenty-two legions under his command and hungry for glory, insisted on accepting the surrender of Sicily in person. When Octavianus objected, he ordered him off the island. Bearing the magic name of Caesar, Octavianus boldly entered the camp of Lepidus and persuaded his legions to desert. Then he stripped Lepidus of his triumviral powers, and committed him to honorary confinement at Circeii. There Lepidus died twenty-four years later.

The Triumphant Return of Octavianus

A sincere and joyous welcome at Rome awaited the homecoming of the victorious Octavianus, who had ended wars in the West, restored the freedom of the seas, and liberated Rome from the danger of famine. Though he

had crushed liberty, he brought the blessing of strong and ordered government. The restoration of the ancient Republican constitution was now beyond hope.

A grateful and idolizing people heaped honors upon Octavianus, even epithets and adorations of divinity: his statue placed in Italian temples, a golden one in the Roman Forum, and the sacrosanctity of a plebeian tribune in addition to the military title of "Imperator Caesar," which he had already usurped.

Octavianus had already attained a success beyond reasonable expectation. Frail in health and utterly lacking in military skill, he had triumphed over seemingly insuperable odds. He owed his success to his own coolness and indomitable courage, good looks and distinguished bearing, his knowledge of men, an ability to take advantage of his opponents' mistakes, and an unusual skill as a propagandist. He had exploited Caesar's name, Cicero's eloquence, and the prestige of the Republican senate. He had also used Lepidus, Marcus Antonius, and Sextus Pompey, the Roman populace, and Caesar's veterans; such loyal friends as Agrippa and Maecenas, and even his own wives.

Art, Architecture, and Literature during the Second Triumvirate

As master of Italy and the West, Octavianus continued Julius Caesar's work of beautifying Rome. To this period belong the first public library, a temple to Apollo on the Palatine, a new theater, the rebuilding of the Regia, the completion of the Basilica Aemilia, and the repair of the temple of Hercules. Agrippa, an engineer as well as soldier and admiral, began the repair of the aqueduct, the *Aqua Marcia* and, as aedile in 33 B.C., the construction of the aqueduct, *Aqua Julia,* and other public works.

Literature: 40–31 B.C.

During this period of military despotism, oratory, being neither useful nor esteemed, had languished and declined. Cicero, Caesar, Calvus, and Hortensius all were dead and in the new age had no peers. Pollio and Messala, the best orators of their day, were second rate.

Of the prose writers the most notable were Sallust, Asinius Pollio, and Varro. Pollio wrote a critical and authoritative history of the Civil Wars from 59 B.C. to the battle of Philippi, an excellent monograph though written in a rather dry, harsh style. It became the main source, now lost to us, of Plutarch's *Lives* of *Caesar* and of *Antony,* and of Appian's *Civil Wars.*

Varro: 116–27 B.C.

The most learned and versatile of all ancient writers was Varro. He wrote with indefatigable industry on a great variety of subjects—history, law, religion, philosophy, education, linguistics, biography, literary criticism, and agriculture. His greatest work was probably the *Antiquities Human and Divine,* which contained a vast array of knowledge as well as many errors. Of his numerous works the only ones to come down to us are his three valuable books on agriculture, six of his twenty-five books on the Latin language, and many fragments of his *Menippean Satires,* a medley of prose and verse on almost every subject under the sun. In 36 B.C., at the age of eighty, he brought out his monumental work on the theory and practice of farming, a treatise of inestimable value for an understanding of Roman social and economic history.

Vergil: 70–19 B.C.

In 38 or 37 B.C. Vergil, the son of a North Italian farmer near Mantua, published his *Eclogues,* ten short pastoral poems in the style of Theocritus idealizing country life, the loves and sorrows of shepherds. Shortly thereafter he began and by 29 B.C. had completed his *Georgics,* a didactic poem in four books, like Hesiod's *Works and Days.* Not intended as a technical handbook, like Varro's, the *Georgics* nevertheless describe with realism and firsthand experience the various activities of the farmer—the plowing, the harvest, the care of vines and orchards, the breeding of cattle, and the keeping of bees. The poem was a hymn of praise to Italy's soil and her sturdy farmers.

Horace: 65–8 B.C.

Another great poet of the age was Horace, son of a fairly well-to-do freedman of Venusia in Apulia. A sincere believer in a good education, his father sent him to school in Rome and later to college at Athens. There he met the noble Brutus and, like many young idealistic Romans studying abroad, he fought for the Republic at Philippi. Afterwards he returned to Rome penniless, and got a job in a quaestor's office which, though boring, gave him the time and means to write poetry. His earliest poems, the *Epodes,* followed by his *Satires,* the first book published in 35 B.C., the second in 30 B.C., firmly established him as a poet of first rank. In 38 B.C. Vergil, much impressed by his genius, had introduced him to Maecenas, who later persuaded Octavianus to give him a small but comfortable estate on the Sabine Hills.

Antonius in the East

Having lost the better part of two years helping Octavianus to win mastery of the West, Antonius returned to the East. The work he did there was the reorganization of the eastern half of the Roman empire, a great work destined to endure for many centuries. In the past the dependent kingdoms of the East had owed allegiance not to Rome but to their patron, Pompey the Great. The Parthian invasion had clearly revealed the weakness of that relationship and the disloyalty of the native kings and dynasts to Rome.

Antonius did not disturb the territorial administration of the provinces of Asia, Bithynia, and, perhaps, Syria; but he assigned the rest of the eastern territories to four feudal or vassal kings dependent on Rome, but strong enough by means of their heavily armed and mail-clad cavalry to guard their frontiers against invasion. This policy was neither original nor new. The Parthian and Armenian kingdoms had long before adopted it to resist the pressure of the Huns and other invading

Graffito from Dura-Europos showing a mail-clad knight and horse. (Courtesy Yale University Art Gallery)

peoples from central Asia (*see* p. 198). The graffito from Dura-Europos shows a knight in full armor—tall helmet with vizor, chain mail, sword, spear, greaves, and the horse protected with armor too. Feudalism had arisen long before the tenth century A.D.

One vassal of Antonius was Cleopatra, who came at his summons to meet him at Antioch early in 35 B.C. To her he gave Syria, Cyprus, and part of Cilicia, territories not more extensive than those given to other vassal rulers but immensely rich. Even these did not satisfy the ambitious queen, who wanted in addition the domains he had given to Herod I, who ruled over Judea. Antonius firmly rejected these demands.

Marriage to Cleopatra had made Antonius

joint ruler of the strongest and most splendid of the eastern kingdoms and permitted him access to the treasures of the Ptolemies to finance his Parthian campaign. The other vassal rulers of the East would also furnish some men, money, and supplies.

The Parthian Campaign: 36 B.C.

At last Antonius was able to set out on his long planned campaign against the Parthians. His plan was not to cross the trackless deserts of Mesopotamia, as Crassus had done, but to invade by way of Armenia, where Canidius was awaiting his arrival with sixteen seasoned legions, 10,000 Gallic and Spanish cavalry, and 16,000 Armenians. The loyalty of Artavasdes, the Armenian king, was essential to the success of the enterprise.

Loyalty was too much to expect from Artavasdes. When Antonius had begun his march of five hundred miles to Phraaspa, the capital city of the Medes (about one hundred miles south of present-day Tabriz in the Ajerbaizan), the treacherous king withdrew his cavalry and allowed the Parthians to attack and destroy two Roman legions left behind the main army to bring up the baggage and the siege train. The lack of siege equipment made the siege of Phraaspa impossible. Food running low and winter near, Antonius retreated to Armenia, harassed all the way by Parthian sneak attacks. He finally straggled back to Syria with a loss of more than 20,000 men and would have lost even more but for his superb generalship and the discipline of the legions.

The lack of trained troops prevented Antonius from resuming operations until 34 B.C., and even then he was able only to overrun Armenia, whose treacherous king he vengefully seized and deposed. He made Armenia a Roman province and formed an alliance with the Medes, who had revolted against their Parthian overlords. The Parthians remained unsubdued and Carrhae unavenged. Alarming reports of trouble in the West compelled Antonius to abandon his Parthian enterprise never to attempt it again.

Despite his failure against the Parthians, Antonius was still strong in the East and the dominant partner in a divided empire. He also had an impressive following of Roman senators, Caesarians, Pompeians, and such staunch Republicans as Cn. Domitius Ahenobarbus, L. Calpurnius Bibulus, and several kinsmen of Cato and Brutus. The two consuls of 32 B.C. were also his adherents.

The Prelude to Actium

Between the master of the East and that of the West a clash was inevitable. Octavianus was the aggressor, who first set the stage for military aggression by hostile and fraudulent propaganda. The truth lies buried beneath a thick hard crust of defamation, lies, and political mythology. Had Antonius instead of Octavianus won the War of Actium,

the official characterization of the protagonists would have been equally fraudulent perhaps but utterly different. Antonius would have been depicted as a sober statesman; not a sex-crazed slave of Cleopatra but a loving husband and father; not a tyrant striving to subject the liberties of the Roman people to an oriental despotism but the savior of the Republic from ruin and destruction.

Of greater moment than the propaganda of Octavianus and the Roman dislike of an alien queen was the threat of a divided empire and the fear that Italy would lose the rich kingdoms of the East. Even now Antonius had hurt the interests and reduced the profits of Roman financiers and tax-farmers by his feudal policy of dividing the East among semi-independent vassal kings. Long had businessmen yearned to exploit the untapped riches of Egypt. It was alarming and repugnant to national honor that Antonius by his territorial donations should have restored to Egypt the territories, opulence, and power once held by Ptolemy Philadelphus. The centrifuge was at work. Antonius had initiated it. It would eventually ruin Rome and Italy. Was it for this that Rome had sent her legions to the Euphrates and the Caucasus?

The Divorce of Octavia

The love life and marriages of Antonius were only pretexts for the coming struggle for power between the rival triumvirs. Historical fiction and romance has depicted Antonius as a libertine and sensualist, who abandoned his virtuous Roman wife for the more dynamic Cleopatra, the foreign and sinister queen who aimed to rule the world.

It is undeniable that Antonius treated Octavia in a foul and shabby manner: although he had married her for political reasons, she was a good wife and had loyally cared for the children of the dead Fulvia as well as her own. His rejection and divorce appeared abominable to many Romans, and for Octavianus constituted a personal insult, a breach of friendship, and an act of war.

It was not easy even for as crafty a politician as Octavianus to go to war against a man as popular as Antonius with both consuls on his side and half the senate. To prove Antonius a menace to Rome was also difficult. Cleopatra was more vulnerable. Against her the propaganda machine could more easily go to work. Was not that detestable Oriental queen plotting to make herself empress of the world? Had she not been heard to say she would some day hand down justice from the Capitol? In all her alleged machinations Antonius was made to seem her doting dupe!

The breach between the two triumvirs constantly widened. In a bitter exchange of letters each hurled recriminations against the other, charges of broken promises, family scandal, and private vices. Poets, orators, lampoonists, and pamphleteers entered the fray at the expense of truth and justice.

The two consuls of 32 B.C., Sosius and Domitius Ahenobarbus, both friends and partisans of Antonius, had earlier received from him despatches requesting the senate's confirmation of all his acts in the East and his donations to Cleopatra and her children. Antonius also promised, for propaganda purposes, to resign from the triumvirate and restore the Republic. Fearing its political repercussions, the consuls withheld the contents of the dispatch though Sosius in a bitter speech before the senate roundly condemned Octavianus and moved a vote of censure against him. A tribune promptly interposed his veto.

A few days later Octavianus appeared before the senate in person with an armed bodyguard. He denounced Antonius and his agents, the consuls. Then he dismissed the senate with the promise to present incriminating evidence against Antonius at the next meeting. The consuls and more than three hundred senators at once fled from Rome to Antonius. Octavianus suffered them to depart.

The Will of Antonius

Meanwhile Plancus, hitherto a strong adherent of Antonius, had with several others deserted Antonius and fled to Rome. The defection of Plancus, who had never yet proved wrong in his choice of a probable winner, was ominous, sensational, and to Antonius most disconcerting. To Octavianus he brought a precious gift, none more urgently needed, namely the knowledge that Antonius had deposited with the Vestal Virgins his last will and testament. Octavianus promptly and illegally extorted that will from the Vestal Virgins and read it at the next meeting of the senate. The will allegedly confirmed the legacies to the children of Cleopatra, declared that Caesarion was a true son and successor of Julius Caesar, and directed that Antonius after death be buried beside Cleopatra in the Ptolemaic mausoleum in Alexandria.*

Genuine or forged, the will gave to Octavianus his greatest propaganda victory. It confirmed the most vicious rumors against Antonius, befuddled his friends, and filled the middle class with loathing and horror.

Octavianus Declares War

Capitalizing on the popular revulsion against Antonius, Octavianus now resolved to mobilize the power of the West against the East. By various means—local agitations, propaganda, patriotic appeals, and some intimidation perhaps—he contrived to secure from the municipalities first of Italy and later of the Western provinces an oath of personal allegiance. Fortified by this somewhat spurious popular mandate, he declared Antonius stripped of his *imperium* and of his consulate of 31 B.C. Late in the fall of 32 B.C. Octavianus declared war on Cleopatra and spent the rest of the winter in preparation.

Antonius himself had meanwhile not been idle. He had for some time been assembling at Ephesus a vast apparatus for war—thirty legions mostly of Italian origin, 12,000 cavalry, 500 ships, and large stores of grain and supplies. Towards the end of 32 B.C. he sailed for Greece and took up battle stations at Actium, at the entrance of the Ambracian Gulf, in which lay the main part of his fleet.

Militarily and materially Antonius should have won the battle of Actium. He was the greatest general of his age and commanded an army numerically equal in both infantry and cavalry to that of Octavianus. He also

* Though regarded as genuine by some classical scholars, more than one historian has judged the will of Antonius to be an obvious forgery.

had one of the biggest and strongest fleets the ancient world had yet seen.

His weakness overbalanced strength. His ships were too heavy and slow, their crews untrained and inexperienced in recent naval warfare. Not one of his admirals was the equal, in skill and daring, of Agrippa, one of the greatest naval strategists in Roman history.

More serious still was the lack of morale of Antonius' troops, if confronted with that patriotic fervor Octavianus seemed able to inspire in the West. While most legionaries admired Antonius as a man and soldier, they hated war against fellow citizens. His officers detested Cleopatra and in private cursed Antonius for not being man enough to send her back to Egypt. They did not know how much he depended upon her for money, grain, and supplies. She in turn feared to let him out of her sight, lest he abandon her and go back to Octavia. Antonius was doomed.

The Battle of Actium: 31 B.C.

The details of the battle of Actium, one of the most famous and decisive of world history, are not known. Its phases, duration, and character are obscure or controversial. Despite the efforts of ancient writers to embellish or dramatize it, it was evidently a miserable affair, scarcely worthy of the name of battle. It took place at sea and involved a pitifully small number of ships. The land armies never fought at all. Actium was famous and decisive only because it marked the end of the Republic and the beginning of the Empire.

The blockade had caused a severe famine and an outbreak of plague in Antonius' camp; his commanders were divided and quarreling among themselves; his troops were paralyzed by treason and desertions. Antonius himself had become negligent and he continued to place undue importance on his ponderous ships instead of reviving his famed leadership on land. Some days later, his legions capitulated to the victorious Octavianus. At the height of the already hopeless battle, Antonius caught sight of Cleopatra's ship heading out to sea.* The distraught Antonius instantly followed the queen. His men, left leaderless, soon succumbed to bewilderment and surrendered.

The victory of Octavianus was so complete that he felt no immediate need to pursue the fugitives to Egypt. He turned his attention to mutinous legions in Italy instead, and crossed the sea to appease their demands for land and money.

It was not until the summer of 30 B.C. that Octavianus, desperate for money, went to Egypt. The legions of Antonius put up only a brief resistance. Alexandria surrendered. While Octavianus was celebrating his recent victory, news arrived that Antonius had committed suicide. A few days later Cleopatra followed suit. Thus passed the last of the Ptolemies, a dynasty that had ruled Egypt for almost three hundred years. Egypt became part of the Roman Empire, and its rich treasures fell into the hands of Octavianus, who had defeated the greatest militarist of the age and was now undisputed master of the world. After a century of civil war, peace had come at last.

* The reason for Cleopatra's precipitate departure is not known. Some attribute it to despair at having received word that Antonius was killed. Others, less romantic, maintain that the battle had clearly taken a turn for the worse and Cleopatra was fleeing to escape capture.

THE EMPIRE BEFORE AUGUSTUS
TERRITORIES ADDED BY AUGUSTUS
TERRITORIES ADDED AFTER 14 A.D.
SHADED BORDERS: TEMPORARY OCCUPATION

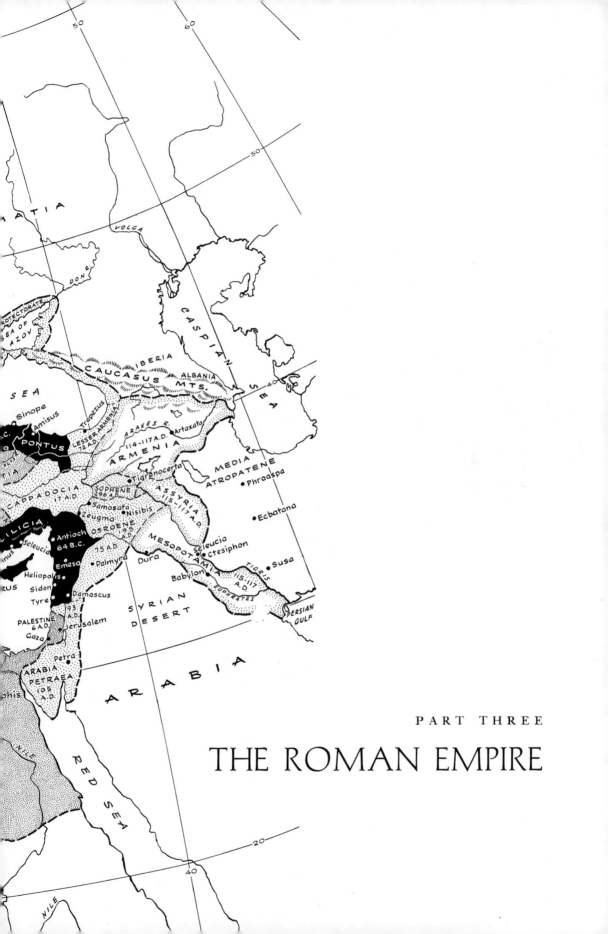

PART THREE

THE ROMAN EMPIRE

THE PRINCIPATE OF

MOST OF THE INFORMATION CONCERNING THE EARLY PRINCIPATE
or Empire comes from the extant books of the *Annals* of Tacitus
(which begin with the death of Augustus in 14 A.D. and end with
the death of Nero); the *Roman History* of Cassius Dio (Books
51 to 60); the *Lives of the Twelve Caesars* (from Julius Caesar
to Domitian) by Suetonius; the *Compendium of Roman History*
by Velleius Paterculus (who ended his work in 30 A.D.); and
an inscriptional transcript of the *Deeds of Augustus* (*Res Gestae
Divi Augusti*), a document written by the emperor, revised after
his death and set up as inscription at Rome, Ancyra (now
Ankara), Apollonia in Galatia, Antioch in Pisidia, and other
places. Also of great importance is a long Greek inscription from
Cyrene, containing five edicts known as the *Edicts of Cyrene*, and
first published in 1927. In addition thousands of Latin and Greek

AUGUSTUS

inscriptions, papyri, and coins survive. Archaeology also provides much information about the social, economic, and cultural life of the period.

After the deaths of Antonius and Cleopatra, Octavianus annexed Egypt to the Roman Empire, but governed it as an exclusively imperial possession through viceroys or prefects and refused to allow members of the Roman senate even to visit there. His first prefect was C. Cornelius Gallus, a Roman knight.

Octavianus made very few other changes in the East, leaving the dispositions of An-

tonius practically unaltered. He accepted the pledges of loyalty and allegiance of the vassal rulers Antonius had enthroned to guard the eastern frontiers, confirmed their titles, and added to their territories. With ambitious plans for the West, Augustus desired peace in the East and therefore sought neither the annexation of Armenia nor the conquest of Parthia. Nor did he attempt to avenge the disaster at Carrhae.

The Triumphal Return to Rome: 29 B.C.

In the late summer of 29 B.C. Octavianus returned to Rome in triumph. The senate ratified all his acts, proclaimed his birthday a future holiday, and decreed the erection of triumphal arches at Brundisium and at Rome. The poets hailed the mighty conqueror. On three successive days he held triumphs for Dalmatia, for Actium, and for Egypt, all surpassing in pomp and splendor the triumphs of Julius Caesar. For the first time since the end of the First Punic War in 241 B.C. the doors of the temple of Janus stood closed as the mute but visible sign of peace on land and sea. After a century of civil war and violence men could at last breathe freely, work, and enjoy peace and prosperity without fear of confiscation, proscription, or violent death.

Although peace reigned within the empire, the imperial frontiers had yet to be pro-

tected lest the barbarians massed beyond the Rhine and the Danube swarm into the rich and peaceful provinces of the empire. Imperial defense called for a policy of aggressive war as yet unprecedented in Roman history.

The Roman armies themselves were an even greater potential menace to internal peace and stability than the barbarians. Under the command of ambitious and ruthless generals they could again turn and rend the state, as they had in the recent past. After Actium Octavianus found himself the master of seventy legions, of which less than thirty would suffice for imperial defense. Over these he must retain supreme and undivided command and disband the rest. He then had to deal with the problem of finding land on which to settle the veterans of more than forty legions without confiscation of private property or higher taxes, as well as with the heavier and more manifold problem of reconstruction: the creation of a strong central government; the revival of the prestige and authority of the senate, whose power Caesar had weakened and the development of a cabinet system of government; the maintenance of control over the army by the chief of state; the creation of an imperial civil service; the regulation of public finance and the administration of the provinces and control over foreign affairs; the problem of finding and securing a suitable successor; the revival of the ancient moral code and the regeneration of the state religion. To carry out all these tasks might well have taxed the strength of a human dynamo.

The sickly Octavianus compensated for his poor health by the willpower, determination, coolness, and political astuteness he had demonstrated from the beginning of his slow and arduous climb to power.

He had returned from the East a popular idol, with a prestige and power such as even Caesar had never possessed. East and West were bound to him in fealty and by oaths of allegiance, and he had supreme command of the biggest and best army in Roman history,

Augustus Imperator: statue (ca. 20 B.C.) from the Villa of Livia at Prima Porta. (Courtesy The Photographical Archives of the Vatican Museums and Galleries, Rome)

as well as access to the revenues and resources of a rich and mighty empire. The confiscated treasures of the Ptolemies might alone have sufficed to provide land and bonuses for his veterans, feed and amuse for a time the populace of Rome, and even revive the economic prosperity of Italy by permitting the removal of taxes and the initiation of a vast program of public works.

In addition to his financial resources, Octavianus had an *auctoritas*, a prestige and dignity unique in Roman history. At first the "soul" of Julius Caesar, "cleansed" of earthly sin and "translated" into a comet, had been called upon to aid Octavianus in his struggle for power. Such "divine" aid was now no longer needed, for Octavianus, a war hero and popular idol, was also the unchallenged leader of a powerful political party and the acknowledged source of all patronage and power.

Special Titles

First among the imposing string of titles Octavianus possessed was *Caesar,* his adopted name. The coinage clearly proves that he retained the name even after Actium. Though then no longer needed, indeed temporarily abjured by him, and almost blotted from the record, it had yet a great future, illustrious, imperial, even absolutist, later becoming a title worn by all succeeding emperors and, in more recent centuries, by the Kaiser of Germany and the Czar of Russia.

The title *Imperator,* also part of his nomenclature, was a proud and ancient title. A commander-in-chief of a victorious army had always been hailed as Imperator, and retained the title until after his triumph. Marius, Sulla, Pompey, and Caesar had frequently held it, Octavianus himself twenty-seven times before his death for victories won either by himself or by his legates. Unlike Caesar, Pompey, and all the other generals of the Republic who had this title bestowed upon them, Octavianus adopted it as a *praenomen* and permanently retained it as part of his official nomenclature, thereby emphasizing his military past. Though repudiated by his immediate successors, Tiberius, Caligula, and Claudius, with and after Vespasian *Imperator* became the standard title of all Roman rulers and survives as the English word "emperor."

Although it never became part of his official nomenclature, outstanding among the titles of Octavianus was *princeps civitatis* ("leader of the state"), a term usually shortened to *princeps,* from which are derived the words "principate" and "prince." Though it later came to signify something like "monarch" or "emperor," it was neither unique nor new: there had been other *principes.* During the Republic the term *princeps* had meant *"dux,"* the victorious general, an ex-consul of patrician or of noble family, who had returned as a leader of the senate, a director of foreign affairs, and a person of great prestige, venerability, or *auctoritas.* Available sources attribute the term to august personages belonging to the earliest and latest days of the Republic: to Atta Clausus Sabinus (consul ca. 495 B.C.), to Cincinnatus (ca. 460 B.C.), Camillus (ca. 401 B.C.), Scipio Africanus (205, 194 B.C.), the elder Cato (195 B.C.), Scipio Aemilianus (147, 134 B.C.), to Marius, Lucullus, Pompey, Julius Caesar, and to many others.

The foundation of the power of Octavianus was the army and the people; his rule rested upon the twin pillars of the proconsular *imperium* and tribunician power. His was *imperium maius,* or superior to that of all provincial governors and army commanders. Rome, Italy, Egypt, and all the provinces in which legions still fought—Spain, Gaul, and Syria—were subject to his overriding command. The *imperium maius* placed in his hands supreme command over the armed forces and prevented the usurpation of power by generals (which phenomenon had brought about the fall of the Republic).

Octavianus had held the consulship continuously from 33 to 23 B.C. In 36 B.C. he had acquired for life the sacrosanctity of a plebeian tribune. Although as a patrician (by virtue of his adoption), he was ineligible for election as an ordinary tribune of the plebs, he exercised all the powers of that formidable office till the end of his life. Another instrument of administrative power was his *auctoritas,* as the coinage amply demonstrates (p. 300).

Although the popular Octavianus could probably have set up a dictatorship or even a military despotism, he determined to share the government with the senate and contented himself with exercising the traditional and constitutional powers of a true magistrate of a restored Republic. He was probably sincere, for his conservative temperament and upbringing made him proud to share power with the scions of Rome's oldest and most illustrious families—the Claudian, Calpurnian, Aemilian, Fabian, or Cornelian.

To make the senate a more effective branch of the government, he carried out in 28 B.C. a purge of about 200 of its unworthiest and most unreliable members, most of whom the triumvirs had introduced between 43 and 31 B.C. Subsequent purges in 18 and 13 B.C. finally reduced the membership from an original thousand to 600. To fill vacancies in the senate he restored the practice of admitting ex-quaestors but restricted the quaestorship to men of senatorial family and of good moral character, to men who had had military training and were possessors of property worth at least 800,000 sesterces (about $70,-000), a valuation later raised to 1,000,000 sesterces (about $90,000). Similarly, he made admission into the equestrian order dependent, as before, upon a property valuation of 400,000 sesterces (about $35,000). To invigorate both orders with new blood, Octavianus adopted Caesar's policy of admitting a few rich and aristocratic residents of the Italian *municipia* and even of the Roman colonies of Gaul and Spain. Future emperors would continue that policy on a much more extensive scale.

The Reorganization of the Government: 27 B.C.

On the thirteenth of January, 27 B.C., Octavianus dramatically appeared before the purged and rejuvenated senate and offered to surrender all his powers to the senate and the Roman people. That solemn and dramatic act seemingly portending the restoration of the Republic aroused, as he probably expected, more trepidation than joy. Overwhelmed by the noble gesture, the senators prevailed upon him to accept proconsular power for ten years over the large and geographically separated single province of Spain, Gaul, and Syria, where most of the legions were stationed.

In the new division of power, the senate resumed control over Rome and Italy and over the provinces of Sicily, Sardinia and Corsica, Illyricum, Macedonia, Greece, Asia, Bithynia, Crete-Cyrene, and Africa.* Augustus governed the "imperial" provinces through his own legates or deputies, while the senate controlled the "senatorial" provinces through proconsuls or propraetors. The princeps probably maintained effective control over the governors of the "senatorial" provinces either through his *auctoritas* or his *imperium maius,* thus retaining as much real power after his so-called restoration of the Republic as he had had before.

Three days after Octavianus' "surrender" of power, the senate met to honor the restorer of the Republic. A laurel wreath was to be placed above the door posts of his house and a golden shield inscribed with his virtues of valor, clemency, justice, and piety, was to be hung up in the senate. An even greater honor was their conferral upon him of the name *Augustus,* of exalted connotation and religious association.

The new Augustus in turn had exalted the senate and augmented its powers. He restored its control over public finance and even the right, for a time at least, of coining money in gold and silver. For the first time in its history the senate became a supreme court to judge cases of extortion in the senatorial provinces and to hear appeals from Italy and the provinces. Though he continued to recognize the popular assemblies as law-making bodies, he permitted the senate to issue decrees having the force of law without ratification by the people. Officially, the senate had become a full partner in the government. Theoretically, it was even more: the ultimate source of the princeps' power. What it had granted it could also take away.

* The so-called "senatorial" provinces were, according to Dio (53.12.2) and (53.13.1), generally peaceful and, unlike the "imperial" provinces, did not require garrison of legionary troops. This distinction did not always hold, for the proconsuls of the senatorial provinces of Africa, Illyricum, and Macedonia, had legionary troops under their command at various times during the early principate.

In reality, as Tacitus and Dio both saw, the restoration of the Republic turned out to be a constitutional window dressing for an imperial regime that was to become almost absolutist. Yet Augustus probably neither realized nor foresaw the unreality of the "restoration" he proclaimed. Even if he had, he was powerless to reverse the forces slowly generated by the conquest of a great empire. Even the old Republic had been unable to cope with those resistless forces, much less its ghost however earnestly called up from the dead.

One such force, which had prospered in the days of Marius, was the army. Without it, there could be no internal order, no external peace. It was now the army of the revolution and Augustus was its revolutionary commander-in-chief, the supreme master of the state as well as its guardian and defender. Control of that army gave him the substance and reality of a power not fully disguised behind the false front of the restored Republic.

He had the right to summon the senate, control its debates, and purge its membership; to preside at elections in the popular assemblies, nominate and recommend candidates, and veto acts of all other magistrates; to control the administration of justice and serve as the highest court of appeal in the empire. In addition he was president of the senate (*princeps senatus*), an office giving him the right to speak first and direct deliberations. Even that ancient and formidable office was not his only means of controlling the senate, the second strongest branch of the government.

Nor would the senate majority have wanted a genuine restoration of the Republic, whose recent history—anarchy, proscription, and civil war—was so frightful. To most senators, control of the army or the problem of imperial defense must have seemed insuperable tasks. Victorious warlords such as Marius or Sulla, Pompey or Caesar might again return to rend the state. Spain, not yet subdued, required pacification; Gaul, settlement and reorganization; Syria required defense against the dreaded Parthians. In the forests and fens beyond the Rhine and the Danube lurked restless barbarian hordes ready to break into the warm and peaceful lands of the empire. Who but Augustus, supreme general of the armies, could now successfully defend the empire without risk of civil conflict or a future struggle for power? Augustus had been the last of the great revolutionary warlords. Rome could ill afford another.

Evolution of a Cabinet System of Government

As early as 27 B.C. Augustus had secured the appointment of a senate committee to assist him in preparing the agenda for meetings of the senate. This committee, consisting of the consuls, one representative from each of the other magistracies, and fifteen senators selected by lot, was to change every six months. As reorganized in 13 A.D. and reinforced by members of the imperial family and from the equestrian order, the committee began to assume functions formerly belonging to the senate. Even as reorganized, it was not a true cabinet. Meeting more or less publicly, it was an administrative, not a policy making, body.

The real predecessor of the later imperial cabinet was not this clumsy, rotating committee of the senate but small coteries of top-flight administrators, close friends of Augustus, high ranking senators, legal experts, and other specialists, who met informally and behind closed doors. They decided the policy of the government, the legislation to be presented before meetings of the senate and the popular assemblies, the candidates it might please Augustus to recommend at the coming elections, the next governor of such and such a province, and all matters pertaining to public finance, foreign affairs, law, religion, and the administration of the empire.

The Imperial Civil Service

One of the outstanding achievements of Augustus was the creation of a permanent civil service, a task begun early in his reign but still uncompleted at the time of his death. The trained and salaried staff he slowly built up was the predecessor of the imperial bureaucracy, which enabled the later emperors to maintain executive control over the Roman world state.

The idea of a civil service was not entirely new. Since the Second Punic War provincial governors, administrators, and even the proprietors of large and scattered estates had employed their freedmen and personal slaves as secretaries, accountants, and business managers. Pompey had engaged such assistance in his administration of the grain supply and in the government of his provinces. Augustus had inherited from Caesar a large corps of trained slaves and personal agents, the nucleus of the complex bureaucratic organization he was later to extend over all the empire.

Never until the principate of Augustus had the need for the civil service been more urgent—in Rome, for the administration of such vital services as the grain supply (*cura annonae*), the grain dole (*frumentatio*), the water supply (*cura aquae*), police and fire protection, the prevention of floods, the construction and maintenance of streets and marketplaces, and the erection and repair of temples and public buildings; in Italy, for the preservation of law and order and for the construction and maintenance of such public works as roads and bridges; in the provinces, for the management of the emperor's private estates, the collection of taxes, the supplying of the armies with provisions and equipment, public works, and the imperial postal system (*cursus publicus*).

Senators in Civil Service

In his civil service organization Augustus employed people of every social class—senators, knights, freedmen, and even slaves. The Police Commissioner (*praefectus urbi*), who had under his command a police force of three cohorts of 1000 men each, was at first always a senator of consular rank; so was the Water Commissioner, whom Augustus appointed in 12 B.C. to supervise, with the assistance of two other senators, the 240 slaves Agrippa had trained to service the aqueducts and water mains of the city. Another board of five senators dealt with the flood problem along the Tiber. Two senators of consular rank presided until 6 A.D. over the vitally important grain commission, which had branch offices at Puteoli as well as in the grain producing provinces.

Most of the senators serving on the commissions just mentioned were of praetorian rank. Ex-praetors outnumbered consulars in the water commission, on the grain dole board set up in 22 B.C., in the commission in charge of public buildings in Rome, and in that appointed in 20 B.C. to supervise the construction and maintenance of roads throughout Italy. Besides, nearly all the provincial governors and legates of the imperial provinces were men of this rank.

Equestrians or Knights in Civil Service

Although Augustus, especially in the early years of his principate, conferred upon senators positions of dignity and prominence, he drew many of his top-ranking administrators from the equestrian class. The knights had acquired valuable experience, especially in the fields of finance, taxation, and commerce, of which senators had little knowledge. For more than a century the knights had been exploiting the natural resources of the empire—mines, forests, and fisheries—had set up large banking, shipping, industrial, and commercial monopolies, and through their tax-farming companies had unmercifully wrung taxes from the provinces.

Now somewhat restricted by the reforms of Caesar and Augustus, they were glad of the opportunity of rendering a more useful and honorable service. Augustus, in turn, welcomed their services because he regarded them as more reliable and less politically dangerous than senators, and more dependent upon him for patronage and future advancement.

The careers open to knights were military, judicial, financial, and administrative. A young knight usually began his career as a prefect of an auxiliary cavalry squadron, advanced to tribune of a cohort or legion, then to prefect of a cohort. A prefect of the engineers (*praefectus fabrum*) could also look forward to a future of some importance.

Military service often varied in length. Knights, such as the historian, Velleius Paterculus, usually served eight years. Others served longer. Some even chose the military life as a career: knights frequently commanded legions on garrison duty, particularly in Egypt, a land forbidden to senators.

After a year or two in the regular army, some knights served as attorneys in the civil administration; others as officers with the Praetorian Guard (the imperial guard—preserver of law and order in Rome and Italy), the urban police or the fire department; or, more frequently still, as procurators, or imperial agents in the provinces.

In the imperial provinces a procurator was the emperor's financial agent, his tax collector and paymaster; in the senatorial provinces, his financial agent, manager of his private estates, and collector of the revenues therefrom. He also served as a special observer. A corrupt and rapacious governor had to be exceedingly wary, lest he be liable to stern retribution at termination of office. The procurator was often more powerful even than a governor of consular senatorial rank.

Procurators might also govern provinces, especially the more backward and turbulent ones, such as Rhaetia and Noricum north and east of the Alps, not to speak of Egypt, the richest and most important of all, the eminence and power of whose prefect even the very proudest senatorial governor might envy.

Second in power to the prefect of Egypt were the two prefects (also of equestrian rank) whom Augustus had in 2 B.C. placed in joint command over the nine cohorts (each 1,000 strong) of the Praetorian Guard. This *praefectus praetorio* later became chief of staff of all armies, head of the civil service, the highest judge of appeals in the Empire, eventually the maker and unmaker of emperors and on occasion ascended the throne himself.

Two other prefectures, created around 6 A.D., were less important, but often served as stepping stones to higher office. One belonged to the commissioner of the grain administration, the other to the prefect of the *Vigiles*, a corps of seven cohorts, each consisting of 1000 former slaves, who patrolled the streets at night and guarded the city against riot or fire.

Freedmen in the Civil Service

The rise of the knights in the civil service was neither as rapid nor as spectacular as that of the freedmen, some of whom ultimately attained positions more powerful than those held by knights, senators, consuls, or provincial governors.

At first, the freedmen performed the more menial tasks. Their willingness to take orders, their subservience and loyalty proved in the end their greatest asset. By dint of hard work, thrift, loyalty, and intelligence the freedman gradually began to forge ahead and occupy positions of opulence and power.

The bureaucratic tasks of imperial correspondence became their monopoly. As a result of the growing needs and complexity of a great empire, the services rendered by freedmen finally proved more essential to imperial administration than military commands or governorships. The routine work of the various bureaus created by Augustus required large numbers of accountants, auditors, secretaries, and clerks. In this vast organization freedmen held the higher and better paid jobs, slaves the more menial and obscure. The secretarial bureaus, as important to the Roman empire as the departments of state, treasury, war, and commerce to a modern state, remained the monopoly of the freedmen class and a source of immense power.

Soon freedmen had entrusted to their control the revenues and disbursements of the empire—gold from Spain and Dalmatia, grain from Africa and Egypt, taxes or tribute from provinces or vassal kings, pearls from the Indian Ocean, and all the wealth ships carried over seven seas.

Watchful, shrewd, quick at arithmetic, versed in the art of flattery, they soon came to determine how much the state should spend on armaments, on aqueducts, temples, palaces, games, and spectacles; how much on roads, bridges, harbors; the weight and fineness of gold or silver coin; the taxes or tribute provinces must pay; even the salaries governors, prefects, procurators, and other civil servants should receive.

Finally certain freedmen in high positions began to receive petitions and requests from every part of the empire—complaints of extortion from provincial councils, applications for offices or priesthoods, prayers for manumission, petitions for imperial decorations. The option of ignoring or bringing such petitions to the emperor's notice gave these freedmen officers positions of real patronage and power.

Augustus sets out for Gaul and Spain: 27 B.C.

Before he had even begun the work of reconstruction, Augustus set out for Gaul and Spain. The conquest of the latter country, though begun two centuries earlier, was still far from complete. The Cantabrians and Asturians, wild and uncivilized tribes in northwestern Spain, had been raiding for years the more peaceful and civilized peoples to the east and south. Though often defeated by Roman arms, they remained unsubdued.

In 26 B.C., three separate Roman armies converged on the Spanish tribesmen. The armies, led by Augustus, succeeded in hacking their way to the coast by means of pitched battles and much guerrilla warfare. But the toil and hardships endured by the princeps wrecked his health and obliged him to entrust the campaign to his lieutenants. They failed. Finally, Agrippa was recalled from the East and sent to Spain where, by authorizing systematic massacres and mass enslavements, he finally subdued the mountaineers (19 B.C.) and brought peace to that ruined land.

The Political Crisis of 23 B.C.

Still frail and weak, the princeps arrived in Rome in 24 B.C., after an absence of two years. The next year began badly. A dreadful illness beset Augustus, and a treason trial and conspiracy by two eminent senators revealed the weakness of the regime. After a miraculous recovery, Augustus took warning and made drastic changes in the government.

On July 1st, 23 B.C., he resigned the consulship, which he had held continuously since 31 B.C. Continued tenure had not only undermined his health but was also making him most unpopular with ambitious young nobles who aspired to the office which was the prerogative of their birth and the summit of their political career. It seemed unwise to incur the continued ill-will of a class whose help the princeps so urgently required in administration.

The Settlement of 23 B.C.

The crisis and settlement of 23 B.C. brought Augustus an increase rather than a diminution of real power. He had resigned the consul's office, but retained consular power and extended his proconsular *imperium* over Rome and the entire empire. He also invoked the powers of a plebeian tribune (*tribunicia potestas*), vague yet formidable, imperial in essence, in origin democratic. The year 23 B.C., in which he assumed full tribunician power, marked for Augustus the beginning of a new phase of his principate, for history the birth of the Roman Empire, the year 27 notwithstanding. Augustus apparently realized the significance of that year, for he dated future public documents from the year 23 B.C.

Besides the powers of an ordinary tribune —personal inviolability, the veto, and the right of intercession (p. 184)—Augustus could summon and present legislation before both the senate and the Tribal Assembly and preside at elections of magistrates, thereby controlling all the main avenues of public life. Tribunician power also made it easier for him to designate a successor.

The Problem of Succession

The political crisis of 23 B.C. and his almost fatal illness drove Augustus to concentrate attention upon the urgent problem of the succession. Legally and constitutionally, the choice of a successor was not his right, but that of the senate and the Roman people, to whom he owed his power. Nevertheless he feared that his failure to deal with the problem might, after his death, bring about a civil war between rival candidates for the throne. Also, he hoped to find a successor in his own family and of his own blood. Unfortunately, he had no sons and only one daughter, Julia, who had been married in 25 B.C. to his nephew C. Claudius Marcellus, Octavia's son, a youth of eighteen. Augustus assiduously promoted the advancement of his son-in-law and, at nineteen, that handsome youth was already a member of the senate. In 23 B.C. he was elected curule aedile and served also as pontiff, and then was scheduled for election to the consulship though ten years younger than the legal age.

The election of Marcellus to the consulate was a virtual certainty. He not only enjoyed the backing of Augustus, but had made himself immensely popular during his aedileship by the magnificence of his games and shows. Augustus might have openly adopted him as his son had he dared to offend the two persons who had helped him most in his own rise to power: Livia and Agrippa. Agrippa, the loyal architect of victory, was on the surface a reliable, self-effacing deputy, but was actually most ambitious, possibly ruthless. Livia, that cool, close-lipped lady, had married Augustus principally to further the interest of her two sons from a previous marriage, Tiberius Claudius Nero and Nero Claudius Drusus. Neither she nor Agrippa would have permitted the young Marcellus to stand in their way. Augustus must have known that, for the adoption never happened.

In 23 B.C., Augustus seemed close to death, Marcellus still too young to succeed. The princeps handed Agrippa his signet-ring, thereby designating him as the successor. The problem of succession seemed settled.

When Augustus recovered, he procured for Agrippa the proconsular *imperium* over all the imperial provinces and sent him to the East to superintend the affairs of Syria and strengthen the defenses against the Parthians. Not long after Agrippa had departed for the East, Marcellus died (23 B.C.).

Augustus was still determined to keep the succession within the family. In 21 B.C., he sent for Agrippa and prevailed upon him to divorce his wife and marry Julia. In 18 B.C. he had extended Agrippa's *imperium* over the senatorial provinces as well and even conferred upon him tribunician power for five years. Agrippa, always the faithful deputy, was now son-in-law, co-regent, and heir presumptive to the Augustan throne. Nor was that all. In 17 B.C. the princeps adopted, under the names of Gaius and Lucius Caesar, the two young sons of Julia and Agrippa, thereby settling the problem of succession not just for one but for two generations to come.

The succession problem apparently settled, the princeps and Agrippa set out to tour the provinces. Both had already traveled extensively. The princeps had been in Gaul and Spain from 27 to 24 B.C., in the East from 22 to 19 B.C., and again in Gaul from 16 to 13 B.C. After his return from the East, Agrippa spent the years 20 and 19 B.C. in Spain, and the period from 17 to 13 B.C. in the East as inspector-general. Their travels had firmly convinced them that imperial defense depended upon a standing army of professional soldiers, well equipped and thoroughly trained.

The Army

After Actium Augustus had demobilized at least 300,000 men and cut the number of legions from over seventy to, perhaps, twenty-eight (or about 160,000 men), not too large an army for the defense of a frontier at least 4000 miles long. Of the twenty-eight legions, at least eight guarded the Rhineland, seven or more the Danubian region. Three legions were in Spain, four in Syria, two in Egypt, one in Macedonia, and one in Africa. Italy itself was now adequately garrisoned by the Praetorian Guard of 9000 men. Augustus had 5000 troops in Asia Minor, 3000 in Judea, and 1200 in Gaul. Besides the legionaries, there was an equal number of auxiliaries organized in infantry and cavalry cohorts of 480 and 960 men respectively.

The recruitment of legionaries, except after a military disaster, was usually by voluntary enlistment. Most of the recruits came not from peninsular Italy, where army life was unpopular and manpower scarce, but from the Celtic districts north of the Po, from the newly conquered Alpine valleys, from southern Gaul, and from Spain. The legionaries either enjoyed Roman citizenship before enlistment or had it conferred upon them shortly afterwards. Some of the finest fighting men now came from the lands of the Rhine and the Danube, though probably not as legionaries, but as auxiliaries. The defense of the empire was no longer the sole responsibility of Italy.

Length of military service varied with category or circumstance. Praetorian guardsmen normally served for 16 years, legionaries for 20, and auxiliaries for 25. Sometimes legionaries and auxiliaries had to stay in the army for 30 years or more, because of military necessity, lack of replacements, or insufficient funds for pensions.

The pay varied with category and rank. For legionary soldiers the pay was ten asses a day or 225 denarii (about $85) a year. They had to buy their equipment, uniforms, bedding, and perhaps even food. Praetorians probably got more, auxiliaries considerably less.

In 13 B.C., Augustus substituted money for land as a reward for discharged veterans. Within the years 7 to 2 B.C. he paid out no less than 400,000,000 sesterces (about 36,000,000 dollars), most of it from his own funds.

The bonus of a praetorian private was 5000 denarii (about 1500 dollars), that of a legionary 3000 (about $1000). A centurion often received a sum which, when added to his savings and loot, enabled him to attain the status of a knight. The auxiliaries did not fare so well. Since their bonus, if any, was small, their greatest reward was the *diploma* of citizenship.

In 6 A.D. Augustus threw upon the state the responsibility of providing soldiers' bonuses by setting up a special fund (*aerarium militare*), to which he contributed 170,000,000 sesterces (about $15,300,000) of his own money and to maintain it applied the revenues accruing from a five percent inheritance tax, a four percent tax on slaves, a one percent sales tax, as well as the gifts and legacies received from his subjects and clients.

The Imperial Roman Navy

The war with Sextus Pompey and the battle of Actium clearly demonstrated the need for a permanent Roman navy. To suppress piracy, defend the shores of Italy, and escort grain transports and trading ships, Augustus created two main fleets, one based at Misenum on the bay of Naples, the other at Ravenna on the Adriatic. He had other bases also, especially at Alexandria, and for a time one at Forum Julii (now Fréjus) in southern Gaul. The fleets, manned by a few slaves or freedmen, but largely by Dalmatians, were under the command of prefects who were sometimes equestrians but more often

freedmen. Auxiliary river flotillas patrolled the Rhine, the Danube, the French rivers and the Nile.

Road Building

Road building went hand in hand with conquest, imperial defense, and provincial communication. Though road building for military purposes did not originate with Augustus, he devoted much attention to it and was the first to extend the network from Italy to the provinces. By 27 B.C. he had completed the repair and reconstruction of the Italian roads, much neglected since the time of Gaius Gracchus, especially the Flaminian Way, main thoroughfare between Rome and the North and a vital artery of the empire. After the conquest of the Alpine and Danubian regions, he began the construction of a road from Trento on the Adige to Augsburg, Germany. Other roads ran through the Alps between Italy and Gaul. The completion of this program brought Switzerland, the Tyrol, Austria, Bavaria, and Gaul into close and rapid communication with Italy.

The Imperial Post (Cursus Publicus)

Road building made possible another Augustan achievement—the imperial postal service (*cursus publicus*) for transfer of official letters and despatches and the carrying of officials, senators, and other privileged persons. The expense of this service—relays of horses and carriages and the provision of hotel service for official guests—fell upon the towns located along the great highways, a grievous burden upon many towns but most conducive to imperial communication and centralization of administration.

Colonization

Another valuable instrument in the work of conquest and empire was the colony, which served several purposes: the settlement of war veterans, the consolidation of conquest, and the Romanization of the provinces. Throughout his political career from 43 B.C. till 14 A.D. Augustus had founded twenty-eight colonies in Italy and perhaps eighty in

This granite bridge, built during the reign of Augustus, is half a mile long, and spans the Guadiana near Emerita Augusta (now Mérida), Spain. (Courtesy Spanish Tourist Office, New York)

the provinces. The Italian colonies, composed mainly of war veterans, were centers of tremendous loyalty to the new regime. Augustus seems to have abandoned Caesar's policy of commercial colonies and founded few, if any, civilian or commercial colonies outside of Italy. Most of his colonies were for settlement of veterans or for military and strategic purposes.

The main function of the Augustan colonies in the provinces was to serve as fortresses or military outposts at strategic points to hold down and secure conquered territory. In the Alps, Gaul, Spain, and Portugal especially, they served as garrisons in wild, uncivilized regions, though they later helped to spread the use of the Latin language and of Roman law among the conquered peoples and became important agents of Romanization. Around some sprang up large and prosperous communities, the original foundation of well-known modern cities, Barcelona, Zaragoza, and Mérida in Spain; Vienne, Nîmes, and Lyons in France; and Tangier in Africa.

Imperial Expansion—the Alps

Imperial expansion kept pace with the forging of the instruments of conquest—armies, fleets, roads, postal service, colonies. After Spain (p. 276) Augustus paid earliest attention to the Alpine districts. Though the Roman empire now extended from Gibraltar to the Euphrates, the Alpine region had remained unsubdued and menacing. Wild and vicious tribes continued to raid their peaceful neighbors to the south and held passes essential to direct communication between Italy and Gaul.

In the year 25 B.C. the princeps sent Terentius Varro Murena against the Salassi, the most dangerous of all Alpine tribesmen. A decisive victory and ruthless enslavement removed the menace. Thereafter, a colony of veterans at Aosta guarded the Great and Little St. Bernard Passes and made possible the construction of a road through the Little St. Bernard leading from Italy to Lyons.

The Roman theater at Mérida, Spain (first century B.C.). It had places for 5,000 spectators. (Courtesy Spanish Tourist Office, New York)

Next came the turn of the northern and eastern Alps. In 17 and 16 B.C. P. Silius Nerva, able governor of Illyricum, began the conquest of Noricum (modern Tyrol, Styria, and Salzburg). The task was completed in 16-14 B.C. by the emperor's two stepsons, Tiberius Claudius Nero and Nero Claudius Drusus who, in a brilliant and converging campaign, consummated the conquest of both Noricum and Rhaetia (East Switzerland and West Tyrol) and all the tribes living near the headwaters of the Rhine and Danube. Noricum and Rhaetia became imperial provinces, at first governed by prefects, after 8 B.C. by procurators. The upper Danube became the northern boundary of the Roman empire.

The Conquest of the Danubian Lands

Long overdue was the conquest of the Balkans. The two provinces of Illyricum (modern Albania and parts of Yugoslavia) and of Macedonia had often been invaded by the Pannonians, who dwelt in what is now Hungary, northern Yugoslavia, and eastern Austria, or by the Dacians and Bastarnae of Romania and northern Hungary. In addition, the Dalmatians of Illyricum, never completely pacified, were usually in full revolt against Roman authority.

The suppression of the Dalmatian revolt and the subjugation of the Pannonians first fell to M. Vinicius, the capable proconsul of Illyricum in 14/13 B.C. He was replaced in the winter of 13/12 B.C. by Agrippa. Agrippa, his health shattered by the rigorous winter campaign, died, leaving his mission unaccomplished. The conquest was finally completed by Tiberius after four hard years of fighting (12-9 B.C.). He had carried the Roman standard to the south bank of the middle Danube and incorporated Pannonia with Illyricum.

The eastern Balkans had also long been a troubled area. In 30 and 29 B.C. M. Licinius Crassus, grandson of the victim of the debacle at Carrhae in 53 B.C., had as governor of Macedonia subdued Thrace (now Bulgaria) and had driven the land-hungry Bastarnians back over the Danube, for which he was granted by a jealous Augustus a long delayed and niggardly triumph. The peace did not last long, for in 13 B.C. Thracian uprisings, an invasion of Macedonia, and massive raids by the Dacians over the Danube compelled Augustus to summon an army from Galatia. Its commander, the able but hard-drinking L. Calpurnius Piso, restored order in the area after three years of fighting (13-11 or 12-10 B.C.). Later, sometime between 9 B.C. and 6 A.D. Cn. Cornelius Lentulus and Sextus Aelius Catus sent armies across the river and transplanted 50,000 Dacians to Moesia, which extended along the south bank of the Danube from Hungary to the Black Sea. In 6 A.D. Moesia became a separate province or military district governed by legates of Augustus.

In establishing the Danube as the northern frontier of the Roman empire, Augustus had achieved greater expansion than even Julius Caesar. The newly annexed Danubian lands, less valuable than Gaul economically, soon proved to be the best recruiting grounds in the entire empire.

Military Operations In Gaul and Germany

In Gaul Caesar's thorough conquest left Augustus nothing more than minor campaigns in Aquitania and administrative reorganization. In 22 B.C. he transferred Gallia Narbonensis to the senate. He divided Gallia Comata into three administrative parts: Aqui-tania, Lugdunensis, and Belgica, each under a separate legate subject, during his principate, to the governor or proconsul, who had his headquarters at Lugdunum (Lyons).

In Gaul peace and quiet, in Germany land-hunger and restlessness. The Rhine, established by Caesar as a defensive line against Germanic invaders from the east, was proving itself untenable. In 38 B.C. the Ubii crossed. Agrippa permitted them to settle at Cologne. In 16 B.C. the Sugambri came, mauled a Roman army and went back home. Their return in 12 B.C. persuaded Augustus to invade Germany and push the frontier to the Elbe and later, if possible, to the Vistula, so as to shorten the frontier line at least 300 miles or more. Shortened defense lines required less manpower.

Augustus assigned the invasion of Germany to his favorite stepson, Drusus, young, brave, intrepid. The assignment was a difficult one: there were no roads through that wild land of forests and swamps. How were supplies to be brought forward? How was ambush to be avoided? Drusus first constructed a line of forts along the Rhine—Vindonissa (near Basel); Bonn, Xanten, Mainz, Strasbourg. Next, he ordered a canal dug from the lower Rhine to the Zuider Zee and the ocean so as to admit the passage of an impressive flotilla of ships which might serve not only to awe the Frisians and other shore tribes, but also to keep the army supplied and carry out such amphibious operations as might be necessary. The strategy succeeded: two campaigns in 12 and 9 B.C. brought Roman arms to the west bank of the Elbe. There Drusus set up a trophy.

The young man's triumph was to be short. On the way back to the Rhine Drusus fell off his horse and broke a leg. Complications set in and a month later he was dead. Buried at Rome with due military pomp, he received the proud but posthumous title of Germanicus.

Tiberius took up the task. He spent two years in the Rhineland consolidating previous gains, pacifying, civilizing, and settling 40,000 Germans on Gallic soil. Two massive silver cups found at Boscoreale near Pompeii and several famous cut gems commemorate his achievements. He had performed his appointed task so well that in 5 B.C. L. Domitius

Ahenobarbus was able to march over the Elbe, negotiate with tribes nearby, and on the east bank erect an altar glorifying Rome's deeds in Germany under the auspices of Augustus.

Twelve B.C., the year of Agrippa's death, was a year of crisis: the military situation was precarious, Agrippa and Taurus were both dead. Agrippa's two sons, Lucius and Gaius, whom the princeps had adopted as his own, were still too young to take part in affairs of state. The far-sighted plans of the princeps to choose a successor seemed to have gone awry.

Although Augustus did not particularly like Tiberius, he took enough of an interest to make him divorce his beloved Vipsania and marry Julia, the young widow of Marcellus and Agrippa. Tiberius did not like her gay and frivolous ways. Nor did she like her new husband, grim, austere, and reserved. Julia, pushed about as a political pawn from one husband to another, soon turned for comfort to more experienced lovers.

Tiberius was enraged less by Julia's misconduct than by the devotion of the princeps to his young adopted sons, Lucius and Gaius. The five-year grant of tribunician power in 6 B.C. neither appeased Tiberius nor averted the impending crisis: bitter and morose, Tiberius retired to Rhodes to sulk for almost a decade. Finally Augustus, himself grown disturbed by Julia's flagrant adulteries, had her exiled to a desert island in 2 B.C. He executed some of her paramours (who were more guilty of conspiracy against the regime than of vice) and banished others. Even Tiberius interceded on Julia's behalf, but unsuccessfully. The princeps would not relent.

Again fate intervened in favor of Tiberius and shattered the princeps' hope of a successor of his own blood. In 2 A.D., the year of Tiberius' return from Rhodes, Lucius Caesar died on the way to Spain. Two years later Gaius, after a treacherous attack in Armenia, died of his wounds. The princeps had no choice but to turn to Tiberius. In grief and frustration he adopted Tiberius as his son in 4 A.D.

Tiberius in Germany and Illyricum

After his adoption and the grant of tribunician power, this time for ten years, and of a special *imperium*, Tiberius resumed command in Germany. To consummate the conquest of Germany, he planned a gigantic pincers' assault upon the Marcomanni, whose energetic king, Maroboduus, had seized possession of Bohemia. The army of the Rhine was to advance from the northwest, while Tiberius himself with an army from Illyricum was to cross the Danube from the south. Everything seems to have suddenly gone wrong. In 6 A.D. a revolt broke out with utmost fury in Pannonia and Illyricum and cut short the grand design. The suppression of that rebellion, gravest of all wars since Hannibal, kept Tiberius occupied for almost three years (6-9 A.D.).

The Disaster of Varus: 9 A.D.

All had gone fairly well in Germany until Augustus sent to the Rhineland P. Quinctilius Varus. Varus had been a fairly successful governor of Judea, but in Germany he proved to be headstrong, rapacious, and incompetent. His fatuous attempt to tax and discipline the Germans provoked rebellion in 9 A.D. when Tiberius was fully occupied in quelling the revolt in Pannonia and Illyricum. Their leader was Arminius, a crafty imitator of Roman methods of warfare who profited greatly from the follies of Varus.

One day in late summer Varus, marching with three legions through the Teutoburg Forest, was suddenly assailed from ambush. Lightning crackled through the trees. Rain poured torrentially. Violent winds broke branches above the heads of his men and blocked their way with fallen trees. For three days fearful, weary, desperate, they plunged blindly through forest and swamp, unable to shake off the relentlessly attacking enemy. Exhausted and panic-stricken, Varus committed suicide. Some of his officers followed suit. Some twenty thousand of his men afterwards surrendered, many massacred on the spot, some put to death by torture. Few escaped.

News of the Teutoburg disaster reached Rome. The princeps first; dazed, sorrowing, broken, old, kept moaning to himself "Quinctilius Varus, give me back my legions."

The Teutoburg debacle and the lack of manpower to replace the three lost legions persuaded the princeps to abandon hope of conquest in Germany and, despite all later successes of Tiberius and Germanicus, to relinquish the ambition of making the Elbe a frontier of the empire in Europe. That decision final, momentous, irrevocable was administratively, though probably not strategically, sound. Sound or not, it may have determined the future of Europe for all time.

Africa and the Red Sea Zone

Augustus' preoccupation with the imperial frontiers did not preclude activity in other areas as well. Egypt, richest of all Augustan annexations and producer of one third of the Roman annual grain supply (5,000,000 bushels), remained relatively quiet except for some skirmishes on the Ethiopian border.

C. Cornelius Gallus, Egypt's first prefect, a distinguished general, elegist, friend of Augustus, of Pollio, and of Vergil, led an expedition against the Ethiopians in 29 B.C.* A later prefect, C. Petronius, repulsed counterattacking invaders from Ethiopia and in two campaigns (27 and 22 B.C.) drove them back into the Sudan, capturing and destroying their holy city of Napata. In agreement with Candace, their queen, the princeps finally fixed the southern boundary of Egypt near the First Cataract, where it remained for the next three hundred years.

About this time (25-24 B.C.) the princeps sent Aelius Gallus, probably prefect of Egypt, on an expedition down the Red Sea against the Sabaeans, who dwelt near Aden and in Saudi Arabia. The purpose of this expedition was to gain naval control of the Straits of Bab-el-Mandeb in order that Alexandrian merchants might break the Sabaean monopoly of trade with India in precious stones, spices, cosmetics, and other commodities. That expedition, though badly handled by Gallus, paved the way for more successful ones later. Strabo the Geographer tells us that from Myos Hormos, a port on the Red Sea, there annually sailed 125 ships, some to Zanzibar

and East Africa, many to western India, others to Ceylon, and some as far east as the shores of the Bay of Bengal and possibly Indo-China. Recent excavations conducted at Pondicherry and Arikamedu in eastern India reveal the amazing scope of this Roman commerce.

North Africa

Caesar had enlarged the old province of Africa Proconsularis by the annexation of Numida. But Augustus, convinced that the enlarged province was too difficult to defend, consigned the western part of it to the kingdom of Mauretania (modern Algeria and Morocco) and placed upon the vacant throne of Mauretania Juba II of Numidia, who had married Cleopatra Moon (or Selene), daughter of Antonius and Cleopatra. Juba, a Latin author in his own right, and a connoisseur of art, proved an enlightened and cultivated ruler. He raised the cultural level of his own country and West Africa, defended his realm against the wild tribes of the desert, and assisted Augustus in the work of founding twelve Roman colonies, of which Tangier was the most notable, along the Moroccan coast.

The Eastern Frontiers

The problems of the Middle East differed widely from those of the West. The East, heir to a very old and advanced civilization, was proud of its traditions, and was still a powerful creative force. The Parthian empire was a territorially compact national state embracing an area of 1,200,000 square miles from the Euphrates to Lake Aral and beyond the Indus. Parthia, moreover, had within recent memory inflicted three stinging defeats upon the Romans, and was still considered a potential menace.

After Actium an insistent clamor arose for a war of revenge against Parthia. Without openly defying the demands of public opinion and the patriotic sentiments of Vergil and Horace, Augustus accepted the logistic impossibility of waging war in Spain, Germany, and along the Danube and of conducting at the same time a major campaign against Parthia. The empire lacked the manpower,

---

* Erected statues of himself and boastful proclamations of his exploits incised on pyramids incurred the wrath of Augustus and condemnation for treason by the senate. He took his own life in 27 B.C.

resources, and communications for such an undertaking. He would try other methods first.

Roman power in the East rested on the loyalty of the provinces of Asia, Bithynia-Pontus, Cilicia, and Syria towards Rome; and the loyalty of these provinces depended, in turn, upon wise and just administration. To assure such administration, Augustus kept firm control over the governors, imperial as well as senatorial, strengthened the laws against extortion, reformed the system of taxation by instituting a census of property at regular intervals. He curbed the power of the tax-farming companies, and gradually transferred the collection of direct taxes to procurators assisted by local tax officials. These reforms made possible in the East a rapid economic recovery and commercial expansion and helped Augustus win the loyalty of the provincial peoples.

The princeps respected local customs, and gave the provinces considerable rights of self-government, encouraging the growth of urban communities out of villages, hamlets, and temple lands. More important still, he allowed the town councils and the councils of the provincial cities and tribes (*concilia* or *koina*) freedom of assembly and the right to express gratitude or homage and bring their grievances to the attention of emperor or senate.

The provincial and city councils, serving as centers of the imperial cult, were of inestimable value in strengthening the ties of loyalty towards Rome. Far from suppressing the worship of himself and of the goddess Roma, Augustus accepted and encouraged it. By 29 B.C. he had permitted Nicaea, Ephesus, Pergamum, and Nicomedia to erect temples dedicated to himself and Roma and to institute quinquennial festivals known as *Romaia Sebasta*. Other members of the imperial family, Livia and Gaius Caesar, also received divine honors. The West soon followed the example of the East except that the Western towns—Cologne, Lyons, Narbo, and Spanish Tarraco—erected altars instead of temples.

Vassal Kingdoms

To strengthen Roman power and neutralize Parthia Augustus continued the policy of Antonius, which maintained vassal kingdoms as buffer states between Parthia and the Roman provinces. After Actium, Augustus had consigned large territories to Amyntas the Galatian (Galatia, Pisidia, Lycaonia, and most of Cilicia). He had also confirmed possession of East Pontus and Lesser Armenia to the enlightened Polemo, and had awarded to the despicable Archelaus the huge realm of Cappadocia. He enlarged Judea, the kingdom of Herod I, the so-called Great (37-4 B.C.), a wily and efficient ruler who built a splendid temple at Jerusalem but was also an accomplished murderer of wives and sons. These were the principal vassal kings.

Eventually all the vassal kingdoms became provinces. When Amyntas was killed in 25 B.C. while rounding up some savage tribes in the Taurus mountains, Rome acquired the vast province of Galatia and Pamphylia. A decade after Herod's death Augustus made Judea and Samaria an imperial province or rather a Syrian sub-province, governed by prefects, the most famous of whom was Pontius Pilate, who held office (26-36 A.D.) at the time of the crucifixion of Christ.

Only in one vassal kingdom, Armenia, had Roman influence deteriorated after the death of Antonius. Subdued and annexed as a province in 34 B.C., Armenia had slipped away from Roman control just before Actium and had come under the brutal rule of Artaxias, who forthwith slew all Roman residents in Armenia. Augustus did not avenge their deaths and, for over a decade, made no effort to recover the region, though it provided the best land routes leading from Parthia to Asia Minor and Syria. He watched and waited.

In 20 B.C. Artaxias was killed. Augustus immediately sent Tiberius into Armenia with an army. He placed Tigranes III, a pro-Roman brother of the late king, on the throne. At the same time he frightened the Parthian king into surrendering the battle standards and all surviving Roman soldiers captured at Carrhae or after. A rattle of the saber temporarily restored Roman prestige in the East and wiped away the stain upon Roman honor.

All was quiet in the East until the death of Tigranes in 1 B.C. The Armenian nationalists, aided and abetted by the Parthians, enthroned a king of their own choice without even consulting Augustus. He at once sent Gaius Caesar, armed with full proconsular power over the entire East, into Armenia at the head of a powerful army. Gaius subdued the Armenians and compelled the Parthians, by show of force and by diplomacy, to recognize Rome's preponderant interests in Armenia. After that magnificent feat, Gaius Caesar died (4 A.D.) of wounds that would not heal.

Parthia, as well as Augustus, had reasons for avoiding war. Torn by the dissensions of rival claimants to the throne and continually menaced by Asian migrations, Parthia was in no position to attack, and willingly endured diplomatic defeat rather than risk actual conflict. Diplomacy and intrigue might succeed; overt aggression would surely fail.

Parthia and Rome also had common economic interests which would be ruined by war. Both were interested in opening the Euphrates valley as a caravan route for trade with India, central Asia, and China. Under joint Parthian and Roman protection Palmyra was rapidly becoming a large and prosperous caravan city with fine streets, parks, and public buildings. Other cities — Petra, Jerash, Philadelphia, and Damascus—were beginning to enjoy the rich benefits of caravan trade.

New Territories and Provinces

As a result of his conquests and expansionist policy, Augustus had, during his lifetime, added to the empire Egypt, Dalmatia, Galatia, Judea-Samaria, Noricum, Moesia, Pannonia, Rhaetia, North Spain, Alpine territories, and Thrace. At the same time he had increased the number of provinces from eleven to twenty-eight, ten of which were senatorial and eighteen imperial (see map p. 265). He created new provinces partly by fresh conquests and annexations and partly by breaking up the large provinces of Gaul, Spain, and Macedonia in order to secure more administrative efficiency and tighter central control over the governors. The senate's control over proud and ambitious nobles with large provinces and huge armies had often proved futile in the past. The Augustan policy, in contrast, was a notable success.

Urbanization of the Provinces

The most striking feature of the princeps' provincial policy was the urbanization of the West. In the East he simply followed the policy initiated by Alexander the Great and continued by the Hellenistic kings, Pompey, Caesar, and Antonius. That policy Augustus extended to Gaul and Spain and revived in Africa. In Gaul hilltop towns, fortified refuges, and market places were dying out, giving place to towns built on the flat-lands, at river bends and fords, and at road junctions.

Augustus had social and political motives for promoting town and city life in the provinces, for the towns served as centers for diffusion of Roman culture. Furthermore, like modern county seats, they often controlled territories within a radius of fifty miles or more and so served the central government as convenient administrative units for the collection of taxes and other useful functions. No doubt, too, Augustus realized that, since the towns owed their privileged position to the central government, they would in turn support the new imperial regime with vigor and enthusiasm.

Financial Reconstruction

Before the principate of Augustus, the civil wars of the late Republic had depleted the funds of the old senate-controlled state treasury, the *aerarium Saturni,* and exhausted its revenues. The old system of tax collection, corrupt and inefficient at best, had completely broken down and the absence of any formal budget, regular estimate of tax receipts and expenditures, or census of taxable property only made an already bad situation worse.

Upon that depleted and exhausted treasury fell burdens both numerous and heavy: funds for the grain administration that furnished free grain to 200,000 proletarian families in Rome; money for public games and religious festivals; funds for the construction and repair of roads and streets; for maintenance of the water supply and sewers, and the police and fire departments of the capital. Maintenance of these services required enormous sums of money. In addition, the ever mounting costs of imperial defense, administration, and the provision of pensions for war veterans rendered a reform of the financial system absolutely imperative.

Despite the urgent need for action, Augustus at first moved most slowly and circumspectly, wishing to avoid in every way the suspicion of ruthlessly trampling upon the ancient prerogatives of the senate. In 28 B.C. he requested a transfer of control over the state treasury from inexperienced quaestors to ex-praetors selected at first by the senate but, after 23 B.C., annually by lot. Because his greater income enabled him to subsidize the state treasury he soon acquired virtual control over all the finances of the state.

Not content with that, Augustus, after 27 B.C., set up for each imperial province a separate account or chest called a *fiscus* (literally "fig basket"), into which he deposited the tax receipts and revenues of the province for payment to the legions. The *fisci* not only helped him, as sole paymaster, to assume complete mastery of the armies, but enabled him to take control over the financial administration of the empire. Years later Claudius united the several *fisci* into a single and central *fiscus,* which then became in fact and in law the main treasury of the Roman empire.

In 6 A.D. Augustus established a third treasury, the *aerarium militare,* to provide pensions for discharged war veterans (*see* p. 278).

Augustus had still a fourth fund, the *patrimonium Caesaris,* of fabulous size, though not strictly a treasury. It consisted of Caesar's private fortune, the confiscated properties of Antonius, the vast treasures of Cleopatra, the revenues from Augustus' private domains in the provinces, and the numerous legacies left him by wealthy Romans. (The legacies alone amounted to the enormous sum of 1,400,000,-000 sesterces, equivalent to at least $125,000,000.) These funds gave him control over the entire financial administration of the empire.

Social Reforms

Augustus' social and religious reforms were conspicuously lacking in either success or permanence. Most were futile, some reactionary. Their purpose was to halt the ravages of degeneracy and vice in high society and promote the moral regeneration of the Roman people, laudable objectives but not to be attained by legislative action or imperial decree.

Most praiseworthy was his attempt to improve the treatment of slaves. According to a story of Dio Cassius, Augustus was dining one day at the home of Vedius Pollio, a rich freedman who had acquired the habit of feeding the lampreys in his fish pond with erring slaves. As Vedius and Augustus were eating, a waiter accidentally broke a precious crystal goblet. Enraged, Vedius ordered that the slave be thrown into the fish pond. The trembling slave knelt before Augustus and begged for his intercession. Augustus, moved, asked Vedius to have fetched all the crystal goblets in the house. When they had been placed before him in glistening array, he sent them all smashing to the floor. Vedius flushed, but said not a word. The point was clear.

In contrast to his attempts to ease the lot of slaves, Augustus assaulted human freedom and dignity by his revival of the law of treason (*maiestas*), vague, flexible and sweeping, comprehending all offenses from conspiracy against the state to insult or even disrespect to the emperor in speech, writing, or deed. Seditious books or libelous pamphlets were burned in public bonfires. Informers (*delatores*) received one fourth of the property of their victims. The law was to become an instrument of tyranny and repression for future emperors.

Less noxious but less effective were the attempts to control promiscuity and regulate marriage and family life. The two Julian laws of 18 B.C. and the *Lex Papia Poppaea* of 9 A.D.* were specifically designed to curb immorality, speed up the birth rate, and revive ancient Roman virtue.

The new laws prohibited long engagements and divorce; required all bachelors and spinsters to marry as soon as possible, all widows below fifty and all widowers below sixty to

---

* This last was a complete and systematic codification of all previous laws and edicts pertaining to marriage and adultery.

marry within three years. Failure to comply carried many penalties and disabilities: partial or complete ineligibility to receive legacies or hold public office and exclusion from public games and spectacles. Married persons who were childless, impotent, or sterile incurred similar disabilities, while those with three or more children could advance rapidly in their public careers and social life. The total effectiveness of the law was somewhat diminished by the conferral of the special and fictitious "right of three children" (*ius trium liberorum*). Persons of influence might claim this right. Thus the unmarried poets Vergil and Horace, Augustus himself with only one child, the Empress Livia with two, the married but childless Maecenas, and even the two bachelor consuls who lent their names to the *Lex Papia Poppaea,* did not have to comply with the provisions of the law.

The new laws made adultery a criminal as well as a private offense. A *pater familias* might kill his adulterous daughter and her paramour; a husband, his wife's lover. A man who refused to divorce a wife caught in adultery or knowingly married an adulteress was equally guilty before the law. Flagrant adulterers suffered penalties varying from fine and loss of property to banishment and even death.

Although Augustus himself finally admitted that his marriage laws neither curbed immorality nor raised the birth rate, his legislation was not wholly without result: it enriched the treasury and favored the rise of a class of informers, who were to remain the bane of social life in future years.

In the field of social legislation three other laws deserve mention—the *lex Fufia Caninia* of 2 B.C., the *lex Aelia Sentia* of 4 A.D., and the *lex Junia Norbana* probably of 17 B.C. The first two prohibited the mass emancipation of alien slaves, who might swell and swamp the ranks of Roman citizens and, through intermarriage, "defile" and "pollute" the "purity" of the Italian race. The Junian Law relegated slaves freed without proper formalities to the status of second class citizens, the so-called Junian Latins. They could attain the privileges of full citizenship only by fulfilment of marriage vows and procreation of children.

Religious Reforms

In his reformation of the ancient state religion Augustus resurrected long neglected ceremonies and priesthoods. It was a difficult undertaking. For the primitive Roman animism, the worship of the spirits of stream, field, house, grove, and cross road, which had gradually merged with Greek anthropomorphism, was past resuscitation. Its revival could only be artificial, unreal, impermanent. The masses of the common people, except perhaps in the most backward and superstitious of Italian communities, had long ago turned to the more exotic and exhilarating religions of Egypt and the Near East. The cultured and sophisticated upper classes had turned to Philosophy—Stoic or Epicurean, Sceptic or Cynic.

As early in his career as 42 B.C. Augustus began his program of temple building. In 28 B.C. he undertook the repair of all temples in Rome (eighty-two, according to his own statement). The previous year had witnessed the dedication of the new temples of the Divine Julius (in the old Forum) and of Apollo (on the Palatine), a fitting tribute since both gods were protectors of the Julian dynasty, givers of victory, and saviors of the state from civil war. In 2 B.C. Augustus had erected a new temple to Mars the Avenger on the newly built Forum of Augustus.

The repair of crumbling temples was a prelude to the revival of many half-forgotten religious rites of Old Rome. In 27 B.C. Augustus reconstituted the college of the Arval (Plowing) Brethren, who once led the people each year at the end of May in the *Ambarvalia,* a solemn yet joyous procession around fields to implore divine blessing on growing crops, and who also conducted the celebration of the festival of a primitive field goddess known as the Dea Dia. Augustus also revived the priesthood of the Flamen Dialis with all its old taboos.

A decade later Augustus invited all Italy to a celebration of the long postponed Secular Games (*Ludi Saeculares*), a public festival of expiation and thanksgiving held, according to Etruscan reckoning, every 110 years. For this occasion Horace composed his

A sculptured marble slab from the Altar of Peace (Ara Pacis), *showing Mother Earth* (Terra Mater). *(Courtesy Metropolitan Museum of Art, gift of the Italian Government, 1939)*

Secular Hymn (*Carmen Saeculare*), which was sung by a choir of fifty-four boys and girls before the temple of Apollo on the Palatine.

The revival of archaic rites may have helped revive the spirit of piety and valor, but could not immediately evoke loyalty or devotion to the new government or create propaganda for monarchic Augustan rule. Accordingly, in 13 B.C., the senate voted to erect an altar of Augustan Peace (*Ara Pacis Augustae*). One of the sculptured panels of this superb monument shows Augustus proceeding in solemn pomp to offer sacrifice; another panel shows Mother Earth seated on a rock and holding on her lap two children and the fruits of the earth. The altar seems to suggest peace with the gods and on earth peace and plenty, blessings which flowed from the martial valor of Augustus and his dauntless devotion to duty.

Augustus was able to push the new religious program with more zeal and vigor after

12 B.C., when he succeeded Lepidus as Pontifex Maximus. By 7 B.C. he had the city divided into fourteen regions and the regions into wards or precincts (*vici*). The *vicomagistri* or ward masters, usually of freedmen status, not only assisted the aediles in fighting fires but officiated at the shrines dedicated to the worship of the *Lares Compitales*, guardian spirits of the cross roads and household. At each shrine the *vicomagistri* also offered sacrifices to the Genius of Augustus, his guiding spirit. These religious demonstrations were spontaneous enough but subtly helped organize public opinion behind the government.

From Rome the new religious policy spread into the towns of Italy and the Western provinces. Some towns had their own copies of the *Fasti Consulares* and the official religious calendar. Many imitated the monuments and sculptures of Rome. Carthage, for instance, had her own reproduction of the Altar of Augustan Peace showing the goddess

Roma seated on a heap of arms, a beautiful symbol of Augustan Rome and of that mighty world state consolidated by Augustus. Many Italian and provincial towns instituted religious colleges composed of six minor officials, mostly freedmen, known as *Seviri Augustales,* for the service of the imperial cult.

The Death of Augustus

At last after a political career of almost sixty years on August 19 of A.D. 14 in the little Campanian town of Nola Augustus died. And death overtook him not unprepared. He was ready, serene, cheerful; not plagued by doubt, guilt, or remorse. Dying, he jokingly quoted to his friends words from a Greek drama: "Have I played my part well? Then clap your hands and take me off the stage." Played his part well? Indeed he had. *Legiones, classes, provincias, cuncta inter se conexa.* So wrote Tacitus. And that neatly sums up the Augustan Age.

Material and Cultural Trends

The Augustan Age witnessed a general quickening of economic life throughout the Mediterranean. The ending of the civil wars, the suppression of piracy at sea and of banditry and lawlessness in Italy, and the Augustan program of road building in Italy and the provinces brought about a remarkable expansion of agriculture, industry, and commerce. Italy was for a time the chief beneficiary of the new expansion, for the East had not yet recovered from the effects of past wars and exploitation, and the Western provinces were still too young to take full advantage of the new order. Italy therefore continued to dominate the Mediterranean world both economically and politically.

Agriculture

The foreign and civil wars, the proscriptions, confiscations of private property, and

The atrium of the house of Menander in Pompeii. In early Republican times, the atrium, *a timber-roofed hall with a skylight in the center directly above a rain-catch basin sunk in the floor* (impluvium), *was the main living room of the Roman house. (Courtesy Istituto Italiano di Cultura, New York)*

Top: *The atrium of the house of the Triclinio (first century B.C.) at Herculaneum. (Courtesy Fratelli Alinari, Florence).* Bottom: *The atrium of the house of the Mosaics at Herculaneum. (Courtesy Istituto Italiano di Cultura, New York)*

Top: *The peristyle of the house of the Vettii in Pompeii (ca. 50 A.D.).*
Bottom: *The unreconstructed peristyle of the house of the Labyrinth at Pompeii. (Courtesy Istituto Italiano di Cultura, New York)*

The slave quarters of the house of Menander in Pompeii. (Courtesy Istituto di Cultura, New York)

the repeated and extensive settlement of war veterans had created surprisingly little change in agricultural conditions in Italy since the second century B.C. (*see* pp. 161–166). Large estates continued to grow bigger at the expense of small farms. The wine and oil plantations described by Varro in his *De Re Rustica* (published in 36 B.C.) were twice as large as those of which the Elder Cato had written in the *De Agri Cultura* ca. 150 B.C. Columella, who published the most authoritative treatise on Roman agriculture, *De Re Rustica* (in twelve books, ca. 50 A.D.), discussed plantations which were larger still.

Modest plantations, many of them owned by the rich city bourgeoisie, were also increasing in number and importance. Excavations around Pompeii, which was buried by the

eruption of Vesuvius in 79 A.D., have revealed over forty villas which varied from 35 to 200 acres. At least thirty had facilities for the making of oil or wine, or both, mainly for local consumption. The largest seems to have been engaged in the production not only of wine, but milk, cheese, and grain, as proved by the discovery of a wine press, a cow stable, a cheese factory, a gristmill, and a bakery. The owners of some of these villas had evidently followed the practice advocated by the Elder Cato and made their estates as self-sufficient as possible.

Some of the Pompeian villas date from the second century B.C., but others, as indicated by the style of the wall paintings found in the houses, belong to the Augustan period. The villas fall into three main types: a combination summer house and farmstead, which the owner visited during the summer months; an ordinary farm house, modest and clean, which served as the permanent residence of a well-to-do farmer; and the large plantation with barracks for the many slaves and a small, plain house for the overseer.

The most celebrated Pompeian villa was at Boscoreale, two miles beyond Pompeii. The storage jars found there indicate an annual wine production of some 20,000 gallons. The spacious house, the wall paintings, the luxurious three-room bath, and the complex water heating system suggest a generous income. The owner probably sold his wine locally at Pompeii and other towns nearby; for Pompeian wine, somewhat raw and quick to deteriorate, was not in great demand in export trade.

The Pompeian wine and olive plantations could not have compared favorably in size or importance with those Campanian and Latian estates that produced for Roman consumption or for world trade. Horace and other contemporary poets speak of the famous wines of Falernum, of Surrentum, of Cales, and of Mount Massicus. In the Falernian district there is said to have been a wine plantation of over 600 acres; at Cales, not far from Minturnae, another which employed some 400 slaves. Cicero tells us that at Casinum, once the site of the Elder Cato's vineyard, a certain Valgus had, by proscribing his neighbors and taking over many farms, finally created an estate with all the likeness of a county.

Many of the really large plantations adhered rigorously to the Elder Cato's ideal of self-sufficiency. In addition to the staples—oil and wine—they raised grain, livestock, and produced immense quantities of meat, hides, wool, clothing, pottery, and farm tools. They

Two frescoes of the early Second Style (first century B.C.), from the Cubiculum *of a villa at Boscoreale, near Pompeii. (Courtesy Metropolitan Museum of Art, Rogers Fund, 1903)*

had their own gristmills, bakeries, pottery works, tanneries, and shops. Such a variety of activities made the plantation a little world of its own and gave it an enormous competitive advantage over smaller estates.

Not all landowners had their property concentrated in single blocks. Some preferred to maintain a number of smaller holdings in different regions, partly to distribute the risk of crop failure and partly to improve operating efficiency. Varro himself owned one plantation near Vesuvius, another at Tusculum, and a horse and mule ranch at Reate. Sextus Roscius in the time of Sulla owned thirteen separate properties. In Pompeii, the owner of the famous House of the Vettii, whose Black Room contained a series of wall paintings depicting the various operations of farm and shop, had many farms in the neighborhood of the city.

The acquisition of new plantations resulted from a desire not only of investing newly accrued capital but also of providing placement for a surplus slave population and its natural increment of from three to seven per cent annually. At this time the procurement of fresh slave labor depended no longer, as in the past, upon war captives or the victims of piracy and kidnaping but upon slave breeding deliberately stimulated by the promise to a prolific female of exemption from work and of manumission after her third child, often accompanied by a handsome bonus.

Ranching. Another favorite form of investment was ranching. The demand for meat, wool, and other animal products made it a profitable enterprise especially since its costs of production were comparatively low. It was possible in Italy to pasture livestock in the open all the year round and on land too rugged for agriculture and therefore procurable at small unit cost. It was also possible to drive livestock to market from the remotest of regions and thereby escape the heavy costs involved in the transportation of grain or wine. Ranching also required less labor. In Varro's day one shepherd, it is said, could look after 80 or 100 sheep and with the help of a couple of dogs many more. More important still, ranching was an excellent investment made to order for a senator, banker, or business man, who had to spend most of his time in Rome.

Ranching has always been conducted on a large scale, then as well as now. The Elder Pliny tells us that in southeastern Italy a single ranch contained 250,000 sheep. Domitia Lepida, whom Nero put to death for her failure to prevent her slaves from disturbing the peace and security of that area, must have owned many more. Etruria and Cisalpine Gaul were also important cattle- and sheep-breeding regions. The northern cities of Parma, Padua, Verona, and Milan were as noted for their textiles as Tarentum, Canusium, Luceria, and Brundisium in the South.

The most interesting of Varro's four books on agriculture is his third, in which he describes the poultry business and the quick and easy returns made by those who supplied the Roman luxury market with peacocks, thrushes, geese, ducks, teal, and numerous other field-fares and edible fowls. One enterprising game and water fowl breeder, failing to find enough space in Etruria for his paddocks and preserves, enclosed large areas in southern Gaul for the purpose.

The Farmer. Contrary to the exaggerated assertions of some ancient writers, the expansion of plantation agriculture and ranching did not result in the total disappearance of the small independent farmer. In large and numerous districts, especially in Etruria, Umbria, Picenum, many parts of the Po Valley, and even in South Italy, the small farmer had successfully held his own. As in the past, small-farm families continued to consume most of what they grew—wheat and barley mainly, but also pigs, chickens, vegetables,

fruits, and perhaps wine and some oil. What they did not require for household use they sold in nearby markets. They thereby made a living, if not much money.

In the late Republic and in the age of Augustus a new kind of farmer appeared—the tenant or *colonus.* Two recent developments may account for his appearance. Among the thousands of war veterans settled on the land were many with no knowledge of or interest in farming. These preferred to rent to tenants who were sometimes free farmers but often freedmen and even slaves. Secondly, some large landed proprietors, like Domitius Ahenobarbus or Pompeius Magnus, owned such extensive tracts of land that they were able to promise farms to thousands of their retainers and landless soldiers. Even the poet Horace rented out part of his estate on the Sabine Hills to five tenant families. Tenant farming, now still in its infancy, was later to become a more general phenomenon.

The rise of tenant farming did not mean the decline of slave labor. The slave-worked plantation was still profitable and Italy was still the best cultivated land in the empire. Not until the late first century A.D. did competition from the western, northern, and eastern provinces gradually compel Italian landowners to cut back production of oil and wine and rent out part of their land to tenants.

Grain Production in Italy and the Provinces. Specialized plantation agriculture, ranching, or poultry raising had not seriously diminished grain production in Italy except in some coastal areas. Grain was still the main crop of all small farms both independent and tenant. Many large and medium size plantations grew considerable amounts. It remained the chief crop in Cisalpine Gaul even after the extension of wine and olive plantations into that area. In Campania, a land of oil, wine, fruits, and flowers, of numerous seaside resorts, parks, and pleasure villas, grain was still a valuable crop according to such contemporary eyewitnesses as Varro and Dionysius of Halicarnassus. The growth and spread of tenant farming favored an even higher grain production in most parts of Italy.

Nevertheless, for centuries Italy had been unable to supply the needs of the city of

Richly painted walls (ca. 60–79 A.D.) of the dining room (triclinium)
*of the house of the Vettii, rich wine merchants of Pompeii. (Courtesy
Fratelli Alinari, Florence)*

Rome to which were added, probably, in the Augustan age, the demands of some of the larger coastal towns. The reason for that inability was not so much the deficiency of Italian grain production as the high costs and slowness of land transportation. Transportation by sea was both faster and cheaper. The chief source of Rome's grain supply was first Sicily and Sardinia, later Egypt, and finally North Africa, which ultimately became as important as all others combined.

Industry

Our knowledge of craftsmanship in the Augustan age is still defective and spotty. The excavations of Pompeii and Ostia have yielded some information about the industrial life of small cities and one port, but little or nothing is known about that of the larger cities and other harbors—Rome, Brundisium, Naples, Puteoli, Capua, Tarentum, and Aquileia—in which excavation is either impossible or has scarcely begun.

The excavation of the so-called Street of Abundance in Pompeii has clearly shown the quickening effect of Augustan peace and prosperity upon industry in Italy. Before the principate that street had been entirely residential; by 79 A.D. (the year of the eruption), the ground floors of most of the houses had been converted into small factories or shops, many of them engaged in the clothing business—fulling, cleaning, and dyeing. The powerful fullers' guild had its display and sales rooms in a large exchange building nearby.

The most interesting of the shops excavated in Pompeii were the bakeries because therein is preserved the equipment used in every step of the ancient breadmaking process—grinding, kneading, and baking. The shops are distributed quite evenly throughout the city, one

Top: *A typical street in Pompeii.* Bottom: *The Street of the Tombs in Pompeii. (Courtesy Istituto Italiano di Cultura, New York)*

in almost every block, some of them fairly large with four or five mills, a kneading machine, and oven. One shop had a capacity of apparently 2,000 loaves per day. With a few slight repairs the mills can still grind wheat into flour. One of the ovens contained, when excavated, the very loaves, now somewhat charred and carbonized, that were baking at the moment of the eruption.

Not even the largest of the Pompeian milling and baking shops (of which there were almost forty) would compare in size with the enormous bread-making establishment of M. Vergilius Eurysaces who, as contractor (*redemptor*) for the state, employed scores of workmen, both slave and free. His tall and ugly monument, still to be seen near the Porta Maggiore, has bas-reliefs representing all the various operations of the bread-making process. Thus Pompeii with its small shops and guilds had a typical small-town economy (not unlike that of a late medieval town) and the fullest description of its crafts producing for local trade would fail to convey an adequate idea of some of the larger industries of Roman Italy that almost reached the stage of mass production and shipped their products

to distant markets from Jutland to the Caucasus, from Britain to India.

The Glass Industry. The thriving glass industry had been revolutionized around 40 B.C. by the Syrian (or Egyptian) invention of the blow pipe which made possible the production not only of beautiful goblets and bowls but even window panes, useful in northern climes at once for admittance of daylight and exclusion of winter's cold. From the glass factories of Campania or of the Adriatic seaport of Aquileia came wares that found their way from Trondheim fiord in Norway to the southernmost borders of the Soviet Union. Augustan Italy enjoyed temporarily an exclusive monopoly of western glass exports. A half century later Gaul began to compete and the factories first of Lyons and finally of Cologne on the Rhine exported small bowls with cut geometrical designs not only to Denmark but to the lands near Danzig (Gdansk) and the tributaries of the Danube and the Theiss.

Arretine Pottery. Italian pottery repeats the history of glass. The factories engaged, at Arretium in Etruria and later at Puteoli, in the manufacture of a table ware known as *terra sigillata,* a red glazed pottery of beautiful ornamentation, had in the time of Augustus and Tiberius achieved mass production and enjoyed an export monopoly from the British Midlands to Arikamedu in southeastern India. One Arretine factory had a mixing vat with a capacity of 10,000 gallons and might well have employed as many as forty expert designers and a much larger number of mixers, potters, and furnacemen. Even then branch factories were being established in southern and eastern Gaul, in Spain, Britain, and on the Danube, which eventually broke the proud monopoly in western and northern Europe and even in Italy itself.

The Metal Industries. Augustan Italy led the world in the manufacture of metal wares. The chief centers of the iron industry were the two great seaports of Puteoli and Aquileia. The iron foundries of Puteoli smelted ores seaborne from the island of Elba and by repeated forging manufactured arms, farm implements, and carpenters' tools which were as hard as steel. Easy access to the rich iron mines of recently annexed Noricum (Austria) stimulated at Aquileia the manufacture of equally excellent farm implements for sale throughout the fertile Cisalpina and for export to Dalmatia, the Danubian region, and even Germany.

For the manufacture of silver ware (plates, trays, bowls, cups, and candelabra) the two leading centers were Capua and Tarentum; for bronze wares (statues, busts, lamp stands, tables, tripods, buckets, and kitchen pots and pans), Capua, where factories employing perhaps thousands of workmen had evolved a specialization and division of labor usually associated with modern industry. The immense export trade of Capua to Britain, Germany, Scandinavia, and South Russia continued unabated until Gaul had established factories first at Lyons, and around 80 A.D., further north in the Belgica and the Rhineland.

Building Supplies and Trades. The extensive building program of Augustus and the large sums spent on beautifying the world's capital stimulated the manufacture or extraction of building and plumbing materials— lead and terra cotta pipes, bricks, roof tiles, cement, marble, and the so-called travertine, a cream-colored limestone quarried near Tibur. Some of these crafts seem never to have developed large-scale factory methods of production. The makers of lead pipes, for instance, were small shop owners who, with the help of a few slaves, filled orders as they came in, buying the lead and making the pipes, and also laying and connecting them.

On the other hand, the making of bricks and tiles had reached the mass production stage especially on senatorial and imperial estates, which competed with private enterprise in the production of materials for public works. Almost nothing is known about the organization of the enterprises which made cement, a mixture of volcanic ash and lime and a cheap and flexible building material in great demand.

The queen of building materials was marble. Not only did the Romans import the famous marble of the Greek Aegean, the fine white purple-veined varieties of Asia Minor, the serpentines and dark red porphyries of Egypt, and the beautiful, gold-colored marble of Simitthus in Numidia but they also began

A red Arretine cup (terra sigillata) *(ca. 10 B.C.–10 A.D.), showing men fighting bears, and bearing the stamp of Marcus Perennius, the factory owner. (Courtesy Metropolitan Museum of Art, gift of J. Pierpont Morgan, 1917)*

Detail of a mold (late first century B.C.) for Arretine bowls, showing vintage by satyrs picking grapes. (Courtesy Metropolitan Museum of Art, Rogers Fund, 1919)

at this time to quarry marble in Italy: the famous white marble of Carrara in Etruria and all those remarkable varieties found in the Piedmont, in Liguria, and near Verona, noted for their colors—brilliant greens and yellows, or mixed reds, browns, and whites.

The Roman Imperial Coinage

The Augustan age not only marked the political and economic unification of the Mediterranean region and a tremendous expansion of industry and world commerce but also witnessed new developments in the creation of a stable and abundant coinage to serve ever-expanding economic needs both within the empire and far beyond its frontiers.

Before Actium the coinage had been in a somewhat confused state. During the mideighties B.C., the mint in Rome had suspended all issues in bronze (an alloy of copper, tin, and lead) because of the scarcity of tin, and in the early thirties had suspended all issues in gold and silver (*aurei et denarii*). Various mints in Italy and the provinces sporadically and inadequately coined money for business and the payment of armies.

In the decade after Actium, Augustus struck coins of various denominations, styles, and types in gold, silver, and bronze: first in the East at Ephesus, Pergamum, Apamea, at Antioch in Syria, and elsewhere; later in the West at Emerita (Mérida) in Spain and at Nemausus (Nîmes) in Gaul.

Sometime after 23 (probably in 19) B.C., Augustus began to lay the foundations of a genuine imperial coinage, one of the most notable achievements of his principate. He reopened the mint at Rome and instituted a college of three mint officials (*tresviri monetales*), who struck (at the joint direction of the princeps and the senate) coins in gold and silver as well as in brass or orichalcum (an alloy of copper and zinc) and in pure copper. The brass and copper coinage (perhaps token money without relation to actual metal value) helped satisfy the empire's long-standing need for small change. In addition to the mintages at Rome Augustus issued, during his stay in Gaul in 16–13 B.C., a huge bronze coinage at Nîmes. A major emission, issued contemporaneously at Antioch in Syria, bore in reverse the legends s c (*senatus consulto*) and c a (*Caesaris auctoritate*) both

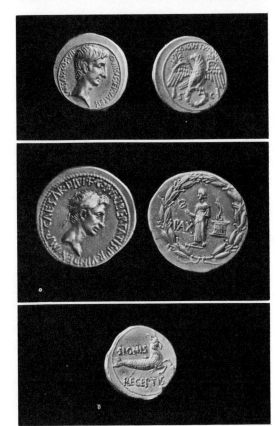

showing that the "clear-cut" distinction between imperial and senatorial provinces is a modern myth. In the coinages at Rome, princeps and senate likewise worked together. One imperial gold *aureus* had the value of 25 silver *denarii,* a *denarius* had the value of four bronze *sestertii* or 12 *asses* during and after the principate of Augustus. Local issues by provincial governors, allied kings, and autonomous cities and tribes in gold (Bosporan kingdom of South Russia) and especially in silver and bronze supplemented the imperial coinage, though with a variously reduced valuation.

The Augustan coinage had an important propaganda or publicity value in addition to its purely economic function, for it provided the new-born regime a flexible yet easily controlled, a subtle yet compelling method of influencing public opinion. Its kaleidoscopic variety of types kept the public informed of the ideals and everchanging policies and objectives of the government. People all over the Empire would use and inevitably look at the coins, which could vaguely yet effectively suggest what the government from time to time wanted to be felt and believed. New coin types appearing as frequently as modern stamps kept before the public eye the exalted figure of Augustus sometimes as an associate of Roma (ROM. ET. AUG), as the victor at Actium (IMP. X. ACT), as the preserver of citizens' lives (CAESAR. COS. VII. CIVIBUS. SERVATEIS), as the defender of the *libertas* of the Roman People (LIBERTATIS. P. R. VINDEX), or as the recoverer of the standards lost to the Parthians in 53 B.C. (SIGNIS RECEPTIS).

As media of publicity and mass propaganda, which must have shifted with each changing nuance of imperial policy and achievement, the coinages were more effective and malleable than the arts, for even the most wonderful works of architecture and sculpture were too stiff and static to serve as propaganda devices. Moreover, comparatively few of the empire's 70,000,000 inhabitants ever saw them whereas people everywhere daily used and handled the coins.

The coinages were also more tractable and amenable to rapidly changing purposes, policies, and resolves of the government than literature, for writers, especially poets, have an unfettered, independent spirit, seldom captive to a despot's shifting moods or yoked in service to the state. Some writers—such as Vergil, to some extent Livy, and occasionally Horace—entered into the spirit of the Augustan age, at times freely and even enthusiastically. Others, such as Tibullus, ignored Augustus entirely, while Asinius Pollio remained unyieldingly opposed, unredeemably republican.

Architecture and Art

In the Augustan principate Roman art, a blend of Italic, Etruscan, and Hellenistic elements, acquired its distinctive Roman and imperial character. The conditions which favored this development were the peace and economic prosperity of the period, the publication of Vitruvius Pollio's classic *De Architectura* (ca. 27 B.C.), which has exerted a profound influence on the architecture of Europe until modern times, and the great building activity of Augustus himself. In his *Gesta* he briefly refers to the temples he had constructed and the 82 he had repaired. Before his death he remarked that he "had found Rome a city of brick and left it one of marble," a claim undoubtedly accurate with respect to temples and public buildings but not to the huge blocks of flimsy tenements constructed of small timber and sun-dried brick.

The most important structures erected during the Augustan principate were the Temple of Divus Julius at the eastern edge of the old Roman Forum; the Temple of Mars the Avenger in the newly constructed Forum of Augustus, the first of the four great imperial forums; the magnificent Temple of Apollo on the Palatine, the first great building in Rome

The upper half of this exquisite cameo of carved onyx (the Gemma Augustea, *first century A.D.) shows the coronation of Augustus, with Livia seated beside him as goddess of Rome and Tiberius stepping from his chariot. The lower half of the cameo depicts prisoners of war. (Courtesy Kunsthistorisches Museum, Vienna)*

to be constructed entirely of the gleaming white Carrara marble.* Also imposing are the Theater of Marcellus, with its three rows of arcades supported by Corinthian columns and with a seating capacity of 20,000; the Baths of Agrippa, the first of a long series culminating in the enormous Baths of Caracalla and Diocletian (all adorned with mosaics, paintings, and statues, and equipped with hot and cold baths, steam rooms, swimming pools, gymnasiums, libraries, and recreation rooms); the huge Mausoleum of Augustus of Etruscan *tumulus* shape (erected beside the Tiber in 28 B.C., it served as the imperial family tomb from the death of Marcellus in 23 B.C. till that of Nerva in 98 A.D.). The Pantheon ("Shrine of all the Gods") was erected by Agrippa in 27 B.C., and, though reconstructed by Hadrian in the second century A.D. (*see* p. 364), still bears on its façade the famous inscription, M . AGRIPPA . L . F . COS . TERTIUM FECIT. After 13 B.C. the Altar of Augustan Peace (*Ara Pacis Augustae*) was erected, whose marble panels contain perhaps the finest sculptured reliefs in the history of art (*see* p. 288).

As portrayers of the leading ideas and achievements of the government (peace, prosperity, victory, religion) as well as masterpieces of art, the panels of the Altar of Peace are equalled only by the celebrated portrait statue of the Augustus from Prima Porta, the cuirass of which portrays the Parthian surrender of the captured standards to Tiberius, the final conquest of Spain and Gaul, the fecundity of the earth (*Terra Mater*), and Jupiter's protecting mantle over all. Similar, if not identical, ideas are conveyed by the marble altar of Carthage (*see* p. 288) showing Roma seated on a heap of arms contemplating an altar with *cornucopiae, caduceus,* and globe (*orbis terrarum*) resting upon it; by the exquisite Vienna cameo (*Gemma Augustea*) and the Grand Camée de France showing respectively a triumph of Tiberius and the ascension of Augustus into Heaven; by two silver cups from Boscoreale showing the submission of the Germanic Sugambri to Augustus and Tiberius

* This temple, completed in 28 B.C., contained two libraries, one for Greek books, the other for Latin.

A highly decorated Roman arch (first century A.D.). (Courtesy Yugoslav State Tourist Office, New York)

(*see* p. 281); and by a silver *patera* of Aquileia, which shows the emperor surrounded by the four seasons and by all the symbols of the fertility, plenty, and prosperity of the Golden Age.

The building activity of the Augustan period was not confined to Rome. A study of the ruins of the cities of northern and central Italy reveals that the Augustan age was a period of economic prosperity and of great building activity by the rich city bourgeoisie. The Western provinces, especially Gaul, copied or borrowed from the newly erected monuments of Rome. To the time of Augustus belong the famous Etruscan-like temple at Nîmes, the so-called Maison Carrée, notable for its harmony, symmetry, and delicate finish; possibly also the lofty Pont du Gard, which rises on three tiers of arches 160 feet above the deep gorge of the river Gard and carries on its top an aqueduct that brought fresh water to Nîmes; an unfortified city gate (Porte de Mars) at Reims; and at

The Maison Carrée at Nîmes, built by Agrippa (16 B.C.). (Courtesy Helga Schmidt—Glassner, Stuttgart)

Orange (Vaucluse) an arch of triumph and an immense theater, whose colonnade and central niche housed a colossal statue of Augustus.

Literature

The Augustan age was one of the great periods of world literature and comparable to that of Pericles in Athens, of Elizabeth I in England, and of Louis XIV in France. It has therefore been usually called the Golden Age because during the Augustan principate Roman literature acquired its highest perfection in form and expression. Although this period did not produce any literary figures, apart, perhaps, from Vergil, of the stature of Homer, Aeschylus, Plato, Shakespeare, or even Lucretius, the term "Augustan Age," as applied to English literature of the early eighteenth century, has come to connote the "correct" and "classical" expression of the gracious elegance and polished *urbanitas* of everyday human life in an aristocratic so-

ciety. It therefore denotes a period in which literature was in perfect harmony with the aims and ideals of the governing class.

Augustan Rome provided conditions highly favorable to literature. After a century of chaos and bloodshed, an era of general peace and ordered government evoked the gratitude, pride, and enthusiasm of the Roman people. It offered themes for literary glorification: a heroic past and a great and glorious present. Already the political capital of the world, it was rapidly becoming the cultural center, attracting students, scholars, and writers from abroad. Dionysius, who taught rhetoric in Rome from 30 to 8 B.C. and wrote *Roman Antiquities (see* p. 77f.) came from Halicarnassus; Strabo the Geographer (64/3 B.C.–ca. 21 A.D.) came from Amaseia on the Black Sea; Diodorus, the author of a universal history *(see* p. 80f.) from earliest times down to the consulship of Caesar (59 B.C.), came from Agyrium in Sicily; and Seneca the Elder (ca. 54 B.C.–ca. 39 A.D.), who wrote two important works on rhetoric (*Controversiae* and

Suasoriae), came from Corduba (Cordova) in Spain. And the two greatest Augustan writers were born not in Rome nor even in peninsular Italy, but in the Transpadana-Vergil near Mantua, Livy in Patavium (Padua).

Unlike the age of Caesar, in which prose writers predominated (Cicero, Caesar, Sallust, Nepos, and Varro), the Augustan age was notable for its poets (Vergil, Horace, Tibullus, Propertius, and Ovid). It was essentially an age of poetry. Even Livy's *Ab Urbe Condita* was no exception, for it was regarded by some critics as an epic in prose form. The *Ab Urbe Condita* began where the *Aeneid* of Vergil left off.

Vergil: 70–19 B.C.

After completing the *Georgics* in 30 B.C. (*see* p. 261), Vergil spent the next decade in the composition of his greatest work, the *Aeneid,* a national epic in twelve books, the first six of which correspond to Homer's *Odyssey,* the last six to the *Iliad.* Written in the smoothest and most beautiful narrative and in stately hexameter verse, the *Aeneid* unfolds the destiny of Rome from the burning of Troy and the landing of the hero Aeneas in Latium to its rise as a great world empire, of which the Augustan age was the culmination. It glorifies as the fulfillment of decrees of fate the achievements of the Roman people from Aeneas to Augustus. Though Aeneas, the legendary ancestor of the Julian family, is nominally the hero, the real theme is Rome, her mission is to rule the world, to teach the nations the way of peace, to spare the vanquished, and subdue the proud. The fulfillment of this mission requires of all its heroes the virtues that made Rome great: courage, piety, devotion to duty, constancy, and faith. Vergil's emphasis upon these virtues was in line with the Augustan reformation of morals and the revival of ancient faith (*prisca fides*).

Vergil expresses confidence in Rome's eternal future and his own immortality in the

The Pont du Gard, an aqueduct near Nîmes (built during the reign of Augustus). (Courtesy Helga Schmidt-Glassner, Stuttgart)

ninth book, where he describes the death of two boys who left their camp by night, fell into enemy hands, and died fighting to the end: "O happy both! If aught my song avails, no day shall erase you from remembering years, while Aeneas' house shall stand on Capitoline's unmoving rock, and he whom Rome calls father shall give commandment to the world!"

On his deathbed Vergil requested the burning of the *Aeneid* for he considered it not yet perfected. Augustus countermanded that request and by ordering its publication passed on to posterity one of the sublimest works of human genius and Rome's greatest literary legacy to the modern world.

Horace: 65–8 B.C.

Horace (*see* p. 261) had a job in the revenue office which he despised but which did enable him to live and write poetry. By 35 B.C. he had composed some of his *Epodes*, bitter, pessimistic little poems in iambic meter (in imitation of the Greek poet Archilochus) and the first book of his *Satires* (which he called *Sermones,* informal "conversations" in colloquial style and in hexameter verse), in which he pokes fun at the vices and follies of the capital. His earliest poems, though caustic, sometimes vulgar, and even obscene, were written in such a clear and incisive style and with such wit and cleverness as to win the admiration of Vergil, who in 38 B.C. introduced him to Maecenas, the rich and powerful confidant of Augustus and for years as illustrious a patron of poets and artists as Lorenzo de Medici of Renaissance times.

At first Maecenas provided Horace an income sufficient to enable him to give up his job and spend his time writing poetry, roaming the streets, and observing life in the metropolis. He later (33 B.C.) presented the poet a house of twenty-four rooms and an extensive estate worked by eight slaves and five tenant families in the Sabine country near Tivoli. There Horace could loaf, drink wine, enjoy the solitude of the country, and write poetry.

In 30 B.C. Horace published his second book of *Satires,* in which he is more mellow and less caustic than in the first. Meanwhile he had begun and for seven years thereafter continued to work on his *Odes.* The first three books, which appeared in 23 B.C., comprised eighty-eight poems of varying lengths and in a score of meters, most of which he derived from Sappho, Alcaeus, Archilochus, and Anacreon and adapted to Roman lyric form.

The *Odes* (*Carmina*) (a monument "more durable than brass and loftier than the pyramids of Egyptian kings"), on which the fame of Horace chiefly rests, touch lightly on many subjects, their variety adding yet another charm to artistry, compactness, pure diction, fastidious taste, and lightness. Some are so-called "wisdom poems" containing moral exhortations which he himself took seriously: since Youth and Beauty touch us and soon are gone, let us enjoy them now; since envious time keeps running out, seize the occasion (*carpe diem,* "snatch the day"). Others discourse on friendship, the brevity of life, religion and philosophy, drinking wine, and making love, which for Horace was a pastime lightly comic, not an all-consuming passion as for Catullus.

Horace was not a descriptive nature poet or a landscape word painter like Vergil in the *Eclogues* and *Georgics,* though now and then, in the manner of Gerard Manley Hopkins, he flashes pictures that sparkle and soon are gone: a snowy mountain glistening in the distance, a vine-clustered elm, a herd of long-horned, black-muzzled cattle grazing peacefully under Campagna's cloudless skies.

Among his *Odes* are the long, solemn, so-called Roman poems, Pindaric in their splendor, wherein he praises the old virtues resurrected by Augustus: moderation and frugality, valor and patriotism, justice, piety, and faith. In proclaiming these virtues as the sole hope of Rome's salvation, Horace anticipated the implementation of the Augustan policy of social regeneration by at least five years.

In his later years, Horace wrote two books of *Epistles,* which were sermons on morals, religion, and philosophy rather than real letters such as those written by Cicero, the Younger Pliny, Fronto, St. Jerome, or Symmachus. Though some of these so-called letters are charming and even entertaining, others seem stodgy, uninspiring, even repellent, but they commended themselves to critics of the English "Augustan Age" because of their wit, geniality, *urbanitas,* pretty phrasings, and paradoxes. The longest and most famous of these letters, the so-called *Art of Poetry (Ars Poetica),* sets forth the principles for writing poetry, especially tragedy. From this Alexander Pope in the eighteenth century drew many of the principles he versified in his *Essay on Criticism.*

The Latin Elegy

The elegiac couplet consisting of a hexameter alternating with a pentameter had served in Greek and Latin literature a variety of purposes—drinking songs, patriotic and political poems, dirges, laments, epitaphs, votive dedications, epigrams, and love poetry. The first Roman to use the elegy extensively for love poetry was probably Cornelius Gallus, whose four books of *Amores*, all lost to us, gave birth to the subjective erotic elegy. After Gallus came Tibullus (54?–19 B.C.), Propertius (50?–ca. 15 B.C.); and Ovid (43 B.C.–17/8 A.D.). For smoothness and elegance Quintilian (ca. 35?–97? A.D.), the Roman professor of rhetoric, liked Tibullus best. Some modern critics would agree.

Of Albius Tibullus there is known only the little he tells about himself in his two books of sixteen elegies addressed to Delia and to Nemesis, two slum-bred tramps who alternately made him swoon with ecstasy or drove him to madness by their vile temper and infidelities. He seems to have been goodlooking, elegant and rich, but rather neurotic and sometimes even morbid. His two passions in life were girls and the peace and beauty of the country. The attraction of the first was often stronger than that of the second. In spite of his problems he was a remarkable poet, clear, brilliant, never trite. His verse was smooth, elegant, musical and he was a master of the elegy of love and of lament.

Some would prefer the Umbrian-born Propertius. His love was Cynthia, well-born, beautiful, gifted. To her he addressed four books of elegies the chief burden of which was how she had bewitched him, and how she was sole cause of his joy and pain. In spite of her charm, her suspicions, rages, and infidelities drove him away to some other girl.

Superior in some ways to Tibullus as a stylist, Propertius is a peculiar poet, bewildering and hard to understand. Frequently he abruptly veers off into some obscure Greek myth, which dulls the most passionate climacteric. Boldest and most original of poets, he yet manages somehow by his recondite allusions to destroy the fine effects achieved by the hard brilliance and sparkle of his verse.

The most sensual and sophisticated of the elegists was Ovid, who came to Rome from the little town of Sulmo in the remote mountain region of the Abruzzi. That graceful and nimble writer fell in with the smart and fashionable Roman set, "whose morals were so congenial to his own."

The two most informative and important of Ovid's works were the *Metamorphoses* or *Transformations* and the *Fasti*, the first written in hexameters, the second in elegiacs. The *Metamorphoses,* a collection of 250 stories in fifteen books, is a store house of information about Greek mythology and the source of inspiration to poets and painters ever since. The *Fasti* or *Calendar* described and explained the origin of the chief religious festivals of Rome.

Among his earliest works were the *Amores* or *Love Elegies,* written in the style of Tibullus, with less sincerity but with more polish and virtuosity and greater mastery of erotic verse. Then came his masterpiece, the *Art of Love,* a pornographic handbook, perversely didactic, which explains all the arts of seduction and surveys all the known aspects of heterosexual experience from rape to incest. This thorough piece of research, which the two Julias (daughter and granddaughter of Augustus) both appreciated, gave offense to the princeps as an insult to the laws dealing with moral reform and the sanctity of marriage. The princeps remembered. Later (8 A.D.), when Ovid became implicated in a scandal involving the younger Julia, Augustus ordered them banished: Julia to some rocky island in the Adriatic, the poet to the cold and barbarous town of Tomi (now Constantza) on the Black Sea (his works removed from the public libraries and consigned to the flames). From Tomi, Ovid wrote with unusual depth of feeling two poems in graceful and melodious verse: the *Tristia* ("Sorrows") and the *Ex Ponto* ("Epistles from Pontus"), in which he complains bitterly of the ice and snow on that dismal, treeless rock and the barbarity of the knife-wearing *Getae*. At Tomi after many years of useless and pathetic begging for permission to return from exile, Ovid finally died (18 A.D.).

Latin Prose Writers

The most notable prose writers of the Augustan age were Asinius Pollio, Augustus himself, Livy, and Velleius Paterculus. All except the last were remarkable for their style, especially Pollio, whose admirably plain, dry, hard style, also somewhat abrupt and elliptic, and his honesty as a historian makes all the more regrettable the loss of his *History of the Civil Wars* from 60 to 42 B.C. Fortunately Plutarch in his *Lives* of Caesar and Antonius and Appian in the *Civil Wars* used Pollio as their main source.

Augustus was also an excellent stylist. In his *Gesta* the princeps wrote with clarity, brevity, and precision without shrinking from a slang or colloquial phrase that might express his meaning more accurately and vividly. This precious document officially records the achievements and honors of Augustus and formulates the constitutional position of the princeps in the reorganized state.

The supreme prose writer of the Augustan age was Titus Livy (59 B.C.–17 A.D.). Of his 142 books on the history of Rome from its founding to the death of Drusus in 9 B.C., there are extant Books I-X (from the landing of Aeneas in Latium to 293 B.C.) and XXI-XLV (218–167 B.C.). Short summaries or epitomes (written probably in the fourth century A.D.) indicate the contents of all the books except CXXXVI and CXXXVII. In a swiftly flowing Ciceronian style blended with Sallustian and poetical phraseology and with great dramatic power Livy records the mighty deeds of the Roman people and Rome's divinely ordered march to world conquest. Beginning with a stern preface in which he denounced the luxury and vices of his own age, he proposed to show that Rome's success and greatness resulted from patriotism and virtue: pious devotion to the gods, valor in war, self-control, constancy, *gravitas*, and the sanctity of family life. (His work was in full accord with the social reforms of Augustus). In spite of numerous defects as a historian: uncritical use of sources, failure to consult documents and other primary sources, ignorance of economics and military tactics, and failure to interpret primitive institutions in their proper social setting, Livy succeeded in giving the world a conception of Roman history and character.

A minor writer of this period was Velleius Paterculus (ca. 19 B.C.–ca. 31 A.D.), who in 30 A.D. hurriedly dashed off two books (part of the first and the second is extant). Though crude, he provides a useful antidote to the prejudice of Tacitus against the Emperor Tiberius.

Jurisprudence

The Augustan age marks the end of the so-called Hellenistic period of Roman legal science or jurisprudence and the beginning of a new period known as the Classical, which lasted till the reign of Diocletian.

The Hellenistic Period: 200–27 B.C. In the Hellenistic period, which began around 200 B.C. and ended with Augustus, Roman legal science had come under the powerful stimulus of Greek jurisprudence, philosophy, and rhetoric which, acting as a catalyst, released the natural and national energy of Roman jurisprudence. This period saw the rise of nonpriestly jurisprudence, and the gradual replacement of state priests and pontiffs by laymen as professional jurists, consultants, and interpreters of the law. One of the earliest secular jurists was Sextus Aelius Paetus Catus, who published the *Tripertita* containing the text of the XII Tables with commentary (*see* p. 126).

The greatest of all legal works published during the Republic was the *Civil Law* (*Ius Civile*) of the Pontifex Maximus, Q. Mucius Scaevola, who was consul in 95 B.C. The *Civil Law* in eighteen books was the first systematic exposition of private law, and down into the second century A.D., served as a model for legal commentators, thereby laying the basis not merely of Roman law but of future European jurisprudence.

The Classical Period. The Classical period saw the creative ideas of the Republic elaborated in great detail. Genius was now slowly giving way to professionalism. As the old Roman families of high pedigree and proud public achievement gradually became extinct, new jurists and legal experts from Italian and even provincial towns came to the fore. Though some jurists held high office in the early principate, after Vespasian's time (69–79 A.D.) another type more commonly appeared, the salaried officials of the Imperial bureaucracy. Many of the jurists were practising consultants, writers, and professors of law.

Responsa. Augustus did not abolish the custom established by the early pontiffs and later jurisconsults of giving expert opinions or rulings (*responsa*) on legal questions. Wishing to preserve that custom, he gave a few select jurists the right to give responses reinforced by his own personal authority (*ius respondendi ex auctoritate principis*). Most praetors and judges respected and accepted these responses, but were under no legal obligation to do so. Unauthorized jurists were still free to give responses and magistrates and judges to accept them. Like so many other innovations of Augustus, official authorization of jurisconsults did not endure beyond the reign of Trajan (98–117 A.D.).

As Roman society became more complex and jurists more active in civil and criminal cases than during the Republic, the demand for legal education increased correspondingly.

Law Schools

In the first century A.D. two law schools sprang into being. One said to have been founded by Capito (*consul suffectus* of 5 A.D.) was actually a foundation of C. Cassius Longinus, who died shortly after 69 A.D., but the school is often called Sabinian after Masurius Sabinus, a famous teacher of Cassius. The other school was probably a foundation of M. Antistius Labeo in the time of Augustus even though it later received the name of Proculian from a certain Proculus, who allegedly taught law during Nero's reign.

The restoration of peace and orderly government after Actium and the economic upsurge that followed laid the groundwork for a brilliant efflorescence of art and literature, which Augustus himself did much to inspire and encourage. Augustan art not only achieved complete Romanization, but acquired an imperial character, as shown by the sculptures on the Altar of Carthage and numerous monuments in Gallia Narbonensis. In Vergil, Horace, Propertius, and Ovid the Latin language was perfected as a poetic medium, and Latin literature became one of the great literatures of the world.

XIII

PRINCIPATE OF THE

THE NEXT PRINCEPS AFTER AUGUSTUS WAS TIBERIUS CLAUDIUS
Nero, or Tiberius Caesar Augustus, a man of fifty-five and much
experienced in war, government, and administration as stepson,
adoptive son, colleague, and heir apparent of Augustus. His
ancestry was ancient and illustrious: both of his parents belonged
to the Claudian family whose history was the history of Rome
herself.

Tiberius

The early life of Tiberius had been neither easy nor satisfying.
Born in 42 B.C., he spent the first two years of his life with his
parents in political exile. In 38 B.C. his mother Livia Drusilla

JULIO-CLAUDIANS

persuaded his father to divorce her so that she could marry Octavianus, who seems to have disliked the shy lad with the slow, halting speech and to have preferred his younger brother, Drusus, who had a more jovial and appealing personality. These early experiences made Tiberius a gloomy man, cynical and resentful.

Nor did manhood bring him respite from trouble. Hard work and successful generalship won him neither recognition nor reward. He found himself repeatedly passed over in favor of younger men. After a fairly satisfactory marriage with Vipsania, Agrippa's

daughter, he yielded to the emperor's insistence that he divorce the woman he loved to marry Julia. To escape from that marriage and from the favoritism Augustus had begun to show towards Julia's sons by Agrippa, Lucius and Gaius Caesar, Tiberius went into self-imposed exile at Rhodes, where he remained for nine years. His adoption by Augustus after the deaths of the young Caesars and his later assumption of tribunician power and the proconsular *imperium* could not efface all the slights, snubs, and indignities he had suffered in the past. At his accession he was still a soured and disillusioned man.

The principate of Tiberius began ominously with the execution of Agrippa Postumus, the grandson of Augustus but a brutal and intractable person whom Augustus had exiled to a barren island in 7 A.D. Unarmed but with the strength of an ox, Postumus savagely resisted the centurion dispatched to the island to put him to death. It is not known who decided or ordered the killing—Augustus, perhaps Livia, or Tiberius. Suspicion fell upon Tiberius. So Tacitus reports in his *Annals* as the "first crime of the new principate" (*primum facinus novi principatus*).

Sources

The most important sources on the reign of Tiberius are the first six books of the *Annals* of Tacitus (ca. 56–ca. 123), the biography of Tiberius by Suetonius (ca. 69–ca. 140), the 58th Book of the *Roman History* of Cassius Dio (ca. 155–ca. 229), and the second and only extant Book of the *Compendium of Roman History* of Velleius Paterculus (ca. 19 B.C.–ca. 32 A.D.), an old staff officer and admirer of Tiberius. A few items of information appear in the writings of Strabo the Geographer, Valerius Maximus, the Younger Seneca, the Elder Pliny, Josephus, and Plutarch.

Tacitus is the best and most reliable source because he himself had excellent sources of information: many primary documents such as the *acta senatus* (Proceedings of the Senate) containing debates and speeches by senators and Tiberius and the *acta diurna* (The Daily Bulletin), which reported the main events of the day and all official decrees and announcements; the brief autobiography of Tiberius and historical works by several of his contemporaries (especially Aufidius Bassus and Servilius Nonianus); the memoirs and letters of the Younger Agrippina; the reports of proconsuls and imperial legates on military operations in Gaul, Germany, the Balkans, the East, and especially Africa; the records and archives of noble families; and the stories and recollections of elderly aristocrats Tacitus may have heard in his youth.

Despite the excellence of his sources and his honesty in reporting the facts, Tacitus often allows his judgment of Tiberius, whom he represents as a tyrant and a hypocrite, to be warped and unbalanced by his hatred of the tyranny he himself had endured under Domitian (81–96). Yet the judgment of Tacitus is not altogether personal. It undoubtedly reflects the consensus of aristocratic opinion, which Tacitus accepted and converted into an enduring work of art by his literary skill and historical research.

Tiberius and the Senate

Ancient writers agree that Tiberius was a good emperor at least in the first decade of his reign. He treated the senate with respect and deference: he attended all its meetings, permitted freedom of speech and debate, and accepted it as a genuine partner in the government. He transferred to the senate an age-old prerogative of the popular assembly: the function of electing the highest magistrates (consuls and praetors). He finally made the senate a supreme court of justice, especially for the trial of influential persons accused of treason and in the case of provincial governors, imperial as well as senatorial, of extortion and corrupt administration in their provinces. Though some treason trials even as late as 20 took place in the regular praetor's courts, Tiberius preferred to have such cases tried in the senate because it was less vulnerable to bribery and intimidation by powerful defendants.

He also made it a practice to consult the senate on all affairs of state—finances, public works, the raising and disposition of armies for imperial defense, the appointment of generals and governors, and the conduct of foreign affairs. In short, the senate received its last chance to act as an effective branch of the government. It failed, not because Tiberius was insincere, but because the senators themselves refused to accept the role he offered them.

The Mutiny of the Legions

Shortly after the accession of Tiberius, the legions stationed in Pannonia (Hungary) and those in the Lower Rhineland mutinied in protest against the long terms of service, wretched pay, and discipline enforced by beatings and brutalities. Tiberius sent his son Drusus to Pannonia to quell the mutiny there, and Germanicus, his nephew, adopted son, and heir, to the Rhineland. Drusus, acting with dignity and courage, successfully restored discipline, but Germanicus resorted to weak emotional displays and theatrical threats of suicide, which inspired little respect.

Germanicus

To restore the morale of the troops, to emulate the deeds of his father, Drusus, and to avenge the defeat of Varus, Germanicus determined to renew the attempt to conquer Germany. In the first summer's campaign he laid waste fifty miles of enemy territory and succeeded only in uniting the infuriated Germans to attack the retreating Roman columns. The next year Germanicus laid waste the entire country between the Lippe and the Ems. That same summer he visited the gruesome site of the Teutoburg Forest disaster (*see* p. 282) and there performed funeral rites for the Roman dead. While marching along the coast of the North Sea to winter quarters on the Rhine, his army encountered high tides lashed by equinoctial gales and suffered heavy losses in men and supplies.

In the year 16 Germanicus led his third expedition into Germany and penetrated as far east as the Elbe. Though he defeated Arminius, the famous German war leader, he was unable to hold Germany in permanent occupation. Again he had to retreat to the Rhine, sending some of his forces overland, and loading others on transports. A violent storm on the North Sea destroyed many ships and men.

Tiberius realized that the military ventures of Germanicus were a drain upon the empire's manpower and resources. His personal knowledge of Germany convinced him of the wisdom of the Augustan policy of making the Rhine a permanent frontier. He therefore called Germanicus back to Rome and renounced the conquest of Germany, preferring to rely instead on the diplomatic talents of his son Drusus. This reversal of policy soon bore fruit. Arminius and Maroboduus, the powerful king of Bohemia,

began to quarrel and then to fight. Maroboduus lost his kingdom and fled to Italy as a refugee. Arminius fell victim to an assassin's dagger. Bohemia became virtually a vassal kingdom of Rome.

After receiving Germanicus at Rome with highest military honors (including a splendid triumph), Tiberius sent him to the Middle East with powers transcending those of all governors and legates in that area. The purpose of the mission was to negotiate with Artabanus III, the ambitious and aggressive king of Parthia, to place upon the now vacant throne of Armenia a king friendly to Rome, and to superintend the annexation of the kingdoms of Cappadocia, Cilicia, and Commagene as imperial provinces. Germanicus carried out these difficult tasks with consummate efficiency and success.

All would have ended well had not Tiberius feared that Germanicus might impulsively embroil the empire in an all-out war with Parthia. To act as a brake upon the war-making proclivities of that brilliant but impulsive youth he sent Cn. Calpurnius Piso to the East as governor of Syria. The choice was most unfortunate, for Piso hated Germanicus and refused to acknowledge him as a superior officer or obey his orders.

Germanicus was guilty of mistakes too. Without authorization from Tiberius he went to Egypt, where he accepted divine honors and opened reserve granaries for the relief of starvation in Alexandria. Although that generous act did not endanger the food supply of Rome, his journey to Egypt seemed contrary to the policy of Augustus and naturally irritated the suspicious and legalistic mind of Tiberius, who complained bitterly before the senate.

On his return to Syria, Germanicus found that Piso had contemptuously disobeyed all his orders and had no alternative but to order him out of the province. Shortly after Piso's expulsion, Germanicus took sick at Antioch. In his illness and delirium he accused Piso of attempting to destroy him by sorcery and poison and, calling upon his wife and children to avenge his murder, died.

The body of Germanicus was hastily cremated and Agrippina, his wife, set out for Rome with the ashes. Piso seized the opportunity to make a bold stroke for the province of Syria but he was defeated and brought to Rome. There he was brought to trial before the senate on three charges: the murder of Germanicus, insubordination in disobeying a superior officer, and his attempt to recover a province from which ordered to depart. Although acquitted of the charge of murder, he was convicted and condemned of the others. Upon hearing of the senate's judgment, Piso committed suicide.

The death of Germanicus left Drusus, the only natural son of Tiberius, next heir to the throne. He was of the same age as his first cousin, Germanicus, whom he had greatly admired and whose children he treated with utmost kindness. Drusus had to deal from the first with Sejanus, for many years the adviser, confidant, and favorite of his father, Tiberius.

Sejanus

L. Aelius Sejanus, one of the most infamous and sinister personalities in Roman history, was of distinguished equestrian family. Talented and cunning, he had stealthily worked his way into the confidence and good graces of Tiberius, who placed him in command of the elite Praetorian Guard. The Guard soon became for Sejanus an instrument of great power and terror especially after he had persuaded the princeps to concentrate all of its nine cohorts, hitherto scattered throughout Italy, in new barracks on the eastern outskirts of Rome. Growing ever more presumptuous, he aspired to marriage within the imperial family and eventual succession to the throne. His first step was the seduction of Livilla, the wife of Drusus. In 23 Drusus died under rather suspicious circumstances, but although Tiberius refused to grant Sejanus permission to wed Livilla, he did not really suspect foul play until long afterwards.

To clear the way to the throne and remove all potential rivals, Sejanus next plotted the ruin and death of Agrippina and her three sons. Deviously and with devilish cunning he aroused the emperor's suspicions of that violent and vindictive woman, whose hatred for Tiberius was public knowledge. The intrigues of Sejanus against Agrippina became increasingly bold in 26, when Tiberius decided to leave the hectic capital and ensconce himself on the lovely and inaccessible island of Capreae (Capri). Sejanus opened his offensive against Agrippina by attacking her friends, charging them with treason and driving them into exile or death by suicide or execution. After the death of the old empress Livia in 29 (at the age of eighty-six), he apparently convinced Tiberius of Agrippina's involvement in a plot against the throne. Thereupon the senate (after two missives from Tiberius) exiled Agrippina to the island of Pandateria and her eldest son Nero to Pontia, where he soon afterwards killed himself. Her second son, Drusus, committed to a prison in Rome in 30, starved himself to death three years later. The only consolation that Agrippina and Drusus might have enjoyed was that they lived long enough to learn of the downfall and death of the agent of their ruin.

Sejanus' attempt to glide gently into power had been a notable success until he overreached himself. In 31 he was consular colleague of Tiberius and received from the senate the proconsular *imperium* through which he was able to extend his patronage by the disposal of honors and provinces. He now formed a double matrimonial connection with the imperial family: he won Tiberius' consent to wed the princess Julia, daughter of Drusus and Livilla, and betrothed his own daughter to the son of Claudius (the future emperor). In Rome the statues of Sejanus and Tiberius stood side by side and altars to clemency and friendship conjointly commemorated their virtues. Only one obstacle now blocked the way to the throne: Agrippina's third son Gaius (Caligula), whom Tiberius had recommended in a missive to the senate as heir to the throne. Sejanus sought to remove that obstacle by a plot against the life of Gaius. Then suddenly something went wrong.

Antonia, daughter of the Triumvir Marcus Antonius and grandmother of the young prince, secretly sent her freedman Pallas to Tiberius, who promptly summoned Gaius to the safety of Capri. Then he sent Naevius Sutorius Macro to Rome to take over command of the Praetorian Guard and convey to the senate a long and wordy letter (*verbosa et grandis epistula*). The letter, read out by the consul, began with mild praise of Sejanus. Praise became criticism, criticism reproof, and the reproof ended in sharp denunciation and a peremptory order for arrest. The senate at once voted condemnation and death. The populace hailed the fall of Sejanus with frenzied joy, pulled down his statues, dragged his body through the streets and flung it into the Tiber. Many of his friends and supporters fell victim to the infuriated mob.

The treason of a long trusted minister was a cruel blow to Tiberius. Others were soon forthcoming: Apicata, the divorced wife of Sejanus, maddened by the execution of her eleven-year-old son and the raping and strangling of her little daughter, committed suicide. Before doing so she wrote Tiberius a letter informing him that Sejanus and Livilla had murdered Drusus, the heir to the throne. The slave attendants of Drusus (a doctor and a eunuch), when put to torture, confirmed the ghastly revelations, and Tiberius realized that he had become the unwitting accomplice in a conspiracy against the state of unknown ramifications. This he resolved to eradicate and destroy.

The Law of Treason (*Maiestas*)

A mighty weapon lay at Tiberius' hand —the law of treason (*maiestas*), not of his own forging but the product of a long process of evolution from the early Republic to the principate of Augustus. *Maiestas* originally covered all offenses against the safety of the state such as betrayal to an enemy or physical assault upon a magistrate. By the time of Julius Caesar the law came to include all offenses against the dignity of the state. In the principate, it covered not only high treason (*perduellio*) but a variety of rather ill-defined charges which ranged from arrogance, sacrilege, and slander to extortion, adultery, incest, rape, and murder.

Under a law of such flexibility it is not surprising that 106 persons should have been brought to trial during the long reign of Tiberius. Tiberius often favored acquittal or disallowed convictions already handed down by the lower courts or by the senate, and not all the charges resulted in convictions. Of twenty-four charges of slander, libel, and similar offenses only six convictions are known. Of the eighty-two remaining cases of *maiestas* sixteen involved high treason in the provinces: three defendants had their indictments quashed before trial, one committed suicide, four won acquittal, and eight were convicted (Tiberius disallowed one of the convictions). Of fifty-two defendants charged with high treason, conspiracy, and mutiny seven had their indictments dropped, one died before trial, fourteen won acquittal, four committed suicide, two had their citizenship revoked, four suffered imprisonment, five banishment, and twelve execution (eight at the express orders of Tiberius). These facts and figures speak for themselves. The principate of Tiberius seems therefore not to have been really a tyranny, much less a reign of terror.*

The Informers (*Delatores*)

The most execrable aspect of the treason trials during the principate of Tiberius was the practice of permitting private citizens to initiate prosecutions for financial rewards (usually one-fourth of the convicted defendant's property). The use of *delatores* or informers was a miserable system of law enforcement because it encouraged unscrupulous persons to trump up charges against the rich, but it was a necessary evil since there was no public prosecutor or state secret police. Tiberius himself once remarked that the abolition of rewards to professional accusers would wreck the entire system of existing law enforcement.

Yet it would be erroneous to suppose that many *delatores* rose from poverty to riches (*ex pauperibus divites*). Of fourteen recorded prosecutors, who later appeared as defendants on charges other than that of calumny, only one had ever informed against more than one person. The informer's pro-

* *See* R. S. Rogers, *Criminals Trials and Criminal Legislation under Tiberius* (Middletown, Conn., 1935) and *Studies in the Reign of Tiberius* (Baltimore, 1943).

fession was apparently not either busy nor lucrative—nor safe. It was invariably one of considerable risk. Tacitus himself reports how lucky some informers were to suffer merely the loss of an expected reward. On several occasions Tiberius had false accusers and calumniators punished, sometimes exiled. They brought ruin upon others, in the end upon themselves (*perniciem aliis ac postremum sibi invenere*).

Tiberius the Administrator

The fame of Tiberius rests chiefly on his knowledge of and skill in imperial administration. He followed the foreign policy of Augustus, relying wherever possible on diplomatic rather than military tactics (*plura consilio quam vi*). He compelled Germanicus (*see* p. 313) to abandon the conquest of Germany and restrained him from involving Rome in a war with Parthia. The Augustan conquests in central Europe and the East required a pause for consolidation. By strengthening the defenses along the Rhine and other frontiers and by suppressing revolts in Gaul, in Thrace, and in North Africa, he kept the empire at peace and at an unprecedented peak of prosperity.

To promote the material welfare of the provinces he kept tribute and taxes at a minimum and, by strict financial economy (the curtailment of expensive spectacles and ambitious building projects), he was able to reduce taxes and yet build up a large surplus in the treasury. In an effort to procure a more honest and efficient collection of provincial taxes, he restricted the tax-farming companies to the collection of customs dues and severely punished all provincial governors guilty of extortion, floggings, and confiscation of private property, or of corrupt administration. Some of the governors found guilty of such injustices committed suicide rather than face the wrath of the emperor.

Tiberius appointed able and conscientious men to govern the imperial provinces. As an incentive to honest administration, he increased governors' salaries and lengthened their terms of office so that they would get increasingly familiar with their duties and with local conditions. Many of the governors held office from five to ten years, some even longer. C. Poppaeus Sabinus was in charge of the newly united imperial province of Macedonia, Achaea, and Moesia for twenty years and C. Calvisius Sabinus was legate of Pannonia for almost twenty-four. As a result of this policy cases of extortion and corruption arose less frequently in the imperial provinces than in the senatorial, where governors normally held office for only one year.

Tiberius encouraged the provincial assemblies (*concilia*) to send delegates to Rome to lodge complaints before the emperor and the senate about the conduct of governors, legates, and procurators in both the imperial and senatorial provinces.

Tiberius prohibited the Gallic cities from issuing silver coins in order that a uniform imperial coinage might be established to facilitate trade and the exchange of goods over wider areas. To expedite frontier defense and encourage travel, communication, and commerce, he embarked upon an extensive road and bridge building program in Gaul, Pannonia (Hungary), Moesia (Bulgaria), North Africa, Egypt, and particularly in Spain, where flourishing cities sprang up at road junctions and terminals.*

The new economic prosperity of the provinces, the efficient collection of taxes, and careful financial administration increased revenues and created a large surplus in the treasury which enabled the emperor to give prompt and liberal relief to stricken areas in both Italy and the provinces. In 17, twelve cities in Asia Minor were severely damaged by an earthquake; Tiberius not only remitted all their taxes for five years, but contributed generously toward their reconstruction. Two years later, he provided subsidies to relieve a famine in Rome. In 33, he attempted to counteract the effects of economic crisis and financial panic by authorizing the senate to promulgate a law requiring all creditors to invest two-thirds of their capital in Italian land, and lent the treasury 100,000,000 sesterces, interest free, to establish a loan fund for the assistance of landowners able to post collateral equal to at

* We learn of this important work only through the numerous inscriptions found in almost every part of the empire.

least twice the amount of the loan. In 36, he spent a similar amount to repair the damage and relieve the distress caused by a disastrous fire on the Aventine. Even after making these and other large grants from the treasury, Tiberius was able to reduce an unpopular sales tax from one to one-half per cent and to leave behind in the treasury the sum of 2,700,000,000 sesterces (3,300,000,000 according to some authorities).

The Death of Tiberius: 37

Tiberius died at Capri in 37, at the age of seventy-seven. He had been one of Rome's finest administrators and, in the opinion of Theodor Mommsen, the ablest ruler the Empire ever had.

Caligula

The next emperor was Gaius, officially Gaius Caesar Augustus Germanicus, better known as Caligula.* He was a scion of three famous families—Claudian, Julian, and Antonian: his father, Germanicus, was a Claudian; his mother, Agrippina, a Julian; one of his great-grandfathers was Augustus, another was Marcus Antonius, so that in his veins there flowed the blood of both the victor and the vanquished of Actium. In his later teens he had lived with his grandmother, Antonia, who threw him into constant companionship with three young Thracian princes, with the young Herod Agrippa I of Judea, and with Ptolemy of Mauretania, a grandson of Antonius and Cleopatra. From them he may have acquired his Oriental conception of absolute monarchy. During his stay at his uncle's court at Capri he practiced the art of dissimulation and obsequiousness, which helped to conceal his sadism, his self-indulgence, and his predilection for taverns and brothels.

After the long, stern, and puritanical reign

* Literally, "Little Boots," a name bestowed on him as a child in the Rhineland by his father's soldiers because his mother, Agrippina, liked to dress him in the uniform of a legionary soldier, complete with little military boots (*caligulae,* the diminutive of *caligae,* "heavy top boots").

of Tiberius, the people welcomed their gay new ruler with gladness and thanksgiving. He delighted the populace by distributing the legacies of Livia and Tiberius, by abolishing the unpopular sales taxes (already slightly reduced by Tiberius), and by his splendid spectacles, games, chariot races, and wild-beast hunts. He even restored to the popular assemblies their ancient right of electing magistrates. He pleased the senate by his deference and courtesy and by his conciliatory attitude toward the nobility. He abolished all impending trials for treason, curbed the infamous activities of the *delatores,* recalled the exiles of Tiberius, and piously had the bones and ashes of his mother Agrippina and his brother Nero brought back from the islands for interment in the mausoleum of Augustus. He adopted his cousin Tiberius Gemellus as his son and heir, shared the consulship with his uncle Claudius, and had his three sisters honored throughout the empire. To cap it all, he stirred the patriotic fervor of all classes by announcing preparations for the conquest of Britain and Germany. A serious illness forced him to postpone this enterprise, and shattered men's hopes for a glorious reign of concord and felicity.

Ancient sources imply (especially Suetonius) that after his recovery Caligula became mentally deranged and succumbed completely to the temptations of supreme power. He began to play the role of an Oriental despot and indulged in acts of cruelty, megalomania, and madness. He insulted and humiliated the senate, stripped it of military control over Africa Proconsularis, and deprived it of its exclusive right of coinage in Italy by removing the imperial mint from Rome to Lyons. He forced individual senators to swear they would lay down their lives for him and his sisters, to wait upon his table dressed as slaves, trot beside his chariot in their togas, and even kiss his feet in homage. Like the Pharaohs of ancient Egypt (whom he greatly admired, and imitated), he asserted the right of eminent domain over the property of his subjects (he introduced taxes in the Egyptian manner on shopkeepers and craftsmen), lived in habitual incest with his sisters, and longed to be worshipped as a god on earth, the *Neos Helios* (Egyptian coins represent him as a sun-god). He loved to sit in the Temple of Castor and Pollux and receive divine worship or converse with Jupiter and the other gods. Eventually he had a temple erected to himself out of public funds and not only appointed his favorite horse (which he believed to be a reincarnation of Alexander the Great's Bucephalus) as high priest of his cult but even adlected him into the senate. In 39 he had a bridge of ships built across the Bay of Baiae and celebrated its completion by riding over it wearing the breastplate of Alexander, meditating vast military enterprises. At the height of the celebration, a great many people became drunk and, as boats overturned, some got drowned.

Financially, Caligula was equally reckless and mad. He squandered money on perfume baths, banquets, and fabulous drinks, and on horse races, shows, and largesses to the populace. His pleasure barges on Lake Nemi contained baths, gardens, gem-studded sterns, and the costliest of furnishings. These and many other extravagances soon exhausted the huge surplus Tiberius had accumulated in the treasury. To obtain new funds he resorted to extraordinary taxes (on foodstuffs, law suits, and the earnings of porters, panders, and prostitutes), to forced legacies, and confiscations. He accordingly revived the treason laws as a means of confiscating money and property.

Among his victims were his father-in-law Junius Silanus, Tiberius Gemellus, his adopted son and heir, Naevius Sutorius Macro, the prefect of the Praetorian Guard, who had helped him to the throne, and several members and partisans of the Claudian family (perhaps because they were agitating for a restoration of the Republic). His uncle Claudius escaped only because he seemed to be a harmless dolt.

Some of Caligula's victims were actually guilty of treason: one of his army commanders in the Rhineland, Cn. Cornelius Lentulus Gaetulicus, conspired to place upon the throne M. Aemilius Lepidus, the widower of Caligula's own dearly beloved sister Drusilla. Caligula had both men executed and exiled two of his other sisters, the Younger Agrippina and Julia Livilla, both of whom were involved in the plot. He also brought Calvisius Sabinus, the governor of Pannonia, to trial for tampering with the loyalty of the army under his command.

After suppressing the conspiracy in the Rhineland, Caligula crossed the Rhine in force in order to discourage future German border raids, but his long-planned invasion of Britain came to nothing more than a march to the Strait of Dover and the erection of a lighthouse (200 feet high) at Boulogne, which remained standing until 1544.

Caligula's Foreign and Provincial Policies

Though Caligula was autocratic and capricious in foreign and provincial affairs, he generally favored the policies of Pompey and Marcus Antonius rather than that of Augustus and Tiberius. In the East, for example, he preferred client kings to provincial governors, who might enter into conspiracies and create armies for rebellion against the throne. He abandoned Greater Armenia as a Roman sphere of influence and allowed Parthia to control it in exchange for Parthian recognition of Rome's interests in the East. He restored Commagene, which Tiberius had annexed as a province, to Antiochus; he made his three young Thracian friends vassal rulers respectively of Thrace, Pontus and the Bosporus, and Lesser Armenia; and placed Herod Agrippa over the whole of the kingdom formerly ruled by his grandfather Herod the Great. In Africa, on the other hand, Caligula deposed and executed Ptolemy, the client king of Mauretania (western Algeria and Morocco), and made his kingdom a Roman province. The murder of Ptolemy provoked a revolt, which Caligula did not live long enough to suppress.

In his policy towards the Jews, Caligula was equally erratic and provocative. In Alexandria, where there was a large Jewish community, he permitted a Greek mob to sack the Jewish quarters and forcibly erect his statues in their synagogues. In 40 the Jews sent a delegation to Caligula but obtained no redress. Meanwhile, Caligula had instructed Petronius, his legate in Syria, to install his statue in the temple at Jerusalem, but Caligula's death relieved Petronius of the necessity of carrying out the order.

Caligula's brief career of extravagance, oppression, murder, and madness came to an abrupt end on January 24, A.D. 41, when Cassius Chaerea, a tribune of the Praetorian Guard, whom he had offended by his obscenities, struck him down in a secret passageway of the palace. The hand that struck was Chaerea's, but the men behind the deed were prominent members of the senate, administration, and army.

Claudius

While ransacking the imperial palace after Caligula's assassination, some soldiers of the Praetorian Guard happened to see two feet sticking out from under a curtain in the balcony. They discovered that it was Claudius, the brother of Germanicus. Instead of killing him as he doubtless expected, they carried him over to their barracks where the troops tumultuously acclaimed him emperor of Rome. He acquiesced, promising each soldier 15,000 sesterces, and, when the senate compliantly conferred the imperial powers upon him, he assumed office under the name of Tiberius Claudius Caesar Augustus Germanicus.

All his life Claudius had had to contend with the most extreme physical and psychological handicaps: persistently poor health, physical deformity, slow mental development, social maladjustment, and timidity. An early attack of infantile paralysis had apparently left him with a grotesque appearance—wobbly head, spindly legs, a gawky look, and a speech defect which made him appear simple-minded. His imperial relations either felt ashamed of him and tried to keep him out of sight or else made fun of him. Caligula often made him act the part of a court buffoon.

His ugliness and social awkwardness drove Claudius to drinking and gambling or into the seclusion of the study. As his mental powers developed under the tutelage of the great historian Livy and through association with Greek scientists and scholars, he be-

came a philologist and antiquarian, and an expert on Roman law and government, and even on Etruscan and Carthaginian history. Unfortunately none of his important historical works has survived.

Sources

The most important writers about the reign of Claudius are Tacitus, Seneca the Younger, Josephus, Suetonius, Cassius Dio, and the Elder Pliny. Both Seneca and Josephus contradict themselves in their appraisal of Claudius. In an earlier essay (*Consolatio ad Polybium*), Seneca praises the emperor highly; in a later one (*Apocolocyntosis*), he condemns him as an idiot and a tyrant, who judicially murdered thirty-five senators and 221 knights.* Josephus was inconsistent too. In his *Jewish War* he described Claudius as a capable, self-reliant leader with a dominating will; in the *Jewish Antiquities*,† as a helpless, bewildered person wholly dependent upon the advice and craft of the Jewish king, Herod Agrippa I of Judea. The first account is more in harmony with contemporary inscriptions and papyri.

Tacitus in his *Annals* (in the extant part of Book XI and in Book XII) depicts the latter part of the Claudian reign (from 47 to 54 A.D.) as a wretched age of lust and corruption: a repulsive, garrulous, and gluttonous old man, a helpless puppet in the hands of base freedmen ministers and two notorious wives,‡ degraded the dignity of the imperial office and his own illustrious ancestry. Though Tacitus honestly reports the

* In the *Consolatio ad Polybium,* Seneca had a favor to ask of Claudius; whereas in the *Apocolocyntosis,* an undignified work filled with rancor and vindictiveness, he not only expresses a grudge, but courts the favor of conservative senators.

† The *Jewish Antiquities* of Flavius Josephus (A.D. 37–100) is a history of the Jews from the creation of the world to 66 A.D. Books XIX and XX, which treat the reigns of Claudius and Nero, are vivid and sparkle with metaphor. He explains the despotism of the Caesars as a result of the lethargy of the senatorial aristocracy.

‡ Valeria Messallina, Claudius' first consort, was notorious for her murders and for her promiscuity and sexual depravity; his second consort, the Younger Agrippina, was like Messallina but more ferocious in criminality (*ferox facinoris*) and atrocious in hatred (*atrox odii*).

facts of great military and administrative achievement and acknowledges industry in the conduct of the government and concern for justice and public welfare, he casts over the entire reign a pall of malicious insinuation and prejudice.

Suetonius, whose biography of Claudius is full of gossip and scandal, depicts the emperor as a mixture of imbecile and tyrant. Unlike Tacitus, Suetonius is lacking in political insight and fails to reveal the great achievements of the reign.

After his accession, Claudius revealed astonishing strength of character and political acumen. He had won the support of the Praetorian Guard by a liberal donative and compelled the senate to accept him as princeps, though many of its members had sworn to abolish the principate and toyed with the idea of restoring the Republic. As a Julio-Claudian and brother of the once popular Germanicus, Claudius enjoyed the support of the army, the urban populace, the Italian upper class, and the people of the provinces.

The Political Philosophy of Claudius

From his study of Roman history and political institutions Claudius learned that Rome owed her greatness to her willingness to devise new institutions to meet new needs: reform, he held, lay at the very root of her tradition, and would be her salvation in the noontide of her power.

Claudius and the Senate

Claudius, like Augustus, showed the senate respect and deference and earnestly desired its collaboration in the governance of the empire. He sat between consuls or on the tribune's bench only when he had something special to propose. He religiously attended all meetings, took his seat as an ordinary senator, and expressed his opinion (*sententia*) only if and when so asked. Though proclaimed *Imperator* at least twenty-seven times for military victories won in his name, he refused the title as well as that of "Father of the Fatherland" (*Pater Patriae*). In 44, he restored to the senate the provinces of Macedonia and Achaea

which Tiberius had made "imperial" in 15. He conferred upon the senate the election of curule magistrates, which Caligula, reversing the policy of Tiberius, had transferred to the popular assembly.

The Centralization of Government

Though desirous of the senate's collaboration, Claudius did not forget that he was the chief executive of an empire which could no longer be exploited as the private estate of a narrow and selfish aristocracy. The time had come for Rome to integrate herself with Italy and with the provinces. Good government and efficient administration must now supersede the ancient privileges of the senate.

In 47-48 Claudius revived the censorship, which had been defunct for sixty-eight years. Assuming the office himself, he purged the senate of some old members and added new ones. A few of the new senators were his own clients, tribal chieftains of Gallia Comata whose families had received citizenship from Julius Caesar. They were richer than most Italian senators and controlled large and devoted clans. The adlection of Gallic senators gave the Gauls political equality with the Italians and made them loyal partners in the new world state. Later emperors recognized the wisdom of such a measure and adopted it on a larger scale.

Claudius struck other blows against the Roman senatorial aristocracy. He weakened the senate's power over the armies by increasing the importance of the military tribunes, who were of equestrian rank, at the expense of the legates, who usually belonged to the senatorial class. He diminished the senate's control even over its own provinces by granting the imperial procurators judicial powers (formerly exercised solely by the proconsular governors) in all cases affecting the *fiscus* and the assessment and collection of taxes.

He transferred the management of the treasury (*aerarium Saturni*) from the board of praetors set up by Augustus to a new one of two quaestors appointed by and responsible solely to himself, to serve for three years at a stipulated salary. From the treasury, now under his control, he diverted to the imperial *fiscus* such important revenues as the five per cent inheritance tax and probably the tax on manumitted slaves. The *fiscus*, now reorganized, though probably not yet consolidated into a central treasury, assumed burdens formerly borne by the *aerarium*. These were the expenses of the grain administration (which had to do with the purchase of provincial grain, its subsidized transport, storage, and free distribution to at least 200,000 recipients at the Porticus Minucia in Rome), the administration of the water supply, the flood control on the Tiber, and the construction and maintenance of roads, canals, and harbors in Italy. Claudius' first object was to weaken senatorial interference and to place all such services under imperial control in order to achieve the administrative efficiency which centralization of government alone could secure.

The Expansion of the Civil Service and the New Cabinet

Centralization of government entailed an expanded civil service and an enlarged secretariat or cabinet. Though Claudius originated neither, he took decisive steps towards the development of the later imperial bureaucracy by his division of the executive into special bureaus or departments (*scrinia*)

The director of each department was a member of the cabinet or advisory council of the emperor. Narcissus, his secretary of state (*ab epistulis*), drafted all laws and decrees sent out over the empire under the imperial seal. Callistus headed the justice department, which consisted of an examiner of petitions sent to the princeps from the provinces (*praepositus a libellis*) and an attorney-general (*praepositus a cognitionibus*), who had charge of judicial investigations and trials. Another important official was Pallas (whom Antonia had secretly sent to report to Tiberius the conspiracy of Sejanus). As head of the treasury department (*a rationibus*), he coordinated all the provincial *fisci* and the activities of the procurators. A fourth was Claudius Polybius, keeper of the records' office and reference library (*a studiis*).

Many of the officials of the imperial administration were freedmen of Greek or Asiatic origin. They were excellent executives and perhaps men of character, though some made use of their positions to enrich themselves. The equestrian class resented them because they were freedmen, the senatorial aristocracy feared their power and influence in the government. Ancient and modern writers have been too closely bound to a biased and hostile tradition when they represent Claudius as dominated by his ministers. Actually he was the master and they his faithful and obedient servants.

Public Works and Welfare

The administrative efficiency thus achieved enabled Claudius to devote attention to public welfare and carry out a vast program of public works. He curbed some evils of money-lending by forbidding usurers to lend to teenage spendthrifts; he abolished sales taxes on food and relieved stricken communities of their tax burdens; and through his control of the imperial mint both prevented excessive inflation and met the expanding needs of trade and industry, to which public works gave an added stimulus.

The public works were of a strictly utilitarian character, economic as well as military. In Rome Claudius completed two aqueducts begun in Caligula's reign and repaired a third. The administration of the water supply was reorganized to eliminate waste, graft, and neglect. In Asia Minor and in Numidia he had two new aqueducts constructed for irrigation purposes. He crisscrossed the western provinces with new highways—in Gaul from the Alps to the Channel, from the Italian Riviera to the Pyrenees, and from the Rhône to the Ocean; in Spain from Narbo to Cartagena, from Barcelona to Seville, thence westwards to Lisbon and to Salamanca and the Asturias of the northwest. Similar work was carried on in Britain, in Dalmatia, and along the Danube; in Thrace, Asia Minor, and Egypt.

Nor did Claudius neglect the development of waterways. A canal between the Rhine and the Meuse gave central Gaul access to the North Sea. In Italy, 30,000 men worked for eleven years on the huge task of draining the Fucine Lake in order to prevent floods, to

reclaim 150,000 acres of swamp land, and to make the Liris navigable.*

The most spectacular of all the Claudian projects was the development of Ostia as the port of Rome. Claudius created, at the mouth of the Tiber, a harbor deep and capacious enough to accommodate grain ships bound from Egypt, North Africa, and Sicily. The ships formerly docked at the deep-water port of Puteoli 138 miles away, and the grain had to be brought to Rome by road, a laborious and expensive haul. Though Ostia was the natural port of Rome, its harbor had become filled with the silt brought down by the Tiber so that seagoing ships had to stand outside and transfer their cargoes to lighters or barges, so that in stormy weather the risk of damage was great.

This project, undertaken by Claudius and completed by Nero, had been a dream of Caesar's and a subject of discussion for ninety years by engineers. Against the advice of his own engineers, Claudius ordered the dredging of a basin of some 200 acres, the construction of concrete breakwaters, a lighthouse, wharves, and unloading installations. Behind and beyond the docks there rose a city of warehouses, granaries, imperial administrative offices, commercial firms, banks, four-story apartment buildings of red or yellow brick, and many stores, restaurants, bakeries, and bars. Here congregated a polyglot population of 100,000 from every part of the world—sailors and shipowners, speculators and merchants, dock hands and craftsmen.

The development of the port of Ostia raised economic problems both difficult and unforeseen. Ships using the port had to leave empty. Rome was a consumer of the world's products, not a producer. Her exports were

* This project, first planned by Julius Caesar and often attempted later but without success, never became a reality till 1875.

insignificant, her imports immense—grain, fruits, fish, meats, hides, oil and wine; minerals of every sort, marble, lumber, glass, paper, dyes, clothing, jewelry; spices, ointments, and perfumes. No sooner had Claudius diverted shipping from Puteoli (the outlet of a rich exporting region of both agricultural and industrial products) than the shipowners complained of losing money because of the lack of return cargoes. To satisfy them and keep vital supplies moving into Rome, Claudius and his successors had to compensate them with special concessions, such as insurance against shipwreck, tax exemptions, the waiving of the succession law, and the grant of citizenship to those engaged for six years in the grain carrying service.

Foreign Policy and Imperial Defense

In foreign policy Claudius, like Tiberius, was a pupil of Augustus and followed Caesar's militaristic expansionism only when and where impelled by the requirements of imperial security and defense. He restored the provinces of Macedonia and Achaea to the senate, and in 46 annexed the turbulent kingdom of Thrace as an imperial province. Annexation of Thrace led to Roman intervention in Romania, in the Crimean peninsula, and everywhere north of the Black Sea as far east as the Don. Claudius made the Black Sea almost a Roman lake.

In the Middle East his policy was at once vigorous and cautious: he fomented internal discord and rivalry in Parthia, perennially Rome's most dangerous enemy. He re-established the Roman protectorate over Armenia, reinstating a friendly vassal king, and, on the death of Herod Agrippa I, annexed Judea as a Roman province. His chief objectives were peace and Roman control over the Eastern trade routes (the Red Sea, the Indian Ocean,

Ruins of an apartment house in Ostia built during the reign of Trajan. (Courtesy Fototeca, Unione Internazionale degli Istituti, Rome)

View of a Campanian harbor, from a wall painting (ca. 50 B.C.) at Stabiae. (Courtesy Anderson, Rome)

and the caravan route through Parthia to India and China).

Early in his reign Claudius had to suppress the revolt which Caligula had provoked in Mauretania by the murder of King Ptolemy. After crushing the revolt in two years of hard fighting, Claudius organized Mauretania into two imperial provinces, Mauretania Caesariensis in the east and Mauretania Tingitana (Tangier) in the northwest. Though the subjugation of Mauretania was a very important and difficult military achievement, it received less fanfare than the conquest of Britain.

The Conquest of Britain: 43

The reasons that impelled Claudius to resume the conquest of Britain, which Caesar and Augustus had renounced, evade certitude. One powerful motive was probably his need for military glory; another undoubtedly was the conviction that the enterprise would arouse strong national sentiment. He may have desired to protect Roman traders and to gain for Rome access to the island's reputed wealth in minerals, timber, cattle, and slaves. Nor were pretexts lacking. Claudius had received invitations to intervene from lesser British chiefs who feared the expansive power of the kingdom Cunobelinus (the Cymbeline of Shakespeare) had established in the southeast, with its capital at Camulodunum (Colchester). After Cunobelinus' death (ca. 40 A.D.), his son Caratacus, hostile to Rome, had extended the kingdom as far as the Wash and the Cotswolds and had stepped forward as the champion of Druidism (which Augustus and Tiberius had attempted to stamp out in Gaul because of its savage and inhuman rites) and as the undisputed leader of pan-Celtic nationalism in its resistance to Roman suzerainty. The existence of that strong British kingdom was a perpetual threat to Roman authority in Gaul.

In 43 A. Plautius landed an army of 50,000 men in Kent and, after defeating the Britons in a two-day battle on the Medway, advanced to the Thames to await the arrival of Claudius, who, taking command, quickly defeated Caratacus and took his capital, Camulodunum, where he accepted the submission of eleven British kings. In tribute of the swift victory, the senate voted Claudius a triumph and the proud name of Britannicus. After the celebration of his triumph in 44, his legates had within the next eight years created a province extending from the borders of Wales to the estuary of the Humber.

Colonization and Urbanization in the Provinces

Hand in hand with conquest and imperial expansion went colonization, urbanization, and extension of Roman citizenship in the provinces. This process, begun by Julius Caesar, continued with restraint by Augustus, slowed down by Tiberius, was resumed on a large scale by Claudius and continued by later emperors at an accelerated rate until the issue of the *Constitutio Antoniniana* (*see above*, p. 394) in 212 by Caracalla, who granted citizenship to all free inhabitants of the empire. Claudius founded a colony in 51 at Camulodunum (Colchester) in Britain, where he erected a temple to Roma and Augustus and established the imperial cult. In 50 he established a colony in Germany at Cologne (a settlement of the Ubii) and another at Trier (Augusta Trevirorum), which later became the capital of Roman Gaul. He founded at least four colonies in Mauretania and several in the Balkans (Apri in Thrace, Emona and Savaria in Pannonia, and Aequum in Dalmatia), and three colonies of veterans in the East. Most of these colonies served at once as military bastions in conquered territory and islands of Roman citizenship. The conversion of rural and tribal communities into organized municipalities (*municipia*) served similar purposes. In Mauretania he incorporated native tribesmen at their request at Volubilis, granting them not only Roman citizenship but many special privileges. He likewise incorporated the Anauni in the *municipium* of Tridentum (Trento) and granted Latin Rights (*ius Latii*) to many other mountain tribesmen in Noricum (the Tyrol), thus supplementing citizenship in one district with Latin Rights in another. In all this work of urbanization and Romanization, Claudius paid attention, as his numerous and prolix edicts and the extant inscriptions and papyri reveal, to the smallest administrative details and exhibited an

Ruins of Volubilis, Morocco. (Courtesy The French Embassy, New York)

amazing knowledge of local conditions. He was hardly the old fogy depicted by biased ancient writers.

The Death of Claudius: 54

The last days of Claudius were tragic. In 48, his wife, Messallina, after numerous and varied infidelities, finally got herself involved in an affair with a handsome young noble, Gaius Silius. Fearing a plot against the throne, Claudius had both of them executed. After pondering the physical attractions of three young ladies, Claudius, intolerant of an unmarried life (*caelibis vitae intolerans*), married his niece Agrippina, a woman of exorbitant ambition. Her adulteries were almost as flagrant as those of Messallina, but she put them to more practical use: power for herself and accession to the throne for Nero, her son by a previous marriage. In 50 she persuaded Claudius to adopt Nero as his son and heir to the exclusion of his own natural son, Britannicus, by Messallina. Three years later Nero married Octavia, Claudius' daughter. Agrippina could now face the future with considerable confidence and optimism.

Claudius died at 54 from an undetermined cause. The story that he died as a result of eating a bowl of poisoned mushrooms served him by Agrippina comes from a hostile source (her arch-enemy Pliny the Elder) and should therefore be accepted with reserve.

Nero

Nero, the last of the Julio-Claudians, was a Claudian by both birth and adoption. On his mother's side he was a great-great-grandson of Augustus and Marcus Antonius; on the side of his father, Cn. Domitius Ahenobarbus, an utterly detestable man (*omni parte vitae detestabilis*), whose family had for five centuries been conspicuous for wealth, arrogance, bloodthirstiness, and tumult. Nero, a strong, well-built boy of nearly seventeen, was fond of sports, poetry, music, and art. Until his accession he had been subject to the imperious will of the domineering Agrippina, who worked and schemed to secure him the throne.

The inauguration of Nero was a joyous occasion. A visit to the barracks of the Praetorians (each was promised 15,000 sesterces), a carefully prepared and well-delivered speech before the senate (in which he promised to follow the policies of Augustus and respect the prerogatives and powers of the senate, keeping for himself only the command of the armies), cheers, pledges of loyalty, and other obsequious effusions highlighted the first day of Nero's reign.

Nero was probably sincere in his desire to be a good emperor, to deserve the loyalty and affection of the people by relieving poverty and oppression, and to govern in collaboration with the senate. To help him in the task of government he had capable assistants and wise advisers—his mother Agrippina, Afranius Burrus, the efficient and dependable commander of the Guard, Pallas, the able and hard-working freedman treasurer, and his old tutor, the philosopher Lucius Annaeus Seneca, who wrote Nero's speeches, sounded out the feelings and wishes of the senate, and assumed many of the burdens of government.

The Quinquennium Neronis: 54–59

According to a reported statement by the later Emperor Trajan (98–117),* the first five years of Nero's reign—the so-called *quinquennium Neronis*—stood out as the best governed period of the principate. Heeding Seneca's sound advice, Nero applied the ideal of clemency extolled by the philosopher in his essay *De clementia* by putting an end to the infamous Star Chamber trials (*intra cubiculum principis*) which Claudius had instituted against senators. Besides respecting the privileges of the senate, Nero provided annuities to assist impoverished senatorial families. On the impetus of the smoothly functioning administrative machinery set up by Claudius, Nero's government maintained peace and prosperity within the empire, guarded its frontiers, kept piracy in check, and restrained the rapacity of tax collectors (*publicani*) and provincial governors by vigorous prosecution of extortion before the sen-

* Aurelius Victor, *De Caes.* 5.2: *quinquennium tamen tantus fuit, augenda urbe maxime, uti merito Traianus saepius testaretur procul differre cunctos principes Neronis quinquennio.* In spite of much argument to the contrary, to Victor's mind the *Quinquennium* referred to the first five, not the last five years of Nero's reign.

ate. Oppressive taxation was mitigated, and Nero himself even proposed (a measure dropped at the senate's insistence) the total abolition of all indirect taxes and customs duties in order to stimulate free trade throughout the empire. The regime evinced also a respectable record of military achievement. Two of the greatest generals of the century—Domitius Corbulo in the East and Suetonius Paullinus in Britain—added fresh laurels to Roman arms.

Yet the period was not devoid of violence, sensuality, and murder. Agrippina was the initiator of Nero's gradual declension towards tyranny and crime. Realizing his youth and immaturity, he had allowed her at first a dominant role in the government: she directed policy; she received embassies; she had her effigy engraved on imperial coins; she set about eliminating family rivals. Early in the reign she contrived the murder of M. Junius Silanus, great-grandson of Augustus and proconsul of Asia, hounded Nero's aunt, Domitia Lepida, to death, and had one of Claudius' freedmen ministers, Callistus, removed from office, and another, Narcissus, summarily executed. She would have committed other murders but for the intervention of Seneca and Burrus, who resented her domineering ways and resolved to thrust her out of the government. They began to undermine her influence by subtly suggesting to Nero that he was old enough to be his own master and make his own decisions.

Nero himself, as he grew older, began to rebel more and more against his mother's domination. He was irked especially by her hypocrisy, her nagging, and her constant reminders that he owed the throne to her. His growing resentment rendered easier Seneca's attempt to circumvent, if not block, that violent and imperious woman.

One day while walking through the palace Nero happened to see a girl of striking beauty. Her name was Acte, a Greek freedwoman and servant of his wife Octavia, whom he had never loved. He fell madly in love with Acte and decided to marry her. Seneca encouraged the love affair in the hope that it would drive a wedge between Nero and his mother and destroy the latter's influence in the government.

Agrippina was furious when she heard of Nero's intention of marrying an ex-slave girl. In a bitter flow of words, she accused him of ingratitude to her and of disgracing the imperial family by his acting and singing in public, his insufferable addiction to chariot racing, and his nightly escapades in the city, where he and a gang of teenage thugs prowled the streets accosting women, beating people up, and frequenting whorehouses and bars. Worst of all, he took it upon himself to dismiss Pallas, the secretary of the treasury, who was her steady supporter and secret paramour.

The feud between Nero and Agrippina became ever more open and savage. The dismissal of her favorite, Pallas, sent her into a cascade of rage. Flinging caution aside, she threatened to depose her ungrateful son and enthrone Britannicus, the natural son and rightful heir of the divine Claudius. She would appeal to the Praetorian Guard, she ranted, and call upon the army. That would teach the foul impostor and Seneca, the lying sneak, and that disgusting Burrus with the truncated hand (*trunca scilicet manu*) not to tangle with the daughter of Germanicus and great-granddaughter of Augustus.

Agrippina's tirades and wild threats aroused Nero's fear of plots against the throne. In 55 he contrived the death of Britannicus (perhaps by poison) in order to remove a possible rival. Four years later he compassed the death of Agrippina because he feared her incessant intrigues against him. Then in 62, his passion for Acte having abated, he divorced and exiled Octavia and married his mistress, the beautiful and seductive Poppaea Sabina.*

After the death of Burrus in 62, Nero acquired a new favorite in Ofonius Tigellinus, a former fish salesman and horse breeder. As head of the fire and police departments and commander of the Praetorian Guard, Tigellinus took a vicious delight in tracking down plots against the throne. His organization of informers, spies, and secret agents helped him to make the latter part of Nero's principate a veritable reign of terror.

* Nero had Octavia murdered later. Poppaea's role in both assassinations evades detection.

His zeal was too much even for Seneca, the apologist of Nero's earlier atrocities. Loaded with wealth and honors, Seneca retired from office. He was not destined to enjoy his retirement long.

The Great Fire of Rome: 64

In 64 there occurred a long period of hot dry weather. One sizzling night in July, a fire broke out in the slums at the east end of the Circus Maximus between the Palatine and Caelian hills. Fanned by a strong southeast wind, the flames leapt from house to house, from block to block, fed by the stores of dry wood and oil. The fire raged for nine days, turning more than half of Rome into a charred and blackened waste. Not only had acres of flimsy apartment houses and some of Rome's most venerated temples and shrines gone up in smoke, but Nero's own palace as well, with its priceless collection of books, manuscripts, and works of art.

Nero had been staying at the time at Antium (Anzio), about 35 miles from Rome. Aroused from sleep, he swiftly sped to the scene of the conflagration. Fearing neither the assassin's dagger nor the blast of the holocaust, he gave all possible aid to the crazed and helpless victims of the fire. After a vain attempt to check the progress of the flames, he converted Mars' Field and his private gardens into shelters for the homeless and hastened the transport of grain supplies from Ostia to feed the destitute. His indefatigable energy in the alleviation of suffering did not spare him from the malicious rumor that he had started the fire in order to acquire the glory of building a new and more beautiful Rome.

After the fire and removal of the debris Nero widened and straightened the streets and had pillared colonnades built on both sides of them to provide shade and lessen the danger of fire. The rebuilt sections of the city had many fountains and open squares. The new houses had to have their façades and first stories built of fire-proof stone and to be separated by alleys, with gardens in the rear provided with fire buckets and supplies of water.

No expense was spared in the rebuilding

The Donus Aurea, *or Golden House, of Nero, built after the fire of 64 A.D. (Courtesy Istituto Italiano di Cultura, New York)*

of Rome. Nero's new palace, the Golden House (*Domus Aurea*), probably rivaled in cost and splendor the great palace of Louis XIV at Versailles. The vestibule was lofty enough to accommodate Nero's colossal statue (120 feet high), and the hall, consisting of three pillared arcades, was almost a mile long. Together with colonnades, gardens, lakes, fields, and game parks it occupied an area of 120 acres between the Palatine and Esquiline hills.

Nero's Persecution of the Christians

According to Tacitus (*Annals* XV 44; written probably as late as 120, perhaps even 123), Nero cast about for scapegoats for the fire in order to avert suspicion from himself. He found them in the Christians, a "detestable sect, which owed its name to Chrestus, who, in the reign of Tiberius, suffered under Pontius Pilate. Suppressed for a while, this dangerous superstition, soon revived and spread not only in Judea but even in the city of Rome, the common cesspool into which everything hateful and abominable flows like a torrent from all parts of the world. When some of these depraved and profligate wretches were induced to confess their guilt, Nero had some of them torn apart by dogs, some nailed to crosses, and others burned alive."*

Some scholars have doubted, others even

* Most modern writers have accepted without question the view that Nero not only outlawed Christianity in a *senatus consultum* but persecuted its adherents. Some have even asserted that he charged them with arson in order to avert the wrath of the Roman populace from himself. That the Roman government, between the reigns of Nero and Nerva, made unrepentant adherence to the Christian faith a crime punishable by death is incontrovertible. A letter of the Younger Pliny (*Epp.* X. 96) to the Emperor Trajan and the latter's reply (ca. 112), Hadrian's rescript to Minicius Fundanus the proconsul of Asia in 122/3, unequivocal statements by Justin Martyr (ca. 100–166) and by Tertullian (ca. 160–ca. 230), and the *Acts of the Christian Martyrs* is sufficient confirmation. That Nero actually charged and convicted the Christians of incendiarism is another matter (Suetonius [*Nero* XVI 2] refers to the Neronian persecution without mention of the fire).

Sestertius of Nero (ca. 65 A.D.). This is perhaps the first representation of Annona, goddess of the grain supply (standing, holding horn of plenty). She is accompanied by Ceres, goddess of agriculture (holding grain in her right hand and torch in her left hand). An altar with a modius is between them, and the stern of a ship is seen in the background. In later coins, Annona appears alone. (Courtesy The American Numismatic Society, New York)

denied, the occurrence of a Neronian persecution of the Christians. They base their doubt, or denial, on the strange failure of contemporary writers—Seneca, Petronius, Juvenal, the Elder and Younger Pliny, Josephus, Martial, and others—to mention so monstrous an atrocity, if it actually occurred. No details of the Neronian persecution were remembered in the Christian tradition. The same scholars have also asserted that the famous Tacitean passage (the sole early evidence of a persecution) contains obscurities and contradictions as well as expressions unusual for Tacitus. They have also pointed out that this passage was unknown to or at least ignored by the later writers—Suetonius, Cassius Dio, and even the Christian writers Tertullian, Lactantius, and St. Augustine—all of whom were otherwise presumably familiar with the works of Tacitus.

According to these scholars, the first writer later than Tacitus known to have used the passage found in the *Annals* was Severus Sulpicius who, around 400, inserted into his *Sacred History* a passage similar in style and content to the Tacitean. The similarity of the two passages (Tacitean and Sulpician) neither proves the existence of the Tacitean in 400 nor excludes the possibility that the latter may have been an interpolation based on the one found in the *Sacred History*. Thus, it is asserted that a Neronian persecution of the Christians remains unproved and open to serious doubt.

The Reform of the Currency

The huge sums spent on the rebuilding of Rome and on Nero's Golden House soon exhausted the funds in the public treasury and rendered a depreciation of the currency imperative. Nero therefore carried out a currency reform and introduced a monetary system that remained essentially unchanged till the reign of Severus (193–211). He reduced the weight of the *aureus* by about ten per cent and the silver content of the *denarius* by a similar amount, thereby bringing both coins into a more stable relation with each other and with the new bronze coins he proposed to strike. The reform also brought the Roman coinage more closely in line with the Greek, thus promoting trade within the empire through the adoption of a more uniform imperial standard. The currency depreciation perhaps served another purpose: it tended to check the serious drain of gold and silver to India and southeast Asia (in payment for luxury imports such as spices and precious stones).

The chief disadvantage of the devaluation was that it forced prices up by about ten per cent and created hardships for people dependent on savings or fixed incomes. It finally compelled Nero to extend the grain dole, formerly limited to the plebs, to all destitute residents of Rome.

Plots against the Throne

Absorbed in the many activities of government, Nero finally became aware of the secret plots taking shape against his life and throne. A confused tangle of motives inspired them: some of the conspirators genuinely hoped for a restoration of the Republic; others hated Nero's despotism and resented his employment of Oriental freedmen in positions of power and influence. The most formidable attempt against the throne was the conspiracy of Gaius Calpurnius Piso in 65, which involved many knights as well as senators. Nero's reprisals were savage: among his numerous victims were leading members of the senate and three of the greatest literary figures of the century—the philosopher Seneca, the poet Lucan, and the novelist and satirist Petronius (*see* p. 332), who obediently cut open their own veins. Two of the most eminent of Nero's victims, though not actually involved in the conspiracy, were the famous general Corbulo and Thrasea Paetus, a Stoic renowned for his austere conduct and high moral principles and the champion of *dignitas* and *libertas,* the traditional virtues of the old Roman aristocracy.

Nero's Concert Tour of Greece: 66–67

Neither fire nor conspiracy nor the arduous tasks of government interrupted Nero's musical career.*

After elaborate preparations, Nero set out in the fall of 66 on a grand concert tour of Greece. He took with him many musicians, chorus singers, and a host of supernumeraries as well as officials, assistants, guardsmen, and soldiers. The tour was a personal triumph. He made numerous appearances as singer, tragic actor, or charioteer at Olympia, Corinth, Delphi, and many other places and came away as the winner of 1808 prizes and trophies. Pleased with the flattering reception extended him by the Greeks and their appreciation of his art, he proclaimed in 67 the liberation of Greece from the governor of Macedonia in words reminiscent of the speech of Titus Quinctius Flamininus in 196 B.C. (*see* p. 145).

Nero's Foreign Policy

The equal, if not the superior, of Tiberius and Claudius as an administrator and statesman, Nero maintained the peace and prosperity of the provinces; chose honest and able governors, holding them strictly to account; and guarded and extended the frontiers, sending good generals to command the

---

* He took his singing seriously and, as recent studies indicate, was probably considered a good singer and cithara player.

legions: Verginius Rufus to the Rhineland, Suetonius Paullinus to Britain, and to the East first Corbulo, then Vespasian.

Two danger spots remained: Armenia and Britain. Armenia, a problem since the days of Marcus Antonius, had engaged the attention of all Nero's predecessors. Rugged, mountainous, and subject to summer's heat or winter's cold, Armenia was hard to conquer, difficult to hold, and impossible to annex while Parthia remained strong and unsubdued. Neither Rome nor Parthia could allow the other to occupy it without loss of security and prestige. The only permanent solution of the Armenian problem, as Julius Caesar had foreseen, was the subjugation of Parthia.

Nero first came to grips with the Armenian problem early in his reign when Vologeses I, the young and aggressive king of Parthia, placed his brother, Tiridates IV, upon the Armenian throne. Nero sent out to the Middle East Cn. Domitius Corbulo, a strict disciplinarian and one of the ablest generals of the century. Corbulo's assignment was difficult and dangerous and, before he could move into Armenia, he had to train and drill the two new and undisciplined legions transferred to his command from the province of Syria. Vologeses made no move because he was occupied by revolts in the eastern part of his kingdom. When ready, Corbulo invaded Armenia, captured and burnt the capital city of Artaxata and occupied the second capital city of Tigranocerta before Vologeses was able to offer opposition. After driving out Tiridates, he placed Tigranes V, a Roman vassal, upon the Armenian throne. The brief period of peace and quiet in the Middle East which ensued offered Nero time to resume the conquest of Britain.

Military Operations in Britain: 60–61

To Britain Nero sent C. Suetonius Paullinus, another able general. In 60, after he had conquered the island of Mona (Anglesey), the main center of Druidism, a dangerous rebellion broke out behind his lines among the Iceni and Trinovantes, who then dwelt between the Thames and the Wash. After the death of their king, who had willed his territory to the Roman people, Roman procurators (acting on behalf of money lenders such as Seneca) confiscated farm lands and reduced the former owners to the level of serfs. They robbed the king's widow, Queen Boudicca (Boadicea), of her land, flogged her, and permitted the raping of her daughters. The outraged queen collected an army and captured the Roman colony of Camulodunum (Colchester). She destroyed the Roman legion sent against her and marched on London, where she caused the massacre of 70,000 Romans. Suetonius Paullinus defeated her army in battle by superior discipline and skill and stamped out the rebellion with ruthless efficiency. The vanquished Boadicea took her own life, and Britain thereafter remained quiet and peaceful, except for a few border raids.

Armenia Again: 61–63

Not so Armenia. After Corbulo had pulled out his army, Tigranes V attacked Media, a powerful Parthian vassal, and started a war he could not finish. Vologeses invaded Armenia in force. He badly mauled and compelled the surrender of a Roman army, which Nero had sent, at Corbulo's request, under the command of the incompetent and cowardly Caesennius Paetus. In 63 Corbulo took command, outmaneuvered and defeated Vologeses, and compelled Parthia to accept Roman supremacy. In return he allowed Tiridates IV to ascend the throne of Armenia (provided that he go to Rome and receive his crown at Nero's hands).

The coronation of Tiridates was a makeshift settlement, as Nero himself clearly saw. Since the permanent solution of the Armenian problem required annexation of the country and the conquest of Parthia itself, he revived Caesar's foreign policy. To soften up Parthia for conquest, he began surrounding her with a ring of vassal states. In the southwest he made Aden a strong fortress, occupied Zanzibar as a naval station, and made plans for the conquest of the Somaliland and of Ethiopia by an expedition up the Nile. In the northeast he established a naval patrol on the Black Sea, liberated the Crimea from Sarmatian domination, and made preparations for a campaign against southwestern Siberia north and east of the Caspian Sea.

His plans were cut short by the revolt of Vindex in 68.

The Revolt of Vindex: 68

Nero had planned to tour Asia Minor and Egypt also, but bad news compelled him to cancel the trip and return to Rome: C. Julius Vindex, the governor of one of the provinces of Gaul, had revolted and raised an army of 100,000 men. Vindex also had the support of Servius Sulpicius Galba, the governor of Nearer Spain, and of M. Salvius Otho, the governor of Lusitania (now Portugal). North Africa and Rome itself were also seething with revolt.

The rebellion received a sudden check when L. Verginius Rufus, the loyal and able governor of Upper Germany, led three legions into Gaul and overwhelmed the raw and undisciplined troops of Vindex at Vesontio (Besançon). The vanquished Vindex committed suicide. Even then Nero was unsafe. The victorious legions of Rufus revolted in their turn and proclaimed their commander emperor of Rome. Rufus rejected the acclamation and placed himself unreservedly at the disposition of the senate.

Fall of Nero: 68

The reasons for the opposition to and rebellion against Nero are not far to seek. He had antagonized the conservative upper class (equestrian as well as senatorial, from which all provincial governors, "imperial" as well as "senatorial," and even "procuratorial," high army officers, procurators, and other administrative officials, were still recruited), by his un-Roman attitudes and activities (as Agrippina pointed out), by his seizure and confiscation of large private estates in Italy and the provinces, especially in North Africa, by his many tyrannies and executions, and by his slow but steady declension towards an Oriental despotism in which he was the true, though perhaps unconscious, imitator of Caligula. Not only that, he had failed to win or hold the loyalty and affection of the legions (which was crucial). He had towards the end of his reign allowed the pay of the troops to fall into arrears, thereby seriously undermining their loyalty and enthusiasm. Furthermore, he had neglected them. Their *Imperator* they had never seen. They did not know him. Much better for him and the perpetuation of his reign had he gone to the Rhineland to see his soldiers rather than on his triumphal tour of Greece.

Meanwhile Galba had not been idle. He sent his agents to Rome to undermine the loyalty of the Praetorian Guard with the promise of 80,000 sesterces to each man. The guards succumbed to the bribe, deserted Nero, and declared for Galba. Soon the armies began to renounce their allegiance. The senate proclaimed Nero a public enemy. Deserted and condemned by all, he persuaded a faithful freedman to plunge a sword into his throat. Thus died Nero, the last of the Julio-Claudians.

Our sources—Tacitus, Suetonius, and Dio Cassius—may have correctly conveyed the feeling of the upper classes towards Nero, but not that of the common people of Rome, Italy, and the provinces. To the nobles he appeared a madman and a fiend. To the masses he was a benefactor and friend, and a champion in their struggle for survival. Never till his reign had they been so well fed or so royally entertained. *Panem et circenses!*

The public's adoration of Nero, and the flowers placed by unknown hands upon his tomb disturbed Galba and later emperors. Otho, Galba's successor, restored Nero's fallen statues and proudly took the name of "Nero"; Vitellius, who overthrew Otho, publicly praised Nero's name and even offered sacrifices to him. Years later the Emperor Domitian also revered his memory and executed some of his surviving foes.

Literature

The reign of Claudius and of Nero marks the beginning of a century of Latin literature traditionally known as the "Silver Age," a term which implies a decline from the excellence achieved in the "Golden Age" of Augustus. The period's main characteris-

tic is the achievement of the "pointed" style by the use of terse *sententiae,* apophthegms, antitheses, paradoxes, and the resort to various other artificial devices for the purpose of startling listeners at public recitations (*recitationes*). The rhetorical schools which dominated Roman education during the principate also tended to foster the affectations and insincerities of most "Silver Age" authors. Nevertheless, in the essays of Seneca, the satires of Petronius and Juvenal, the epigrams of Martial, and, above all, in the histories of Tacitus, the "Silver Age" reached heights of excellence unparalleled in the history of Roman literature.

Seneca

Seneca (ca. 4 B.C.–65 A.D.), the most noted literary figure of the Julio-Claudian principate, was born at Corduba, Spain, and came to Rome while still a boy. There he studied rhetoric and philosophy, and became a lawyer. An astute politician, he made millions from banking and viticulture. He was also one of Rome's most notable Stoic philosophers and a copious and versatile writer. His extant works are numerous and varied: a spiteful burlesque on Claudius (*Apocolocyntosis*); a long treatise on natural science (*Quaestiones Naturales*) nine tragedies, typically Euripidean in plot and theme; ten essays (misnamed *Dialogi*), containing a full exposition of Stoic philosophy, such as *De Ira* (*On Anger*), *De Vita Beata* (*On the Happy Life*), and *De Otio* (*On Leisure*); prose treatises (*De Clementia* and *De Beneficiis*); and one hundred and twenty-four *Moral Epistles* (*Epistulae Morales*), brilliant exponents of a Stoic philosophy at once spiritual and humane.

Lucan

Lucan (A.D. 39–65) was Seneca's nephew. He, too, was born in Corduba, Spain, brought to Rome in infancy, and educated in a rhetorical school. His sole extant work is the *De Bello Civili* (often called *Pharsalia*), a violent and pessimistic epic poem in ten books, which narrates the war between Caesar and Pompey. It displays a strong Republican bias and a violent hostility towards Caesar. Despite its irrelevant digressions and tiresome repetitions, it is a remarkable poem because of its violence and sincerity. Suspected of complicity in Piso's conspiracy against Nero, Lucan committed suicide.

Petronius

Another of Nero's literary vicitims in 66 was the novelist and satirist Petronius, whom Tacitus mentions as the "arbiter of social graces" (*elegantiae arbiter*) at Nero's dissolute court. His *Satyricon* is frequently described as a picaresque novel, probably in sixteen books, of which are extant only fragments of the last two. Written in the form of the Menippean satire with prose interspersed with verse, they describe the adventure of three depraved young freedmen in the taverns and brothels in the port towns of southern Italy. The best-known episode is the *Cena Trimalchionis,* an uproariously funny caricature of a dinner-party given by the wealthy freedman Trimalchio, who, like his vulgar freedmen guests, gets drunk, forgets his recently acquired elegance, and brags about his wealth and enormous estates, or tells smutty jokes.

Martial

Another satirist who began to write during Nero's reign (though most of his writing belongs to the reign of Domitian) was the epigrammatist Martial (ca. 40–104). Born at Bibilis near the Tagus in Spain, he came to Rome in 64 and began addressing epigrams (sharp little poems, often indecent) to rich people for his dinner. His twelve books of epigrams (1561), attack, with shrewd insight, the shams and vices of people in all walks of life. In one of his letters (*Epistles* 3:21) Pliny described Martial as a man of wit, sharp and biting, who mixed salt with honey, and especially candor.

Columella

Another writer of that period was Columella, born at Gades (Cadiz). Columella wrote (ca. 50) twelve books (the tenth is in hexameters), *De Re Rustica,* the classic work on Roman agriculture. From personal knowledge (he owned estates in Italy at Ardea, Carseoli, Alba, and Caere), he described the various aspects of farming, the breeding and care of livestock, and the duties of the farm manager.

Pliny the Elder

Pliny the Elder (ca. 23–79 A.D.) also discussed farming occasionally in his huge, unscientific *Natural History* (in 37 books), the sole survivor of 160 volumes on such subjects as oratory, marksmanship, and Rome's wars in Germany. In his *Natural History* he discusses an amazing array of topics: geography, anthropology, zoology, botany, and mineralogy. This work, a mine of misinformation and superstition, and Seneca's *Quaestiones Naturales* were the chief sources of scientific knowledge during the Middle Ages.

RISE AND FALL OF THE

THE YEAR FOLLOWING THE DEATH OF NERO WAS PROBABLY ONE of the most memorable in the history of the Roman people. It marked not only the end of the Julio-Claudian line of emperors but the rise of the Flavian dynasty, though the three immediate successors of Nero—Galba, Otho, and Vitellius—belonged to neither family. The change of dynasty was not the sole or the most important change in that terrible year of anarchy and civil war during which large Roman armies repeatedly fought each other and four emperors died by the sword. Nor did its significance lie wholly in the discovery that emperors could be created elsewhere than in Rome.*

The significance lay rather in the reinforcement and culmina-

---

* The Spanish legions had declared their general, Galba, emperor of Rome.

FLAVIAN DYNASTY

tion of trends and tendencies which had
been slowly evolving since the time of
Caesar and Augustus: the progressive decay
of the old senatorial aristocracy; the growing
political power of the armies stationed on the
frontiers of the Rhine, the Danube, and the
Euphrates; the centralization of executive
power in the imperial bureaucracy; the wider
participation of Italy and the provinces in the
government and administration of the empire; and the slow evolution of a truly integrated world state. Of the new emperors
Galba alone could boast of an ancient Roman
pedigree, while Otho, Vitellius, and Ves-

pasian were all of Italian family and belonged
to the newly rising aristocracy of office.

Galba

Galba, the first to succeed Nero,
reigned for only a few months. Though of an
old senatorial family, he had little talent for
practical politics, and since he was already in
his early seventies when he came to the
throne, he was already too old to learn the
half-conscious secrets of empire (*arcana imperii*). Before fully consolidating his power,
he attempted two contradictory and impos-

sible things: balancing the budget and winning the support of the armies. He alienated the Roman populace by cutting down the grain dole, the Praetorian Guard by his failure to pay the promised donatives, and the armies on the Rhine, already hostile and sullen, by his unwise act of recalling their beloved commander, Verginius Rufus, and replacing him with the elderly and unpopular Hordeonius Flaccus. The two armies mutinied and proclaimed one of their commanders, Aulus Vitellius, emperor of Rome.

Even then Galba might have saved his life and throne by adopting Verginius Rufus as heir and co-regent. He chose instead the aristocratic L. Calpurnius Piso Licinianus, who was very acceptable to the senate, but totally devoid of popularity or of political and military experience, and unknown to the armies. Galba's choice turned a former friend and supporter, Marcus Salvius Otho, into a jealous and dangerous enemy who hurried off to the camp of the praetorians and by liberal promises of money persuaded them to proclaim him emperor. They promptly murdered Galba and Piso.

Otho

Although Otho, the next emperor, had the support of the Praetorian Guard and the Roman populace and soon won recognition by the senate, the armies on the Rhine, who had already declared for Vitellius, marched against him. Otho blocked the Alpine passes against them, but he was too late. Though he proved himself a fairly good strategist by defeating part of their forces at Bedriacum after a daring encircling movement, the Danubian legions on whom he chiefly depended had not all arrived on time to help him in his premature attack on superior Vitellian forces based at Cremona. Defeated after a long, hard-fought battle, he lost his nerve and terminated his short reign by suicide.

Vitellius

The victor of Cremona was one of the most inept and helpless emperors ever to disgrace the Roman throne. During his brief reign (seven months) he spent 900,-000,000 sesterces on dinners alone. Having thus emptied the treasury, he was unable to pay his troops their promised rewards, and allowed them to make good their loss by looting and plundering Italy. Yet his reign was not entirely without significance. He was the first of Roman emperors since Tiberius not to owe elevation to the throne wholly or in part to the Praetorian Guard, whose monopoly of emperor making had now been definitely broken.

One emperor was already created by the armies of the Rhine. Now those stationed in the East were about to create another, Titus Flavius Vespasian, whom Nero had in 66 sent to Judea to suppress an uprising of the Jews. Leaving his son Titus in charge of the siege of Jerusalem, Vespasian himself hastened to Egypt in order to prevent the shipment of grain supplies to Rome, while his adjutant, C. Licinius Mucianus, the governor of Syria, marched with 20,000 men through Asia Minor to invade Italy.

Meanwhile the armies of the Danube had also declared for Vespasian and an army of 50,000 men was already on the march to the Italian frontier. They seized the Alpine passes, which Vitellius had neglected to block, and without waiting for the arrival of Mucianus from Asia Minor met and routed the Vitellian forces in a bloody night battle near Cremona. They stormed the city, sacked and burnt it and massacred its inhabitants. After that frightful outrage, they marched on Rome, where Vitellius had already begun to negotiate terms of abdication with Vespasian's elder brother Flavius Sabinus, Prefect of the City by Otho's appointment.

Vitellius' attempt to abdicate was most unacceptable to his own soldiers. They rioted, murdered Sabinus, burned down the Temple of Jupiter, and forced Vitellius to renounce his intended abdication. Whereupon the Danubian army now within sight of the city broke in, annihilated the rioting troops, killed Vitellius, and proceeded to repeat in Rome the atrocities they had committed at Cremona. Fortunately, the army of Mucianus had arrived on time to restore order and prepare for the coming of Vespasian, now proclaimed emperor by the senate.

Vespasian: 69–79

The accession of Vespasian ended the nightmare of 69 with its civil wars, bloodlettings, and pillage. A new day of peace and tranquillity was dawning almost as glorious and as welcome to the Roman people as the day of the Augustan victory at Actium which had brought to an end the strife, anarchy, and civil wars of the dying Republic. Vespasian, of course, lacked the glamor and prestige of Augustus, nor was his reign quite as memorable. It did, nevertheless, usher in a new phase in the history of the Roman Empire and many of the policies typical of the second century.

Among the many problems Vespasian had to solve were the following: the restoration of peace and the suppression of rebellions in Germany, Gaul, and Judea; the reform of the army; imperial defense and provincial administration; the centralization of government; the expansion of the civil service; the balancing of the budget and the rehabilitation of imperial finances; and, finally, the regulation of the succession to the throne.

Titus Flavius Vespasianus, sprung from an ordinary, hard-working, middle-class family of Etruscan descent, was born on a farm in 9 A.D. in a small hamlet near the hilltop town of Reate in the Sabine country. His grandfather had been an auctioneer, his father an honest and upright tax collector in Asia Minor and, after his retirement, a money lender in Switzerland. He later returned to Italy, married into a family slightly above his own social station, and settled down on a medium-sized farm near Reate.

Young Vespasian had received a fair education and was able to make jokes not only in Latin but even in Greek, some rather corny and at times slightly obscene. He was also good at arithmetic, and his unusual understanding of finances brought him to the notice of Narcissus, the freedman finance minister of Claudius. Claudius later procured for him several important military commands in Germany and in Britain, where he captured twenty towns and conquered the Isle of Wight. Under Nero he became governor of Africa Proconsularis and later the commander of the legions ordered to suppress the Jewish revolt in Palestine.

A marble lifesize bust of Vespasian (ca. 75 A.D.), from the Museo delle Terme. (Courtesy German Archeological Institute)

Coming to the throne in 69 at the age of sixty, bald, wrinkled, and tough, he had behind him much administrative and military experience. He knew the needs of the empire thoroughly for he had been, in one capacity or another, in Thrace, Spain, Gaul, Germany, Britain, Africa, Syria, and Egypt. A rugged, hard-bitten old soldier, he had the respect of the armies and could command their loyalty and obedience. They accepted his reforms without murmur or dissent. He was a tireless worker and, although he often took his time making up his mind on a specific course of action, he carried out his decisions with determination and inflexibility. Knowing from past personal experience the value of money, he gave Rome for the first time in many years a good business government and took endless pains in balancing the budget. Such was the man who rescued Rome from the brink of financial and political disaster and made possible more than a century of peace and prosperity.

The Restoration of Peace

Most urgent was the task of breaking the rebellions in Germany, Gaul, and Judea. Julius Civilis, a German tribal chieftain, had served in the Roman army and was thoroughly acquainted with Roman methods of warfare. Towards the close of the reign of Vitellius, he persuaded his tribe, the Batavi, who supplied eight cohorts of auxiliary troops to the Roman army of the lower Rhine as well as some legions, to rebel in support of Vespasian. Then, throwing off all pretense of allegiance to Rome, he proclaimed the national independence of Germany and prevailed upon other German tribes on both sides of the Rhine and the German nationals serving in the Roman army to join him in creating a German national state.

Following his example, the Celtic tribes in Belgium and northeastern Gaul—the Nervii, the Tungri, and most especially the Treveri and the Lingones—also rose in revolt and similarly attempted to establish a Gallic national state with capital at Trèves. The Celtic uprising failed because the Sequani and most of the other Gallic tribes, now more or less Romanized, refused to break away from Rome.

Both the German and the Celtic national movements collapsed in the spring of 70 when there arrived in the Rhineland strong Roman reinforcements under the command of the able Q. Petilius Cerialis, who subdued the Treveri and Lingones and forced the Batavi to submit to Rome.

Meanwhile, in the Middle East, Titus, Vespasian's eldest son, had stormed and captured Jerusalem. He slew thousands of Jews and sold many more into slavery. A relief on the Arch of Titus erected by Domitian in the Roman Forum to commemorate the capture and destruction of Jerusalem, shows a triumphal procession bearing the seven-branched candlestick, the table of the shew bread, and other spoils taken from the Temple.

Reform of the Army

The part played by the provincial armies in the havoc of 69 had clearly indicated to Vespasian the urgent need for a reform of the army. First he struck from the Roman

A relief from the Triumphal Arch of Titus (81 A.D.), showing the spoils from Jerusalem. (Courtesy Fratelli Alinari, Florence)

The Arch of Titus in Rome, commemorating the capture of Jerusalem. (Courtesy Fratelli Alinari, Florence)

army lists the legions that had supported the German and Celtic national movements just suppressed. Next he stopped the practice of recruiting some of the legionary and most of the auxiliary troops from the frontier regions in which they served, where they were apt to sympathize with the national aspirations of their own people. To counteract such nationalistic tendencies he either formed new auxiliary units of mixed tribal and national origin—Spanish, Gallic, Dalmatian, Danubian, Anatolian, and African—or transferred units to frontiers far removed from their homeland and under the command of Italian officers.

As Rostovtzeff has shown, Vespasian departed radically from the policy first initiated by Marius of recruiting the legions from the "unruly, discontented, and highly inflammable elements" of the Roman and Italian proletariat. He extended legionary recruitment from Italy to the more cultured and educated youth of Gaul and Spain, where military academies for the training of future officers (*collegia iuvenum*) became ever more common. Thus Vespasian's military reforms not only made the army more truly the servant and defender of the empire but went hand in

hand with his broader policy of Romanizing and urbanizing the provinces.

Provincial Policy

Surpassing even Sertorius, Caesar, Augustus, Tiberius, and Claudius, Vespasian inaugurated a new age of municipalization in the Roman world that lasted until about 260. Completing the work of former centuries, he made Spain an integral part of the new world state by extending Latin Rights to about three hundred and fifty Spanish cities and towns. Even Dalmatia began in his reign to assume an aspect of urbanization and municipalization never before known. The Danubian provinces were the last regions in the Roman world to receive Roman Citizen colonies (*coloniae deductae*) and, during Vespasian's reign, benefited from a policy of colonization inaugurated long before in the historic year of 338 B.C. (*see* p. 104f).

Vespasian did more to make the Western provinces full partners in the government and administration of the empire than to use them as recruiting grounds or to grant Roman citizenship to office-holders in the newly chartered *municipia*. He went beyond Claudius or any of his predecessors in employing the local aristocracy of Gaul and Spain in imperial administration and in his expanded civil service. He used his powers as censor to add numerous members of the municipal aristocracy of southern Gaul and of Baetica in southwestern Spain to the rolls of the Roman senate, whose ranks had become depleted by the persecution of former emperors and by the recent civil war of 69. By utilizing the talents and services of the Gallic and Spanish provincials, Vespasian had given them a stake in the military defense of the empire and in the maintenance of peace, order, and tranquillity in the West.

Vespasian greatly strengthened the military defenses of the northern frontiers by restoring the number of legions serving along the Rhine to eight and by his creation of two new military provinces in Upper and Lower Germany, both entirely separate from the administration of the Gallic provinces. Along the Danubian frontier he built numerous military roads and new stone fortresses, at Günsburg, for example, at Vindobona (now Vienna) and at Carnuntum between what are now Vienna and Budapest. More important still, he wiped out that dangerous salient in the defense line in southwest Germany and Switzerland at the headwaters of the Rhine and the Danube by the annexation of a triangle of land called the *Agri Decumates* (now largely occupied by the Black Forest).

Vespasian sent three men of great renown to resume the conquest of Britain, which Claudius and Nero had left unfinished. The first was Petilius Cerealis (71–74), who had vanquished Civilis in Germany. Advancing from his headquarters at Lincoln, Petilius invaded Yorkshire and Lancashire, subduing all the tribes living between the Humber and the Tyne. It was he who probably founded York (Eboracum) and made it the headquarters of all future military operations in Britain. The successor of Cerealis was Julius Frontinus (74–77/8), who wrote a great book, still extant, on military science and tactics. He invaded the mountainous districts of Wales, built forts along the Usk and the Severn and established a large military camp at Chester (Deva) which existed for centuries.

The best known of all the three great governors of Britain was Cn. Julius Agricola (77/8–84), about whom his own son-in-law, Tacitus, wrote a famous biography, the *Agricola*. On completing the conquest of Wales begun by Frontinus, he advanced north and secured the ground already won by a chain of forts between the Solway and the Tyne. Between 81 and 83 he invaded Scotland, where he built another chain of forts between the Firth of Forth and the Clyde, as well as several military roads. Domitian recalled him from Britain, just as he was planning an invasion of Ireland, for the very good reason that Rome needed all the troops she could spare to beat off a threatened invasion of the Danube Valley (*see* p. 346).

The Middle East

In the Middle East, which he knew well from firsthand experience, Vespasian attempted with the limited means at his disposal to remedy some of the fundamental weaknesses in the defensive arrangements of his predecessors. The chief defects in the Eastern defense system had been primarily the lack of natural boundaries; a long exposed frontier of some three hundred miles stretching from Syria to the Black Sea; the attempt to contain the expansionism of Parthia by placing Roman puppets on the throne of Greater Armenia and by maintaining a chain of vassal kingdoms to protect that long frontier extending from the Lebanon to the Black Sea; the absence of any legionary troops or camps to guard the easy crossings of the Middle and Upper Euphrates at Zeugma, Samosata, or Melitene; and, finally, the total dependence for Middle Eastern defense upon the slow-moving and poorly disciplined legions based in the distant province of Syria.

To rectify some of the dangerous weaknesses of Rome's position in the Middle East, Vespasian attempted to maintain peaceful relations with Parthia, even to the extent of resigning control, direct or nominal, over the kingdom of Greater Armenia. His least friendly act towards the Parthians was his refusal to cooperate with them in repelling the Alani, a Sarmatian tribe living beyond the Caucasus, who had overrun Media Atropatene and Greater Armenia and were then a threat to the very existence of the Parthian state. Instead he unilaterally occupied the Darial Pass and in 75 built a fortress near Tiflis in what is now the Caucasus province of the Soviet Union.

Some of his other measures were even less pleasing to the Parthian king. First, he strengthened Roman control over the great caravan city of Palmyra and made Judea a separate procuratorial province with one full legion stationed at Jerusalem. He extended the province of Syria from the northern edge of the Lebanon to the upper reaches of the Middle Euphrates by the annexation of the kingdom of Commagene, whose king he deposed and further north created a huge province in Anatolia by adding Cappadocia and Lesser Armenia to the former province of Galatia. There he stationed two legions, one to guard the vital Euphrates crossing at Melitene, the other the important road junction of Satala, whence roads led to Trebizond and to other naval bases on the Black Sea. Thus Vespasian, except at Zeugma and Samosata, now legionary strongholds, diminished the responsibility of Syria for the Roman defense of the Middle East against Parthian attempts to cross the Euphrates.

Vespasian's Relations with the Senate

Vespasian, like Augustus, Tiberius, and Claudius before him, and the so-called "good" emperors after him, treated the senate with the utmost deference and respect, even extending financial assistance to impoverished but deserving members of ancient and illustrious lineage. Yet he did not treat the senate as an equal partner in the government of the empire. Though the senate remained a sounding board of upper-class Roman and Italian opinion and therefore exerted a powerful influence upon the character of even the most autocratic imperial regime, it had nevertheless since Tiberius been steadily declining as an effective organ of the government. The extent of its decline was marked in 73, when Vespasian, following the example of Claudius, assumed the censorship which gave him the power to remove objectionable and recalcitrant senators and replace them with

new men from Italy and the Western provinces, who would co-operate and obey. The new men were usually of demonstrated ability and staunch supporters of the regime.

The Expansion of the Civil Service

The weakening of the senate resulted in a steady concentration of power and function in the imperial executive and in the expansion of the civil service, whose value as the sole means of preserving continuity of administration under rapidly changing emperors came to light more clearly than ever before in 69.

In his selection of civil service officials Vespasian made two important innovations: he replaced freedmen, who under Claudius had held some of the highest positions, with equestrians or knights; and appointed more and more Italians and provincials. The reasons for these innovations are clear: the knights usually had considerable business and administrative experience and, having private sources of income, were naturally less tempted than freedmen to embezzle public funds. The provincials brought with them a knowledge of local conditions that must have been most useful in the administration of a highly diversified empire.

Financial Administration

Vespasian's greatest claims to fame was his success in handling financial problems—balancing the budget and restoring the public finances, which had been thrown into chaos by Nero's extravagance and the civil wars of 69. Besides personal frugality, native shrewdness, financial experience, and an unusual ability to drive hard bargains, Vespasian had a firm control over the armies so that he did not need to buy their loyalty or obedience by large donatives. Nor would he tolerate graft or embezzlement of public funds by government officials. Also, he ruthlessly imposed new and heavier taxes on the provinces and drastically cut down public expenditures.

Using his powers as censor, Vespasian had a careful census taken of the financial resources of the empire. He discovered that the provinces after a century of peace and pros-

Despite a reputation for meanness, Vespasian spent money freely on imperial defense, on roads, bridges, and fortifications in the provinces, on public buildings in Rome, and on education. After repairing the damage wrought in Italy by the civil war of 69, he commemorated the end of the Jewish War by beginning construction in Rome of the Forum that bears his name with the Temple of Peace in the center, the Arch of Titus, and the gigantic *Amphitheatrum Flavium* or Colosseum† a name most fitting for a structure with a seating capacity of 50,000 spectators and built of travertine stone faced with stucco. Though used as a quarry by generations of Renaissance architects, the Colosseum of the Flavians still stands as a symbol of the might and majesty of Imperial Rome and as one of the great man-wrought wonders of the world. Another great architectural achievement of the reign was the completion in 71 of a new temple to Capitoline Jupiter.

As an encouragement to literature and education, Vespasian liberally subsidized poets and prose writers. From public funds he endowed schools and established a chair of literature and rhetoric, of which M. Fabius Quintilianus, the celebrated Spanish rhetorician, was the first incumbent (*see* p. 370).

The Opposition to Vespasian

Despite his conspicuous achievements and services to the empire, Vespasian never fully escaped the opposition of Republican-minded senators and of the Stoic and Cynic

perity were able to pay much more tribute than formerly exacted from them. He assigned certain "free" cities and islands previously immune from taxation, such as Rhodes, Samos, and Byzantium, to provinces and forced them to pay taxes. He restored to the senate the province of Greece, to which Nero had granted freedom and immunity from taxes, and took back under imperial control the richer provinces of Sardinia and Corsica. He asserted the government's claim to land seized surreptitiously by private owners or occupied illegally by squatters and took back, on behalf of the *fiscus,* many estates given by former emperors to their friends and reorganized for revenue purposes the other imperial estates especially those containing mines, quarries, fisheries, and forests. In Spain, for example, he revised and codified the leasing of mining properties in accordance with principles long ago worked out by the Hellenistic monarchs and perhaps put into practice by the Elder Cato (p. 156). In short, no source of revenue, however unorthodox or unsavory (such as a tax on public latrines*) was beneath Vespasian's notice.

* When his own son Titus squeamishly objected to the latrine tax, he is said to have offered him a coin to smell and asked if it stank of urine. To this day public *pissotières* in Paris go by the name of *vespasiennes,* in Rome by that of *vespasiani.*

† The Colosseum owes its name, not to its own size, but to the size (125 feet high) of the statue of Nero which stands at the entrance. It was placed there by the Emperor Hadrian, who removed it from the court of the Golden House.

The Amphitheatrum Flavium or Colosseum (ca. 80 A.D.). (Courtesy Fotocielo, Rome)

philosophers. Many senators objected to his numerous consulships, by which he sought to enhance the nobility of his family, to his assumption of the censorship, his practice of admitting Italians and provincials into the senate, and his ill-concealed intention of founding a new dynasty by handing down the office of princeps to members of his own family. The senatorial opposition was more vocal than dangerous and Vespasian paid little attention to it. Far more irritating were the attacks of the Stoic and especially of the Cynic philosophers, who finally nettled him into ordering their expulsion from Rome.

Vespasian's Death: 79

In the spring of 79, after a decade of hard and continuous work, Vespasian died and the hour of death did not deprive him of his sense of humor. As he lay dying he muttered, "Dear me, I think I'm becoming a god!"

Before his death Vespasian believed he had settled the perennial problem of the succession to the throne. He had carefully prepared his son Titus to succeed him by giving him army commands, the proconsular *imperium* and tribunician power, by sharing the censorship with him for one year and the consulate for seven. He had also appointed him sole prefect of the Praetorian Guard.

Titus: 79–81

After Vespasian's death, the senate at once conferred upon Titus the usual honors and titles of the principate, though not without some qualms and misgivings. Titus

The Amphitheater at Pompeii (80 B.C.), the oldest surviving amphitheater in Italy. (Courtesy Istituto Italiano di Cultura, New York)

was handsome, charming, genial, and generous enough, but his moral conduct had reportedly not been of the best. He had associated rather freely with the wilder elements of Roman aristocratic society and a love affair with Julia Berenice, a sister of the Jewish king, Herod Agrippa II, revived memories of Antony and Cleopatra.

Yet once seated on the throne, Titus became the ideal princeps, eager to promote the welfare of his subjects and much beloved by the people. He recalled the philosophers exiled by his father and halted all treason trials. He rewarded informers with public flogging and enslavement or exile to unhealthy islands. He sent away his former mistress, Queen Berenice, to avoid giving offense to the senate. He entertained the people with splendid games and shows to the amazement and delight of the Roman populace. He celebrated the dedication of the almost completed Colosseum by holding a festival lasting a hundred days and commemorated the opening of the Baths of Titus with elaborate gladiatorial contests.

Three catastrophes marred that brief but brilliant reign. In August of 79 Vesuvius, after centuries of quiescence (except for a severe earthquake in 63) suddenly burst forth into violent eruption. The ground quaked and heaved and the light was blotted from the sky, tons of smoking pumice and volcanic ash rained down upon and buried the two Campanian cities of Pompeii and Herculaneum. Next, a plague, like none ever seen before, descended upon Campania. In Rome another great fire broke out, raged for three days, gutted the Capitol, the Pantheon of Agrippa, the newly built Temple of Capitoline Jupiter, and thousands of private homes. These disasters, occurring as they did in rapid succession, put to the severest test the energy and philanthropy of Titus.

In September of 81, after a reign of twenty-six months, Titus died at his father's Sabine home at the age of 42. The Roman people mourned the death of their beloved ruler, and the senate showered him with posthumous praises and honors. Deification followed.

Domitian: 81–96

Leaving his brother's deathbed, Domitian rode in haste to Rome. He went to the barracks of the Praetorian Guard to be acclaimed as emperor. The armies acquiesced, the senate approved. Neither had much choice for the son of Vespasian and brother of Titus had no rival claimants to the throne. It became his, not through any special education or previous military or administrative experience, but by accident of birth. Under Vespasian and Titus he had been pushed, almost like Claudius, into the background. Rejected, neglected, ignored, he consoled himself by writing Greek verse and studying the *Acta* or *Deeds* of Tiberius, whose reserve, grimness, and austerity he much admired and later imitated.

Soon after taking office, Domitian incurred the senate's displeasure and hostility, which his autocratic behavior did little to soften or assuage. To appear before them in the regalia of a triumphant general was an affront to their dignity* and his seventeen consulships and his exercise of the censorship for life (*censor perpetuus*) not only defied all tradition but revealed his intention of establishing an absolute dictatorship. Worse still, he outdid even Caligula and Nero by permitting and encouraging poets, courtiers, and even civil servants to address him as Lord and God (*Dominus et Deus*).

He trampled underfoot the ancient prerogatives of the senate by elevating knights to positions of power formerly reserved to senators. He appointed knights to his judicial *consilium* to sit in judgment on senators and even named a knight proconsul of the senatorial province of Asia. Acts such as these were more intolerable than his autocracy and his impious pretentions to divinity. No wonder, after his death, the senate damned his memory and ordered the removal of his statues from public places.

* His triumphal robes marked him as an *Imperator* with power to command. In non-military attire he would have been a *princeps* seeking advice.

Perhaps Domitian owed his reputation for despotism and tyranny not so much to the fact that he was essentially an evil man or a bad emperor as to his failure in public relations. Had he been a shrewder politician and more vocally dedicated to *Libertas, Mos Maiorum,* or Roman ideals, with a few Ciceronian platitudes thrown in, he might easily have won over the senate without loss of real or actual power. He might even have saved his memory from the venom-dipped pens of Tacitus and the Younger Pliny.

Domitian as an Administrator

As an administrator Domitian had a long and respectable record of achievement. He kept the populace happy, well fed, and amused. Three times he distributed among them largesses (*congiaria*) amounting to a total of 225 denarii a head. For their amusement he organized splendid spectacles—wild beast hunts, mimic sea and land battles, gladiatorial contests in the Colosseum and chariot races in the Circus Maximus. He built a Stadium and an Odeum in Mars' Field to encourage competitions in the Greek manner not only in sports but in literature. He completed the Colosseum and the Arch and Baths of Titus and restored the Pantheon and Baths of Agrippa and the fire-gutted temples of Serapis and Isis (in front of which he placed imported Egyptian obelisks). He erected a beautiful new temple to the deified Vespasian, a huge temple to Jupiter the Guardian (*Juppiter Custos*) and, most magnificent of all, a temple to Jupiter Optimus Maximus on the Capitol, with columns of Pentelic marble, gold-plated doors, and roof tiles overlaid with gold leaf. Not neglecting himself, he built a grand imperial palace on the Palatine and a huge mansion on Mount Alba overlooking the placid waters of the Alban Lake.

In Italy he constructed a road from Sinuessa to Cumae, and established in Britain, as well as along the Rhine and Danube, numerous fortresses and garrison camps. He raised the pay of legionary soldiers from 300 to 400 denarii per annum, and also fought, between 81 and 93, several costly wars.

Where he got the money for all this is a mystery. He apparently never tapped new sources of revenue nor accepted legacies from testators having five or more children. He canceled debts owing to the state for more than five years and, unlike Vespasian, gave clear title to occupiers of public land in Italy. Unlike Nero, he never debased the coinage. To explain how he was able to hand on to his successors a fairly full treasury, it must be assumed that he had his father's financial ability, and was an efficient administrator and a strict collector of provincial taxes. In addition he probably raked into the *fiscus*, now reorganized and centralized, the proceeds of considerable property confiscated from persons condemned for treason against the state, of whom there were probably not a few in the latter part of his reign, as we shall later see.

The Rebellion of Saturninus: 89

Treason trials occurred more frequently after the rebellion of L. Antonius Saturninus, the governor of Upper Germany and commander of two legions wintering in the double camp at Moguntiacum (Mainz). On January 1, 89 he seized the army savings and payroll and used it to bribe his legions to proclaim him emperor and the Chatti, a strong German tribe dwelling east of the middle Rhine, to invade Roman territory. To crush that revolt Domitian at once sped north with his Praetorian Guard, having ordered Trajan (the future emperor) to bring up a legion from Spain. Both got there too late for the battle. L. Appius Maximus Norbanus, the loyal governor of Lower Germany, aided by a sudden thaw which broke up the ice over the Rhine and prevented the Chatti from crossing to help the rebels, suppressed the rebellion and killed Saturninus. Nevertheless Domitian did not slacken the pace of his march to the Rhine.

After his arrival, Domitian ruthlessly punished the officers and accomplices of Saturninus and expanded the Roman territory to the east of the Rhine and to the north of the river Main. He sent the severed head of Saturninus to Rome and rewarded Maximus Norbanus with a second consulate, the loyal and victorious legions with extra pay and privileges. He himself later celebrated a double triumph, not over the Roman Saturninus,

of course, but over the Chatti and the Dacians, against whom he advanced after having secured the Rhine frontier by shortened defense lines, watchtowers, and fortifications.

The Dacian Frontier: 85–93

The Danube had been for years a more difficult and disturbed frontier than the Rhine. The Germanic Suebian tribes to the north of the river, the Marcomanni and Quadi in what is now Czechoslovakia, the Sarmatian Iazyges of the Hungarian Plains between the Danube and the Theiss, the Dacians of Romania, and the Sarmatian Roxolani of Moldavia and Bessarabia with their fearsome armor-clad cavalry were all extremely dangerous enemies. The Dacians, now united by their young and aggressive king Decebalus (85–106) into a strong and warlike state, were particularly menacing.

In 85 the Dacians crossed the Danube, invaded the Roman province of Moesia and, after overwhelming Roman forts and garrisons near Adamclisi in the Dobrudja, defeated and killed the governor, C. Oppius Sabinus. After his arrival on this battlefront, Domitian placed his Praetorian Prefect, Cornelius Fuscus, in charge of military operations, transferred another legion to Moesia, and divided the province into two parts, Upper and Lower Moesia. After expelling the Dacians, he ordered that three parallel defense lines (each forty miles in length and interspersed at mile intervals with garrisoned forts) be constructed across the Dobrudja.

Not content with that, Domitian sent Fuscus across the Danube to invade Dacia, in the forests of which Fuscus met disaster and death. A miserable remnant of his army got back safely over the river. Two years later, in 88, after careful preparations Domitian ordered a second invasion of Dacia. He sent his legate Tettius Julianus at the head of a powerful army, which met and defeated the Dacians with immense slaughter at Tapae not far from the Iron Gates. Fuscus was avenged.

Tapae unfortunately was not decisive nor was it followed by the total conquest of Dacia, for Saturninus had chosen that moment to rebel in the Rhineland. The Marcomanni, Quadi, and Iazyges thereupon broke their treaties with Rome, cast off allegiance, and declared war. The Roman army, led by Domitian himself, suffered so sharp a reverse that he gladly came to terms with Decebalus, the Dacian king. Decebalus agreed, in 89, to surrender all Roman captives and accept vassalage. In return, Domitian recognized him as the legitimate king of the Dacians, granted him an annual subsidy, and furnished him Roman engineers skilled in the art of building roads and fortresses.

The Dacian peace treaty, though dictated by expediency, was of immense value to Rome. It turned Decebalus into a benevolent neutral, if not an active ally, when the Iazyges irrupted into Pannonia in 92, attacked and cut up a Roman legion. It also helped Domitian isolate the hostile Marcomanni and Quadi by alliances with the Germanic tribes living to the north of them, with the Semnones east of the Elbe and the powerful Lugii of Silesia. Domitian was able to stabilize the Danubian frontier by concentrating nine or ten legions along the river in strongly fortified camps at Vindobona (Vienna), at Carnuntum, at Aquincum (Budapest), and at Troesmis near modern Braila. By 93, peace prevailed again along the entire Danubian frontier.

Conspiracies and Treason Trials

The rebellion of Saturninus so upset Domitian that he developed a serious persecution complex and saw conspiracies forming against him everywhere. Spies and informers began to play upon his fears. In 89 he banished philosophers and astrologers from Rome but later struck out most savagely against prominent senators, some able provincial governors, and even members of the imperial family. Among his victims were the governors of Asia and Britain, the Prefect of Egypt, and two prefects of the Praetorian Guard. In 95 he put to death his own cousin, Flavius Clemens, a gentle and inoffensive person, on a trumped-up charge of atheism, probably, in fact, a form of Christianity. He drove his niece Domitilla, Clemens' wife, into exile.

The Murder of Domitian: 96

When Domitia, the emperor's wife, found out that she was going to be the next victim, she enlisted the secret aid of the two new praetorian prefects. They persuaded Domitian to grant audience to Domitilla's former but devoted butler, a certain Stephanus, who pretended to have secret information about an alleged conspiracy. Admitted to the emperor's bedroom, he handed him a document. As Domitian unfolded the document, Stephanus stabbed him in the groin with a dagger concealed in an arm bandage. The wounded Domitian staggered to his bed and groped frantically under the pillow for the dagger he always kept there. The dagger was gone.

GOLDEN AGE OF THE

ASSASSINATION HAD REMOVED A TYRANT BUT DID NOT DESTROY the principate. Within its own ranks, the senate found a successor to Domitian: M. Cocceius Nerva, sixty years old, long past his prime and poor in body, personality, and spirit. Generous donatives paid or promised kept both the Praetorian Guard and the provincial armies temporarily satisfied and acquiescent.

Nerva: 96–98

Though Nerva's family contained several distinguished jurists, it was not an old one and had gained social acceptance only because his maternal uncle had married a woman of Julio-Claudian birth, an ennobling but a tenuous link. Nerva himself

ROMAN EMPIRE

had not won much distinction as a jurist or as a public speaker, had never governed a province or commanded an army, though he had done fairly well politically. Being a safe and innocuous man and willing to cooperate with any regime, he had had one statue erected to him in the Forum, another on the Palatine during Nero's reign. He had reached the consulship in 71 under Vespasian and again in 90 under Domitian. He also held several priesthoods. In all his past career he seems to have preferred security to fame.

The senate regarded Nerva as the ideal ruler for many reasons: his deference; his vow never to put a senator to death unless condemned by a senatorial court; his restoration to the senate of the administration of the grain dole; his suspension of the hated law of treason (*maiestas*); and his recall of senatorial exiles, and the suppression of informers.*

Nor did Nerva successfully resist the demand for punishment of Domitian's assassins. When members of the Praetorian Guard besieged his palace clamoring for vengeance

* The more agile and astute of these nevertheless managed somehow to hold positions of immense power and even serve as members of his kitchen cabinet.

against Domitian's killers, that old man meekly allowed them to take the life of their former prefect and several other conspirators.

Farm Credit and Child Welfare: 97

In his handling of social and economic problems Nerva showed understanding, initiative, and statesmanship of a high order. The most pressing problem was the agricultural crisis in Italy and the rapid decline of the rural population.

The farm crisis was neither of recent development nor unrelated to the progressive economic decay of Italy in general. The main causes were the competition with Italy of Gaul and Spain in both industry and scientific agriculture. A good example of provincial industrialization was the establishment (see p. 298) of glass factories at Lyons and Cologne, of metalworking shops at Lyons and Gressenich, and pottery works at Montans, La Graufesenque, Bassanac, and Lezoux, which rivaled Arretium (Arezzo) in the production of that beautiful red-glazed tableware known as *terra sigillata*.

In breaking Italy's sales monopoly of industrial products throughout the empire, provincial competition brought about in Italy industrial stagnation, unemployment, a decline of buying power, and a decreased demand for the products of Italian scientific agriculture. At the same time the provinces, especially Gaul and Spain, were also competing with Italy in the making of oil and wine, upon which the prosperity of Italian scientific agriculture had chiefly depended. Gaul could now produce as fine a wine as Italy's best, both in the Provence and at Bordeaux. Spain produced almost as good a wine and perhaps a better kind of oil, and the oil of North Africa made up in quantity what it lacked in quality. A visible testimony of the volume of the oil and wine exports of those provinces even to Rome itself is Monte Testaccio on Tiber wharf, a mound of broken pottery more than a hundred feet high and over a half a mile in circumference. Most of the broken jars date from 50 to 250 A.D.

Provincial competition was not the sole cause of the Italian agricultural crisis: another was the rising costs of labor. The price of slaves had mounted after the cessation of foreign wars and the suppression of piracy and kidnaping. Slave-breeding farms helped, but did not entirely meet the demand. The loss of markets combined with mounting labor costs compelled many owners to mort-

The Alimenta, a bas-relief of one of the balustrades of the Forum of Trajan. (Courtesy Fratelli Alinari, Florence)

gage land and slaves. The owners of very large estates, such as the Younger Pliny, resorted to renting at least part of their land to tenants (*coloni*) who, like the present day sharecroppers, farmed the land for a stipulated share of the crop. For the far more numerous owners of medium-sized estates, such a solution meant the abandonment of intensive farming, a much reduced income, and considerable hardship. The only solution of their problem, as they saw it, was the institution of a farm loan scheme backed by the imperial government, by which they could obtain credit on fairly easy terms. Nerva understood the problem and had the courage to attempt a solution.

Nerva's attempt to solve the Italian farm problem was not entirely without precedent. To assist wine producers in Italy, Domitian had years earlier forbidden the planting of new vineyards in Italy and had decreed the destruction of half the existing vineyards in the provinces. Nerva went much further in his program of farm relief and public welfare. In 97 he used the *fiscus* as a farm loan bank, which lent money to landowners at probably five per cent interest payable annually to local agencies specifically set up for the maintenance and education (*alimenta*) of free-born boys and girls. Nerva's relief program, expanded later by Trajan, his successor, not only extended farm credit at low rates of interest but encouraged the rearing and education of children in Italy.

The Succession

Another of Nerva's statesmanlike acts was his adoption of M. Ulpius Trajanus, the military governor of Lower Germany, as son, heir, and co-regent. The choice, whether dictated by fear, pressure of events, or by wise counsel offered in secret conclave, was excellent. A year after the adoption Nerva died (he was the last Roman emperor to be buried in the mausoleum of Augustus).

Trajan: 98–117

Two difficulties hamper the historian in his effort to describe Trajan's reign. One

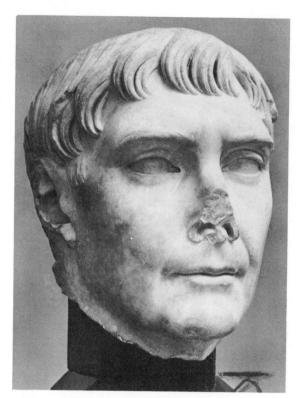

A marble lifesize head of Trajan (98– 117 A.D.). (Courtesy Ostia Museum)

is the poverty of literary sources, another the uniformly laudatory character of the few that do exist. Suetonius ended his *Lives of the Twelve Caesars* with Domitian's death in 96; there also Tacitus ended his *Histories*. In his other works—the *Dialogus,* a treatise on oratory, the *Agricola,* a biography of his father-in-law and a geographical and ethnographical description of Britain, and the *Germania,* a purely ethnographical treatise on Germany (all three were published if not written after Trajan's accession), and his later works, the *Histories* and the *Annals*—Tacitus makes penetrating and often critical remarks about Trajan and his reign. Compared with Tacitus' works, the *Letters* of the Younger Pliny, and particularly the published abridgement of a panegyric he delivered before the senate in 100 and the lectures of the Greek rhetorician, Dio Chrysostomus of Prusa, Bithynia (ca. 45– 115 A.D.), on the ideal kingship, are laudatory and shallow. The eleventh-century epitome of the sixty-eighth book of Dio Cassius is a miserable source, while the often hostile com-

The lower part of the marble Column of Trajan. (Courtesy G. E. Kidder Smith, New York)

Trajan, the first emperor of provincial origin, was born in Spain at Italica near Seville in the rich province of Baetica. He was proud of his father, whom Vespasian had admitted not only into the senate but into the Roman patriciate. The consulship, the Syrian command, the proconsulate of Asia, and numerous triumphal honors followed in swift succession.

Before his adoption by Nerva, Trajan too had had a long and distinguished military career under Vespasian and Domitian on the Rhine, the Danube, and the Euphrates, in Syria and in Spain. As governor of Lower Germany he had won, during Nerva's reign, the proud title of *Germanicus;* under his own auspices he would win still others: *Dacicus* and *Parthicus* (Conqueror of the Dacians and the Parthians).

After Nerva's death, two years spent in inspecting and strengthening defenses along the Rhine and the Danube preceded Trajan's long awaited and much acclaimed arrival in Rome. Well might both populace and senate have acclaimed such an imperator: the majestic figure, the rugged face, the iron gray

The Forum of Trajan. (Courtesy Istituto Italiano di Cultura, New York)

ments found in Jewish sources—the *Mishna, Talmud, Midrash,* and the *Oracula Sibyllina* —do not furnish an adequate antidote to the panegyrical character of our extant literary sources.

The best sources consist, therefore, of numerous inscriptions, papyri, coins, and two famous monuments — Trajan's Column in Rome and the Arch at Beneventum. That imposing column of Parian marble one hundred feet high, erected in Trajan's Forum at Rome, has a spiral frieze of 155 pictures and 2,500 figures commemorating his Dacian Wars. The Arch of Beneventum commemorates Trajan's Eastern Wars and the completion of the great Via Traiana, which ran from Beneventum to Barium (Bari) and Brundisium. Other monuments in Italy and the provinces portray various achievements of his reign.

hair—a battle-hardened soldier in the prime of life, not a callow unpredictable youth like Caligula or Nero, nor a feeble, scraggy old man like Galba or Nerva. His very appearance commanded respect.

Trajan's Administration

Towards the senate Trajan was tactful, respectful, often gracious, even indulgent—the attitude of "the Optimus Princeps," a title bestowed as early as 100, stamped on the coinage in 105, but not officially assumed till 115. Centuries later, the senate bestowed on every new emperor the supreme compliment: "Luckier than Augustus, better than Trajan" (*Felicior Augusto, melior Traiano*).

The senate with which Trajan had to deal was different in attitude and composition from that of the early Empire. Severely chastened by Nero and Domitian, it gladly accepted him as being at least "better than the worst" (*melior pessimo princeps*). Change of attitude arose out of change of composition. As inscriptions and papyri show, the senate of Claudius and Vespasian contained few members of provincial origin. Under Trajan provincial senators made up slightly over forty per cent of the total, more and more of whom now came from the Eastern provinces.

Enjoying, as he did, the support and affection of the senate, the people, and the provincial armies, Trajan was able to carry out

The Arch of Trajan at Beneventum (114 A.D.). (Courtesy Fratelli Alinari, Florence)

Coin of Trajan (ca. 105 A.D.). Ob verse: *Head of Trajan.* Reverse: *Trajan's bridge over the Danube.* *(Courtesy The American Numismatic Society, New York)*

his administrative program without distraction or fear. In Rome the building projects, the flood control works on the Tiber, the repair and extension of the Circus Maximus, and the construction of aqueducts, baths, temples, and triumphal arches testify to his energy and organizing ability. Most wondrous of his works was the Forum Traianum, the largest and most splendid of all imperial fora, with marble colonnades, gilded horses and countless statues, the Basilica Ulpia, libraries, and that magnificent Column surmounted by a colossal statue of Trajan himself.

In Italy he repaired the Appian, Aemilian, and Latin Ways, built a causeway over the Pontine Marshes, and constructed the great Trajan Way from Beneventum to Brundisium. Some of his bridges are still in use. At Ostia he added to the anchorage and shelter hitherto provided African grain ships by the harbor of Claudius (*see* p. 322) by the construction of a second harbor octagonal in shape and seventy acres in extent. He created a new harbor further north at Civitavecchia, another at Terracina sixty miles south of Ostia, and another at Ancona, on the east coast, the embarkation port for Dalmatia and the Danubian region.

To stimulate the birth rate as well as relieve the farm crisis in Italy, Trajan expanded Nerva's *alimenta* program and made children eligible for the monthly grain dole and occasional distributions of money (*congiaria*). He restricted emigration from Italy, founded colonies of veterans near Rome, and compelled provincial senators to invest at least one-third of their capital in Italian farm land. A liberal farm loan policy encouraged the reclamation of waste lands and enabled landless peasants and manumitted slaves to acquire farms and homes of their own.

The measures Trajan took to improve economic conditions in the provinces were equally impressive: roads, bridges, harbors, and aqueducts in almost every province. He built a great stone bridge over the Danube at Drobetae near the Iron Gates. Over the Tajo (Tagus) near Alcantara in Spain he built a beautiful high-span bridge which still exists. He constructed aqueducts in Dalmatia, at Miletus, Smyrna, and Antioch in the Middle East, and harbor works at Ephesus; and had a navigable canal dug from the Nile to the Red Sea. In Africa he founded the military colony of Timgad (Thamugadi), which with its markets, baths, temples, theaters, and a library of 23,000 volumes, became the pride of Roman Africa.

In his efforts to increase efficiency, Trajan introduced changes in the administration of cities and municipalities in Italy and the provinces which set the dangerous precedent of interference with municipal affairs and led, a century later, to the decay of local initiative in financial matters. His motives were good, and his intervention seemed justified at the time.

Some cities in Italy and the Eastern provinces had become involved in financial troubles in spite of fairly large revenues—rents from suburban farms and urban real estate, fines imposed on lawbreakers, fees accompanying applications for citizenship, the sale of hunting and fishing licenses and, in some cases, tolls and harbor dues. These revenues often failed to meet the expenditures on games, religious festivals, embassies to Rome, and ambitious building projects. The financial disabilities of some municipalities were further aggravated by the responsibility for collecting taxes for the imperial government and making up for arrears or deficiencies.

To help the municipalities solve their financial problems Trajan sent agents or inspectors (*curatores* or *correctores*). In 111 he sent the Younger Pliny to Bithynia. In 109 he sent a certain Maximus to Greece to investigate and regulate the affairs of Athens, Sparta, and Delphi, and an imperial legate to the Italian Transpadana.* The advice of these agents, though tendered in a polite and friendly way, was not to be ignored.

The Dacian Wars: 101-106

Public works and administration were not Trajan's sole employment nor his greatest claim to fame. The army, which had been his life, continued to be his chief delight. In 101 he set out on an invasion of Dacia, with whose king Decebalus Domitian had concluded the treaty of 89, convenient, expedient, but gálling to Roman imperial pride.

The conquest of Dacia proved neither swift nor easy. In that land of mountain and forest defended fanatically by the Dacian nationalists led by their wily and Roman-hating king, Trajan suffered a severe reverse at Tapae near the Iron Gates. He prudently withdrew to winter quarters on the Danube. That winter Decebalus, aided by the Roxolani, invaded Lower Moesia, where he did much damage before finally withdrawing.

In the spring of 102, Trajan again invaded Dacia. He crossed the Carpathians via the Red Tower Pass and, after several successful battles, finally occupied the capital city of Sarmizegethusa, where he stationed a permanent garrison. Decebalus surrendered unconditionally and agreed to become once more a Roman vassal. Trajan then returned to Rome to celebrate his triumph and added Dacicus to his titulature.

In 105 Decebalus broke the peace agreement and attacked the Iazyges, Rome's allies in the Hungarian plains. He massacred Roman garrisons in Dacia and again invaded Moesia. Embarking from Ancona, Trajan hastened to the lower Danube with thirteen legions, crossed the stone bridge (which his architect Apollodorus had built) and broke Dacian resistance (in 106). After the suicide of Decebalus, Trajan annexed Dacia as a province, made Sarmizegethusa a colony (*Ulpia Traiana*). He settled numerous veterans and colonists from all over the empire, ancestors of the present-day Romanians. Fifty thousand Dacian war prisoners ended their days as gladiators in the Roman arena. Vast streams of Dacian gold made possible magnificent public works in Rome, Italy, and the provinces and temporarily so disturbed the ratio between gold and silver that the emperor slightly increased the copper content in silver coins in order, probably, to restore the balance.

The Parthian Wars: 113-117

After seven years of peace a war of Trajan's own making broke out with Parthia. Chosroes, the new Parthian king, provoked Trajan by deposing without Rome's consent his nephew Axidares, the king of Armenia, and enthroning the latter's elder brother, Parthamasiris (probably to remove a potential claimant to the Parthian throne). Trajan's reaction was swift: he set sail for the East in the fall of 113.

The following spring he invaded Armenia, which offered no opposition. Near Erzerum in central Armenia Parthamasiris belatedly sought and gained audience with Trajan. He laid his crown at the emperor's feet in the hope of formal investiture, but Trajan was adamant. Parthamasiris was deposed and Armenia declared a Roman imperial province.

The swift and bloodless conquest of Armenia spurred Trajan on to seize yet another province, since the Parthian king was too distracted by revolts throughout his immense kingdom to offer effectual resistance. On the way back from Armenia to Antioch Trajan marched triumphantly through Upper Mesopotamia, where Parthian vassals either came to terms or fled precipitously before his advance. In 115 he resumed operations along the Upper Euphrates. The annexation of two provinces and the official acceptance of the title of *Optimus Princeps* proclaimed the success of the campaigns of 114 and 115.

Still not content, Trajan crossed the Tigris in 116, and overran the Parthian vassal kingdom of Adiabene, which he annexed as the province of Assyria. Next he invaded Parthia

---

* Trajan evidently regarded the Transpadana as an imperial province since he sent a legate of praetorian rank to govern it and a commissioner to superintend its finances.

itself, besieged and captured Ctesiphon on the Tigris, and occupied the winter palace of the Parthian kings. At his approach Chosroes fled in haste, leaving behind his golden throne. Trajan added yet a fourth province to the empire and assumed the title of *Parthicus*.

Longing to be a second Alexander, Trajan went down to the mouth of the Tigris, receiving on the way the submission of a powerful Parthian vassal, whom he accepted as a Roman client king. Within two years he had extended Rome's dominion from the headwaters of the Tigris and Euphrates to the Persian Gulf. Trade routes to the Far East were now within his grasp and passage to India might have been his next move. As he gazed wistfully upon the waters of the Persian Gulf and watched a ship sailing eastwards, he mused resignedly: "Oh, had I been younger, I should have liked to go to India too." Instead, he went up the Euphrates to Babylon and there received disturbing news.

The empire, which Trajan had extended to the furthest limits yet attained, was suddenly convulsed by simultaneous revolts. Seleucia, Mesopotamia, Assyria, even Armenia, all were in revolt and powerful Parthian armies were returning to reoccupy lost territory. The Sarmatians and Roxolani along the Danube were again on the move. In Britain Roman garrisons were in retreat from the borders of Scotland.

The most serious revolts were those of the Jews in Cyrenaica, Mesopotamia, Adiabene, Cyprus, and Egypt, which were marked by savage massacre. Trajan acted with resolution and promptness; but without the help of his able marshal and comrade in arms, Lusius Quietus the Moor, he would have failed to restore the rapidly deteriorating situation. Trajan himself pacified southern Mesopotamia by his capture and ruthless destruction of Seleucia on the Tigris, while his marshal reconquered northern Mesopotamia and later, as governor of Judea, stamped out all Jewish riots in Palestine. His other marshals were less successful in suppressing the revolts in Cyrenaica, Cyprus, and Egypt. Nor was Trajan able to hold all his Parthian conquests: in 116 he surrendered the province of southern Mesopotamia to a Parthian prince, nominally a Roman vassal, and lost the entire province of Assyria, along with part of Greater Armenia.

The Death of Trajan: 117

Three years of hard campaigning in the desert and the strain of recent months had overtaxed Trajan's strength. He was then past sixty. On the road back from Ctesiphon he became ill and during the winter at Antioch, where he was busily preparing for another campaign in Mesopotamia in the following spring, he grew steadily worse. Reluctantly he abandoned his plans of campaign and set out for Rome leaving Publius Aelius Hadrianus to take command in the Middle East. He never put out to sea. At Selinus in Cilicia he suffered a stroke and died a few days later (August 9, 117).

The Effects of Trajan's War

Trajan, one of the greatest of Roman *Imperatores,* was the first to realize at least in part Caesar's plans to conquer Dacia and Parthia. Marcus Antonius had tried but never succeeded, Nero had aspired but never tried. Under Trajan the Roman empire reached the high tide of territorial expansion; after him there was to be a slow and inexorable ebb.

The costs of imperial expansion were high. Trajan paid the price in health; the empire, in manpower and resources. Moreover, Trajan had expanded the empire beyond defensible limits and in the process had weakened, if not totally paralyzed, the capability of three strong buffer states, Dacia, Parthia, and Nabataean Arabia.* Rome would later have to absorb and repel the mass invasions of the Goths and other Germans, the Alans, and Iranian nationalists who, impelled by the relentless pressure of the Huns from central Asia, would break and burst through the brittle, overextended defenses of the Roman empire on the Rhine, Danube, and Euphrates. Trajan's paralyzing of the defensive powers of the Dacians, Nabataeans, and Parthians spelled disaster for the Roman empire of the future.

* The last had been occupied and made a province in an easy campaign of 106.

Hadrianus Augustus: 117–138

No sooner had news of Trajan's death reached Antioch than the armies of Syria proclaimed Hadrian, their commander-in-chief, emperor of Rome. Several days later the senate officially confirmed the acclamation. The rumor that Hadrian owed his throne to a forged instrument of adoption carried little weight against acclamation by the army and the senate's ratification.

Inscriptions, papyri, coins, and excavated monuments together with the *Historia Augusta*, a late biography of second and third century emperors beginning with Hadrian, reveal many important facts about Hadrian's life and principate but leave many problems unsolved. Tacitus, too, though indirectly, is an important source of information.

Hadrian's birthplace is disputed. According to the *Historia Augusta* he was born in Rome in 76, but his family on both sides belonged to Italica, the same Spanish town where Trajan was born. An orphan at the age of ten, he became a ward of Trajan, his father's cousin and closest male relative. He received an excellent education and acquired a strong and lasting love of Greek studies, Greek art and philosophy, to which interest he owed his half-contemptuous nickname of Graeculus ('Greekling'). He became a man of refined artistic tastes, an intellectual with a keen, penetrating intelligence.

Nor was Hadrian's training wholly academic. Healthy, well-built, and strong, he liked the outdoor, strenuous life and was inordinately fond of hunting. Like Plato's philosopher king, he had a long military and official career as military tribune, quaestor, plebeian tribune, praetor, and consul. He had seen military service in Spain, Pannonia, Moesia, Germany, and Parthia. In the First Dacian War he was Trajan's quaestor, in the Second, the commander of a legion. He was governor of Lower Pannonia in 107, and governor of Syria in 117. To facilitate his climb to power, he married Trajan's grandniece, Vibia Sabina, a strikingly beautiful but frustrated woman, whom he probably would have divorced had it not been for his ambition.

Hadrian had fallen heir to a difficult task, not rendered lighter by inevitable comparison with his illustrious predecessor, from whom he had in actual fact inherited a legacy of disturbance and revolt in Cyrenaica, Egypt, and Cyprus, in Mauretania, on the lower Danube, and in Britain. The man who helped him quell those revolts was his trusted friend, Marcius Turbo, who replaced Trajan's great Moorish marshal, Lusius Quietus. Three other marshals also made way for new men more in sympathy with the policies of the new regime.

With the new regime came also a change in foreign policy. Convinced that Trajan's wars of expansion were a drain upon the empire's manpower and resources, at the outset of his reign Hadrian abandoned all recent conquests east of the Tigris and Euphrates, allowed Greater Armenia to revert to the status of a vassal kingdom, and made peace with Parthia.

Popular frustration and anger over the retreat from the East gave rise to the rumor that Hadrian also planned to evacuate Dacia with its thousands of Roman colonists and had demolished the superstructure of Trajan's great bridge over the Danube. According to the rumor, levelheaded friends convinced him that the public would not stand for so gross a betrayal of the empire.

If Trajan had sought to emulate, by wars of conquest, the deeds of Caesar, so Hadrian

Coin of Hadrian. The obverse side bears the magic legend, HADRIANUS AUGUSTUS, and the reverse shows Roma, seated on a cuirass, holding victory and a cornucopiae. (Courtesy The American Numismatic Society, New York)

found precedent for his program of peace in the policy of Augustus, though he did not adopt the magic legend of HADRIANVS AVGVSTVS on his coins until the year 123, which happened to be the one hundred and fiftieth anniversary of the senate's conferral of the name 'Augustus' upon Octavianus.

The new 'Pax Augusta' did not please everyone—especially not Lusius Quietus and the three former marshals, who had admired Trajan's dynamic policy and disapproved of Hadrian's new frontier policy. Mild expression of disapproval and annoyance led to overt acts of treason which finally called forth senatorial condemnation. The four were executed without Hadrian's sanction or knowledge; or so he averred. He wished his reign to be one of clemency and mercy and not stained with the blood even of trouble-making consulars.

To many highranking Romans his disavowals sounded evasive and hollow. Reluctantly, therefore, and under a heavy cloud he set out on his much-deferred journey to Rome. After a long stopover at Byzantium or at Nicomedia and an extended tour of inspection of the Danubian frontiers, he finally arrived in Rome early in July of 118.

A day or so after his arrival, he appeared before the senate—a tall, bearded,* imposing figure—and solemnly promised the assembled dignitaries that no senator would henceforth be put to death without prior condemnation by a senatorial court.†

The senate pacified, Hadrian began to court the favor of the masses with a double liberality (*congiarium*) and a vast remission of debts and tax arrears. Day after day there hung over the Forum the smoke of burning account books as debts amounting to fifty million dollars were obliterated, an unavailing gesture of generosity—which brought

* The beard set a fashion for a long succession of Roman emperors.

† He kept the promise for twenty years.

A bas-relief found in the Roman Forum, from the time of Hadrian, showing the burning of records of debts to the State. (Courtesy Fratelli Alinari, Florence)

small comfort to him or his entourage. Hadrian's anger at the public's ingratitude was so great that he left Rome again.

Hadrian's Travels

The year 121 found Hadrian in Gaul and the Rhineland. The next year he went to Britain, where he inspected plans for the construction of a wall (which bears his name) from Solway Firth to the Tyne to keep marauding tribesmen of the North from raiding farmlands south of the Scottish border. On the way back from Britain he passed through Gaul and thence to Spain, where he spent the winter. In the spring he led a punitive expedition against the Moors, who had been raiding Roman towns in Morocco. There he received news that the Parthians had again broken the peace, and he set sail for Ephesus.

His dramatic arrival in the Middle East, backed by impressive troop concentrations, inspired Chosroes to negotiate rather than fight. The war ended, Hadrian went on to hear petitions and complaints. He punished misgovernment of the provinces, arranged for the construction of municipal temples, baths, aqueducts, and theaters, and built an enormous temple at Cyzicus.

In 128 he visited North Africa, where he inspected the imperial estates (saltus) and studied ways and means for more efficient exploitation. He spent the following winter in Athens, where he presided at games and festivals, codified laws, completed and dedicated a huge temple to Olympian Zeus, the Olympeion, which the tyrant Peisistratus had designed seven centuries before. In the suburbs of Athens he built a new city, named Hadrianopolis and in it erected a pantheon, the Stoa, a gymnasium and a library, and another great temple, the Panhellenion, which he romantically dedicated to an ancient ideal —Greek unity. In the spring of 129 he again toured Asia Minor, stopping at Smyrna, Ephesus, Cyzicus, Bithynia, Antioch, and Palmyra. Towns, temples, libraries, baths, and aqueducts sprang up wherever he went.

Yet he displayed a singular lack of understanding in Jerusalem where, although he found the city in ruins and a wretched population living in hovels and destitution, he resolved to found a Roman colony called Aelia Capitolina and, on the site of the Jewish Temple, he erected a shrine to Jupiter Capitolinus. This act provoked one of the bloodiest rebellions in history.

Meanwhile, heedless of what he had done, Hadrian went to Egypt to reorganize its economic life and visit the monuments of its glorious past. There he founded a beautiful new city Antinoopolis on the east bank of the Nile.*

The Jewish Revolt

Hadrian returned to Rome to learn that the Jews had rebelled in the fall of 132 and were waging guerrilla war against the Roman army of occupation. Led by a famous guerrilla strategist, Bar Kokhba, "Son of the Star," the Jews captured Jerusalem, slaughtered an entire Roman legion, and for a time seemed about to drive the Romans out of Palestine. Hadrian hastened back to Syria, assembled reinforcements from the other provinces, and summoned the able Julius Severus from Britain to take command. Severus began systematically isolating strongholds and inhabited places and starving out the defenders. He slaughtered half a million people, and enslaved as many more. When the revolt was finally quelled in 135, peace and desolation descended upon a ruined land.

Frontier Defense

Hadrian's renunciation of Trajan's aggressive foreign wars and his surrender of some recent conquests did not constitute a neglect of frontier defense. He was the first emperor to erect on a large scale fixed frontier defenses such as Hadrian's Wall in Britain. He extended fortifications for 345 miles in South Germany behind continuous lines of ditches

* Hadrian had had a companion, Antinoos, a handsome Bithynian youth whom he adored as the embodiment of the Greek ideal of beauty. The youth drowned in the waters of the Nile. After his death, Hadrian worshipped him as divine, built shrines and temples to him, struck coins bearing his likeness, and set up statues and busts of him all over the empire.

and oakwood palisades nine feet high. These fortifications, with their garrisoned forts and watch towers, not only protected the frontier from enemy raids and even mass attacks, but marked the frontier and served as check points for the control of trade between the Roman and the barbarian world.

The Reform of the Army

Nor did Hadrian neglect the army. His reforms in discipline, recruitment, and tactics were of lasting importance. Discipline was for him almost a cult and to secure it he personally inspected army posts all over the empire; watched soldiers drill, march, maneuver; inspected equipment, dress, baggage, and mess kitchens; ordered fatigue marches during which, dressed as a common soldier, he marched along with the men, carrying his own knapsack. To no emperor were the armies more devoted and under none were they more disciplined and efficient.

One of Hadrian's most important army reforms was the progressive removal of distinction between the legions and the auxiliary corps (*auxilia*) with respect to training, equipment, and composition. For the first time both consisted of Roman citizens and non-citizens, recruited more and more in the frontier regions in which they were to serve. Many of the new recruits were soldiers' sons born near the permanent camps and to them Hadrian granted the right, hitherto withheld, of inheriting their fathers' property.

In addition to the *auxilia*, which garrisoned the permanent forts strung out along the frontiers, Hadrian began to levy, especially in the German and Danubian provinces, in Britain, and in Morocco, many auxiliary units of a new type called *numeri*. These were small mobile corps, some of them light in-

The Interior of the Praetorium *or Central Fortress at Lambaesis (Lambèse, Algeria), which Hadrian (or perhaps, Trajan) made the permanent headquarters of the Roman Army in North Africa. (Courtesy The French Embassy, Information Division, New York)*

fantry, some cavalry, others mixed, while some consisted of mounted scouts known as *exploratores*. Though often commanded by Roman ex-centurions, the *numeri* retained their native languages, arms, and methods of fighting.

Hadrian's greatest reform in battle tactics was the introduction of an improved form of the old Macedonian phalanx. In offensive operations the *auxilia* would launch the initial attack while the phalanx of the legions advanced later to deliver the final blow. If the enemy attacked first, the *auxilia* would take the brunt of the initial assault. The legions held in reserve in camps behind the frontier forts would then advance to destroy the exhausted forces of the enemy. Hadrian's tactics were to remain standard military strategy, except for minor modifications, for over two centuries.

The Provinces

Extensive travels and detailed reports from procurators and other agents afforded Hadrian an intimate knowledge of conditions in the provinces. No detail of provincial administration seemed too small for his personal attention, especially when it involved the defense of the weak against the strong, the poor against the rich (*humiliores contra honestiores; tenuiores contra potentiores*). To reduce the cost of living of the poor of Athens, he limited the export of olive oil and regulated the price of fish. He granted tax relief and financial assistance to cities in Asia Minor stricken by earthquake or famine. In Egypt he relieved peasants working on imperial estates from high taxes, high rents, and compulsory labor exacted by contract farmers (*conductores*) and imperial procurators, and guaranteed longer and more secure tenure so that they who had hitherto lived in misery and squalor became self-supporting and independent farmers.

Similarly in North Africa Hadrian encouraged settlers to take up land on imperial estates and, wherever possible, to convert virgin and waste land to productive use by the planting of olive orchards. The settlers enjoyed two benefits: low rents—in some cases none at all until the orchards began to bear—

and the right of appeal to the emperor when exploited by *conductores* or oppressed by procurators.

Under Hadrian, urbanization of the empire reached its peak. Even the primitive frontier provinces of Dacia and North Africa, former villages and settlements around military camps and castles were now becoming full-fledged self-governing towns and cities. Hadrian founded and built such cities as Hadrianopolis in Thrace (now Adrianople near the Turkish-Bulgarian border); Hadrianuthera and Stratonicea in Asia Minor; Antinoopolis in Egypt; Colonia Julia Hadriana Avenio (now Avignon) in Gaul; and many in the Danubian provinces.

The extension of Roman citizenship kept step with the diffusion of culture and civilization. Large-scale gift of Roman citizenship to the provinces first came into play under Caesar and Augustus, who granted Latin Rights to the Romanized parts of Spain and southern Gaul. Latin Rights (*Ius Latii* or *Latium*), of which the law of contracts (*ius commercii*) was the most valuable, became the first step towards the acquisition of full Roman citizenship. Before Hadrian, two kinds of provincial communities enjoyed citizenship: self-governing towns or *municipia* and Roman citizen colonies founded by Rome. In the second century it became the fashion for provincial *municipia* to petition the emperor to grant them the status of colony, which was considered a mark of distinction though it conferred no special legal or material benefit.

Though Hadrian made much use of the fiction of the titular colony, its inventor was Pompeius Strabo, a consul during the Italic or Social War (90–88 B.C.). It made its first important appearance during the principate of Claudius, who elevated Vienne, Trèves, and other towns in central Gaul to colonial status. Hadrian applied the device to the *municipia* of Dacia and North Africa.

Another Hadrianic device, but of more recent origin, was Greater Latinity (*Latium Maius*), which conferred citizenship upon all members of town councils or local senates (*decuriones*), as well as upon magistrates. This device was probably not, as commonly asserted, a sign of municipal decay, nor was it employed simply to make officeholding more attractive but to speed the growth of Roman citizenship everywhere and transform the Roman empire into a genuine world commonwealth.

The Reorganization of the Imperial Bureaucracy

The growing administrative needs of the Roman world commonwealth as well as Hadrian's passion for efficiency led to an expansion and reorganization of the imperial bureaucracy. The qualities he demanded from civil servants were not unlike those required in most modern states. He insisted that holders of public office be able, well-trained, and competent, loyal to the emperor and devoted to the state. He paid them well and gave rewards for hard work, initiative, and efficiency.

Vespasian had reversed the policy of Claudius, by employing knights instead of freedmen in high administrative positions. Hadrian followed Vespasian's lead and appointed knights as directors of the four executive departments created by Claudius (*see* p. 321)—imperial correspondence (*ab epistulis*), justice (*a libellis*), treasury (*a rationibus*), and the research and library service (*a studiis*). To enhance the prestige of these offices, he bestowed upon the knights such resounding titles as *vir egregius, vir perfectissimus,* and that of *vir eminentissimus* held by the prefect of the Praetorian Guard. Gradations of salary also differentiated the various executive offices. Procurators, for example, received 60,000, 100,000, 200,000, or 300,000 sesterces per year, according to their rank. Four equestrian prefects commanded even higher salaries.

To these government departments Hadrian added two new ones of cabinet rank, both pointing not only to an increased centralization of government but to wider equestrian participation in government service. One of the new departments resulted from his reform of the vitally important system of the so-called imperial post and communications (*cursus publicus*), formerly a financial and administrative burden laid upon municipalities in Italy and the provinces. Hadrian lightened this burden by his reorganization of the system as a state institution controlled by a central bureau in Rome headed by an equestrian prefect of vehicles (*praefectus vehiculorum*).

The other new department owed its origin to an overhauling of the tax collecting system, especially that pertaining to the collection of the five percent succession tax (*vicesima hereditatum*), which Hadrian, in line with policies set by Caesar, Augustus, and Tiberius, transferred from tax-farming companies to a state agency presided over by an equestrian procurator. The procurator, assisted by numerous agents throughout the empire, collected these and many other taxes, direct and indirect.

In the reorganization of the imperial bureaucracy Hadrian departed from the policy of Augustus by separating the civil and military careers of equestrian officials and by appointing knights without prior military experience to civil service jobs. He probably wanted to attract into government service people of legal and philosophical interests to whom army life seemed irksome and distasteful.

In lieu of the now optional military training, Hadrian required knights seeking high administrative positions to begin their civil service career by accepting such minor jobs as agents or attorneys of the treasury (*advocati fisci*), a newly created class of officials sent all over the empire to prosecute cases of tax evasion and delinquency.

Hadrian's separation of civil and military careers was probably a poor idea, since it deprived high government officials of requisite military experience and control over the army and left them helpless when confronted, as they were to be in the third century, by a formidable group of army commanders totally ignorant of civil government. In this instance Hadrian's yearning for administrative efficiency proved injurious to the future stability of the state.

Reorganization of the Cabinet

Having a mania for organization, Hadrian converted the informal conclave of palace friends and advisers, such as Augustus and his successors had consulted, into a genuine cabinet and permanent council of state (*consilium principis*). It consisted of the heads of the various departments of the government, the chief prefects, and several distinguished jurists. Besides serving as the chief policy-making body of the empire, it also acted as a supreme court whose function was to hear cases involving senators and high-ranking officials and to advise and assist the emperor in the creation and interpretation of civil and criminal law.

Legal Reforms

Of all the reforms of Hadrian the greatest and most enduring were in the field of law. One such reform gave the unanimous opinions (*responsa*) of distinguished jurists the force of law binding upon judges trying similar cases. Only when the opinions conflicted could judges reach their own decisions. These responses later entered into the literature of Roman law, becoming enshrined at last in the *Digest* and *Code* of Justinian I.

More important still was the redaction and codification of the *Praetorian Perpetual Edict*. Ever since early Republican times, each incoming Urban Praetor had drawn up and posted edicts setting forth the laws and court procedure he intended to follow during his year of office. The Praetor for Aliens (*Praetor Peregrinus*) as well as the provincial governors had followed suit. Since the praetors normally retained the laws and procedure of their predecessors, adding new ones as need arose, the edicts tended to perpetuate many obsolete rules, contradictions, and obscurities, all of which seemed intolerable to Hadrian's logical and legalistic mind. He therefore commissioned Salvius Julianus to draw up a permanent edict (*edictum perpetuum*) binding upon all present and future praetors without alteration or addition unless authorized by the emperor or by decree of the senate.

The statutes of the emperors (*constitutiones principum*) thereafter became increasingly important as sources of law. These consisted of imperial edicts (*edicta*) issued by virtue of his *imperium*; his judicial decrees (*decreta*) or decisions; his rescripts (*rescripta*) or responses to written inquiries on specific points of law; and his mandates (*mandata*) or administrative directives issued to officials subject to his orders.

To ease the crowded calendar of the praetors' courts in Rome and expedite the administration of justice in Italy, Hadrian divided the peninsula into four judicial districts each presided over by a circuit judge of consular rank (*juridicus consularis*) to try cases of inheritance, trust, and guardianship, and probably to hear appeals from the municipal courts. Though the innovation was both salutary and necessary and not intended simply to reduce Italy to the status of a province, it evidently displeased the senate, at whose insistence Hadrian's successor, Antoninus Pius, unwisely abolished it. Marcus Aurelius had to revive it later.

Social Reforms

As the supreme source of law and justice, Hadrian exerted his authority for the protection of the weak and helpless in accordance with Stoic philosophical principles and the ideas of Seneca and the Cynics, in whose eyes even a slave was a person. Hadrian made it illegal for a master to kill, torture, or castrate a slave, or sell him as a gladiator or for any lewd or immoral purpose. He also deprived the father of a family of the power of life and death over his children and safeguarded the right of minors to inherit and own property.

In the field of social welfare and education Hadrian continued the policy of Nerva and Trajan of using state funds for the maintenance and education of children of poor families in Italy and appointed a superintendent of child welfare (*praefectus alimentorum*) to administer the distribution of such funds. He also provided funds for secondary school education in many municipalities of the empire and for pensions for retired teachers. Continuing Vespasian's policy, he endowed rhetorical, philosophical, technical, and medical schools in both Rome and the provinces.

Public Works in Rome and Italy

In addition to the building projects completed in the provinces, Hadrian built, repaired, or restored hundreds of buildings in Rome, five of which are outstanding. One was the double-apsed temple of Venus and Roma probably designed by Hadrian himself. It was the largest of Roman temples and, because of its enormous vaulted roof of gold-plated bronze tiles, one of the most spectacular. Another was the gigantic temple erected in honor of Trajan and Plotina after her death in 122. A third was the enormous villa he built for himself at Tibur (Tivoli) by the banks of the Anio. It sprawled over 160 acres of ground and consisted of numerous buildings—palaces, libraries, baths, arcades—constructed in every variety of architecture, ingenious, unsymmetrical, often extravagant, and crammed with enough works of art to fill every major museum in Europe.

Across the Tiber there arose another architectural marvel of the age, Hadrian's tomb, a colossal mausoleum, massive, solid, round, over a thousand feet in circumference. On its summit a bronze four-horse chariot stood poised for flight; inside were walls faced with Parian marble, huge columns of Eastern marble or Egyptian porphyry, mosaic floors, and numerous statues. In the Middle Ages that massive structure long served as a fortress and was known as the Castle of Sant' Angelo, a name it still bears.

The greatest of Hadrian's structures was the Pantheon, constructed by Apollodorus. It is the best preserved of all ancient buildings and is the oldest still in use. It has been a Christian church since 609 and an Italian national monument since the nineteenth century. The portico with its sixteen Corinthian columns is the sole remnant of the original Pantheon constructed by Agrippa in 27 B.C. and destroyed by fire during the reign of Titus. The rotunda has an interior diameter of 132 feet; the walls are 20 feet thick; the apex of the domed roof is a round opening 26 feet in diameter, the sole and sufficient source of light.

That dome, the largest ever built, is so constructed that it does not require supporting columns. It was the model for all later domes

A plastic reconstruction of the zone of the great peristyles of Hadrian's Villa at Tivoli. (Courtesy Photo Alterocca, Terni, Italy)

The Mausoleum of Hadrian (Castel Sant' Angelo). (Courtesy Istituto Italiano di Cultura, New York)

such as those of the church of the Holy Wisdom in Constantinople, St. Peter's Cathedral in Rome, and the Capitol in Washington.

The Last Years of Hadrian

After the Jewish War Hadrian returned to Rome (135) never to leave Italy again. He spent his last years at his beautiful villa of Tivoli in the lonely Campagna but could not enjoy himself. The man who had traveled so much and seen and done so much had lost all zest for life. Loneliness and despair had come over his mind; a wasting disease racked his body.

As his illness grew worse and death seemed at hand, he turned his attention to the problem of choosing a successor. His first choice was his friend, Lucius Ceionius Commodus Verus, and he spent large sums of money to win the support of the soldiers and the people for the adoption. The money was wasted, for Lucius Verus died early in 138. Hadrian next adopted a rich and virtuous senator, Titus Aurelius Antoninus, whom he required to adopt in turn as his sons, Marcus Annius Verus, a youth of seventeen (who later became the Emperor Marcus Aurelius) and a seven-year-old boy, Lucius Aelius Verus, the son of the late Lucius Verus. After doing this, Hadrian felt that he had followed the example of Augustus in securing the succession not just for one, but for two generations to come. His last and only wish was to die in peace.

Death came, but not soon enough for him. Maddened by pain, he longed to take his life. He begged his doctor to give him a dose of poison; the doctor took one himself. He ordered a slave to stab him in the heart; the slave ran away. Finally at Baiae on July 10th, 138, nature granted his wish. His son and heir, Antoninus, had his body placed in the Mausoleum and, against the opposition of the senate, secured his deification. Another god had now entered the Roman Heaven, and Antoninus won for himself the new name of Pius.

Antoninus Pius: 138–161

Despite its length (23 years), the reign of Antoninus Pius was singularly uneventful. The empire remained at peace; no foreign wars or internal revolts disturbed the outward calm. The Emperor himself was a man of peace and the possessor of almost every known virtue. According to the *Historia Augusta,* he was tall and handsome, dignified and courteous, eminently talented, eloquent, scholarly, and industrious, just, honest, deeply religious, tolerant of others, a cool appraiser of himself, and withal most benevolent and serene. He had few enemies and many friends.

The life of Antoninus had always been simple, but never unpleasant; disciplined, but never strenuous; never dangerous or insecure. He was born and raised at Lanuvium, a

The Pantheon (117–125 A.D.). (Courtesy Fototeca Unione, Rome)

famous old Latin town, but his family came from Nemausus (Nîmes) in southern Gaul, a rich aristocratic old family that owned numerous estates in Italy and valuable brick yards near Rome. Of all his estates the one at Lorium in the drear Campagna pleased him most. He spent a great deal of time there, personally managing the property. He fed his chickens, entertained his friends, hunted and fished. Rome and its palaces and Hadrian's Tivoli held little attraction for him.

His Early Career

Having held all the offices of a normal senatorial career, Antoninus intended after his second consulship in 120 to retire to his country estates and enjoy himself. Instead, Hadrian made him a district judge of Italy and, in 135/6, proconsul of Asia, where he distinguished himself as an administrator. His expert knowledge of law and his skill in administration led to further appointments, none of which were solicited by him. Hadrian made him a member of the Imperial Council and, finally, his successor and colleague.

Antoninus and the Senate

Antoninus' first act as emperor was to frustrate the attempt of the senate to damn the memory and annul the edicts and acts (*acta*) of Hadrian, whose normative, philhellenic, and cosmopolitan policies they had always disliked and whose approval of the execution of high-ranking generals and senators they abhorred.* Pointing out that the annulment of Hadrian's acts would have

* In 136 four consulars, including Hadrian's brother-in-law, Servianus, were tried and condemned to death by the senate on charges of conspiracy and treason.

Interior of the Pantheon. (Courtesy Fratelli Alinari, Florence)

meant a repudiation of his own adoption and succession to the throne, Antoninus prevailed upon the senate to decree divine honors for his predecessor. In return, he agreed to abolish the four hated judgeships of Italy and to spare the lives of senators proscribed by the dying Hadrian. Thus his relations with the senate began most harmoniously.

Antoninus further improved his relations with the senate by his deferential attitude, by his attendance at meetings, by seeking its advice on policy, and by rendering financial assistance to needy senatorial families. Even more gratifying was his reversal of Hadrian's policy of treating Italy as one of the provinces.

Public Works

Antoninus allotted to Italy a generous share of the money earmarked for public works and social welfare: harbor improve-ments ordered at Puteoli, Ostia, Caieta, and Terracina, baths constructed at Ostia and an amphitheater at Capua; endowments provided for education and child welfare, and liberal distributions of food and money to the Roman populace. Last, but not least, he sponsored elaborate games and spectacles.

Nor did he entirely neglect the provinces. Under his reign of peace the upper and middle classes prospered although the masses of exploited peasants everywhere and particularly the *fellahin* of Egypt continued to be under the heel of poverty. Though blind to the sufferings of the millions, Antoninus gave ready ear to the desires and petitions of the ruling classes of the cities of Greece and Asia Minor and of some Aegean islands. He frequently reduced their taxes or canceled their debts and came to their aid when they were stricken by earthquake, fire, or flood. Furthermore he spared them the heavy burden of the

Roman emperor surrounded himself with such an array of legal talent, five jurists being members of the Imperial Council. There was the illustrious Salvius Julianus who, under Hadrian, had codified the *Praetorian Perpetual Edict* and whose influence upon the history of Roman jurisprudence can be compared only with that of Labeo. Scarcely less illustrious were some of Salvius' pupils, L. Volusius Maecianus, for example, the teacher of Marcus Aurelius and the author of a sixteen-volume work on trusts. There were also the famous Sextus Pomponius, who wrote a thirty-two volume commentary on the Provincial Edict, and especially Ulpius Marcellus, brilliant and sharp.

Antoninus himself had an intimate knowledge of both the minutiae and the spirit of the law. He clarified the laws dealing with inheritance, the protection of the legal interests of minors, and the manumission of slaves. He increased penalties against masters who killed or mistreated their slaves, and imposed a severe punishment on kidnaping, hitherto a frightful scourge in Italy and the provinces. Conversely, he reduced penalties for army deserters and released captives after ten years of hard labor in the mines; he permitted Jews the right of circumcision and restricted the persecution of Christians. Of more general interest was his ruling that a man must be considered innocent until proved guilty and in cases where the opinions of the judges were evenly divided, the prisoner must receive the benefit of the doubt. Antoninus had anticipated Blackstone by many, many centuries.

A marble portrait head of Antoninus Pius (138–161 A.D.). (Courtesy Metropolitan Museum of Art, Fletcher Fund, 1933)

imperial travel train by staying at home, content to let his power and beneficence radiate from Rome or Lorium like the peaceful glow of a late summer's afternoon.

Financial Administration

Despite his huge expenditures on charity and public works in Rome, Italy, and the provinces, Antoninus had before his death succeeded, through sound financial administration and personal frugality, in leaving behind in the treasury a surplus of 2,700,000,000 sesterces (about 135 million gold dollars), the largest surplus since the death of Tiberius.

Legal Developments

An even prouder achievement was his contribution to Roman law. Never had a

Foreign Policy

Antoninus, the living symbol of the might and majesty of the Roman state, possessed a prestige and authority far transcending the imperial frontiers. Embassies came to him from Bactria and India. His name was heard in central Asia and China. Eastern kings sought his advice and a letter to the king of Parthia dissuaded an invasion of Armenia. He awarded thrones to some, enlarged the territories of others. Even the Quadi of Bohemia accepted a king he nominated for them.

Despite that, the power of Rome was waning. Its shaky foundations rested solely on Trajan's military exploits and on Hadrian's indefatigable efforts to make the Roman army an efficient, hard-hitting force. Antoninus, in his efforts to save money, allowed this force to grow soft and deteriorate, while the nations beyond the frontiers—Germans, Huns, Iranians, and Arabs—were gradually acquiring military capability by copying Roman arms and tactics. The superior equipment and training that had once made one Roman legionary a match for several Germans or Parthians was now no longer a Roman monopoly. Even such a minor uprising as that of the Moroccan tribesmen was not suppressed without considerable difficulty. Simi-

The reverse side of a coin showing Antoninus Pius, placing a tiara on the head of the king of Armenia. (Courtesy The American Numismatic Society, New York)

The Temple of Antoninus and Faustina in the Roman Forum. (Courtesy Istituto Italiano di Cultura, New York)

lar revolts were occurring from time to time in Britain, Germany, Dacia, South Russia, Asia Minor, Egypt, and Palestine.

In the only two frontier zones—Britain and Germany—where Antoninus did exhibit energy or initiative he was simply following a policy of Hadrian's. In Scotland he pushed the frontier about 75 miles to the North and had a wall of turf and clay constructed between the firths of Forth and Clyde, a distance of some 37 miles, which was about half the length of Hadrian's Wall between the Solway and the Tyne. The purpose of the Antonine Wall, with its nineteen forts spaced two miles apart, was to overawe the natives living north and south of it and check cattle rustling or smuggling. In southwest Germany he shortened the defense line (*limes*) by pushing it forward from 20 to 30 miles, and strengthened it with new forts and watchtowers made of stone.

The Death of Antoninus

The defenses Antoninus erected in Britain and Germany stood firm to the end of his reign, but not long after. The policy of static defense and of isolationism and the failure to keep the army in top form had left the empire poorly equipped to roll back the tide of massive assault which broke after his death. Perhaps he dimly realized his mistake as he lay dying at Lorium in March, 161. In his delirium he talked fretfully about the empire and all the lying kings who had betrayed him. Too late to undo the harm, he turned over on his side and quietly died.

The Dual Monarchy: Marcus Aurelius and Lucius Verus

After Antoninus came Marcus Aurelius, one of the most remarkable and certainly the noblest of Roman emperors. He was a Stoic philosopher and, though not a Christian, most Christ-like in his spirituality and dedication to peace. It is one of the ironies of history that so peace-loving a man had to spend the greater part of his reign in fighting the empire's battles against German and Parthian onslaughts upon its frontiers.

Marcus Aurelius was born in Rome in 121 of rich and illustrious Spanish parentage. He enjoyed all the educational advantages money, rank, and high favor could bestow. He was only six when Hadrian insisted that he be adopted by Lucius Commodus Verus. Later he was to be adopted by Antoninus Pius, upon whose demise he was to become emperor of Rome.

Educational and Cultural Background of Marcus Aurelius

Marcus had never gone to public school. He was taught by private tutors from the three R's to grammar, literature—Greek as well as Latin—, science and mathematics, music, dancing, painting. The sports he learned included ball-playing, of which he was very fond, boxing, wrestling, hunting, and fishing.

The next stage in the education of Marcus was the study of rhetoric and Roman law, the former taught by Cornelius Fronto (ca. 100–ca. 166 A.D.), the famous rhetorician and advocate from Africa, the latter by the illustrious legal authority, L. Volusius Maecianus. Herodes Atticus (ca. 101–177 A.D.), a Greek sophist and rhetorician of incredible wealth, came from Athens to teach him Greek oratory. These were the most distinguished of his teachers, of whom he had altogether almost a score—four grammarians, four rhetoricians, one jurist, one painter, and finally eight philosophers, all experts in their special fields. But the greatest and the most beloved of all was the rhetorician, Fronto, with whom he corresponded for many years.

At this time rhetoric was more than the art of elegant speaking and writing; it embraced, as Cicero and Quintilian had insisted, all the disciplines necessary to produce a fully cultured man. In Fronto's eyes, it was the perfect and sufficient preparation for life. Never had the study of rhetoric for its own sake been more assiduously pursued than in the age of Marcus Aurelius, when Hermogenes of Tarsus (fl. 160–180 A.D.) reinforced the lofty ideals set forth during Domitian's reign in the *Institutio Oratoria* of Quintilian (ca. 35–97 A.D.). Hermogenes' digest of Hellenistic and Roman rhetoric, extant in five treatises, has had a powerful influence upon the art of public speaking from the Italian Renaissance to modern times.

By the time of Hadrian rhetoric had undergone an evolution in both function and character. No longer as useful in courts of law and in politics as formerly, it began to acquire a new and important function as a means of public entertainment and adult education.

Rhetoric had always been essentially a Greek art. Even by the second century most of its professors were Greeks who for money, fame, or both, made platform appearances all over the empire (as did Lucian), or set up studios in Athens or Pergamum, in Ephesus or Smyrna, in Antioch or Alexandria, in Italy, Gaul, or Spain. Most of them eventually turned up at Rome, which had become the cultural center of the empire. A few were sincere practitioners of the art, but many were smart charlatans, who with a little native wit, a plethora of words, and much effrontery captivated semi-educated but well-dressed and affluent audiences.

At this time rhetoric had undergone a change in character and style. Ever since Hadrian had announced a personal preference for Ennius over Vergil and for Cato over Cicero, the rhetoricians of the age exerted themselves to resurrect the archaic style and vocabulary of Cato and Gaius Gracchus and to detect in the slang and colloquialism of the street corner or country crossroad survivals of earlier Latin, which they fancied had a freshness and vigor absent from the more polished and artificial language of Cicero, Seneca, or the Younger Pliny.

The high priest of the new rhetoric was Fronto, the Latin tutor of Marcus Aurelius. After coming to Rome, Fronto had won a Ciceronian reputation as a lawyer and public speaker. Although his eloquence cannot be appraised, since none of his speeches are extant, many of the letters he wrote to Marcus, preserved in a palimpsest, reveal an amazing poverty of thought, an arid pedantry not redeemed by elaborate similes and other tricks of style.

One of Fronto's pupils, Aulus Gellius, carried the archaizing tendency even further in his *Attic Nights,* a handbook written for Latin readers and packed with antiquarian learning. His passion for erudition, mainly literary and grammatical, and the large excerpts culled from a score of authors no longer extant have made his work, in spite of its colorless style, a mine of information about the ancient world.

Another such treasure is the more famous handbook, *The Travel Guide to Greece,* by Pausanias. Without its aid, many historic sites and monuments would probably have remained undiscovered or their significance unexplained. His work also reveals the contemporary craze for travel. The affluence, prosperity and splendor of the East under the enlightened rule of the Antonines is the main theme in many of the fifty-five extant speeches of Aelius Aristides of Smyrna (117–189 A.D.) and especially in the famous panegyric addressed in 154 to Rome. His description of the cities with their paved and lighted streets, miles of shady porticoes, libraries, scientific and medical schools, gymnasia, markets, and theaters must have greatly stimulated the urge for travel and sightseeing. Tourists, some rich and cultured, flocked to Greece, Asia Minor, or Egypt, where they scratched their names on famous monuments, ambled into art museums, or attended lectures by noted philosophers, sophists, or rhetoricians. Having swiftly passed from one famous site to another in Greece or Asia Minor, they would then cross over to Egypt to have a look at the pyramids or the temple of Karnak.

Even the stay-at-homes could enjoy, vicariously, the pleasure of travel and adventure by reading the *Golden Ass,* by the African-born Lucius Apuleius. A weird extravaganza about a traveler magically transformed into a donkey with human intelligence, this novel is nevertheless famous for its beautiful rendition of the story of Cupid and Psyche.

The more educated and sophisticated reader now had at hand the dialogues of Lucian (ca. 120–180 A.D.), a sophist and satirist born in Syria near the Euphrates. He had once been a traveling lecturer and entertainer. Later he wrote Menippean mixed prose and verse satire. In Platonic dialogue form and in idiomatic Attic, he made fun of the Olympian gods, Cynic and Stoic philosophers, fake sophists and rhetoricians, and of all the superstitions and miracle-mongering of the age. Occasionally the humorist turned moralist and displayed a spirituality not unlike that of Marcus Aurelius, though less intense or sublime.

The Philosophical Training of Marcus Aurelius

Such might have been the complete educational and literary background of Marcus Aurelius had Fronto had his way, but to Fronto's disgust his introspective and philosophically inclined pupil had even before puberty turned from rhetoric to the philosophy of Stoicism. He studied under Junius Rusticus, who lent him a copy of the *Discourses* of Epictetus (ca. 55–135 A.D.), a Phrygian slave, lame, of feeble health, and horribly treated by a freedman in Nero's court. Later freed, Epictetus taught philosophy in Rome until exiled in 90 by Domitian because of his uncompromising Stoic resistance to tyranny. Even in exile (at Nicopolis in Epirus) he attracted such distinguished pupils as Arrian (ca. 95–180 A.D.),* who took down in shorthand and later published the lectures of Epictetus under the titles, *Discourses* and *Enchiridion*. These teach that all men are sons of God and, because they have within them a spark of divinity, they belong to a universal brotherhood.

With Epictetus there came a change in Stoicism. It became a religion as well as a philosophy. It was no longer simply an intellectualized restatement of the ancient Roman moral code with its emphasis on courage in war, fortitude, temperance, piety, and patriotism—the simple virtues of a practical and warlike people—but a religious faith, more universal and spiritual, and more mystical than the older Roman Stoicism of Scipio the Younger, of Cato and Cicero, and even of Seneca.

The most sublime expression of Stoicism, except possibly for the *Hymn to Zeus* by Cleanthes (ca. 310–232 B.C.), is contained in the *Meditations* of Marcus Aurelius. While

* In imitation of Xenophon, Arrian wrote a hunting book (*Cynegeticus*), an *Anabasis of Alexander,* the best authority on the life of Alexander the Great, a study on the Black Sea (*Periplus of the Euxine*), and a book on India (*Indica*).

encamped along the Danube during the Second Marcomannic War (169–175), Marcus spent his nights writing down in Greek his reflections—scattered, disjointed, and unaffected soliloquies or dialogues between himself and the Universal Power. In the *Meditations* (*Ta eis heauton*—"To Himself"), he strongly reaffirmed the traditional Stoic virtues as the basis of morality, from which the spirit is propelled into direct communion with the divine and unapprehensive resignation to its will. "Thy will be done" are Christian words, but they also sum up the philosophy of Marcus Aurelius.

Persecution of the Christians

The most controversial aspect of the reign of Marcus Aurelius concerns his alleged persecution of Christians. It is known that adherents of the Christian faith did suffer martyrdom at that time: Justin Martyr (who adapted Platonic and Stoic philosophy to Jewish and Christian theology) died in Rome along with six companions; other Christians died at Scyllium in Numidia; and at Lyons and Vienne in the Transalpina numerous Christians (forty-seven in Lyons) were tortured to death at the demand of an angry, bloodthirsty mob.*

Like most pious orthodox Romans of his time, Marcus Aurelius regarded the Christians as not only a depraved and superstitious sect but an illicit and subversive organization dedicated to the overthrow of the Roman way of life. The wilful and obstinate refusal of the Christians to obey a magistrate's order to sacrifice to the gods of the state was regarded as opposition to the efforts of the emperors to restore the ancient Roman culture and religion as a means of strengthening the empire against the barbarians from without and disintegration from within. The com-

* There were sporadic persecutions of the Christians during the second century. St. Ignatius (ca. 50-107 A.D.), the bishop of Antioch, and St. Simeon of Jerusalem were both killed during the reign of Trajan. Telephorus, the bishop of Rome, is known to have suffered martyrdom during the reign of Hadrian. In 155 A.D., under the reign of Antoninus Pius, Polycarp, the bishop of Smyrna, and eleven other Christians met with a violent end at the hands of an angry mob in Smyrna.

mon people accused the Christians of atheism, incest, and even cannibalism and made them the scapegoats for the calamities that were falling on the state. When angry mobs, as at Lyons and Smyrna, demanded vengeance, the officials often yielded to those demands.

Marcus Aurelius as Emperor and Soldier

Marcus Aurelius was not only a scholar and philosopher, but a man of action, an able administrator and commander of armies. The first two years of his reign were filled with crises: a serious Tiber flood, an earthquake in Cyzicus, a famine in Galatia, a revolt in Britain, a German crossing of the Rhine, and an invasion of Armenia and Syria by the young Parthian king, Vologeses III. Marcus, therefore, halted his studies and put away his books. His first act as emperor was to insist on appointing Lucius Verus as his colleague, equal in honor, titulature, and power, even against the opposition of the senate, who regarded Verus as a frivolous young man addicted to pleasure and self-indulgence.

The Parthian War: 161-165

Marcus Aurelius sent Verus out to the East, where Verus cleverly combined pleasure with a thorough reorganization of the undisciplined and demoralized army of Syria and Cappadocia. He had as his subordinates two able generals. One was Statius Priscus, who invaded Armenia, captured and burnt down its capital of Artaxata; the other was the Syrian-born Avidius Cassius, a hard-bitten martinet, who whipped the Syrian army into shape, crossed the Euphrates, and invaded Mesopotamia capturing in rapid succession Edessa, Nisibis, Ctesiphon, and Seleucia, which he burnt to the ground. Both emperors jointly shared the triumph, though Aurelius, the actual author of the winning strategy, was unwilling to deprive Verus of the glory of victory.

Then suddenly two disasters struck. Soldiers returning from the fire-gutted ruins of Seleucia brought back with them a frightful plague. It forced the retreat of the victorious armies of the East, then infected Asia Minor,

Egypt, Greece, and Italy, destroying as much as a third of the population in some places, and finally decimating the armies guarding the frontiers along the Rhine and Danube. The defenses along the Danube had already been weakened by extensive troop withdrawals for service in the East; there now burst through them a host of Germans—the Marcomanni, the Quadi and many others, reacting at last to the slow but relentless pressure which had for centuries been building up from the vast heartland of Eurasia. Pouring through the sparsely guarded frontiers, they overran the provinces of Rhaetia, Noricum, and Pannonia, pressed down through the Julian Alps into North Italy, besieged Aquileia, the big seaport at the head of the Adriatic. Never since the Cimbrian and Teutonic invasions in the days of Marius (*see* p. 188) was Italy in greater danger.

War on the Danube Front: 167-175

Ignoring an outbreak of famine in Rome, Marcus Aurelius took energetic measures. He announced to the senate that he and Verus must at once take off for the northern front. The treasury having been depleted by the expenses of the Parthian War, Marcus raised money by selling the gold vessels and art treasures of the imperial palaces to avoid increasing taxes: drafted slaves, gladiators, and brigands into the army, hired German and Scythian tribes to harass the enemy rear, blocked the Alpine passes and fortified towns in the danger zone. Then he hurried north to relieve Aquileia and reoccupy Noricum and Pannonia. At his approach the enemy retreated and asked for a truce. It was granted —reluctantly—only because a fresh outbreak of the plague had wrought havoc in the Roman army and almost destroyed the garrison at Aquileia. In 169, their mission accomplished, both emperors set out for Rome. On the way, Lucius Verus, stricken with apoplexy, suddenly died.

Marcus Aurelius, now sole princeps, had to contend with a host of troubles: the main enemy—the Quadi, Marcomanni, and Iazyges —remained unsubdued and menacing; the Parthian king again invaded Armenia; in 169 the Chatti invaded the frontier regions of the

A relief from the Column of Marcus Aurelius, showing Roman soldiers crossing a river. (Courtesy Fratelli Alinari, Florence)

Another relief from the Marcus Aurelius Column, showing the storming of a Sarmatian stronghold. (Courtesy Fratelli Alinari, Florence)

upper Rhine, while the Chauci attacked the Belgica; the rebellious tribesmen of Morocco harassed the shores of Africa and Spain, crossed the straits, and invaded Baetica; the herdsmen of the Nile delta rose in revolt and were subdued only by the timely intervention of Avidius Cassius; and worst of all, in 170 the Costoboci of eastern Galicia joined forces with the Sarmatians, crossed the lower Danube, broke into Moesia, overran the Balkans, and invaded Greece as far south as Attica, where they plundered the Temple of the Mysteries at Eleusis before being driven back.

In the fall of 169 Marcus Aurelius again returned to the Danubian front determined to destroy the main enemy—the Marcomanni, Quadi, and Iazyges—one by one, finally annex their lands, and bring to pass the grand strategy of Julius Caesar, which Augustus and Tiberius had abandoned. In 172 he crossed the Danube, attacked the Quadi first, then the Marcomanni, and finally the Iazyges. He forced each in turn to return all the Roman prisoners they had taken, make reparations for the damages they had inflicted on the provinces, and evacuate a strip of territory ten miles wide running along the north bank of the Danube.

A sculptured record of this long Marcomannic War survives on the spiral frieze of the Marcus Aurelius column in the Campus Martius. Some of the 116 reliefs show Roman soldiers transporting baggage and war material, convoying booty and captives, crossing turbulent rivers, or storming German and Sarmatian strongholds. Others depict the emperor himself, calm and self-assured, riding with his troops, consulting with his aides, receiving foreign envoys, or accepting the obsequious attentions of conquered foes.

With the subjugation of the Iazyges, the Sarmatians, and the Costoboci not yet complete, Marcus Aurelius had again to turn against the Quadi, who had already violated their treaty obligations. While thus engaged, he received disturbing news from the East.

The Usurpation of Avidius Cassius: 175

In the East Avidius Cassius, the able governor of his native Syria, but a violent and ruthless man, misled by the false rumor

of the death of Marcus Aurelius, had himself proclaimed emperor. Marcus hastily concluded peace with the still unsubdued Quadi and Iazyges, summoned his wife Faustina and young son Commodus to Sirmium, and prepared to set out with them to the East. Before his departure, he addressed his troops and in a dramatic speech of mingled pathos, irony, and clemency promised to pardon the rebel. Presently a legionary showed up bearing the head of Cassius, which the emperor refused to look at but ordered reverently buried.

The death of Cassius would seem to have removed the need for Marcus to go to the East, but he went anyway, desiring perhaps to make a display of Roman power, receive expressions of loyalty, and remove disloyal officials from their posts. On his way through Asia Minor he suffered the loss of his dear wife, Faustina, Antoninus' daughter, a woman he had loved for thirty years and the mother of his thirteen children.

After traversing Asia Minor, Syria, and Egypt, greeted everywhere by acclamations of loyalty, he arrived in Rome in 176, a sad and lonely man, bereft of his wife and one of his best generals; he resolved never again to make a man governor of the province of his birth and at once to recognize, as heir and successor, his son Commodus, a remarkably handsome and athletic youth but totally unlike his father in character and ideals. Marcus seemed not to realize that a good lion killer does not necessarily make a good emperor.

In Rome Marcus Aurelius celebrated his German and Sarmatian triumphs. In the course of the celebration he unveiled the famous Marcus Aurelius equestrian statue which still stands on the Roman Capitol, the prototype of most later equestrian statues, and laid the foundation stone of the Marcus Aurelius column in the Campus Martius.

Return to the Danube: 178-180

Rumors of fresh troubles along the Danube caused the emperor to hasten north in 178 (followed later by his son Commodus). Leading his men himself, he crossed the Danube and, after a long and strenuous campaign known as the Third Marcomannic War,

The equestrian bronze statue of Marcus Aurelius, the prototype of the Gattamelata of Donatello and all later equestrian statues. (Courtesy Fratelli Alinari, Florence)

crushed the resistance of the Quadi and Marcomanni. He established a new legionary camp on the Danube at Castra Regina (Regensburg in Bavaria) and proceeded to create two new provinces—Marcomannia and Sarmatia—by annexing that vast territory extending as far north as the Erzgebirge and as far east as the Carpathians, in order to shorten and strengthen the northern frontiers against future barbarian assaults. While engaged in this mighty task, Marcus Aurelius suddenly caught a dangerous infection (possibly the plague) and died in his camp at Vindobona (Vienna) on March 17, 180. His last words were "Go to the rising sun; my sun is setting."

The most permanent result of the Danubian campaigns consisted not in the victories of Marcus Aurelius over the Germans and Sarmatians, but in the transplantation and settlement of thousands of Germans in the war-torn and plague-devastated provinces of Dacia, Moesia, Rhaetia, Pannonia, Dalmatia, Gaul and even Italy. This measure not only temporarily relieved the pressure on the frontiers of the Rhine and of the Danube but finally altered the entire racial composition of the Roman empire.

The Second Century in Review

The death of Marcus Aurelius marked the end of a century described by Gibbon as the happiest and most glorious in the history of mankind, and by others as an age of decline and decadence. Although the second judgment is more widely held than the first, it probably reflects a mistaken view of the nature of human society, not unlike that of the historian Annaeus Florus (ca. 130 A.D.), who referred to the Roman Empire as a period of old age (*senectus imperii*) as if a society were subject, like a biological organism, to birth, growth, old age, and death.

Actually the second century brought to fruition tendencies implicit and even evident in the first. The Antonines continued the process initiated by Caesar and Augustus of centralizing the government without fundamentally altering the character of the principate or destroying the prestige of the senate.

The Function and Composition of the Senate

In two ways did the senate of the second century slightly differ from that of the first: composition and function. The change in function was not a revolutionary development, for the division of power between senate and princeps had been from the start more or less of a farce, a clever fiction of its author, Augustus (*see* p. 273). Many of the functions performed by the senate of the Republic had been relinquished to the princeps by default because of the senate's inability to control the army, the mainspring of power. Loss of that control by Commodus and by the emperors of the third century (except Septimius Severus and Diocletian), made their reigns difficult and short.

Senatorial membership was no longer confined to the aristocracy of Rome and Italy but open to the best families of Gaul and Spain and, especially since Trajan, to those of Africa, Syria, Greece, Asia Minor, the Danubian provinces, and to men of merit everywhere. Rome had become the spiritual symbol of a world state which embraced the civilized parts of three continents. Her economic and cultural influence penetrated far

Roman ruins at Sufetula (Sbeitla, Tunisia): three temples, a theater, baths, and a Christian basilica. (Courtesy The French Embassy, Information Division, New York)

beyond the imperial frontiers. As a spiritual and cultural power, the Rome of Marcus Aurelius was at its zenith.

Economic Changes

Never in the history of the ancient world had prosperity and wealth been more widely diffused. Italy had lost its proud monopoly of the Augustan Age to the economic upsurge and competition of the provinces, all of which now shared fully in the benefits of the universal peace (*Pax Romana*). Incomes soared and gave rise to an unprecedented urge to travel which was further encouraged by the construction of a huge network of excellent roads. The provinces were urbanized and cities appeared: Mainz, Strasbourg, Cologne along the Rhine, Vienna, Budapest, and Belgrade on the Danube, London, York, and Gloucester in England, and some such as Timgad later buried beneath the sands of North Africa. A traveler in Asia, Africa, Spain, or Gaul might then see temples, theaters, libraries, baths, and fine homes differing only in size and splendor from those of Rome. Products of farm and shop moved freely over land and sea. Ships sailed to India and, in 166, Greek merchants even appeared at the Chinese imperial court.

Behind the apparent prosperity, a serious weakness existed in the financial structure of the empire. In spite of the large surplus Antoninus Pius had reportedly left behind in the treasury, Marcus Aurelius found himself obliged to sell the palace jewels and treasures in order to finance the Danubian campaigns and to debase the silver currency by raising its copper content to approximately thirty-four per cent.

In times of peace the revenues of the empire barely covered expenditures. The mounting costs of government and imperial bureaucracy, the donatives given to the troops, the vast sums spent on education and public welfare, monuments and public buildings, and relief to stricken communities normally left nothing in reserve to meet unexpected civil or military emergencies. The cancellation of arrears and reduction of taxes together with an inefficient system of tax collection kept the state perpetually on the brink of bankruptcy.

Instead of increasing the regular taxes and extending their collection to every part of the empire, the emperors often resorted to extraordinary taxation, confiscations of capital, requisitions of money, food, and transport for the army, or compulsory labor. These levies not only imposed hardship upon the municipalities and the rich men made responsible for their collection, but sometimes drove the tenants on the imperial estates such as the *saltus Burunitanus* of North Africa or the herdsmen of Egypt into strikes, revolt, or flight.

The Failure of Ancient Technology

Yet it would be erroneous to suppose that the crippling burden of taxation, the large-scale exploitation and consumption of wealth, bad financial policies, and the prodigious demands of a world-wide military establishment and of a vast bureaucratic machine alone provide an adequate explanation of the economic crisis of the Late Roman Empire. The root of the trouble lay rather in the persistent failure of Graeco-Roman society to transform pure science into technology. Although the Greeks had an impressive record of achievement in the history of theoretical science and mathematics and in the Hellenistic period owed to Archimedes (ca. 287–212 B.C.), to Hero of Alexandria (?ca. 150 B.C.), and others the invention of many mechanical contrivances such as the endless chain, the compound pulley, the lifting crane, the steam engine, and the reaction turbine, they never succeeded in putting these inventions to practical use to save labor, increase productive capacity, and build an industrial civilization capable of bearing the financial load of a highly centralized bureaucratic state.

The clue to the ancient failure to transform science into an industrial technology may be found not only in the slave syndrome (which had been breaking down since Augustan times) and the aristocratic leisure-class contempt for work, but principally in the failure of ancient education. The undue emphasis upon rhetoric to the exclusion of science and practical technological training was designed to produce lawyers, administrators, and professors of rhetoric rather than scientists and industrial engineers and technicians. The rapid disappearance of slave labor and the shortage of free labor made the need for industrial technology and for labor-saving machines particularly acute in the age of the Antonines.

Literature

Some historians of Latin literature have indicted the age as decadent because it failed to produce a Cicero, a Vergil, or a Horace. It was not from mental fatigue that the best minds of the second century turned away from the older genres of a literature limited, as it was, by rigid tradition to a few well-worn themes. Instead they moved into other fields such as administration, law, public speaking, business, and science.

Nor was literature in a broader sense either lacking or completely feeble—indeed the second century was the golden age of jurisprudence, medicine, theology, and geography. To Salvius, who codified the *Perpetual Edict,* to Scaevola, to Papinian, to Ulpian, and to Paul, five of the greatest jurists of all time, modern Europe owes a vast debt as the chief architects of Roman civil law. The *Institutes* of Gaius (issued ca. 160 A.D.), a masterly introduction to Roman law, has made a lasting contribution to legal studies. The greatest name in medicine was Galen (ca. 130–200 A.D.), whose encyclopedic work reigned in undiminished authority until the time of Harvey. Another great name was Ptolemy (ca. 121–151 A.D.), whose theories on astronomy and geography remained unchallenged till overthrown by Copernicus.

Some of the ablest men of the age were the Christian writers, who wrote with remarkable intellectual power and fiery zeal. The most notable were Ignatius of Antioch (50–107 A.D.), the first great ecclesiastic and the father of Christian orthodoxy; Irenaeus of Lyons (ca. 130–202 A.D.), the powerful advocate of Christian unity, denunciator of heresy, and the father of systematic theology; Tatian (ca. 120–172 A.D.) "the Assyrian," whose *Life of Christ,* a harmony of the Four Gospels, was read in Syrian churches for almost three centuries; and, finally, toward the end of the second century, Tertullian of Carthage (ca. 160–230? A.D.), whose vigorous Ciceronian eloquence, wit, and biting satire transformed Christian polemic into Latin literature and Latin into the enduring language of Western Catholicism.

The second century A.D. Roman amphitheater at Pula is one of the best preserved in the world. (Courtesy Yugoslav Tourist Office, New York)

The granite aqueduct at Segovia, Spain, was constructed in the time of Trajan, and is still in use. (Courtesy Spanish Tourist Office, New York)

The amphitheater at Verona, the third largest in the Roman world. (Courtesy Fratelli Alinari, Florence)

Two interior views of the famous amphitheater at Thysdrus (El-Djem) in Tunisia (third century A.D.). (Courtesy Embassy of Tunisia, Washington, D. C.)

The Arch of Marcus Aurelius (163 A.D.) at Tripoli. (Courtesy Fratelli Alinari, Florence)

Architecture

Nor is there evidence of decadence in the monumental architecture of the age, which symbolized the might of Imperial Rome. The temples erected by Trajan and Hadrian, the Pantheon, the massive mausoleum of Hadrian, the columns of Trajan and of Marcus Aurelius, the beautiful high-span bridge which rises 180 feet above the Tagus, are compelling structures—poetic, bold, and of monumental grandeur. As imposing as the Pont du Gard at Nîmes (*see* p. 305) is the magnificent aqueduct (94 feet high) which Trajan's engineers constructed of granite at Segovia in Spain. The splendid amphitheater at Pola (Pula) in Istria is comparable in size and state of preservation to the earlier amphitheater at Nîmes, though inferior in size to the two gigantic third-century structures at Verona, Italy and Thysdrus (El-Djem) in Tunisia. The great temples of Jupiter Heliopolitanus and of Venus (or Bacchus) at Baalbek in Syria and the splendid arch of Marcus Aurelius at Tripoli also testify to the monumental achievements of the age.

Mosaics, Coins, and Medallions

The numerous mosaics of the period, which are found all over the empire especially in the villas of North Africa, are not only very valuable documents on the social and economic life of the region, but exhibit remarkable taste and workmanship in an art destined to have a future even more brilliant. The coins and medallions of this period are among the finest in history. The art of medal-engraving, which had its genesis in Hadrian's issue of a series of bronze medallions, reveals a love of symbolism and allegory and a skill and technique comparable to that of the most beautiful coinages in the ancient world.

A floor mosaic, found in a large villa near Uthina (Qudna) in Tunisia, depicts life on an African estate during the early second century A.D. (Courtesy Bardo, Tunis)

This Roman mosaic, now at the Bardo, came originally from *Thuburbo Majus*, 35 miles southwest of Tunis. It represents a Greek dramatist, possibly Menander, reading plays before two facial masks. (Courtesy Embassy of Tunisia, Washington, D. C.).

Medallions of the time of Hadrian, used as ornamental details of the Arch of Constantine. (Courtesy Fratelli Alinari, Florence)

THE THIRD CENTURY

THE PERIOD FROM THE DEATH OF MARCUS AURELIUS IN 180 TO the accession of Diocletian in 284 is one of the most difficult, confusing, and misunderstood periods of Roman history. More intensive future studies may render much present information obsolete or incomplete. The main difficulty is that the obscure and anonymous forces of the time were not understood or perceived by contemporary witnesses.

Cassius Dio (ca. 153–240? A.D.) wrote a history of Rome (up to his own times) in the Thucydidean Greek compressed style. His later and most valuable books (except 79 and 80) are untunately preserved only in epitomes supplemented by fragments often tantalizingly obscure. Valuable information about the period from 180 to 238 is contained in the eight extant books of Herodian and the *Historia Augusta* (though some of the

biographies of the latter are more romantic fiction than history). Preserved in Justinian's *Corpus Iuris Civilis* are numerous fragments of third century legal works which, together with coins, papyri, inscriptions, and archaeological material, are all excellent primary sources. Although these sources have not yet been fully explored or interpreted, they constitute the bulk of information about the third century. One very important inscription, which throws much light on Rome's wars with Parthia, was discovered and photographed in 1936. Incised in Greek and two Persian dialects on the so-called Kaaba of Zoroaster, near Persepolis, it is a lengthy report by Shapur I (241–272), the second ruler of the new, revolutionary, Arsacid-overthrowing dynasty of Persia. In it Shapur boasts about the extent of his domains, domestic affairs and administration, the cities he captured, and his victories over Roman emperors, especially Gordian III and Valerian I. This is a most valuable document comparable to the annals of the Assyrian kings, the Behistun inscription of Darius I, and the *Monumentum Ancyranum* of Augustus.

The reverse side of a coin, showing Hercules (with the features of Commodus) placing his right hand on trophy. HERCVLI ROMANO AVG SC. (Courtesy The American Numismatic Society, New York)

Commodus: 180–192

The third century really began with the reign of Commodus, the unworthy son of Marcus Aurelius, who is variously described as a voluptuary, degenerate (he reputedly kept in one wing of his palace 300 beautiful young girls and in another as many handsome teenage boys), and buffoon. Though he outraged the upper-class sense of propriety by staging lion and tiger hunts in the Colosseum, he delighted the crowd by his feats. He developed such skill with the javelin that he could hit the neck of an ostrich at fifty paces. He delegated important responsibilities of the empire to various favorites, but murdered them as soon as they fell from favor. He exhausted the treasury by his wild extravagance and mad career of vice and dissipation, and betrayed the empire by a hastily concluded peace with the Germans and Sarmatians.* He came to an ignominious end at the muscular hands of his favorite wrestling partner who was also the willing accomplice of his mistress and her friends.

Pertinax and Didius Julianus: 193

The next emperor, Pertinax, attempted to restore order and refill the treasury. He reduced taxes, granted full possession and ten years' remission of taxes to occupiers of war-torn and plague-depopulated

---

* Even while it was within his power to consummate Marcus Aurelius' dream of extending the frontiers to the Elbe and the easily defensible Carpathian mountain chain.

land, and put up for sale the treasures Commodus had accumulated in his palace—fine silks and costly robes and cloaks, gladiatorial paraphernalia and chariots, and most of the human resources of pleasure and vice. Unfortunately, like Galba, Pertinax alienated the Praetorian Guard by his failure to make promised payments and by his attempt to make them submit to strict discipline. Several hundred guardsmen marched on the palace and murdered him.

The guardsmen thereupon auctioned off the throne to a fabulously rich senator, M. Didius Julianus, who promised each man the sum of 25,000 sesterces (about 1,250 dollars). Helpless, the senate confirmed the nomination.

Goaded to action by this outrageous affront to the august imperial office, the Roman people assailed Julianus with vile names and pelted him with stones as he made his way in and out of his palace under armed escort. Then they thronged into the Circus, where they passed a resolution calling upon Pescennius Niger, the governor of Syria, to rise in arms and seize the throne. The legions of Syria saluted the governor as emperor. Simultaneously the armies of Britain and the Danube declared for their respective commanders, Clodius Albinus and Septimius Severus, and made a dash for Rome. Septimius got there first and with boldness and decision seized the throne. At first Julianus attempted to resist Severus and then to negotiate, but deserted by the praetorians who had sold him the throne and deposed by the senate, he sought refuge in the palace, where a guardsman found him and put him to death.

The Reign of Septimius Severus

Septimius Severus was born in 146 at Leptis Magna, an African town not far from Tripoli. He had had an active career: a student of literature and philosophy in Athens, a lawyer in Rome, a tribune of the people, a praetor in Spain, and governor of Gallia Lugdunensis (Lyons) and finally of Pannonia. Though he spoke Latin with an African accent, he was well-educated and loved the company of poets and philosophers.

The Basilica at Leptis Magna, erected by Septimius Severus.
(Courtesy The German Archeological Institute)

His second wife was a rich and beautiful Syrian woman named Julia Domna, who was very intelligent but quite promiscuous. She bore him two sons—Caracalla and Geta.

Severus moved swiftly to consolidate his power. He seized the various treasuries, restocked the depleted granaries of the city, and avenged the murder of Pertinax, whose name he assumed. He increased the pay of his own troops to make sure of their continued loyalty, and disbanded the Italian Praetorian Guard, replacing it with 15,000 of his best legionary soldiers who had been recruited largely in Illyria and Thrace. The change in the composition of the Guard helped to remove the special privileges of Italy in the choosing of emperors and in the government of the empire.

The War against Pescennius Niger: 193–194

Severus thereupon set about dealing with one rival at a time. He temporarily acknowledged Albinus as Caesar and adopted successor, thus securing his rear as he advanced against Niger. Niger had meanwhile won the support of Roman Asia and Egypt and had seized Byzantium as a base from which he could threaten the Danubian provinces of Severus. In a swift and savage campaign, Severus put Byzantium under siege, advanced into Asia Minor and broke Niger's control of the Bosporus by victories at Cyzicus and Nicaea. At Issus in Cilicia he inflicted upon Niger's army a loss of 20,000 men and captured Antioch. Niger was overtaken and killed as he attempted to escape to the Parthians across the Euphrates. Severus inflicted terrible punishment upon the cities which had actively assisted Niger: Antioch and Neapolis (in Palestine), and especially Byzantium, which capitulated after a two-and-a-half-year siege.

War against Parthia: 194–195

After Niger's defeat and death, Severus attacked Parthia, whose king, Vologeses IV, had not only offered assistance to Niger but had tampered with the loyalty and allegiance of the king of Osrhoene, a Roman vassal in western Mesopotamia. In 194/5 Severus overran Osrhoene, northern Mesopotamia, and Adiabene (the modern Azerbaijan). Here the campaign came to an abrupt end: Albinus had amassed an army in Britain for the impending conflict with Septimius.

Albinus had been growing suspicious of the emperor's sincerity in acknowledging him as Caesar and successor. Supported by a large following in the senate, he decided to make a bid for supreme power. To enforce his claim, he crossed over into Gaul and set up headquarters at Lyons. Here Severus hastened and the two armies, each consisting of some 150,000 men, fought a furious battle which ended in the defeat and suicide of Albinus. Severus allowed his victorious troops to sack and burn the city of Lyons and carried out a ruthless extermination of the adherents of Albinus.*

Financial Reforms

The confiscations of property belonging to political enemies in both East and West were so enormous that Severus created the *res privata principis,* a new treasury department separate and distinct from the *fiscus,* the regular imperial treasury, and from the *patrimonium Caesaris.* The new treasury, administered by a procurator, gave the emperor a stronger control not only over the financial administration of the empire but over the army, whose annual pay he probably raised from 375 to 500 *denarii* per man (this increase can be explained by the inflation that had raged since the reign of Commodus). Financial difficulties also obliged Severus to reduce the silver content of the *denarius* to fifty percent. Nevertheless, his financial administration was actually sounder than that of many of his predecessors and brought about a temporary revival of economic prosperity and a fairly respectable surplus in the treasury.

Septimius as Administrator

Although Septimius was a usurper who owed his throne solely to his control of a

powerful and victorious army, he did not set out to establish a revolutionary regime. Like Augustus, another *dux* who usurped political power by military force, Septimius sought legitimization of his regime, but did so not by extorting legal sanction from the senate or by resort to the Augustan pretence of concealing naked force behind a façade of constitutional government, but by invoking the imperial cult which, after a century of evolution, had reached its peak of development during the enlightened monarchy of the deified Antonines. He accordingly adopted as his "father" the last and most brilliant star in the imperial firmament, Marcus Aurelius, and proclaimed himself the "brother" of Commodus, whose *memoriae damnatio* he compelled the senate to revoke. He officially proclaimed as his successor his son, Caracalla, and bestowed upon the youth the august name of Marcus Aurelius Antoninus.

The Severan policy towards the senate was neither wholly new nor revolutionary. He was not the first to substitute knights for senators in most of the key administrative positions. He continued Trajan's policy of increasing the representation of the Eastern and African provinces in the senate by new elections. He did not restore to the senate the legislative and policy-making functions of which it had earlier been deprived. As the result of a process of evolution dating back to Augustus, the senate had become simply a sounding board of policies formulated by the princeps and his Imperial Council, which had now become the true successor of the old Republican senate. Since its inception, the Council had grown in membership and now included not only many of the leading senators and equestrians but the best legal minds of the age—Papinian, and later, Ulpian and Paulus.

Legal Reforms

Even the legal reforms of Septimius were implicit in those of Hadrian, especially in the Julianus redaction of the *Perpetual Edict.* The major Severan reform was the abolition of the regular standing jury courts (*quaestiones perpetuae*) of Republican times and the transfer to the jurisdiction of the Urban

---

* Among whom were twenty-nine members of the senate, who had their property confiscated.

Prefect (*praefectus urbi*) of major criminal cases in Rome and within a hundred-mile radius.* Such cases as arose throughout Italy, as well as appeal cases from the provinces, came under the jurisdiction of the Praetorian Prefect (*praefectus praetorio*).

The powers of this official were greatly increased: he also presided over the grain administration, was commander-in-chief of all armed forces stationed in Italy, and was vice-president of the Imperial Council, the supreme court of the Empire and its highest policy making body. From 197 to 205 the senior praetorian prefect was C. Fulvius Plautianus, a man of extreme ambition, arrogance, and cruelty, who wielded almost autocratic power because of his overpowering personality and his influence over the emperor. He finally fell from favor and was assassinated.

* Paradoxically, the abolition of the old jury courts was actually a return to the Republican practice of relegating criminal trials to the executive branch of the government.

The next senior prefect was the distinguished jurist, Papinian.

Another Severan innovation was the introduction of different scales of punishment for the two social classes into which the citizen body was now divided—the *honestiores*, consisting of senators, knights, all municipal magistrates, and soldiers of all ranks and the *humiliores*, or proletariat. A privileged person might be exiled, an underprivileged one sentenced to hard labor in the mines for the same crime. Furthermore, *honestiores* had the right of appeal to the emperor, *humiliores* had not. This change in criminal procedure continued to be reflected in the feudal society of the Middle Ages.

Provincial Administration

In general, the provincial policy of Septimius Severus was a corollary of that of Hadrian and the Antonines, who had begun to raise the status of the provinces to equal

Ruins of Cuicul (Djemila, Algeria); on the extreme left is the Temple of Septimius Severus, on the right, the Arch of Caracalla. (Courtesy The French Embassy, Information Division, New York)

that of Italy. Severus continued this policy, not out of hatred for Italy, but purely because of political and dynastic motives. His disbanding of the Italian Praetorian Guard and his adlections of Oriental and African senators had been measures undertaken principally to consolidate his regime. He stationed one of his newly created legions in Italy, the other two in Mesopotamia thus showing that he regarded Italy as not more secure than one of the most exposed frontier provinces of the empire. Though he spent money liberally in Rome and Italy on public works, on the feeding and amusement of the Roman populace, and on the resumption of Nerva's alimentary and educational program (which Commodus had suspended), he spent equally vast amounts in Africa and Syria. Thus the Severan regime was the consummation of a policy begun by earlier emperors leading to a balance, equalization, and fusion of the Greek, Latin, and Semitic elements of the Graeco-Roman world.

As a precaution against the dangerous concentration of power in the hands of provincial governors who might prove as dangerous as Pescennius Niger and Clodius Albinus, Septimus followed the policy of Augustus, Trajan, and Hadrian and partitioned large, legion-filled provinces. He divided Syria and Britain into two separate provinces and detached Numidia from Africa, thus creating smaller provinces and correspondingly weaker provincial governors.

Military Reforms

Owing his power entirely to the army, Septimius made a historic contribution to it, not only by increasing its size from thirty to thirty-three legions, but by making army life as attractive as possible to the common soldier. The Praetorian Guard, though no longer composed solely of Italians, Western provincials, and Macedonians, continued to be an elite corps, trained in the best Roman tradition, and still remained a renowned training school for future army officers. The so-called "barbarization" of the army was a much later development.

In his reorganization of the army, Severus replaced senators with knights, who were often ex-centurions promoted from the ranks. The commanders of the legions were no longer senatorial *legati* but equestrian prefects with *legatus* rank, some of them eligible for provincial governorships. Severus democratized the army by making it possible for a common soldier of ability and initiative to pass from the centuriate to the rank of tribune, prefect, and *legatus,* and eventually to the high office of praetorian prefect, if not emperor. Even ordinary veterans became a privileged class, with good jobs in the civil service awaiting them after discharge.

Septimius made army life more attractive by allowing junior officers to organize social clubs, to which all contributed for drinks, entertainment, and financial insurance during service and after discharge. He legalized marriages between soldiers defending the empire's frontiers and native women living near forts and encampments, thus abolishing anomalous marriages long in existence, but not officially countenanced.

Foreign Policy

In foreign policy too Septimius adhered closely to his predecessors. He continued the historic war against the Parthian empire without realizing that such a policy had become untenable and even dangerous, in view of changed world conditions. He was unaware that the steppes of Central Asia had for centuries been the spawning ground for vast hordes of Huns and other barbarian tribes who would one day descend like an avalanche upon both the Roman and Persian empires. These hordes were already exerting heavy pressure against the Alans, who dwelt between the Urals and the Caspian. Pushed westwards, the Alans were in turn forcing the Goths and other Germanic tribes against the northern and western barriers of the Roman empire. Even without pressure from the East, the Germans had for centuries been seeking outlets for their surplus population in the warm and sunny lands of the south. The resources and manpower of the empire, though huge, were inadequate for waging war simultaneously against the Germans and the Parthians.

Another dangerous consequence of the

Severan resumption of war against Parthia was the further weakening of the weak and ineffectual Arsacid dynasty, which had held sway over Parthia ever since 238 B.C., and its final overthrow in 227. As a result of Roman assaults the Arsacid dynasty eventually gave way to the more dynamic and revolutionary Sassanid dynasty and the new Persian empire founded by Ardashir I (224–241), who was succeeded by his son, Shapur I (241–272), the most formidable opponent of Rome in the Middle East since the days of Mithridates VI of Pontus. Shapur I so harassed the Romans that only after his death were they able to muster enough force to drive out the Germans who had burst in over the northern and western frontiers.

The new Persian dynasty of Ardashir and Shapur was rendered formidable by its highly centralized administration and the might of its army, especially its heavily mailed cavalry. An even greater threat to Rome lay in its expansive Iranian nationalism and the revival of the ancient Zoroastrian religion and its organization as a national church.* Shapur tolerated and even favored the fiery crusading zeal of Manichaeism, which blended the orthodox Zendism of Zarathustra (660?–583? B.C.) with elements of Christianity, Judaism, and Buddhism.

Mani, the founder of Manichaeism and the greatest religious personality in Persia since Zarathustra, was a mystic and fanatic contemporary with the great Shapur and, like Shapur himself, was one of the most dynamic personalities of the third century. Mani (Manes or Manichaeus) began to preach around 240 A.D. at Ctesiphon, the capital of the Sassanid dynasty. Convinced that he was a Messiah sent to save mankind from sin and darkness, he revealed the cosmic conflict between the two rival kingdoms of Light and Darkness, of God and Satan, of spirit and matter. In the course of this conflict, the two realms, originally separate from each other, became fused by an event called "the seduction of the demons." The Prince of Darkness

* A rock relief at Nasq-i-Rustam (near Persepolis, Persia) shows Ahura Mazda, the God of Light, conferring sovereignty upon King Ardashir, who transformed the ancient religion of Zarathustra into a state religion.

used parts of the divine substance Light, stolen by the demons, to build the earth and all things contained therein, including man. Thus man was created by Satan and made part of Satan's realm. Fortunately, man received the divine injunction to set free the Light imprisoned within him and help restore it to the realm of Light. Thus, in this cosmic process, which must end in the victory of Light over Darkness, man has to free himself from evil (sin, sex, and sorcery) by chastity, righteousness, and reason. Only by living the ascetic life might man overcome Satan and enter into the kingdom of Light.

Although Mani had successfully preached this doctrine throughout the reign of Shapur, he finally suffered death at the instigation of the orthodox Zoroastrian priests. His martydom kindled the fire of Manichaeism which swept with devastating fury through the Middle East, Central Asia, and even China. In North Africa, Saint Augustine was to be one of its most notable adherents during the ten years preceding his conversion to Christianity. Manichaeism survived the persecutions of Diocletian and, centuries later, the crusades of the Prophet, and did not die out completely until long after the coming of Genghis Khan.

The Second Parthian War: 197–199

Shortly after having destroyed his rival, Clodius Albinus, Septimius returned to the East to resume warfare against the Parthians. In 197 he drove them out of Osrhoene and Adiabene and a year later captured Ctesiphon, which he burned to the ground. Again he annexed Mesopotamia as a province to be governed, like Egypt, by an equestrian prefect. The chief permanent result of this unfortunate campaign was the further weakening of the power of the Arsacid dynasty to maintain itself against the revolutionary upsurge of Iranian nationalism.

The War in Britain: 208–211

In the last years of his reign Septimius, accompanied by his sons Caracalla and Geta, led an expedition into the heart of Scotland but failed in his attempt to bring the natives

The Arch of Septimius Severus (193–212 A.D.). (Courtesy Fratelli Alinari, Florence)

A view of the Roman Forum, showing, in the foreground, the Temple of Vespasian (left), The Arch of Septimius Severus (center), and the Temple of Saturn (right). (Courtesy Italian State Tourist Office, New York)

to battle. They resorted instead to guerrilla tactics and inflicted heavy losses upon the Roman army. Despite the losses and the apparent failure of the whole campaign, Septimius achieved important results: the display of Roman power and the thorough reconstruction of Hadrian's Wall effectively discouraged future invasions of England from the North and gave Britain almost a century of peace. Septimius was not to see Rome again: he died at York in 211.

Caracalla: 211–217

Septimius dead, Caracalla and Geta together ascended the throne, but their attempt at joint rule, in accordance with their father's dying wish, proved hopeless. Each lived in mortal dread of the other until Caracalla treacherously lured Geta to their mother's apartment and there murdered him, "drenching his mother's breast with a slaughtered brother's blood" (Herodian III, 4). Then he carried out a pitiless extermination of Geta's supposed friends and supporters, among them the illustrious jurist and praetorian prefect Papinian. To silence the murmurs of the soldiers over Geta's killing, he increased their pay from 500 to 750 *denarii*, an expenditure which exhausted the treasury and compelled him to raise more revenue by doubling the tax on inheritances and the manumission of slaves and by slightly deflating the currency. He issued a new coin called the *Antoninianus*, supposedly a double *denarius* but actually not equal in weight.

Caracalla, who got his name from a long Gallic cape he used to wear, was a fairly good soldier and strategist and had some of the instincts of the statesman. The most historic act of his reign was the extension of citizen-

The Arch of Caracalla at Volubilis, Morocco. Similar Caracalla arches are to be seen at Theveste (Tebessa, Algeria) and at Cuicul (Djemila, Algeria). (Courtesy The French Embassy, Information Division, New York)

A marble portrait head of Caracalla. (211–217 A.D.). (Courtesy The Metropolitan Museum of Art, Samuel D. Lee Fund, 1940)

a common front to the barbarians beyond the frontiers. Had this offer of marriage been accepted, Caracalla might have saved both the Romans and the Iranians from future disaster.

German and Parthian Wars

What Caracalla had failed to achieve by diplomacy he tried to accomplish by war. In 213 he left Rome, never to return.* The major part of his reign was spent in war, and Caracalla proved himself a real soldier emperor: he ate and marched with his men and helped them dig trenches, build bridges, and fight battles.

Caracalla first proceeded to the Rhaetian *limes* to attack the Alemanni, a formidable but newly organized confederacy of mixed resident and displaced tribes that had migrated westward and settled along the right bank of the upper Rhine. After decisively defeating them on the Main, he built and restored forts, repaired roads and bridges, and extended a 105-mile stone wall from six to nine feet high and four feet thick along the Rhaetian frontier, which successfully withstood barbarian assault for the next twenty years.

After similarly strengthening the defenses in Pannonia and along the lower Danube, Caracalla proceeded to the East. He brutally suppressed an uprising in Alexandria and resumed the war against Parthia.† In 216 he marched across Adiabene and invaded Media but, after sacking several fortified places, he withdrew to winter quarters at Edessa. There he made preparations to mount a more vigorous offensive the following spring, but he did not live to witness the consummation of his plans. On April 8, 217, while traveling from Edessa to Carrhae to worship at the temple of the Moon, he was stabbed to death at the instigation of the praetorian prefect, M. Opellius Macrinus.

The most unfortunate result of Caracalla's abortive campaign against Parthia was the

ship in 212 to all free inhabitants of the empire, thus culminating a process initiated by Julius Caesar. By his promulgation of the famous *Constitutio Antoniniana*, Caracalla obliterated all distinction between Italians and provincials, between conquerors and conquered, between urban and rural dwellers, and between those who possessed Graeco-Roman culture and those who did not. Henceforth every free inhabitant of the Roman empire was a Roman citizen.

Another manifestation of Caracalla's statesmanship was his proposal of marriage to the daughter of Artabanus V of Parthia in order to bring to pass his dream of uniting the Roman and Parthian empires. He hoped that the two great civilizing powers might present

---

* He never witnessed the completion of the gigantic Baths of Caracalla, the ruins of which are among the most impressive from the ancient world.

† The occasion of the war was the rejection of the offer of his hand to the daughter of Artabanus V.

The Baths of Caracalla. (Courtesy Fratelli Alinari, Florence)

further weakening of an already decrepid regime and its final overthrow in 227 by the aggressive Persian dynasty of Ardashir I and Shapur I, who immediately set about recovering all the territories once ruled by the Achaemenid dynasty of ancient Persia (ca. 560–330 B.C.).

Macrinus: 217–218

M. Opellius Macrinus, the ringleader of the plot against Caracalla, secured the acclamation of the army and ascended the throne. He was a Mauretanian by birth, an *eques* in rank, and the first princeps without prior membership in the senate to reach the throne. He had a little business ability but was otherwise quite an insignificant personality. To affiliate himself to the Severan dynasty he adopted the name of Severus, bestowed that of Antoninus upon his young son Diadumenianus, and even ordered the senate to proclaim Caracalla a god. Realizing that he needed some military prestige in order to hold the loyalty of the army, he embarked upon a war with Parthia. But he proved to be a poor general. After a few minor successes and two major defeats, he lost the respect of the army by his agreement to surrender to the Parthians the prisoners he had captured and to pay a large indemnity. This inglorious settlement together with his unwise decision to reduce the pay for new recruits ultimately cost him his life and throne.

Heliogabalus: 218–222

The women of the Severan family were not disposed to permit a man like Macrinus occupy the throne of the Antonines. Julia Maesa, after the death of her sister, the empress Julia Domna, had gone with her two daughters, Soaemias and Mamaea, to live in Emesa, a Syrian town just north of Damascus and not far from the Lebanon. Here Varius Avitus, the fourteen-year-old son of Soaemias, served as high priest of the Syrian Sun-God, Elagabal, and therefore received the name of Elagabalus or, more fittingly, Heliogabalus.

Knowing how the army cherished the memory of Caracalla, the wily and unscrupulous Maesa concocted the rumor that Varius Avitus was the natural son of Caracalla and therefore a real Severus. She presented him to the legions of Syria who, further convinced by the offer of a large donative, saluted him as emperor under the name of Marcus Aurelius Antoninus. Macrinus, deserted by most of his troops and defeated in battle, fled, but was later hunted down and killed.

A year later, Heliogabalus arrived in Rome, wearing a purple silk robe, rouge on his cheeks, a necklace of pearls, and a bejeweled crown. He had brought from Emesa a conical black stone—the cult image of Elagabal—which he enshrined in an ornate temple on the Palatine and worshipped with the weirdest rites, prostitutions, and perversions, to the accompaniment of drums, cymbals, and anthems sung by Syrian women. What shocked the Roman public even more than any of these strange rites was his endeavor to make the Syrian Sun-God, Elagabal, the supreme deity of the Roman state.

In order to devote more time to his priestly duties and debaucheries, he entrusted most of the business of government to his grandmother and appointed his favorites to the highest public offices—a professional dancer, for example, as praetorian prefect, a charioteer as head of the police and fire department, and a barber as prefect of the grain administration.

Maesa, realizing that the idiotic conduct of Heliogabalus would lead to his downfall and the ruin of the Severan family, tactfully suggested that he ought to adopt Gessius Bassianus Alexianus, her other grandson, as Caesar and heir to the throne. When Heliogabalus saw that Alexianus, whom he adopted under the name of Marcus Aurelius Severus Alexander, was preferred by the senate and the people, he regretted his decision and twice attempted to get rid of the boy.

Maesa and Mamaea appealed to the Praetorian Guards who seized Heliogabalus and his mother, Soaemias, in their hiding place: a latrine. They cut off their heads and dragged the corpses through the streets to the Aemilian bridge. There they tied weights to them and hurled them into the Tiber.

Alexander Severus: 222–235

The ascension of Alexander Severus was greeted with rejoicing. Though only fourteen, he was studious, talented, and industrious. Actually, his mother, the dominating Julia Mamaea, held the reins of power. She was virtually, even to the end of his reign, the first empress of Rome.

The reign of Alexander marked the revival of the prestige, if not the power, of the senate, whose support Mamaea sought to enlist in order to strengthen the arm of the civil government in controlling the unruly and mutinous armies. She accordingly set up a council of sixteen prominent senators to serve nominally as a regency though actually, perhaps, only in an advisory capacity. Senators also probably held a majority in the enlarged Imperial Council. The president of both councils was the praetorian prefect, normally of equestrian rank, but now elevated while in office to senatorial status in order that he might sit as judge in trials involving senators without impairing the dignity of the defendants. At this time the praetorian prefect was the distinguished jurist, Domitius Ulpianus. Thus the new regime not only enhanced the dignity of the senate but enlarged the powers of the praetorian prefect.

Social and Economic Policy

The government seems to have tried to win the goodwill and support of the civilian population by providing honest and efficient administration. It reduced taxes, and authorized the construction of new baths, aqueducts, libraries, and roads. It subsidized teachers and scholars and lent money without interest to enable poor people to purchase farms. One major reform was the provision of primary school education all over the empire, even in the villages of Egypt. Another was the legalization, under government supervision and control, of all guilds or colleges (*collegia*) having to do with the supply of foodstuffs and essential services to the people of Rome. Under this category fell wine and oil merchants, bakers, and shoemakers. In return, the guilds enjoyed special tax favors and exemptions and the benefit of legal counsel at public expense.

The Military Problem

The fatal weakness of Alexander's regime was its failure to control the armies. In 228 the Praetorian Guard mutinied and murdered, in the emperor's palace itself, their prefect, Domitius Ulpianus, because he seemed too strict. The Mesopotamian army mutinied and murdered their commander. Another excellent disciplinarian, the historian Dio Cassius, would have suffered the same fate, had not Alexander whisked him off to his homeland of Bithynia.

Never had the need for disciplined armies been greater than in 226/7. The new Iranian regime of Ardashir I was waging a war of aggression against Rome: he had already overrun Mesopotamia and was threatening the provinces of Syria and Cappadocia. In 232, after a futile diplomatic effort, Alexander himself had to go to the East. He planned and executed a massive three-pronged attack which should have ensured a decisive victory, but, because of poor generalship and excessive caution, it resulted only in heavy losses on both sides and at best produced nothing more than a stalemate. Alexander returned to Rome to celebrate a splendid but dubious triumph.

Meanwhile the Alemanni and other German tribes had broken through the Roman defenses and were pouring into Gaul and Rhaetia. Alexander hurried north, accompanied by his mother. After some early successes, he foolishly followed his mother's suggestion and bought peace from the Germans with a subsidy. His men, who would have preferred to use some of that money themselves, were disgusted. Under the leadership of the commander of the Pannonian legions, Maximinus the Thracian, they mutinied in 235 and killed both Alexander and his mother, thus terminating the Severan dynasty and ushering in almost a half-century of civil war.

Maximinus the Thracian: 235–238

The next emperor was Maximinus the Thracian, an ignorant peasant of tremendous size and strength who was reported capable of consuming 46 pints of wine and 40 pounds of meat a day. He had come up from the ranks and the soldiers under his command feared, respected, and admired him. He knew their moods and aspirations and, after they had saluted him as emperor, he doubled their pay. They followed him deep into Germany and, near Württemberg, defeated the Germans, taking thousands of prisoners and vast quantities of booty. After defeating the Sarmatians, Dacians, and perhaps even the Goths on the lower Danube, Maximinus laid plans for the total conquest of Germany.

The chief problem facing Maximinus was that of obtaining money to pay his troops. He sent his collectors all over the empire. They plundered all classes, especially the rich, whom they reduced to beggary. One particularly ruthless procurator created a violent reaction in North Africa: big landowners, faced with the loss of their estates, fomented a rebellion. They killed the procurator, repudiated Maximinus, and proclaimed the extremely rich but elderly M. Antonius Gordianus as emperor and his son of the same name as co-emperor. The senate, which had always hated the Thracian boor, hailed the nomination with delight and declared Maximinus a public enemy. When the two Gordians had lost their lives, the younger by falling in battle against Maximinus' governor of Numidia, the elder by suicide, the senate then appointed two of its members, M. Pupienus Maximus and D. Calvinus Balbinus as joint emperors, and a grandson of Gordian I as Caesar. The rejuvenated senate of Alexander Severus acted with amazing resolution and speed. For a time its prestige was high.

Events in Africa and Italy forced Maximinus to set out on an immediate march on Rome. Finding his way barred at Aquileia, he laid siege to the city but failed to take it. Finally, his own men, starving and desperate, mutinied and killed both Maximinus and his son. They acclaimed the two senatorially appointed emperors, Balbinus and Pupienus, whose arrival in Rome was hailed with delirious joy. The joy did not last. Less than two months after the death of Maximinus the Praetorian Guard killed the two emperors and acknowledged Gordian III, a boy of thirteen, as the new emperor.

Gordian III: 238–244

At the accession of the boy emperor two powerful and dangerous enemies had begun or were about to assail the weakened frontier defenses of the empire. The Goths, a North Germanic people originally from Sweden, had in the second century migrated from the basin of the Vistula to the Ukraine and the coastal regions of the Black Sea. They were now streaming over the lower Danube and, in alliance with the Sarmatians and the Carpi, were overrunning Moesia and Thrace. In the Middle East the Persians were invading the provinces of Mesopotamia and Syria. In 241 the mighty Shapur was marching towards Antioch on the Orontes.

Rome might well have suffered a disaster of unparalleled magnitude had not Gordian III been able to count on the loyalty, experience, and brilliance of his own father-in-law, C. Furius Timesitheus, the praetorian prefect, who was not only a fine army commander but a superb organizer. In 242 they set out from Rome together and, after stabilizing the situation on the Danube, proceeded to Syria, where they relieved Antioch and recovered the Roman provinces. They were on the point of taking the Persian capital of Ctesiphon when Timesitheus died. His death threw Gordian III to the tender mercies of Philip, an Arab sheik from the Jordan, who, after his appointment as praetorian prefect and co-regent, took advantage of a threatened food shortage and engineered a mutiny, which resulted in the death of Gordian.

Philip the Arab: 244–249

The first act of the usurper was to make peace with Shapur. The terms were that Rome might retain the provinces of Mesopotamia and Little Armenia in exchange for waiving all interest in Greater Armenia and the payment of 500,000 denarii either as indemnity or as ransom for prisoners captured by the Persians.

Though he courted the goodwill of the senate and gave painstaking attention to the government, Philip was neither a good emperor nor a competent general. After a minor victory over the Dacian Carpi, he returned to Rome in 247 to make preparations for the celebration of Rome's thousandth anniversary. Even during the magnificent festival, the Goths and Carpi were thundering across the Danube and the revolting Danubian legions had proclaimed one of their commanders emperor. Two other pretenders appeared in the East. These calamities compelled Philip to send his ablest general, C. Decius, to the

Danube. After restoring discipline in the army, Decius drove the Goths back over the Danube. Out of respect for him as a disciplinarian and general, the soldiers saluted Decius as emperor, who promptly marched into Italy against Philip. In 249 a great battle was fought near Verona, during which Philip was defeated and slain. Thus ended the principate of Philip the Arab, the first Oriental to occupy the imperial throne.

Decius: 249–251

Meanwhile the Goths, led by their able king, Kniva, poured through huge gaps torn in the Danubian defenses into Dacia, Lower Moesia, and Thrace, where they besieged and destroyed fortified cities, massacred the inhabitants, took thousands of prisoners, and seized immense quantities of plunder. The invasion brought Decius hurrying from Rome. Though he inflicted a severe defeat on one of the Gothic armies, his forces were too weak, his marches too slow, and the support he received from his sluggish subcommander, Trebonianus Gallus, too dubious and ineffectual to enable him to overtake and destroy the enemy. Finally, in 251, Kniva succeeded in luring Decius into a trap on boggy ground at Abrittus near Adamclisi in the Dobrudja, where the Romans suffered one of the most disastrous defeats in their history. Decius and his son were slain. Gallus, proclaimed emperor by the soldiers, made a disgraceful treaty with the Goths which permitted them to return home with all the plunder and high-ranking Roman prisoners they had captured together with the guarantee of an annual payment of tribute by Rome.

Few emperors have aroused more controversy in ancient and modern times than Decius. Pagan Latin writers, who usually were prejudiced in favor of the senate, praised Decius highly because he maintained cordial relations with the senate. In their eyes he was an admirable ruler, an excellent administrator, a brilliant general, and a man of boundless energy and iron will. Christian writers (Lactantius, for example, called him "an execrable animal") have condemned him because he instituted the first systematic persecution of the Christians all over the empire. Pagan writers generally justified the persecution because the Christians belonged to a subversive organization which refused to recognize the state religion and obstructed the defense of the empire by preaching peace (*see* p. 372).

Gallienus: 253–268

The next two emperors, Gallus (251–253) and Aemilianus (253), reigned only briefly. Both were assassinated by mutinous soldiers as the army continued to hold sway over the Empire. After the death of Aemilianus, Valerian I was proclaimed emperor. He named his son, Gallienus, associate emperor and gave him full command of the West. The two reigned together until the death of Valerian in 260.

The Age of Gallienus was one of the most critical in the history of the Roman people. It witnessed the culmination of the destructive trends originating in the past. It laid the groundwork for future recovery. It began in catastrophe: the barbarians were breaking through the shattered and weakly defended frontiers along the Rhine and the Danube. Two large confederations of German tribes, the Franks of the lower Rhine and the Alemanni of the upper Rhine, were overrunning Gaul and Spain. On the upper Danube the Alemanni and the Marcomanni swept through the Roman provinces and poured into Italy. On the lower Danube the Goths were devastating the Balkans, Asia Minor, and the islands and coast lands of the Aegean. In the Middle East the Persians had invaded the provinces of Mesopotamia, Syria, and Cappadocia. Scarcely a province escaped the havoc wrought by invasion: the widespread destruction of property, the sacking and burning of cities, and the massacre and enslavement of citizens.

Pirates infested the seas as in the days before Pompey; bands of robbers and thieves raided the countryside; earthquakes rocked both Italy and Asia Minor. At the height of the barbarian invasions a plague broke out in Egypt and infected the entire empire, where it raged for more than fifteen years. The death toll was staggering: two-thirds of the population of Alexandria died and as many as 5,000 a day in Rome alone. It created a shortage of farm and factory labor and production fell sharply. Worse still, it severely depleted the ranks of the army. The impact of all these blows occurring simultaneously or in rapid succession broke the resistance and shattered the unity of the empire.

A more immediate source of disintegration was the army itself. Septimius Severus had permitted regular and auxiliary troops to marry and live outside the barracks. Alexander Severus had permitted them to hold and cultivate land in the vicinity of the camps. Although these innovations gave the soldiers a stake in the land and an incentive to defend it, they also tended to make them neglect their military duties and the repair of frontier fortifications. Worse still, the armies soon acquired the dangerous and disruptive spirit of localism and separatism, and they came to consider the defense of their own provincial districts more important than the defense of the empire as a whole. This localist spirit, together with the constant desire for more pay, fanned the ambitions of high ranking officers; during the reign of Gallienus alone eighteen usurpers made vain attempts to seize the throne.

Foreign Affairs

Alarming reports from the Middle East began to reach Rome. The year before the accession of Valerian, Shapur had engineered the assassination of the Roman client king of Armenia and replaced him with his own puppet thereby opening the way to the conquest of Roman Asia Minor. He at once invaded Mesopotamia and Syria. In 253 he knocked out a Roman army of 60,000 men and broke the stubborn defense of Dura-Europos on the Euphrates. He thereupon entered Syria and Cappadocia, capturing Antioch and thirty-six other cities and towns. Shortly after that, the Goths plundered cities along the eastern and southern shores of the Black Sea and began a naval attack upon the coasts of Asia Minor.

A rock relief at Naqsh-i-Rustam (near Persepolis, Persia), showing the Roman Emperor Valerian kneeling in chains before Shapur I of Persia. (Courtesy Thames & Hudson, Ltd., London from Costa & Lockhart, Persia, 1958)

The gravity of the situation impelled Valerian to leave Rome, probably in 256, and appear in the East, where he proved utterly incompetent. Despite a few minor skirmishes (described on his coinage as major victories), he failed to restore Roman prestige. Frustrated and depressed, he took out his resentment on the Christians and subjected them to hideous persecution. Finally, in desperation, he sent his plague-stricken army to meet the main Persian army at Edessa. The results were disastrous both to his army and himself. He fell into the hands of Shapur in 260 and ended his days in captivity, one of the most pathetic figures in Roman history.

Meanwhile Gallienus, constantly at war since 254, had been busy clearing the Alemanni and the Franks out of Gaul and the Rhineland. He beat back further attempts to cross the river, and strengthened the fortifications. Further south the Marcomanni and the Alemanni, who had been hammering away at the Danubian defenses, broke through and pushed down into Italy. The former had penetrated as far as Ravenna in 254, the latter reached Milan four years later. Gallienus first halted the Marcomanni by concluding an alliance with them and granting them land south of the Danube in Upper Pannonia, and in 258/9 crushed the Alemanni near Milan. The next year he had to suppress two dangerous rebellions in Pannonia where the legions, irked by his continued absence on the Rhine, had thrown their support first to one pretender to the throne, then to another.

The situation in the Rhineland had rapidly deteriorated during his brief absence. The Alemanni had crossed the upper Rhine and invaded the Rhone valley and the Auvergne.

The Franks had surged over the lower Rhine and had overrun Gaul, Spain, and even Morocco. The Saxons and the Jutes, who dwelt along the coasts of Germany and Denmark, had begun roving the seas and raiding the shorelands of Britain and Gaul. Nor was that all. In 259 the legions on the Rhine in fear and desperation mutinied and renounced their allegiance to their absent emperor in favor of Postumus, the general whom Gallienus had left in command of the Rhineland. The armies of Spain and Britain later followed suit.

Gallienus did not recognize the usurpation of Postumus but, hampered by the German and Gothic invasions of the Danubian provinces as well as by the rebellions of other pretenders to the throne, he could do no more than compel Postumus to confine himself to the Western provinces. Left alone, Postumus drove the Franks and the Alemanni out of Gaul, energetically defended the frontiers, issued his own coinage, and established an efficient administration. Gallienus himself could not have done better.

The Eclipse of Roman Power in the East

After their defeat and capture of Valerian in 260, the triumphant Persians plundered Antioch, occupied all of Mesopotamia, overran Cilicia and Cappadocia, and cut across Asia Minor to the Black Sea. They might have occupied all of Asia Minor permanently, had they maintained their military organization. Instead, they broke up into small looting bands easily cut off and isolated.

All the while Rome was preparing her counterstroke. Macrianus, one of Valerian's old generals, aided by his lieutenant Callistus, had rallied the shattered remnants of Valerian's army. Putting some of the troops aboard transports, Callistus made landings along the Cilician coast, where he surprised and defeated thousands of Persians and captured Shapur's baggage train together with his harem. That embarrassing loss impelled Shapur to evacuate Asia Minor and retreat to Ctesiphon with all his plunder and hordes of captives. On the way back, he came into conflict on the banks of the Euphrates with an unexpected enemy, Odenathus, the Roman client sheik of Palmyra. That disastrous

encounter left Shapur crippled for a long time. To the end of his reign, the war-weary Shapur devoted himself to internal affairs and to his ambitious building projects, leaving the future of Asia Minor to Odenathus and Gallienus.

Palmyra was an oasis in the Syrian desert. It lay astride the main caravan routes from the Mediterranean to Central Asia and to the Persian Gulf; and piled high in its market place were goods from China, India, Persia, and Arabia such as textiles, spices, perfumes, jewelry, and precious stones. By the second century it had become one of the major cities of the Middle East with fine wide streets and thruways, shady porticoes, stately arches, and magnificent public buildings.

Since the time of Trajan, Palmyra had been an important recruiting ground for the Roman army. The famous Palmyrene cohorts of mounted archers and armored cavalry had rendered invaluable service all over the empire. Later on, the Severi, who gave Palmyra the rank of titular colony and adlected some of its leading citizens into the senate, allowed these units, though officially part of the Roman army, to serve as a semi-independent Palmyrene army in Syria and along the Parthian frontier. That was the army with which Odenathus humbled the pride of the mighty Shapur on the western banks of the Euphrates.

The hostility of Odenathus towards Shapur arose chiefly from the Persian conquest of the Characene, the annexation of which shut off Palmyra's access to the Persian Gulf and injured her caravan trade. When Shapur haughtily refused to negotiate, Odenathus followed up his initial victory by driving the Persians out of Mesopotamia and Armenia. In 263 and again in 267 he invaded Persia and laid siege to Ctesiphon, though without success.

The services which Odenathus had performed for Rome on his own initiative were not lost upon the shrewd and opportunistic Gallienus, who showed his gratitude by rewarding him with flattering high-sounding titles and by making him commander of all the Roman forces in the Middle East.

Macrianus, meanwhile, had broken with Gallienus and had persuaded the army to proclaim his two sons, Macrianus and

Quietus, joint emperors. The long-suffering East hailed them with delight and all might have gone well had the elder Macrianus been content to limit his ambitions to the East. He resolved instead to reach out for the rest of the empire. Leaving Quietus behind in the East, he and his elder son set out for the Danube. There they were defeated and killed by Aureolus, whom Gallienus had sent to intercept them. Then Odenathus hunted down and put to death the other pretender, along with his praetorian prefect, Callistus.

In his second campaign against Persia in 267, Odenathus turned from the siege of Ctesiphon to drive out the Goths, who had invaded Asia Minor by land and sea, had laid waste the rich cities of Chalcedon and Nicomedia, and destroyed the great temple of Diana at Ephesus. He failed to overtake them for they had already boarded ships at Heraclea Pontica with all their loot and captives. Shortly after that, an unknown assassin stabbed Odenathus to death. His widow, the beautiful, gifted, and intelligent Zenobia, assumed power in Palmyra and held it until the reign of Aurelian.

The Last Battles of Gallienus: 268

Much encouraged by their success in the previous year, the Goths began the largest invasion of the empire of the third century. An armada of 500 ships (some say 2,000) put to sea and a land army reported at 320,000 men invaded the Balkans and the Aegean area, ravaged Greece, and captured the cities of Sparta, Argos, and Athens. The invaders passed north through Epirus and Macedonia and finally arrived at Naissus (modern Nish) in Moesia. There in 268 Gallienus intercepted them and, in the bloodiest battle of the third century, destroyed 50,000 of them. This victory might have been the end of the Gothic peril, had not Gallienus been compelled to break off pursuit and hasten back to Italy to suppress the rebellion of Aureolus, the cavalry general to whom he had entrusted the defense of Italy against Postumus. Gallienus defeated Aureolus in battle near Milan, only to be assassinated by his own staff officers, all of them Illyrians who may have felt that Gallienus had not devoted enough energy to the defense of the Danubian lands.

The Reforms of Gallienus

The reforms of Gallienus laid the foundation of future recovery and prepared the way for the reforms of Diocletian and Constantine. Their purpose was to strengthen the hands of the central government in restoring discipline in the armies, in preventing the rise of usurpers, and in defending the empire against the attacks of the barbarians.

The most radical of the reforms of Gallienus was the exclusion of senators from all high army commands and their replacement by equestrian prefects, many of whom were now coming up from the ranks. This reform was no doubt intended to prevent possible rebellions and attempts by ambitious senatorial commanders to usurp power. It also aimed at the restoration of military discipline and efficiency through the substitution of professional officers willing to endure the hardships of army life on the frontiers and capable of enforcing strict military discipline. The reform not only completed the process of democratizing the army and dealt a heavy blow to the prestige of the senate but, more important, it helped take the army out of politics, making it once again the servant rather than the master of the state.

Equestrians also gradually replaced senatorial governors in most of the imperial and occasionally even in the senatorial provinces. In provinces where armies were stationed equestrian governors held command, senatorial governors did not. Thus in equestrian provinces there was a merger of civil and military authority, but in the senatorial provinces, a separation.

The most revolutionary of the strictly military reforms of Gallienus was the replacement of fixed frontier fortifications by a system of defense in depth. The second century system of fixed frontier defenses first devised by Domitian (when he created the famous German *limes*) and further developed by Hadrian, was too rigid to withstand a mass assault and too extended to permit easy defense. Gallienus maintained that system as the first line of defense, but also fortified cities behind the frontier capable of absorbing and containing enemy forces after they had broken through the outer defense line.

The new strategy also called for a mobile army to be stationed at strategic points well behind the frontier lines and capable of moving at a moment's notice to the scene of greatest danger. Since the strategic points in the West were Aquileia, Verona, and especially Milan, the reform made Italy once more a center of great military importance. On the other hand, it reduced the political importance of the city of Rome and the senate because the emperors found themselves compelled to transfer to the great military centers not only the mint and arms factories but their own residences as well. Where the emperor was, there Rome was also.

The conception of mobile defense demanded the replacement of the slow moving legion, hitherto the main offensive weapon, by a cavalry corps which was to operate independently of the infantry. The new cavalry corps consisted of Moorish bareback-riding javelin men, Dalmatian horsemen, Osrhoenian and Palmyrene mounted archers, and the heavily man-and-horse armored cavalry of the Persian type (*cataphractarii*). Gallienus regarded this cavalry corps so highly that in 263 he placed it on a par with the Praetorian Guard. Its commander soon rivaled and later eclipsed the praetorian prefect and, though only of equestrian rank, became the most powerful man in the empire next to the emperor. Claudius Gothicus, Aurelian, Probus, and Diocletian were later to use this command as the springboard to the principate.

Of all his imperial predecessors, Gallienus seems to have most closely resembled Hadrian. He had the same keen intelligence, indefatigable energy and capacity for swift decision. Gallienus shared Hadrian's love of poetry and the arts, and his admiration for Greek culture, literature, and philosophy.* Both emperors were reformers and innovators, and both displayed a hostile attitude towards the senate and a cynical disregard of outworn tradition. Both laid foundations upon which later emperors built.

Claudius Gothicus: 268–270

The next emperor, Claudius II, was a member of that group of brilliant young Illyrian officers whom Gallienus had promoted from the ranks. His first task as emperor was to drive back the Alemanni, who had invaded Italy as far as Lake Garda. Then he rounded up the Goths who had escaped Gallienus, as well as those who had later invaded the Balkans. He enrolled some of the captured Goths in the Roman army, he settled others on abandoned farms in Thrace, Moesia, and Macedonia. So thoroughly had he liquidated the Gothic menace that it did not again recur on a mass scale for more than a century. For this great contribution to the empire's reconstruction he received the richly deserved title of Claudius Gothicus.

Aurelian: 270–275

When Claudius died of the plague, the army chose as his successor another brilliant Illyrian officer, Lucius Domitius Aurelianus, whom Claudius had put in command of the cavalry corps during the Gothic war. Born and raised in the country, Aurelian had developed great physical strength. He became a tough, fearless soldier and, later, a skillful general whose harsh discipline earned him the nickname, *Manu ad ferrum* ("Hand on Steel"). So severe were his punishments that he seldom had to inflict them.

The tasks awaiting Aurelian were numerous and difficult. He had to secure the long Danubian frontiers from attack and Italy from invasion, restore both the Western and

* Gallienus planned to found in Campania an ideal Platonic state (Platonopolis) and install as its ruler his court favorite, the Hellenized Egyptian Plotinus (205–270 A.D.), who taught at Rome from ca. 253 till his death in 270. Plotinus, the last great philosopher of antiquity, was the founder of Neo-Platonism, a revival of Platonism in an age when all philosophy tended to assume a religious character. Plotinus maintained that the vital and creative principle in man and the universe is Soul. The highest function of the human soul is Reason, the faculty of using ideas—through sensation, recollection, imagination, and thought—to obtain knowledge. Just as Reason is above the human soul, so above the World Soul is Divine Mind. Still higher than the Divine Mind is The One (or God) which can be apprehended neither by thought nor Reason but only through an ineffable mystic experience.

The Wall of Aurelian (271–275 A.D.), Rome. (Courtesy Fratelli Alinari, Florence)

Eastern provinces to the Roman Empire, and solve various political and economic problems, among which was the regulation of the ruined and disorganized coinage.

The immediate task was to rescue Italy from the invasion and depredations of the Juthungi, kinsmen of the Alemanni living north of the upper Danube. At Aurelian's approach they attempted to retreat quickly with their plunder, but he caught them from ambush at the river and destroyed half their army. He next defeated the Asdingian Vandals, who had invaded Pannonia, and forced them to supply 2,000 cavalrymen for the Roman army. Meanwhile the Juthungi, aided by the Alemanni and the Marcomanni, once more invaded Italy, besieged Milan, and occupied Piacenza. There they set an ambush for Aurelian and defeated his army which had been wearied by the long march from the Danube. The invaders could easily have marched on and taken Rome had they kept together instead of spreading out into scattered marauding bands, which Aurelian easily destroyed. His victories on the Metaurus and near Ticinum sent the invaders scurrying back to Germany.

Aurelian, free for other tasks, returned to Rome to suppress a serious revolt of the mint officials who were aggrieved at the emperor's efforts to check their profiteering out of debased coins. Aurelian immediately closed the mint for a time as a preliminary step towards his projected reform of the coinage. In order to protect Rome from future barbarian assault and capture, he began in 271 the construction of a brick wall around the city. The wall, which was twelve miles long, was twenty feet high and twelve feet thick. It had eighteen gates as well as many sally ports and towers for artillery. Convinced of the impossibility of permanently holding Dacia with its irreparably broken defenses, Aurelian withdrew all the garrisons and most of the civilians from the province. The withdrawal not only shortened the frontier defense line of the empire but released troops for service elsewhere. The evacuated civilians were resettled in the ravished and depopulated provinces of Pannonia, Moesia, and Thrace, and Dacia was abandoned to the Goths.

The Reconquest of the East: 272–273

With Italy and the Danubian provinces temporarily safe from attack, Aurelian was free to attempt the reconquest of the East. The enemy he had to conquer was not the Persian king, but Zenobia, the ambitious and strong-willed queen of Palmyra, who matched the Egyptian Cleopatra in intellect and personality and far surpassed her in beauty and virtue. Zenobia not only maintained a court of Oriental pomp and splendor but gathered about her scholars, poets, and artists.*

Taking advantage of Aurelian's preoccupation in Italy and on the Danube, Zenobia seceded from the Empire and extended Palmyra's dominion over Egypt and Asia Minor as far north as Bithynia. She had concluded an alliance with the Persians but received little help from them.

Aurelian entrusted the reconquest of Egypt to Probus, and himself advanced through Asia Minor. He encountered little opposition until he reached Antioch on the Orontes, where he was engaged in battle by the Palmyrene army of mounted archers and heavy cavalry. He overcame them and proceeded to Emesa, where he engaged a Palmyrene army of 70,000 men. The Romans won a second resounding victory and set out under the broiling desert sun for the city of Palmyra, eighty miles away. Well prepared for a siege, Palmyra resisted long and stubbornly. It finally capitulated when the panic-stricken queen attempted to flee to Persia for help. Brought before Aurelian, the captured queen saved her life by accusing her chief adviser, Longinus, and her other advisers and friends of inspiring the aggressions. Longinus died like a true philosopher. Aurelian was most lenient with the people and city of Palmyra. He stationed a small garrison there and at once set out for Europe.

He got as far as the Danube when word came that Palmyra had risen in rebellion and massacred the garrison. Aurelian's return was swift, his vengeance terrible. Not one man, woman, or child escaped his wrath. He had Palmyra's treasures carted away, tore down the walls, and reduced the once proud and powerful city to a desolate desert village, which it has remained to this day.†

---

* Her chief adviser was Dionysius Cassius Longinus (213?–273 A.D.), the celebrated rhetorician and philosopher who probably was the author of the famous treatise, *On the Sublime*.

† Soon after, he suppressed a rebellion in Alexandria with similar ruthlessness and finality.

The Reconquest of Gaul: 273–274

The reconquest of Gaul was less difficult. After the murder of Postumus in 268, the Gallic succession passed first to Victorinus and then to Tetricus. Tetricus was a harmless old senator who could neither keep out the German invaders nor maintain authority over his own army officers. His opposition to Aurelian was halfhearted and ineffectual. When his subordinates finally compelled him to fight, he deserted his brave men and surrendered to Aurelian. He was forced to walk through the streets of Rome in Aurelian's triumphal parade together with a more spirited captive, the gorgeous Zenobia, queen of the East. After the triumph, Aurelian treated both captives with unparalleled leniency and dignity. He appointed Tetricus chief inspector of Lucania (*Corrector Lucaniae*) in southern Italy and presented Zenobia with a villa at Tivoli, where she ended her days as the wife of a Roman senator.

Upon his recovery of the lost provinces, Aurelian received the proud title of *Restitutor Orbis* ("Restorer of the World").

Economic Reforms

In 274 Aurelian grappled with another gigantic task: the restoration of internal stability. The most pressing problem was the regulation of the coinage, which had depreciated so much since 267 that people had to use *denarii* and *Antoniniani* by the sackful (3,125 double *denarii* to the sack). Aurelian reduced the official valuation of the *Antoninianus* or double *denarius* from eight *sesterces* to one in order to bring it in line with the eightfold rise in the price level after 267.* He also closed down all local mints and permanently abolished the senatorial mint at Rome, a blow against municipal autonomy and the prerogative of the senate.

To relieve the distress in Rome which had resulted from the rise of food prices Aurelian placed the breadmaking industry under the direct control of the state, which sold wheat

---

* Whether the change actually halted inflation is debatable.

for milling to the bakers' guild and fixed the price of bread. He suspended the monthly grain dole, and arranged instead for the daily distribution of two pounds of bread to all eligible citizens. For the same citizens he instituted regular distributions of pork, oil, salt, and possibly wine.

Following the example of Alexander Severus, Aurelian placed all guilds or colleges engaged in the transport and processing of food and other necessities under state control, thereby making them agencies of the government.*

Religious Trends

Two developments of Eastern inspiration and impulse approached their culmination during the reign of Aurelian. The monarchistic tendency in government, and the monotheistic trend in religion began at this time to achieve a sure dominance, and even a certain interrelation. The rapid changing of emperors during the third century had not destroyed the monarchy, it served rather to transform the principate into autocratic absolutism. The trend towards monotheism in religion was equally pronounced. The rise of the universal cosmopolitan state, together with the far-reaching influence of Oriental culture and of the westward-spreading Eastern cults had precipitated the decline of the old national and local polytheism and the rise of a more universal and monotheistic religion. Even the imperial cult lost its potency as a moral basis for imperial unity and power and gave way before the twin emergence of autocracy and monotheism.

In Rome, Aurelian erected a resplendent temple to the Unconquered Sun (*Sol Invictus*) and established a college of pontiffs of senatorial rank to superintend the worship of this supreme god of the universe and divine protector of the Roman state. A single divine power was now to watch over the single earthly ruler.

---

* This extension of bureaucratic control over economic life should not be interpreted as an anticipation of modern state socialism, for the ancient economy had never been either socialistic or capitalistic in the modern sense.

Unfortunately for Aurelian, the new divinity did not save him from the fate of many other third century emperors. A crooked secretary, caught in a lie and fearing for his life, forged a list of the chief officers of the Guard and spread the false rumor that Aurelian planned their execution. The "condemned" officers acted swiftly; they murdered Aurelian at Caenophrurium, between Perinthus and Byzantium, in the fall of 275.*

Tacitus: 275–276

Contrite and dismayed, the army leaders deferred to the senate in the choice of the next emperor. After some hesitation and delay, the senate nominated its own leader, M. Claudius Tacitus, a man in his middle seventies. In spite of a fairly successful campaign against the Goths and Alans in Asia Minor, he too fell victim to a conspiracy of his own soldiers. His six-month reign marked a fleeting resurgence of senatorial power which, meteor-like, rose, briefly flashed, and was gone forever.

Probus: 276–282

After Tacitus' death, the power of making and breaking emperors reverted to the army. It soon disposed of Florianus, the late emperor's half-brother, who had seized the throne without consulting army or senate. The army of the East had already proclaimed emperor the mighty Probus, another great Illyrian, who was the equal of Aurelian as a general and perhaps his superior in intellect and culture. Probus continued the work of imperial consolidation by restoring peace and order in the provinces.

The first task was the liberation of Gaul from the Franks and the Alemanni who, after Aurelian's death, had overrun the entire province, seized some seventy cities, and laid waste countless fertile fields. Within a year the invaders were in full retreat, with the victorious Probus in relentless pursuit, killing

---

* When the truth finally came to light, the horror-stricken officers repented. Only it was too late.

them by the tens of thousands and driving the rest back into the wilds of Germany. Probus built strong redoubts along the eastern bank of the Rhine opposite the Roman cities on the western bank. He also recruited 16,000 German soldiers for the Roman army, and assigned them in small units to the various provinces. Except for the rebellions of two disloyal and ambitious generals (which he firmly suppressed), Gaul remained quiet throughout the reign of Probus.

In 278 Probus cleared the Alemanni and Burgundians out of Rhaetia and the Vandals out of Pannonia. He settled on abandoned land in Thrace some 100,000 Scythians and Bastarnae who had been dislodged from their South Russian homelands by the Goths.* He subdued the Isaurian brigands of southern Asia Minor and established colonies of veterans there to keep the peace and breed young recruits for the Roman army. Finally he liberated Egypt from the Blemmyes who had invaded from the Sudan.

Among the economic reforms of Probus was an edict countermanding Domitian's edict of ca. 91 (which prohibited the further plantings of vines in Italy and ordered the destruction of half of the existing vineyards in the provinces). Probus authorized and encouraged vine plantations in the Danubian provinces, in Gaul, and even in Britain. To protect his soldiers from the deteriorating effects of idleness in the barracks, he set them to work reclaiming waste and swamp lands, planting vineyards, digging drainage ditches, and building roads. That tedious work, together with the normal army discipline, which Probus never relaxed even in time of peace, aggravated the latent discontent of the men. While working on a drainage project near Sirmium in southern Pannonia, word came of the mutiny in Rhaetia and the proclamation as emperor of the praetorian prefect, Marcus Aurelius Carus. This report fanned their discontent into open mutiny, and Probus, one of the ablest and most conscientious rulers of the century, fell victim to their hate.

Carus and his Sons, Carinus and Numerianus: 282–285

Carus, the new emperor, was another Illyrian. He too was a professional soldier and a fairly competent general. Upon his accession, he conferred the rank of Caesar on his two sons, Carinus and Numerianus. Leaving Carinus in charge of the defense of Italy and Gaul, he set out for the East with his other son. Early in 283, after defeating the Quadi and the Sarmatians, who had come over the Danube, he marched against the Persians. He crossed the Euphrates, and took Seleucia, then crossed the Tigris and took Ctesiphon. This series of successes came to an abrupt halt with his mysterious death attributed, by available sources, to a bolt of lightening. It is far more likely that Carus fell victim to foul play at the hands of his praetorian prefect, Arrius Aper, who later secretly arranged the assassination of Numerianus.

A council of war was held to pick a successor. The army of the East ignored the claims of Carinus, who was generally despised for his known addiction to vice, and nominated instead one of their own officers, Diocles. The first act of the new emperor (who is better known as Diocletian) was to run Aper through with his sword. Carinus, who had been left in charge of Italy, refused to acknowledge Diocletian as his colleague and marched against the army of the East. The two armies clashed in Moesia in the valley of the Margus (Morava). In the fierce battle that ensued the superior army of Carinus had almost achieved victory when Carinus himself received a dagger's thrust through the heart.* His victorious but leaderless army accepted Diocletian as their emperor. Thus by a quirk of fate the best man was found in 285 to finish the reconstruction for which Gallienus, Claudius II, Aurelian, and Probus had worked and died.

* The Bastarnae were a Germanic people who lived originally in Galicia and Bucovina, but after 200 B.C. migrated to the lower regions of the Danube and Dniester. They began to disturb the Roman frontiers in the time of Augustus, were later suppressed by Marcus Aurelius, and finally permitted by Probus to settle south of the Danube.

* The dagger was wielded by a tribune whose wife Carinus had seduced.

THE DOMINATE OF

THE HALF CENTURY BETWEEN THE DEATH OF ALEXANDER Severus and the accession of Diocletian had witnessed a series of disasters unparalleled in history—massive barbarian assaults simultaneously launched against every frontier in Europe and Africa, a disastrous war between Rome and the resurgent Sassanid kingdom of Persia, mutinies in numerous Roman armies, the secession of provinces, the violent and sudden death of more than a score of emperors, famine, and plague. A gigantic mobilization had rolled back the tide of invasion and checked the dissolution of the Empire, but the work of reconstruction was still to be done.

The dominate of Diocletian (284–305), which ended the principate and opened the last phase of the history of the Roman people, was a culmination of the trends which had begun with the accession of Septimius Severus. The dominate (a word de-

DIOCLETIAN

rived from *dominus,* "lord and master," and synonymous with absolute monarchy or autocracy) was the goal towards which the Roman world had been moving for more than three centuries. It was welcomed by people of every class and station in the Roman world. It seemed the sole guarantee of peace, order, and security. Even the soldiers, sickened by decades of foreign invasion, civil war, and social chaos, accepted the autocracy of the dominate with relief and enthusiasm.

Most sources of information about the fourth century, while generally superior to those of the third, have unfortunately been neither thoroughly investigated nor analyzed. Typical of that neglect has been the failure to evaluate the work of Zosimus, the excellent Greek writer who, in 600 or thereabouts, published his *New History,* a narrative in six books on Roman history from 270 to 410. It was a continuation as well as a supplement of the *Histories* of Ammianus Marcellinus, the last great Latin historian of Rome who, in imitation of Tacitus, wrote a reliable, penetrating, and elegant history of Rome from Nerva to Valens (378) in thirty-one books. Only the last eighteen books, which cover the period from 353 to 378, are extant.

The secondary sources include the biography of Diocletian at the close of the *Historia Augusta* and several *breviaria*, brief historical surveys in Latin, the last parts of which are of real value since they record events of the authors' own time. Of these the best are the *Caesars* of Aurelius Victor, short biographies of the emperors from Augustus to Julianus Apostata; the *Breviary* of Eutropius, which ends with the year 369; the *Breviary* of Rufius Festus, which ends with the year 371; and the anonymous *Epitome of the Caesars,* which ends with the death of Theodosius I in 395.

The works of the Christian writers are valuable sources because they contain careful verbatim citations of many documents which otherwise would have been lost—imperial constitutions and edicts, proceedings of church councils, imperial correspondence, and letters written by bishops and other church officials. Lactantius in his Latin tract *On the Deaths of the Persecutors,* which maintained that emperors who persecuted the Christians were doomed to a painful death, has preserved a faithful firsthand record of certain events from the accession of Diocletian to the death of Maximinus Daia in 313. Years later, St. Athanasius (ca. 296–373), the Bishop of Alexandria, wrote many document-filled tracts, the most important of which were his polemics against the adherents of the Arian heresy.

The most valuable sources are the numerous works of Eusebius (ca. 264–340), a bishop of Caesarea in Palestine, who was the first of the great Greek Fathers of the Late Empire and the most learned and prolific writer of his age. In addition to several commentaries on the Bible, he wrote a *Universal History,* in which he fixed the dates of all important events from Abraham to Constantine. In his *Life of Constantine* he eulogized the emperor's piety and devotion to the Christian Church, and in his *Chronicle (Chronica),* the forerunner of all chronicles published in the Late Empire and the Middle Ages, he registered events from Abraham to the Council of Nicaea in 325. The most important of his works was the *Ecclesiastical History,* which contains an authoritative history of the Christian Church down to the Council of

Nicaea as well as a valuable collection of documents and an eyewitness account of the Great Persecution under Diocletian.

The primary sources include inscriptions, papyri, coins, archaeological materials, and especially the imperial *constitutiones** preserved in inscriptions, papyri, various juristic and literary works, in the Theodosian Code (published in 438 during the reign of Theodosius II: 408–450), and in the Justinian Code (first published in 529 during the reign of Justinian I: 527–565). The two most important inscriptional texts are Diocletian's famous *Edict on Maximum Prices,* and the great Paikuli inscription of Narses I of Persia (293–302), wherein the king recounted his triumphs and the acts of homages paid him by Roman envoys and the vassal kings of Asia.

The Rise of Diocletian

Diocletian was born in ca. 245 in Dalmatia probably near Salona (now Split, Yugoslavia), the son of a humble scribe or freedman. His obscure birth did not prevent him from achieving a brilliant army career: he was a cavalryman under Gallienus, a *dux* or cavalry commander in Moesia, and commandant of the imperial mounted bodyguard. His excellent military record is nevertheless overshadowed by his genius as an organizer, administrator, and statesman. He was greatly aided by excellent advisers and generals, who assisted him to restore the Empire to its former greatness.

The chief problems facing Diocletian

* The *constitutiones principum* ("Statutes of the Emperors"), which had the validity of laws, included (a) *edicta* or edicts (official proclamations of the Emperor as a Roman magistrate which were valid during his term of office for the whole empire); (b) *decreta* or decrees (court decisions of the Emperor having the force of law); (c) *rescripta* (written responses to written inquiries on specific points of law). Although the *constitutiones* were originally valid only during the principate of their author, they later remained in force as sources of public and private law unless revoked by a later imperial constitution. The Emperor also became a source of law through the responses of eminent jurists to whom he had delegated the *ius respondendi* (see p. 309).

were the strengthening of the power and authority of the central government, the defense of the frontiers, the recovery of the rebellious and seceding provinces, and the removal of those conditions which favored constant attempts to seize the throne. This work, begun by Aurelian and Probus, had been halted by their assassination. Armies could again mutiny and proclaim emperors; usurpers not only could but did arise again, provinces seceded. The danger of secession was particularly acute in Gaul, which was suffering from repeated invasion by the Franks, Burgundians, and Alemanni and the resulting devastation and famine. Here the Bagaudae had revolted, bands of peasants driven to desperation by the triple scourge of invasion, imperial taxation, and landlord exploitation.

Diocletian's first act was to find a general who could take over the defense of the West and permit him to concentrate his energies upon the protection of the threatened Danubian and Eastern frontiers. His choice fell upon Maximian, an old comrade in arms, whom he elevated to the rank of Caesar and sent to Gaul. Although Maximian was a rude Illyrian peasant, violent, ruthless and cruel, he was a capable general and fanatically loyal to Diocletian.

In Gaul, Maximian quickly crushed the rebellion of the Bagaudae and, by two brilliantly executed land campaigns, drove the Germans out of Gaul into the forested wilds east of the Rhine. In recognition of these victories Diocletian raised Maximian to the rank of Augustus in 286. Maximian was to rule jointly with Diocletian and to be second only in personal prestige and authority.

Maximian had not been so successful at sea. To clear the Channel and the North Sea of the Frankish and Saxon pirates who had been raiding the shores of Gaul and Britain, he established a naval base at Boulogne and placed in command of the Roman fleet a certain Mausaeus Carausius. Carausius, a native of the German Lowlands and an experienced and daring sailor, overcame the pirates within a few weeks. His ambition stimulated by his naval exploits, he enlarged his fleet with captured pirate ships and men, seized Boulogne and Britain, and conferred upon himself the title of Augustus. Since

Diocletian was too occupied to do more than protest, and Maximian's fleet was wrecked at sea, Carausius maintained undisturbed sway over Britain for seven years as Emperor of the North.

Diocletian himself had meanwhile not been idle. He had gone from province to province, inspecting frontier defenses and repelling invasions. He had displayed the might of Rome on the Danube and Euphrates: in 289 he had defeated the Alemanni in Rhaetia, the Sarmatians and Goths in Pannonia and Moesia, and the Arabic invaders of Syria. In 291 he had defeated the Blemmyes, who had invaded Egypt from the Sudan. In 290 he had made Greater Armenia once more a vassal Roman kingdom and placed upon its throne Tiridates III, a scion of the now defunct Arsacid Parthian line of kings and a Roman protégé. He also persuaded the Persians to abandon claim to the former Roman province of Mesopotamia.

The Tetrarchy: 293–312

Diocletian was convinced that the dual *imperium* had proved itself to be a successful military and political experiment. In order to strengthen imperial control of the armies and forestall usurpers such as Carausius, Diocletian resolved in 293 to create a tetrarchy. Two Caesars were to be appointed, one to serve under Diocletian in the East, the other under Maximian in the West. Diocletian selected as his Caesar, Gaius Galerius, a rough Illyrian soldier, and now an experienced general and brilliant strategist, but as a person most uncultured and brutal. Maximian's choice was another Illyrian of humble origin, C. Flavius Julius Constantius, commonly called Chlorus or "Pale Face," who proved himself an excellent general, a prudent statesman, and the worthy father of the future Constantine the Great.

The tetrarchy, probably an adaptation of a Persian institution, proved to be an ingenious system. It was held together by the personality and authority of Diocletian, and doubly strengthened by adoption and marriage; for each Caesar was the adopted heir and son-in-law of his Augustus. The tetrarchy was in-

A Roman lighthouse at Dover, England. (Courtesy British Travel and Holidays Association, New York)

for protecting the Eastern part of the Empire from Nicomedia on the Sea of Marmara. In spite of this division of responsibility, the Empire remained a territorial and administrative whole.

The tetrarchy also provided for a quiet and orderly succession to the throne. On the death or abdication of an Augustus, his Caesar, also his adopted son and heir, would take his place and would in turn select a new Caesar. The system permitted the Caesars to gain experience in war and government before taking office as Augusti.

The Tetrarchy in Action

The tetrarchy fully jutisfied Diocletian's expectations as each of the four rulers set about restoring peace and unity in his own part of the Empire.

Constantius immediately began operations against the usurper Carausius. He captured Boulogne, and subdued the Franks and other German allies of Carausius that dwelt beside the North Sea. He transported many of the captives to eastern Gaul for peaceful farming and for future service in Roman armies. In 293, Carausius was assassinated by an ambitious and treacherous rival.

In 296, Constantius invaded Britain and reestablished Roman dominion from Land's End to Hadrian's Wall. Then he began reorganizing defenses and restoring prosperity: he provided protection for shipping in the Channel, the North Sea, and the Atlantic, and erected a series of strong and well distributed forts to safeguard the southern and eastern shores against Saxon pirate raids. He placed all these forts, together with a powerful new fleet, under the command of a new official known as the Count of the Saxon Shore.

Constantius then returned to the Continent, where he drove the German invaders back over the Rhine and strengthened the *limes* of the Rhineland with many redoubts and fortifications. His spectacular victory over the Alemanni near Langres in 298 brought Gaul many years of quiet and prosperity. He afterwards made his capital city of Trèves one of the most important and loveliest cities in the Western empire.

divisible in operation and power; laws were promulgated in the names of all four rulers, and triumphs gained by any one of them were acclaimed in the name of all. On the other hand, each member of the tetrarchy had his own separate court and bodyguard and had the right to strike coins bearing his own image and titulature.

Each Augustus and Caesar had assigned to him those provinces and frontiers that he could conveniently and adequately defend from his own capital: Maximian protected the upper Rhine and upper Danube from Milan; Constantius shielded the middle and lower Rhine, Gaul, and later Britain from Trèves (Trier); Galerius guarded the middle and lower Danube from Sirmium on the Save; and Diocletian assumed responsibility

Galerius and Diocletian were equally busy on the Danube and in the East and no less successful. In the years 293–6 Galerius had defeated the Goths, Marcomanni, Sarmatians, and Bastarnians, and had settled captured Iazyges and Carpi in depopulated Pannonia. He had built forts along the Danube, and had cleared and irrigated land for farming in the southern Danubian basin.

After helping Galerius in the defense and fortification of the lower Danube, Diocletian suppressed an uprising in Egypt where two usurpers, Achilleus and Lucius Domitius Domitianus had, in 296, proclaimed themselves respectively Corrector and Augustus.* Diocletian recaptured Alexandria after eight months and put Domitianus, Achilleus, and their Manichaean or social revolutionary partisans to death: then he abolished the Alexandrian provincial mint and totally reorganized the administration of Egypt.

Taking advantage of Diocletian's preoccupation with Egypt. Narses, king of Persia, opened hostilities against Rome: he overran the kingdom of Armenia and invaded Syria. Galerius, summoned from the Danube by Diocletian in 297, rushed to the East, but at Callinicum, not far from Carrhae, he impetuously attacked the Persians with insufficient forces. He suffered a disastrous defeat which resulted in the loss of Mesopotamia. The next year, reinforced by fresh levies from the Balkans, Galerius advanced into Armenia and routed Narses at Erzerum. Galerius, whose immense booty included the king's harem, followed up his success by the reconquest of Mesopotamia, and the capture of Nisibis and the Persian capital of Ctesiphon.

The loss of his wives and children obliged Narses to accept harsh peace terms. He agreed to surrender Mesopotamia which now extended to the upper Tigris, and five small provinces beyond the Tigris. He acknowledged as Roman protectorates Greater Armenia and the kingdom of Iberia south of the Caucasus. He also agreed that merchants traveling between the Roman and Persian empires must pass through the Roman customs center of Nisibis. The victory of Galerius was so complete that the Persians did not risk war with Rome for another fifty years.

The existence of the tetrarchy had been fully justified by the victories of Constantius in the West and of Galerius in the East, by the construction of strong defenses in Britain, along the Rhine, Danube, and Euphrates, in Egypt and Mesopotamia, and by the systematic settlement of captured barbarians to repopulate and help defend lands adjacent to the frontiers. That four-headed, seemingly decentralized, but actually united power, greatly contributed to the recovery and stabilization of the empire and laid the constitutional foundations for a state destined to endure more than a thousand years.

Diocletian's Reforms

In addition to consolidating the military defenses of the empire, Diocletian carried out sweeping reforms in almost every department of the government. These reforms, though brilliant and original, were not wholly without precedent, for they were not the innovations of a radical but rather the continuation by a confirmed conservative of the work of Augustus, Claudius, Hadrian, Septimius Severus, Gallienus, and Aurelian. Diocletian's reforms not only left intact the ancient structure of the Roman state, but strengthened and affirmed the development of absolute monarchy.

Court Ceremonial

A regime which plans large scale reforms must first secure recognition from the army and the people. It must surround itself with an aura of such power, pomp, and sanctity that an attempt to overthrow it must appear not only treasonous but sacrilegious. Diocletian assumed the title of Jovius as Jupiter's earthly representative sent to restore the Roman Empire. He bestowed upon his colleague, Maximian, the name of Herculius,

* A new text in A. E. R. Boak-H. Ch. Youtie, *The Archive of Aurelius Isidorus* (1960) no. 62 mentions the Corrector Aurelius Achilleus and the Augustus L. Domitius Domitianus as two different persons. This document disposes of previous attempts to prove that the two names belonged to one and the same person.

the earthly Hercules and helper of Jovius. Together they demanded the reverence and adoration due to gods. Everything about them was sacred and holy—their palaces, courts, and bedchambers. Their portraits radiated a nimbus or halo, an outer illumination effluent from an inner divinity.

In order to dazzle his subjects with his power and majesty and infect them with a feeling of mystery and awe, Diocletian adopted an elaborate court ceremonial and etiquette, not unlike that prescribed at the royal court of Persia. The emperor became less accessible and seldom appeared in public. When he did, he wore the diadem and carried the scepter. He arrayed himself in purple and gold sparkling with jewels. Those to whom he condescended to grant audience had to kneel and kiss the hem of his robe. This act of adoration was incumbent also upon members of the Imperial Council (consilium), which acquired the name of the Sacred Consistory (sacrum consistorium) from the necessity of standing while in the imperial presence.

Provincial Reorganization

To strengthen the central government and prevent rebellions by powerful and ambitious governors, Diocletian carried out a complete reorganization of the provinces. He divided the larger ones into smaller units, thereby increasing the total number from about 50 to 100 or so. By depriving practically all the governors of their military functions, Diocletian not only reduced their power and independence and exercised closer administrative supervision of the provinces but increased the central government's control of patronage and power of appointment, from which every government, ancient and modern, has derived its main source of strength and stability. Even more drastic but quite in line with a policy initiated by Septimius Severus was Diocletian's abolition of Italy's former privileged status. He made her subject to imperial taxes and cut her territory up into sixteen provinces.

To enable the imperial government to control the provincial governors more effectively, Diocletian grouped the provinces in twelve administrative districts known as dioceses. Each diocese fell under the supervision of a so-called vicar (vicarius), a deputy of one of the four praetorian prefects, each one of whom was in turn an administrative assistant of a member of the imperial tetrarchy. The vicars supervised all governors within their respective dioceses (consulares, correctores, and presides), even those of senatorial rank—except the three proconsuls of Africa, Asia, and Achaea. The vicars themselves were of equestrian rank and, like all governors (except those of Mauretania and Isauria in Asia Minor), were purely civilian officials whose main function was the administration of justice.

Diocletian assigned command over the armies and garrisons stationed in the provinces to professional military men known as dukes (duces). To assure close supervision and the mutual restraint of ambitious impulses he made the dukes dependent for military supplies and provisions upon the governors and other civilian officials. In some dioceses several dukes might serve under the command of a higher officer known as a count (comes).

Military Reforms

Despite all Gallienus had done, military reform continued to be a pressing necessity. Throughout the third century there were never enough legions to fight major wars without a substantial withdrawal of troops from the frontier defenses. Except for the Praetorian Guard, an elite but relatively small corps, there was no standing army. Nor had Gallienus been able to correct the weakness of the cavalry. With characteristic energy, Diocletian set about solving these most difficult problems.

In order to strengthen the defense of the frontiers, he decreased the size of the legion from 6,000 men to 1,000. The number of legions was thus increased from 39 to 65 or more and the cavalry and auxiliary units correspondingly, although the increase in total armed strength was only from 400,000 to probably 500,000 men. The increased number of legions permitted a more even distribution of the troops available for frontier defense.

Porta Nigra, a fortified city gate in Trier, Germany (late third or early fourth century A.D.). (Courtesy Deutscher Kunstverlag, Munich)

Diocletian also divided the army into two main and distinct branches, the *limitanei*, who served as border or frontier (*limes*) guards, and the *comitatenses* (from *comitatus*, originally "the emperor's escort," but now designating a mobile field force consisting largely of cavalry), which was stationed at strategic points well behind the frontiers and capable of moving at a moment's notice to any point of danger. The *comitatenses* had higher physical standards, better pay and food, and more privileges. Also they were required to serve only twenty years instead of twenty-five.

Another military problem, which arose from the manpower shortage, was the recruitment of soldiers. Though the old obligation of universal military service still obtained, in theory, the government actually could not afford to call too many men away from agriculture, industry, transportation, and other essential services.

Diocletian resorted to various methods to secure the required number of recruits: the draft, the enforcement of hereditary obligations, the hiring of mercenaries, and volun-

tary enlistment. He enforced the draft against male persons not engaged in essential occupations and, of course, against able-bodied beggars and tramps. He compelled the sons of German settlers to enlist in the army upon reaching the proper age as well as the sons of veterans and even of soldiers still in active service. He enforced a modified form of the draft against landowners, requiring them to fill a legally fixed quota of recruits each year from their tenants and dependents. They might, in lieu of men, present a sum of money sufficient for the hiring of an equivalent number of mercenaries.

Voluntary enlistment was not uncommon because it frequently afforded an escape from something more unpleasant than army life or provided a means of securing legal advantages, such as immunity from municipal obligations or exemption from taxes, not enjoyed by the average civilian. A prisoner of war, for example, might enlist to escape death or enslavement and even a municipal senator or town councillor might choose army life in preference to an unbearable burden of taxes and other irksome responsibilities.

Financial Reforms

The endless series of frontier wars, the expansion of the army, the doubling of the number of provinces and governors, the establishment of four separate imperial capitals, and the creation of a vast civil bureaucracy devoured enormous sums of money and put the finances of the state under a heavy strain. Another source of financial stress was Diocletian's own mania for building. In addition to highways and fortifications in almost every province and the military installations (arms factories, depots, and arsenals), he embellished the four imperial capitals with splendid palaces, basilicas, and baths. Trèves received its famous Basilica and the Porta Nigra, the most elaborate city gate preserved from the Roman world. Rome acquired an arch of triumph, a new senate house, and the colossal baths of Diocletian with recreational facilities to accommodate 3,600 persons at a time. Salonika commemorated the victories of Galerius with a splendid triumphal arch. Salona, where Diocletian spent his last days, was the site of an enormous fortress-like palace, a wonder of the ancient world. The raising of money to finance these and other ambitious projects necessitated a reorganization of the entire financial and fiscal system.

The reorganization of the financial system consisted of two major reforms: a revision of the tax collecting system and the introduction of a new and stable currency. These reforms were the most enduring achievements of Diocletian's reign, wherein he proved himself superior to Augustus as an administrator, and more clever than Vespasian as a financier.

His reforms were necessary because of the failure of the ancient world to translate science into an industrial technology capable of producing the required amount of wealth to bear the financial burden of a highly centralized and bureaucratic state such as that of the Roman Empire.

Tax Reform

He swept away the obsolete and financially unsound system of indirect taxes, provincial tribute, and testamentary bequests upon which Augustus and his successors had depended as sources of revenue. To create and maintain a steady and adequate flow of revenue into the treasury, Diocletian also abolished the irregular emergency levies and requisitions of the third century and replaced them with a regular income tax on production. Though certain traditional and local taxes continued to be payable in money, the new taxes were payable in kind, that is, in the form of agricultural products such as grain, oil, wine, or manufactured goods, the so-called *annona*, which previous emperors had requisitioned irregularly and then only to make up for unexpected deficiencies in the regular revenues.

The main effect of Diocletian's tax reform was to convert these emergency levies, which varied in amount from region to region and from time to time, into an ordinary annual tax collectable from the entire empire. The new tax was periodically estimated, fixed in advance, and announced by an imperial decree or indiction (*indictio*), which specified the taxes to be collected from the empire as a whole and from each diocese and province. Later the term "indiction" came to mean the period between two assessments, which occurred every five years between 297 and 312 but thereafter every fifteen. The cycle became so well established as a regular institution that it came to constitute an actual system of chronology.

The tax system of Diocletian introduced in 287, elaborated in 297, and perfected by 312, despite much study and research, remains obscure and perplexing. There is reason to believe that the system was not consistent in practice nor uniformly applied to every region or diocese of the empire. Apparently, Diocletian shrank from the task of ironing out all regional social and economic differences and of imposing upon the entire empire a single, simple, and uniform system.

Capitation (Capitatio)

The core of Diocletian's tax reform was capitation, a very complex institution which varied greatly from diocese to diocese within the next two centuries. Derived from *caput*, "head," it was a species of poll or personal tax which had existed before Diocletian and in some dioceses even after. As a result of his reform, there arose another but more important form of capitation, which in some dioceses supplanted, absorbed, or integrated the older personal capitation, in others existed side by side with the latter as a distinctly separate tax upon rural property.

Diocletian's form of capitation was not an individual or personal tax but a method of assessing or evaluating for taxation purposes the totality of rural wealth and property in the empire. It included all such concrete elements as land, labor, crops, and livestock, and the ideal unit of assessment was the *caput*, which may be defined as that quantity of labor, whether of an independent peasant owner, tenant (*colonus*), sharecropper, or hired hand, required to render parcels of land varying in area with geographical location, climate, soil fertility, or type of crop capable of producing crops of equivalent taxable value.*

A Syriac translation of a fifth century Romano-Syrian lawbook indicates that in some provinces (Syria, for example) the unit of assessment was probably not the *caput* but a surveyor's unit of measurement called the *jugum*. In Syria at least, the *jugum* comprised an area respectively of 20, 40, and 60 Roman acres (*jugera*) of grain planted land graded according to soil fertility, or five acres of vineyards, level ground having on it 225 mature olive trees, or mountainous terrain bearing 450. In other words, the *jugum* was that quantity of land required to produce crops having an assessable value equal to that of the *caput*.

In the ideal system of *jugatio-capitatio*, a *jugational* form of capitation, the two units, *caput* and *jugum*, though equivalent and even interchangeable, represented two distinct taxes. By combining the two units, the tax assessors were able to calculate all the natural physical, human and animal resources of a community, province, or diocese. Unfortunately, the perfect jugational form of capitation did not apply fully to any diocese of the empire except possibly Asia Minor and

Pontus, both of which were adjacent to Diocletian's capital of Nicomedia and therefore under his personal supervision. A less perfect and elaborate form of the system existed probably in Thrace, Illyria, and Gaul. In Egypt, land and personal taxes were kept separate until sometime between 349 and 359 in the reign of Constantius II. In North Africa, the surveyor's unit was not the *jugum,* but the *centuria* of 200 acres. Though North Italy fell under Diocletian's system of taxation and paid the *annona* as a *regio annonaria,* the capitation tax was not assessed in conjunction with the *jugum*; in central and southern Italy (then known as *regio suburbicaria*), which supplied Rome with meat, wool, wine, wood, and lime, the unit of measurement was the *millena,* about which almost nothing is known.

The Effects of the Tax Reform: The Decay of the Municipal Middle Class

The beneficial effects of Diocletian's tax reform were notable. Knowing several years in advance what the approximate tax receipts would be, the government could plan and control its expenditures and curb the excessive spending that had formerly wrought havoc with the coinage. At last the government could draft an annual budget, without which any attempt to stabilize the coinage would have been useless and absurd.

The reform also helped the taxpayers by distributing the burden fairly and equitably and by announcing in advance how much they had to pay. The government was able not only to bring about a temporary stabilization of the economy but to lay the groundwork for a fiscal system which endured for more than a thousand years. It probably tended to stimulate production, especially in agriculture, where the collection of taxes in kind was an intelligent recognition of an economic fact of long standing. For decades farmers, unable to sell surplus produce for cash, had been growing only enough food for their families or for barter with their neighbors. They now had to produce more so as to have a surplus with which to pay their taxes.

The defects of Diocletian's tax reform had

---

* A woman was rated as half a *caput,* and animals proportionately lower.

equally momentous historical consequences. It tended to destroy the local municipal bourgeoisie and to create conditions favorable to the rise of serfdom, the most characteristic of medieval institutions. In a sense, Diocletian's reign marks the end of the ancient world and the beginning of the Middle Ages, especially in the West.

When Diocletian, following the policy of Septimius Severus, threw the onus of collecting the capitation tax on the municipal senates or councils, he unwittingly contributed to the ruin of the municipal middle class—business men and landowners—who had in the past played an important role in the social, economic, and cultural life of the early Empire. As municipal magistrates and municipal councillors or *curiales* (members of the *curia* or municipal senate), members of the city bourgeoisie had not only freely spent their own money to beautify their cities and towns, but had appropriated municipal funds for public works, baths, public entertainment, and food for the indigent. They also served as collectors of imperial taxes and provided for the feeding and bedding of troops in transit and for change of horses for the imperial post. They performed many of these functions for the state at their own expense. Indeed, the emperor Majorian (457–461) once called them the nerves and vital organs of the state, but this pronouncement was more descriptive of their role in the second and third centuries. By the fourth century they had already lost the power to save themselves let alone serve the state.

When Diocletian made the municipal senators responsible for the collection of taxes within their territories, he drove them into bankruptcy and ruin. They had to make up arrears and deficiencies out of their own pockets. Powerless to compel senatorial landlords to pay their share, they attempted to shift the burden to the poorer and more helpless classes, by whom they came to be regarded as oppressors and tyrants. Their office became a cruel burden from which they sought release as soldiers, tenants on large estates, and in later times as priests or monks.

In a desperate attempt to keep the curiales at their jobs, later emperors issued 192 laws, the earliest of which bound them to their councils and made their status hereditary. Thus the tax reforms of Diocletian contributed to the ruin and enslavement of the urban bourgeoisie and to the decay of town and city life in the Western part of the empire.

The tax reform of Diocletian also brought misery for the tenant farmer or *colonus*. It drove him to change landlords or else become a robber or a tramp. Since land without labor to cultivate it could not produce taxes, the government of Constantine the Great promulgated, in 322, a law permanently binding tenant farmers to the soil and thereby created the famous *colonatus,* the perpetual and hereditary status of a *colonus* or serf. A landlord could not sell the land without the serf nor the serf without the land. This institution persisted in the Byzantine Empire for almost 300 years and in parts of Western Europe for more than twelve centuries. In Eastern Europe it lasted until the twentieth century.

The Reform of the Coinage: 286

By his reform of the coinage Diocletian succeeded in ending the frightful monetary chaos of the third century and created a fairly reliable coinage in silver and gold, which served as a model for his successors. In 286 he replaced the old *aureus* with a new gold coin at the rate of 60 to the standard gold pound of 327 grams and a new silver coin, the *argenteus,* at 96 to the pound and roughly equivalent to the *denarius* of Nero's time. To answer the need for small change he struck silver-washed bronze coins of three weights and denominations, the heaviest often known as the *follis,* the lightest being the silver-coated *denarius,* which probably had a nominal valuation of 50,000 to the gold pound and was roughly equivalent to 20 *follis* coins.

The most enduring of the new coins was the *aureus.* After Constantine had decreased its weight in 324 from 60 to 72 to the pound, it became known as the *solidus* (and later the Byzantine *bezant*). It circulated freely throughout the Roman world and even the Persian empire and persisted both in the Byzantine Empire and in the medieval West for more than a millennium. Its name still survives in the Italian *soldo* and the French *sou*. By 296, as a result of Diocletian's currency reform, a money economy became re-established in the Roman world, and finds of Roman coins in Germany, Ireland, Scotland, Scandinavia, India, Ceylon, and even in Iceland indicate the extension of money economy to regions far beyond the imperial frontiers.

The Edict on Ceiling Prices: 301

Unlike the *solidus,* the silvered bronze or billon currency underwent further depreciation, resulting in turn in a sharp rise of prices. To combat the inflation Diocletian issued his famous *Edict of Maximum Prices* in 301. This Edict is the most important and instructive document available on Roman economic life. It has been reconstructed from numerous Greek and Latin inscriptional fragments found largely in the Eastern part of the empire but recently also in Italy. It set a ceiling on the prices of over a thousand different items, from wheat, barley, poultry, vegetables, fruits, fish, and wines of every variety and origin, to clothing, bed linen, ink, parchment, and craftsmen's wages.

In a remarkable preamble to the law, Diocletian sharply condemned speculators and profiteers who robbed the people and especially soldiers and government workers, and invoked harsh penalties against them. Though the law worked well for a time, it eventually failed to prevent monopolists from creating an "economy of scarcity" or profiteers from removing goods from the sales counters and selling them on the black market. The chief defect of the law was that it was a half measure; it failed to regulate prices because the government did not own and control the means of production. The extensive tracts of agricultural land owned and exploited by the state since the time of Septimius Severus and the several large arms factories and textile mills operated by the government were the exception, not the rule. The Edict had to be relaxed to encourage production and distribution and was finally revoked by Constantine.

The Last Persecution of the Christians: 303–311

Far less effective than the *Edict on Prices,* was Diocletian's persecution of the Christians, which brought his reign to a tragic and bloody close. What influences drove him to shed their blood and shatter the forty-year religious truce proclaimed by Gallienus in his edict of toleration in 260 has been a subject of much speculation.

Some scholars have held that the Christian persecution was a natural and logical outcome of Diocletian's own conservative and reactionary policy; that having assumed the title of Jovius as Jupiter's earthly delegate he felt it his duty to restore not only Rome's former military glory and power but her ancient faith and moral code. The Christians, a supposedly subversive and hostile sect, had made numerous converts who infiltrated the army, the civil service, and even the imperial court. Furthermore, their tightly-knit organization was so perfected as to constitute a veritable state within the state. It is possible that Diocletian deferred dealing with this menace until after his victory over Persia and the completion of his tasks of internal reorganization.

Other scholars have argued that Diocletian was never a religious fanatic concerned with the triumph of any sect or principle but was rather a cool, clear-headed statesman who worked hard to promote the peace and prosperity of the empire. Remembering the failure of the Decian and Valerian persecutions, from which the Christians had emerged with greater strength and solidarity than before, Diocletian would naturally have refrained from embroiling the empire in a disruptive persecution of at least one-tenth of its most active and industrious population. Some pressure, force, fear, or event must have driven him to abandon his previous policy of religious toleration and embark upon one of the longest and bloodiest of anti-Christian persecutions in the history of the Roman Empire.

According to the Christian writer Lactantius, who stayed at Diocletian's court in Nicomedia as tutor of the young Constantine, the real instigators of the persecution were Galerius, Diocletian's Caesar in the East, and Hierocles, the governor of Bithynia, who in a pamphlet addressed to Diocletian directed the heavy artillery of Neoplatonic philosophy against the Christian religion.

The persecution began in 299. At a public sacrifice offered to determine the will of the gods from an inspection of the entrails of the slaughtered animals, the augurs reported that the presence of hostile influences had frustrated and defeated the purpose of the sacrifice. Diocletian, suspicious and furious, gave orders that all persons in the imperial palace —including his own wife—offer sacrifice to the traditional gods of the state and, upon refusal to do so, be beaten. He next permitted Galerius to post orders that all officers and men in the army be required to offer sacrifice on pain of dismissal from the service. After that he drafted an edict which ordered the destruction of the Christian churches and the surrender and burning of sacred books, prohibited Christian worship at any time or place, and restricted the rights of prosecution and defense formerly enjoyed by Christians in courts of law. Still Diocletian shrank from unleashing a bloody persecution.

One evening in the winter of 303, without having waited for the official proclamation of the edict, the imperial police suddenly entered, ransacked, and demolished the Christian cathedral which stood opposite the emperor's palace in Nicomedia. The edict was posted throughout the city the next day. An enraged Christian tore down one of the posters, was arrested, and burned at the stake. Within the next fifteen days two fires of unknown origin broke out in the imperial palace in Nicomedia. Numerous Christian suspects were imprisoned, tortured, and killed. At the same time, revolts ascribed to Christians in Syria and Cappadocia, though easily suppressed, led to the proclamation of two more edicts; one ordered the imprisonment of the clergy, the other sought to relieve the overcrowding of the prisons by offering liberty to all who would consent to make sacrifice to the gods of the state and condemned to death those who refused.

After his visit to Rome, where he had just celebrated the twentieth anniversary of his accession, Diocletian became very ill and ceased to attend to public affairs. According

Restoration of the Palace of Diocletian at Split, Yugoslavia. (Courtesy Yugoslav State Tourist Office, New York)

Peristyle of the Palace of Diocletian at Split, Yugoslavia. (Courtesy Yugoslav State Tourist Office, New York)

to Eusebius, Galerius seized the opportunity to draft and publish a fourth edict which required all Christians to offer the customary sacrifices under pain of death or hard labor in the mines.

None of the four edicts, except perhaps the first, was enforced everywhere with equal severity. In Gaul and Britain Constantius limited himself to merely pulling down a few churches whereas Galerius and Maximian were far more zealous in their domains. When Diocletian abdicated, in 305, the persecution was at its height.

The Abdication

On May 1st, 305, in the presence of the assembled troops at Nicomedia, Diocletian formally abdicated. With tears in his eyes he took leave of his soldiers, telling them that he was too old and sick, probably from a stroke, to carry on the heavy tasks of government. On the same day at Milan in fulfill-

ment of a promise previously extracted by Diocletian Maximian also resigned. Diocletian nominated Constantius Chlorus and Galerius as the new Augusti, with senority for Constantius, who received as his special provinces Gaul, Britain, Spain, and Morocco. Galerius took the Balkans and most of Asia Minor. Galerius, in turn, nominated his nephew Maximinus Daia as his Caesar in the East and ruler over the provinces in the rest of Asia Minor, Syria, and Egypt, while Constantius chose Flavius Valerius Severus, who was to rule over Italy, Roman Africa, and Pannonia.

After their abdication, the two ex-Augusti went into retirement. Maximian, fuming over his enforced abdication, went to Lucania to await the first opportunity to snatch back his Empire. Diocletian retired to his enormous fortress palace at Split, where he spent the last eight years of his life weeding turnips and cabbages in his garden and listening to the gulls screaming above the whitecaps of the Adriatic.

XVIII

CONSTANTINE : THE

DIOCLETIAN HAD SOARED FROM OBSCURITY TO BECOME ONE OF the greatest of Roman emperors. He had displayed the might of Rome throughout the world and by his reforms rescued her from chaos and set her upon the road to recovery.

Despite those achievements, he lived to see the disintegration of the tetrarchy and the recognition of a religion he himself had persecuted. He saw his own great fame fade into obscurity before the blazing light of Constantine's rising sun, and died in the belief that he had lived and worked in vain never realizing that the mighty structure he had raised was destined to endure.

Constantine the Great was the bastard son of Constantius Chlorus and his common-law wife, Helena, whom he had met in Bithynia. After living together for some years, Constantius abandoned her in 289 in order to marry Theodora, the step-

FIRST CHRISTIAN EMPEROR

daughter of the emperor Maximianus. Constantine grew up at Diocletian's court in Nicomedia, where he learned at first hand the secrets of empire and developed into a strong and handsome man.

Although Constantius was nominally the senior Augustus, Galerius was the actual master of the empire. He still basked in the glory of his victories over Persia in 298. His two Caesars, Maximinus Daia in the East and Flavius Valerius Severus in the West, were both obligated and blindly devoted to him. Through them Galerius was able to control the major portions of the empire. The pres-

ence of the young Constantine at his court gave him an additional advantage, both as a hostage in any future dealings with Constantius and as his spokesman and advocate with the army. The power of Galerius was now at its height.

The Rise of Constantine: 306

An invasion of England by the Scottish Picts in 306 provided Constantius a sound and plausible reason for requesting the return of his son. Unwilling to forego Constantine's

Colossal head of Constantine, and an allegorical statue of a province. (Courtesy Fratelli Alinari, Florence)

services and perhaps suspecting a coup d'état, Galerius procrastinated as long as he could, but finally consented to let the youth go, and signed the necessary travel papers. Fearing that Galerius might change his mind, Constantine stealthily disappeared one night and, after a swift journey during which—to forestall possible pursuit—he killed or lamed all the post horses he had to leave behind, he reached his father at Boulogne and with him sailed to Britain. After a swift and easy victory over the Picts, Constantius died at York (where Septimius Severus had died almost a century before). The army proclaimed Constantine Augustus in his father's place.

Constantine at once wrote Galerius requesting recognition as an Augustus. Galerius did not reject this petition outright since he did not wish to risk civil war. He compromised by granting Constantine the title and rank of Caesar. The young man quietly accepted in the interests of peace and the preservation of the tetrarchy established by Diocletian, whom he still greatly respected. Nor was he much perturbed by the subsequent elevation of Severus, henchman of Galerius, to the rank of Augustus. Confident that time was on his side, Constantine kept strengthening his position by winning fresh victories over the Alemanni and the Franks, whose captured kings he cast into foul dungeons or threw to the lions in the arena at Trèves.

The Usurpation of Maxentius: 306

Maximian's son Maxentius was greatly incensed by the news of Constantine's elevation. Who had a better right to the throne than himself, the legitimate son of an ex-Augustus? He naturally felt aggrieved to find his way to the throne blocked by Galerius, who personally detested Maxentius because of his lethargic temperament and unmilitary bearing. At the latter's instigation Severus ordered the dissolution of the Praetorian Guard because it had supported and abetted an uprising in the Roman pig market. Severus also attempted to impose the capitation tax on Rome and Lower Italy. His injudicious action permitted Maxentius to foment popular uprisings and stage a successful and almost bloodless coup d'état.*

Meanwhile, Maximian, chafing to recover the throne, left his estate in Lucania and set out to win over the army. He also tried, unsuccessfully, to persuade Diocletian to resume office.

Galerius had recognized Constantine, though semi-officially and against his will, but he had no intention of recognizing either Maxentius or his father Maximian. He not only hated them both personally, but regarded them as a threat to the stability of the Diocletian tetrarchy which he represented. Accordingly, Galerius ordered Severus to march on Rome. The march ended in a fiasco, for Rome closed her gates against him and secret agents undermined the loyalty of his own army. Finally, by some clever ruse, Maxentius and his father lured Severus into their hands and had him killed.

Events now began to follow one another with startling rapidity. Galerius marched into Italy and upon Rome. The invasion failed. Rome was too strong to be taken by storm and too well supplied with food to be starved into surrender. Some of his exhausted legions mutinied, others deserted. To escape the fate of Severus, Galerius beat a hasty retreat. For some obscure reason, Maxentius neither pursued Galerius nor attempted to destroy his looting, undisciplined, and disorganized army. All he did was to assume the title of Augustus.

Maximian

In 307, Maximian also took the title of Augustus. He became estranged from his son, Maxentius, for some obscure reason. He went to the court of Constantine at Trèves, betrothed his teenage daughter Fausta to him, and endeavored to win his support in the coming battle against both Galerius and

---

* The sole victim was the city prefect, a strong partisan of Galerius.

Maxentius. He even offered to recognize Constantine as Augustus. Constantine ignored the offer. He could afford to wait.

The disappointed Maximian returned to Rome late in 307. His frustration appears to have affected his reason for, after a wild, impassioned speech to the imperial troops, he attempted in their presence to rip the purple off his son's shoulders. The soldiers sided with Maxentius and the old man again went back to Constantine's court leaving Maxentius master of Rome.

Seeing the tetrarchy tottering to a fall and the impending collapse of Diocletian's grand design, Galerius with rare statesmanship decided to call a meeting of Augusti and Caesars at Carnuntum on the Austrian Danube and persuaded Maximian and Diocletian to attend. The decisions reached at this conference appeared momentous at first. Maximian reluctantly consented to go back into retirement. Licinius, an old army man and comrade of Galerius, became Augustus in place of Severus. Maxentius, who had seized power illegally, was declared a public enemy. Constantine and Maximinus Daia, neither of whom attended the meeting, had to accept the inferior status of Caesars, both angry at the sudden elevation of the unknown Licinius. The decisions, therefore, really satisfied no one except Galerius and Licinius.

After the Carnuntum meeting the turbulent old Maximian again went to visit Constantine, who received him with honor and respect but did not appoint him to any important offices. Frustrated by what he regarded as shabby treatment, Maximian took advantage of Constantine's absence on a campaign against the Franks in 310 and at Arles proclaimed himself emperor for the third and last time. Constantine, outraged at such treachery on his own territory, hurried back from the Rhine with unexpected speed and laid siege to the usurper. Maximian was forced finally to surrender at Marseilles. Later, according to official sources, he hanged himself in his own room.

Constantine's Repudiation of the Herculian Dynasty

After the death of Maximianus Herculius, Constantine repudiated the Herculian dynasty as the basis of his claim to rule and sought a new sanction by announcing his descent from the renowned Claudius Gothicus. In place of Hercules he adopted as his patron deity the Unconquered Sun (Sol Invictus), who was identified in Gaul, it seems, with Apollo. This deity had also been the protector of Claudius Gothicus and Aurelian. Constantine's claim of descent from Claudius Gothicus enabled him to assert not only his right to the throne by inheritance but his right to undivided rule over the whole Empire as well. Fortified by this new sanction, he was now ready to wage open war against Maxentius, whom he formally declared a usurper and a tyrant.

Constantine's first hostile act against Maxentius occurred in 310 with the annexation of Spain, which had been Rome's chief source of food since the defection of Africa in 308. The loss of Spain therefore created serious problems for Maxentius in Rome—famine, food riots, street fighting, and a death toll of 6,000 people. The situation forced Maxentius to send an expedition for the reconquest of Africa. The success of this expedition not only solved the problem of the Roman food supply, but left Maxentius free to take up the challenge of Constantine. He charged the latter with the murder of his father Maximian and prepared for war. War was postponed only by the pressure of events taking place in other parts of the empire.

The Edict of Religious Toleration: 311

After the abdication of Diocletian, the persecution of the Christians continued only in the dioceses of Galerius (Illyricum, Thrace, and Asia Minor) and particularly in those of Maximinus Daia (Syria and Egypt). Maximinus ordered punishments ranging from mutilations and hard labor in mines and quarries to execution for men, women, or children who refused to participate in pagan sacrifices. He also attempted to counteract the influence of the Christian Church by organizing a pagan church and priesthood with a similar hierarchy of priests, charitable institutions, and local temples subordinated to the great city temples.

Finally, in 311, while in the clutches of a mysterious disease, Galerius became convinced of the futility of the Christian persecutions. As senior Augustus he issued his famous Edict of Toleration which granted Christians all over the empire freedom of worship and the right to reopen their churches provided they pray for him and the state and do nothing to disturb public order. He explained his change of policy by stating that it was better for the Empire for people to practice some religion than none at all. A few days after the proclamation of this edict, Galerius died.

After the death of Galerius, the four remaining Augusti kept the empire divided by their mutual jealousy and hate. Maximinus Daia at once overran and seized the Asiatic provinces of Galerius and threatened Licinius' control over the Balkans. In anticipation of war with Maxentius, Constantine made an alliance with Licinius and betrothed him to his sister Constantia. Meanwhile, Maximinus came to a secret understanding with Maxentius.

Constantine's Invasion of Italy: 312

Constantine launched his long awaited invasion of Italy. In the spring of 312 he set out from Gaul with an army of nearly 40,000 men and crossed the Alps. Near Turin he met and defeated a large force of armored cavalry despatched by Maxentius for the defense of Upper Italy. Then, in swift succession, he captured the cities of Turin, Milan, Aquileia, and Modena, and advanced against Rome. Maxentius had originally intended to defend the city behind the almost impregnable walls of Aurelian.

Had Maxentius adhered to his original strategy, which had earlier succeeded against Severus and Galerius, he might have won. Constantine's army, the smaller of the two, was too weak either to take the city by storm or to conduct a long siege. Whether through belief in religious "omens" or through fear of a popular uprising, Maxentius changed his plan and went out to meet Constantine in open battle.

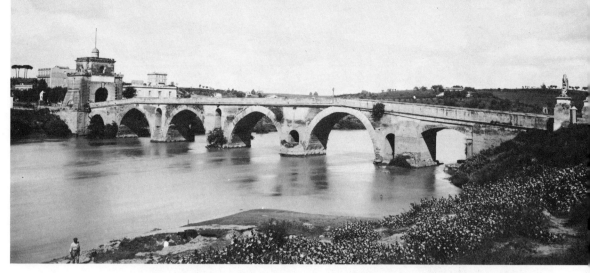

The Ponte Molle, formerly the Milvian Bridge. (Courtesy Fratelli Alinari, Florence)

The Battle of the Milvian Bridge: 312

Maxentius led out his army and crossed the Tiber over a pontoon bridge hastily constructed to replace the old Milvian Bridge, which he had ordered destroyed as a defensive measure in accordance with his earlier strategy. The pontoon bridge consisted of two sections held together by chains which could be quickly cut apart to prevent pursuit by the enemy. He advanced along the Flaminian Way as far as *Saxa Rubra* ("Red Rock") about ten miles north of Rome. There Constantine had encamped the night before.

Lactantius tells us that on the night before the battle a vision appeared to Constantine bidding him place upon the shields of his soldiers the ancient symbol of victory which was also the emblem of Christ, a monogram consisting of an X with a vertical line drawn through it and ending in a loop to represent the first two Greek letters of Christ's name. With less plausibility, Eusebius asserts that Constantine told him years later that sometime before the battle he saw in the sky across the sun a flaming cross and beneath it the Greek words ἐν τούτῳ νίκα ("By this sign thou shalt conquer", or as handed down in the more familiar Latin form: *in hoc vince* or *in hoc signo vinces*), Constantine obeyed the omen and went forth to battle.

Constantine attacked first with the cavalry. The infantry followed and forced the enemy troops into a tight pocket with their backs to the rain-swollen Tiber. Unable to stand their ground, many plunged into the river, others stampeded onto the shaky pontoon bridge which parted under their weight and collapsed, hurling Maxentius and thousands of his men into the swiftly running stream.

Next day Constantine entered Rome in triumph. In the forefront of the procession a soldier carried the head of Maxentius (whose body had been fished out of the river) fixed on a spear. The jubilant throng hailed Constantine as liberator. The senate damned the memory of Maxentius, declaring his acts null and void, and proclaimed Constantine senior Augustus of the entire empire. Though the senate undoubtedly hailed the event as the triumph of *Libertas,* the true victor was the Church Militant. A victory statue of Constantine had a cross placed in his right hand. The Constantine Arch of Triumph inscriptionally attributes the victory to the intervention of an unnamed divine power (*instinctu divinitatis*) and to his own magnitude of mind (*mentis magnitudine*).

While Constantine himself ascribed his victory to the intervention of Christ, he was obviously too keen a statesman to attempt to impugn or trample under foot the religious beliefs of perhaps eighty percent of his subjects, not to mention the senate, the imperial

The Triumphal Arch of Constantine. (Courtesy Fratelli Alinari, Florence)

bureaucracy, and the army. One victory, however brilliant and decisive, could not in one day change the cherished beliefs of a thousand years. As emperor, he continued to hold the ancient Roman office of Pontifex Maximus. The Arch of Triumph represents the Unconquered Sun as Constantine's patron deity. A set of gold medallions struck in 313 shows the heads of Constantine and the Sun side by side. A silver medallion struck in 315 represents a blending of typical Roman and Christian symbolism: it shows the emperor with the Christogram on his helmet, the Roman she-wolf on his shield, and a cruciform-headed scepter in his hand. Constantine continued to strike coins in honor of Mars, Jupiter, and even Hercules until 318; and coins in honor of the Sun until 323. Thus Constantine's reign was a link between the Roman Empire that was soon to pass and the Christian Empire that was to come.

The conquest and possession of Rome was for Constantine a tremendous moral and psychological triumph but he had no intention of staying there. Actually the city had been steadily losing her pre-eminence since the time of Hadrian, if not earlier. She might have regained some of her former power had Maxentius won, but when he lost both

throne and life Rome too lost all hope of recovering her ancient imperial power. Before his departure, Constantine abolished the Praetorian Guard, once the maker of emperors, and dismantled their barracks. The abolition of that famous regiment ended the predominance of Illyrians in army and government.

As senior Augustus, Constantine ordered Maximinus Daia to discontinue his persecution of the Christians in the Middle East. Daia obeyed. In 313 Constantine instructed his proconsul in Africa to restore to the churches all confiscated property, to furnish Caecilianus, the newly elected bishop of Carthage, funds for distribution among the orthodox bishops and clergy in Africa, Numidia, and Mauretania, and to exempt them from all municipal burdens or liturgies. That done, Constantine left Rome for Milan to attend a conference with Licinius.

The Edict of Milan: 313

At the Milan conference of 313, which gave rise to the famous Edict of Milan, there not only took place the long expected marriage of Licinius and Constantia, but the two emperors reached a general agreement regarding complete freedom of religion and the recognition of the Christian Church or rather of each separate local church as a legal "person."*

The publication of an actual Edict of Milan is open to some doubt, but the agreements reached included not only the Edict of Toleration of Galerius but all the Western rescripts of Constantine concerning the restitution of property and exemption from public burdens in favor of the churches. Licinius applied this Magna Carta of religion not only to his own domains in Europe but also to the Middle East which was soon to be liberated from the persecutions of Maximinus Daia.

The End of Maximinus Daia: 313

Maximinus Daia, though depicted by Christian writers as a slave to vice, was undoubtedly a man of some principle, military competence, and statesmanship. Since the publication of the Edict of Galerius, he had sporadically persecuted the Christians in his dominions or subjected them to humiliating indignities. Constantine's order to desist was obeyed, but with neither alacrity nor enthusiasm.

Since becoming a Caesar, Daia had met many disappointments. Diocletian had treated him as a barbarian; he received no invitation to attend the conference at Carnuntum; Galerius had ignored or brushed aside his demand for recognition as an Augustus; Licinius had long waited for the opportunity to declare war against him for seizing the provinces Galerius had possessed in Asia. After the defeat and death of his ally Maxentius, Daia stood alone against the combined forces of Constantine and Licinius. Constantine's departure for Gaul to repel a Frankish invasion of the Rhineland presented Daia an excellent opportunity to attack Licinius. He resolved to strike.

In the dead of winter, Daia moved down

* In much the same sense as used to describe big corporations in America, which have secured exemptions and immunities from public regulation by claiming to be legally "persons" within the meaning of the due-process clause of the Fourteenth Amendment of the Constitution.

from the snow-bound highlands of Asia Minor with an army of 70,000 men. He crossed the Bosporus and laid siege to Byzantium, which capitulated in eleven days. Licinius rushed from Milan with a smaller but better trained army. The two forces met near Adrianople. Defeated in the battle, Daia made his escape disguised as a slave. Licinius pursued him into Asia Minor, where he took sick and died. With the East now in his hands, Licinius granted the Christians complete religious freedom and, as he had agreed at the Milan conference, restored to them their confiscated churches and properties.

The Empire Divided: 313–324

Once again the empire was divided, as it had been in the days of Marcus Antonius and Octavianus, and had to undergo a long and bitter struggle between two rival dynasts. Neither Constantine nor Licinius liked or trusted each other. To avert or postpone the inevitable struggle, Constantine strove to create a buffer state between their two domains: he appointed Bassianus to serve as Caesar over Italy, Africa, and Pannonia. The choice of Bassianus, who was married to Constantine's stepsister Anastasia and had a brother named Senecio at the court of Licinius, seemed perfect but proved unacceptable to Licinius. Deeply suspicious of his rival's designs, Licinius persuaded Senecio to incite Bassianus to a revolt against Constantine. The latter discovered the plot in time, had Bassianus executed, and demanded the surrender of Senecio. When Licinius rejected the demand, Constantine attacked in 316. He defeated Licinius with heavy losses in Pannonia but fought to a draw in Thrace. As neither wished the inconclusive struggle to continue, they arranged a truce in which Licinius agreed to abandon his claim to any territory in Europe but Thrace and Constantine agreed to waive his claim to the right as senior Augustus of legislating for Licinius' part of the empire.

The compromise peace was neither destined nor intended to last. After a few years of apparent harmony and cooperation, relations between the two emperors began slowly

The Basilica of Constantine (ca. 310–320 A.D.), Rome. (Courtesy G. E. Kidder Smith, New York)

to deteriorate. Mutual antagonisms and rival ambitions widened the rift. Constantine did not really want peace: his claim of direct descent from Claudius Gothicus established his title to undivided rule over the empire as a matter of manifest destiny. Licinius unintentionally helped to fulfill this destiny by his divergent religious policies. His reversal of the policies agreed upon at Milan presented Constantine a ready-made, though specious, pretext for war.

Unlike Licinius, Constantine had become a devoted Christian ever since the battle of the Milvian Bridge. The benefits which Constantine at this time bestowed upon the Church were to render thanks to God for the aid he believed he had been given in battle. In turn he recognized the Christian Church on earth and made it an effective partner of the state.

Although he hesitated to make Christianity the state religion because of the predominance of pagans in the population, army, and bureaucracy, he authorized measures which went far beyond the Edict of Milan, granting Christians ever more privileges and immunities. An important feature of his religious policy was to permit the Pope of Rome and the orthodox clergy to determine correct doc-

trine and discipline and to enforce their decisions by the authority of the state. In a constitution published in 318, he recognized the legality of decisions handed down by bishops' courts. In a rescript of 321 he not only legalized bequests by Roman citizens to the Christian Church, but assigned to it the property of martyrs dying intestate. In the same year he proclaimed Sunday a public holiday and day of rest for people working in law courts and factories.* Symbolic, too, of Constantine's acceptance of Christianity was his adoption after the battle of the Milvian Bridge of the *labarum,* a standard consisting of a long-handled cross with a *Chi Rho* monogram at the top.

The Donatist Schism

Such being his general policy, Constantine took a serious view of the schism which, shortly after his conversion, was rending the Church in Africa and destroying unity in the state. The schism derived its name from Donatus, the fanatical leader of a radical

* The proclamation could have been interpreted either way: by a Christian as "the Lord's Day," by a pagan as "the holy day of the Sun."

group of dissident and non-conformist clergy-men. This group had protested strongly against the election of Caecilianus as metropolitan bishop of Carthage on the ground that he was too ready to pardon and restore to clerical office those who had betrayed the faith during Diocletian's persecution.* Contrary to the will of the Roman Pope the Donatists had elected as bishop of Carthage Donatus himself who, during the persecutions, had endured six years of incarceration in a foul dungeon and had survived nine stretch-ings on the rack without flinching.

The African dispute rose to a crescendo of fanaticism when Constantine denied the Donatists a share in the benefactions he had recently granted the clergy and congregations of Africa. In 313 they petitioned him to select bishops from Gaul as a panel of im-partial judges to arbitrate the dispute. He chose three Gallic bishops and requested the Pope to preside over their meetings. The Pope converted that tribunal into a regular council by adding fifteen Italian bishops. When the council decided in favor of Caecili-anus, the Donatists appealed to Constantine to convene a larger and more representative council. Fearing the evil effects of the schism

* They had surrendered the Holy Scriptures for burning.

upon church and state, Constantine sum-moned bishops from all over his part of the empire to hold a council at Arles in 314. The Council of Arles confirmed the earlier judgment.

The adverse decision of the Council of Arles was inacceptable to the Donatists. They appealed to the emperor to judge their case himself. At last he agreed. After much delib-eration, he reaffirmed the decisions of the councils and ordered the military suppression of the Donatists and confiscation of their churches. In 321, Constantine realized that persecution only heightened their fanaticism and increased the turmoil in Africa, and ordered the persecutions to cease, scornfully leaving the Donatists "to the judgment of God." His first attempt to restore peace and unity in the Church had failed dismally.

Through his concessions to the Church, Constantine actually won a political victory of historic and enduring importance. He had subordinated the Church to the civil au-thority of the state and had compelled it to acknowledge his right to adjudicate theo-logical disputes, to summon church councils, to exile bishops, confiscate churches, and to assume for himself the towering position of *Isapostolos*, "an equal of the Apostles" and elected servant of God.

Ruins of the Basilica at Volubilis, Morocco.
(Courtesy The French Embassy, Information Division, New York)

The Arian Heresy

Similar religious problems confronted Licinius, but he handled them differently. At first he faithfully observed the decisions reached at Milan but, when the Arian heresy arose in Egypt and threatened to disrupt the peace and unity of his realm, he resorted to systematic persecution of the Christians.

The seeds of the Arian heresy took root, as did those of the Donatist schism, during Diocletian's persecution. Like Donatus, Bishop Melitius of Lycopolis strongly disapproved of the readmission of wavering and renegade Christians by St. Peter, the Bishop of Alexandria. Melitius became the leader of a large group of dissenters, of whom Arius later became the most heretical.

Tall, gaunt, and of melancholy look, Arius was an ascetic of exemplary life and faultless moral character. His speech was soft and gentle, but of unusual persuasive power. His unorthodox views regarding the nature of Christ set the entire East aflame from the Cyrenaican desert to the Balkans and threatened to shatter the structure of the Christian Church and destroy its authority.

The doctrine that Arius set forth in his sermons was that Christ was not "of the same substance" (*homoousios*) with the Father but of "similar substance" (*homoiousios*). Since He was the Son of the Father, He must therefore have been subsequent and posterior. Though begotten before all worlds, there must have been a time when He was not.

That unorthodox doctrine, though not substantially different from occasional utterances of the three great Church Fathers of the early third century—Origen, St. Dionysius of Alexandria, and, in his old age, Tertullian—shocked and angered St. Peter's successor, Bishop Alexander, who held the more orthodox belief that the Son was of the same substance with the Father; and that all the three Persons of the Trinity—the Father, Son, and the Holy Spirit—were one in time, substance, and power, representing the three aspects of the Almighty Power of the Universe.

Arius, excommunicated and expelled from the diocese of Egypt, went first to Palestine to see Eusebius, the eminent church historian and Bishop of Caesarea; next to Nicomedia, the see of another Bishop Eusebius, who wielded strong influence at the court of Licinius. Arius made a powerful impression upon both bishops, as well as upon the empress Constantia herself and upon other persons high up in affairs of church and state throughout Asia Minor.

Through their influence, two synods were convened—one in Bithynia, another in Palestine—which condemned the excommunication of Arius by the Bishop of Alexandria and declared the Arian doctrine to be in accord with Holy Scripture and the teachings of Christ. The synods therefore drew up resolutions demanding that Alexander revoke the excommunication of Arius and reinstate him as a priest in good standing. Alexander not only rejected the demand, but summoned a synod of one hundred Egyptian and Libyan bishops which reaffirmed his excommunication of Arius and excommunicated two pro-Arian bishops in Libya for good measure.

The controversy raged throughout the East. Vitriolic letters and pamphlets went from diocese to diocese, and Arius himself composed popular songs to win the support of the common people.

Then Licinius' patience snapped. Never really sympathetic towards the Christians, he now saw in their controversies a disruptive element all the more dangerous in view of his impending power struggle with Constantine (on whose behalf he perhaps suspected they were saying their prayers). Accordingly, in 320, he banned all church synods and restricted church services to open air assemblages beyond the gates of the cities. In some cities the churches were actually demolished. Women were forbidden to attend religious services with men and Christian adherents were dismissed from his court, the army, and civil service. Some of the more zealous provincial governors ordered bishops, Arian as well as anti-Arian, to be arrested, imprisoned, and even executed.

The Defeat and Death of Licinius: 324

Although the Christian persecutions may have provided Constantine with a moral issue in his war against Licinius, he found a more immediate cause in the Gothic invasion of Moesia and Thrace in 323. To repel the invasion, Constantine had no other recourse but to trespass upon the Thracian domains of Licinius. Licinius made an angry protest; Constantine rejected it. Both sides at once mobilized: Constantine amassed an army of 120,000 infantry, 10,000 cavalry, and 200 ships; Licinius had 150,000 infantry, 15,000 cavalry, and 350 ships.

In the middle of 324 Constantine attacked and defeated the land forces of Licinius at Adrianople. His fleet, under the nominal command of his teen-age son Crispus, destroyed or dispersed the ships Licinius had deployed to guard the Dardanelles. Having thus gained undisputed mastery of the sea, Constantine crossed the Bosporus in force, overtook the remaining forces of Licinius at Chrysopolis, and crushed them. Licinius surrendered, but an appeal by his wife Constantia moved Constantine to spare his life. He was exiled to Salonika. Six months later, Constantine had him put to death for treason. Constantine was now sole emperor over an empire that became united for the first time in almost forty years. The new slogan of empire came to be "one ruler, one world, and one creed."

The Council of Nicaea: 325

The military victory had reunited the empire politically, but did not so quickly and decisively restore the religious unity which Constantine had striven to bring about.

In all his efforts to promote religious unity, Constantine labored under one distinct handicap: he failed to understand the point of the controversy between Arius and the Bishop of Alexandria. Since his chief aim was to achieve harmony within the state, it made little difference to Constantine whether the Father, Son, and Holy Spirit represented one indivisible godhead or were three separate deities. Accordingly, he wrote to Arius and Bishop Alexander urging them to get down to fundamentals and abandon their battle of words over abstruse and unimportant points of theology. His letter naturally failed to end the controversy.

The dispute entered a more acute phase: at a church council meeting at Antioch, late in 324, the orthodox clergy took control and excommunicated Arius, Bishop Eusebius of Caesarea, and two other supporters. They arranged for another synod meeting to be held at Ancyra in Galatia, the see of one of the most violently orthodox bishops in Asia Minor.

Still hoping for an amicable solution of the problem, Constantine canceled the prejudiced Arian-packed council at Ancyra and summoned an ecumenical council at Nicaea, to which bishops from all over the empire might travel at state expense and at which he himself would be present.

On May 20, 325, some 300 bishops gathered at Nicaea in Bithynia. Present, or represented, were the bishops of Rome, Alexandria, Carthage, Antioch, Caesarea, Arles, Cordova, Ancyra, Nicomedia: some renowned for learning; others, for virtue and character; others, for stoic endurance of suffering and persecution. In prayerful suspense, they awaited the Emperor's entrance.

In his brief opening address, Constantine avowed his own devotion to God and exhorted the assembled bishops to work together to restore the unity of the Church. All else, he declared, was secondary and relatively unimportant. He then turned the council over to them, reserving for himself only the right to intervene from time to time to expedite debate and deliberation.

The Council of Nicaea defined the doctrine and completed the organization of the Catholic Church. Its decisions affected not only the problems of 325, but Christianity for all time. It formulated the Nicaean Creed which, except for some minor modifications adopted at the Council of Constantinople in 381, has remained the creed of most of the Christian Church to this day. It reaffirmed the doctrine of the indivisible Trinity, excommunicated Arius, and ordered the burning of his books. Easter was fixed to fall on the first Sunday after the first full moon following the spring equinox, and twenty canons were formulated for the regulation of church discipline and government throughout Christendom. In short, the Council of Nicaea marked the gradual replacement of paganism by Christianity as the established religion of the Roman Empire. It marked too, one might say, the end of the period known as ancient history and the beginning of the Middle Ages.

Constantine's Secular Policies

Not only in his religious dispensations, but in his military, social, and economic measures as well does Constantine appear to have marked the end of the ancient world and the beginning of the Middle Ages (though not all scholars would agree).

In completing the military reorganization of Diocletian, Constantine weakened the frontier garrisons (*limitanei*) by transferring some of the best troops to enlarge and strengthen the mobile field armies (*comitatenses*), to which he added a new elite corps composed of some infantry, but mainly of cavalry, known as the Palace Guards (*palatini*). He greatly accelerated the enrollment of Germans in the imperial armies and their appointment to high military commands and often to the highest offices in the state. He replaced the Praetorian Guard, which he had disbanded in 312, with a personal bodyguard of crack troops, most of whom were German. To this bodyguard he gave the peculiar name of "Palace Schools" (*scholae palatinae*).

Another important military development was the reorganization of the high command and the complete separation of military and civil functions. Constantine replaced the praetorian prefects with two supreme commanders known as Master of the Infantry (*magister peditum*) and Master of the Cavalry (*magister equitum*). Similarly, he abrogated the authority of the provincial governors over the dukes and counts, who commanded the frontier garrisons.

Though stripped of their military functions, the praetorian prefects were still very powerful dignitaries. Each exercised the powers of deputy emperor in one of the four great prefectures of Gaul, Italy, Illyricum, and the East. After 331, all judicial decisions handed down by them were final and were not subject to appeal even to the emperor.

They supervised the administration of the imperial postal system, the erection of public buildings, the collection and storage of taxes, the control of craft and merchant guilds, the regulation of market prices, and the conduct of higher education. Even more important, their executive control over the recruiting and enrollment of soldiers, military installations, and the provision of supplies acted as a powerful brake upon ambitious army commanders.

Another powerful dignitary was Master of the Offices (*magister officiorum*). After 320, he became the supreme head of all departments of the executive and a permanent member of the Supreme Council of State (*sacrum consistorium*). His duties and functions were numerous and varied: as secretary of state, he directed foreign affairs and diplomacy and was grand master of all state ceremonial; he was administrative chief of the imperial postal system and of arms factories and arsenals; he was supreme commander of the emperor's mounted guards, head of the imperial bureau of investigation, and chief of the secret police (*agentes in rebus*), which not only directed espionage throughout the empire, but controlled the movement and deployment of troops.*

Currency Reforms

Constantine's reform of the currency was also of great future importance. He stabilized Diocletian's gold *solidus* at 72 to the pound, and issued a new silver coin, the *miliarense* (denoting a thousandth part of the gold pound). These constructive measures brought about a gradual revival of money economy for the next two centuries, enabled the government to collect most of Diocletian's taxes in cash, and stimulated trade not only within the empire but far beyond the imperial frontiers. Centuries later, it provided the Byzantine Empire with the financial stability and resources to beat back the repeated onslaughts of the Islamic Caliphate.

* Constantine's revived *agentes in rebus* may have served as the model for all secret police and espionage agencies until modern times.

A mosaic found at Carthage, showing a season of the year in each corner and depicting life on the manorial estate of Julius. (Courtesy The Bardo, Tunis)

The Feudal System, Serfdom, and the Guilds

Three of the most characteristic institutions of the medieval period had their origins in the reign of Constantine: feudalism, serfdom, and the guild system.

Though the catastrophes of the third century—civil war, barbarian invasion, plague, inflation—had brought misery, ruin, famine, and death to millions of people, they did not prevent or halt the acquisition of vast estates by powerful senatorial families and imperial bureaucrats. Those who had wealth—whether by inheritance or later acquisition—bought land, still the safest and most fashionable form of investment, often at sacrifice prices, or else leased, or simply appropriated large fertile tracts formerly belonging to private individuals and even to the imperial government.

The tax reforms of Diocletian and Constantine, though excellent in many respects, had not made things easier for the small landowner or the tenant. Unable to bear the excessive tax burden, small individual farmers and even entire peasant villages were often glad to surrender their holdings in return for whatever protection they could obtain against invading barbarians or rapacious tax

officials (these marauders could be defied by powerful barons behind their fortified keep-like villas, as illustrated by numerous mosaics found in North Africa).

Numerous emperors, from Constantine to Justinian I, deplored on moral grounds the *patrocinium* movement (the forerunner of medieval feudalism), whereby the poor and helpless secured the patronage and protection of the rich and powerful by surrendering their lands. Although a few emperors attempted to halt this pernicious trend by legislation, most eventually succumbed to the evil because they needed immediate tax revenues or guarantees thereof regardless of whether they derived from free peasant owners or serfs ground under the heel of a feudal lord.

Adding insult to injustice, Constantine had by 332 bound the tenants (*coloni*) to the land by law and authorized their exploiters to collect from them taxes due to the government, to draft their sons into the army, and to exercise over them the tyrannies of police and judge. He thereby sanctioned the transformation of the *colonus* into the serf, and laid the pattern of medieval feudalism. In another century or two, the new landed aristocracy became the inheritors of a ruined and disintegrating empire. Their state was kingly, their estates—often the size of small kingdoms—were little worlds in themselves, self-sufficient, self-contained. Mosaics found in North Africa, Italy, and Gaul reveal their way of life: their large and beautiful villas and their retinue of slaves, serfs, and armed retainers. A beautiful mosaic found at Carthage shows the master of a villa riding a spirited horse on a hunting expedition while his wife sits majestically out in front of the henhouse, accepting from the *coloni* the fruits and tributes of the seasons—a pair of ducks, a young goat, a sack of fish, and baskets of flowers, fruit, and ripe olives. Similarly, a bas-relief of the famous Igel column near Trier shows six *coloni* bringing their master such gifts as a hare, a string of fish, an eel, a chicken, and a basket of fruit.

City dwellers, especially merchants and craftsmen, fared little better than the *coloni*. Every five years, if not annually, they had to pay regular taxes in money or in kind. In addition, there were special emergency taxes payable in labor or products. Their attempt to escape these oppressive taxes brought down upon them the heavy hand of the government, which tied them to their jobs by forcing them to belong to associations variously known as colleges, corporations, or guilds. In 314, Constantine made membership in the shipowners' corporation a compulsory and hereditary obligation. Later, he compelled other essential workers and craftsmen, such as millers, bakers, butchers, shoemakers, carpenters, and bricklayers, to stay at their jobs for life and train their sons to follow the same trade. The corporations of the late Roman Empire gave origin to the Byzantine and probably some Islamic guilds but whether to those of medieval Italy, France, and Spain is a question still much disputed.

The Founding of Constantinople: 324–330

Next to Constantine's conversion to Christianity, the most memorable and enduring achievement of his reign was the founding of Constantinople, on the site of the ancient Greek city of Byzantium. Constantine's choice of site for an Eastern capital and a second Rome reveals intuitive genius: there Europe meets Asia. The Black Sea flows through the straits leading to the Mediterranean. Through the city passed roads linking the Middle East and Asia Minor with the Balkans and Western Europe—roads with easy access to two of the main battle fronts of the empire, the lower Danube and the Euphrates. Situated on a promontory, protected on two sides by the sea and by strong land fortifications on the third, Constantinople occupied an almost impregnable position, which remained invulnerable for more than a thousand years. It also has an excellent deep water harbor (later called the Golden Horn), the entrance to which could be quickly and easily closed against attack by sea. Ideally located for trade, it captured the commerce of the world passing east and west, north and south—furs from the North and spices from the Orient, fine wines and luxuries of every kind that added zest and elegance to life.

Beyond whatever military, strategic, and commercial possibilities he may have foreseen, Constantine had yet another reason for choosing that site as his second world capital: no place seemed more suited to become the center of the new anti-Rome Christian theology. Predominantly Christian, Constantinople became the first mother of churches—the Holy Peace, the Holy Wisdom (Hagia Sophia), and the Church of the Twelve Apostles.

In all else save religion, Constantine made the new capital (which he named after himself) an exact replica of Rome. The new capital had to have a senate. Though the Roman senate had actually become quite an effete institution during the dominate of Diocletian and Constantine, it was nevertheless one hallowed by an ancient and glorious past. A new senate house was therefore erected in the most exclusive part of the new city, and Constantine summoned to its meetings not only the heads of Rome's most illustrious families, but the grandees of the Eastern provinces.

The new Rome must also have a *Populus Romanus,* privileged and exempt from taxation, and, above all, a *plebs*—one, as in

Rome, recipient of free entertainment, of free bread baked from the best Egyptian wheat, and of free rations of pork, bacon, oil, and even wine.

To beautify the new capital, Constantine ransacked ancient temples and shrines—even Delphi, from which he removed the Tripod and the statue of Apollo. His confiscations (amounting perhaps to 60,000 pounds of gold) made it possible for him to build in Constantinople an enormous imperial palace, a huge hippodrome, a university, public schools and libraries, and magnificent Christian churches.

The Death of Constantine I: 337

Domestic tragedy marred an otherwise glorious reign. In 326, Constantine had his eldest son Crispus, a youth with a brilliant military future, put to death on a trumped-up charge of raping his stepmother, the Empress Fausta (who it appears had fallen in love with him but secretly wanted him removed as a possible rival of her own three sons—Constantine II, Constantius II, and Constans). In the same year the empress herself died, scalded in a hot bath after the emperor's mother, Helen, had revealed the lurid story of her affair with a slave.

In 337, while preparing to lead an army against Persia in retaliation for unprovoked aggression against the Roman protectorate of Armenia, Constantine fell ill. Feeling the relentless approach of death, he summoned the Arian Bishop Eusebius of Nicomedia to administer to him the sacramental rite of baptism. While still arrayed in the white robes of a Christian neophyte, Constantine died. His tomb was the mausoleum connected with the Church of the Twelve Apostles.

XIX

BYZANTIUM: AN

CONSTANTINE I, BY HIS REMOVAL OF THE SEAT OF THE EMPIRE from Rome to Byzantium, carried further a process which Hadrian had begun two hundred years earlier: the shifting of balance from the western to the eastern half of the Empire. The Eastern Mediterranean was bordered by the richest provinces, which had constituted since the time of Alexander the Great a homogeneous cultural region where Greek speech and Greek thought had predominated, and where now a decisive influence was exerted on the development of Christianity. In dividing the Empire between his sons Arcadius and Honorius in 395, Theodosius I (379–395) shattered the *Imperium Romanum* for all time. Western Rome collapsed eighty-one years later under the onslaught of the Germanic peoples. The Eastern Empire, consolidating its position, continued to exist for another thousand years.

EPILOGUE

The Eastern Empire

Constantinople was destined to become the guardian of the Graeco-Roman heritage throughout the Middle Ages. In spite of many vicissitudes and invasions by barbarian peoples, Constantinople successfully accomplished this mission; the idea of Empire, spiritualized as it was by Christian ethics, had received a new and vigorous lease of life. As a State of many nations, the Byzantine Empire (which after the loss of its southern and eastern provinces was increasingly dependent on the Greek element) never surrendered its claim to sovereignty over the entire civilized world. Sustained efforts were made to spread the civilization of Greek Christianity to the barbarian peoples of the North and East and even to the Abyssinians.

The Imperial absolutism (*dominatus*) established by Diocletian was made effective also in New Rome. As the successor of the Latin *Imperatores,* the ruler of the Byzantine Empire regarded himself as the "Father" of all the princes of the world; he became the *Autocrator,* or undisputed master. His acts now had ecclesiastical significance. Ever since Constantine the Great had ordered his body interred in the Church of the Holy Apostles, the first church of Constantinople, as a "thirteenth apostle," the Emperor was the Elect, the Vicar and Envoy of Christ on earth. He ranked with the Apostles (*Isapostolos*), and in him all power was concentrated. He was the central figure of an elaborate ceremonial. Even high officials, ambassadors and foreign princes had to prostrate themselves in his presence (*proskynesis*). His palace, consisting of innumerable buildings, halls, courts, gardens and churches, was considered a holy place. On his election by the army and senate the circus factions and populace acclaimed him with shouts of "Holy! Holy! Holy!" The Emperor was clothed in the finest purple cloth and invested with the scepter and diadem. At important ceremonies his purple shoes were not to tread on anything but porphyry. However lowly the origin of the Elect of Christ, as soon as he inhabited the holy palace as the bearer of the Imperial insignia and officiated at the services in St. Sophia, his person became sacred.

Yet, only about thirty-four in the line of one hundred and seven Eastern Emperors died a natural death, for here, as in Rome, the succession was not fixed by constitutional laws. Some outstanding rulers, by their popularity, secured the succession of their sons or widows to the throne. Such imperial dynasties, however, were swept away by revolts, palace intrigue, open violence, or murder, before getting firmly entrenched. Energetic military leaders, administrators or diplomatists made numerous—and successful—bids for the throne. Many times was the diadem worn by an usurper.

How little the nationality of the ruler mattered is evident from the fact that until the middle of the eleventh century there were Eastern Emperors of Latin, Asiatic, or Graeco-Slav stock. Only the last dynasties, the Comneni and Ducas (1057-1185), the Angeli (1185-1204) and Palaeologi (1261-1453), considered themselves true Greeks.

The Emperor was the central figure, governing his Empire through a hierarchy of highly-trained civil servants. But the Patriarch of Constantinople, the first priest of the Eastern Empire, gradually acquired a position second only to that of the Emperor. Since the time of Constantine, ecclesiastical disputes were referred to the arbitration of the Emperor. Justinian I, a zealous advocate of the unity of the Church, made permanent its subjection to the temporal power. Once Christianity was accepted as the religion of the State, the Church became part of the secular hierarchy and the civil service. The theological principles of the Emperor were compulsory for all loyal Christians of his realm.

The monastic institutions, however, expressed the religious temper of the lower classes and had no little share in shaping those typical features of the Greek Orthodox and Oriental Churches, mysticism and otherworldliness. Small and regional sects like the Copts and Syrian Christians, with principles opposed to the compulsory State religion, sprang up everywhere. Their members probably constituted the greater part of the population, though they were persecuted and suppressed by the orthodox authorities with such ruthlessness that they did not put up any effective resistance. When Leo III (717-741) took measures against iconolatry he provoked a struggle which raged with unparalleled violence for more than a hundred years and shook the very foundations of the Empire. (It finally ended with the victory of the *Iconodules*.)

Dogmatic differences and the dispute for precedence with the Popes of Rome led to an estrangement from the West and culminated, after repeated clashes, in the final Schism of the Church (1054). The Patriarch of Constantinople rose by degrees to supreme power in the Eastern Church, but had to be content with the position of Court Bishop to the Imperial Palace. The Pope, on the other hand, did not recognize any secular power over him or the Christian Church, and became the strongest spiritual force in a Western World that was gradually achieving a new cultural unity.

In spite of its subordination to the temporal power, however, the Eastern Church had tremendous influence throughout the territories of the Byzantine Empire. It is characteristic that the spiritual life of the Byzantine people concentrated more and more on the Church and its controversies. It was mainly around such issues that a public opinion developed which even the Emperor had to take into account. The Greek educational institutions were superseded by Christian schools and universities in which not only the Scriptures and Christian literature were taught, but also Greek poetry and prose, Isocrates and the Attic orators, mathematics, astronomy, natural science, and medicine. Philosophical inquiry was fostered chiefly by a study of Aristotle and Plato. These links with classical Antiquity proved an unfailing inspiration to Byzantine thought. Byzantine scholars and poets, steeped in the vast heritage of ancient Greece, produced works of note in history, philosophy, technical subjects, astronomy, mathematics, natural history, rhetoric, grammar, lexicography, religious and secular poetry. The result was an unique blending of Latin, Greek, and Oriental elements.

Constantinople was ideally located for the centralized administration of the Eastern Empire and for the strategic control of the Levant. Situated at the cross-roads of important land and sea trade routes, it was, by the same token, a key position in the Em-

pire's defence. Theodosius II (408-450) fortified the landward side of the town by a double wall studded with 118 towers and stretching for more than three miles from the Sea of Marmara to the Golden Horn. The Emperor Theophilus (829-842) completed the defence scheme by throwing up earthworks along the northern and southern shores. Built, like Rome, on seven hills, and numbering more than half a million inhabitants, the capital must have presented an imposing spectacle with its barracks, arsenals, and docks, its innumerable churches and convents, its large squares and palaces lavishly adorned with ancient statues and bas-reliefs. Travellers extolled the wonders of this international city in their accounts, and an echo of their boundless admiration still rings in the words of Geoffroy de Villehardouin (about 1150-1213), who writes that the Crusaders could not see their fill of the wonder that was Constantinople.

Justinian I

Byzantium experienced its first period of greatness and expansion under Justinian I (527-565), a native of Illyricum. Of Latin speech and still under the exclusive influence

The Hagia Sophia or Holy Wisdom of Constantinople (ca. 532–537 A.D.). (Courtesy G. E. Kidder Smith, New York)

The interior of the Hagia Sophia of Constantinople. (Courtesy Max Hirmer, Munich)

of the Roman Imperial tradition, Justinian commissioned the compilation of the Corpus Juris, which eventually spread the formative influence of Roman law among all Christians and even Islamic peoples. His conquests in Persia and Spain, his extermination of the Ostrogoths in Italy and the Vandals in Africa secured for the Byzantine Empire its greatest extension, and reinstated it as the first power in the Mediterranean in spite of rapacious Balkan invasions of Slavs and Bulgars. Following the earlier Roman defensive system of the *limes,* Justinian protected his frontiers by a belt of citadels stretching from Tunis through Egypt to the Euphrates, and across the mountains of Armenia to the Black Sea, and from there up along the Danube.

But if Justinian I overtaxed the resources of his Empire in the pursuit of his ambitious aims, he none the less greatly encouraged the arts and sciences. Byzantine art was derived from late Graeco-Roman and Early Christian art. The latter had turned from the plastic and naturalist Graeco-Roman

forms to flat, simple patterns and decorative effects as a means of expression, especially so in the provinces of Egypt, Syria, and Asia Minor where Oriental influence was strong. In Byzantium this yearning for otherworldliness found expression in the union of scintillating materials and sombre, mysterious colors, while the classical forms were subdued in a severe idealism far removed from all sensual connotations. In St. Sophia, the "Temple of Holy Wisdom" in Constantinople, built anew from 532-537, the color scheme of the walls and piers that are richly clad with veined marble and variegated stones combines with the magical blaze of light from the soaring cupola and the vaults decked with glass mosaics on a gold ground to produce an overpowering effect. The plan of St. Sophia is a logical development from ancient architecture and engineering; its gorgeous play of light and color, on the other hand, is Sassanian in principle, recalling the splendor surrounding the Zarathustrian King of Kings. To the Byzantine people, the dome of their chief church was the vault of heaven descended amongst them. Even certain types of mosques imitated this pattern, as did St. Peter's of Rome when rebuilt during the Renaissance.

St. Sophia combines the Roman basilica with a central dome. The Church of the Holy Apostles, on the other hand, as rebuilt in 536-546, was the prototype of domed churches on a Greek cross plan. St. Mark's, in Venice, was copied from it. Byzantine influence extended to Italy, and particularly to Ravenna, which was the seat of the Byzantine Exarchs. In Ravenna, the art of mosaic reached a monumental grandeur in the churches of San Apollinare Nuovo, San Vitale (a polygonal building crowned by a cupola), and in the Baptistry. Large proportions and a ritual solemnity were characteristic of miniature painting, in which the Graeco-Roman elements were modified by the Syrian and Sassanian tendency to abstract the essentials as may be seen from the Codex Cosmas. What the art of sculpture as such lost in interest is outweighed by the virtuosity displayed in ivory carvings, especially in the Imperial and Consular diptychs. Goldsmiths' work and enamelling reached a high degree of perfection and, together with silk weaving, were remarkable for choice of materials and workmanship.

Increased pressure from the North and East seriously menaced the Byzantine Empire during the two centuries after Justinian I. Anarchy spread under Phocas, who had usurped the throne in 602, and the Slavs and Avars succeeded in occupying nearly all that remained of the Balkans and large parts of Greece. Heraclius I, the son of an Exarch of Africa, overthrew the usurper in 610, but could not prevent the Persian conquest of Syria, Palestine and Egypt. Then Heraclius summoned the faithful to a crusade and advanced with his army beyond Ctesiphon, the enemy's capital. It was the first time that a crusade was effective for political aims: the Sassanian state was reduced to impotence. At the same time Heraclius conquered the Slav invaders of the Balkan provinces and strengthened the Empire by dividing it up into military districts (*themata*). Another means of consolidating the Empire was the colonization of the Balkans and Asia Minor with large numbers of veterans turned yeomen. These soldier settlements were founded on a primitive Christian co-operative basis. It may well be that they were the prototypes of the well-known communistic village Zadruga of the early Yugoslavs.

The Onslaught of Islam

The Empire had enjoyed but four years of peace (629-633) when the tidal wave of Islam broke. Omar, the Caliph, conquered the tottering Empire of the Sassanids, the Byzantine provinces of Egypt, Syria, Palestine,

Interior of the Basilica of Saint Paul Outside the Walls (380 A.D.). Etching by G. B. Piranesi 1749. (Courtesy Metropolitan Museum of Art, Jacob S. Rogers Fund)

and Mesopotamia, and, in 637, entered Jerusalem. The Mohammedan armies soon overran also the Byzantine provinces of North Africa, Morocco, Spain and Sicily. In 672, the Arab navy was strong enough to attempt the assault of Constantinople itself, was repelled, but repeated the attack every summer until the year 678. Constantinople was able to avail itself of a novel weapon invented by Callinicus, a Syrian technician. By means of a suction-and-delivery pump he was able to ensure a wider effective range of "Greek Fire," which is mentioned as early as under Anastasius I (491-518) as an explosive mixture which ignited even in water, and consisted of nitre, light rock-oil, and quicklime.

While the new fire-ships were pouring burning destruction on the Arab squadrons, the inhabitants of Constantinople successfully withstood the simultaneous onslaught of the Avars and Slavs by means of smaller, portable pumps. The Arabs suffered heavy losses, were compelled to abandon the siege of Constantinople; and Caliph Mo'awiya concluded a treaty of non-aggression for thirty years. Hardly had the Arab threat been averted when a new enemy approached from the north. In 680 the Bulgars, a Ural-Altaic people, finally crossed the Danube, and subjugated the Slavs in the region between this river and the Balkan range. The warlike Bulgars thrust south for many years. Their Tsars, conscious of their power as builders of great empires, claimed to be recognized as equals by the Byzantine Emperors.

Recovery of the Empire

Throughout the vicissitudes of the eighth century the Byzantine Empire succeeded in preserving its territories intact. The last Arab siege of Constantinople had been staved off early in 718 and the city's plague-ravaged population had been replenished by new immigrants from Asia Minor and Syria. The revival of the Western Empire by Charlemagne in the year 800, and his immediate claim to be the Protector of the Christian population in the Holy Land, dealt a serious blow to Byzantine prestige. Yet the Eastern Empire was to make a full recovery. The reinstatement of Orthodoxy (842) gave rise

to active missionary work coordinated, as always in Byzantium, with political aims. The first Slavonic national Church was founded in Moravia by Cyril and Methodius in 862; the Cyrillic alphabet, developed from the Greek, is still used in Russia and the Balkans. Bulgaria was won over to the Orthodox Church by the conversion of Prince Boris in 864; and most of the Yugoslavs were drawn into the orbit of Byzantine civilization. In southern Italy, which was in sore distress owing to the decline of Frankish rule and the advance of Islam, Byzantium once more gained a foothold. In the first few decades of the tenth century drastic reforms and the eclipse of the Abbasid Caliphate enabled the Eastern Empire to consolidate its position so as to make it once again the leading Christian State.

Byzantine Culture

This renascence of the Empire marks the beginning of a new era of Byzantine culture, which was to last until the conquest of Constantinople by the Crusaders (1204). New forces were at work in every sphere. The sciences were taken up with renewed vigor at the new University of Constantinople, founded by Caesar Bardas in 863 and counting among its staff Leo, the famous mathematician. Classical studies were revived: the legacy of the ancients was collected in comprehensive encyclopedias, while historiography and literature flourished once more. The arts, after their long quiescence due to the Iconoclasts, revived. Painters and illuminators gradually turned away from copying ancient and early Christian models, and became absorbed in creating icons conceived in a spirit of mysticism. The mosaic figures of saints, realistic and yet charged with deep emotional significance and solemn hieratic dignity, were set against a sparkling gold ground in their appointed places in church. Divested of all detail not relating to attributes proper to the particular saint, this Byzantine art of the middle period, from which ancient Russian art derives, is liturgical in the true sense. Church architects made use of the drum, a vertical cylindrical wall, to raise the dome higher. Most churches were given the form of a Greek equilateral cross and had a central dome. The exterior walls were decorated with blind arcades and colored stones. This was the prototype of the Russian churches in stone until the seventeenth century, and came into use throughout the area under the sway of the Orthodox Church. The Byzantine crafts connected with the fine arts experienced a development similar to that of painting. Goldsmith's work, cloisonné enamelling, and silk and gold fabrics with their light effects, all of which served the needs of a Court and Church fond of magnificent display, showed a tendency to ever increasing uniformity and rigidity of design.

Downfall of the Empire

In the second half of the tenth century the spirit of conquest carried the Byzantine Empire forward for the last time. The retaking of Crete in 961 and Cyprus in 965 made Constantinople once more the mistress of the Eastern Mediterranean. In the East, the Empire's frontiers were extended as far as northern Syria and Mesopotamia, and in the North as far as the Lower Danube. Basil II (976-1025), a brilliant strategist, destroyed the powerful West Bulgarian Empire in a war lasting twenty-nine years (990-1018) and added Armenia and Georgia to the reconquered provinces, consolidating at the same time the Byzantine possessions in southern Italy. The conversion of the Russians under Grand Duke Vladimir (988), who was baptized when he married Anna, the Emperor's daughter, was to make Byzantine civilization the decisive influence in the destinies of the Eurasian plains. The achievements of Basil II and his predecessors were rendered futile both by the decline of the Macedonian dynasty, which became extinct in 1056, and by dissensions between the civil administration assisted by the villagers and the generals, who had the support of feudal landowners. Armenia, Mesopotamia, and the Italian possessions were irretrievably lost. After the defeat of the Byzantine army in the battle of Manzikert in 1071 the Turkish Seljuks established themselves in Asia Minor

with the help of defecting Byzantine soldier-colonists. The loss of the eastern provinces which had been the chief source of manpower for the Byzantine army, and the changes of population in Asia Minor, were soon to prove fatal.

The Crusades

It is true that Alexius I (1081-1118) saved the Empire from complete anarchy and decline, inaugurating the rule of his house, the Comneni. This dynasty, while investing Byzantine culture with new glory, reduced the authority of the State by its policy of favoring feudal landowners. The Norman peril forced the conclusion of an alliance with Venice, and later with Genoa and Pisa, obtained only by granting them trading privileges so generous as to weaken considerably the economic position of Constantinople. The Comneni failed to seize on the Crusades, that sudden demonstration of renewed strength of the West, as a means to buttress their Empire and bring about a rapprochement with the Latins. Instead, Alexius I and his successors tried to gain political advantages in Hungary and Asia from the victories won by the Crusaders, sometimes even in collusion with Islam. This resulted in bitter hatred between the Latin West and the Orthodox East, still further widening the gulf that had divided Christendom since the Schism of 1054.

When in 1202 Flemish, French, German, and Italian princes and knights gathered at Venice for the Fourth Crusade, Enrico Dandolo, the aged but active Doge, thought the moment propitious for dealing the Byzantine Empire a decisive blow and seizing the monopoly of the Levant trade. On April 12, 1204 the Crusaders forced their entrance into Constantinople from land and sea. For three days and nights they sacked the town, burning houses and churches and destroying many irreplaceable monuments of antiquity in a senseless fury of vandalism.

On the ruins of the Eastern Empire the Crusaders erected a feudal state of western type under a Latin Emperor, Baldwin I of Flanders. Venice acquired all the coastal areas and islands of strategic importance, thus forging a chain of Venetian ports and maritime bases from the Adriatic to Constantinople.

The conquest of the great city on the Golden Horn made a deep impression on the peoples of the European West. But the Crusaders were not capable of creating a state that would afford effective protection to Eastern and Western Christendom against the Mohammedans. The sack of Constantinople had deprived the Byzantine Empire of its material basis of existence. Yet the Imperial idea survived with continued vigor. In Bithynian Nicaea, the ancient seat of kings, not far from the Sea of Marmara, Theodore Lascaris founded a new Empire in 1206, which came, within a short time, to include all the Greek portions of western Asia Minor and extended to northern Greece. Michael VIII (1259-82), the founder of the last Byzantine dynasty, the Palaeologi, reconquered Constantinople with the help of the Genoese, and overthrew the weak Latin Empire (1261). Under the Palaeologi Constantinople once more became a center of the sciences and the arts, and this last renascence of the Greek spirit saw the birth of a proud national consciousness. The late Byzantine art of the fourteenth and fifteenth centuries had a wider range of subjects, and revealed a novel sense of depth as well as an animation of form and color similar to that which the naturalism of the Trecento at the same period developed in Italy.

The restored Empire was, however, a feudal rather than a constitutional state and no longer a match for the hostile powers which were advancing from all sides. The two maritime rivals, Genoa and Venice, contended tenaciously for their trading monopoly, even engaging in violent naval actions in the very harbor of Constantinople. Under Stephen Dushan (1331-55), Serbia reached as far as the Gulf of Corinth and the Aegean Sea, while the Ottoman Turks, the successors of the Seljuks, occupied the whole of Asia Minor, and in 1354 founded their first settlement on the Gallipoli peninsula as mercenaries and allies of the usurping Emperor, John (Cantacuzene) VI. The Ottomans soon spread to the Balkans. In 1361 they captured Adrianople; in 1389 they defeated the Serbs in the battle on the field of Kossovo; and in 1393 conquered the Bulgars, so that at the end of the fourteenth century all that remained of the Byzantine Empire were the hinterland territories of the capital on the Sea of Marmara, Salonika, and a bridgehead in the Peloponnese. In 1396, Sultan Bayezid I (1389-1403) defeated Sigismund of Hungary and an allied army of German and French knights at Nicopolis.

Thereupon Bayezid demanded from the Emperor the surrender of Constantinople and tried to starve the city into submission. It was at this moment that the Mongol hordes of Tamerlane approached from the East, and dealt the Ottomans an annihilating blow on the plain of Angora in 1402. The Christian States of the Balkans, disunited, failed to take advantage of the situation. As early as 1422, the Turks had recovered and resumed their attack on Constantinople, but were repulsed by the desperate defenders. In the course of a few decades, however, the fate of the Balkan countries was sealed. Salonika fell in 1430; almost the whole of Serbia was annexed in 1438, with the Ottomans advancing as far as the gates of Belgrade and laying waste Transylvania. It was too late then, for the Latin West, to stem the Mohammedan tide which was surging into Europe, too late for the Eastern Empire to obtain sufficient reinforcements by a union of the Churches in 1439.

Triumph of Islam

After the defeats of the Hungarian commander John Hunyadi and the Crusaders near Varna (1444) and on the field of Kossovo (1448), all hope was lost. The youthful and active Sultan Mohammed II (1451-81) dealt the final blow to the spiritual center of the Eastern Empire. In March 1453, he advanced on Constantinople with an army of 100,000 men. Constantine XI prepared to defend the town with a small force of 7,000 men, 5,000 of whom were said to be Greeks and 2,000 Latins. On April 11, the Turkish batteries, which included an immense piece weighing nearly ten tons, took up their positions. On the following day the Sultan's fleet appeared off Galata. In spite of their small number the defenders again and again repelled the fanatical besiegers, and succeeded in protecting the walls against the shattering impact of the cannon balls by means of a coating of soft mortar and crushed tiles. On the night of the May 29 the Ottomans launched the main assault. The Greeks succeeded in holding up the first attack on the Romanus Gate, where the Emperor himself had taken position. Mohammed then sent in his best troops, the Janissaries, supported by heavy artillery fire. Despite the heroic resistance of the Greeks, the Turks secured a footing on the walls and by entering through a narrow gateway, the *Kerkoporta*, took the Emperor and his troops in the rear. In the meantime the artillery had made a huge breach in the wall near the Romanus Gate, and the besiegers poured into the city. The last Byzantine Emperor died a hero's death fighting side by side with his soldiers.

After a brief struggle, the victors sacked the town, and destroyed the sacred objects. The inhabitants, who had taken refuge in St. Sophia, were dragged into captivity. At midday, Mohammed rode through the Gate of Adrianople to St. Sophia where a mullah proclaimed the Mohammedan creed from the pulpit. The Sultan himself jumped onto the altar and said his prayers there. Thus the Cathedral of Justinian I passed into the hands of Islam. It only remained to proclaim the transfer of the Imperial power from the Byzantine Empire to the Sultanate by a symbolic act. The decapitated head of the last Emperor of New Rome was exhibited on the Augusteum until nightfall.

The last rallying points of Greek independence disappeared with the conquest of Athens in 1458, the Peloponnese in 1460, the Empire of Trebizond in 1462, Naxos in 1566, and Cyprus in 1570. In conformity with Islamic practice, Mohammed II did not attempt the complete enslavement or extermination of his Christian subjects. With wise moderation he conceded wide powers of ecclesiastical and civil jurisdiction to the Patriarch of Constantinople, enabling the Orthodox Greeks to continue practicing their religion and even to survive as a nation. Politically, however, the Eastern Church now gravitated to independent Moscow, the "Third Rome." Of the many Greek scholars who emigrated to Italy and Spain where they spread their knowledge of Greek civilization and played a considerable part in the renascence of Western Europe, the best known are Theodore Gaza, grammarian and philosopher, Constantine Lascaris, the grammarian, and John Argyropulus, the philosopher. Nor should Domenico Theotocopuli (El Greco), the great Cretan painter, be forgotten.

It would be difficult to overrate the significance of Late Roman civilization in world history. It is the key to the understanding of the spiritual and political history both of Russia and the Mohammedan world. The late Roman and Byzantine administrative system is the source of the medieval and modern bureaucracies and methods of taxation. European Court etiquette and Court dress as well as medieval chivalry and military organization were largely inspired by Byzantine example. The theology of the Greek East was an enormous achievement; and its active mysticism has never ceased to exert a stimulating influence on the more passive attitude of its western counterpart. Consequently, much of what the peoples of the Balkan countries, Russia, and the Mohammedan world have again adopted from the West in recent centuries must be looked upon as their own heritage, an original achievement of Near Eastern Roman civilization, albeit modified by Western humanism from Charlemagne to modern existentialism.

BIBLIOGRAPHY

REFERENCE AND GENERAL WORKS

Aymard, A. and J. Auboyer, *Rome et son Empire (Histoire générale des civilisations*, Vol. II., 3rd ed.) Paris, 1959.

Bailey, C., *The Legacy of Rome*. London, 1923.

*Barrow, R. H., *The Romans*. Harmondsworth, 1949.

Boak, A. E. R., *A History of Rome to 565 A.D.*, 4th ed. New York: The Macmillan Co., 1954.

Cambridge Ancient History, Vols. VII–XII. Cambridge, 1926–1939.

Cary, M., *A History of Rome Down to the Reign of Constantine*, 2nd ed. London, 1954.

*De Burgh, W. G., *The Legacy of the Ancient World*. Harmondsworth, 1953.

Dudley, D. R., *The Civilization of Rome*. New York: New American Library of World Literature, Inc., 1960.

Durant, Will, *Caesar and Christ*. New York: Simon and Schuster, Inc., 1944.

Geer, R. M., *Classical Civilization: Rome*, 2nd ed. Englewood Cliffs, N. J.: Prentice-Hall, Inc., 1950.

Glotz, G., ed., *Histoire romaine*. 4 vols. Paris, 1926–1947.

*Grant, M., *Ancient History*. London, 1952.

Hadas, M., *A History of Rome*. New York: Doubleday & Co., Inc., 1956.

Laistner, M. L. W., *The Greater Roman Historians*. Berkeley: University of California Press, 1947.

Lewis, N. and M. Reinhold, *Roman Civilization*. 2 vols. New York: Columbia University Press, 1955.

McDermott, W. C. and W. E. Caldwell, *Readings in the History of the Ancient World*. New York: Holt, Rinehart & Winston, Inc., 1951.

Maschkin, N. A., *Römische Geschichte*. Berlin, 1953.

Niese, B. and E. Hohl, *Grundriss der römischen Geschichte. (Handbuch der Altertumswissenschaft*, 5th ed.) Munich, 1923.

Oxford Classical Dictionary, ed. M. Cary and Others. New York: Oxford University Press, 1949.

Pareti, L., *Storia di Roma e del mondo romano*. 4 vols. Turin, 1952–1955.

Pauly-Wissowa-Kroll, *Real-Encyclopädie der Altertumswissenschaft*. Stuttgart, 1894–1962.

Piganiol, A., *Histoire de Rome*. Paris, 1946.

*Robinson, C. A., *Selections from Greek and Roman Historians*. New York: Holt, Rinehart & Winston, Inc., 1957.

*Scullard, H. H., *From the Gracchi to Nero: A History of Rome from 133 B.C. to A.D. 68*. London, 1959.

Swain, J. W., *The Ancient World*, Vol. II. New York: Harper & Brothers, 1950.

Van Sickle, C. E. A., *A Political and Cultural History of the Ancient World*, Vol. II. Boston and New York: Houghton Mifflin Company, 1948.

GEOGRAPHY

Ashby, T., *The Roman Campagna in Classical Times*. London, 1927.

Bagnani, G., *The Roman Campagna and its Treasures*. London, 1929.

Cary, M., *The Geographic Background of Greek and Roman History*. Oxford, 1949.

"Italy," Topography, *Encyclopaedia Britannica*, 14th ed., art.

Ludwig, Emil, *The Mediterranean: Saga of a Sea*. New York: McGraw-Hill Book Co., Inc., 1942.

Newbigin, M. I., *The Mediterranean Lands*. London, 1924.

Newbigin, M. I., *Southern Europe*. New York: E. P. Dutton & Co., Inc., 1950.

Philippson, A., *Das Mittelmeergebiet*, 4th ed. Leipzig, 1931.

Rose, J. H., *The Mediterranean in the Ancient World*. London, 1932.

Semple, E. C., *The Geography of the Mediterranean Region*. New York: Holt, Rinehart & Winston, Inc., 1931.

Siegfried, A., *The Mediterranean*. New York: Duell, Sloan & Pearce, Inc., 1948.

Thompson, J. O., *History of Ancient Geography*. Cambridge, 1948.

PALEOLITHIC MAN AND ART

Boule, M. and H. V. Vallois, *Fossil Men*. London, 1957.

This bibliography provides a list (in no sense complete) of modern and accessible publications in English and other languages. They do not necessarily support (they often controvert) the views expressed in the text. Books with an asterisk prefixed are obtainable at moderate cost, the majority being paperbacks.

Braidwood, R. J., *Prehistoric Men*. Chicago: Chicago Natural History Museum, 1948.

Breuil, H. and H. Obermaier, *The Cave of Altamira*. Madrid, 1935.

Breuil, H., *Four Hundred Centuries of Cave Art*. Montignac, Dordogne, 1952.

Brodrick, A. H., *Early Man*. London and New York, 1948.

Brodrick, A. H., *Prehistoric Painting*. London, 1948.

Brodrick, A. H., *Lascaux: A Commentary*. London, 1949.

Burkitt, M. C., *The Old Stone Age*, 3rd ed. New York: New York University Press, 1955.

Burney, C. B. M., "Radiocarbon Dating Results from the Old World," *Antiquity*, 26 (1952), 35 f.

Clark, J. G. D., *From Savagery to Civilization*. London, 1946.

Flint, R. F., *Glacial Geology and the Pleistocene Epoch*. London and New York, 1947.

Frobenius, L. and D. C. Fox, *Prehistoric Rock Pictures in Europe and Africa*. New York: Museum of Modern Art, 1937.

Hawkes, C. F. C., *The Prehistoric Foundations of Europe to the Mycenaean Age*. London, 1940.

*Hawkes, C. F. C. and J. Hawkes, *Prehistoric Britain*. Harmondsworth, 1949.

Herskovits, M., *Man and his Work*, 2nd ed. New York: Alfred A. Knopf, Inc., 1955.

Kroeber, A. L., *Anthropology*, 2nd ed. New York: Harcourt, Brace & World, Inc., 1948.

*Laming, A., *Lascaux Paintings and Engravings*. Harmondsworth, 1959.

Libby, W. F., *Radiocarbon Dating*, 2nd ed. Chicago: University of Chicago Press, 1955.

Luquet, G. H., *The Art and Religion of Fossil Man*. New Haven: Yale University Press, 1930.

Maringer, J. and H. G. Bandi, *Art in the Ice Age*. New York: Frederick A. Praeger, Inc., 1952.

McCown, T. D. and Sir Arthur Keith, *The Stone Age of Mount Carmel*. 2 vols. Toronto: Oxford University Press, 1937–1939.

Osborn, H. F., *Men of the Old Stone Age*. New York: Charles Scribner's Sons, 1924.

*Raphael, M., *Prehistoric Cave Paintings*. New York: Pantheon Books, Inc., 1946.

Sergi, S., "The Paleanthropi in Italy: the Fossil Men of Saccopastore and Circeo," *Man*, 48 (1948), 75 f., 91 f.

Vallois, H. V., "Fontéchavade Fossil Man," *American Journal of Physical Anthropology*, 7 (1949), 339 f.

Vaufrey, R., *Le paléolithique italien*. Paris, 1928.

Windels, F. and A. Laming, *The Lascaux Cave Paintings*. London, 1949.

Wright, W. B., *The Quaternary Ice Age*. London, 1937.

Zeuner, F. E., *Dating the Past*, 2nd ed. London, 1950.

Zeuner, F. E., *The Pleistocene Period, its Climate, Chronology, and Faunal Succession*, 2nd ed. London, 1959.

NEOLITHIC, BRONZE, AND IRON AGES IN EUROPE AND THE MIDDLE EAST

Aaberg, N., *Bronzezeit und früheisenzeitliche Chronologie*. Stockholm, 1930.

Akerström, A., *Der geometrische Stil in Italien*, *Acta Instituti Romani Regni Sueciae*, 9. Lund, 1943.

Bradford, J., "Buried Landscapes in Southern Italy," *Antiquity*, 20 (1946), 191 f., 23 (1949), 65 f., 24 (1950), 84 f.

Bradford, J., *Ancient Landscapes in Europe and Asia*. London, 1957.

Braidwood, R. J., *A Synoptic Description of the Earliest Village-Culture: Human Origins*. Chicago: University of Chicago Press, 1939.

Braidwood, R. J., *The Near East and the Foundations of Civilization*. Eugene: University of Oregon Press, 1952.

Childe, V. G., *The Bronze Age*. London: Cambridge University Press, 2nd ed. 1957.

Childe, V. G., *The Danube in Prehistory*. New York: Oxford University Press, 1929.

Childe, V. G., *The Dawn of European Civilization*, 6th ed. London, 1952.

Childe, V. G., *New Light on the Most Ancient Near East*, 4th ed. London, 1952.

Childe, V. G., *Prehistoric Migrations in Europe*. Oslo and Cambridge, 1951.

*Childe, V. G., *What Happened in History*. Harmondsworth, 1954.

Clark, J. G. D., *Prehistoric Europe: the Economic Basis*. New York: Clarke & Way, Inc., 1952.

Dillon, M., "Italic and Celtic," *American Journal of Philology*, 65 (1941), 124 f.

Dixon, P., *The Iberians of Spain and their Relations with the Aegean World*. New York: Oxford University Press, 1940.

Duhn, F. von, *Italische Gräberkunde*. 2 vols. Heidelberg, 1924, 1929.

Grbic, M., "Preclassical Pottery in the Central Balkans," *American Journal of Archaeology*, 61 (1957), 137 f.

Hansen, H. D., *Early Civilization in Thessaly*. Johns Hopkins University Studies in Archaeology, 15. Baltimore, 1933.

Hencken, H., "Indo-European Languages and Archaeology," *American Anthropologist*, 57 (1955).

Heurtley, W., *Prehistoric Macedonia*. London: Cambridge University Press, 1939.

Hubert, H., *The Greatness and Decline of the Celts*. London, 1934.

Hubert, H., *The Rise of the Celts*. London, 1934.

Jacobsthal, P., *Early Celtic Art*. Toronto: Oxford University Press, 1944.

Kashnitz-Weinberg, G. von, *Italien, Sardinien und Malta*. (*Handbuch der Archäologie, 2.1, Handbuch der Altertumswissenschaft*.) Munich, 1950.

Laviosa-Zambotti, P., *Le più antiche culture agricole Europeë*. Milan, 1943.

Laviosa-Zambotti, P., *Les origines et la diffusion de la civilisation*. Paris, 1949.

Laviosa-Zambotti, P., *Il Mediterraneo, l'Europa, l'Italia durante la preistoria*. Torino, 1954.

Mehrhart, G. von, "Donauländische Beziehungen der früheisenzeitlichen Kulturen Mittelitaliens," *Bonner Jahrbücher*, 147 (1942), 1 ff.

Messerschmidt, F., *Bronzezeit und frühe Eisenzeit in Italien*. Berlin and Leipzig, 1935.

Montelius, O., *La civilisation primitive en Italie*. Stockholm, 1904.

Petroni, G., *La preistoria*. Milan, 1937.

Piggott, S., *British Prehistory*. London, 1949.

Powell, J. G. E., *The Celts*. London, 1958.

Quagliati, Q., *L'Apuglia preistorica*. Tranni Vecchi, 1936.

Randall-MacIver, D., *Villanovans and Early Etruscans*. New York: Oxford University Press, 1924.

Randall-MacIver, D., *The Early Iron Age in Italy*. New York: Oxford University Press. 1927.

Randall-MacIver, D., *Italy before the Romans*. New York: Oxford University Press, 1928.

Rellini, U., *Le origini della civiltà italica*. Rome, 1929.

Rellini, U., *La più antica ceramica dipinta in Italia*. Rome, 1934.

Rostovtzeff, M. I., *Animal Style in South Russia and China*. Princeton: Princeton University Press, 1929.

Saeflund, G., *Le terremare delle provincie di Modena, Reggio Emilia, Parma, Piacenza*. (*Acta Instituti Romani Regni Sueciae, 7.*) Lund, 1939.

Sauer, C. O., *Agricultural Origins and Dispersals*. New York: American Geographical Society, 1952.

Spekke, A., *The Ancient Amber Routes and the Geographical Discovery of the Eastern Baltic*. Stockholm, 1957.

Stevenson, R. B. K., "The Neolithic Cultures of South-East Italy," *Proceedings of the Prehistoric Society*, 17 (1947), 85 ff.

Suess, E., *Le incisioni rupestre in Val Camonica*. Rome, 1939.

Thieme, P., "The Indo-European Language," *Scientific American*, 199, 4 (1958).

Vouga, P., *Le néolithique lacustre ancien*. Neuchâtel: Université de Neuchâtel, 1934.

Whatmough, J., *The Foundations of Roman Italy*. London, 1937.

THE ETRUSCANS

Alexander, Christine, *Jewelry, the Art of the Goldsmith in Classical Times*. New York: Quaritch, 1928.

Andren, A., *Architectural Terracottas from Etrusco-Italic Temples*. Lund and Leipzig, 1939/40.

Beazley, Sir J. D., *Etruscan Vase-Painting*. Toronto, 1947.

Ducati, P., *Le problème étrusque*. Paris, 1938.

Fell, R. A., *Etruria and Rome*. London, 1924.

Grenier, A., *Les religions étrusque et romaine*. Paris, 1948.

Hanfmann, G. M. A., *The Etruscans and Their Art*. Rhode Island Museum Press, 1940.

Hopkins, Clark, "Oriental Evidence for Early Etruscan Chronology," *Berytus*, 11 (1955), 75–84.

Johnstone, M. A., *Etruria Past and Present*. London, 1930.

Pallottino, M., *Art of the Etruscans*. New York: Vanguard Press, 1955.

*Pallottino, M., *The Etruscans*. Harmondsworth, 1955.

Pallottino, M., *Etruscan Painting*. Geneva, 1953.

Randall-MacIver, D., *The Etruscans*. New York: Oxford University Press, 1927.

Renard, M., *Initiation à l'étruscologie*. Brussels, 1943.

Riis, P. J., *Tyrrhenika: an Archaeological Study of the Etruscan Sculpture in the Archaic and Classical Periods*. Copenhagen: Levin, 1941.

Riis, P. J., *An Introduction to Etruscan Art*. Copenhagen: Levin, 1953.

Seltman, C. T., *Greek Coins*, 2nd ed. London, 1955.

Shaw, C., *Etruscan Perugia*. Baltimore: The Johns Hopkins Press, 1939.

Ullman, B. L., "Early Greek Alphabets with Especial Reference to Phrygian," *Classical Studies Presented to Edward Capps*. Princeton: Princeton University Press, 1936, 333 f.

EARLY ROMAN SOCIETY

Adams, L., *A Study in the Commerce of Latium from the Early Iron Age through the Sixth Century B.C.* Thesis. Bryn Mawr College, 1921.

Bloch, R., *Les origines de Rome*, 2nd ed. Paris, 1959.

Ciaceri, E., *Le origini di Roma*. Milan-Genoa-Rome-Naples, 1937.

Devoto, G., *Gli antichi Italici*. Florence, 1951.

Ducati, P., *L'Italia antica*. Milan, 1937.

Ducati, P., *Come nacque Roma.* Rome, 1939.

Dumézil, G., *Naissance de Rome.* Paris, 1944.

Dumézil, G., *L'héritage indoeuropéen à Rome.* Paris, 1949.

Gagé, J., *Huit recherches sur les origines italiques et romaines.* Paris, 1950.

Gilmore, H. W., "Cultural Diffusion Via Salt," *American Anthropologist,* 57 (1955).

Gjerstad, E., *Early Rome.* 3 vols. Lund, 1953, 1956, 1960.

Homo, L. P., *Primitive Italy and the Beginnings of Roman Imperialism.* New York: Alfred A. Knopf, Inc., 1929.

Homo, L. P., *Roman Political Institutions from City to State.* New York: Alfred A. Knopf, Inc., 1929.

Last, H., "The Servian Reforms," *Journal of Roman Studies,* 35 (1945), 30 ff.

Mattingly, H., "Historical Revision: Servius Tullius and the Comitia Centuriata," *Proceedings of the Cambridge Philological Society,* 179 (1948), 15 ff.

Meyer, Ernst, *Die Indogermanenfrage.* Marburg, 1948.

Müller-Karpe, H., *Vom Anfang Roms.* *(Deutsches Archäologisches Institut, Römische Abteilung, Supplement 5.)* 1959.

Nichols, J. J., "The Reform of the Comitia Centuriata," *American Journal of Philology,* 77 (1956), 225 ff.

Oro, A. dell', *La formazione dello stato patrizio-plebe.* Milan-Varese, 1950.

Paribeni, R., *All' alba della storia d'Italia e di Roma.* Milan, 1951.

Paribeni, R., *La famiglia romana.* Rome, 1948.

Robathan, D. M., *The Monuments of Ancient Rome.* Rome, 1950.

Rose, H. J., *Primitive Culture in Italy.* London and New York, 1926.

Ryberg, I. S., *Early Roman Traditions in the Light of Archaeology. (Memoirs of the American Academy in Rome),* 7 (1929).

Ryberg, I. S., *An Archaeological Record of Rome from the Seventh to the Second Century B.C.* Philadelphia: University of Pennsylvania Press, 1940.

Stroux, J., "Die Foruminschrift beim Lapis Niger," *Philologus,* 86 (1931), 460 ff.

Tilly, B., *Vergil's Latium.* London, 1947.

Westrup, C. W., *Family Property and Patria Potestas.* Copenhagen: Levin, 1936.

Westrup, C. W., *Introduction to Early Roman Law.* 5 vols. Copenhagen: Levin, 1934–1954.

THE ROMAN REPUBLIC

Accame, S., *Il dominio romano in Grecia della guerra acaica ad Augusto.* Rome, 1946.

Adcock, Sir F. E., "Consular Tribunes and their Successors," *Journal of Roman Studies,* 47 (1957), 9 ff.

Afzelius, A., "Die römische Eroberung Italiens," *Acta Jutlandica,* 14.3 (1942).

Altheim, F., *Lex Sacrata: Die Anfänge der plebeischen Organisation.* Amsterdam, 1940.

Altheim, F., *Römische Geschichte.* 2 vols., 4th ed. Frankfurt, 1951/53.

Altheim, F., *Römische Geschichte.* 3 vols., 2nd ed. Berlin, 1956.

Badian, E., *Foreign Clientelae 264–70 B.C.* New York: Oxford University Press, 1958.

Baker, G. P., *Hannibal.* New York: Dodd, Mead & Co., 1936.

Beloch, K. J., *Römische Geschichte bis zum Beginn der punischen Kriege.* Berlin and Leipzig, 1926.

Bikerman, E., *The Maccabees,* trans. by M. Hadas. New York: Schocken Books, Inc., 1947.

Bleicken, J., *Das Volkstribunat der klassischen Republik.* Munich, 1955.

Boddington, A., "The Original Nature of the Consular Tribunate," *Historia,* 8 (1959), 356 ff.

Botsford, G. W., *Roman Assemblies from Their Origin to the End of the Republic.* New York, 1909.

Broughton, T. R. S., *Magistrates of the Roman Republic.* 2 vols. New York: American Philological Association, 1951/52.

Brown, R., "A Study of the Scipionic Circle," *Iowa Studies in Classical Philology,* 1 (1934), 13–90.

Buchan, J., *Caesar.* London, 1932.

Burck, E., *Die Erzählungskunst des T. Livius.* Berlin, 1934.

Carcopino, J., *Autour des Gracques.* Paris, 1928.

Carcopino, J., *Sylla ou la monarchie manquée.* Paris, 1931.

Carcopino, J., *Cicero and the Secrets of his Correspondence.* 2 vols. London, 1951.

Cary, M., *A History of the Greek World from 323 to 146 B.C.* 2nd Ed. London, 1951.

Coleman-Norton, P. R., *The Twelve Tables,* 3rd ed. Princeton: Princeton University Press, 1950.

Coleman-Norton, P. R., "Cicero's Contribution to the Text of the Twelve Tables," *Classical Journal,* 46 (1950), 51 f., 127 f.

Collins, J. H., "Caesar and the Corruption of Power," *Historia,* 4 (1955), 445 ff.

Cornelius, F., *Untersuchungen zur frühen römischen Geschichte.* Munich, 1940.

Corradi, G., *Le grandi conquiste mediterranee.* Bologna, 1945.

*Cowell, F. R., *Cicero and the Roman Republic.* Harmondsworth, 1956.

Cross, G. N., *Epirus.* London, 1932.

D'Arms, E. F., "The Classes of the Servian Constitution," *American Journal of Philology*, 64 (1943), 424 ff.

De Beer, Sir Gavin, *Alps and Elephants*. London, 1955.

Debevoise, N., *A Political History of Parthia*. Chicago: University of Chicago Press, 1938.

De Francisci, P., *Arcana Imperii*. 3 vols. Milan, 1948.

Degrassi, A., *Fasti Consulares et Triumphales* (*Inscriptiones Italiae*, XIII, 1). Rome, 1947.

Degrassi, A., *Fasti Capitolini*. Turin, 1955.

Düll, R., *Das Zwölftafelgesetz*. Munich, 1953.

Frank, T., "Roman Historiography before Caesar," *American Historical Review*, 32 (1926/27), 232 ff.

Frisch, H., *Cicero's Fight for the Republic*. Copenhagen: Levin, 1946.

Gelzer, M., *Die Nobilität der römischen Republik*. Berlin and Leipzig, 1912.

Gelzer, M., *Pompeius*, 2nd ed. Munich, 1959.

Gwosdz, A., *Der Begriff des römischen princeps*. Diss., Breslau, 1933.

Hadas, M., *Sextus Pompey*. New York: Columbia University Press, 1930.

Hanell, K., *Das altrömische eponyme Amt*. Lund, 1946.

Hansen, Esther V., *The Attalids of Pergamum*. Ithaca: Cornell University Press, 1947.

Hard, H. P., *The Topography of Punic Carthage*. Diss., Columbia University, 1934.

Hardy, E. G., *Roman Laws and Charters*. New York: Oxford University Press, 1912.

Haskell, H. J., *This Was Cicero*. New York: Alfred A. Knopf, Inc., 1942.

Haywood, R. M., *Studies on Scipio Africanus*. Baltimore: The Johns Hopkins Press, 1933.

Hill, H., *The Roman Middle Class in the Republican Period*. New York: The Macmillan Co., 1952.

Holleaux, M., *Rome, la Grèce, et les monarchies hellénistiques au IIIe siècle av. J.-C.* Paris, 1921.

Holmes, T. R., *Caesar's Conquest of Gaul*. New York: Oxford University Press, 1911.

Holmes, T. R., *The Roman Republic and the Founder of the Roman Empire*. 3 vols. New York: Oxford University Press, 1926.

Jacobs, K., *Gaius Flaminius*. Diss., Hoorn, 1937.

Kienast D., *Cato der Zensor*. Heidelberg, 1954.

Klotz, A., *Livius und seine Vorgänger*. Leipzig and Berlin, 1941.

Laidlaw, W. A., *A History of Delos*. New York: Oxford University Press, 1931.

Larsen, I. A. O., "The Origin and Significance of the Counting of Votes," *Classical Philology*, 44 (1949), 177 ff.

Leifer, F., *Studien zum antiken Ämterwesen*. (*Klio*, Supplement 23.) Leipzig, 1931.

Lepore, E., *Il Princeps ciceroniano*. Naples, 1954.

Lübtow, U. von, *Das Römische Volk*. Frankfurt a. M., 1955.

Meltzer, O. and U. Kahrstedt, *Geschichte der Karthager*. 3 vols. Berlin, 1877–1913.

Meyer, Eduard, *Caesars Monarchie und das Principat des Pompejus*. Stuttgart-Berlin, 1922.

Meyer, Ernst, *Römischer Staat und Staatsgedanke*. Zürich, 1948.

Münzer, F., *Römische Adelsparteien und Adelsfamilien*. Stuttgart, 1920.

Niccolini, G., *Fasti dei tribuni della plebe*. Milan, 1932.

Niccolini, G., *Il tribunato della plebe*. Milan, 1932.

Nocera, G., *Il potere dei comizi e i suoi limiti*. Milan, 1940.

Norden, E., *Aus altrömischen Priesterbüchern*. Lund, 1939.

Oost, St. J., *Roman Policy in Epirus and Acarnania in the Age of the Roman Conquest of Greece*. Arnold Foundation Studies 4. Dallas: Southern Methodist University Press, 1954.

Rosenberg, A., *Einleitung und Quellenkunde zur römischen Geschichte*. Berlin, 1921.

Rudolph, H., *Stadt und Staat im römischen Italien*. Leipzig, 1935.

Scullard, H. H., *A History of the Roman World, 753–146 B.C.* 3rd ed. London, 1961.

Scullard, H. H., *Roman Politics, 220–150 B.C.* Toronto, 1951.

Scullard, H. H., *Scipio Africanus in the Second Punic War*. London, 1930.

Sherwin-White, A. N., *The Roman Citizenship*. Toronto, 1939.

Siber, H., *Die Plebejischen Magistraturen bis zur Lex Hortensia*. Leipzig, 1938.

Skard, E., *Sallust und seine Vorgänger*. Oslo, 1956.

Smith, R. E., *The Failure of the Roman Republic*. New York: Cambridge University Press, 1955.

Staveley, E. St., "The Reform of the Comitia Centuriata," *American Journal of Philology*, 74 (1953), 1 ff.

Staveley, E. St., "Provocatio during the Fifth and Fourth Centuries B.C.," *Historia*, 3 (1954/55), 412 ff.

Staveley, E. St., "The Constitution of the Roman Republic," *Historia*, 5 (1956), 74–119.

Staveley, E. St., "The Political Aims of Appius Claudius Caecus," *Historia*, 8 (1959), 410 ff.

Strasburger, F., *Caesars Eintritt in die Geschichte*. Munich, 1938.

Tarn, W. W., *Hellenistic Civilization*, 3rd ed. London, 1952.

Taylor, L. R., *Party Politics in the Age of Caesar*. Berkeley: University of California Press, 1949.

Taylor, L. R. and T. R. S. Broughton, "The Order of the Consuls' Names in the Early Lists," *Memoirs of the American Academy in Rome*, 19 (1949), 1 ff.

Taylor, L. R., "Annals of the Roman Consulship on the Arch of Augustus," *Proceedings of the American Philosophical Society*, 94 (1950), 511 ff.

Torr, C., *Hannibal Crosses the Alps*. London, 1935.

Van Ooteghem, J., *Pompée le Grand, bâtisseur d'Empire*. Brussels and Paris, 1954.

Van Ooteghem, J., *Lucius Licinius Lucullus*. (*Mémoires de l'Académie Royale de Belgique*, 43.4.) 1959.

Vogt, J., *Novus Homo*. Stuttgart, 1926.

Von Fritz, K., "The Reorganization of the Roman Government in 366 B.C. and the So-called Licinio-Sextian Laws," *Historia*, 1 (1950), 3–44.

Von Fritz, K., *The Theory of the Mixed Constitution in Antiquity*. New York, 1954.

Walbank, F. W., *Philip V of Macedon*. London, 1940.

Walbank, F. W., *A Historical Commentary on Polybius I*. New York: Oxford University Press, 1957.

Wilkin, R. N., *Eternal Lawyer*. New York: The Macmillan Co., 1947.

Wirszubski, C., *Libertas as a Political Idea at Rome during the Late Republic and Early Principate*. New York: Cambridge University Press, 1950.

Yeo, C. A., "The Founding and Function of Roman Colonies," *Classical World*, 52 (1959), 104 ff., 129 ff.

IMPERIAL ROME

Albertini, E., *L'empire romain*, 3rd ed. Paris, 1938.

Alföldi, A., *The Conversion of Constantine and Pagan Rome*. New York: Oxford University Press, 1948.

Altheim, F., *Niedergang der Alten Welt*. 2 vols. Frankfurt a. M., 1952.

Anderson, H. A., *Cassius Dio und die Begründung des Principates*. Berlin, 1938.

Balsdon, P. V. D., *The Emperor Gaius*. New York: Oxford University Press, 1934.

Baynes, N. H., "Constantine the Great and the Christian Church," *Proceedings of the British Academy*, 15 (1929), 341 ff.

*Baynes, N. H., *The Byzantine Empire*, 2nd ed. New York: Oxford University Press, 1943.

Baynes, N. H. and H. Moss, *Byzantion: An Introduction to East Roman Civilization*. London, 1948.

Baynes, N. H., *Byzantine Studies*. London, 1955.

Bersanetti, G. M., *Studi sull' imperatore Massimino il Trace*. Rome, 1940.

Bersanetti, G. M., *Vespasiano*. Rome, 1941.

Besnier, M., *L'Empire romain de l'avènement des Sévères au concile de Nicée*. Paris, 1946.

Boak, A. E. R., *Manpower Shortage and Fall of the Roman Empire in the West*. Ann Arbor: The University of Michigan Press, 1955.

Buchan, J., *Augustus*. New York: Houghton Mifflin Company, 1937.

Bury, J. B., *A History of the Later Roman Empire, 395–565*. 2 vols. London, 1923.

Charlesworth, M. P., *The Roman Empire*. Toronto, 1951.

Crook, J., *Consilium Principis; Imperial Councils and Counsellors from Augustus to Diocletian*. London, 1955.

Damarau, P., *Kaiser Claudius Goticus*. (*Klio*, Beiheft XXXIII.) Leipzig, 1934.

Gerkan, A. von, "Zur Einwohnerzahl Roms in der Kaiserzeit," *Römische Mitteilungen*, 55 (1940), 149 ff.

Gerkan, A. von, "Weiteres zur Einwohnerzahl Roms in der Kaiserzeit," *Römische Mitteilungen*, 58 (1943), 213 ff.

Gerkan, A. von, "Grenzen und Grössen der vierzehn Regiones Roms," *Bonner Jahrbücher*, 149 (1949), 5–65.

*Gibbon, E., *Decline and Fall of the Roman Empire*. London, 1954.

Grant, M., *From Imperium to Auctoritas*. London, 1946.

Hammond, M., *The Augustan Principate in Theory and Practice*. Cambridge, Mass.: Harvard University Press, 1933.

Hammond, M., *The Antonine Monarchy*. (*Papers and Monographs of the American School in Rome*, 19.) 1959.

Hasebroek, J., *Untersuchungen zur Geschichte des Kaisers Septimius Severus*. Heidelberg, 1921.

Henderson, B. W., *The Life and Principate of the Emperor Hadrian*. London, 1923.

Henderson, B. W., *Five Roman Emperors*. London, 1927.

Holmes, T. R., *The Architect of the Roman Empire*. 2 vols. New York: Oxford University Press, 1928–1931.

Homo, L. P., *Vespasien, l'empereur de bon sens*. Paris, 1949.

Honigman, E. and A. Maricq, *Recherches sur les Res Gestae Divi Saporis*. (*Mémoires de l'Académie Royale de Belgique*. Classes des Lettres, 47, 4.) Brussels, 1953.

Jones, A. H. M., *Constantine and the Conversion of Europe*. London, 1948.

Kahrstedt, U., *Kulturgeschichte der römischen Kaiserzeit*. Bern, 1958.

Katz, S., *The Decline of Rome and Rise of Medieval Europe*. Ithaca: Cornell University Press, 1955.

Klinger, F., *Tacitus über Augustus und Tiberius*. Munich, 1954.

Kraft, H., *Kaiser Konstantins religiöse Entwicklung.* Tübingen, 1955.

Lambrechts, P., *La composition du sénat romain (117–192 A.D.).* Antwerp, 1936.

Lambrechts, P., *La composition du sénat romain (193–284 A.D.).* Antwerp, 1937.

Lepper, F. A., *Trajan's Parthian War.* New York: Oxford University Press, 1948.

Levi, M. A., *Nerone e i suoi tempi.* Milan, 1949.

Lissner, Ivar, *The Caesars: Might and Madness.* Trans. by J. M. Brownjohn. New York: G. P. Putnam's Sons, 1958.

Lofstedt, E., *Roman Literary Portraits.* Uppsala, 1959.

Lot, F., *The End of the Ancient World.* New York: Alfred A. Knopf, Inc., 1931.

Marsh, F. B., *The Founding of the Roman Empire,* 2nd ed. New York: Oxford University Press, 1927.

Marsh, F. B., *The Reign of Tiberius.* New York: Oxford University Press, 1931.

Mattingly, H., *Roman Imperial Civilization.* London, 1957.

Momigliano, A., *Claudius, the Emperor and his Achievement.* New York: Oxford University Press, 1934.

Ostrogorsky, G., *History of the Byzantine State,* 2nd ed. New York: Oxford University Press, 1956.

Paribeni, R., *Optimus Prinseps: Saggio sulla storia e sui tempi dell' Imperatore Traiano.* Messino, 1926–27.

Parker, H. M. D., *A History of the Roman World from A.D. 138 to 337,* 2nd ed. London, 1958.

Perowne, St., *Hadrian.* London, 1959.

Pflaum, H. G., *Essai sur le cursus publicus sous le Haut Empire romain. (Mémoires de l'Académie des Inscriptions, 14, 1.)* Paris, 1950.

Pflaum, H. G., *Les procurateurs équestres sous le Haut Empire romain.* Paris, 1950.

Pippidi, D. M., *Autour Tibère.* Bucharest, 1944.

Platnauer, M., *The Life and Reign of the Emperor Septimius Severus.* New York: Oxford University Press, 1918.

Rogers, R. S., *Criminal Trials and Criminal Legislation under Tiberius.* New York: American Philological Association, 1935.

Rogers, R. S., *Studies in the Reign of Tiberius.* Baltimore: The Johns Hopkins Press, 1943.

Rostovtzeff, M. I., *The Social and Economic History of the Roman Empire,* 4th ed. Revised by P. M. Fraser. New York: Oxford University Press, 1959.

Runciman, St., *Byzantine Civilization.* New York, 1958.

Salmon, E. T., *A History of the Roman World from 30 B.C. to 138 A.D.,* 3rd ed. London, 1957.

Scrammuzza, V., *The Emperor Claudius.* Cambridge, Mass.: Harvard University Press, 1940.

Seston, W., *Dioclétian et la Tétrarchie.* (Ecoles Françaises d'Athènes et de Rome, 162.) Paris, 1946.

Smith, C. E.; *Tiberius and the Roman Empire.* Baton Rouge: Louisiana State University Press, 1942.

Stähelin, F., *Kaiser Claudius.* Basel, 1933.

Stähelin, F., *Die Schweiz in römischer Zeit,* 3rd ed. Basel, 1948.

Starr, C. G., *Civilization and the Caesars.* Ithaca: Cornell University Press, 1954.

Stein, A., *Der römische Ritterstand.* Munich, 1927.

Stein, E., *Histoire du Bas-Empire.* 2 vols. Brussels and Paris, 1949–1960.

Syme, R., *The Roman Revolution.* New York: Oxford University Press, 1952.

Syme, R., *Tacitus.* 2 vols. New York: Oxford University Press, 1958.

*Ure, P. N., *Justinian and His Age.* Harmondsworth, 1951.

Van Berchem, D., *L'armée de Dioclétien et la réforme constantinienne.* Paris, 1952.

Vogt, J., *Konstantin der Grosse und sein Jahrhundert.* Munich, 1949.

Walbank, F. W., *The Decline of the Roman Empire in the West.* New York: Abelard Schuman, Limited, 1953.

Warmington, E. H., *The Commerce between the Roman Empire and India.* London, 1928.

*Wheeler, M., *Rome Beyond the Imperial Frontiers.* Harmondsworth, 1955.

Winspear, A. D. and L. K. Geweke, *Augustus and the Reconstruction of Roman Government and Society.* Madison: University of Wisconsin Press, 1935.

THE ROMAN PROVINCES

Abbott, F. F. and A. C. Johnson, *Municipal Administration in the Roman Empire.* Princeton: Princeton University Press, 1926.

Albertini, E., *Roman Africa.* Alger, 1932.

Alföldi, A., *Die Vorherrschaft der Pannonier im Römerreich.* Frankfurt, 1930.

Bell, H. I., *Egypt from Alexander the Great to the Arab Conquest.* New York: Oxford University Press, 1948.

Bouchier, E. S., *Life and Letters in Roman Africa.* New York: Oxford University Press, 1913.

Bouchier, E. S., *Spain under the Roman Empire.* New York: Oxford University Press, 1914.

Brogan, O. K., *Roman Gaul.* London, 1953.

Broughton, T. R. S., *The Romanization of Africa Proconsularis.* Baltimore: The Johns Hopkins Press, 1929.

Chilver, G. E. F., *Cisalpine Gaul: Social and*

Economic History from 49 B.C. to the Death of Trajan. New York: Oxford University Press, 1941.

Collingwood, R. G. and N. Myers, *Roman Britain.* New York: Oxford University Press, 1937.

Gsell, S., *Histoire ancienne de l'Afrique du Nord.* 8 vols. Paris, 1913–1928.

Jones, A. H. M., *The Cities of the Eastern Roman Provinces.* New York: Oxford University Press, 1937.

Magie, D., *Roman Rule in Asia Minor.* Princeton: Princeton University Press, 1950.

Miller, S. N., *The Roman Occupation of South West Scotland.* Glasgow, 1952.

Mommsen, T., *The Provinces of the Roman Empire.* 2 vols. 2nd ed. by F. Haverfield. New York, 1909.

Pârvan, V., *Dacia, an Outline of the Early Civilizations of the Carpatho-Danubian Countries.* London, 1928.

*Richmond, I. A., *Roman Britain.* Harmondsworth, 1955.

Starcky, J., *Palmyre.* Paris, 1952.

Stevenson, G. H., *Roman Provincial Administration,* 2nd ed. New York: Oxford University Press, 1949.

Sutherland, C. H. V., *The Romans in Spain.* London, 1939.

Thouvenot, R., *Essai sur la province romaine de Bétique.* Paris, 1940.

LATIN LITERATURE

Adcock, F. E., *Caesar as Man of Letters.* London, 1956.

Altheim, F., *Literatur und Gesellschaft im ausgehenden Altertum.* Halle, 1948–1950.

Bagnani, G., *Arbiter of Elegance.* Toronto, 1954.

Bardon, H., *La littérature latine inconnue.* 2 vols. Paris, 1952–56.

Beare, W., *The Roman Stage.* London, 1955.

Duckworth, G. E., *The Complete Roman Drama.* New York: Random House, 1942.

Duckworth, G. E., *The Nature of Roman Comedy.* Princeton: Princeton University Press, 1952.

Duff, J. Wight, *A Literary History of Rome,* rev. ed. New York: Barnes & Noble, Inc., 1953.

*Frank, T., *Life and Literature in the Roman Republic.* Berkeley: University of California Press, 1930, 1956.

*Godolphin, F. R. B., *The Latin Poets.* New York: Modern Library, Inc., 1949.

*Grant, M., *Roman Literature.* New York: Cambridge University Press, 1954; Harmondsworth, 1958.

Guinagh, K. and A. P. Dorjahn, *Latin Literature in Translation.* New York: Longmans, Green & Co., 1953.

Hadas, M., *A History of Latin Literature.* New York: Columbia University Press, 1952.

Hadzsits, G., *Lucretius and His Influence.* London, 1935.

Highet, Gilbert, *Juvenal the Satirist.* Oxford, 1954.

Highet, Gilbert, *Poets in a Landscape.* New York: Alfred A. Knopf, Inc., 1957.

Hunt, H. A. K., *The Humanism of Cicero.* Melbourne, 1954.

Lind, L. R., *Latin Poetry in Verse Translation.* New York: Houghton Mifflin Company, 1957.

MacKendrick, Paul L. and H. M. Howe, *Roman Classics in Translation.* Madison: University of Wisconsin Press, 1952.

Murphy, C. T., Guinagh and Oates, *Greek and Roman Classics in Translation.* New York: Longmans, Green & Co., Inc., 1947.

Norden, E., *Das römische Literatur.* Leipzig, 1954.

Rand, E. K., *The Building of Eternal Rome.* Cambridge, Mass.: Harvard University Press, 1943.

Wilkinson, L. P., *Ovid Recalled.* London, 1955.

ROMAN EDUCATION

Bonner, S. F., *Education of a Roman.* Liverpool, 1950.

Dobson, J. F., *Ancient Education and its Meaning.* London, 1932.

Gwynn, A., *Roman Education from Cicero to Quintilian.* New York: Oxford University Press, 1926.

Haarhoff, T., *Schools of Gaul: A Study of Pagan and Christian Education in the Last Century of the Western Empire.* New York: Oxford University Press, 1920.

Marrou, H. I., *A History of Education in Antiquity,* 3rd ed. New York: Oxford University Press, 1956.

Smith, W. A., *Ancient Education.* New York: Philosophical Library, Inc., 1956.

PHILOSOPHY

Arnold, E. V., *Roman Stoicism.* London, 1911.

Bailey, C., *Epicurus.* New York: Oxford University Press, 1926.

De Witt, N. W., *Epicurus and his Philosophy.* Minneapolis: University of Minnesota Press, 1954.

Dudley, D. R., *A History of Cynicism.* London, 1937.

Reesor, M. E., *The Political Theory of the Old and Middle Stoa.* New York, 1951.

Wenley, R. M., *Stoicism and Its Influence.* Boston: Longmans, Green & Co., Inc., 1925.

RELIGION

Altheim, F., *Griechische Götter im Alten Rom.* Giessen, 1930.

Altheim, F., *A History of Roman Religion.* New York: E. P. Dutton & Co., Inc., 1938.

Altheim, F., *Terra Mater.* Giessen, 1931.

Bailey, C., *Phases in the Religion of Ancient Rome.* Berkeley: University of California Press, 1932.

Cumont, F., *Oriental Religions in Roman Paganism.* La Salle, Ill.: Open Court Publishing Co., 1911.

Dumézil, G., *Les mythes romaines.* 2 vols. Paris, 1942, 1943.

Evans, E. C., *The Cults of the Sabine Territory.* Rome: American Academy in Rome, 1939.

Fowler, W. W., *The Religious Experience of the Roman People from the Earliest Times to the Age of Augustus.* New York: The Macmillan Co., 1911.

Grenier, A., *The Roman Spirit in Religion, Thought, and Art.* New York: Alfred A. Knopf, Inc., 1926.

Halliday, W. R., *Lectures on the History of Roman Religion.* Liverpool, 1922.

Laing, G. J., *Survivals of Roman Religion.* New York: Longmans, Green & Co., Inc., 1931.

Rose, H. J., *Ancient Roman Religion.* London, 1948.

Turchi, N., *La religione di Roma antica.* Rome, 1939.

Westrup, C. W., *On the Antiquarian-Historical Activities of the Roman Pontifical College.* Copenhagen, 1929.

CHRISTIANITY

Carrington, P., *The Early Church.* 2 vols. London, 1957.

Cochrane, C. N., *Christianity and Classical Culture. A Study of Thought and Action from Augustus to Augustine.* New York: Oxford University Press, 1952.

Davies, J. G., *Daily Life in the Early Church.* London, 1952.

Glover, T. R., *The Conflict of Religions in the Early Roman Empire,* 10th ed. New York and London: Charles Scribner's Sons, 1923.

Halliday, W. R., *The Pagan Background of Early Christianity.* Liverpool, 1925.

Lebreton, J. and J. Zeiller, *Histoire de l'église de la fin du 2me siècle à la paix constantinienne.* Paris, 1946.

Musurillo, H. A., *The Acts of the Pagan Martyrs.* New York: Oxford University Press, 1952.

Nock, A. D., *Conversion: the Old and New in Religion from Alexander the Great to Augustine of Hippo.* New York: Oxford University Press, 1933.

SOCIAL AND ECONOMIC LIFE

Carcopino, J., *Daily Life in Ancient Rome,* edited with bibliography and notes by Henry Rowell. New Haven: Yale University Press, 1941.

Charlesworth, M. P., *The Trade-Routes and Commerce of the Roman Empire,* 2nd ed. New York: The Macmillan Co., 1926.

*Dill, Sir Samuel, *Roman Society from Nero to Marcus Aurelius,* 2nd ed. Meridian Books, Inc., 1919.

Forbes, R. J., *Metallurgy in Antiquity.* Leiden, 1950.

Forbes, R. J., *Studies in Ancient Technology.* Leiden, 1955, 1958.

Frank, T., *An Economic History of Rome,* 2nd ed. Baltimore: The Johns Hopkins Press, 1927.

Frank, T., *An Economic Survey of Ancient Rome.* 4 vols. Baltimore: The Johns Hopkins Press, 1933–1940.

Frank, T., *Social Behavior in Ancient Rome.* Cambridge, Mass.: Harvard University Press, 1932.

Friedländer, L., *Roman Life and Manners in the Early Empire.* 4 vols. New York: Oxford University Press, 1908–1913.

Heichelheim, F. M., "Man's Role in Changing the Face of the Earth in Classical Antiquity," *Kyklos,* 9 (1956), 318–355.

Heichelheim, F. M., "On Ancient Price Trends from the Early First Millennium B.C. to Heraclius I," *Finanzarchiv* (Tübingen), 15 (1955), 498–511.

Heichelheim, F. M., "Römische und Byzantinische Sozial- und Wirtgeschichte," *Historia Mundi,* 4 (1956), 397–488.

Heichelheim, F. M., *Wirtschaftsgeschichte des Altertums.* Leiden, 1938.

Jefferson, Loane H., *Industry and Commerce of the City of Rome (50 B.C. to A.D. 200).* Baltimore: The Johns Hopkins Press, 1938.

Mattingly, H., *The Man in the Roman Street.* New York: The Numismatic Review, 1947.

Singer, C. J., *A History of Technology.* 2 vols. New York: Oxford University Press, 1954, 1956.

Sirago, V. A., *L'Italia agraria sotto Traiano.* Louvain, 1958.

Toutain, J., *The Economic Life of the Ancient World.* London, 1930.

Westermann, W. L., *The Slave Systems of Greek and Roman Antiquity.* (Memoirs of the Philosophical Society, 40.) Philadelphia, 1955.

Wheeler, M., *Rome Beyond the Imperial Frontiers.* London, 1954.

Yeo, C. A., "The Development of the Roman Plantation and Marketing of Farm Products," *Finanzarchiv* (Tübingen), 13 (1952), 321–342.

Yeo, C. A., "The Economics of Roman and American Slavery," *Finanzarchiv*, 13 (1952), 445–485.

Zimmermann, C. C., *Family and Civilization.* New York and London: Harper & Brothers, 1947.

LAW AND GOVERNMENT

Arrangio-Ruiz, V., *Istituzioni di diritto romano*, 11th ed. Naples, 1952.

Arrangio-Ruiz, V., *Storia del diritto romano*, 6th ed. Naples, 1950.

Arrangio-Ruiz, V., *Studi in onore di.* Naples, 1950, 1951.

Berger, A., *Encyclopedic Dictionary of Roman Law. (Transactions of the American Philosophical Society*, 43.3.) Philadelphia, 1953.

Buckland, W. W., *A Textbook of Roman Law from Augustus to Justinian*, 2nd ed. London, 1932.

Buckland, W. W., *A Manual of Roman Private Law*, 2nd ed. London, 1939.

Buckland, W. W. and Sir A. McNair, *Roman Law and Common Law*, 2nd ed. London, 1952.

Daube, D., *Forms of Legislation.* New York: Oxford University Press, 1957.

Declareuil, J., *Rome, the Law Giver.* London and New York, 1927.

De Francisci, P., *Sintesi storica del diritto romano.* Rome, 1948.

De Francisci, P., *Spirito della civiltà romana*, 2nd ed. Rome, 1952.

De Martino, F., *Storia della costituzione romana.* Naples, 1951.

Jolowicz, H. F., *Historical Introduction to Roman Law*, 3rd ed. London, 1952.

Jolowicz, H. F., *Roman Foundations of Modern Law.* New York: Oxford University Press, 1957.

Kaser, M., *Das altrömische Jus.* Göttingen, 1949.

Kaser, M., *Römische Rechtsgeschichte.* Göttingen, 1950.

Kaser, M., *Eigentum und Besitz im altrömischen Recht*, 2nd ed. Göttingen, 1956.

Kaser, M., *Das römische Privatrecht.* 2 vols. (*Handbuch der Altertumswissenschaft*, 10.3.3.) Munich, 1955, 1959.

Kunkel, W., "Herkunft und soziale Stellung der römischen Juristen," *Forschungen zum römischen Recht*, 4, 1952.

Kunkel, W., *Römische Rechtsgeschichte*, 2nd ed. Vienna, 1956.

Radin, M., *Handbook of Roman Law.* Minneapolis: University of Minnesota Press, 1927

Riccobono, S., *Lezione di storia del diritto romano.* Messina, 1951.

Schulz, F., *Principles of Roman Law.* Oxford University Press, 1936.

Schulz, F., *Classical Roman Law.* Oxford University Press, 1951.

Schulz, F., *History of Roman Legal Science*, 2nd ed. Oxford University Press, 1953.

Schwind, F. and H. Kreller, *Römische Recht.* 2 vols. Vienna, 1950.

Siber, H., *Römisches Verfassungsrecht.* Lahr, 1952.

Taubenschlag, R., *The Law of Greco-Roman Egypt in the Light of the Papyri.* 2 vols. New York and Warsaw: Herald Square Press, Inc., 1944, 1948.

Turner, J. W. C., *Introduction to the Study of Roman Private Law.* London, 1953.

Wolff, H. J., *Roman Law: An Historical Introduction.* Norman: University of Oklahoma Press, 1951.

THE ROMAN COINAGE

Bernhardt, M., *Handbuch zur Münzkunde der römischen Kaiserzeit.* 2 vols. Halle, 1926.

Kraay, C. M., "Caesar's Quattuorviri of 44 B.C.: the Arrangement of the Issues," *Numismatic Chronicle*, 14 (1954), 18 ff.

Mattingly, H. and E. S. G. Robinson, "The Date of the Roman *Denarius* and Other Landmarks in the History of the Roman Coinage," *Proceedings of the British Academy*, 18 (1933), 211–268.

Mattingly, H., "The First Age of the Roman Coinage," *Journal of Roman Studies*, 34 (1944), 65 ff.

Mattingly, H., *Roman Coins.* London, 1960.

Robinson, E. S. G. and R. A. G. Carson, *A Guide to the Exhibition of Roman Coins in the British Museum.* London, 1952.

Sydenham, E. A., *The Coinage of the Roman Republic.* London, 1952.

ART AND ARCHITECTURE

Anderson, W. J. and R. P. Spiers, *The Architecture of Ancient Rome*, Vol. I. New York: Charles Scribner's Sons, 1927.

Blake, Marion E., *Ancient Roman Construction in Italy from the Prehistoric Period to Augustus.* Washington, D.C.: Carnegie Institution, 1947.

Boethius, A., *Roman and Greek Architecture.* Göteberg, 1948.

Ducati, P., *L'arte in Roma dalli origini al sec. VIII.* Bologna, 1938.

Lugli, G., *Roma antica, il centro monumentale.* Rome, 1946.

Maiuri, A., *Roman Painting.* Skira, 1953.

Platner, S. and T. Ashby, *A Topographical Dictionary of Ancient Rome*, 2nd ed. New York: Oxford University Press, 1929.

Richter, G. M. A., *Roman Portraits*. New York: Metropolitan Museum of Art, 1948.

Robathan, D., *The Monuments of Ancient Rome*. Rome, 1950.

Robertson, D. S., *A Handbook of Greek and Roman Architecture*, 2nd ed. London, 1943.

Scheffold, K., *Pompejanische Malerei*. Basel, 1952.

Scherer, M. R., *Marvels of Ancient Rome*. Greenwich, Conn.: Phaidon Publishers, Inc., 1955.

Strong, E., *Art in Ancient Rome*. 2 vols. New York: William S. Heinemann, 1929.

Swindler, M. H., *Ancient Painting*. New Haven: Yale University Press, 1929.

ROMAN ARMS AND ARMIES

Adcock, Sir F. E., *The Roman Art of War under the Republic*. Cambridge, Mass.: Harvard University Press, 1940.

*Birley, E., *Roman Britain and the Roman Army*. Kendal, 1953.

Cheeseman, G. L., *The Auxilia of the Imperial Roman Army*. New York: Oxford University Press, 1914.

Coussin, P., *Les armes romaines*. Paris, 1926.

Echols, E., "The Roman City Police," *Classical Journal*, 53 (1957/58), 377 ff.

Liddell-Hart, B. H., *A Greater than Napoleon: Scipio Africanus*. London, 1926.

Liddell-Hart, B. H., *Strategy*. New York: Frederick A. Praeger, Inc., 1954.

McCartney, E. S., *The Military Indebtedness of Rome to Etruria*. (Memoirs of the American Academy in Rome, 1.) 1917, 121 ff.

Nilsson, M. P., "The Introduction of Hoplite Tactics at Rome: Its Date and Consequences," *Journal of Roman Studies*, 19 (1929), 1 ff.

Parker, A. M. D., *The Roman Legions*, 2nd ed. New York: Oxford University Press, 1958.

Smith, R. E., *Service in the Post-Marian Roman Army*. Manchester, 1958.

Starr, C. G., *The Roman Imperial Navy*. Ithaca: Cornell University Press, 1941.

Tarn, W. W., *Hellenistic Military and Naval Developments*. London, 1930.

Thiel, J. H., *Studies on the History of Roman Seapower in Republican Times*. Amsterdam, 1946.

Thiel, J. H., *A History of Roman Seapower before the Second Punic War*. Amsterdam, 1954.

Wallinga, H. T., *The Boarding Bridge of the Romans: Its Function in the Naval Tactics of the First Punic War*. Groningen, 1956.

Webster, G., *The Roman Army*. Chester, England, 1956.

INDEX

This index is not designed to be a concordance of all proper names occurring in the text.
Most Romans, except emperors and authors (who are entered under their conventional names), are listed under their *gens* name: e.g. Julius for Caesar.
For given names the following conventional abbreviations are employed: A. for *Aulus*, C. for *Caius* or *Gaius*, Cn. for *Cnaeus* or *Gnaeus*, D. for *Decimus*, L. for *Lucius*, M. for *Marcus*, P. for *Publius*, Q. for *Quintus*, S. for *Sextus*, T. for *Titus*.

invasions of, 371, 398, 400, 402; Hannibal in, 129; made a province (united with Illyria), 203, 222, 251, 255; ranching, 293; reattached to Italy, 255; as recruiting ground, 205, 224, 251; revolts in, 205; road building in, 152; taxation of, 415; writers from, 235, 259, 303

Cissus, naval battle off, 145

Citizenship (*see also* Latin Rights): as birthright (of early plebeians), 56, (of Roman Citizen colonists), 105, 194; granting of (to Latin and Italian *municipia*), 104-105; (to Italians south of the Po), 195, 199; (to soldiers serving in Roman armies), 248; (to certain Gaulic and Spanish towns), 248-49, 283, 318, 337, 359; (to African and Balkan provincials), 322, 337, 359; (to provincial town councilors), 359; (to all free inhabitants of the empire: *see Constitutio Antoniniana*), 392; obligations of, 64, 104, 105; rights and privileges inherent in, 57, 87, 104, 359

Civil Service (*see also* Freedmen; Knights; Prefects; Procurators): Augustan institution, 268, 271-73; departments and functions, 239-40, 272, 273, 329, 388, 432; expansion of, 319, 338, 339, 360-61, 386-87, 412, 432; freedmen in, 273, 319, 338; knights in, 272-73, 339; provincials in, 339; senators in, 272, 386; slaves in, 272

Civitavecchia, harbor of, 352

Classes, see Army

Classis (division of citizens for military and voting purposes), 56, 64, 83, 126

Claudian *gens*: ancestor of, 55; characteristics of, 55, 101, 106, 115, 118, 172, 173, 223, 238, 257, 270, 308; notable representatives of, 55, 86, 101, 106, 115, 118-19, 131-32, 134, 154, 172-73, 223, 308, 317; radicalism, 86, 101, 172, 223-24, 228-29, 318

Claudius I (Tiberius Claudius Caesar Augustus Germanicus), Emperor: accession, 317, 318; advisers, 317, 319, 324; character and personality, 316, 317-18, 319; colonies founded by, 322; centralization of government by, 318, 411; conquest of Britain, 322, 338; expansion of civil service, 319, 339, 360; financial policy, 284, 318-19; foreign policy, 320, 322; municipalization, 322, 337; philosophy of government, 318; public works, 319-20, 352; scholarship, 33, 317; urbanizing activity, 322; wives, 317, 323

Claudius II Gothicus (M. Aurelius Claudius Augustus), Emperor: liquidation of Gothic menace by, 401; Constantine's claim of descent from, 424, 428

Claudius, Appius (Atta Clausus), 55

Claudius Appius, the Decemvir, 86

Claudius Caecus Appius, the Censor: reform of voting system by, 101, 173; builder of Appian Way, 106-107

Claudius Caudex, Appius (consul), 115, 116

Claudius, Q. (tribune of the plebs), 224

Claudius Marcellus, C. (consul), 238

Claudius Marcellus, M. (consul), 131, 132, 143

Claudius Marcellus, M. (praetor, consul, governor of Spain), 154

Claudius Marcellus, M. (consul), 238

Claudius Marcellus, C., 274, 280; death of, 275; Theater of, 301

Claudius Nero, C. (praetor, consul), 134

Claudius Nero, Tiberius (consul), see Tiberius, Emperor

Claudius Polybius (freedman cabinet minister of Claudius I), 319

Claudius Pulcher, P. (consul, Roman admiral), 118-19

Claudius Pulcher, Appius (consul, censor), 172, 173, 175

Claudius Quadrigarius, Q. (annalist), 79

Cleanthes (Stoic philosopher), 370

Clausus Sabinus, Atta (consul), 269

Cleomenes III (king of Sparta), 144

Cleonymus of Sparta, invasion of Italy by, 107

Cleopatra I, Queen of Egypt, 141, 144

Cleopatra VII, Queen of Egypt: ancestry, 141, 243; character and ambitions, 243, 255, 260, 262; death of, 263; descendants, 262, 281, 315; marriage with Caesar, 243; propaganda against, 261, 262, 263; relations with Antonius, 255, 260, 262, 263; territorial donations from Antonius, 260, 261, 262

Cleopatra Moon (Selene) (daughter of Cleopatra VII and Antonius), Queen of Mauretania, 281

Clientage and clients (*see also Patrocinium*): nature and origin of, 55; obligations and rights of, 55, 60; relationship to the primitive *gens*, 55, 60; to individual patrons, 55, 57, 74, 83, 166; and rise of plebeian class, 57

Climate: of Italy, 4-5; changes in prehistoric times, 6, 7-11, 16, 22

Clodia (sister of Clodius), 235, 237, 238

Clodius (Claudius) Pulcher, P. (tribune): ancestry and character, 217, 223; banishment of Cicero and Cato by, 223-24; as demagogue and political gangster, 223, 228-31, 234; grain distribution law, 224; death and funeral, 234-35

Clodius Thrasea Paetus, P. (consul), 328

Clusium, *see* Chiusi

Cohortes (*see also* Army): introduction by Marius, 189; prefects of, 272

Coinage (*see also Antoninianus*; *As*: *Aureus*; *Denarius*; *Sestertius*; *Solidus*; *Victoriatus*; and esp. Mints): Etruscan, 32; Gallic, 225-26; Italian Confederate, 194; Massilian, 128; Roman Republican, 128, 143, 165-66, 249; Roman Imperial (control over), 270, 298-99, 403; (depreciation of), 327, 353, 376, 386, 391, 403; (illustrations of), 165, 168, 239, 246, 247, 299, 320, 327, 352, 355, 367, 383;

(use as historical sources), 112, 225, 267, 299, 350, 352, 355, 357, 383, 385

Collegia (guilds) (*see also* Associations): of bakers, 394, 403-04, 434; exemptions and tax benefits enjoyed by, 394; of fullers (Pompeii), 294; membership, 434; state regulation and control of, 394, 403-04, 432, 434

Collegia iuvenum, as military academies, 337

Colline Gate, battle at, 201-02, 205, 209

Cologne (Colonia Agrippinensis): Agrippa's settlement of Ubii at, 279; altars for imperial cult at, 282; as Claudian colony, 322; glass factories at, 296, 348; urbanization of, 322, 376

Coloni and *colonatus*: genesis of, 293, 304, 349; on Horace's estate, 293, 304; on Imperial estates, 349, 416, 433-34; military service required from, 413; revolts of (*see also* Bagaudae), 376; taxation of, 409, 415, 433; transformation to serfdom, 416, 433-34

Colonies and colonization: (early period) Etruscan, 30; Greek, 30, 33, 48; Latin, 104-05; Massilian (Marseille), 121; Phoenician and Carthaginian, 112, 113; (Roman Republic) agricultural, 179, 180, 184, 218; Caesarian, 248; commercial, 179, 248, 277; Gracchan, 179, 180; Latin, 105, 126, 154; military, 104, 105, 126, 152; Roman Citizen, 105, 152, 184; transmarine, 179, 184, 248; veteran, 184, 191, 248; (Imperial period) Augustan, 276-77; Claudian, 322, 359; military and strategic, 277, 322; as Romanizing and urbanizing agents, 248, 277, 322, 337, 335, 357, 359; titular, 359; veteran, 248, 277, 353

Colosseum (Amphitheatrum Flavium), 34, 340, 341, 342, 343, 384

Columella (L. Junius Moderatus Columella (writer), 162, 290, 331

Column: of Marcus Aurelius, 372, 373; of Trajan, 350

Comata, *see* Gaul

Comitatenses (mobile field forces), 413, 432

Comites (*see also* Count; Duke): comrades of a provincial governor, 122; supreme commanders of a group of military districts, 412; (*see* Count of Saxon Shore, 410)

Comitia Centuriata (Centuriate Assembly): ancient organization, 61, 63-65; as *Comitiatus Maximus*, 65, 101; as court of appeals, 65, 82, 87, 88 (see also Court); functions of, 64-65, 85, 86, 87, 88, 89, 90, 100, 101, 126, 142, 202, 310; reorganization, 126, 199-200; tribal basis of, 64, 126; voting procedure, 64, 126, 200; wealth and property as basis for gradation into classes (*see Classes*)

Comitia Curiata (Curiate Assembly): antiquity of, 60; functions during the kingship, 60-61, 65, 72; the Republic, 84, 89; superseded by *Comitia Centuriata*, 61, 89, 101; voting procedure, 61, 64

Comitia Tributa (Tribal Assembly) (*see also Concilium Plebis Tribu-*

individual, 54, 56, 60; religion of, 56, 65, 68, 71, 74; status of women in, 36, 41, 42, 87, 173, 216, 223, 234, 243, 250, 256, 257, 261, 262, 274, 285, 293, 309, 312, 316, 317, 323, 324, 325, 355, 362, 373, 385, 388, 393, 394, 409, 420, 430, 435

Famine, 256, 311, 314, 327, 371, 424

Farmers, small, plight of, 84, 125, 160, 164, 172, 173, 293, 349

Fasces, 29, 82, 88, 100, 243

Fasti (of Ovid), 305

Fasti (lists of eponymous magistrates, *see also Annales Maximi*), 80, 81, 86, 88, 99

Fausta (wife of Constantine I), 423, 435

Faustina (wife of Marcus Aurelius), 373

Felsina (Etruscan settlement near Bologna), 30

Festus (S. Pompeius Festus) (grammarian), 86

Feudalism: forerunners of, 196, 260, 433; traces in early societies, 29, 55, 93, 196, 260

Fidenae (Tiber town opposite Veii), 48, 51, 91

Fides (faith), 55, 74, 116, 303, 304; temple of, 175

Fines: imposition of, 172, 213; limitation of, 85-86

Fire: Gallic, 387 B.C., 47, 98; of 64 A.D., 325; of 80 A.D., 342

Fiscus, fisci: control of, 318; created as separate provincial treasuries, 279; expenditures, 319, 340; as a farm loan bank, 349; officers and attorneys (*advocati*), 360, 386; reorganization by Claudius, 319, 344; sources of revenue, 284, 319, 340, 344; unification as single imperial treasury, 284, 344, 386

Flamen ("kindler of the sacred flame"), 66, 72, 100, 285

Flaminian Way (*Via Flaminia*), 125-26, 130, 152, 276, 425

Flamininus, *see* Quinctius

Flamininus, C. (consul, plebeian tribune, censor): conqueror and colonizer of North Italy, 125-26, 184; defiance of the senate, 125, 174; reforms of the Centuriate Assembly, 126; at Trasimene, 129-30

Flaminius, C. (consul), as builder of New Flaminian Way, 152

Flavius Clemens, T. (consul), execution of by Domitian, 345

Flavius Fimbria, C. (*legatus* of L. Valerius Flaccus), 200

Flora (spirit of springtime and flowers), 66

Florence (Italy), 202, 205, 219

Florianus (M. Annius Florianus Augustus), Emperor, 404

Florus (L. Annaeus Florus, historian), 375

Fordicidia, see Religious feasts and festivals

Fortifications (*see also* Army; Limes; Walls): construction, 338, 344, 357-58, 368, 392, 410, 411, 414, 439; maintenance and repair, 397; replacement by mobile field forces, 400-01, 413, 432

Fortuna (goddess of chance), 70

Fora: (Forum of Rome) excavations under, 23, 48, 81; public and political center, 86, 101, 165, 175, 199, 222, 223, 228, 239, 244, 245, 250, 251; (Imperial Fora) Forum of Augustus, 285, 300; Forum of Trajan, 352; Forum of Vespasian, 340

Forum Julii (Fréjus, southern France), 276

Fossa people and culture, 23-24, 48

Franks (invaders of Gaul), 397, 398, 404, 409, 422, 423

Freedmen: assignment to voting tribes, 199; government assistance to, 352; government service (imperial cabinet), 319, (civil service), 273, 319, 324, 339, 360, (navy), 276; social and civil status, 285; wealth, 319

Fregellae, rebellion and destruction of, 177, 181

Frentani (Umbro-Sabellian tribe, central Italy), 106

Frontinus (S. Julius Frontinus) (governor of Britain, writer on military tactics), 338

Fronto (M. Cornelius Fronto) (rhetorician, teacher of Marcus Aurelius), 304, 369

Fucine Lake (western Abruzzi) drainage of projected by Caesar, 248; attempted by Claudius, 320

Fulvia (wife of Clodius, Curio, and Marcus Antonius), 234, 238, 250, 256

Fulvius Flaccus, M. (consul): ardent Gracchan partisan, 176, 180, 181; campaign for Italian citizenship, 177, 193; land settlement activities in Gaul, 177, 205

Fulvius Nobilior, M. (consul, patron of Ennius), 171

Fulvius Plautianus, C. (consul, praetorian prefect), 387

Furius Camillus, M. (dictator): conquest of Veii, 90, 91; exploits during Gallic Sack of Rome, 99; later fame, 190, 269

Furius Sabinus Aquila Timesitheus, C. (praetorian prefect), 396

G

Gabinius, A. (tribune, consul), 213, 214, 224

Gades (Cadiz, Spain): ancient Phoenician colony, 112, 134; chief Carthaginian seaport in Spain, 113, 120; made a Roman ally, 134; promised status of *municipium*, 153; temple of Hercules at, 227

Gaius (jurist): fragments of XII Tables preserved by, 86; *Institutes* of, 377

Gaius, the Emperor, *see* Caligula

Gaius Caesar (grandson of Augustus): adoption by Augustus, 275, 280; Eastern campaigns of, 280, 283

Galatia (central Asia Minor): conquered by Gauls, 94; nominal Roman ally, 197; made a province by Augustus, 282, 283; made part of Anatolia by Vespasian, 339; stricken with famine, 371

Galba (Servius Sulpicius Galba), Emperor: as governor of Nearer Spain, 329; principate of, 333, 334

Galen (Claudius Galenus of Pergamum) (writer on medicine), 377

Galerius (C. Galerius Valerius Maxi-

mianus Augustus), Emperor: adopted by Diocletian as Caesar, 409, 410; Eastern triumphs of, 411, 414, 421; Edict of Toleration, 424, 427; march against Maxentius, 423, 424; persecution of Christians by, 417, 418, 419; triumphal arch of, 414

Gallia Cisalpina, *see* Cisalpine Gaul

Gallia Comata, *see* Gaul

Gallia Narbonensis (The Province): geography, 184, 224; invasion by Cimbri and Teutons, 188; made a Roman province, 184, 188, 203, 226; as province (of Caesar), 223, 224, 227, 229, 238; (of Lepidus), 254; Roman monuments in, 301, 302, 303, 307, 380; senatorial province, 279

Gallia Lugdunensis (main administrative province of Gallia Comata), 279

Gallienus (P. Licinius Egnatius Gallienus Augustus), Emperor: battles of, 398, 400; compared with Hadrian, 401; edict of Christian toleration, 417; military reforms, 401, 412; policies of, 399, 400; revolts against, 399, 400

Gallus, *see* Cornelius

Gallus, *see* Trebonianus

Gaul: (prehistoric) Paleolithic, 8-16; Neolithic, 20-21, 91-92; (Celtic *see also* Celts), 91-97, 224-26; agriculture, 224-25; coinage, 225-26; crafts, 225; geographical divisions, 224; invasions (Cimbrian), 190, (Germanic), 226-28, (Roman), 177, 184, 227-31; mines, 224; towns, 226; tribes, 184, 226, 227, 228, 229, 230, 231; trade, 163, 225; (Roman) agriculture, 163, 293, 348, 405; cities, 226, 322; colonization, 184, 191, 248, 277, 322, 359; conquest, 177, 184, 227-31, 241; economic competition with Italy, 163, 293, 296, 348; Germanic invasions, 395, 397, 398, 399, 409, 410, 423; industries, 225, 296, 348; legions stationed in, 275; mints (imperial), 298, 314; nationalist tendencies, 336, 399; persecutions of Christians, 310, 419; provinces, 184, 227-31, 238, 251, 253, 254, 255, 256, 279, 283, 338, 419; public works, 301, 302, 303, 319, 380; revolts, 314, 334, 336, 399, 403, 405, 409; Romanization, 248-49, 361; senators from, 248, 270, 318, 338, 375; trade, 163, 296, 348; urbanization, 248-49, 283, 322, 337-38, 359, 376

Gauls, *see* Celts

Gellius, Aulus (antiquarian, essayist, grammarian), 86, 369

Gellius, Cn. (annalist), 79

Geneva, 224, 248

Genoa (Genua), 134, 152

gens (*see also* Clients), 54, 55, 60, 62

Gergovia (capital of the Arverni): Gallic hilltop *oppidum*, 226; siege of, 233

German, Germans: invasions (of Italy), 189, 371, 398, 402, (of Gaul), 188, 226, 228, 229, 279, 395, 397, 404-05; serving in Roman armies, 231, 401, 402, 405, 413, 432; settlement on Roman territory, 279, 374, 398, 401, 411

Malaga (Malaca, Spain), 134, 153
Malaria in Italy, 160
Mallius Maximus, Cn., 189, 193
Malta: Neolithic subterranean temples in, 18, 21; early colony of Carthage, 112; occupied by Romans, 129
Mamertines (see also Messana), 115, 116
Mamilius Limetanus, C. (tribune), jury law of, 186
Mancinus, see Hostilius
Mani and Manichaeism, 389, 411
Manilius, C. (tribune), see Lex Manilia
Maniple (manipulus): basic tactical unit of early Roman legion, 133; abolished by Marius, 189
Manlius Capitolinus, M. (consul, alleged savior of the Capitol from the Gauls), 98
Manlius Torquatus, L. (consul), 217
Manlius Vulso Longus, L. (consul), 117
Mantua: birthplace of Vergil, 259, 303; Etruscan foundation, 30; Terramare settlement, 22
Marcellus, see Claudius
Marcius Coriolanus, Cn. (dictator), 90
Marcius Philippus, L. (consul), 193
Marcius Turbo, Q. (Hadrian's favorite marshal), 355
Marcomanni (Germanic tribe): Bohemia seized by, 280, 344, 371; defeated (by Marcus Aurelius), 371, 373, (by Galerius), 411; Italy invaded by, 397, 398
Marcus Aurelius (M. Aurelius Antoninus Augustus), Emperor: adoption by Antoninus Pius, 363; Arch of, 379, 380; character, 368, 371, 373; Christian persecutions under, 370; circuit judges restored in Italy by, 361; Column of, 372, 373, 380; Danubian Wars of, 371-74; death, 374, 382; education in rhetoric and philosophy, 368-70; Meditations of, 370; memory and cult, 386
Maremma (coastal region of Etruria), 173
Margus (Morava) River, battle by, 405
Marius, C. (consul): character, 186, 190, 192, 208; early career, 155, 186; family connections, 186, 212, 216; military commands, 187, 188-89, 194; novus homo, 167, 220; political offices, 186, 187, 191, 200; partisans, 192, 199-200, 201, 206, 222; reform of the army, 188-89, 337; struggle with Sulla, 197-200
Marius Minor, C. (consul), 201
Marmara, Sea of, 141, 410, 439, 444
Maroboduus (king of the Marcomanni), 280, 311
Marrucini (Italic tribe in central Apennines), 100, 104, 194
Mars (Mavors or Mamers), 51, 66, 69, 71, 100, 115, 426; temples of, 248, 285, 300
Mars Field (Campus Martius, Rome), 64, 244, 325, 343, 373
Marseille (Massilia): ancient Greek settlement in, 30; alliance with Roma, 121, 128, 133; coinages, 128, 226; commerce, 95, 121, 163, 225; exiles at, 211, 235; siege by Caesar, 240, 241

Marsi: in Samnite Wars, 102, 106; in Italian War, 194, 195
Marsic War, see Italian War
Martial (M. Valerius Martialis) (epigrammatic poet), 327, 331
Marzabotto: founded by Etruscans, 30; occupied by Gauls, 97
Massicus, Mount (Campania), 291
Massinissa (king of Numidia): ally of Rome in Second Punic War, 135, 136; aggressions against Carthage, 155-56; character, 155, 184, 196; death and successors, 184
Master of the Horse (magister equitum): chief assistant of a dictator, 82, 130, 244, 245; imperial Master of the Cavalry, 432
Master of the Infantry (magister peditum), 432
Master of the Offices (magister officiorum), 432
Massurius Sabinus (jurist), 307
Mauretania (see also Morocco): colonization by Rome, 277, 281; native rulers of, 187, 281, 315, 316; Roman protectorate, 281; Roman province, 316; numeri in, 358; rebellions in, 367, 373, 393
Mausoleum: of Augustus, 301, 349; of Hadrian, 362, 363, 380
Matera (Lucania), pottery of, 19
Maxentius (M. Aurelius Maxentius Augustus), Emperor, 422-23, 424-25
Maximian (M. Aurelius Valerius Maximianus Herculius Augustus), Emperor: associate emperor in the Diocletian tetrarchy, 409-10; abdication, 419; resumption of office, 423; death, 423
Maximinus Daia (Galerius Valerius Maximinus Daia Augustus), Emperor: Caesar of Galerius in the East, 419, 421; Christian persecutions of, 424, 426; rivalry with Licinius, 424, 427; defeat and death, 408, 427
Maximinus Thrax (C. Julius Verus Maximinus Augustus), Emperor, 395
Media Atropatene (modern Azerbaijan), 261, 329, 338-39, 392
Mediterranean race, 18
Melitene, legionary camp at, 339
Melpum (Etruscan settlement near Milan), 30
Memmius C. (tribune), 185, 192
Menander (writer of Greek New Comedy), 171, 381
Menippus of Gadara (Greek satirist), 331, 369
Mercenaries: Carthaginian, 115, 118, 120, 136; Hellenistic, 108, 147; Roman, 371, 413
Mercury, 71
Mérida (Emerita, Lusitania, Spain), 278, 298
Mesolithic period, 16, 18, 20
Mesopotamia: belonged to Seleucid empire, 139, 140; invasions by Roman armies, 208, 234, 333-54, 371, 385-86, 411; northern part (annexed by Trajan), 353, (abandoned by Hadrian), 355, (reannexed by Septimius Severus), 388, (lost to the Persians), 395, 396, 397, 411, (recovered by Diocletian), 409, 411; southern part annexed by Trajan, 354
Messallina, Valeria (wife of Claudius), 317, 323

Messana (Messina, Sicily), 115, 116
Messapic (dialect spoken in southeastern Italy), 23
Metaurus river, battles of, 134, 402
Metallurgy (see also Mines): Carthaginian, 112, 113; Celtic, 92, 225; Etruscan and Villanovan, 24, 25, 31, 49, 92; Roman, 296-97, 348
Metellus, see Caecilius
Micipsa (king of Numidia), 184
Middle class, see Knights
Milan (Mediolanum): prehistoric and Etruscan, 21, 30, 97; Roman colony, 152; German invasion, 398; imperial capital for the West, 410, 414; Conference and Edict of, 426, 427, 428, 430
Milo, see Annius
Milvian Bridge, battle at the, 425, 426, 428
Minerva, 35, 58, 69-70, 71
Mines and Mining: in Britain, 112, 322; in Etruria and Elbe, 31, 42, 89, 297; in Gaul, 225; in Macedonia, 148; in Noricum, 297; in Spain, 112, 113, 121, 134, 153, 154, 340; regulations governing, 154, 340
Mints (see also Coinage): control of, 298, 319, 403; location of, 298, 315, 403, 411; officials, 273, 298
Minturnae: Roman colony, 105; slave-worked plantations around, 166, 291
Minucius Rufus, M. (consul, master of the horse), 130, 131
Misenum (on Bay of Naples): Treaty of, 257; naval base, 276
Mithridates VI Eupator (king of Pontus): conquests and aggressions, 196-97; massacres in Asia and Delos, 197; wars with Rome, 200-01, 206-08, 215, 389; death, 215
Mithridates of Pergamum, 243-44
Modena, see Mutina
Moesia: geographical location, 279, 314; invasions of, 344, 353, 373, 396, 400, 431; made a province, 279, 283; subdivided by Domitian, 344; settled with captive barbarians, 374, 401, 403; road building in, 314
Mogontiacum, see Mainz
Moldavia (between Carpathians and Dniester), 344
Mommsen, Theodor (German epigraphist and historian), 55, 57, 60, 221, 237, 315
Monarchy: early, 58-60; fall of, 81-84
Money lenders, see Usury
Monte Testaccio, 348
Monumentum Ancyranum, see Res Gestae
Moral code (see also Mos maiorum), 56, 73-75, 170, 303, 304, 306, 370
Morocco (see also Mauretania and North Africa): Carthaginian exploration and colonization, 111; conquest by Marius (105, B.C.), 187; municipalization, 322; native rulers, 187, 281, 315; numeri in, 358; protectorate of Rome, 281; provincial status, 316, 322, 419; unrest, rebellion, and invasion, 357, 367, 373, 399
Mos maiorum (see also Moral code), 56, 73-75, 303, 304, 306, 343, 370
Mucius Scaevola, P. (consul, jurist): adherent of Stoicism, 170; Grac-